Getaways
For
Gourmets
In the Northeast

By Nancy and Richard Woodworth

Wood Pond Press
West Hartford, Conn.

Prices, menus, hours, and days closed in restaurants and inns change seasonally and with business conditions. Places in this book are assumed to be open year-round, unless otherwise noted. Readers are advised to call or write ahead to avoid disappointment. Prices quoted were correct as this edition went to press. They are offered as a relative guide to what to expect and are, of course, subject to change.

Lodging rates are for double occupancy and include breakfast, unless specified to the contrary. EP (European Plan) means no meals. MAP (Modified American Plan) means breakfast and dinner.

The authors value their reputation for credibility and have personally visited the places recommended in this book. Unlike others, they do not ask the owners to fill in information forms or to approve the final copy. No fees are charged for inclusion.

Readers' comments and suggestions are welcomed.

Cover Photo: Breakfast table overlooking the water outside Five Gables Inn at East Boothbay, Me.

Cover Photo by George W. Gardner.

Copyright © 2000, 1997, 1994, 1991, 1988 and 1984 by Nancy and Richard Woodworth.

Library of Congress Catalog No. 84-51593.

ISBN No. 0-934260-86-9.

Published in the United States of America.
Sixth Edition.

Contents

1. **Brandywine Valley, Del-Pa.** 1
   A Feast for All the Senses

2. **Bucks County, Pa.-N.J.** 21
   Romance Along the River

3. **Cape May, N.J.** 47
   Two for B&B, Tea and Dinner

4. **Hudson Valley, N.Y.** 67
   Mecca for Gourmets

5. **Finger Lakes, N.Y.** 97
   The Pleasures of the Grape

6. **Niagara-on-the-Lake, Ont.** 128
   Wine, Orchards and Shaw

7. **Saratoga Springs, N.Y.** 154
   The Summer Place to Be

8. **Montreal, Que.** 173
   A Tale of Two Cities

9. **Burlington, Vt.** 205
   A Culinary Sense of Place

10. **Woodstock and Hanover, Vt.-N.H.** 224
    Quintessential New England

11. **Southern Vermont** 245
    Old Inns, New Style

12. **The Tri-State Berkshires, Mass.-N.Y.-Conn.** 269
    A Tradition of High Tastes

13. **Ridgefield, Conn.** 307
    An Enclave of Elegant Eateries

14. **Southeastern Connecticut** 323
    Down the River and Along the Shore

15. **Newport, R.I.** 349
    In Pursuit of Pleasures

16. **Providence, R.I.** 371
    Cinderella of Cuisine

17. **Cape Cod, Mass.** 395
    New Capers on the Old Cape

18. **Nantucket, Mass.** 423
    The Ultimate Indulgence for Gourmets

19. **Boston, Mass.** 449
    Baked Beans to New Cuisine

20. **Monadnock Region, N.H.** 480
    A Step Back in Time

21. **Southern Maine** 497
    Sophistication by the Sea

22. **Portland, Me.** 518
    Bounty by the Bay

23. **Mid-Coast Maine** 538
    Where the Real Maine Starts

24. **Down East Maine** 564
    Lobster, Plus

About the Authors

Nancy Webster Woodworth began her dining experiences in her native Montreal and as a waitress in summer resorts across Canada during her McGill University years. She worked in London and hitchhiked through Europe on $3 a day before her marriage to Richard Woodworth, an American newspaper editor, whom she met on a ski tow at Mont Tremblant in Quebec. In 1972 she started writing her "Roaming the Restaurants" column for the West Hartford (Conn.) News, which led to half of the book *Daytripping & Dining in Southern New England* (1978), since published in two other editions. She is co-author as well of *Weekending in New England, Inn Spots & Special Places in New England, Inn Spots & Special Places in the Mid-Atlantic, Inn Spots & Special Places in the Southeast, Waterside Escapes in the Northeast,* and *The Restaurants of New England.* She and her husband have two grown sons and live in West Hartford, where her ever-expanding collection of cookbooks and food and travel magazines threatens to take over the entire kitchen and den.

Richard Woodworth was raised on wholesome American food in suburban Syracuse, N.Y., and except for four years at Middlebury College, spent much of his early life in upstate New York. He was a reporter for daily newspapers in Syracuse, Jamestown, Geneva and Rochester before moving to Connecticut to become editor of the West Hartford News and executive editor of Imprint Newspapers. He is editor and publisher of Wood Pond Press and co-author of *Inn Spots & Special Places in New England, Inn Spots & Special Places in the Mid-Atlantic, Inn Spots & Special Places in the Southeast,* and *The Restaurants of New England.* With his wife and sons, he has traveled to the four corners of this country, Canada, and portions of Europe, writing their findings — from a cross-country family expedition by station wagon to exchanging houses with a family in England — for newspapers and magazines. Between adventures and writing ventures, he tries to find time to weed the garden in summer and ski in the winter.

Excerpts from several of the authors' guidebooks may be seen on-line at **www.getawayguides.com.**

Introduction

Between the terrine and the truffles, dining out provides many an adventure. The best of these adventures is what this book is about.

It is written not by food critics who wax poetic or devastate with every precious bite. Rather it is written by travelers who like to eat and explore and who, as journalists and guidebook authors, are in a position to evaluate hundreds of restaurants and share their findings.

Ours is a highly personal guide to the best and most interesting places in 24 of the Northeast's most appealing destination areas for gourmets. They are the "best" as defined locally, by restaurateurs and chefs, and by our tastes.

We don't think haute cuisine should mean haughty cuisine. As journalists, we seek out the new and are skeptical of the old if it rides on pretension or reputation. As diners, we like to be comfortable in restaurants where the food is good and meals an adventure. We don't mind paying a lot if the experience is worth it, but we prefer the unusual or distinctive place and we expect our money's worth.

We also steer you to more than good restaurants. We point out the most choice places in which to stay. We highlight other attractions of interest to food-lovers, such as specialty-food shops, kitchen stores, bakeries, wineries, herb gardens and special museums – more than ever in this newly expanded edition.

Through photographs as well as our reporting, we try to give you a feel for our destinations before you arrive. We want you to know what to expect, and what it will cost.

In the years we have spent researching six editions of this book, we have eaten in as many restaurants as time and budget have allowed. For most of those mentioned here in which we haven't dined, be assured that we'd like to, having visited and talked with the people involved.

In preparing earlier editions of this book, we were struck by how young some of the best restaurants and lodging facilities really are. With the easing of the recession of the early 1990s, many newcomers have emerged. And prices generally have risen to pre-recession levels, although many restaurants now offer less-expensive cafe and bistro menus or venues. Diners realize these days that good eating need not be beyond their aspirations or pocketbooks

For this edition in particular, we've noted a trend to more healthful eating. There's a lighter and often a vegetarian accent on many gourmet menus these days. Many restaurants offer light fare and encourage so-called grazing.

New chapters in this edition cover dining in Providence, R.I., and Portland, Me.

The continuing evolution is the nature of the business – and the hazard for a guidebook that aims to keep up with the times rather than stick with the tried and true. We find the food and lodging scene so fluid at the turn of the millennium that we would rather risk a few non-survivors than not share news about promising newcomers.

So here we are, many meals and miles (and pounds) later, having traipsed across the Northeast in sun, rain, and snow, from early morn to midnight. Some places we loved; some we tolerated. Some we can't wait to get back to; some may never see us again.

But all had a certain something that earned them a place in this book.

Our hope is that you enjoy the partaking as much as we did the finding.

Nancy and Richard Woodworth

New Year's calling treats are on display for Yuletide at Winterthur.

Brandywine Valley

A Feast for All the Senses

Mention the Brandywine Valley and most people think of gardens, house museums and art, probably in that order. And with good reason, for the region is unsurpassed on the East Coast in its extraordinary combination of the three.

This is an area of unusual visual appeal, especially during spring when the gardens burst into bloom, and in summer, when the renowned mansions and art museums are at their crowded peak.

But the area straddling the Delaware-Pennsylvania border north of Wilmington is more than a treat for the eyes and more than a seasonal tourist destination. It's a feast for all the senses – especially so during the holiday season, which arrives early and leaves late.

Experiencing a Brandywine Christmas is like coming upon an oasis of color and sensation in the midst of a stark Andrew Wyeth landscape. Simply incredible are the museum treasures within half a dozen miles of each other in this valley that the du Ponts and the Wyeths have made famous. All the museums put on their best holiday spread, and Yuletide at Winterthur is the year's highlight for food lovers, who see feasts recreated from yesteryear. The area's food treats include wines and locally grown mushrooms.

Strangely for such a touristy area, this region lagged in providing country inns and good restaurants in which travelers could rest their weary bones and sate their appetites between expeditions to the valley's attractions. The situation is much improved lately, however.

Dining

The Best of the Best

Krazy Kat's, Route 100 and Kirk Road, Montchanin, Del.

As distinctive as the Inn at Montchanin Village of which it is the centerpiece, this polished and uniquely styled restaurant occupies the former blacksmith shop in the restored village that once housed workers at the du Pont powder mills. Owner Missy Lickle chose the unlikely name for an eccentric old maid who once lived there "and was crazy as a cat," in the words of her grandmother. The theme turns up at the entry in a local artist's cartoon-like portrait of a gawky feline with a goofy grin, in cat sculptures clad in Japanese robes in each of the front windows, in gilt-framed portraits of cats attired in royal or military regalia on the walls and on the brocade vests worn by the wait staff. The theme broadens in the low-slung chairs with zebra-print cushions at tables set with beige over zebra-print cloths and stunning china designed by a Connecticut artist in the colorful jaguar jungle pattern. The tables seating 55 in two rooms are large and well spaced, the walls radiate a warm salmon color, and a fire burns in one of the original forges up near the ceiling.

It's an enchanting setting for exceptional contemporary American fare overseen by executive chef Fred Kellerman, who came here from Philadelphia.

A bowl of four varieties of olives and a basket of breads arrive with the dinner menu. One of us started with the zesty bluepoint oyster gratin teamed with prosciutto, tri-color bell peppers, shallots and parmesan cheese. The other sampled the salad of field greens, a first-rate mixture dressed with toasted pinenuts, stilton cheese and a zippy roasted garlic vinaigrette. Main courses range from blackberry-braised cornish game hen with sweet white corn flan and green leek and shiitake ragoût to herb-grilled veal chop with roasted red pepper and rosemary oil vinaigrette, marinated asparagus soufflé and parsnip chips. The signature sautéed crab cakes were bound with a shrimp mousseline and served with honey-jalapeño tartar sauce and sweet potato fries. The sautéed Chesapeake rockfish was of the melt-in-the-mouth variety, sauced with bluepoint oysters in a tomato-fennel cream and accompanied by crisp haricots verts and flavorful dark wild rice. Our bottle of Sterling sauvignon blanc ($19, from a well chosen and affordable list honored by Wine Spectator), was poured in the largest wine glasses we've seen, surpassed in size only by the balloon-size globes used here for red wines.

The dessert recitation included a walnut-praline tart and crème de cassis crème brûlée. We settled for the intense raspberry and mango sorbets, architecturally presented with enormous blackberries and an edible orchid in an almond tuile.

Although a place for serious dining and undeniably elegant, the feline motif and lack of pretension imparts a refreshing light-heartedness. Both the meal and the setting were among the happiest of our travels.

(302) 888-2133. Entrées, $22 to $27. Lunch, Monday-Friday 11 to 2. Dinner nightly, 5:30 to 9:30. Jackets requested.

Dilworthtown Inn, Old Wilmington Pike at Brinton Bridge Road, Dilworthtown, Pa.

In the quaint hamlet of Dilworthtown, this old wood, stone and brick inn has a

Zebra-print cushions on chairs contribute to distinctive look at Krazy Kat's.

classic continental menu and what is considered to be the area's best wine list. Its 800 selections start at $19 and rise rapidly into the triple digits. We counted more than 110 cabernets from the Napa Valley alone.

The original 1758 inn and its late 18th-century wing were restored in 1972 into a warren of fifteen small dining rooms, a bar and a lobby complete with plate-glass windows and plantings in a mini-atrium. Each room features rich, handmade chestnut tables covered with woven mats and flanked by tavern-style chairs. Lighting is from gaslight chandeliers and candles. The dining areas, which use no electricity, have eleven wood-burning fireplaces, including three walk-in hearths and a beehive bake oven. Tuxedoed waiters lend sophistication and elegance. In season, diners may eat outside in the original stable area, surrounded by the remains of stone walls.

The leather-bound, eight-page dinner menu starts with a dozen appetizers. Included are two standbys, shrimp cocktail with rémoulade sauce and the house pâté of creamy duck liver with black truffles and port wine syrup. The chef shows his reach with saffron crayfish risotto, pan-seared crab and mushroom galette with caramelized tomato and mango chutney, and confit of pheasant and fingerling potato pierogi with black truffle butter.

Among the entrées are three kinds of steaks, including grilled ostrich tenderloin and the chef's duet of filet mignon and stuffed Australian lobster tail. Otherwise, expect such contemporary continental updates as roasted Chilean sea bass with lobster tarragon sauce and pan-seared breast of Hudson Valley duck with crispy confit. The kitchen is at its best with its legendary nightly specials. Appetizers could be ginger-crisp lobster drizzled with a Thai apricot sauce, and grilled portobello mushrooms with herbed polenta and white truffle sauce. Main courses include grilled mahi-mahi with melon and pineapple salsa, medallions of New Zealand venison with juniper berries, and veal osso buco.

Desserts range from chocolate mousse to crème caramel. They include wonderful homemade sorbets and ice creams of exotic flavors (the white-chocolate/macadamia-nut is a favorite).

Except for the creative specials, the inn preserves the traditional, according to co-owners Robert Rafetto and James Barnes. That's fine with the clientele, who rate it their favorite all-around spot for consistency, charm and service. *(610) 399-1390. Entrées, $17.25 to $34.95. Dinner nightly, 5:30 to 9:30, Saturday from 5, Sunday 3 to 9.*

The Farm House Restaurant, 514 McCue Road, Avondale, Pa.

This once rather ordinary-looking restaurant in the 18th-century farmhouse that doubles as the clubhouse at Loch Nairn Golf Course is on the way up in culinary circles. Owners Virginia and Hank Smedley have enhanced two small and atmospheric dining rooms off a spacious lounge with barnwood walls, country artifacts, baskets hanging from the beams, candlelight and fresh flowers. We particularly liked the looks of the canopied outdoor patio, glamorously set for dinner with white linens on large tables flanked by heavy wooden chairs. There's also a stunning new contemporary function facility that relegates the "farmhouse" image to history.

The crab cake's reputation made this a must stop for lunch. We were seated in rather formal surroundings and faced a rather daunting menu strong on dinner-type fare. Yes, there are salads and sandwiches, although caesar salad with pan-fried oysters and sautéed salmon on a warm croissant are not typical golf-club style. A basket of sundried tomato-basil bread and garlicky focaccia staved off hunger as we studied the three dozen possibilities, augmented by such specials as a sampler of smoked fish from the restaurant's smokehouse. But it was the crab cake we were after. It turned out to be an unpriced special, sautéed to lock in the flavor, then broiled and served over whole-grain mustard sauce. Thick with tender crabmeat, with no filling and absolutely luscious, it came with roasted peppers, snow peas and potatoes, and was well worth the $14 price tag that showed up on the bill. We also sampled the rich mushroom soup ($4) and an appetizer of chicken liver pâté ($6) with fresh figs, apple slices and crostini rounds. Service was so leisurely that we ran out of time for dessert. The choice included key lime pie, chocolate mousse torte, crème brûlée and cheesecake laced with grand marnier.

Dinner is a similarly elegant, leisurely affair. The menu pairs the luncheon appetizers with more substantial entrées, varying from poached salmon to veal madeira. The range is indicated by cashew-crusted trout florentine, panned breast of chicken with smoked scallops, tenderloin steak au poivre and pan-seared venison rack chop served on roesti potatoes with a confit of tomatoes and herbs. *(610) 268-2235. Entrées, $18.50 to $24. Lunch daily, 11 to 3. Dinner, 5 to 9.*

Maxwell Creed's, 503 Orchard Ave. at Route 1, Kennett Square, Pa.

What a transformation! And what food! This exciting new restaurant evolved in 1998 from the Market Place deli hidden behind Phillips Place. Gone is the deli, its space having been supplanted partly by a bar. The old specialty-food section in front is now a reception area with bar seats, a handful of dining tables and wall shelves artfully stocked with chafing dishes, pans, vine wreaths, books and magazines. Beyond is a low-ceilinged dining room with barnwood walls accented by local art, an end wall bearing a colorful mural of a courtyard scene, and dark green-clothed tables seating about 40. A two-level brick patio out front accommodates another twenty in season.

Such is the stylish yet homespun setting for inspired fare offered by talented local chef Ray Maxwell, a graduate of the Restaurant School in Philadelphia, and

Ken Creed and chef Ray Maxwell are partners in Maxwell Creed's restaurant.

restaurateur Ken Creed, former golf pro and bon vivant who oversees the front of the house. Chef Ray makes creative use of locally cultivated mushrooms, the house specialty. He's partial to such exotica as ostrich and buffalo, and flies in fresh moonfish every Thursday from Hawaii. Interestingly, Ken and the wait staff finish most dishes at tableside.

The signature starter at both lunch and dinner is a complex mushroom soup, served in the shell of a roasted acorn squash and topped with jarlsberg cheese. Ours tasted more sweetish than savory, but was a worthy preliminary for a lunch that also included an assertive smoked wild mushroom and duck salad and a sensational crab and cheese sandwich, made with custard batter-dipped bread that looked and tasted like french toast. Everyone raves about the crab cakes topped with citrus hollandaise, available at both lunch and dinner. Ditto for the grilled vegetable napoleon layered with portobello mushrooms, fresh mozzarella and four kinds of vegetables.

For dinner, expect starters like a memorable poached pear and blue cheese salad over bitter greens dressed with a port wine vinaigrette, the sampler of house-smoked delicacies finished with apple chutney and herbed crostini, and a crab cocktail with zesty mango dressing and plantain chips. Creamy mushroom and garlic butter, shaped like a floret, accompanies the sourdough and mixed grain rolls. Main courses could be Chilean sea bass en papillote, chicken "gran champion" (an award-winning concoction stuffed with truffles and basil and served over a sherry-caramel sauce – the chef *is* partial to sweets), ostrich filet with bosc pears and madeira demi-glace, and free-range buffalo steak topped with smoked portobello and roasted red peppers.

Most diners finish, at least the first time, with the specialty dessert called strawberries Henry VIII. Plump berries are mixed with white and brown sugar and lemon juice, flamed with cognac and finished with ground pepper, then served over cinnamon ice cream. Other choices might be key lime tart, mixed berry crumble and triple chocolate terrine with chocolate shavings on top.

The select wine list is priced from the twenties up.

(610) 388-9450. Entrées, $15.95 to $25.95. Lunch, Tuesday-Saturday 11:30 to 2. Dinner, Tuesday-Sunday 5 to 9 or 10. Sunday brunch, 11 to 3.

The Gables at Chadds Ford, 423 Baltimore Pike, Chadds Ford, Pa.

Once part of a dairy farm, this handsome stone and frame barn is now a stylish restaurant specializing in California cuisine with an Asian accent. Jack McFadden, area restaurateur for 30 years and known recently for successes at the nearby Marshalton Inn and The Restaurant and The Bar in West Chester, invested more than $1 million into what he considers his best effort so far. "I call this my grown-up restaurant," he said. His loyal following agreed.

The place is named for the 23 gables added to the barn in an 1897 Victorian facelift. An interior design aficionado who did the architectural renderings himself, he scouted up three art deco bronze chandeliers and matching sconces for the bar area, where a grand piano greets arriving customers and the metal milking stools are cushioned with a deep red faux ostrich skin. Leaded glass windows separate the bar from the 120-seat dining room. Jack calls the decor "barn chic." The linens are white, the floors heartpine, the walls are white wood and brick and crackle painted with gold tint, and dining is by candlelight. A sparkling new upstairs room with a 2½-story ceiling handles functions and overflow.

The extensive menu is the kind upon which every item appeals. We'd happily make a dinner of such appetizers as ahi tuna with wasabi and soba noodle salad, sautéed escargots with mushroom ragoût, crab cakes with fried leeks and soy-coconut sauce, and a frisée salad with panko-encrusted chèvre, pinenuts and raspberry vinaigrette. The duo of dumplings – tuna and cilantro, vegetable and ginger – are as good as they get.

Or you could make a meal of pastas like creamy crab ravioli or linguini with shrimp and scallops. Main courses range from Thai marinated grouper with wilted greens and citrus-glazed salmon with ancho chile rice to sautéed duck breast with fig and black currant chutney, grilled pork tenderloin with port demi-glace and roasted lamb with red pepper cabernet butter.

Desserts include crème caramel, chocolate mousse and fresh fruit napoleon. Like the rest of the meal, they are presented on oversize white plates garnished and decorated to the hilt.

(610) 388-7700. Entrées, $17.95 to $23.95. Lunch, Tuesday-Saturday 11:30 to 2:30. Dinner, Tuesday-Saturday 5:30 to 10:30. Sunday, brunch 11 to 2:30, dinner 5 to 9.

Sovana Bistro & Pizza Kitchen, 696 Unionville Road, Kennett Square, Pa.

"What the Brandywine Valley needs is a good bistro," was the lament we heard time after time. "These old farmers have plenty of money and will spend it on good food," one innkeeper advised.

Young chefs Nick Farrell and Frank Delvescovo heeded the call, launching this jaunty establishment in 1998 in the Willowdale Town Center shopping complex off Route 82 north. The pair man the grills and ovens in an elongated open kitchen, nicely separated from the high-ceilinged main dining area by a divider holding wine bottles (stored for regulars) and a prominent horse saddle mounted in front. It's a soaring, stark space painted pale green. Exposed ducts shine beneath a skylight. A large wall mural conveys the local landscape, showing houses from the area.

Nick found the name Sovana in an Italian travel guide and turned to Tuscany for much of the culinary inspiration. The dinner menu is made for grazing. You might order a first course of sautéed calamari with roasted tomato chili sauce, shrimp and vegetable tempura or pan-seared tuna loin over asian greens with a wasabi mustard dressing. There's a choice of five salads, including one with lump crabmeat and avocado on organic greens with a dijon vinaigrette. Jumbo shrimp, roasted tomatoes and asparagus topped with melted mozzarella turn up on a featured pasta dish. Or how about a pizza of prosciutto, goat cheese, roasted peppers and arugula? The options seem endless.

Main courses tempt, perhaps grilled salmon over couscous topped with citrus-mango salsa, pan-seared tuna with a white port-ginger sauce, and roasted veal rib chop with prosciutto, sage and peas. Order these and you're advised to skip the pastas and pizzas, even those that come in small as well as large sizes. You may well be too sated for dessert.

Expect similar treats for lunch, or settle as we did for the tasty broiled crab burger with dijon mustard sauce.

(610) 444-5600. Entrées, $15 to $23. Lunch daily, 11 to 2:30. Dinner nightly, 5 to 10. BYOB.

Half Moon Restaurant & Saloon, 108 West State St., Kennett Square, Pa.

Exciting New American cuisine and remarkably reasonable prices are the hallmarks of this hot spot built – literally – by young restaurateur Scott Hammond from an old candy kitchen. With a few helpers, he constructed the 35-seat mahogany bar in the front of the long, high-ceilinged downtown storefront, which became a popular watering spot for a young crowd. He also built the booths and tables in the rear, where diners both casual and serious gather away from the hubbub to enjoy the inspired fare of Tennessee chef John Stewart, once the private chef for Gov. Lamar Alexander.

Scott named the place for a favorite after-ski haunt in Montana with the intention of opening a microbrewery called Total Eclipse. The restaurant proved so successful that the brewpub plans were shelved in favor of a major expansion calling for a large new kitchen and an indoor-outdoor rooftop dining area.

From a menu made for grazing, we enjoyed the spiced bluefish wrapped in a potato crust with a shrimp and crawfish court bouillon, julienned mixed vegetables and melt-in-the-mouth mashed potatoes, and cashew-encrusted chicken sautéed with chèvre, served with assertive curried vegetables and jasmine rice. With a bottle of Lost Horizon chardonnay, the dinner tab for two came to less than $40.

At least one-quarter of the changing menu is devoted to "grazers," many with a cajun or Southwest bent. Consider the crab nachos, the stuffed portobello with crab and crawfish imperial, the gator and crawdads creole over cheese grits, and even the rattlesnake and rabbit rellenos (described on the menu as a poblano chile pepper "stuffed with R&R sausage, feta and jack cheeses, covered with a chipotle corn batter and baked"). Or sample escargots in exotic mushroom sauce over a saffron potato cake, a crispy ginger-fried lobster salad with watercress and plum dressing, a crab cake sandwich, grilled elk chop gremolata, chocolate-chip cheesecake or apple-cranberry tart. The tastes are great, and so are the values.

(610) 444-7232. Entrées, $11.95 to $19.95. Lunch, Monday-Friday 11:30 to 5:30. Dinner, Monday-Friday 5:30 to 10, Saturday 6 to 10.

The Back Burner, 425 Hockessin Corner, Hockessin, Del.

Started as a cooking school, this quickly became a local favorite for innovative American cuisine in a country setting, and in a 1997 readers' choice poll was ranked the best restaurant in Delaware. The barn-style establishment, casual but sophisticated, is part of the fantastic Everything But the Kitchen Sink culinary complex. "This area was farmland when we opened," said owner Missy Lickle. "We began a cooking school and started serving lunch to get people out here." A full-fledged restaurant was the next step, followed by a thriving deli and takeout operation called The Back Burner to Go.

The dining-room menu here changes every week. For dinner, you might find crab cakes mousseline with wasabi vinaigrette, baked salmon served over "eggplant caviar," grilled calves liver, pan-roasted chili-rubbed pork tenderloin, filet en croûte with brie, and dijon-crusted roasted rack of New Zealand lamb. Start with baked brie or crab-stuffed mushrooms, signature appetizers. Finish with chocolate-amaretto cake or tiramisu.

Lunch time produces a variety of interesting salads (how about one of blackened chicken?), hefty sandwiches and half a dozen entrées ranging from quiche of the day to mustard-crusted Atlantic salmon or grilled garlicky shrimp and sea scallops.

The wine and beer lists are as good as everything else about the place.

(302) 239-2314. Entrées, $17.95 to $24.95. Lunch, Monday-Saturday 11:15 to 2:15. Dinner, Monday-Thursday 5 to 9, Friday-Saturday 5:30 to 9:45.

More Dining Choices

Buckley's Tavern, 5812 Kennett Pike (Route 52), Centreville, Del.

Immensely popular locally is this tavern built in the late 1700s, all spiffed up with a pretty, white-linened interior dining room and an airy garden-room addition. The singles head for the tavern, where snacks and light entrées are available all day, or the open-air bar on two upper levels outside.

Lately, the former tavern and dinner menus have been combined into one extensive, interesting menu appealing to a variety of tastes, including those who want "shared plates and finger foods," to whom this establishment seems to be increasingly catering. At a recent dinner, one of us enjoyed oriental spring rolls and a half serving of an addictive pasta of farfalle with smoked salmon and roquefort. The other liked the caesar salad and porchetta (sliced pork roasted with garlic and rosemary, served on an onion roll with roasted peppers). With a Round Hill chardonnay and a slice of key lime pie, the tab came to a modest $40 before tip.

You also could try, as we did on another occasion, one of the handful of entrées, ranging from shrimp and andouille sausage diablo to grilled filet of beef in a roasted shallot and port wine demi-glace. We liked the crab cakes, their flavor heightened by a dill mayonnaise laced with orange, and the linguini with smoked chicken and red peppers. Votive candles cast shadows on bare, rich wood tables flanked by comfortable, cushioned chairs as we lingered over a Hogue Cellars chardonnay from Washington State.

With a wine store operated by Collier's of Wilmington in the front of the building, you would expect Buckley's selection to be excellent. It's also very reasonably priced, and many wines are available by the glass.

The special cappuccino-pecan-praline ice cream was a hit among desserts. They included a light lemon-ginger cake and chocolate cups filled with raspberry mousse, served on a pool of crème anglaise. The cheesecake studded with black raspberries and strawberries is to die for.

(302) 656-9776. Entrées, $11.95 to $19.95. Lunch, Monday-Friday 11:30 to 2:30, Saturday to 3. Dinner nightly, 5:30 to 9:30 or 10. Sunday brunch, 11 to 3.

Chadds Ford Inn, Routes 1 and 100, Chadds Ford, Pa.

Three generations of Wyeth works grace the dining rooms of this restaurant, which was founded in 1736 and looks it. And Andrew and Betsy Wyeth have been known to dine here.

Acquired in 1998 by a group that also owns Buckley's Tavern and the Marshalton Inn nearby, the place is popular with passing tourists. People started beating down the doors for lunch at 11:30 on the Saturday we were there, and the two long dining rooms on either side of the center entry hall soon were filled. So were three upstairs dining rooms. Only the tavern had empty tables and they filled up later, no doubt. Service by a young staff is geared to handling the crowds, however.

One yellow rose in a slender vase adorned our table, nicely set in beige and brown. The candles were lit at noon, though they were scarcely needed with sunlight streaming through the alcove windows. The low beamed ceiling and wainscoting enhanced the Wyeths on the walls.

It was here we first learned that the area's popular snapper soup is not made with red snapper but with snapper turtle. Thick and spicy, it tastes like the turtle soup we've had in New Orleans. From a wide-ranging menu that has become overly New Americanized with the change in ownership, we also enjoyed the creamy oyster pan roast served over a cornmeal biscuit. The grilled chicken salad platter served with fresh fruit was another good choice.

The dessert tray, long considered a strong point, looked a bit listless at our latest visit. It held old favorites like pecan and pumpkin pies as well as chocolate mousse cake and a strawberry-kiwi tart.

At night, the historic atmosphere is grand, the presentation stylish and the service leisurely, at least the midweek evening we dined. The new menu is categorized under small bowls, big bowls, small plates and big plates, and reads like something from a new millennium bistro rather than the 265-year-old Brandywine Creek "tavern at Chad's fording place," as described on the back cover. Gone were the mustard-sauced Australian loin of lamb and the tender grilled venison steaks topped with port wine and plum sauce that we had enjoyed a few years earlier. In their place were trendies like braised lamb shanks, grilled duck breast with apricot glaze and herb-seared tuna steak served over orzo. The only holdovers from old seemed to be shepherd's pie and beef wellington. The locals weren't entirely happy. Tourists would not realize the difference.

(610) 388-7361. Entrées, $14.95 to $22.95. Lunch daily, 11:30 to 2. Dinner, 5:30 to 10 or 10:30, Sunday 4 to 8.

Hartefeld National, 1 Sheehan Road, Avondale, Pa.

The name of this big new place is as confusing as its location, tucked away behind mushroom and mulch farms and with signs that steered us the wrong way. You will know you're there when you reach the showy fieldstone clubhouse and the valet tries to park your car. Golfers and other sporty types are much in evidence at the much-ballyhooed public golf course and apparent residential development.

Everyone in the area recommended the setting, especially that of the two-tiered **Grille,** the main dining room with tall windows onto the rolling fairways. Paneled in rich wood with sports photos on the walls, it's contemporary, spacious and clubby. The principals also own the acclaimed Columbus Inn in Wilmington, so they bring a solid food background to the operation.

Lunch is popular with daytrippers as well as golfers. The vast menu has something for everyone, from quesadillas and turkey cobb salad to grilled yellowfin tuna and crab marinara over linguini. Corned beef and cabbage, chicken pot pie with dumplings and veal meatloaf revive memories of earlier times.

At night, the chefs combine lunch appetizers and low-priced "country casual fun food" with more elaborate offerings. Among the last are a salad of grilled portobellos stuffed with crabmeat and main courses like crab-crusted fillet of swordfish with horseradish beurre blanc and grilled veal chop with a port wine demi-glace. The cigar-friendly Walker Cup Room caters to golfers, and there's an Irish Pub adjacent to the dining room.

(610) 268-8800 or (800) 240-7373. Entrées, $16.95 to $24.95. Open daily, 11 to 9.

Pizza, with Pizzazz

Pizza by Elizabeths, 4019A Kennett Pike, Greenville, Del.

Two Elizabeths – Greenville residents Betty Snyder and Betsy LeRoy – own this gourmet pizza parlor in the heart of du Pont country. No ordinary pizza parlor, this. In the midst of a high-style shopping plaza called One Greenville Crossing, the place is a beauty in beige and green, with a Mediterranean terra-cotta tile floor, oversize dried-flower wreaths on the walls and an array of booths and tables. The pizza toppings are displayed in containers at the pizza bar. Baking in a wood-fired oven makes the crusts crisp and chewy. The beverage list includes not only Evian and cappuccino but Samuel Adams beer and a connoisseur's selection of wines, priced up to $60.

Pizzas come in regular and mini sizes. You can try creations named after famous Elizabeths, from $9.50 for the basic Barrett Browning to $14 for the Crocker (with crabmeat, asparagus and brie). The Taylor combines goat cheese, rosemary, sautéed onions, sundried tomatoes and black olives. Or you can create your own pizza from a selection of six sauces and about four dozen toppings. Seasoned breadstick appetizers with dips, green salads and cookies and a few rich desserts make up the rest of the menu.

(302) 654-4478. Pizzas, $5.50 to $14. Open daily, 11:30 to 9 or 10.

Lodging

The Inn at Montchanin Village, Route 100 at Kirk Road, Montchanin, Del. 19710.

The sophisticated yet light-hearted style of its Krazy Kats restaurant (see above) extends to the sumptuous accommodations in this charming complex that evolved from a 19th-century du Pont workers' village. In 1991, local preservationists Missy and Daniel Lickle inherited the twenty-acre village established by her great-great-great grandfather, Eleuthére Irenée du Pont. Rather than sell to developers, they had the vision and resources to restore the site into a lodging and dining destination of distinction.

Guest accommodations were dictated by the idiosyncrasies of a row of turn-of-the-century duplexes, dependencies, a schoolhouse and a railroad station. They were part of a thriving village for workers who toiled at the nearby du Pont powder mills along the Brandywine, today part of the nearby Hagley Museum.

Most of the planned 37 rooms and suites in eleven stone, stucco and stick-style buildings are one- or two-bedroom suites with sitting areas and wet bars. Our

Comfortable furnishings and fireplace are typical at the Inn at Montchanin Village.

quarters in Belin, which turned out to be fairly typical, contained a cozy downstairs sitting room with plump sofa and chair covered in chintz, a TV/VCR atop a gas fireplace and a kitchenette area in the corner with wet bar, microwave and mini-refrigerator, complete with automatic icemaker and stocked with soft drinks and mineral water. Coffee and end tables were charmingly painted with flowers and rabbits. Everything was jolly looking and colorfully decorated in mix-and-match patterns that flow together. Up steep stairs was a skylit bedroom with a king bed dressed in Frette linens, about the most comfortable we've had the pleasure of luxuriating in, and a stunning, huge, all-marble bathroom. The latter came with a chandelier, a deep tub embedded in marble, a separate shower encased in thick clear glass and, if you turned on the right switch, heated towel racks. Wood-look venetian blinds covered the windows, padded hangers and ironing equipment were in the closet, and a country window had been painted whimsically on the wall beside a real window.

The inn's distinctive cowbird logo – a crow perched on the back of a leaping cow – was everywhere (monogrammed on the terry robes, embedded in the marble above the bath). The bed was turned down with chocolates and a copy of the weather forecast, and a thermos of ice water was placed beside. The only downside was traffic noise from the busy intersection out front.

Breakfast the next morning beside the front windows in Krazy Kat's was a feast of fresh orange juice, muffins, and a choice including eggs benedict and an omelet with smoked bacon, brie and chives, tasty walnut-raisin toast, garlicky browned potatoes and garnishes of large blackberries.

Afterward, Missy Lickle led a tour of the heart of the steeply sloping complex sandwiched between main road and train track (golf carts are lined up to transport luggage from parking areas as well as guests of limited mobility). All is artfully landscaped and full of surprises, from picket fences to pocket gardens to gas lights to porches with wicker rockers. Room sizes and configurations differ, but each appeals in its own right. Some have poster beds and some are kingsize. The Jefferson offers wicker porches front and back and a bathroom walled in travertine marble up to the vaulted ceiling. Missy, who decorated with goods from her huge gourmet emporium known as Everything But the Kitchen Sink, incorporated fine period and reproduction furniture, Staffordshire figurines, colorful fabrics and a sense of whimsy.

Like the outbuildings of a plantation, the character of Montchanin derives from the visual harmony of the entire village, rather than in any particular structure.

Almost next door are Winterthur and the Hagley Museum, and not far away are the Brandywine River Museum and Longwood Gardens. "We're surrounded by treasures and have everything right here," says Dan Lickle. "How could we miss?" *(302) 888-2133 or (800) 269-2473. Fax (302) 888-0389. Eleven rooms and 22 suites with private baths. Doubles, $160 to $180. Suites, $190 to $500.*

Whitewing Farm, 370 Valley Road, West Chester, Pa. 19382.

Overnight guests can partake of the good life in this stylish B&B fashioned from the former estate of the treasurer of the du Pont Company. Local contractor/ architect Edward DeSeta and his wife Wanda moved in 1992 with their three children and no intention of running a B&B. An innkeeper/friend who had overbooked called breathlessly one day to ask the DeSetas to put up her guests in their pool house. "All you have to do is serve them breakfast," Wanda recalls being told. "And I've been serving breakfast ever since." Mighty good breakfasts, we might add, to go with comfortable accommodations and elaborate common and sporting facilities that would do many a larger establishment proud.

Consider: A sprawling fieldstone and clapboard mansion dating to 1796 and four outbuildings transformed into seven private guest rooms and a suite. Forty-three acres of rolling property backing up to Longwood Gardens. A swimming pool with a jacuzzi, a stocked, twelve-foot-deep fishing pond, ducks quacking around lily ponds and a waterfall, a ten-hole chip and putt golf course, a tennis court flanked by a trellised pavilion, a greenhouse and showy perennial gardens for the growing of flowers. The DeSetas use a golf cart to transport guests around the property.

The family quarters are upstairs in the mansion, but the lovely downstairs is shared with guests. A knockout country kitchen with french doors onto a terrace was created from five small rooms. From it come the cookies and pumpkin bars that greet arriving guests, as well as gourmet breakfasts served on the terrace or in the formal dining room. Unfolding one after another are a paneled reading room with fireplace and TV, a living room full of substantial antiques and some of the couple's diverse collections, a huge beamed game room with fireplace, pool table, TV and even a small kitchen for refreshments, and a large sun porch overlooking the grounds.

Except for a spacious suite above the kitchen in the mansion, the accommodations are in four outbuildings, where guests are left pretty much on their own. After showing guests to their rooms, members of the busy DeSeta

Spring daffodils brighten pond area in front of Whitewing Farm.

family go their various ways, although they're up early for the breakfast hour that starts at 7:30.

Two comfortable guest rooms are in the converted stables, and three in the carriage house. Renovated for the purpose, each has a queensize bed (one is kingsize), modern bathroom (shower only) with marble floor, TV and a veritable library of books. They're decorated in a hunt theme with pale yellow walls, splashy fabrics and thick green carpeting.

Our quarters in the Gatehouse Suite included a skylit living room with a fireplace and sofabed, a book-lined den with one plush chair in front of the TV, a skylit bedroom with kingsize bed, a beauty of a bathroom done in marble with a bouquet of rosebuds (this in autumn) reflected in the mirror on the vanity, a modern kitchen and a terrace with a gas grill. We could understand why a Texas family considers it home during their annual six-week summer stay.

Two simpler rooms were fashioned from the former men's and women's changing facilities in the Pond House. The decor is garden style, the bed headboard is a picket fence and a patio with wrought-iron lounge chairs faces the idyllic pond, with its frogs croaking and its fountain lit at night. Recently upgraded, they now have built-in cabinets for the TV and marble floors for the bathrooms.

The DeSotas are not through. In 1999, they were about to add two guest rooms in another structure and a health club and breakfast room in an old hay barn. Ed had just acquired a 1930 Ford Model A sedan and a 1938 Ford pickup truck in which to taxi guests. These joined two antique carriages and two sleighs they keep in a new barn they built across the street. Ed was crazy about his new horse named "A Little Bit Tipsy," a companion for the cow his wife bought him for his birthday.

A cook prepares and the DeSotas serve a breakfast worthy of the site. Orange juice, cream cheese and raspberry coffee cake and made-to-order omelets were the fare when we were there. Ed sometimes gets so involved in conversation he forgets to serve. "We have guests who come here and never leave the property," says he. After a stay here, we understand why.

(610) 388-2664. Fax (610) 388-3650. Seven rooms and two suites with private baths. Doubles, $125 to $169. Suites, $195 to $259.

Fairville Inn, Route 52 (Kennett Pike), Box 219, Mendenhall, Pa. 19357.
Fortuitously situated in the heart of museum country, this luxurious B&B is now lovingly tended by Tom and Eleanor Everitt, New Jersey natives who gave up the life of corporate nomads in 1999. They took over a going establishment and started "putting our own stamp on it," in Tom's words.

Their first move was the addition of a hot breakfast entrée every day. In addition to the traditional fresh orange juice, cereal, yogurt and pastries, they offer a farmer's omelet, vegetable frittata or, the day of our latest visit, pancakes with strawberry topping, garnished with blueberries and pineapple. With breakfasts like this, they envisioned the need for a larger breakfast room, which they planned to create by expanding into the front office and reception area. Their breakfast cook also bakes the tortes and scones for afternoon tea, which is a culinary treat as well.

A private residence until 1986, the original 1826 house contains a spacious living room with a stunning copper table bearing some of the magazines displayed throughout the inn, the breakfast area with pink and white linens and copper utensils hanging about, an office/reception area and four upstairs guest rooms. "We want to move toward more of an English country manor look for the public rooms," said Tom.

The most choice accommodations are the ten out back in the Carriage House, built by an Amish family, and in a nearby barn named the Spring House. They were designed by the former owner's uncle, architect Rodney Williams, founder of Vermont's famed Inn at Sawmill Farm.

Each is the epitome of elegant comfort. Accented with barnwood, beams and occasional cathedral ceilings, eight rooms have gas fireplaces. All boast rear decks or balconies looking across three acres of fields toward a pond. Lamps with pierced shades cast pleasant shadows. All possess spacious full baths (ours had two vanities and a separate dressing area; the towels were thick and matched the decor), king or queen beds, oversize closets, unobtrusive TVs, phones, elegant country furnishings, crisp and colorful chintzes, and flowers from a prolific garden. Each of the two spacious suites has a balcony with wrought-iron furniture, a sitting room with a loveseat, and a bedroom with a kingsize canopy bed and two wing chairs by the fire.

(610) 388-5900. Fax (610) 388-5902. Thirteen rooms and two suites with private baths. Doubles, $140 to $180. Suites, $195 to $200. Two-night minimum most weekends.

Hamanassett, 725 Darlington Road, Box 129, Lima, Pa. 19037.
The 19th-century mansion and 48 hilltop acres that served as headquarters for the Lima Hunt is now a B&B run by a retired school teacher who has lived here since her marriage in 1949. Evelene Dohan, mistress of the manor and jack of all trades, offers huge common rooms and six comfortable upstairs guest rooms and a suite, all with private baths, sitting areas and TV/VCRs and most with oversize beds. All are quite spacious, nicely furnished in traditional, unshowy decor and impart a much-lived-in air. A two-bedroom suite comes with a formal living room.

Main 1826 house at Fairville Inn.

A two-room affair with two double beds and a living room would be a suite anywhere else, but because the rooms are "connected through an open archway, it is not a suite," Evelene insists with the precision of a school marm.

With the grace of an heiress, she goes about making her guests feel at home in this house in which she raised five children. There's plenty of home to enjoy: a formal living room/library with fireplace, where the shelves are stocked with more than 2,000 volumes; a cozier Green Room parlor with another fireplace outlined in Delft tiles; a huge, plant-filled solarium to end all solariums, and a majestic front loggia outfitted with lounge chairs overlooking the gardens. Guests stroll through the formal English boxwood gardens with statues of Psyche and Aphrodite and inspect the colorful flower gardens everywhere.

Elaborate breakfasts are taken at individual lace-covered tables in a chandeliered dining room open to the solarium. Evelene "studied at the Cordon Bleu, so cooking doesn't bother me." She prepares an extravagant buffet of juices, stewed fruit and melon, cereals, Virginia ham, turkey sausage, Philadelphia scrapple, creamed mushrooms with basil sauce and assorted pastries from croissants to sticky buns, all homemade except for the English muffins. A couple of hot dishes might be tomato-mushroom omelets and pancakes with raspberries from the garden,

Guests depart well-fed and restored, returning down the winding driveway pasts forests and gardens to Route 1, a half mile and another world away.

(610) 459-3000. Six rooms and one suite with private baths. Doubles, $100 to $125. Suite, $120 to $170. Two-night minimum required. No credit cards. Closed mid-July to mid-August.

Hedgerow Bed & Breakfast Suites, 268 Kennett Pike (Route 52), Chadds Ford 19317.

Massed plantings of impatiens brighten the facade of the handsome Victorian home that had been in owner John Haedrich's family since the 1950s. When John and his wife Barbara took possession in 1988, friends asked why they didn't open it as a B&B. With a "house full of kids," John said, it was more practical to use their rear carriage house instead.

The Haedrichs started modestly by offering two guest rooms sharing a bath in the air-conditioned carriage house, set well back from the road beyond a spreading sycamore that shades much of the back yard. They now use the entire carriage house, which looks like a small house. Upstairs are two rambling suites. Downstairs are a deluxe suite and common facilities, including an inviting parlor and a stylish dining room open to a designer kitchen.

We'd happily settle into the spiffy Longwood Suite, the latest ground-floor addition with its own entrance and screened patio, hand-inlaid cherry parquet floors and antique Victorian furniture made in Chester County. The entry hall with a floor of slate from Brazil opens into an elegant living room with a sofabed, a corner fireplace, a wet bar with mini-refrigerator and microwave, and french doors onto the patio. To the side is a large bedroom, lovely in white and pale green, with a kingsize iron and brass bed. At one end is an alcove with a writing desk and a marble-top bureau. At the other end is a smaller alcove with closet space and a vanity with wash basin. Beyond the living room is a two-part bathroom containing a whirlpool tub in one section and vanity in the other.

Upstairs, the original two bedrooms now form the Winterthur Suite with a sitting room, a queen four-poster in one bedroom and two twin beds in a sun porch. The Brandywine Suite has a sitting room, a queen canopy in the bedroom and an alcove with a twin bed.

All accommodations come with TV, phone and central air conditioning.

From her dream of a kitchen, Barbara has supplemented her original hearty continental breakfast with main dishes like bacon and eggs or baked french toast. The meal is served in the dining room looking onto a brick terrace and, beyond, a gazebo and fish pond.

(610) 388-6080. Fax (610) 388-0194. Three suites with private baths. Suites, $135 to $170 for two; $20 each additional. Two-night minimum stay.

Museums and Gardens

Because of their restaurants and gastronomic appeal, the area's favorite landmarks are of special interest:

Winterthur Museum, Garden and Library, Route 52, Winterthur, Del.

Four generations of du Ponts lovingly cared for this noted country estate that today combines art, history, beauty and learning. Henry Francis du Pont, collector and horticulturist, created an unrivaled collection of early American decorative arts, now on display in period settings in the vast mansion-museum, and a matchless 20th-century naturalistic garden. A research library and the new Galleries, with special exhibitions on two floors, also are open to the public.

For food lovers, it is at its best during the annual **Yuletide at Winterthur,** when the mansion- is decorated with Christmas trees, flowers and the appropriate foods of each era represented in the rooms. The tour focus is holiday dining and entertaining of the 18th and 19th centuries, as well as the ways the du Ponts entertained in the home they occupied until 1951. Interestingly, most of the food is so well preserved (some of it freeze-dried by the Smithsonian Institution) that it not only looks real but smells so, too.

Yuletide celebrations are recreated in more than twenty period rooms, from a parlor prepared for an evening musicale to a nursery ready for an infant's holiday christening. When we visited, the du Pont dining room was set up for Christmas meals as the family would have had them in the 1930s and 1940s. Other rooms are set for anything from a Maryland hunt breakfast to a late 18th-century tea party in Philadelphia and a 19th-century charity dinner in Manhattan. Several rooms are ready for the New Year's Day calling – an occasion when the ladies stayed home to entertain the gentlemen who made the rounds to call (the 300 or so du Ponts in the area continue the family custom to this day, our guide said).

If all this makes you hungry, stop after the tour in the Pavilion Cafeteria in the Visitor Pavilion, where breakfast and lunch are available in a large and handsome room, with floor-to-ceiling windows looking onto the gardens. A salad bar has just about everything you could imagine. The restaurant devotes one section to a fancy garden setting where afternoon tea and Sunday brunch are served.

(302) 888-4600 or (800) 448-3883. Monday-Saturday 9 to 5, Sunday noon to 5. Prices vary from $8 to $21. Yuletide at Winterthur: Nov. 17 through Jan. 2, reservations required, adults $13.

Longwood Gardens, Route 1, Kennett Square, Pa.

For years the 350-acre private preserve of Pierre S. du Pont, the horticultural legacy he left is the area's single most popular showplace. The year-round focal points are the Crystal Palace-type conservatories in which spring begins in January and the spectacle changes monthly through Christmas. How appealing they were on the blustery December day we first visited, brightened by 3,000 perfect poinsettias in red, pink and cream, unusually large and grown singly and in clusters. Outdoors after dark, 400,000 lights glitter in Longwood's trees and colorful fountains dance to music of the season. The indoor plants alone – from bonsai to cacti to impatiens to orchids – are so lush and spectacular as to boggle the mind as to what's outside the rest of the year, which, we discovered on later visits, is plenty.

Longwood's large shop is filled with items for the gardener – small pots of herbs, orchids, tiles, garden chimes, books, placemats and cookbooks, many with an herbal theme. Packets of Brandywine bayberries smell heavenly; tins of various sizes are decorated with flowers and horticultural notes.

Meals are available at the Terrace Restaurant (garden admission required). A formal, sit-down restaurant plus a cafeteria that can accommodate 300 at a time, it is done in fine taste, with walls of windows looking onto the gardens and black wrought-iron furniture on delightful dining terraces. The cafeteria does its own baking and boasts mushroom specialties, chili, deli sandwiches and local wines and beers. A separate line leads to the desserts, among them a luscious hazelnut torte and, at one visit, a celestial cheesecake topped with almonds, whipped cream and all kinds of fruit, including kiwi, in a decorative pattern. Lunch and brunch (and dinner on the nights the gardens are open) are served in the plant-filled dining room. You could start with double mushroom soup with pernod and tarragon, go on to wild mushroom salad, and for your main course have sliced tenderloin of beef with zinfandel sauce. Finish with a pastry or one of the Terrace sundaes.

(610) 388-1000 or (800) 737-5500. Daily, conservatories 10 to 5, outdoor gardens 9 to 6, to 5 November-March. Extended holiday hours in December. Adults, $12 ($8 on Tuesday).

Hagley Museum, Route 141, Wilmington, Del.

The aroma of fresh cookies emanates all year from the wood-burning stove in a typical worker's house, part of this fascinating restoration of the early mill community where E.I. du Pont started the du Pont Company as a gunpowder manufacturer in 1802.

Eleutherian Mills, the first du Pont family home in Delaware, is furnished to reflect the tastes of five generations of du Ponts. We particularly liked the basement keeping room, left as it had been furnished by Louise du Pont Crowninshield, who died in 1958. The formal dining room is remarkable for its scenic American wallpaper, a curious hand-blocked print with Spanish moss adorning trees around Boston Harbor. At Yuletide, it's set for a Twelfth Night celebration. A children's tea set with silver spoons is a highlight of the master bedroom in this house, which impresses because it feels like a home rather than a museum. (The French garden outside has espaliered fruit trees and organic fruits and vegetables – in season, it's not only beautiful, but also functional.)

In keeping with the period, the simple Belin House Coffee Shop on Blacksmith Hill offers sandwiches, beverages and homemade desserts daily from 11 to 4. With lemonade and a piece of pie, you can quite imagine yourself back nearly 200 years in time.

(302) 658-2400. Daily, 9:30 to 4:30, March 15 through December; same hours weekends and one tour at 1:30 on weekdays, January to March 14. Adults, $9.75.

Brandywine River Museum, Route 1, Chadds Ford, Pa.

This special place made famous by the Wyeth family is extra-special during the holiday season when you not only can gaze at paintings but watch an elaborate model-train layout, enjoy Ann Wyeth McCoy's fabulous collection of dolls, see a ram made of grapevines, magnolia leaves, cattails and goldenrod, and eat roasted chestnuts.

Inside a century-old gristmill with white plastered walls and curved glass windows are three floors of beamed galleries that make up a permanent repository of the works of artists inspired by the Brandywine Valley. The paintings of three generations of Wyeths – Andrew, who lives nearby, his father N.C. and his son Jamie – fill the second floor. The newly restored studio of N.C. Wyeth is a treasure trove for Wyeth fans.

An attractive cafeteria-style restaurant has bentwood chairs and little round tables on a floor of old paving bricks in a glass tower that affords a great view of the Brandywine River. It's open from 11 to 3, serving main dishes, salads and wine or beer. Try the Brandywine melt, an open-face sandwich of roast beef, turkey, coleslaw and swiss cheese. The ploughman's lunch brings sausage pâté, cheese and breads.

Museum volunteers put out a marvelous cookbook, named *For the POT* after the Jamie Wyeth painting of a chicken in a pot that graces the cover. It has unusual recipes, many calling for Chester County mushrooms, and several of the Wyeths have contributed their specialties. A raspberry meringue, called "Berried at Sea" from the Andrew Wyeth painting of almost the same name and sent by Betsy Wyeth, sounds out of this world.

(610) 388-2700. Daily, 9:30 to 4:30. Adults, $5.

Gourmet Treats

P.U.F.F., Rockland Road, Montchanin, Del., stands for Pick Up Fine Foods and means exactly that. Run by the sister of the owner of the Inn at Montchanin Village across the street, the delectable little food emporium occupies the restored du Pont Train Station, now listed on the National Register. Expect anything from quiche and dill tuna salad to brie in phyllo, blueberry-lemon bread, oatmeal raisin cookies – all the makings for a picnic or a take-home supper.

The main street (Route 52) of Centreville, Del., has several nice shops. **The Troll of Scandinavia,** 5808 Kennett Pike, makes up good sandwiches for $3.35 (small) or $4.95 (large) – one of the most popular is London broil. At one visit, chef-owner Hebba Lund's soup of the day was pumpkin-mushroom and the chocolate-hazelnut torte with raspberry filling looked delectable. We sampled the famous confetti cheese spread with carrots and celery and found it worth the raves. Next door, **Communiques** is a great card and stationery store with a difference – an interesting selection of gifts, a coffee stand where you can sip a sample or something larger, and special events from art classes to poetry readings. Across the street is **Wild Thyme,** an exceptional garden and gift shop.

In tony Greenville, Del., you can pick up a sandwich or salad at the deli at **Janssen's,** a fine, family-owned market catering to the carriage trade at 4021 Kennett Pike. We liked the Brandywine chicken salad sandwich on a hard roll and another chicken version with almonds and grapes in pita. Nearly adjacent is the **Wine & Spirit Co. of Greenville,** offering hard-to-find beverages.

Just a shopping complex away in 2 Greenville Crossing at 4001 Kennett Pike is **The Country Mouse Cafe** with a selection of more than 100 cheeses and pâtés. The original emphasis on cheeses and pâtés as been expanded to embrace breakfast and lunch items, salads to go, smoked Virginia meats and more in a pleasant cafe with seating inside and out.

Across the road at Powder Mill Square are more treats: **Brew Ha Ha!** (part of a local coffee and newsstand chain, with great pastries as well as fancy coffees) and **Einstein's Bagels** (countless bagels and more coffee). New at 3801 Kennett Pike is the **Brandywine Brewing Company,** featuring award-winning handcrafted beers and regional American cuisine in a casual brewpub atmosphere.

Worth a side trip is the hamlet of Dilworthtown, Pa., northeast of Chadds Ford, and Audrey Julian's **Dilworthtown Country Store,** chock full of American country crafts and folk art. It's been a country store since 1758 but took on its sophisticated form a decade or so ago. The owner shops craft shows to find unusual things – we fell for a tin wreath of sassy spotted cows with "Welcome" in the center and treated ourselves to an anniversary present.

Another worthy side trip is to the hamlet of Glen Mills, Pa., where across the tracks from the train station lies a good-looking Victorian building known as **Pratt and Company.** Inside, Joy Juliano and Margaret DeMarco display collectibles, gifts and period home furnishings in several rooms. The store closes for the better part of a week in early November to prepare for its special Christmas extravaganza, featuring handmade gifts reflecting the spirit of Christmases past. Gorgeous Christmas items (especially the stockings), pretty linens and dried flower arrangements abound.

Offbeat Gourmet

Phillips Place, 909 East Baltimore Pike (Route 1), Kennett Square, Pa.

This area is a center for the cultivation of mushrooms (about 80 mushroom growers are located within a 25-mile radius) and good place to find out about them is at Phillips Place, which offers a small mushroom museum, where you can see them growing at all stages. The museum has a new film, which it says justifies the admission charge, but unless you're really into mushrooms, you'll likely find it a letdown. The adjacent Cap and Stem Gift Shop offers gift items with a mushroom motif, from bumper stickers to neckties. The shop offers a variety of fresh mushrooms for sale and for mail-order. You also can pick up recipes for mushrooms and pamphlets about them. Did you know that mushrooms are high in potassium? Did you know they are 99 percent fat-free? Maybe you don't want to know all these things, but the complex is fun, anyway.

(610) 388-6082. Daily, 10 to 6. Adults, $1.25.

A Gourmet Mecca

Everything But the Kitchen Sink, 425 Hockessin Corner, Hockessin, Del.

For those with a devotion to things culinary, the best side trip of all is to Hockessin Corner and this incredible complex. It's located in a warren of old warehouse buildings beside the railroad track, just off Route 41 on Old Lancaster Pike. In 1977, Missy Lickle opened a small gift shop in two sections of onetime coal bins. Now she has more than 10,000 square feet to work with, which accounts for The Back Burner Restaurant and takeout operation, a cooking school and room after room of kitchenware, a fabulous array of china, MacKenzie-Childs and Lynn Chase dinnerware, cookbooks, gadgets, gourmet foods, paper goods, table linens and even adorable baby clothes. We've never before seen such an interesting and unusual selection in one place.

(302) 239-7066 or (800) 731-7066. Weekdays, 9:30 to 5, Thursday to 7, Saturday 10 to 5, Sunday noon to 4.

A Boutique Winery

Chaddsford Winery, Route 1, Chadds Ford, Pa.

Eric Miller explains why he started his winery in this location and why he expends much effort making elegant chardonnays that are finished in French oak barrels and retail for up to $29 a bottle: "Well, this isn't Disneyland, you know. We've got a lot of traveling connoisseurs who know their wines."

The area's first boutique-style winery, opened in a converted 18th-century barn in 1983, imports most of its grapes from vineyards in Chester County and elsewhere. Its production has increased ten-fold to 30,000 cases a year.

Eric, who comes from a winemaking family (his father owns Benmarl Vineyards in New York's Hudson Valley), and his wife Lee, author of a book about wine, live next door in a house whose image is imprinted on some of the labels that mark their bottles. Their expanding operation includes a private tasting room where they cater dinner parties. A meritage-style cabernet sauvignon/merlot blend called Merican is offered for $32. The winery bottles spiced apple wine ("good with ham," they say) and a sangria ($8.99). The Chaddsford white ($7.99) is great to accompany a picnic lunch on the winery's pleasant outdoor deck.

After hearing the Millers talk about their chardonnay ("it's a good dinner companion and keeps your mouth fresh for the food") and tasting it ("showing honey and vanilla in the nose"), we splurged and laid down a bottle for a special occasion.

(610) 388-6221. Daily, noon to 6. Closed Mondays in January-March.

Daffodils are sign of spring outside Black Bass Hotel in Lumberville.

Bucks County

Romance along the River

There's something very special about the Delaware River section of Bucks County, Pa., and neighboring Hunterdon County in New Jersey.

In both look and feel, from the sturdy stone houses to the profusion of daffodils marching down to the river in springtime, it's the closest thing this side of Great Britain to the Cotswolds we love. There's a welcome sense of remoteness and romance along the River Road, a narrow and winding route that thwarts fast-moving vehicular traffic and invites visitors to take to their feet. There are real country inns, both chic and quaint, and more good dining places than one has aright to expect. And there's the great river with its historic canal and towpath, which shapes the area's character and raises the rationale to laze along, whether by foot, bicycle or canoe.

We're obviously not alone in our love affair with Bucks County, a meandering mosaic of suburbia and seclusion stretching north from the Philadelphia exurbs almost to Easton. Places like New Hope, the artist colony, are wall-to-wall people on summer weekends. More to our liking is the scenic rivershed area stretching above New Hope to Upper Black Eddy, especially in spring or fall.

Consider Lumberville, Pa., for instance. It's so small that you can drive through in less than a minute and canoe past in a few, yet so interesting that a stroll through with stops can take a couple of hours. From our base at Lumberville's 1740 House, we walked the towpath down to Stockton and Phillips Mill, checking out inns and restaurants along the way as we rekindled memories of the British countryside (after all, the area was settled by the English Quakers and names like Solebury, Chalfont and Wycombe persist).

This chapter generally focuses on the strips of Bucks County and Hunterdon County along the river north of New Hope – and places within walking distance of the river. Thus we stress river towns like Lambertville, which has been revitalized to the point where "there's a restaurant for almost every family," according to one local foodie.

Because liquor licenses are limited, inns and restaurants without them – most of them in Hunterdon County – invite guests to bring their own wines. These can't make a profit on liquor, so to survive they have to be extra good with their food, explained one restaurateur.

And good they are. New restaurants are emerging to compete with the old, and several inns have outstanding dining rooms. At peak periods, dinner reservations often are hard to come by. Most inns require at least two-night minimum stays on weekends.

So book well ahead and prepare to relax. Here's a perfect place for a gourmet getaway, especially for anyone with an iota of British blood in his body and a bit of romance in his heart.

Dining

The Best of the Best

Anton's at the Swan, 43 South Main St., Lambertville, N.J.

Anton Dodel launched this fine establishment in 1990 in the Swan Hotel. The New York Times cited Anton's as one of the year's ten best in New Jersey, and it has earned high marks ever since.

Trained at La Bonne Auberge in New Hope and at our late favorite Panache in Cambridge, Mass., Anton is, in his words, spontaneous and eclectic. His short menu changes monthly. The one we salivated over mentioned entrées like steamed salmon on a tamarind-peanut sauce, sautéed lobster with apples and braised fennel, roasted pork loin with persimmons and wild mushrooms, and grilled rack of lamb with potato, apple and celery root pureé.

Starters could be an oyster and vegetable tart, a salad of duck with grilled figs and white beans, a wild-mushroom napoleon with spinach cream and grilled pork sausage with bacon and swiss chard. Polenta sticks fried in goose fat and sugar-snap peas might accompany the skillet-roasted beef tenderloin. "This restaurant is not for those who worry about butter and fat," says Anton. He makes his own butter and says it's much fresher than the norm.

Dessert always includes something chocolate and always a flan, but you might find a poached pear in caramel sauce or a cornbread pudding.

Wall of mirrors and paneling are backdrop for dining at Anton's at the Swan.

All this good eating takes place in a subdued room with paneled wainscoting, a wall of mirrors, hurricane lamps atop white-linened tables and windsor chairs.

Anton rebuilt the hotel's kitchen in order to produce a sophisticated menu and style, "one like a well-established restaurant in France." He cooks more casual fare for the Swan's popular bar, where some regulars eat four or five times a week on fare ranging from a grilled portobello mushroom sandwich or a potato and onion pizza to sautéed shrimp with scallions and yam salad or New York strip steak with scalloped potatoes.

If you want to try a sampling of Anton's high-end fare, consider his special prix-fixe menu, $38 for appetizer, entrée, dessert and coffee.

Anton's choice wine list is priced from the high teens to $140.

(609) 397-1960. Entrées, $23 to $30. Dinner, Tuesday-Saturday 6 to 10, Sunday 4:30 to 8.

Hamilton's Grill Room, 8 Coryell St., Lambertville, N.J.

Former Broadway set designer Jim Hamilton and his daughter Melissa opened this gem, hidden at the end of an alley in the Porkyard complex beside the canal and towpath. Jim, an architect who designs restaurants, installed an open grill beside the entrance and built the wood-fired adobe pizza oven himself. Chef Melissa has turned over the Mediterranean grill concept to executive chef Mark Miller, and Jim says the food has never been better.

Hamilton's created the option of grazing portions to let weekday diners try "a little of everything." Nearly half the entrées are available in standard and smaller portions (at about half the price). You might start with a fennel and roasted tomato soup, an arugula salad with apples, saga cheese and hazelnut vinaigrette or pan-seared scallops with sweet pepper pesto. Or graze with half portions ($10 to $15) of entrées like grilled tuna with capers and golden raisins, grilled salmon with a leek and seaweed salad and garlic-crusted rack of lamb.

The menu is similar but pricier on weekends, when the open grill yields things like a mixed grill of lobster, sea scallops and fish of the day, and seared salmon on a bed of coarse salt with ginger, red pepper and leek marmalade.

Our meal began with a menu standby, grilled shrimp with anchovy butter, and a crab cake on wilted greens and sweet red pepper sauce. Main courses were an exceptional grilled duck on bitter greens with pancetta and honey glaze and grilled ribeye steak au poivre with leek aioli. The oversize plates were filled with fanned razor-thin sliced potatoes and grilled zucchini and green and red peppers. The signature grappa torta and the grand-marnier cheesecake were fine desserts, and two biscotti came with the bill.

Patrons dine at a lineup of faux-marble tables in the mirrored grill room, beneath angels and clouds surrounding a huge gilt mirror on the ceiling of the Bishop's Room, around a changing decorative focal point in the dining gallery and, in season, outdoors around the fountain in the courtyard.

Hamilton's is BYOB with a twist. It serves its regular menu weekends at the Wine Bar annex, a small house across the courtyard for folks who want liquor service. In the main grill, the white wine we toted was stashed in a pail full of ice, and red wines and even water are poured in large hand-blown globes made locally.

Another Hamilton twist is nearby: the new Fish House extravaganza (see below).

(609) 397-4343. Entrées, $17.75 to $28. Dinner nightly, 6 to 10, Sunday 5 to 9. BYOB.

La Bonne Auberge, Village 2, New Hope, Pa.

"Four-star everything," report people who have eaten at this destination restaurant and consider it comparable to the best in New York or Philadelphia. Those doing the reporting happen to be from New York or Philadelphia, where they expect four-star dining and are willing to pay for it. Many of the people around New Hope aren't.

There's no denying the food. The restaurant "seems a strong contender for 'best in Bucks,'" wrote Bon Appétit magazine. "Chef Gerard Caronello, originally from Lyons, makes the kitchen sing. His gracious, soft-spoken wife, Rozanne, sees to things up front. It all translates into some very good French."

There's no denying the setting, either. The pretty stone house is surrounded by nicely landscaped grounds and formal gardens atop a hill at the edge of the Village 2 condominium complex (through which you must pass – and can easily get lost, coming or going). The contemporary, airy, wood-paneled dining room at the rear is gorgeous, its large and well-spaced tables dressed in pink and flanked by upholstered armchairs. Wines are stacked in a corner cabinet, windows look out onto the gardens, and salmon-colored napkins stand tall in twin peaks in the wine glasses.

Downstairs is a cozy hideaway bar that even some regular diners don't know about. Nestled in wing chairs in a candlelit corner, couples sipping after-dinner cognacs (at $12 and up a snifter) might think they've died and gone to heaven.

Count on spending upwards of $200 on dinner for two with a bottle of wine. The printed menu rarely changes. Except for melon glacé or avocado vinaigrette (both $10), appetizers start at $13 for escargots provençal. The three soups (tomato, cream of watercress, and leek and potato) are $10. So is the house salad. Big-spenders can go for beluga caviar ($60).

Skylit dining room is elegant at La Bonne Auberge.

Entrées are $35 to $38, except for grilled chicken dijonnaise, which is $30. The French classics (sautéed salmon au poivre, dover sole with a truffle-champagne sauce, escalopes of veal with morels, rack of lamb provençal and entrecôte of beef) are prepared to perfection, we understand.

Desserts are in keeping, and the wine prices sting, starting in the $30 range.

In addition to the regular menu, on Wednesday and Thursday evenings the chef offers a four-course, table-d'hôte menu with a limited choice for $55. It's considered quite a deal.

For more than twenty years, La Bonne Auberge has been doing very nicely with a loyal clientele that appreciates the best.

(215) 862-2462. Entrées, $30 to $38. Dinner, Wednesday-Saturday 6 to 9, Sunday 5:30 to 8:30. Jackets required.

The Frenchtown Inn, 7 Bridge St., Frenchtown, N.J.

The food is inventive and good, the service friendly yet flawless, and the setting comfortable in this elegant restaurant with a handsome grill room on the side. Young chef-owner Andrew Tomko, a culinary graduate of Johnson and Wales University, was executive chef at the Inn at Millrace Pond in upstate Hope for six years. He and his wife Colleen returned to their home area to buy this restaurant launched to wide acclaim by founding chef Robert Long. They retained the staff, cooking style and some of the menu favorites, and barely missed a beat. They live upstairs with their children, and hoped someday to fulfill their predecessor's plan to convert the third floor into a nine-room B&B.

Arriving for a Friday lunch without reservations, we found the front dining room with its planked ceiling, brick walls and carpeted floors full. We were seated in the more austere columned dining room in the rear, outfitted with pink and green wallpaper, crisp white linens and Villeroy & Boch china, two sets of wineglasses and fresh flowers on luxuriously spaced tables. Although we could have been happy ordering anything on the menu, we can vouch for an unusual and airy black bean soup, the charcuterie plate of pâtés and terrines (small but very good), the corned beef sandwich on brown bread and a sensational salad of duck and smoked pheasant with a warm cider vinaigrette on mixed greens. A layered pear-raspberry tart with whipped cream was a perfect ending.

A later visit produced a memorable (and reasonable) dinner in the white-linened Grill Room, where singles were eating at the bar and dinners options range from an oriental tofu stir-fry to a whole quail stuffed with apricot brioche. A salad of baby lettuces and goat cheese, an appetizer of crispy rock shrimp with wasabi and mustard oils, and an exotic cavatelli tossed with broccoli rabe and sweet Italian sausage were enough for two to share. With a raspberry sorbet for dessert and a bottle of Preston fumé blanc, we were well satisfied for less than $50.

That was barely half what you'd expect to pay for one of the remarkable dinners in the more formal dining venues just across the hall, where main courses range from seafood à la nage to filet of beef wrapped in puff pastry. Choices might include sesame-coated yellowfin tuna and jumbo shrimp a ginger-soy marinade, roast breast of organic chicken over a fricassee of mushrooms, spinach and lobster meat, and roast squab stuffed with westphalian ham over pumpkin risotto with baby tatsoi and red wine jus. The food comes from the same expert kitchen.

(908) 996-3300. Entrées, $21.95 to $27.95. Lunch, Wednesday-Saturday noon to 2. Dinner, Tuesday-Friday 6 to 9, Saturday 5:30 to 9:30. Sunday, brunch noon to 2:45, dinner 5:30 to 8:30.

Manon, 19 North Union St., Lambertville, N.J.

Dining here is reminiscent of the south of France, which comes as no surprise when you learn that young chef-owner Jean-Michel Dumas grew up in Provence. He and his American wife Susan gave a provençal name to the storefront charmer they have run since 1990.

An air of whimsy reigns, from the colorful exterior of burnt orange and blue-green with gingerbread trim to the ceiling painted like Van Gogh's starry night. With a relocated and expanded kitchen, there's more room for Jean-Michel to work his culinary wizardry. There's also an additional table in the intimate, 36-seat dining room in front, as well as a garden terrace with a few tables in back.

Jean-Michel, who was a chef at the Inn at Phillips Mill in New Hope, relies on fresh ingredients cooked simply and served in robust portions. The menu often starts with his trademark anchovy relish and an assortment of raw vegetables, the house pâté, escargots in pernod and salads of mesclun with warm goat cheese or watercress with pear, belgian endive, walnuts and roquefort. Soup of the day could be garlicky mussel or pistou.

Typical seafood entrées are red bouillabaisse, roasted monkfish with pernod and tomato fondue, and fillet of salmon on a bed of spinach with a lobster-mushroom sauce. Others include calves liver with a honey-shallot confit and bercy sauce, filet of beef with a duck liver mousse and madeira sauce, and rack of lamb with herbs of Provence. Desserts might be a classic crème caramel, tarte tatin, chocolate mousse, marjolaine or nougat ice cream with raspberry sauce.

The best deal is a three-course, prix-fixe dinner available on Wednesday and Thursday. The $22 tab is all the more pleasant because you can bring your own wine. Similar fare is offered at wallet-pleasing prices for Sunday brunch.

(609) 397-2596. Entrées, $18.50 to $25. Dinner, Wednesday-Sunday 5:30 to 9 or 10. Sunday brunch, 11 to 2:30. No credit cards. BYOB.

Church Street Bistro, 11½ Church St., Lambertville, N.J.

This space hidden behind Mitchell's bar has proved a launching pad for restaurateurs who moved on to bigger and better things. The latest is Patrick Given, who started here as sous chef under Europe-trained chef David Kiser, an instructor at the French Culinary Institute in Manhattan. Patrick took command a couple of years later and, consensus had it, the "new bistro cuisine" became even better.

Two areas separated by a divider sport a country bistro look with white-clothed tables, spaced nicely apart, and accents of copper pots. The setting is serene and the feeling authentic French. There's an outdoor courtyard for dining in summer.

The short dinner menu changes seasonally and offers some of the area's more interesting dishes, with an emphasis on low-fat preparation. Patrick employs organic produce, farmed seafood and hormone-free veal, poultry and beef for what he calls "cuisine du marché." Starters might include herb-crusted calamari over baby field greens with a lemon-balsamic vinaigrette and sundried tomato-basil pesto, grilled portobello mushrooms with gorgonzola cheese in a roasted garlic cream sauce, and a bouchée of duck confit with caramelized onion, kalamata olives and goat cheese.

Main courses range from grilled tilapia with fire-scorched red peppers, braised celery, kalamata olives and capers to grilled Australian sirloin of lamb with a roasted shallot lamb jus. Typical are grilled Atlantic salmon with tomato-coriander sauce, black pepper-crusted Chilean sea bass with shiitake mushrooms in a ginger-soy-mirin glaze and a cassoulet of red beans and stewed tomato with wild boar sausage, duck confit and garlic sausage.

Desserts might be warm apple tart with homemade vanilla ice cream, pumpkin cheesecake and ginger crème brûlée. The well-chosen wine list is affordably priced.

(609) 397-4383. Entrées, $19 to $25. Lunch, Wednesday-Saturday noon to 3. Dinner, Wednesday-Monday 5 to 9 or 10. Sunday brunch, noon to 3.

The Landing, 22 North Main St., New Hope, Pa.

The only restaurant right in New Hope with a river view is set back from the main street in a small house with windows onto the water and a brick patio around back. Christopher and Leslie Bollenbacher, owners since 1976, are known for offering the best and most consistent food in town.

Inside on either side of a quite luxurious small bar are two dining areas. The front room, welcoming in barnwood, contains booths and two tables for two with wing chairs at each. The rear room has picture windows overlooking the river.

Chef Matthew Levin offers riverside dining at The Landing.

The spacious riverside patio is the place to be in season, the length of which has been extended lately with the addition of patio heaters. It's brightened with colorful planters and umbrellas, dignified by tablecloths at night and made practical by an enclosed bar at one side. A gardener has obviously been at work around the exterior. There's equal talent in the kitchen led by chef Matthew Levin, a Culinary Institute of America graduate who trained at Philadelphia's renowned Brasserie Perrier.

The changing menu (which arrived in a picture frame when we ate there) is creative. Entrées range from peppercorn-crusted yellowfin tuna with curried carrot broth, sautéed red snapper provençal and Moroccan-crusted soft-shell crabs with curry turmeric sauce to grilled filet mignon of veal with mustard sauce and mustard-crusted loin of lamb with sweet tomato-thyme jus.

Typical starters are smoked salmon terrine with sweet corn salad and caviar dressing, escargots in puff pastry with hazelnut-garlic emulsion, steamed Nova Scotia mussels with baguette croutons, and Alaskan king crab and mango salad with pickled ginger.

Desserts are luscious: orange crème caramel touched with cinnamon and caramel, black and white chocolate torta with a tart raspberry pureé, and an extra-rich dark chocolate mousse terrine with a mandarin orange coulis.

The Landing claims to have the largest wine list in Bucks County.

(215) 862-5711. Entrées, $21.95 to $27.95. Lunch daily, 11 to 4. Dinner nightly, from 5. Closed Monday and Tuesday in winter.

Away from the Fray

Three highly regarded restaurants are a few miles removed from the mainstream, a bit "inland" in New Jersey.

The Sergeantsville Inn, 600 Rosemont-Ringoes Road, Sergeantsville, N.J. This historic restaurant was reopened in late 1999 after being closed for two years. Joe and Sandy Clyde closed their highly rated Clyde's in New Brunswick "to get out of the city" and take possession of an old favorite in the tranquil Hunterdon County countryside.

The landmark fieldstone building, where we enjoyed a memorable lunch many years back, appeals more than ever with a new culinary dynamic amid its intimate stone-walled rooms. It seats about 100 diners in a tavern, a couple of fireside dining areas on the main floor and a basement wine cellar plus – beyond and accessible only via stairs up from the wine cellar – the town's old ice house. To serve the last, the staff has quite a trek descending and then ascending from the kitchen.

Chef Joe is known for his game dishes. Sliced antelope steak with wild mushroom demi-glace, grilled filet of kangaroo with balsamic demi-glace, venison london broil, and pan-seared filet of wild boar dusted with cilantro and cumin were on the menu at our October visit. So was farm-raised ostrich. All were teamed with purple mashed potatoes and a root vegetable gratin. Other tastes were tempted by shrimp jasmine, pan-seared tuna with a wasabi ponzu, poached Atlantic salmon with roasted pepper pesto, and pan-seared breast of duck glazed with sweet soy and served with a vegetable wonton and a sweet potato cake.

Each entrée comes with a choice of mesclun salad, soup du jour or Joe's perfectly seasoned tomato bisque, which he considers his signature item. Those with hearty appetites can begin with carpaccio garnished with shaved locattelli cheese and drizzled with porcini mushroom oil, tuna tartare, gin-cured salmon over mesclun greens or a mozzarella stack alternating layers of tomato, red onion and roasted peppers.

Expect desserts like apple strudel, berries with sabayon and tiramisu. The tavern features a martini and cigar bar.

(609) 397-3700. Entrées, $16 to $25. Lunch, Monday-Friday 11:30 to 2:30. Dinner nightly, 5 to 10 or 11. Sunday, brunch 11 to 2:30, dinner 4 to 9.

The Harvest Moon Inn, 1039 Old York Road, Ringoes, N.J.

A handsome 1811 Federal stone house surrounded by five acres of landscaped grounds is the setting for some of the area's finest meals. Stanley and Theresa Novak moved here from New Brunswick, where he was executive chef at the acclaimed Frog and the Peach restaurant.

Stanley, who formerly worked at Brooklyn's River Cafe, is widely known for innovative American cuisine, presented in the architectural style. He seats 120 in two Colonial-style dining rooms warmed by fireplaces, and teaches cooking classes in his kitchen. At night, he offers both a restaurant and a tavern menu. His fans like the fact that both are available in either venue except on Saturday.

The regular dinner menu is short but complex and wide-ranging. Typical appetizers might be plantain and crab fritters with a mango salsa, lobster and mussel stew in a saffron broth and grilled lamb sausage with curried couscous. Among salads are bibb lettuce with peaches and figs in a creamy lavender-honey vinaigrette and julienned smoked salmon with baby red mustard greens, baby tatsoi and crisp wasabi sweet peas.

For main courses, consider cracked pepper-seared tuna with sweet corn and shrimp fritters, sautéed Peking duck breast with a sesame-crusted vegetable spring roll and crisp duck confit, grilled pork medallions in a cassis demi-glace and grilled beef tenderloin with diced portobello mushrooms in a sage demi-glace.

Desserts vary from banana and praline mousse charlotte to assorted sorbets with fresh berries. One extravagance is pistachio and milk chocolate roulade with pistachio crème anglaise and milk chocolate ice cream in a pistachio florentine cookie cup.

The extensive tavern menu offers salads, pastas, pizzas and sandwiches, some of which are repeated on the lunch menu. Wine Spectator has honored the wine list.

(908) 806-6020. Entrées, $21.95 to $28.95. Lunch, Tuesday-Friday 11:30 to 2:30. Dinner, Tuesday-Saturday 5 to 9:30 or 10, Sunday 1 to 8. Closed Monday.

The Cafe, Route 519 at Route 604, Rosemont, N.J.

Lola Wyckoff and Peg Peterson moved their little cafe from Lambertville to a general store dating from 1885 in Rosemont. They have a lot more room to offer "fresh food at its simple best," as their business card attests.

It's a casual, drop-in kind of place where the floors creek, the chairs tilt and the service, we found on more than one occasion, is somewhat laid-back. Shelves are filled with the cookbooks they use, plus items for sale like gourmet foods, Botanicus soaps and striking ceramics, some done by one of the waitresses. A case along one side displays cheeses, desserts and baked goods. Things get more formal for dinner when candles, cloth napkins and 1940s cloths are on the tables.

Stop in for a breakfast burrito or the Adirondack breakfast, muesli and a bran muffin, which "gives you the strength to climb mountains," says the menu. For a leisurely breakfast we found a couple of omelets – the Russian peasant (with caviar) and the cranberry and brie – worth waiting for. The addictive "potatoes from heaven" were grilled with olive oil, rosemary, garlic, onions and cayenne.

For lunch, we've enjoyed an excellent ham and black-bean quesadilla and a hefty turkey sandwich on whole wheat from a menu that included eggplant and mozzarella boboli, pasta with wild mushroom sauce and roasted red pepper ravioli with olive oil and garlic, most in the $6 to $9 range.

At dinner time, you can still find sandwiches and omelets as well as sophisticated entrées. Try rice paper-wrapped salmon with lime glaze, broiled flounder with sweet and hot Moroccan tomato sauce and preserved lemon, grilled lemon-thyme chicken with olive bulghur or grilled steak with balsamic glaze. Pasta choices might include pasta Wilhemina, named for the resident ghost, with chicken, broccoli, mushrooms and garlic, or fettuccine with lobster and corn in jalapeño cream. Mocha pot de crème and cranberry flan are popular desserts, and Peg's cheesecakes (maybe rum-raisin or espresso) are also in demand.

The Wednesday night ethnic dinners are a steal, generally $15 for three courses. The foods of Burma, Cuba and Belgium were scheduled in weekly succession at a recent visit. How about the Burmese offerings: coconut-chicken soup or split-pea fritters, chicken curry with lemongrass or gingered pork stew, and mango mousse or semolina cake with coconut? Here's a kitchen with reach.

(609) 397-4097. Entrées, $15 to $19. Open weekdays at 8, weekends from 9; dinner, Wednesday-Sunday to 9. Closed Monday. No credit cards. BYOB.

Seafood Theatrics

The Fish House, 2 Canal St., Lambertville, N.J.

Restaurant/theater designer Jim Hamilton's latest marquee attraction in his hometown is this one-of-a-kind food emporium transformed in late 1999 from an old factory beside the canal in downtown Lambertville.

The simple name is deceptive yet quite descriptive. It's a happening mix of seafood restaurant, raw bar, diner, gourmet food market, chef's table and sideshow on two floors around a central open kitchen. From the wraparound mezzanine, diners can watch the cooks at work as they feast on the likes of sautéed soft-shell crabs, slow-roasted salmon, oyster pan roast and whole fish of the day. That is, if they can take their eyes off the fanciful 50-foot-long mural depicting an underwater wedding on one wall or the waterfall cascading down another wall.

"We saw a niche market for fish in this area," said Jim. "This is the way people are eating today." He responded with a casual dining space with wooden tables and a diner-style counter on the main floor and a more formal, tableclothed setting upstairs. Other attributes are an extensive raw bar, a chef's table for ten off the open kitchen and glass display cases where "all our larder" from crab cakes and packaged meals to olive oils and condiments is for sale. The retail area also includes items from breads to flowers. Outside is a garden terrace for seasonal dining.

Lured back from the New York Yacht Club to oversee the operation was Paul Ripley, executive chef, who originally worked with Melissa Hamilton at Hamilton's Grill Room. His opening dinner menu was short but sweet. Starters were mussel-scallion soup, pan roast of the day, a raw bar selection and house-smoked salmon corn blinis with crème fraîche. Main dishes included grilled Scottish salmon with stewed white beans, seared tuna with cod cake and tomato broth, whole fish with aged sherry vinaigrette and lobster "any way." Herb-roasted chicken and T-bone steak also were available. Desserts were a fruit tart, bread pudding with vanilla caramel sauce and chocolate truffle cake.

(609) 397-6477. Entrées, $14 to $24. Lunch and dinner daily, 11:30 to 10. Retail shop open from 10.

Offbeat Gourmet

Loafers American Bistro, 10 Bridge St., Frenchtown, N.J.

A restaurant that specializes in all-American meatloaf normally would not be considered gourmet, but this one is. Loafers gives new direction and dimension to the genre. Consider: salmon and clam loaf topped with creamy dill sauce, turkey and stuffing loaf with mushroom sherry sauce, Tex-Mex loaf topped with salsa and guacamole, Greek loaf (seasoned lamb layered with feta cheese and egg-plant), jambalaya loaf (chicken, crawfish and sausage), Thai loaf (peanuts, walnuts, almonds and pecans with rice on sesame noodles), pecan and rice vegetarian loaf. You get the idea.

Rick Baxter started making different kinds of loaves for friends of various ethnic persuasions in New York, and the idea gradually evolved in 1996 into a basement bistro with a seemingly obscure name and theme. "People call us the meatloaf place and think we do just meatloaf," says Rick, who has a full-time chef. "But we do far more than that. Once people understand the concept, they realize how complex these loaves are and how much work and time they take."

We were intrigued enough by the concept, which extends to terrines and pâtés, to stop in for lunch. A cup of meatloaf chowder with an appetizer of country pâté (veal, calves liver and pork) with dijon and crostini was plenty for one. The other tried the Tex-Mex loaf served in a pita with salsa and a side of nut slaw with grapes, coconuts, walnuts and pineapple. They were so good that we ordered the jambalaya loaf and a sauerbraten loaf (marinated steak with a ring of mashed potatoes and stuffed with sweet and sour cabbage) to take home for dinner. The loaves aren't inexpensive ($7 to $10 by day, $10 to $13 or more for specials like cassoulet at night). Nor is that all you can get. There are little pizzas, pierogies and salads for starters; a couple of non-loaf entrées like Garden State veggie ring and rotisserie chicken, and addictive garlic-mashed potatoes, shoestring fries and sautéed squash with jícama for accompaniments. Desserts run to ambrosia crumbles, bread pudding, banana cheesecake, and blueberry and peach buckle. A dessert sampler of any three is $9.50 for two people.

Whether the concept will catch on, we don't know (Rick has started accepting mail-orders and applications for franchises). Nor do we know how often we'd want to eat here, although the funky decor could keep one interested for days. The place is full of artifacts, from an old Coke machine to weigh scales laden with bananas to antique photos on the walls. Check out the men's room, stocked with old barber shop and shaving accessories, and the ladies' room, a millinery fantasy. Rick and crew take Tuesdays off to redecorate. As with the loaves, there seems to be no limit to the possibilities.

(908) 996-0900. Entrées, $10 to $13. Open Wednesday-Sunday, 11:30 to 8 or 9; Thursday-Sunday in winter. Breakfast on weekends from 9. BYOB.

Wine Bars and Pubs

The Boat House, 8½ Coryell St. at the Porkyard, Lambertville, N.J.

In the old ice house for the porkyard is an elegant bar, where cocktails are served, fifteen wines are featured by the glass and the walls are paneled with old twelve-foot-high doors. Appetizers are no longer served, since there's full food service at Hamilton's Grill across the alley. Hamilton's and the Boat House team up to provide food and drinks at the adjacent Wine Bar on Saturdays. Here you might get a glass of Columbia Crest chardonnay for $3.50 or a Simi cabernet for $6. This is also is a good, albeit an expensive, place to pick up a bottle or two of wine for BYOB dinner in a Lambertville restaurant if the liquor stores are closed. Our Mouton Cadet white bordeaux and a Ridge zinfandel came to a cool $27.

(609) 397-2244. Open Monday-Saturday from 4, Sunday from 2.

The Swan, 43 South Main St., Lambertville, N.J.

This is another great place to have a drink and maybe a burger, a wood-grilled pizza, a cheese plate with apples or a few more elaborate dishes up to $15. The public rooms bear the theatrical stamp of designer Jim Hamilton and are filled with art and antiques collected by owner James Bulger. The main bar contains comfortable leather chairs to sink into and a greenhouse wall looking out onto a small garden with a fountain, which is spotlit at night. A pianist entertains on weekends.

You can't beat the prices: our two after-dinner stingers came to about $6. Wines are available by the glass, and there are some exotic imported beers and ales. The bar menu is fulfilled from 5 to 11 p.m. by Anton's at the Swan, the fine restaurant in the other side of the building.

(609) 397-3552. Grill entrées, $6.50 to $15. Open Tuesday-Saturday 4 to 1, Sunday 3 to 10.

Inn of the Hawke, 74 South Union St., Lambertville, N.J.

Two young sisters took over this oft-changing inn, formerly known as the Wilson Inn and later the Elephant and Castle, a short-lived English pub. Melissa and Doreen Masset made cosmetic changes to turn the huge first floor into what they call a country neighborhood pub, with a long horseshoe-shaped bar in the center room and a couple of dining rooms on either side. One looks onto an outdoor courtyard that's great for sipping some of the draught beers that are featured.

A short menu changes daily. It ranges from fish and chips and a ploughman's lunch to roasted pork loin and grilled strip steak. Upstairs are seven redecorated Victorian guest rooms, four with private baths.

(609) 397-9555. Entrées, $5.75 to $18.95. Lunch daily, noon to 5. Dinner, 5 to 10; late-night menu to midnight. Sunday, brunch 11 to 4.

Left Bank Libations, 32 Bridge St., Lambertville.

The newest drinking establishment in a town that zealously protects its licensees is ensconced on the ground floor of the restored Lambertville House. Owned and operated by the hotel, the upscale lounge is open to the public. Plush sitting areas and tables flank a copper-topped bar in a dark and intimate room with a rich library look. Seats on the ornate front porch overlook the passing street scene. The well drinks are top brands, and priced accordingly.

(609) 397-4745. Open Monday-Thursday 5 to 11:30, Friday and Saturday 3 to midnight, Sunday 3 to 11:30.

Dining and Lodging

EverMay on the Delaware, River Road, Box 60, Erwinna, Pa. 18920.

The culinary tradition at this charming country inn continues under the ownership of antiques dealers William and Danielle Moffly, who live on the premises. They and chef William Finnegan have maintained the inn's reputation for stellar contemporary American fare.

Dinner is served only on Friday, Saturday and Sunday nights at one seating, and is in such demand that usually you must book far in advance. The six-course meal costs $62, with little choice except among two entrées.

The main dining room has been enhanced by matching draperies and upholstered chairs. Our favorite is the small rear porch-conservatory, its tables for two set with white over fabric cloths and little electric candles bearing lamp shades. The room is narrow (a bit too narrow, we thought, since you could overhear others' conversations and the waiter's recitation of every course to every table). Also, a chilly evening was made chillier by the stone floors and the wide expanse of windows.

But not to quibble. The meal was one of the best we've had, nicely presented and paced. Hors d'oeuvre of smoked trout salad, sundried-tomato crostini and country pâté with green peppercorns were served first. After these came in order a suave chicken and leek soup, sautéed chanterelles on a saffron crouton, and a salad of boston and mache lettuces, garnished with violets and toasted walnuts and dressed with a fine balsamic vinaigrette.

Thank goodness all these courses were small, for we needed room for the main courses: tender lamb noisettes wrapped in bacon and topped with a green peppercorn butter, and Norwegian salmon poached in white wine, served with

Rear porch/conservatory dining room overlooks gardens at EverMay on the Delaware.

hollandaise sauce and garnished with shrimp. These came with thin, crisp asparagus from Chile, a mixture of white and wild rice, and sprigs of watercress.

A cheese and fruit course of perhaps St. André, montrachet and gorgonzola precedes dessert. Ours was a perfect poached pear, set atop vanilla ice cream, with butterscotch sauce, golden raisins and pecans. Yours might be a candied pear tartlet with crème fraîche and a dried cherry compote.

About twenty chardonnays are on the well-chosen, primarily California wine list, which contains some not-often-seen vintages.

EverMay is more than a memorable dinner. It's an inn with eighteen rooms (one named for Pearl S. Buck, longtime resident of the area) on the second and third floors, a newer loft suite on the fourth floor, and in a carriage house, cottage and barn. They are furnished in Victoriana, as befits the era when the structure became a hotel (the original house dates from the early 1700s). All have telephones, and many have queensize beds. Fresh flowers and a large bowl of fruit are in each room, and at bedtime you may find fruit, candy and a liqueur in a little glass with a doily on top.

Two new deluxe rooms in the barn offer kingsize beds, spacious sitting areas with Vermont Castings fireplaces, and baths with whirlpool tubs and separate showers. Another room in a cottage offers a cathedral ceiling and Vermont Castings stove.

A fire burns in the fireplace in the double parlor, and decanters of sherry are placed on tables in front of the Victorian sofas. Afternoon tea with watercress or cucumber sandwiches and cookies is served at 4 p.m. here or on the brick terrace out back.

Although continental, the complimentary breakfast is quite special, with orange juice, flaky croissants and pastries, one with cream cheese in the center. The pièce de résistance at our visit: a compote of strawberries, red grapes, bananas and honeydew melon, garnished with a sprig of mint and dusted with confectioners' sugar – colorful and tasty.

EverMay also has one of the strangest tubs in which we've bathed. It's in the carriage house and is, we assume, a Victorian number, with oak trim around the rim. It's narrow, so long that a six-footer can stretch out and so deep that you can barely see out. We would not recommend it for anyone with a touch of arthritis – it could take a crane to get you in or out.

We would recommend EverMay's cooking to anyone, however. It's so good that it could practically cure what ails you.

(610) 294-9100. Fax (610) 294-8249. www.evermay.com. Eighteen rooms and suites with private baths. Doubles, $135 to $350; two-bedroom suite, $340.

Prix-fixe, $62. Dinner by reservation, Friday and Saturday at 7:30, Sunday at 6:30. Jackets requested.

The Inn at Phillips Mill, 2590 North River Road, New Hope, Pa. 18938.

Depending on the season, hanging pots overflowing with fuchsias, wooden casks filled with all colors of mums or holiday greenery mark the entrance to this small and adorable yet sophisticated inn. When you see its facade of local gray stone, smack up against an S-turn bend in River Road, with its copper pig hanging over the entrance, you would almost swear you were in Britain's Cotswolds.

Inside, that impression is heightened, as you take in the low-ceilinged rooms with dark beams, pewter service plates and water goblets, and a gigantic leather couch in front of a massive fireplace, on which you can recline while waiting for your table. Candles augment the light from the fireplace, and arrangements of fresh and dried flowers are all around.

At our latest visit, two stalwarts – chef Richard Rohal and pastry chef Roz Schwartz – were back at their early stomping grounds. The classic French menu is short and to the point, the prices reasonable and the results comforting – often exceptional. A wild mushroom ragoût in puff pastry and a salad of goat cheese and roasted onions on frisée might be among appetizers. We started with a springtime special, Maryland crabmeat in half an avocado. It was indeed special, garnished with shredded carrots and black olives.

Main courses range from seared Chilean sea bass with choron sauce to garlic-crusted rack of lamb. We have never tasted such a tender filet mignon with such a delectable béarnaise sauce (and artichoke heart) nor such perfect sweetbreads in a light brown sauce as at our first visit. At our second, the sautéed calves liver in a cider-vinegar sauce and the filet of veal with roasted garlic and scallions were excellent, too.

A basket of crusty French bread (with which you are tempted to sop up the wonderful sauces) and sweet butter comes before dinner. Save room for one of the super desserts – once a lemon-ice cream meringue pie, about six inches high and wonderfully refreshing, and later a vanilla mousse with big chips of chocolate and fudge sauce.

Sometimes it is hazardous to bring your own wine. The host at a table of four next to ours was wondering where his bottle of Clos du Val had gone when we noticed the waitress on the verge of pouring it into our glasses. We caught her in time and reconciled ourselves to our modest bottle of California zinfandel.

Upstairs are four cozy guest rooms and a suite, cheerily decorated by innkeeper Joyce Kaufman (her husband Brooks is an architect who did the restoration of the 1750 structure). The rooms are usually booked for weekends far in advance. One has its own sitting room. Honeymooners ask for the third-floor hideaway suite, where fabric covers the ceiling. Most beds are four-posters or brass and iron and are covered with quilts. They don't advertise it, but sometimes the Kaufmans rent a cottage in back of the inn, and share their small swimming pool with house guests.

A continental breakfast (juice, flaky croissants and coffee) is delivered to your room in a basket.

(215) 862-9919 (dining) and 862-2984 (lodging). Four rooms, one suite and one cottage with private baths. Doubles, $80; suite, $90; cottage, $135.

Entrées, $16 to $26. Dinner nightly, 5:30 to 9:30 or 10. BYOB. No credit cards.

Golden Pheasant Inn, 763 River Road, Erwinna, Pa. 18920.

A more romantic spot than the large solarium of the Golden Pheasant is hard to imagine. Beneath the stars is an array of tables dressed in mauve and white, hanging lamps, green plants and ficus trees, planters of colorful flowers and tiny twinkling lights all around. The place is so dim that we had to ask for an extra candle to read the menu. The canal bank beyond is illuminated at night, and it's all rather magical.

Well-known local chef Michel Faure from Grenoble and his wife Barbara have refurbished the two inner dining rooms to the inn's original 1850s period, brightened with accents of copper pots, oriental rugs and their extensive Quimper collection from Brittany. The bar is in the front of the wallpapered main dining room, which contains a working fireplace. The inner Blaise Room claims hardwood floors, a beamed ceiling, recessed windows and exposed stone walls. The family live upstairs, and they have renovated seven guest quarters to offer "a taste of France on the banks of the Delaware," according to Barbara.

She has decorated the rooms with country touches, antiques and four-poster beds, one so high that you need a stool to climb up. We're partial to the main-floor suite with its private deck and a stereo set. Also popular is a cottage suite with a porch, a plump canopy bed, a sitting room, kitchenette and a newly added fireplace.

Overnight guests enjoy a rear patio beside the canal.

The geese along the canal don't end up on the menu, though pheasant often does, roasted and flambéed with calvados, shallots and apples. Michel, who worked in a number of well-known restaurants, including Philadelphia's Le Bec Fin and New Hope's Odette's, presents classic French fare rich with sauces.

Start with the pheasant pâté, snails sautéed in hazelnut-garlic butter, bay scallops sautéed with saffron sauce or Michel's acclaimed lobster bisque. Entrées vary from grilled tuna fillet with a tomato-basil-garlic sauce grilled filet mignon with béarnaise sauce. Lump crab cakes come with a light mustard hollandaise, and sautéed pork with a coarse dijon mustard and sage sauce. Cassoulet of seafood bears a lobster sauce. Roasted boneless duck might be sauced with raspberry, ginger and rum.

Desserts include cappuccino cheesecake, pecan pie, crème caramel, home-made sorbets and a specialty, Belgian white chocolate mousse with a raspberry coulis.

A three-course Sunday brunch is available for $18.95. Michel offers periodic cooking classes, followed by a sampling of each dish.

(610) 294-9595 or (800) 830-4474. Fax (610) 294-9882. Five rooms and two suites with private baths. Doubles, $95 to $125. Suites, $135 to $175.

Entrées, $18.95 to $24.95. Dinner, Tuesday-Saturday 5:30 to 9. Sunday, brunch 11 to 3, dinner 3 to 8.

Hotel du Village, 2535 North River Road at Phillips Mill Road, New Hope, Pa. 18938.

The French name is a bit misleading, since the chef-owner is Algerian and his hostelry is English Tudor in an early boarding-school setting. The dining room is in the former Lower Campus building of Solebury School and looks exactly like one in an English manor house, with a glowing fire at each end, a beamed ceiling, small-paned windows and a fine Persian carpet on the floor. Crisp linens, candles and fresh flowers add to the luxurious feeling.

Country French cuisine is the forte of Omar Arbani, who arrived in Bucks County in 1976 from Algeria by way of culinary endeavors in France, Denmark, London and Washington, D.C. Partial to fine sauces, he shuns nouvelle to provide "the kind of home-style country cuisine you'd find in the restaurants of Bordeaux or Burgundy on a Sunday afternoon," in the words of his wife Barbara, a former New Jersey teacher, who manages the dining room, bar and inn.

The menu seldom changes and prices remain among the more reasonable in the area. Favorite appetizers include escargots, shrimp sautéed in garlic butter, clams casino and mushrooms rémoulade, as well as lamb sausage, one of the few additions to the menu since we first dined here in the 1980s. Main courses range from fillets of sole richelieu and frog's legs grenouille to duckling montmorency with cherries and steak au poivre. Our tournedos Henry IV, with artichoke heart and béarnaise sauce, was heavenly. So were the sweetbreads financière, with green olives, mushrooms and madeira sauce. Potatoes sautéed with lots of rosemary, crisp beans and grilled tomato with a crumb topping were worthy accompaniments.

Bread was piping hot and crusty – grand when spread with the house pâté ($5.95 for a small crock as an appetizer). Moist black forest cake, crammed with cherries, and café royale were sweet endings to a rich, romantic meal.

The pre-dinner drinks were huge and one of us, who shall be nameless, ordered a bottle of Mill Creek merlot, which was ever so smooth. The trouble was he had forgotten his glasses and thought the price to be $20; when the bill came it was twice what he had expected. Moral: bring along your glasses.

Hotel du Village serves dinner by candlelight in the elegant main dining room, paneled in rare American chestnut pieced together from other sections of the building, in an adjacent room that was originally a sun porch and in a cozy bar. A new addition across the back houses a larger bar and a huge banquet facility.

Accommodations in twenty rather spare rooms in a converted stable in the rear reflect their boarding-school heritage, although all have king or queensize beds and air-conditioning. Guests enjoy continental breakfast and access to a pool, two tennis courts and pleasant grounds.

(215) 862-9911. Fax (215) 862-9788. Twenty rooms with private baths. Doubles, $90 to $110.

Entrées, $15.95 to $20.95. Dinner, Wednesday-Saturday from 5:30, Sunday 3 to 9. Restaurant closed mid-January to mid-February.

The Black Bass Hotel, 3773 River Road (Route 32), Lumberville, Pa. 18933.

The food has been upgraded and updated lately at the venerable Black Bass, an inn dating from the 1740s and every traveler's idea of what a French countryside inn should look like. The late Harry Nessler, founding innkeeper of the 1740 House just down the road, liked to recall how one of his guests, Pierre Matisse, told him that the Black Bass "looks just like the inns my father painted."

Lunch may be a better bet than dinner here because (1) you should take advantage of the fact the dining room with its long porch and a new ground-level dining terrace overlook the river, (2) the food can be inconsistent, although we've had both a good dinner and a good lunch here over the years, and (3) prices at dinner are quite a bit steeper, of course.

Wander around the dark and quaint old inn and look at all the British memorabilia collected by longtime innkeeper Herbert Ward, as well as the pewter bar that came from Maxim's in Paris. We enjoyed our lunch of New Orleans onion soup and the house salad. The soup, thick with onions and cheese, came in a proper crock; the crisp greens in the salad were laden with homemade croutons and a nifty house dressing of homemade mayonnaise, horseradish, dijon mustard and spices. Famished after a lengthy hike along the towpath, one of us devoured seven of the nut and date mini-muffins that came in a basket. The lengthy lunch menu ranges from omelet of the day to oven-roasted cashew-coated grouper with slow-cooked baked red beans and sautéed bananas.

The dinner menu is also extensive, varying from a vegetarian pumpkin stew with chiles, spices and grilled polenta to chargrilled New York strip steak with foie gras butter and a shallot confit. The Charleston Meeting Street crabmeat has been a fixture on the menu of years. Other possibilities include potato-crusted tilapia with the house smoked salmon beurre blanc, coffee-lacquered duck with pear-ginger chutney or veal shank osso buco. Start with a warm wild mushroom terrine or seared diver scallops with tasso and a fava bean cream. Finish with a brandy and ginger pear tart with crème fraîche, walnut pie with bourbon cream, or homemade ice creams or sorbets.

Lighted stamped-tin lanterns hang from thick beams in the various dining rooms, which are filled with antiques, collections of old china in high cabinets, and fancy wrought iron around the windows. The wood chairs look as if they've been around since 1740. It's a wonder they don't fall apart.

Upstairs are seven guest rooms sharing two baths and three suites, all with antique furnishings. Some have ornate iron balconies, upon which continental breakfast may be served overlooking the river.

(215) 297-5770 (dining) and 297-5815 (lodging). Fax (215) 297-0262. Seven rooms with shared baths and three suites with private baths. Doubles, $80 weekends, $65 midweek. Suites, $150 and $175 weekends, $125 to $150 midweek.

Entrées, $21.95 to $26.95. Lunch, Monday-Saturday 11:300 to 3. Dinner, 5:30 to 9:30. Sunday, brunch 11 to 2:30, dinner 4:30 to 8:30.

Lodging

Lambertville House, 32 Bridge St., Box 349, Lambertville 08530.

Lambertville's landmark hotel, which had been closed for eleven years, was grandly restored in 1997 in keeping with its place on the National Register. New Hope developer George Michael added contemporary amenities as he returned the four-story structure to its original luster. His wife Jan directed the stylish furnishing and decorating that helped the boutique hotel quickly win a four-diamond AAA rating. Son Brad became the innkeeper and set about attracting the high-end market, 70 percent of which turned out to be corporate.

The restored 1812 facade is a knockout, with a two-story, wrought-iron trimmed veranda along the stone front and the stucco walls above and beside painted beige with green and burgundy trim.

An elevator serves the 24 guest rooms and suites on the top three floors, each with marble bath and jetted tub/shower (the six suites contain double whirlpool tubs and separate showers). All but three classified as premium rooms have flick-of-the-switch gas fireplaces. Beds are queen or kingsize. Rooms come with a writing desk and a single wing chair, some with an ottoman. The formal furnishings are period antiques and reproductions. Touch-pad telephones with data ports, remote-control TVs hidden in armoires or in cupboards over the fireplaces, waffle-weave robes, granite-top vanities or pedestal sinks, Gilbert & Soames toiletries, make-up mirrors, hair dryers and bottles of San Pellegrino mineral water are among the amenities. Instead of a do-not-disturb sign, a stuffed pussycat hangs on the inside door handle with a little note to "put the cat out" to avoid being disturbed.

The six courtyard suites, two on each floor, are larger and have balconies overlooking the rear courtyard. The one we saw had a queen poster bed with an elegant quilt and a see-through fireplace serving bedroom and bath area, which Brad called "the tub room." It contained a large jetted tub for two and a wicker chair, and opened onto a balcony as well as a bathroom with a glass shower.

A complimentary continental-plus breakfast is offered in a quaint basement breakfast room designed to look like a French kitchen with tiled floor, tiled fireplace, original rafters and wall sconces. Quiches are added on weekends.

Behind the inn is a lovely, landscaped courtyard with a goldfish pond. Hibiscus was blooming in large pots here at our October visit. It's a popular place for breakfast or a drink in nice weather.

Two more guest rooms, retail shops and conference facilities are offered in a couple of buildings beyond the courtyard. The inn's main floor contains a reception foyer beside a stone wall, an elegant cocktail lounge called Left Bank Libations and upscale retail shops, including the Greene & Greene Gallery.

(609) 397-0200 or (888) 867-8859. Fax (609) 397-0511. Twenty rooms and six suites with private baths. Weekends, doubles $192 to $259, suites $272 to $299. Midweek, doubles $162 to $222; suites $232 to $272.

Chimney Hill Farm Estate & Old Barn Inn, 207 Goat Hill Road, Lambertville, N.J. 08530.

Three deer were grazing in the back yard one day we revisited this elegant retreat. "There are lots more," said Terry Anderson, owner and innkeeper with her husband Rich. "They ate every chrysanthemum and daisy off our porch this fall. We also have a brood of wild turkeys, rabbits and big fat groundhogs."

The animals are appropriate at this opulent manor house, sequestered atop a wooded hill beyond a high-rent residential area on the southeast edge of Lambertville. It was once a working farm, and the restored gardens put in by former owner Edgar W. Hunt, an internationally known attorney, are quite spectacular in season.

The inside of the house borders on the spectacular as well. Vacant when it was acquired by two aspiring innkeepers in 1988, they first put it on display as a designer show house.

The Andersons inherited most of the furnishings for the eight original guest rooms, which they have been enhancing ever since. All but one have king or queensize beds and plump seating, and four have fireplaces. Each is awash in splashy fabrics, all Schumacher or Colfax & Fowler. The smallest room has space enough only for a double bed and one chair. The rear Terrace Room is bigger with tapestry fabrics, kingsize bed, a large bath with clawfoot tub and its own balcony. We liked the looks of the Hunt Room master suite, where the covers and canopy on the step-up queen bed match the gently swagged curtains, and the sofa and the oriental carpet pick up the theme.

We also like the sunken main-floor sun porch, with windows on three sides and floors, fireplace and walls of fieldstone. Warmth and color come from ficus trees and the floral chintz that covers four wicker loveseats angled around a huge glass cocktail table. The splashy sun porch makes the attractive living room pale in comparison.

Breakfast is served by candlelight at six tables for two in the 1820 dining room that was the original room in the house (the wings were added by attorney Hunt in 1927). Terry offers fresh fruit, cereals and plenty of homemade pastries, from muffins with farm-made raspberry jam to croissants filled with fruit or cream cheese. Baked french toast is one of the additional treats on Sunday mornings. In the afternoon, port and cream sherry await in the butler's pantry, where tea, cider and snacks also are available. In each guest room is a "gift snack pack" with candy, goldfish and peanuts.

In 1999, the Andersons completed their long-planned expansion, joining a carriage house connected by a courtyard to a restored 1800 barn. The carriage house contains a party facility designed for weddings. Much larger is the barn, with a conference/board room and four luxury suites, each more showy than the last. Two on the main floor have queen beds, sitting areas with loveseats, TVs in armoires, corner gas fireplaces, guest convenience areas with refrigerator and microwave, and baths with bubble-jet tubs and body showers. French doors open onto small patios. Upstairs are two larger, two-level suites. One, named in French for Magic Night, has a see-through fireplace facing both a living room with TV and a bath area with a large whirlpool tub beneath a brass chandelier in the corner, a bathroom with two-person shower and a spiral staircase to a loft with a Shaker queensize poster bed and another TV in a cabinet. The crowning glory is Suite 4, otherwise known as "the Steam Room," with the same features but with mood lights in the jacuzzi and something called a stereo steam room in the shower. The surround-sound stereo or CD music lulls guests as they steam and bake.

On the grounds, the Andersons would planning to add some alpacas, llama-like animals from Peru, to "enhance the farm aspect."

(609) 397-1516 or (800) 211-4667. Fax (609) 397-9353. www.chimneyhillinn.com. Eight rooms and four suites with private baths. Weekends: doubles, $145 to $195; suites, $235 to $295. Midweek: doubles, $125 to $189, suites $157 to $195.

The Woolverton Inn, 6 Woolverton Road, Stockton, N.J. 08559.

Built in 1792 as a manor house by pioneer industrialist John Prall Jr., whose mill is nearby, this is an engaging B&B on ten bucolic acres – where curious black-faced sheep check out guests from a field next to the parking area. Its location off a country road, atop a hill away from the river, assures a quiet night.

Three energetic new owners from Chicago have infused the inn with personality and pampering touches, both of which had been lacking in the past. They also set about upgrading some of the existing accommodations and added five new luxury rooms and suites.

"We want this to be welcoming and to capitalize on our rural, farm setting," said Mark Smith, co-owner with two friends, Carolyn McGavin and Matthew

Verandas and ornamental trim mark facade of The Woolverton Inn.

Lovette. "We hope guests find less of a business feeling and more a sense of visiting friends."

The friendly trio immediately added featherbeds and Egyptian cotton sheets to the eight bedrooms in the main house, all now with private baths – the lack thereof had been a shortcoming when we stayed here a decade earlier. They also were adding more comfortable sitting areas in the rooms. Plush towels, monogrammed terrycloth robes, fresh flowers and bedside chocolates already were the norm. Letitia's Repose, made from two rooms that shared a bath, offers a jacuzzi tub, a king fishnet-canopy bed and fireplace. Two other rooms on the second floor are quite spacious and come with kingsize featherbeds. Eventually, the new owners plan to reconfigure five small rooms on the third floor into four larger rooms.

At our latest visit, two guest rooms in the Carriage House, where the owners also live, were being converted into a luxury suite with kingsize bed, sitting area with a sofabed beside the fireplace, whirlpool tub and a separate shower for two. It also has its own private garden, a showcase for Mark's green-thumb talents.

Expected to be ready for spring 2000 were two rear "cottages" – actually built to look more like rustic barns, a re-creation of the historic farm outbuildings on the property. Each contains two guest suites with fireplaces, telephones and whirlpool tubs. In the planning stage were additional rooms in an existing 18th-century barn.

Guests have the run of the grounds, a pastoral retreat far from road noise and protected from suburban encroachment. A large and elegant living room is where snacks are offered. The trio hoped eventually to host afternoon tea here.

The dining room is the scene of elaborate breakfasts, served from 9 to 10. "We all cook and take turns in the kitchen," says Carolyn. A quiche of onions, apples, Canadian bacon and gruyère cheese was featured the day of our visit, along with homemade muffins and "pineapple upside up" cake. Matthew's fruit dish of apple-blueberry streusel baked in parchment paper is a favorite starter.

As you depart, the inn's two amiable sheep, Betty and Pâté, will likely mosey up to the fence to bid farewell.

(609) 397-0802 or (888) 264-6648. Fax (609) 397-4936. www.woolvertoninn.com. Twelve rooms and one suite with private baths. Weekends: doubles, $115 to $275, suite, $250. Midweek: doubles, $105 to $190, suite, $180.

1740 House, River Road, Lumberville, Pa. 18933.

This new, built-to-look-old motel-type inn was among the first of its genre in 1967 and continues relatively unchanged, although it naturally has lost some of the personality imparted by its founder, the inimitable Harry Nessler, who was a presence on site and manned the front desk until his death at age 92.

Robert John Vris, the innkeeper's grandson, assumed ownership and kept everything the same, except for dropping the dinner service that helped make the 1740 House special for so long.

He continues to offer 24 spacious, individually decorated rooms on two floors overlooking the canal and, beyond the towpath, the Delaware River. And the place maintains its charms: Glass doors open onto your own brick patio or balcony. There are kingsize or twin beds, and real wooden coat hangers that detach from the rod. The chambermaid knocks on the door to turn down the bed and give you fresh towels. You can laze in a tiny swimming pool or paddle the canal beneath your room in the inn's canoe.

A complimentary breakfast is served buffet-style from 8:30 to 10 in a cheery, flagstone-floored garden dining room, where if it's busy you'll share tables. Guests help themselves to juice, cereal, croissants and a hot dish like scrambled eggs or creamed chipped beef, and toast their own English muffins or homemade bread.

This is a place to savor the peace and quiet of the river from your balcony or porch, to read in your room (there's no television) or in a couple of parlors, to meander up River Road to the center of Lumberville and walk the canal towpath or cross the footbridge to an island park in New Jersey.

(215) 297-5661. Fax (215) 297-5956. Twenty-four rooms with private baths. Doubles, $80 midweek, $125 weekends. No credit cards.

Isaac Stover House, 845 River Road, Erwinna, Pa. 18920.

A showplace. That's the way to describe this 1837 Federal-Victorian mansion on twelve acres facing the Delaware River. Two British-born New Yorkers purchased the property in 1999 from Sally Jessy Raphael. The radio-TV personality had opened it first as a frilly Victorian B&B, representative of the later third-floor added to the original Federal structure. She eventually closed the place, only to reopen it in 1995 after redoing the entire house to showcase the Federal period. Then she closed it permanently in 1997.

Along came Sooze Plunkett-Green and Jane Brinton, who tired of their careers in the entertainment industry. "We figured if we were going to be on stage, we might as well come down and make breakfast," said Sooze with her droll British sense of humor.

The house was virtually empty, and the partners spent nearly six months furnishing and redecorating. "We have finished the parlors and added our touches," said Sooze. "It's eclectic English decor, with a touch of whimsy – more like the English country home that we would live in." She was thrilled that among the first guests were "two fashion guys who said it was like staying in someone's home and not a stuffy inn."

Isaac Stover House occupies showplace Federal-Victorian mansion.

The women offer six guest rooms. Four on the second floor have private baths, one across the hall. Two on the third floor share a bath. The rooms were in transition from the times we had seen them, but they have queen beds, down comforters and decorative accents of ivy in one, birds in another.

The main floor remains a designer's dream, from the deep formal parlor to the rear porch outfitted in wicker, from the taproom paneled in pecan wood for lively happy hours and convivial breakfasts to the showplace kitchen with custom-designed "critter" tiles and a huge fireplace. From said kitchen, the innkeepers dispense a pot of tea or a glass of sherry in the afternoon and breakfast in the morning, taken at small round marble tables in the taproom. The sideboard holds "a spa breakfast" of juices, granola and smoked salmon. To that is added the choice of a full English breakfast, with eggs, sausages or bacon, mushrooms, potatoes and fried green tomatoes.

(610) 294-8044. Fax (610) 294-8132. Four rooms with private baths and two rooms with shared baths. Doubles, $125 to $195 weekends, $125 to $150 midweek.

Bridgeton House, River Road, Box 167, Upper Black Eddy, Pa. 18972.

The Delaware River literally is the back yard of this comfortable B&B, just beyond a landscaped terrace and on view through french doors and the third-floor balconies. Although smack up against the road, the onetime wreck of an apartment house built in 1836 was transformed by Bea and Charles Briggs and reoriented to the rear to take advantage of the waterside location.

A parlor with a velvet sofa looks onto the canal. Fresh or dried flowers, a decanter of sherry and potpourri grace the dining room, where breakfast is served. Following a fruit course (perhaps baked pears in cream or a fresh fruit plate) comes a main dish: waffles with strawberry butter, eggs roxanne or mushroom and cheese omelets. Fresh lemon breads, muffins and apple cake accompany.

Upstairs are nine guest rooms and suites overlooking the river. Each is exceptionally fashioned by Charles, a master carpenter and renovator, and interestingly decorated by Bea. Some have four-posters and chaise lounges. All have country antiques, colorful sheets and fresh flowers. There are telephones in all the rooms, and most have TV/VCRs. Our main-floor room included a private porch with rockers and lovely stenciling, a feature throughout the house, done by a cousin who also did the nude paintings scattered about.

What Bea calls Bucks County's ultimate room is a huge penthouse suite with a kingsize bed beneath a twelve-foot cathedral ceiling, a black and white marble fireplace, a marble bathtub, black leather chairs, a stereo/TV center, a backgammon table and a full-length deck looking down onto the river.

(610) 982-5856 or (888) 982-2007. Fax (610) 982-5080. Six rooms and four suites with private baths. Peak season: doubles, $169 weekends, $129 midweek; suites, $189 weekends, $169 midweek; Penthouse, $279 weekends, $249 midweek. Rest of year: doubles $119 weekends, $99 midweek; suites, $169 weekends, $149 midweek; Penthouse, $249 weekends, $225 midweek.

York Street House, 42 York St., Lambertville, N.J. 08530.

This large Georgian brick home was opened as Lambertville's first B&B in 1983 after it had been glamorized as a designers' show house. It wasn't the first time it had received wide publicity – the Massey Mansion was featured in 1911 in House and Garden magazine shortly after a local coal merchant had built it as a 25th wedding anniversary gift for his wife.

Today's visitors are greeted by an imposing brick mansion set back from the street with pillared verandas on the front and side, nicely restored by new owners Beth Wetterskog, full-time innkeeper, and partner Nancy Ferguson, an emergency room physician at a Trenton hospital. They bought the house unfurnished and have been gradually renovating the rooms and furnishing them as they go along. Amazingly, they did the plumbing and carpentry themselves.

Mercer tiles compliment the working fireplaces in the main-floor common rooms and an original Waterford chandelier glitters over down-stuffed furniture in the living room, where there's an unusual chaise for two that's so comfy that "once you get on you don't get off," Nancy advised. Besides the living room, guests spread out on the side porch overlooking the largest yard on the block, which was decked out in welcoming tiny white lights at our latest October visit.

Crystal knobs open the walnut doors to five large guest quarters. Three on the second floor have remodeled baths. Three on the third floor that shared two baths were converted into two rooms, each with private bath.

All with queen or kingsize beds, they are outfitted with TVs and telephones. Still the favorite is the second-floor front room with a lace canopy step-up queen bed, two wing chairs in the corner, an extra sink in another corner and – a startling sight in the bathroom – a free-standing toilet in the front bay window of what once was a dressing room. The partners were redoing in Victorian gingerbread a side bedroom with a wicker bed, window seat and a clawfoot tub in the bathroom beneath original stained-glass windows.

Signs in each room warn of a $150 fine for violation of the B&B's no smoking policy.

A full breakfast is served in the fireplaced dining room. Fresh-ground coffee accompanied croissant french toast the morning of our visit.

(609) 397-3007 or (888) 398-3199. Fax (609) 397-9677. www.yorkstreethouse.com. Five rooms with private baths. Doubles, $130 to $189 weekends, $95 to $125 midweek.

Gourmet Treats

River Road Farms, just up River Road from EverMay in Erwinna, Pa., is a complex of buildings centered by a picturesque red wood and fieldstone barn built in 1749. **Chachka,** an interesting food and gift shop in the barn, is chock full of crystal and porcelain, much of it from Portugal. The real draws here, though, are all the "food accents" and the wild and wonderful preserves and relishes made by owner Richard deGroot, the "Gentleman Farmer," who lives next door. From hot or sweet pepper relish to carrot relish to Colonial cranberry ketchup to pickled cocktail radishes (yes, radishes), the relishes cost $3.69 and up. Most of his preserves, plum-rhubarb with amaretto, pumpkin marmalade with rum, blood orange marmalade with cointreau, banana strawberry with framboise – have you ever heard of such neat combinations? – are in the $5.89 range for ten ounces. All are topped with calico bonnets so they make great hostess gifts. Pastas, sauces and condiments like a *very* hot Thai garlic sauce (opened for tasting – we nearly choked) are dotted around. Chachka also hosts outdoor festivals with seasonal food and entertainment on special weekends.

Open daily for tastings of its 100-percent vinifera wines is **Sand Castle Winery,** run by two brothers from Czechoslovakia, high on a hill above 755 River Road in Erwinna. Paul and Joe Maxian started with riesling and chardonnay before adding cabernet sauvignon and pinot noir. They lead tours through their underground wine cellar in a new building patterned after a 10th-century Czech castle. The tastings are unusual in that each wine is paired with a food that compliments it, such as cheese, chocolates, herbs and fruit. The 72-acre vineyard, largest in Pennsylvania, yields about 42,000 gallons of wine annually.

Across the Delaware River in Ringoes is **Unionville Vineyards,** 9 Rocktown Road. Riesling is its biggest seller among nine varieties produced from grapes grown on 26 acres. Cited as New Jersey's best winery by the New York Times, it's open for tours and tastings Thursday-Sunday from 11 to 4.

Lumberville General Store, River Road, Lumberville, Pa., is a true country store dating to 1770 and run by genial, laid-back proprietor Gerald Gordon. On jumbled shelves you can find anything from ketchup to chicken soup, with more upscale things like Perrier, Pennsylvania Dutch preserves, antiques and Crabtree & Evelyn goods. A post office is at the rear, upstairs is an art gallery and outside are bike rentals. At the deli counter you can get good sandwiches, soups, chili, vegetarian lasagna and pasta salads.

In New Hope, the **New Hope Cheese Shop** at 20 North Main St. purveys all kinds of usual and unusual cheeses, Tuscany toast with sundried tomatoes and wild onions, and cornichons to go with its pâtés. The smoked-salmon mousse is layered with spinach and topped with grape leaves and a fresh mozzarella roll has pepperoni or pesto sauce. **Taste of Honey** at 15 North Main St. stocks kitchen items, wine accessories, teapots, placemats and paper goods, cookie jars and whimsical gifts for those who have everything.

A special place for gourmands at 39 North Main is **Nice & Spicy,** which lives up to its name. Mike and Jennie Barkala, a pair of ex-engineers with a passion for cooking, offer 90 kinds of spices and herbs, more than 40 varieties of loose teas, imported organic pastas, grinders and mills, herbal wreaths, cookbooks and quite an assortment of dried fruits and nuts.

Gerenser's Exotic Ice Cream at 22 South Main dispenses exotica in such flavors as English mincemeat, African violet, Hungarian tokay, Swedish ollalaberry, Polish plum brandy, Greek watermelon, Indian mango, Jewish malaga and ancient Roman ambrosia. All ice creams are made on site, as they have been for more than 50 years. Next door is **C'est La Vie,** which styles itself as a "true Parisian boulangerie and patisserie" and offers an outdoor riverside terrace upon which to enjoy its specialties.

Across the river in Lambertville, N.J., is the **River Horse Brewery** at 80 Lambert Lane, near the Porkyard complex. This small microbrewery produces some highly regarded handcrafted ales and lagers. It offers a walking tour of its kegging and bottling operation, a tasting room and a shop with items for beer lovers.

At **Lambertville Trading Co.,** 43 Bridge St., "when we grind coffee, the whole street smells," says Dean Stephens, who ran the Black Bass Hotel for a time and started selling herbs and spices to the public and to many restaurants, whose chefs rave about them. Since then, he's added a cappuccino bar where you can sip mochacchino and sample a dessert (maybe a chocolate-cranberry tart or brandied apricot mousse) amid a selection of food baskets, cream cheese spreads for bagels, chocolates, preserves, cans of almonds and such.

Two very well-stocked wine shops on the New Jersey side of the river help you handle the BYOB situation at area restaurants. **Welsh's** at 8 South Union St. in Lambertville and **Phillips'** on Bridge Street in Stockton offer shelf after shelf of rare French and Italian vintages, plus wines from most California wineries (about 75 percent of Richard Philips's 20,000 bottles are from California, including those from every boutique winery we have ever visited or heard of and many we haven't). A good selection of whites is kept refrigerated in both establishments. Prices are fair and the staffs are well versed to help you choose. Welsh's also has an incredible selection of cognacs, armagnacs and single-malt whiskeys.

Of interest among the antique and shopping emporia centered around Lahaska are the **Cookery Ware Shop** at Peddler's Village, which claims the area's most extensive collection of cookware and accessories, and **Just Food by BrownGold,** Route 202, Buckingham. Chef Marc BrownGold, formerly at New York's Tavern on the Green, left Hamilton's Grill in Lambertville to open this prepared foods shop featuring smoked fish, fresh roasted deli meats, breads, baked goods, salads and entrées to go.

Bargain Gourmet

Rice's Sale and Country Market, 6326 Greenhill Road, New Hope, Pa.

For the benefit of weekend visitors, this famed market is now open Saturdays as well as the traditional Tuesdays. It's like no other open-air flea market we've seen, and provided a high point on one of our Bucks County expeditions. Amish specialties, fresh produce, seafood, meats, honeys, spices and kitchenware are available, but foods aren't the best part – the incredible bargains on quality merchandise are. We did all the Christmas shopping (Jantzen and Ralph Lauren sweaters, a set of knives, perfume, a watch and a pretty homemade wreath) that two hours and our checkbook would allow. Everything from fine luggage to Evan Picone apparel is offered. Many of the same purveyors and bargain-seekers come weekly to this great flea market, which has been going strong since 1860. It's located off Route 263 northeast of Lahaska (watch for signs).

(215) 297-5993. Open Tuesday and Saturday, 7 to 2.

Lineup of front verandas, a Cape May trademark, is on view from Mainstay Inn.

Cape May, N.J.

Two for B&B, Tea and Dinner

Victoriana, bed and breakfast inns, and dining par excellence. That's the combination that makes Cape May a model of its genre and draws visitors in increasing numbers each year from March through Christmas.

Cape May has shed its mantle as a long-slumbering seaside city that time and Atlantic City had passed by. Its potential was recognized in 1976 when it was designated a National Historic Landmark city, one of five in the nation – an honor it had shunned only a few years earlier. Now its Victorian heritage is so revered that Cape May celebrates a ten-day Victorian Week in mid-October, plus a week-long Tulip Festival, a Dickens Christmas Extravaganza, a Cape May Music Festival, Victorian dinners, a Victorian fair, and various inn and house tours. Most are sponsored by the Mid-Atlantic Center for the Arts, a community organization and promoter that launched an annual Cape May Food and Wine Festival in 1997.

The B&B phenomenon started here in the late 1970s as preservationists Tom and Sue Carroll restored adjacent Victorian landmarks into museum-quality guest houses, setting a national standard and launching a trend that has inspired the opening of more than 80 B&Bs locally.

Besides enhancing the Victorian structures in which they are housed, some of Cape May's B&Bs elevate the level of breakfast and afternoon tea to new heights – in formal dining rooms and parlors, or on the ubiquitous front verandas that are occupied everywhere in Cape May from early morning to dusk or later. The sumptuous breakfast and afternoon-tea ritual draws many couples year after year, and has resulted in publication of a number of Cape May cookbooks.

Where upscale B&Bs open, restaurants are sure to follow. "Our businesses attracted a clientele that demanded good food," says Nan Hawkins of the Barnard-Good House, whose breakfast feasts are the most lavish in Cape May.

Adds Dane Wells of the Queen Victoria B&B: "When my guests arrive, I tell them I know why they're here – for the food. Seven or eight of the best restaurants in New Jersey are within a few blocks of our inn."

Since the late 1970s, more than two dozen restaurants have emerged and, remarkably for a resort town, most have survived. Besides stability, many offer creative food and convivial ambiance. Some are small (make that tiny) and, lacking liquor licenses, allow patrons to bring their own wine. Prices, in many cases, are pleasantly lower than in other resort areas.

The result is that thousands of visitors come to experience the ultimate in bed and breakfast, tea and dinner in this, the culinary capital of South Jersey.

Dining

At peak periods, many restaurants are booked far in advance. Some of the most popular do not take reservations, which may mean a long wait for a table. Some also require a minimum of one entrée per person. Be advised that parking at many Cape May restaurants is difficult to impossible. Parking meters on the street gobble up quarters every half hour until 10 p.m. A few restaurants offer valet parking.

The Best of the Best

410 Bank Street, 410 Bank St.

A gumbo of New Orleans, Caribbean and French dishes, many grilled over mesquite wood, is the forte of this restaurant that consistently ranks as best in town in the annual New Jersey Monthly readers' poll. (The owners' companion Italian restaurant, **Frescos,** is next door and some reviewers think it's even better.)

Dining is pleasant on the recently enclosed garden courtyard, surrounded by plants, tiny white lights and Victorian lamps. If you can't eat there, settle for one of the narrow, vine-covered porches or the small, intimate dining rooms done in Caribbean pastel colors inside the restored 1840 house. Owners Steve and Janet Miller are theater-set designers, so both inside and outside are quite dramatic.

For appetizers, we passed up the menu's crawfish bisque, crab terrine and blackened sea scallops with rémoulade sauce for excellent specials of seviche and mesquite-grilled quail. After those, both our entrées of blackened red snapper with pecan sauce and yellowfin tuna in Barbadian black-bean sauce with a hint of sesame and ginger, served with crisp vegetables and rice pilaf, were almost too much to eat. We had to save room for the key lime pie, which was the real thing.

Patrons dine New Orleans-style on enclosed outdoor courtyard at 410 Bank Street.

Other favorite entrées include mesquite-grilled mako shark with chile-cream sauce, blackened catfish fillet in a lime-jalapeño sauce with bananas and tomatoes, Chilean sea bass creole, cajun shellfish gumbo file, sautéed soft-shell crabs grenobloise, grilled Jamaican filet mignon with twin island sauces and rasta pudding, and rack of lamb with the chef's own foie gras. A French-style roast is offered nightly.

For desserts there are chocolate-pecan pie with amaretto purée, triple-chocolate ganache with grand marnier sauce, hazelnut cheesecake with raspberry purée and a Louisiana bread pudding with hot bourbon sauce that's the best around.

Service is by knowledgeable waiters attired in tropical shirts and bow ties. With the Key West-like atmosphere and a menu like this, who'd guess that the chef, Henry Sing Cheng, is Chinese? Experts consider him the top chef in town.

(609) 884-2127. Entrées, $23.50 to $30.95. Dinner nightly, 5 to 11, May to mid-October. BYOB.

Waters Edge, Beach Drive and Pittsburgh Avenue.

Chef-owner Neil Elsohn and his wife Karen, the hostess, run this sleek, hotel-style dining room in front of La Mer Motor Inn. Neil graduated from the New York Restaurant School in 1985 with the highest marks in the history of school.

His contemporary American menu is so beguiling that, upon first discovering it shortly after the restaurant's 1987 opening, we canceled our dinner reservations elsewhere that night. Known for eclectic, bold and original cooking, Waters Edge has been at the cutting edge ever since. It won New Jersey Monthly's award as best New American restaurant in South Jersey in 1999.

The somewhat off-the-beaten-path establishment has winning ingredients – a well-tailored aspect of banquettes and booths dressed in white cloths with rose-colored runners and flickering votive candles, inspired cuisine, a select wine list, and an outdoor deck with the ocean beyond. We were impressed with our initial dinner: an appetizer of strudel with escargots, mushrooms, pinenuts and an ethereal garlic-cream sauce; abundant house salads with romaine and red-leaf lettuce, yellow cherry tomatoes, julienned leeks and a zesty vinaigrette; poached fillet of salmon with smoked salmon butter, lime and salmon caviar, and sautéed sea scallops with tomatillos, cilantro and grilled jícama, followed by key lime ice cream.

At a subsequent visit, we grazed happily through appetizers and salads, the one-main-course-per-person minimum having been dropped in favor of a $21 per-person minimum. The scallop chowder was wonderfully creamy, dotted with thyme and flecked with prosciutto, and full of scallops and potato. The spicy pork and scallion empanada with pineapple-ginger chutney, encased in a radicchio leaf, was a standout. So was the house green salad with three medallions of Coach Farm goat cheese and a suave balsamic dressing. We also relished the fusilli with grilled tuna, oriental vegetables and szechuan vinaigrette, and grilled chicken salad with toasted pecans, grilled red onions, mixed greens and citrus vinaigrette. A Silverado sauvignon blanc poured in oversize wine globes enhanced a delectable feast, capped by an icy grapefruit and champagne sorbet as a finale.

The entire menu is printed nightly. One recent evening's choices ranged widely from grilled tuna with blackened tomatillo salsa and lime crème fraîche to roast rack of cervena venison with port-plumped dried cherry sauce. The mixed grill was all duck: grilled breast, confit leg and grilled sausage, with coffee-grand marnier glaze. Desserts include a tangy lemon tart with strawberry coulis, chocolate molten cake with vanilla cream and berries, raspberry cheesecake with citrus anglaise, and bittersweet chocolate-walnut pâté with espresso and vanilla sauces.

In season, a lounge menu is offered in the spacious bar. The brunch menu contains some exotic choices. The meal is quite salubrious when taken on the outdoor deck with ocean beyond.

(609) 884-1717. Entrées, $23 to $32. Dinner nightly from 5, mid-June to Columbus Day; Wednesday-Sunday in off-season and weekends in winter. Closed January to Valentine's Day.

The Ebbitt Room, 25 Jackson St.

The intimate, candlelit dining room in the restored Virginia Hotel is elegant in peach and gray. Swagged draperies, crisply linened tables, art-deco wall sconces, potted palms and birds of paradise standing tall in vases enhance the setting.

Named for the original owners of Cape May's first hotel, the Ebbitt Room has become known for some of the best food in Cape May. In a town where restaurants get noisy and hectic, this remains an oasis of calm and professionalism, one worthy of owner Curtis Bashaw's aspirations for a small boutique hotel.

Dinner starts with exceptional, crisp-crusted hot rolls and an appealing choice of appetizers. Ours were an eggplant and gorgonzola crostini served with red onion pesto and a very zesty caesar salad, served on black octagonal plates. The roast cornish game hen was heavily herbed and rested on a bed of caramelized vegetables on a parsley-flecked plate. The filet mignon was served with a grilled three-onion salad and roasted potatoes. On another occasion we liked the shrimp margarita, flamed in tequila and served with avocado cream sauce and roasted tomato salsa, and the pan-roasted quail with grapes and green peppercorns. These came with a medley of zucchini and carrots, and potatoes shaped like mushrooms.

For dessert, we enjoyed an upside-down fig cake and pecan-praline cheese-cake. Others are a decadent Valrhona chocolate cake and crème brûlée. The good wine list leans to the expensive side. Service by young waitresses is graceful, competent and ever so solicitous. And the live music emanating from the piano bar with a side porch dressed in fancy wicker and flowers lends a glamorous air to this fine addition to the Cape May dining scene.

Although longtime chef Christopher Hubert moved on in late 1999, the tradition of top-notch, progressive American fare continued under his sous chefs, whom he trained personally.

(609) 884-5700 or (800) 732-4236. Entrées, $20 to $28. Dinner nightly, from 5:30.

Daniel's on Broadway, 416 South Broadway, West Cape May.
Meals here have been likened to dining in a private home, but with a difference. It's not your ordinary dining. Nor is it your ordinary home. The owner is a terrific cook, and the house is a beauty. Harry and Kristin Gleason saw this when it was a private residence and "it was "exactly what we wanted." In 1998 they opened it as a restaurant that captivated Cape May with its style and charm, winning honors as the best of the year, in the estimation of Atlantic City magazine. "Stunning in every way– food, atmosphere, service, everything," hailed the Philadelphia Inquirer.

Harry said he "wanted a change" after running his family's restaurant outside Valley Forge, Pa. The handsome house, which had been home briefly to Swallows restaurant some years earlier, suited his purposes. He built an addition onto the previous kitchen in the rear portion of the handsome yellow Victorian/Colonial house, which dates to the 18th century and is situated on a nicely landscaped lawn. Five diminutive dining areas on two floors seat a total of 95 amidst swagged windows, antique chandeliers, ornate six-foot mirrors, and splashy floral arrange-ments. Well-spaced tables are set with cream cloths, large stemware and shaded oil lamps. Framed French posters of different wines and liqueurs grace the walls of the main floor. Upstairs, a corner room comes with a colorful mural on the ceiling. A favorite is the rear room with rustic beams and huge Colonial hearth.

Chef Harry offers contemporary American fare, artfully composed and presented. Homemade breads – perhaps poppyseed rolls with onion and garlic and focaccia with herbs and caramelized onions – are paired with butter and an addictive lemon-dill-garlic-cream cheese spread. They stave off hunger as you study the menu. For appetizers, the chef might sear peppered ahi tuna with sesame aioli, scallion-infused oil and wasabi and accompany with vegetable confetti, or glaze coconut beer-battered shrimp with Jamaican rum and serve with grilled mango. The Tuscan salad is a tomato tower layered with mozzarella, prosciutto and basil, drizzled with balsamic vinegar and extra-virgin olive oil.

Signature entrées are grouper Charleston (sautéed with lobster, corn, leeks and plum tomatoes in a lobster-sherry sauce), duet of duck (caramelized breast and confit of duck strudel with a red currant and port wine reduction) and filet mignon (stuffed with stilton cheese, sauced with shiitake mushrooms in red wine and served with herb mashed potatoes and fried spinach. Other possibilities range from grilled opah and jumbo shrimp with creole cream sauce and polenta andouille sticks to Southwest mixed grill of spice-rubbed filet, bacon-wrapped pork tenderloin and grilled quail with roasted garlic sauce.   ·

Desserts are as delightful to look at as they are to taste. Chocolate lava cake in a ramekin, frozen grand-marnier soufflé and triple berry napoleon are sure winners.

(609) 898-8770. Entrées, $23 to $27. Dinner nightly, from 5. Sunday brunch 11:15 to 1:30. Closed in January. BYOB.

Union Park, 727 Beach Drive.

The restaurant in the 85-year-old Hotel Macomber, about to be condemned and the residence of a couple of ghosts, was revived in 1996 by new owners and gets great reviews. The ghosts turn up now and then in the kitchen and brighten and dim the crystal chandeliers in the dining room after hours, the staff advised.

Not to worry. A new spirit has been infused by Crystal and Charles Czworkowski. She was a hotel general manager and he an attorney in Boston, before they moved to the town where she had summered with her parents to buy and operate the 34-room beachfront hotel.

Although Crystal was manning the hotel's front desk at our visit, her heart is in the dining room beyond, a stunningly beautiful, high-ceilinged space evocative of the Cape May of the 1930s. The setting is cool and summery with white-clothed tables, white inlaid-tile ceiling, white crinoline covering the windows and cherrywood-backed chairs that innkeepers say are the most comfortable in town. Tables are set European style, forks face down. Service is in the French style, one server per diner delivering each course simultaneously to the entire table.

Chef Michael Giampa, formerly of the Striped Bass and Brasserie Perrier in Philadelphia, features contemporary fare and showy presentations. Buried amid the complexities of the dinner menu are three signature dishes named for the owners' young children.

Follow their lead and order the tenderloin of veal Casimir topped with lobster or Caskia's vegetarian ravioli of eggplant and sprouts. Other summer favorites are pan-roasted Alaskan halibut with an olivada broth, steamed breast of free-range chicken on a bed of crisp bok choy, and a signature roasted rack of Wyoming lamb with dijon herb crust, often presented wigwam style with asparagus spears perched over garlic-mashed potatoes.

Specialty appetizers are caramelized diver scallops with a coconut-cucumber salad and a light ginger dressing, pan-roasted European quail with a cherry purée, and a stratified parfait of smoked salmon and chilled lump crabmeat with crème fraîche and sweet red onions, two chives rising like antenna with a dollop of black caviar between.

Crystal makes the extravagant desserts, among them daughter Cezanne's apple cloud. Crisp phyllo squares hold sliced apples sautéed in port and brown sugar, flanked by a scoop of homemade vanilla ice cream and a pool of hot caramel sauce. Somewhat similar is a phyllo basket of bananas sautéed in dark rum. The triple chocolate terrine comes with a tangy raspberry-cranberry coulis and the warmed fallen chocolate soufflé with crème anglaise.

(609) 884-8811. Entrées, $24 to $28. Dinner nightly, from 5, Mother's Day to October. Closed weekdays in off-season and mid-December to mid-March. BYOB.

Pristine white dining room at Union Park is cool and summery.

The Washington Inn, 801 Washington St.

By far the best of the large restaurants in town, this has become even better with the new dynamic lent by David and Michael Craig, sons of the founders. And although it offers no lodging, the glamorous and atmospheric establishment has the feeling of an inn. Check out the upstairs ladies' room, which an innkeeper termed the nicest in the entire state. Beautifully decorated in florals, it has a window seat and fresh flowers on the vanity. The men's room is no slouch, but the map on the wall identifies old "Cape May, N.Y.," not New Jersey. Personal touches abound, not the least of which is the beautiful mahogany bar that founder Arthur Craig crafted for the lounge.

The attractive white 1840 Colonial plantation house is surrounded by banks of impatiens. Inside all is pretty as a picture. The Craig brothers redecorated, picking up the colors from their striking, custom-designed floral china. They seat 130 in five dining areas, including a candlelit wicker-filled front veranda done up in pink, a Victorian conservatory filled with greenery, dark and elegant interior rooms, and a romantic, enclosed brick terrace centered by a fountain trickling over an array of plants. Off a Victorian cocktail lounge is another enclosed, L-shaped veranda with more wicker.

Executive chef Mimi Wood's American/continental menu blends the traditional with the more creative. Start with her signature sea scallops wrapped in bacon, or perhaps garlicky escargots with tomato and fennel tapenade or a crab cake with a creamy roasted pepper sauce. At a recent visit, we liked the sound of her specials, creamy mustard scallop bisque, shrimp louis and grilled portobello mushroom stuffed with shiitakes, crabmeat and smoked gouda.

For main courses, she might stuff flounder with crab imperial and top it with a brandy lobster cream sauce, and pan sear sesame-crusted salmon with ginger-mirin beurre blanc and a dollop of wasabi. A sauté of shrimp and scallops tossed with tomatoes and garlic, served over pepper-speckled linguini, is called Jewel of

Provence. The grilled Kansas sirloin might be flavored with cambozola, roasted vidalia onions, cracked pepper and red wine reduction. The rack of lamb, rubbed with olive oil and herbs, is served with a pineapple-mint essence.

The menu ends with "romantic international coffees." Desserts could be frozen key lime pie, crème brûlée, strawberry napoleons and lemon-glazed cheesecake with raspberry sauce.

David Craig likes to show the 10,000-bottle basement wine cellar, which holds an inventory of 850 titles and won the Wine Spectator Grand Award. The wine list has a table of contents, includes a page of chardonnays, and offers a Virginia red and a Lebanese wine, with a number of offerings priced in the teens.

More than 300 recipes are published in the fine new *Washington Inn Cooks for Friends* cookbook. The Craigs also started Craig Bros. Lobster Bake Co., offering on-site clambakes for fifteen to 500. They were preparing one for 300 people on the beach at Atlantic City the October weekday we were last there.

(609) 884-5697. Entrées, $18.95 to $31.95. Dinner nightly, 5 to 10, May-October; Wednesday-Sunday 5 to 9, rest of year.

Tisha's, 714 Beach Drive.
This little winner in the Solarium Building juts out over the ocean beside Convention Hall. Pretty in pink and white to match the glorious sunsets beyond, it seems to be mostly big windows beneath a high ceiling, with close-together tables and a few art and floral accents on the walls.

It's a summery backdrop for interesting fare prepared by chef-owner Paul Negro, whose fisherman-father often provides the day's catch and whose mother, Tisha, persuaded him to open a restaurant in nearby Wildwood in 1988. He jumped at the chance to move into the thick of the Cape May scene, where he's been a seasonal fixture since 1995.

Interestingly, the menus change every two weeks and are prepared before the season opens. They're published in booklet form so you can check your dining date here to see what is offered that evening." What is offered in the way of three appetizers and eleven entrées from fortnight to fortnight doesn't seem to be repeated, making for a remarkable repertoire. In addition, several specials are offered nightly.

Terrific bread and excellent salads, one caesar and one tossed with balsamic vinegar, come with the entrées. At one visit, we enjoyed pork tenderloin with a dijon-caper cream sauce and clams aglio over penne pasta. An autumn dinner produced grilled lamb chops with mint sauce and grilled duck with raspberry sauce, each teamed with sautéed yellow and green squash, carrots, onions and roasted potatoes.

Tiramisu and an apple crisp with ice cream proved worthy endings and, a nice touch at our first visit, the chef sent out complimentary cordials of frangelico.

From lobster ravioli to scallops rockefeller, shrimp alfredo to grilled veal chop, profiteroles to strawberry fondue, the choices never fail to impress. Indeed, the guest reviews of local restaurants, as written in one inn's book at our latest visit, were decidedly mixed from one to the next. There was unanimity on only two: Tisha's and the Washington Inn received the most glowing reports, with nary a complaint about either. Now that's high praise.

(609) 884-9119. Entrées, $17.95 to $26.95. Dinner nightly, from 5. Closed Tuesday and Wednesday in off-season and November-March. BYOB.

Walls of windows yield ocean views at Tisha's.

The Mansion House, 311 Mansion St.
"Sorry we missed the last 143 years," said the sign hailing the arrival in spring 2000 of an upscale seafood restaurant. Perry and Susan Collier were transforming a Civil War-era summer cottage built after the original Mansion House, a huge Cape May hotel, burned in 1857. They own the popular Collier's Liquor Store at the other end of the edge-of-downtown block.

The Colliers added a dining porch and a modern kitchen to the small two-story house that now seats about 50 for fine dining. Keeping it in the family, son Aaron is the restaurant manager.

The menu was being finalized by chef Joe Lotozo, whose food we loved when he was at the old Bayberry Inn in a corner of the Congress Hall hotel. Later the first chef at the Ebbitt Room in the Virginia Hotel, he planned to feature "eclectic seafood" here in the traditional and contemporary American style.

(609) 884-0200. Entrées, $18 to $28. Dinner nightly, from 5. Closed January and February.

Budget Gourmet

Louisa's, 104 Jackson St.
Tops on everyone's list for value is this tiny storefront restaurant that packs in the cognoscenti, who covet its twenty seats despite the fact that for years no reservations were taken and long waits were the norm. Lately, reservations for the week were accepted starting Tuesday at 4 p.m. and were usually gone within two hours.

From a postage-stamp-size kitchen, Doug and Louisa Dietsch – he does the cooking, she does the managing and the desserts – offer some of the most innovative dinners in town. Formerly with the National Geographic Society, he has a natural touch for cooking and a rare way with herbs.

Feeling as if they're sharing their meal and their conversation with everyone in the place, patrons crowd together on molded plastic chairs of vibrant colors at hand-painted tables. Watercolors compete for wall space with photos of New Jersey Devils hockey players.

The changing menu, posted nightly at the door and deceptively simple in terminology, might offer curried carrot soup, smoked fish rillettes, and hot and spicy ginger-sesame noodles to start. Entrées could be soft-shell crabs, scallops with tamari and scallions, grilled salmon, grilled polenta with savory greens and grilled chicken with rosemary, but never a red-meat dish.

For dessert, how about plum cobbler, peach oatmeal crisp, chocolate-banana bread pudding or mango upside-down cake?

We understand that some people come for a week to Cape May and contentedly eat almost every night at Louisa's. It certainly makes it easier now that they can book their table in advance.

(609) 884-5882. Entrées, $11.50 to $17. Dinner, Tuesday-Saturday 5 to 9, March-October. No credit cards. BYOB.

More Dining Choices

Cucina Rosa, 301 Washington St. Mall.

David Clemans, who has a reputation as one of the best cooks in town, opened this authentic and popular Italian restaurant in 1993 after selling the John F. Craig House, his B&B of many years. Former lodging guests may have lamented his move, but locals applauded since they now get to share the fruits of his culinary prowess. "This is my last permitted insanity, according to my wife," says David, who named it for her late grandmother. Here he teams with his stepson, Guy Portewig, who's the chef.

"We take relatively standard southern Italian dishes and make them very carefully," says David. Everything is done from scratch, from the marinara and meat sauces to semolina bread.

Prices are gentle. Appetizers range from eggplant parmigiana to spicy sausage with peppers, onions and sauce. We enjoyed clams oreganata, the house favorite, and the shrimp rosa, wrapped in pancetta and baked on spinach and ricotta. That and the zesty seasonal salad made a mighty good meal.

Those with hearty appetites can choose from quite an array of main dishes, from seafood fra diablo to veal piccata or parmigiana. Widely acclaimed is the chicken portofino, stuffed with mozzarella cheese and Italian sausage specially made for the restaurant, rolled and baked with tomato sauce and served with spaghetti. Other treats are shrimp scampi and grilled lamb chops.

Desserts are David's forte. He makes fruit pies that change daily, lemon cheesecake and a rich chocolate cake. He also offers tartuffo, spumoni and some of the best cannolis ever.

The 64-seat restaurant is at a corner location along the pedestrian mall, with tables spilling out onto a canopied terrace in season. The interior decor is soft and romantic in rose and green tones, with candles flickering on white-clothed tables.

(609) 898-9800. Entrées, $12.95 to $18.95. Dinner nightly, 5 to 10, Sunday 4:30 to 9:30. Closed January to mid-February. BYOB.

Cabanas On the Beach, 429 Beach Ave.

"Upstairs/downstairs...together again," advertised this promising newcomer that took over the space long known as Restaurant Maureen in 1999. The beachfront establishment offers sophisticated dining upstairs and a downstairs bar with a blues/bistro menu. For years, the bar and restaurant had been separate – sometimes to the detriment of both. New owner Mark Beltz integrated the two floors, but retained separate themes. He divides his time between this and the Old Swedes Inn in Swedesboro, which he has owned for twenty years.

The place got off to a rocky start, but business picked up after prices were lowered to fit locals' – and vacationers' – pocketbooks. Executive chef Michael Wenal, a Johnson & Wales culinary graduate, offers contemporary American fare with a decided international accent.

The stress is on seafood, as in entrées of seared scallops with daikon radish, miso dashi, asparagus and soba noodles; seared tuna with coconut milk and red curry, cashew butter and lo mein noodles, and sauté of shrimp with tasso ham, black beans, wild mushrooms and plantains. Meat eaters are well served by roast moulard duck breast with port wine and plums, grilled beef tenderloin with balsamic vinegar demi-glace, and rack of lamb with pistachio-mint pesto.

Typical starters are scallop seviche with wilted green papaya, seafood terrine with green onion sauce and grilled quail with a vidalia onion-mango compote. Chilled jerked beef and chayote salad with guava fruit vinaigrette is a summer tempter, while scallop and goat cheese purses were offered in fall. Among desserts are a rich chocolate-espresso torte, pear-almond tart and crème brûlée.

The downstairs is billed as an art deco bar where blues musicians play nightly. It combines family dining by day with late-night music and food into the wee hours.

Meanwhile, Maureen and Steve Horn, who ran the upstairs (and occasionally both floors) for twenty years, planned to return from Long Boat Key, Fla. Always in the vanguard, they had their eyes on a contemporary fine-dining restaurant and martini bar in nearby Wildwood, which is said to have the best collection of 1950s motels in America. Maureen sees retro as hot, so planned to open there in 2000.

(609) 884-4800. Entrees, $19 to $28. Dinner nightly in summer, 5 to 10:30. Downstairs open daily, noon to 2 a.m. Closed Tuesday and Wednesday in shoulder season and Monday-Thursday in winter. Closed January to mid-February.

Frescos, 412 Bank St.

New Jersey Monthly magazine once sent two writers to cover what they said "may well be New Jersey's leading center of gourmet restaurants." What did they rate best? Frescos, with three and one-half stars of a possible four. That was one-half star more than their second-best rating, 410 Bank Street. Frescos has slipped a bit in the estimation of locals, but the reviewers' accolades keep it near the top, New Jersey Monthly determining it to be the best fine Italian restaurant in South Jersey in 1999.

Crayons are on the tables for doodling on the paper overlays that cover the white-clothed tables in the restored Victorian summer cottage run as an Italian restaurant by Steve and Janet Miller of 410 Bank Street next door. Faux-marble columns and unusual art involving three-dimensional fish accent the spare white dining rooms, where brown leather chairs flank tables that are rather close together. We prefer the narrow wraparound porch, its tables for two far enough apart for private conversations.

The pasta dishes are Cape May's most extensive, ranging from ricotta cheese ravioli with marinara sauce to shrimp with feta and tomatoes over homemade fettuccine. Friends who dined here rated at 9.5 on a scale of 10 both the linguini with white clam sauce and fresh littlenecks, and the fusilli with a sauce of tomatoes, anchovies, black olives, capers and garlic. Seafood and meat choices include grilled tuna with a smoked almond-basil pesto and yellow sundried tomatoes, grilled swordfish with a crabmeat-mushroom cream sauce, duck breast with mission figs and port wine demi-glace, and osso buco served with root vegetables.

We hear the key lime-cream-filled cannoli is even better than the signature dessert: a layered, rum-soaked sponge cake with imported mascarpone cream and grated chocolate.

(609) 884-0366. Entrées, $18.95 to $28.95. Dinner nightly, 5 to 11, April to mid-October. BYOB.

Peaches at Sunset, 1 Sunset Blvd., West Cape May.

Arguably Cape May's prettiest restaurant is this establishment with an offbeat name, derived from chef-owner George Pechin's nickname and its location at the head of Sunset Boulevard in West Cape May. "Peach" Pechin and partner Craig Needles started in 1983 with a small sidewalk cafe in downtown Cape May. Their debut as a gourmet-to-go cafe quickly evolved into a serious small restaurant, one that finally gained the space it deserved with this location.

A nicely restored Victorian house, striking in peach with green trim, holds Peaches at Sunset. Two small dining rooms are divided by a walnut-trimmed aquarium full of tropical fish beneath a stained-glass panel and a tropical design on the ceiling. Peach-colored napkins stand tall in wineglasses at each table. Dining is al fresco on a raised rear deck leading to a gazebo with a few pint-size tables.

Peach calls his fusion cooking Pacific Rim-influenced American cuisine. The dinner menu offers about a dozen entrées, among them avocado crab cakes with a Thai sweet and sour sauce, Chilean sea bass with an orange molasses and chipotle glaze, and grilled Norwegian salmon with black bean, corn and tomato salsa. Twin breasts of duck might be flavored with ginger and mango. The chef's favorite is his baby rack of lamb rubbed with a compress of garlic, kosher salt and thyme.

For starters, consider the creamy clam chowder that we once savored during lunch at Peaches Café or the signature roasted garlic served with mascarpone cheese on grilled sourdough bread. Other tempters are steamed New Zealand mussels in a spicy Thai coconut curry sauce and oriental chive pancakes with a rosette of smoked salmon, garnished with crème fraîche and salmon caviar. Finish with bourbon-pecan pie or crème caramel.

(609) 898-0100. Entrées, $18.95 to $25.95. Dinner nightly from 4:30, May-October; weekends rest of year. BYOB.

Lodging

Since bed and breakfast is so integral to the Cape May experience, we concentrate on a few of the more than 80 in town, particularly those with bountiful breakfasts. Most require minimum stays of two to four nights, do not allow smoking inside, and access is only via push-button combination locks installed in the doors. Breakfasts tend to be lighter in summer, more formal and filling the rest of the year. The Cape May ritual is for the innkeepers to serve – and often sit with – guests at breakfast, and later to help with dinner plans as they review the menus during afternoon tea or beverages. So integral is the food element that many inns keep logs in which guests write comments on local restaurants. Some of the reports are scathingly at odds with previous entries.

The Mainstay Inn, 635 Columbia Ave., Cape May 08204.
Mainstay owners Tom and Sue Carroll began the B&B movement in Cape May at the Windward House, now under different ownership, and purchased this showy Italianate villa in 1975. It was built in 1872 for two gentlemen gamblers and, says Tom, is one of the few Victorians in town that went through 100 years with no transitions. It later became a guest house run by a Baptist minister who never got rid of anything, and the collection is there for all to view.

Tours of the museum-quality inn are offered, lately daily from 11 to 1:30 (self-guided, $3 to benefit MAC) and sometimes more elaborately, four days a week at 4 ($7.50, when visitors join guests for tea). Except in summer, when iced tea is served on the veranda, tea time is inside and formal. The tea is served from a copper container and accompanied by cucumber sandwiches, cheese straw daisies, toffee squares, spiced shortbread, chocolate-chip meringues and the like.

The twelve guest rooms in the main inn and the 1870 Cottage next door have private baths, some with copper tubs and marble shower stalls, many lately upgraded with marble floors and Corian shower surrounds – but still in the Victorian style. The rooms are handsomely and formally appointed with lace curtains, stenciling, brass and iron bedsteads, armoires and rockers. The Carrolls constantly refurbish the antiques throughout and have amassed an important collection of Victoriana. The president of the National Trust said he has never seen "so painstakingly and lovingly restored and preserved" an historic house.

Across the street in the Officers' Quarters, an old World War I officers' house, are four luxury, two-bedroom suites with double jacuzzis, fireplaced living rooms, TVs with VCRs, kitchenettes and private porches. Outfitted in more contemporary style, the suites are designed for couples traveling together and for those who seek privacy. Modest antiques, stenciling, bright colors and plants "give a whole different atmosphere here than in the inn," says Tom. Guests in the Officers' Quarters have continental breakfast delivered to their rooms, since the Carrolls have their hands full serving elaborate breakfasts in the main inn.

They're still hands-on innkeepers, here daily for breakfast and afternoon tea. That testifies to their success as perhaps the nation's longest-running innkeepers – 30 years in 2000. "We don't know anybody who has done this longer," says Tom. Ever involved, he also heads the board of MAC, the ubiquitous Mid-Atlantic Center of the Arts.

In summer, breakfast is continental-plus, served buffet-style on the veranda. Other seasons it is formal and sit-down at 8:30 and 9:30 seatings around the table for twelve in the dining room. Strawberry french toast, chicken-pecan quiche, ham and apple pie, California egg puff and macaroni mousse are some of the offerings. Lately, Sue has been doing less with breakfast meats and more with fruits like banana-pineapple crisp, cranberry-apple compote, orange crunch and banana-cream coffee cake.

So sought-after are Sue's recipes for her breakfast and tea goodies that she has published eight editions of a small cookbook called "Breakfast at Nine, Tea at Four." It has sold about 25,000 copies.

(609) 884-8690. www.mainstayinn.com. Twelve rooms and four suites with private

baths. Doubles, $170 to $275 mid-May to mid-October and all weekends; $95 to $185 midweek rest of year. Officers' Quarters: $245 to $310, peak season and all weekends, $145 to $235 midweek mid-October to mid-May. Three-night minimum in season and most weekends. Officers' Quarters open year-round; inn closed January to mid-March.

Barnard-Good House, 238 Perry St., Cape May 08204.

Breakfasts are *the* claim to fame of Nan and Tom Hawkins, whose morning feast was judged the best in the state by New Jersey Monthly magazine.

Nan never serves plain juice. "It's blended with maybe strawberry or lime juice, sometimes five different kinds." That's followed by a soup course: perhaps fresh peach, blueberry or, in fall, a hot cider soup topped with croutons and whipped cream. In lieu of soup she might serve fresh pears poached in kahlua with sour cream and chocolate curls, or hot apple crunch with applejack brandy. Breads could be brioche, butternut squash rolls, potato biscuits or "dogbone scones," shaped by a dogbone cutter that Nan uses to make dog biscuits for all the dogs in her family at Christmas.

The main course might be shrimp and spinach roulade ("everybody oohs and ahs," says Nan) or a mushroom soufflé with goat cheese. Or you might have swiss enchilada crêpes filled with chili, chicken and tomato, with a side dish of corn pudding. How about ratatouille in cheese puffs with a side of bulghur with mushrooms? Or chicken and apple strudel with pistachios? Or a Norwegian ham pie with sweet-potato pancakes?

For dessert – "why *not* for breakfast?" laughs Nan – there might be applesauce spice cake, sour-cream brownies or brandy crêpes with homemade ice cream. The question struck a chord, for she and her family published a cookbook of 200 recipes called *Why Not for Breakfast?*

"I create as I go," says Nan, for whom cooking is a passion. She spends hours preparing for the next breakfast after serving the last. Guests dine family-style at a lace-covered table in the formal dining room. "My ego trip is seeing the joy of my guests in the morning," she says.

In the late afternoon, she puts out more goodies like chocolate-banana cake and lemon mousse in a meringue shell to accompany tea or beverages in the parlor or outside on the veranda.

Upstairs, the Barnard-Good offers five guest quarters, all air-conditioned and with king or queensize beds. They are arty and as eclectic as the kitchen repertoire. You might find a bed canopy topped by a straw coolie's hat and strings of wooden beads separating the rooms in the Hawkins Suite. Tom hand-painted a gold dragon on a dresser there, and climbing wisteria on the mansard-roof walls in the third-floor Daily Room. Little candies are in every room.

(609) 884-5381. Three rooms and two suites with private baths. Doubles, $110 to $175, mid-June to mid-September; $100 to $165, in off-season. Closed November-March.

The Virginia Hotel, 25 Jackson St., Cape May 08204.

Its gingerbread restored and its interior pristine, the Virginia, built in 1879 as Cape May's first hotel, was reopened in 1989 as what general manager Curtis Bashaw, son of the owner, calls a deluxe "boutique" hotel. Newspapers hang from a rack outside the dining room, and a pianist plays in the pleasant piano bar during the dinner hour in the highly regarded Ebbitt Room.

Upstairs on the second and third floor are 24 guest rooms that vary widely in

Virginia Hotel offers fine dining in elegant Ebbitt Room.

size and shape. Like the public rooms, they are furnished in a simple yet sophisticated manner, which we find refreshing after all the elaborate Victoriana one encounters in Cape May. On your way upstairs check the stained-glass window in the landing; a local craftsman spent a year looking for old glass with which to restore it.

Bedrooms are equipped with modern baths with new fixtures (a couple with separate glass-enclosed sit-down showers), telephones, and remote-control TVs and VCRs hidden in built-in cabinets. The restful decor is mostly soft peaches and grays. Room service is available, and terrycloth robes are provided. There are eleven standard-size rooms, eleven deluxe and two extra-premium at the front of the second floor with private balconies. Five come with a plush sofa and two upholstered chairs each, though one premium room with a kingsize bed has room for only one chair. The wraparound balcony on the second floor gave our expansive room extra space and was a pleasant setting the next morning for a continental breakfast of fresh juice, fruit, danish pastries and croissants, delivered to the room at precisely the time specified.

The front of the main floor harbors a pleasant library/parlor as well as the richly appointed piano bar, which opens onto a side porch furnished in fancy wicker.

Curt sees this as the prototype for other small luxury hotels that he and his father want to develop along the East Coast. For another example, check out nearby Congress Hall, dating to 1816 and once of the nation's largest summer hotels. It's now undergoing a multi-million-dollar renovation under Curt's auspices, to produce 100 renovated hotel rooms in 2001.

(609) 884-5700 or (800) 732-4236. Fax (609) 884-1236. www.virginiahotel.com. Twenty-four rooms with private baths. Doubles, $190 to $325 in July and August and weekends Memorial Day to mid-October. Rest of year, $135 to $275 weekends, $90 to $260 midweek. Three-night minimum weekends in season, two-night minimum midweek in summer and weekends rest of year.

The Queen Victoria, 102 Ocean St., Cape May 08204.

Dane and Joan Wells are among Cape May's original innkeepers and are among the few who still live on the premises. Over the years, they had much experience learning what their guests wanted in their lovely 1881 corner property that has twelve rooms with private baths.

They used that experience in 1989 to refurbish a Victorian house and a carriage house next door with eleven luxury suites offering the niceties that many today seek: queensize brass or iron canopy beds, sitting rooms or areas, mini-refrigerators, whirlpool baths, air-conditioning and television. They also are decorated in a simpler, more comfortable style than the Cape May norm, outfitted with Arts and Crafts-style furniture but still authentic, since Joan once was executive director of the Victorian Society of America. They're named after neighborhoods in London; Dane is partial to the Greenwich, which, "if all the good eating at the restaurants here gets you, has a gout stool."

In 1995, they renovated a property across the hotel and opened it as **Queen's Hotel,** an elegant historic hotel. It has eleven rooms with whirlpool tubs or glass-enclosed marble showers, TVs, telephones, in-room coffeemakers, affordable prices and more privacy. "Twenty percent of our guests have been looking for this kind of thing," said Dane, which he likened to a hotel's concierge floor. "It's for the person who wants historic surroundings without all the B&B trappings."

Now with the largest B&B operation in Cape May, the Wellses still aren't finished. Lately they have enhanced the bathrooms in the original house, some of which are in their third incarnation. These have been updated with large glass-enclosed showers, tile and marble floors, and marble-topped sinks for extra shelf space. Gas fireplaces also are being added where possible.

Each house has a living room, one in the original building with a piano and a fireplace and the newer one with TV, games and jigsaw puzzles. Pantry areas are outfitted with the makings for tea, popcorn, sherry, and such.

Breakfast is an event, offered in the splendor of Victorian dining rooms at each house. Always available are juice, fruit compote, homemade granola, homemade muffins and a basket of toasting breads featuring Wolferman's English muffins. Other options might be baked stuffed french toast with sausage patties, spinach or corn casserole, or baked eggs and cheese with curried fruit. Afternoon tea brings crackers and a dip, maybe blue cheese or salmon, plus cookies and brownies.

Eighty of the house favorites are compiled in "The Queen Victoria Cookbook," exceptionally good-looking and outstanding in its genre. The recipes, scaled to serve twelve, are geared to entertaining.

In 2000, the Wellses launched winter weekend dinner packages. Chefs from some of their favorite local restaurants prepared elaborate dinners for up to twelve guests in the inn's dining room.

(609) 884-8702. www.queenvictoria.com. Fifteen rooms and six suites with private baths. Doubles, $95 to $230; suites, $140 to $290. Lower midweek, November-March.

Manor House, 612 Hughes St., Cape May 08204.

This impressive, gambrel-roofed house with warm oak and chestnut foyer and striking furnishings seems almost contemporary in contrast to all the high Victorian B&Bs in Cape May. Guests spread out for punch, cider or tea in a front room with a striking stained-glass-front player piano or a library with two plush loveseats in front of a fireplace.

Innkeepers Nancy and Tom McDonald, who had stayed as guests here many times, considered the B&B a model and acquired it in 1995. They maintained the tradition of good food, and added a secluded lower-level room with kingsize bed, full bath and private entrance.

Upstairs are eight guest rooms and a suite, all now with private baths. They are furnished in antiques, with brass and wood king or queensize beds, handmade quilts and light Victorian print wallpapers. A third-floor suite stretches across the front of the house with a sitting area and a whirlpool tub by the window in the bathroom. There are handmade "napping" signs for each door knob and Nancy plays "cookie fairy" at night, stocking the cookie jar with treats, including her favorite chocolate chip-pecan hearts, every night.

The McDonalds serve sumptuous breakfasts, employing many of the former innkeepers' recipes. Among favorites are "asparageggs" (poached eggs and asparagus on homemade English muffins with mornay sauce), a corn and egg pie with jalapeño cheese and tomato relish, vanilla whole-wheat waffles, a french toast sandwich with raisin bread stuffed with cream cheese, apple crêpes and corn quiche. Juice, fresh fruit and sticky buns, a house signature, round out the meal. Afternoon tea time brings cheese spreads, bean dip, salsa, coconut-macadamia bars and chocolate streusel bars.

(609) 884-4710. Fax (609) 898-0471. Nine rooms and one suite with private baths. Doubles, $135 to $190, suite $220. Off-season, doubles $90 to $115, suite $150. Closed in January.

The John F. Craig House, 609 Columbia Ave., Cape May 08204.

This attractive Carpenter Gothic cottage has long been known for some of the best breakfasts in town, and owners Frank Felicetti, formerly a lawyer in Wilmington, Del., and his wife Connie continue the tradition. They live in the house, so are more involved than was former owner David Clemans, who was on hand to prepare breakfast but transferred day-to-day operations to his staff. David, who now runs the Cusina Rosa restaurant, left most of the furnishings for the new owners.

Blended coffees and teas are put out for early-risers at 7:30. Breakfast is served by candlelight at 8:30 or 9:45 in the attractive dining room with its lace tablecloth and scallop-shell wallpaper. There are always seasonal fruits on the table as well as homemade muffins and buttermilk coffee cake. The entrée, which comes out on a piping-hot plate garnished with fruit, could be anything from blueberry-stuffed french toast with ricotta cheese and almond flavoring to a bacon and gruyère cheese casserole to eggs with scallions in a ramekin. Homemade sourdough or dark molasses herb breads accompany. Frank does the cooking, while Connie serves.

She also bakes the pastries and goodies for afternoon tea, perhaps baked brie with almonds and brown sugar, oatmeal-preserve bars, almond cake squares or molasses-spice cookies. The couple gathered the recipes from their families.

The house, which comes in two sections, contains nine air-conditioned guest quarters. They are done in typical Cape May style, with lots of wicker and oriental rugs, lace curtains and elaborate wallpaper. Guests have use of the parlor and the requisite Cape May porches.

(609) 884-0100 or 877-544-0314. Fax (609) 898-1307. Eight rooms and one suite with private baths. Doubles, $85 to $165. Suite, $125 to $185. Closed January-February.

The Southern Mansion, 720 Washington St., Cape May 08204.
Cape May's largest and most elaborate mansion, the 30,000 square-foot Italianate villa known locally as the George Allen Estate is a showy small hotel in the making. Barbara Bray and Rick Wilde, newly wed and barely turned 30, poured sweat equity and millions of dollars into restoring the 100-room house built in the mid-19th century for a Philadelphia department store owner and occupying much of a two-acre square block in the heart of Cape May.

With 30 bathrooms, ten fireplaces, shiny Honduran mahogany floors, twelve-foot-high molded ceilings, cast-bronze chandeliers, 23 gold mirrors and 5,000 square feet of verandas and solariums, this was hardly your typical South Jersey beach house, as Barbara was quick to point out. Amazingly, the original furnishings, chandeliers and artworks were intact, many stored in the basement and ready to outfit ten more guest rooms added in a new wing.

Financing the restoration with house tours (daily at 1, for $10 and much in demand) and the backing of her father, a Philadelphia physician, Barbara opened in 1995 with the first of fifteen ample guest rooms on three floors of the main house. They vary widely but come with an assortment of ornate, step-up king and queen beds, televisions cosseted in armoires, gilt-edged mirrors and chairs, gold damask bedspreads and draperies, velvet recliners and settees, writing desks and telephones with modems. Some of the bathrooms are small with clawfoot tubs; others have huge walk-in tiled showers with seats. The sink in one room is installed right in the room between two halves of an armoire.

The larger, more deluxe rooms in a new wing are the ultimate with kingsize beds, some with fireplaces, porches and double jacuzzis. One we saw has a poster bed of honduran mahogany matching the floor, fabric draperies puddling to the rich wood floor, oriental rugs, a Victorian settee and a TV hidden in a carved teak armoire. The bathroom has a two-person shower with tiled fish designs and a marble seat. Most deluxe is a bi-level suite with its own solarium.

Beside the wing is an Italianate pool with columns and a waterfall.

The main floor has a catering kitchen, an enlarged solarium restaurant seating 160 for sit-down dinners, and a ballroom with six gold mirrors that "looks like Versailles," as Barbara envisioned it. The bright aqua and butter-yellow ballroom of the main house is now a parlor with sofas, tables bearing vases of long-stemmed roses and end walls of 23-carat gold-leaf mirrors reflecting into infinity. Beyond is a sunken solarium where a full breakfast is offered for house guests. Typical entrées are eggs Chesapeake with hollandaise sauce, strawberry-yogurt pancakes and three-berry belgian waffles. When we were there, it was set for a mouth-watering buffet lunch of crab cakes and salads for one of the corporate retreats to which the inn caters. Afternoon tea and wine and cheese with crudités are served in the parlor later in the day.

Sometime in 2000, Barbara planned a full-service restaurant for house guests in the enlarged solarium. Already, chef Brian Parker was preparing prix-fixe dinners on Saturday nights ($65 for four courses). The fare included lobster bisque or coconut shrimp with mango salsa, caesar salad, and perhaps lobster alfredo, jerked red snapper, filet of beef or grilled veal chop."

"We'll offer the amenities of a hotel but retain the antiques and charm of a B&B," said Barbara, now a mother of two and relieved of day-to-day operations by a general manager. Then, with a sweep of her arm as she surveyed the nearly completed scene, she added: "We did it. I mean, we really did it."

(609) 884-7171 or (800) 381-3888. Fax (609) 898-0492. Twenty-four rooms and one suite with private baths. Summer and weekends off-season: doubles, $200 to $305, suite $325 to $360. Off-season: doubles, $190 to $285 weekends, $140 to $275 midweek. Suite, $300 to $325 weekends, $265 to $290 midweek. Two-night minimum weekdays and three nights weekends in July and August. Two-night minimum weekends rest of year.

Gourmet Treats

As the restaurant capital of New Jersey, according to the New York Times, this seaside town now hosts the annual **Cape May Food and Wine Festival** the last week in September. Sponsored by the Mid-Atlantic Center for the Arts, it involves three days of dine-around dinners, food tastings, a lobster bake, seminars and cooking classes, featuring signature dishes from leading local restaurants. There's even a "restaurant relay." Teams from local restaurants race against the clock and each other to determine who sets the fastest table, folds the fanciest napkin and delivers a cocktail through an obstacle course without spilling a drop. A highlight is a three-hour, self-guided tour of eight selected restaurants, in which participants get to taste house specialties (300 tickets available at $20). The Chefs' Dine-Arounds are like progressive dinners and wine tastings, with each of five courses at a different restaurant, and a different combination of restaurants available each night (tickets $85, including trolley shuttle). One night is a lobster bake in Convention Hall

Traditionally, Cape May always seemed to be strangely lacking in specialty-food shops, and our informant at the Visitor Center said someone would make a killing by opening one. Happily, Rhona Craig of the Washington Inn satisfied some of the need. Her **Love the Cook & Company** is an incredible gourmet store and cook shop at 408 Washington St. Mall. Even in expanded quarters, it's so chock full of more than 10,000 kitchen items that browsers can barely get by on a busy day. From gadgets to cookbooks to dishware to olive oils and a few specialty foods, you can find it here.

For an extensive selection of wines to carry to the BYOB restaurants, most visitors head for **Collier's Liquor Store** at 202 Jackson St., just north of the Washington Street Mall.

La Patisserie, 524 Washington Mall, is the place for lovely fruit tarts, many breads and all kinds of sweets from chocolate croissants to raspberry puffs and cranberry squares.

Mon Frère French Bakery, 315 Ocean St., next to the Acme Market in the Victoria Village shopping plaza, isn't much to look at, but the breads are baked on the premises. Everything from boules and baguettes to fruit tarts is first-rate.

What's a beach town without saltwater taffy? **Fralinger's,** the original taffy emporium from Atlantic City, opened a Victorian candy store at 324 Washington St. Mall. Although we're not into fudge and taffy, we're certainly impressed by its elegant fixtures and wallpaper borders. The same block of the mall also offers **Laura's Fudge** and **Morrow's Nut House & Fudge.**

For the ultimate omelet, head for **McGlade's,** a small restaurant with a large deck practically over the ocean (from which on some days you can watch dolphins playing). If you can face lunch after a mammoth plate full of the Uncle Tuse's omelet (with about a pound of bacon, tomatoes and sharp cheddar) plus a load of delicious homefries ($7.50) or the shrimp and garlic omelet ($8.95), you have more of an appetite than we do (we can't even eat an omelet each here, so choose one to share). We know some Cape May innkeepers who love McGlade's for dinner (entrées $13 to $18.95 – BYOB). It's on the pier beside Convention Hall, just behind Morrow's Nut House.

For shopping, we always check out the **Whale's Tale** at 312 Washington St. Mall. A gift shop extraordinaire, it purveys everything from gourmet cookware and nifty coffee mugs to shell magnets and an outstanding collection of cards and children's items.

Our last stop on the way out of town is always the **Lobster House Fish Market** at Fisherman's Wharf. Among the largest enterprises around, this includes a restaurant that does one of the highest volumes in the nation, an outdoor raw bar, a moored schooner for lunches and cocktails in season, a takeout counter and one of the best seafood markets we have seen. We drool over the exotic varieties of fresh fish, which can be packed in ice to travel. We like to take home items like snapper-turtle soup, lump crabmeat, oysters rockefeller or clam pies to remember Cape May by.

Tea Time

The Twinings Tearoom, 1048 Washington St.

Think tea and, at least in Cape May, thoughts turn to the Victorian era and B&Bs. So the Mid-Atlantic Center for the Arts, the epicenter of all things cultural and promotional in Cape May, decided to take advantage.

Twining's Teas furnished the teapots for the first exhibit in MAC's new Carriage House Gallery, its latest restoration. The association was a natural, so Twinings provided the seed money for MAC to open a tearoom and lunch restaurant in 1999 at its Emlen Physick Estate.

The location at the rear of the 1876 carriage house is perfect. There are 22 seats inside, set amid the old horse stables paneled in dark longleaf yellow pine. Outside are 55 more on a festive brick patio beneath a tent with a rollup canopy for pleasant days and heat to ward off any chill. Here, in Cape May's only tearoom, you can enjoy a leisurely tea luncheon. The $15 tab includes a choice of four finger sandwiches and quiches, pasta or potato salad, breads and sweets, along with hot and iced tea, lemonade or coffee. A slightly reduced version of same is available later in the day as "elegant afternoon tea." The flower-bedecked setting is indeed elegant, with crisp linened tables and polished service.

The idea was not only to provide visitors a place for lunch or tea, but also educational: a place for tea tastings, pairings of teas and foods, events like mother-daughter teas – "to revive traditions that have been lost," in the words of Bill Ten Eyck, deputy operations director.

In addition to changing exhibits in the gallery, the gallery shop features teas, unusual teapots, china and silverplate serving pieces and cookbooks.

(609) 884-5404 or (800) 275-4278. Tea luncheon, 11:30 to 2, prix-fixe, $15. Afternoon tea, 2 to 4:30, $12.50.

Culinary Institute of America students serve breads to diners at The American Bounty.

Hudson Valley
Mecca for Gourmands

Barely an hour's drive north of New York City lies an area that represents a different world, one often overlooked by travelers destined for Manhattan's urban attractions.

The central Hudson Valley remains surprisingly rural, at times rustic. It is a mixed-bag area of noted mansions and historic houses, hip boutiques and hippie pursuits, winding country roads and a mighty river with seemingly unending, interesting traffic. Steep mountains and rushing streams abound on the west side of the Hudson. The east side, which is our focus here, is a rolling tapestry of pastoral vistas as well.

It also is an area of fine restaurants, one of which we would go so far as to say could give any restaurant in the country a run for its money. That is The American Bounty, one of four esteemed restaurants at the storied Culinary Institute of America in Hyde Park.

The array of restaurants followed the arrival of the relocated institute in 1972. The CIA created a demand for better food supplies in the area as well as a pool of teaching chefs and a ready entourage of culinary students who needed places to serve their required eighteen-week externships. For its 50th anniversary in 1996, the CIA listed 38 food-related places in the area owned by its alumni, running the gamut from gourmet restaurants to McDonald's and Dairy Freeze franchises.

Between meals, you will find plenty to do. The Hudson Valley is the nation's oldest wine-growing region, and more than twenty wineries offer tastings and/or tours. The valley is known for its great estates and house museums. Rhinebeck, Red Hook and Millbrook are villages of particular appeal to visitors. Following your own pursuits will spur an appetite for things culinary.

Dining

The Culinary Institute of America

A former Jesuit seminary high above the Hudson River at Hyde Park became the home of the nation's oldest and foremost school for professional culinary training when The Culinary Institute of America moved in 1972 from New Haven, Conn. It has been a mecca for gourmands ever since, not only for chefs but also for visiting professionals and knowledgeable diners who sample the fare cooked by students in four cutting-edge restaurants.

This is not a traditional college campus, you find upon arrival as you watch budding chefs in tall white hats scurry across the green, most clutching their knife kits. It couldn't be when you learn the rallying cry for the hockey team is "mirepoix, mirepoix, roux roux, roux; slice 'em up, dice 'em up, drop 'em in the stew!"

The bustling, red-brick classroom building has an institutional tinge, but the aromas wafting from The American Bounty or The Escoffier restaurants at either end of the long main hall are tantalizing, hinting at glories to come.

The restaurants are the final courses in 21 months of study for the institute's 2,000 candidates for associate and bachelor degrees, who arrive and graduate in cycles every three weeks. They work in the kitchens and then serve in the dining rooms.

Casual visitors don't get to see much behind-the-scenes action, except through windows into the kitchens off both restaurants. Tours for the public ($4, by reservation, Monday at 10 and 4) and bus groups afford a glimpse into the mysteries of 36 specialty and experimental kitchens, the pantry and the former chapel, which is now the student dining room and used for large banquets and graduation ceremonies. Visitors may catch glimpses of the General Foods Nutrition Center (first of its kind in the country), the Shunsuke Takaki School of Baking and Pastry, the Conrad N. Hilton Library and the Danny Kaye Theatre.

Open regularly to visitors here is an expanded gift shop and bookstore named after Craig Claiborne, stocking specialty-food items and more than 1,300 cookbooks on every culinary subject imaginable. They may inspire you to try at home some of the dishes cooked up in the CIA restaurants.

Or you can eat informally or take out from the CIA's new **Apple Pie Bakery Cafe,** which opened in early 2000 just inside the main building. Open weekdays from 8:30 to 6, it offers soup, salads, sandwiches and baked goods at a counter as well as marble-top tables seating 80.

 Meal reservations for the four major restaurants may be made with the hospitality desk at (914) 471-6608, weekdays 8:30 to 6.

Keep in mind that this is a school and the always-changing staff is in training. The dining experiences vary accordingly, but we have yet to be disappointed.

The American Bounty Restaurant, The Culinary Institute of America.
We've had lunch at Lutèce, the five-star restaurant in New York, and we've had lunch at the CIA's American Bounty, and we liked The American Bounty better.

Arched opening frames view of cloister-style dining room at The American Bounty.

Not only did we find the food more interesting and more attractively presented, but the staff is pleasant and helpful, and the cost less than half.

Opened in 1982 for the presentation of American foods (before they became trendy) and wines, The American Bounty complements the noted, more formal Escoffier Restaurant at the other end of the building.

The high-ceilinged restaurant is the institute's largest. It is stunning, from its etched-glass doors to its cream and green draperies with a floral motif, gathered back from high arched windows. The seminary heritage is evident in the two cloister-style dining rooms, seating 110 people at tables spaced well apart.

A changing array of America's bounty is in front of the window onto the Julia Child Rotisserie Kitchen, through which you can see ducklings turning on the spit as white-clad students near the end of their training.

The menu changes slightly with every meal. Seldom have we had such a dilemma making choices as we did for a springtime lunch, confronting such appetizers as spicy barbecued lamb empanadas with a poblano salsa and New York State foie gras sautéed with concord-grape sauce and fried grapes.

We settled for tomato and celery mousse on cold tomato hash, a heavenly dish decorated with a floret of mayonnaise and a sprig of fresh dill, and a sampling of the day's three soups served in tiny cups: chilled strawberry, the clam chowder and "New Orleans gumbo Ya-Ya." With these appetizers was passed a basket with at least nine kinds of bread and rolls (bran muffins, corn sticks, cloverleaf rolls and biscuits were some), served with a crock of sweet butter.

For main courses, because of the season we ordered fresh asparagus on sourdough toast with creamed salmon and sweetbreads, and "baked fresh seafood variety, new garden style." The former had perfectly crisp asparagus arranged like a fan on crisp sourdough; the sauce was suave and rich. The seafood was served in an iron skillet and was pretty as a picture, rimmed by tomato wedges. Crabmeat, clams, mussels, salmon and more were topped with butter and crumbs and baked. Vegetables, served family style, were stuffed cherry tomatoes, yellow squash and tiny red potatoes.

Desserts include strawberry and rhubarb cobbler with vanilla bean ice cream, a key lime tart with toasted meringue and coconut sauce and, at one visit, sautéed Hudson Valley apples with praline ice cream in a walnut lace cup and pear-blueberry cobbler with Wild Turkey ice cream. We tried the popular Mississippi river boat, a shell of pastry filled with an intense chocolate mousse with kiwi fruit on top and, weird sounding but very good, fried strawberries – huge fat ones in a sort of beignet, served with a sour-cream and orange sauce.

Prices for all this are fairly reasonable. Two people having appetizers, entrées and desserts plus a bottle of wine can have a memorable lunch of dinner-size proportions for $50 to $60.

At night, when dining is by candlelight, typical entrées range from sesame-crusted salmon with grilled shrimp, peas and spiced bean thread in a lemongrass-infused carrot broth to a rotisserie special of maple-glazed duck leg, braised duck breast and seared Hudson Valley foie gras.

Service, of course, is correct and cordial – after all, these students are *graded* for this. But, as you might expect, it can be a bit slow. Not to worry. The food is worth the wait.

Entrées: lunch, $11.75 to $15.95; dinner, $13.95 to $21.95. Open Tuesday-Saturday, lunch 11:30 to 1, dinner 6:30 to 8:30.

The Escoffier Restaurant, Culinary Institute of America.

The great French chef Auguste Escoffier would be pleased that some of his traditions are being carried on in the restaurant bearing his name.

The dining room is pretty in pale pinks and raspberry tones, with comfortable upholstered chairs and elaborate chandeliers and wall sconces. On spacious tables set with ten pieces of flatware at each place, the gigantic wine glasses – globe-shaped for red, hurricane-shaped for white and a flute for champagne – take an inordinate amount of room. With classical background music, it reminds one of a small, select and comfortable hotel dining room and seats about 90.

Menus change seasonally, service is tableside and the prices are the institute's highest. If you come for lunch, expect to spend upwards of three hours and not have any appetite for dinner that night.

The classic French menu has acquired nouvelle touches since we first lunched here in 1978. Gone are the escargots bourguignonne and onion soup. In their place are appetizers like duck terrine with pistachios and truffles, a flan of local wild mushrooms and smoked sturgeon with caviar and accompaniments. Main courses include a signature dover sole meunière, fillet of pompano with citrus sauce, boneless quail enclosed in chicken mousseline with périgourdine sauce, and Gascony-style duck leg confit with torte of prune and apples, sautéed royal trumpet mushrooms and an Armagnac black pepper sauce. We remember fondly an entrée of sweetbreads topped with two large slices of truffle and a subtle sauce. Another winner was chicken in a spicy curry sauce, accompanied by a large tray of outstanding chutneys, the tray decorated with white napkins folded to point up at each corner, giving it the appearance of a temple roof.

Dining room of St. Andrew's Cafe is light and airy.

Overfull diners have been known to moan as the dessert cart laden with noble tortes, rich cakes and more rolls up. But how can one resist at least a taste of a silky coffee-kahlua mousse or an incredible many-layered pastry square, filled with whipped cream and raspberries?

After partaking of the meal, could anyone possibly have room for a full dessert? Our waiter, a former teacher whose wife was putting him through school, replied: "That's nothing. Some people have two or three."

Entrées: lunch, $13.25 to $18.50; dinner, $19.50 to $28. Open Tuesday-Saturday, lunch 11:30 to 1, dinner 6:30 to 8:30.

St. Andrew's Cafe, The Culinary Institute of America.

The institute's best-kept secret had been this cafe, transformed in 1985 from the old Wechsler Coffeehouse and stressing low-fat nutritious food. Dropping in for what we expected might be a quick snack, we were astonished to partake of a memorable three-course lunch, all specially designed to be less than 1,000 calories.

It was a secret, that is, until it moved front and center into the CIA's new General Foods Nutrition Center, behind the main building. All here is state of the art as the CIA seeks to change Americans' eating habits through greater awareness of nutrition and the availability of healthful and delicious meals. That's public-relations jargon for what this cafe produces, "good food that's good for you."

The cafe has gone upscale in decor. Ceramic vegetables on a breakfront in the foyer greet diners, who may see the tiled kitchen through windows behind the bar. Beyond is an expansive, 65-seat room with generally well-spaced tables set with white linens, heavy silver and, surprise, salt shakers that were notably missing in the old coffeehouse. A coffered ceiling, arched windows and upholstered rattan chairs contribute to a light, comfortable setting.

The remarkable appetizers and desserts are what we most remember from two lunches here. We started the first with a Mediterranean seafood terrine with the seafood in chunks, on a wonderful sauce, and a smoked-duck salad with raspberry vinaigrette, a beautiful presentation including about six exotic lettuces topped with raspberries, ringed by sliced pears. A later visit produced a crabmeat quesadilla with a jícama and citrus salad and an extravagant plateful of carpaccio of fresh tuna and oriental mushroom salad.

Hearty breads like rye, sunflower seed and whole wheat along with butter curls were offered no less than four times – surely the fourth would have blown the calorie limit.

Among main courses, barbecue-grilled chicken breast with black bean sauce and roast medallions of lamb with wild mushrooms and a potato pancake kind of affair came with crisp young asparagus garnished with sesame seeds. These were preceded by salads of fancy greens, including endive, and tender peeled tomatoes. Garnishing the chicken dish was a peeled-back tomatillo filled with fresh salsa.

Desserts were, once, a pumpkin torte with cinnamon sauce and glazed pineapple madagascar, a concoction with rum, honey and peppercorns. The second visit yielded a Hudson Valley pear strudel with amaretto glacé and a remarkable warm apple sauté with graham-cracker crisps and apple pie glacé. The latter was so ample and eye-catching when we saw it at the next table that we thought it must have been prepared for a visiting dignitary (not so).

All this, with a glass of wine and a beer, came with tip to about $40 for lunch for two. And, according to the computer printout that you can request for a technical but interesting diet analysis, only the cappuccino took our meal over the 1,000-calorie limit.

The dinner menu, which also changes every few days, offers similar style and heartier main courses. We figured one couldn't spend more than about $25 for a dinner of pheasant consommé with wild-mushroom ravioli, seared sea bass with beluga lentils and merlot sauce, and brandy and prune glace profiteroles with fudge sauce. Wines by the glass, beers and natural juices are available.

As well as eating delicious food cooked with a minimum of salt, sugar and fat, you are given solicitous service such as is rarely found nowadays. If we lived nearby, we'd be tempted to eat here every week.

Entrées: lunch, $6 to $15; dinner, $9 to $16.50. Open Monday-Friday, lunch 11:30 to 1, dinner 6:30 to 8:30.

The Caterina de Medici Dining Room, The Culinary Institute of America.
Offering a varied menu of regional Italian cuisine, this is the newest and smallest of the institute's public restaurants and has been closed to visitors whenever we've been there (as often is the case for lunch, we were told).

The room honors the Renaissance patron whose greatest contributions to European culture and culinary history were her gifts of Florentine cuisine and refinements – among them the use of the fork, the cultivation of the green bean, the creation of ice cream and the introduction of sauce-making to the French.

Today, CIA students serve up prix-fixe meals that reflect a trend toward Italian cucina fresca. The antipasti might be grilled calamari with arugula, stuffed portobello mushrooms or zucchini frittata with parmesan crisps. For main dishes, how about baked cod with pancetta, veal cutlet stuffed with prosciutto and parmesan, or leg of lamb with artichokes? Dessert could be hazelnut torte with ricotta and chocolate, or a selection of homemade gelatos and sorbets.

All is elegant in high-ceilinged dining room at Xaviar's in Garrison.

Italian wines are featured, of course, in this venture's stated attempt to prove to Americans that there's more to Italian cuisine than Pizza Huts. One recent grad advised that some of his peers considered it the CIA's best restaurant.

Prix-fixe: lunch $21.95, dinner $27.95. Open Monday-Friday, lunch 11:30 to 1, dinner 6:30 to 8:30.

The Best of the Best

Xaviar's, Route 9D, Garrison.

This restaurant, launched in 1983 by Peter X. (for Xaviar) Kelly when he was 23, did so well that he opened a second restaurant across the Hudson, **Xaviar's at Piermont** (506 Piermont Ave.), plus an adjacent and more casual **Freelance Cafe and Wine Bar.** In 1998, he opened his biggest and most ambitious venture yet, the 250-seat **Restaurant X and Bully Boy Bar** in Congers.

Both Xaviar's earned the highest ratings in the Zagat Restaurant Survey, near-perfect 29s, the first ever awarded in New York, Peter says proudly. (There are now six restaurants in the country with 29 ratings, and his are two.) In 1996, the two Xaviar's added an "extraordinary" rating (the first outside Manhattan) from the New York Times, which praised the kitchen's artistry and declared Xaviar's a destination for those "seeking something close to perfection in this life."

The Garrison restaurant is in the ballroom of a clubhouse overlooking the grounds at the Highlands Country Club. The long room with 25-foot-high ceilings holds two dozen or so well-spaced tables. It's a sight to behold, decked out in white Versace china and linens, white fanned napkins, gleaming wineglasses, crystal candle-holders and white candles, with a Baccarat crystal stallion here and a silver pheasant there. Arrangements of exotic flowers in crystal vases on each table, on the fireplace mantels, on sideboards and even in the rest rooms add color – the bill from the florist must be staggering. Light is provided by candles everywhere and blazing fireplaces at each end. Music by a harpist adds to the romance.

In a space like this, Peter says, "you couldn't do anything else but grand dining." So the self-taught chef – the tenth of twelve children in a Yonkers family – ultimately canceled his weeknight dinners of long standing to concentrate on special-occasion dining on weekends only. Dinner is prix-fixe, $80 for six courses and a pairing of six wines, with a choice between two menus. The staff suggests that a party of two order both menus to best sample Peter's culinary prowess.

Part of the special-occasion dining at Garrison is the Sunday brunch buffet, $38 including champagne. The buffet, lavish as you'd expect, is supplemented by any number of foods passed from the kitchen.

Wine Spectator gave its Best of Award of Excellence to the Xaviar's wine cellars, which contain more than 750 selections.

Peter, very much a hands-on chef, tends to cook weekends in Garrison and during the week in Piermont.

We consider ourselves fortunate to have sampled a number of his dishes, each a triumph of taste, texture and presentation. Consider his lobster ravioli in saffron sauce, garnished with the ends of lobster tails (they look like butterflies so that's what Peter calls them) and bearing a mound of caviar in the middle and two long chives on top. Or the seared sea scallops, served with potato pancakes and raspberry vinaigrette with a few fresh raspberries for good measure. Or the New York State foie gras, surrounded by sliced kiwi, strawberries and sliced pears and served with a glass of sauternes. Best of all – in fact, one of the best dishes we've had anywhere – is the seared Pacific tuna tartare with wasabi and soy sauce, resting on an oversize plate, the rim garnished all the way around with dollops of red, gold and black caviar.

Finger bowls were presented before our main courses: mignon of venison with grand veneur sauce and the best spaetzle we've tasted, and saddle of veal with wild mushrooms and pommes parisienne, garnished with a tomato carved to look like a rose. Both came with tiny, barely cooked haricots verts.

Desserts here are exceptional as well. One of us had an ethereal hot raspberry soufflé, light as air. The other tried the grand assortment, nine little samples including hazelnut dacquoise, chocolate-chestnut terrine, frozen caramel mousse, raspberry sorbet and praline ice cream. A plate of petits fours, chocolate strawberries and chocolate truffles finished a meal to remember.

The silverware that came and went with each course was as noticeable as all the extra touches that went into food and presentation. "We try to give people a little more than anyone else does," explains Peter. Indeed they do.

Xaviar's at Garrison, (914) 424-4228: Prix-fixe $80, dinner, Friday and Saturday 6 to 9; Sunday brunch, seatings at 11:30 and 2. Xaviar's at Piermont, (914) 359-7007: Prix-fixe, $55; lunch, Wednesday-Sunday noon to 2; dinner, Wednesday-Sunday 6 to 9.

Harrald's, 3110 Route 52, Stormville.

Reservations are essential at this unlikely-looking establishment, for eighteen years rated one of the dozen or so five-star Mobil Guide restaurants in the country and widely revered since its opening in 1971. We tried unsuccessfully two weeks ahead to reserve for a Friday – "we only have thirteen tables," the host reminded. There are two seatings on Saturdays, and the leisurely meal takes three hours.

Yellow lanterns and meticulous landscaping give something of a Japanese look to the Swiss-Tudor house that reflects the tastes and work of proprietor Harrald Boerger. He proudly introduces his wife, Ava Durrschmidt, "the only woman chef-owner in the United States of a five-star restaurant," who explained in a Swiss-German accent her philosophy that "simplicity is elegance." Until recently, hers was a kitchen in which men were not allowed to cook.

Three-foot-high blackboard menus are wheeled to the table, outlining the night's variations on seasonal dishes that rarely change. Dinner is prix-fixe ($65 for six courses, with a $40 option for three courses on Wednesdays and Thursdays). It's served in three small, intimate rooms by waiters who perhaps intimidate more than the outgoing and down-to-earth Harrald, who usually visits each table during the course of the evening. The experience is designed to make guests think they are dining in a home rather than a restaurant, he says.

Owner Harrald Boerger at Harralds.

The meal might start with a choice of home-smoked rainbow trout (the house specialty), crab cakes, a galantine of veal and diced tongue with cashews and green peppers, and a poached egg en cocotte with diced chicken, ham, mushrooms and truffles. The soup course involves a classic French onion with emmenthaler cheese and a choice of one hot and one cold each evening, perhaps a light toasted almond crème and a cold Russian-Polish specialty called okroshka.

A mixed green salad with the house vinaigrette or country herb dressing precedes the main course. Typical choices are poached or sautéed trout au bleu with dill sauce, veal roast with pan gravy and dumplings, steak au poivre, stuffed free-range poussin, canard au cassis and zuricher rahm schnitzel served with four kinds of mushrooms.

Prior to dessert and coffee, a cart brings a selection of fresh fruits, cheeses, nuts and a glass or two of good port. Dessert could be chocolate sabayon cake, chocolate mousse made with Swiss Lindt chocolate, linzer torte or fresh fruit topped with whipped or heavy cream.

Before dinner, you might have drinks on the terrace or stroll the park-like grounds. The trout come from an outdoor tank that looks like a wishing well and has water so fresh it's poured as drinking water – "people bring containers to take some home," says Harrald. Another special touch is a small 200-year-old farmhouse used as a wine cellar with an extensive, 250-vintage selection that is "cheaper than any place I know, because wines should be affordable." Outside the wine house is an old-fashioned swing. Harrald explains: "My wife said she'd like a swing for her birthday. So I built her one for $12."

Harrald does not advertise because it embarrasses him and he doesn't need to. "I put the money I save back into serving our guests," he says. "We're giving them the very best of the best."

Local reviewers variously praise individual items as the best they've had, but it is the entire experience – from soup to nuts, as it were – that earned Harrald's its five stars year after year. Even after the new producers of the Mobil Guide changed their criteria and reduced his rating to four stars (he was chagrined to learn of it in the newspapers), Harrald remained philosophical. "We've had our day (in the stars)," he said. "But we're not going to change a thing."

(914) 878-6595. Prix-fixe, $65. Dinner, Wednesday-Saturday 6 to 9 (two seatings Saturday at 6 and 9:15). Closed January to mid-February. Reservations and jackets required. No credit cards.

Le Pavillon, 230 Salt Point Tpke. (Route 115), Poughkeepsie.

An unlikely looking brick Victorian house on the outskirts of town is home to an intimate, country-French restaurant run by chef-owner Claude Guermont, who was born in Normandy and apprenticed himself to a French chef at age 14. After a stint as an instructor at the CIA's Escoffier Restaurant, he opened Le Pavillon in 1980 against the prevailing wisdom that a fine restaurant could not survive in the area. In 1985, he wrote *The Norman Table,* an acclaimed cookbook of 200 regional recipes from his native land. And lately his restaurant vaulted into the highest echelons in the Zagat survey.

You enter through a vestibule lined with clippings ("Chef has never really left Normandy," headlines one) into a brick and beamed bar. Dining is by candlelight in two intimate dining rooms, each accommodating 30. French posters and art, white service plates bearing a discreet Le Pavillon logo, black candles in small hurricane lamps and white linens contribute to a charming setting.

The French menu is pleasantly priced, available à la carte or $32 prix-fixe for three courses (no à la carte on Saturdays). "I try to stay with local products, make everything here and try to be a little contemporary – not entirely classic or nouvelle," Claude says.

Among appetizers, his crisp frog's legs with garlic sauce and escargots simmered in brandy-garlic sauce are highly rated. So are his Normandy-style onion soup, the shrimp and lobster bisque with sherry and the changing preparation of fresh Catskill foie gras.

The ten or so entrées could include salmon wrapped in potato slices with lime sauce, sautéed sweetbreads with capers, coq au vin, rare roasted squab with cognac sauce, veal kidneys in spicy brandy mustard sauce and steak au poivre. Trout soufflé, cassoulet, rabbit, quail, pheasant and New Zealand venison might be available as specials.

Desserts are hot soufflés and crêpes suzette, as well as French pastries, profiteroles, homemade sorbets and the like. Le Pavillon's award-winning wine list ranges widely from Hudson Valley vintages to French châteaux.

(914) 473-2525. Entrées, $17.95 to $24.95. Prix fixe, $32. Dinner, Monday-Saturday 5:30 to 10.

McKinney & Doyle Fine Foods Cafe, 10 Charles Colman Blvd., Pawling.

The highest accolades go to this cafe, a fortuitous outgrowth of the well-known **Corner Bakery.** "Excellent," declared the New York Times critic. "An all-time favorite," swooned the Poughkeepsie Journal reviewer. Partners Shannon McKinney and Brian Doyle moved to expanded quarters in the center of Pawling from a smaller bakery that had attracted national notice. Shannon mans the bakery and oversees the wine list, while Brian handles the restaurant operation.

And a fine restaurant it is. Sophisticated, stunningly executed fare is served in a comfortable, homespun atmosphere. In 1999, the old-fashioned, high-ceilinged storefront underwent a dinner-time transformation. After the bakery closes at 5,

Shannon McKinney and Brian Doyle run Fine Foods Cafe and Corner Bakery.

a new curtain with a mural screens the bakery cases and a handful of tables are available for cocktails from a full-service bar. The adjacent dining room takes on a softer, gentler ambiance with upholstered booths replacing a hodgepodge of tables and booths that originated in an old Pawling pub. Exposed brick walls hold local memorabilia and art displays. Many and changing are the touches of whimsy: words of dining wisdom here and there; a shelf bearing bricks, shutters, a clothes-line with pins and an old flag; a beehive in a ficus tree, and a window display with an amusing picture of chefs exercising amid an array of spring-form pans. Brian lends his decorating skills and laconic wit to a space that exudes personality.

His kitchen talents are equally diverse. For dinner, you might start with a mashed potato pancake with smoked salmon and tomato butter or a jumbo shrimp martini with "a cool Tanqueray cocktail sauce (extra dry)." The best bread ever with sweet butter and an exceptional house salad of greens with stilton and pears one night, delicate beets and roasted pecans the next, come with. The main event could be cognac-spiked sweetbreads and lobster medallions with asparagus points and artichokes, crisp lemon-pepper duck breast with peach chutney and ginger rice cakes, and mustard-enhanced lamb loin with leek purée and parisienne potatoes. Be sure to save room for one of the bakery's fabulous desserts, perhaps chocolate grand marnier layer cake, sweet pear "upside down" pie or Bailey's Irish cream mousse cake.

Interesting fare also is offered at lunch, perhaps a wonderful soup of shrimp and scallops in a creamy sauternes-leek broth, a pan-seared duck salad, Shannon's "hogbreath vegetarian chili" with grilled jalapeño cornbread or a sandwich of roasted chicken and apricot salad served on a just-baked baguette. Brunch brings a panoply of egg dishes, banana pancakes, almond french toast, sandwiches and salads, and, at our visit, corned-beef hash served in its own cast-iron skillet with a shirred egg and bakery toast.

The award-winning wine list is affordable, with many available by the glass. The adjacent bakery dispenses all kinds of baked goods as well as a variety of foods to take out under the logo of McKinney & Doyle.

Oktoberfest beer-tasting dinners, wine tastings, a Christmas madrigal dinner, art exhibitions, mail-order – it takes their Word of Mouth newsletter just to follow all that these enterprising guys are up to.

(914) 855-3875. Entrées, $17.50 to $23.50. Lunch, Tuesday-Friday 11:30 to 3. Dinner, Tuesday-Sunday 6 to 9. Weekend brunch, 9 to 3.

California Spirit

Cascade Mountain Winery & Restaurant, Flint Hill Road, Amenia.

Why is a winery listed under dining choices? Because this out-of-the-way place is a gem, known as much for its creative food prepared from local ingredients as for its award-winning wines and a funky, California kind of spirit. In fact, we almost felt we were on a Napa Valley hillside the first sunny autumn day we lingered on one of several decks overlooking the apple orchards, enjoying a bottle of seyval blanc and some appealing luncheon fare.

The chef works in a newly renovated kitchen just off the winery's homey dining room, and cooks his best at Saturday night dinners designed to "show off our local wines and food products." Dinner is à la carte, with a handful of changing entrées ranging from pan-seared striped bass with parsley sauce to filet mignon with the winery's Couer de Lion wine sauce.

We got a tantalizing taste of the fare at lunch, nursing the winery's vintage seyval blanc. Our party of four enjoyed a thick butternut-squash soup, a gingered carrot soup, a clear leek soup with roasted garlic and a foie gras pâté with cranberry chutney. Then we dug into excellent pan-browned trout with lemon and capers, a pâté and Old Chatham Sheepherding camembert plate, a mustardy maple chicken salad with green and red grapes, and the signature grilled chicken breast – grilled right on the deck – stuffed with Coach Farm goat cheese in puff pastry. An apple-pear crisp, a plum tart with lavender crème anglaise, spiced maple cheesecake with gingersnap crust and a chocolate-raspberry marjolaine ended a leisurely, memorable meal. The bill was written on the back of a wine label.

After lunch, we stepped gingerly around workmen to enter the main winery downstairs. It's an unexpectedly small and primitive affair, considering the merit of the output (it made the strongest showing of any winery east of the Rockies at a couple of wine competitions). The chief workman turned out to be William Wetmore, owner-winemaker and author of four novels, a jack-of-all-trades who produces almost as many red wines as whites because of his grape-planting decisions more than two decades ago. He oversees the winery, while son-in-law Walter Yahn manages the restaurant and its Sunday lunchtime piano jazz sessions.

A couple of typewritten sheets inside cellophane wrappers pointed out salient facets of winemaking for self-guided tours. Visitors taste wines in the crowded and convivial downstairs setting, where no one takes things too seriously. How could they, at a place where a couple of favorite bottlings are called Heavenly Daze and Pardonnez-Moi? The latter is billed as a dry red wine "for social emergencies," but is also a play on the word chardonnay. The Wetmore family named their beaujolais-style red release Coeur de Lion, meaning heart of the lion, after 60 Minutes documented the drinking of red wine as good for the heart. Such is the homespun fun of Cascade Mountain Vineyards, a place full of integrity. *(914) 373-9021. Entrées, lunch $12 to $15, dinner, $21 to $26. Lunch daily except Wednesday, noon to 3. Dinner Saturday by reservation, 6 to 8. Restaurant closed November-March.*

More Dining Choices

Cripple Creek Restaurant, 18 Garden St., Rhinebeck.

Artistry of the performing as well as the culinary kind embellish this restaurant that took center stage under new ownership in 1999. The food is flavorful, seasonal and mostly indigenous, with an emphasis on organically raised meats, grains and produce from area farms. CIA-trained chef David Bruno calls the fare "regional American with Asian and French influences." Co-owner Bing Yang is responsible for the Asian influence, while partner Dennis Giauque, accompanist for two of the Three Tenors and assistant conductor of the Metropolitan Opera, reflects a musical heritage. Manager Patrick Hayes, a former concert pianist, has a master's degree from the Juilliard School of Music.

The new team took over the failing Cripple Creek Café when their planned new Rhinebeck restaurant – Bing's, advertised as a New York supper club – burned to the ground three days before it was to open. They enhanced the L-shaped room with taupe walls, gray carpeting, white over black linens, black chairs and accents of faux marble. White fabric billows beneath the ceiling, and a corner built-in bookshelf displays books, vases, a small picture of Dennis with Luciano Pavarotti and, at our autumn visit, a display of loose teas and pine cones that we and others thought were chocolates. An outdoor patio is available in season.

Classical music plays in the background, but that is about the only musical accent as the owners bide their time for opening the planned supper club. Patrick said that even then, they would continue to operate Cripple Creek.

The food was terrific but the service languid during a mid-week lunch. The day's roasted garlic and potato purée soup was teamed with half a grilled vegetable and mozzarella sandwich. Homemade potato crisps and a small salad of rice and cranberry beans accompanied this and the other sandwich, an extra-assertive grilled spice-rubbed pork loin with apricot mustard on peasant bread. The delicate and ever-so-flavorful pear tarte tatin with hazelnut ice cream was worth the wait.

Dinner fare is creative and portions substantial. Expect main dishes like pan-seared sea scallops with French green lentils and baby bok choy, sautéed arctic char on jonah crab potatoes with braised fennel, and rosemary-marinated roast lamb on soft polenta with vegetable marmalade. Starters could be cranberry bean and smoked bacon soup with crème fraîche or house-cured duck confit on a ragoût of white beans, garlic and escarole. Finish with a chocolate grand marnier terrine, the house selection of berry ices or ice cream in a honey crisp, or a sampler plate of most of the day's desserts.

(914) 876-4355. Entrées, $15 to $25. Open daily except Tuesday, noon to 9.

Calico Restaurant & Patisserie, 9 Mill St. (Route 9), Rhinebeck.

A perfect five-star rating from the Poughkeepsie restaurant reviewer followed the opening of this snug little hideaway in a twenty-seat storefront across from the famous Beekman Arms. The stars were for the food offered by CIA grad Tony Balassone, an alumnus of Le Pavillon in Poughkeepsie, and the baked goods of his wife Leslie.

It retained its five-star rating in a follow-up 1999 review, although it doesn't get nearly the press of its high-profile neighbor across the street. "This small treasure proves that when the food is supreme and the service is fabulous, you don't need a million-dollar renovation," the reviewer wrote. "The statement is made by the highest-quality cuisine."

The patisserie in front opens at 7 a.m. for croissants and brioche. Come lunch time, the kitchen offers a handful of interesting choices, perhaps seafood chili with cornbread, house-smoked salmon fillet served on a mixture of greens and roasted porcini mushrooms, pizza of the day and sliced flank steak on a toasted baguette. The gratinéed vidalia onion soup laced with Anchor Steam ale makes a good starter. So does the roasted garlic soup with crème fraîche and an herbed brioche crouton.

At night, Tony prepares such treats as sautéed flounder served atop a spinach, shrimp and portobello mushroom hash; a classic bouillabaisse, breast of free-range chicken stuffed with spinach and goat cheese, and rack of New Zealand lamb with mint-infused eggplant and vegetable stew.

Start with a whole roasted garlic head served with gratinéed Coach Farms goat cheese, pesto sauce and croutons. Finish with one of the more than twenty exceptional desserts from the pastry case.

Artifacts and calico items adorn a shelf above the pale blue wainscoting of this pure and simple place beloved by the locals. It has a full liquor license. The wine list features boutique vineyards and good values.

(914) 876-2749. Entrées, $16.95 to $19.95. Lunch, Wednesday-Sunday 11 to 3:30. Dinner, Wednesday-Sunday 5:30 to 9:30 or 10:30.

Le Petit Bistro, 8 East Market St., Rhinebeck.

Two of his staff took over where retiring chef-owner Jean-Paul Crozier left off, and their loyal fans report this long-running charmer is better than ever. Head waiter Brendan Callan moved into the kitchen and partner Dan Bleen manages the front. Brendan has quietly updated the fare, although he insists the menu remains the same. And Yvonne Crozier stayed on, so regulars still get a hug and a kiss upon arrival.

Pine walls and floors give the 40-seat dining room and half-circle bar at the side a country-French look. Except for globe lamps inside wooden frames, the decor is simple and the atmosphere convivial and intimate.

The French menu starts with classics like onion soup, pâté maison, smoked trout and escargots bourguignonne. English Dover sole, offered meunière or grenobloise, is a house specialty. Sea scallops with crushed black peppercorns and cream sauce, duck with chef's choice of sauce, veal scaloppine, frog's legs, rack of lamb provençal and steak au poivre are among the choices. Grilled tuna niçoise, poulet marengo and rainbow trout with crabmeat and grenobloise sauce were specials at a recent visit.

Desserts include crème caramel, mocha mousse, raspberry frappe and peach melba.

(914) 876-7400. Entrées, $17.75 to $23.95. Dinner, Thursday-Monday 5 to 10, Sunday 4 to 9.

Tuscan mural moved with chef Jason Thomas to relocated Xe Sogni.

Xe Sogni, Route 44, Amenia.

Here's the recipe for one remarkable Italian osteria. Enter the CIA at age 17, train at the Old Drovers Inn, work for your father in a gelato manufacturing company and buy out the other partner. Turn the front of the building into a restaurant, tuck an open kitchen into a corner, and cook up "Italian soul food" that changes every few days.

The recipe spelled success for Jason Thomas. With his father Michael as partner ("he's the worrier; I'm the cook") and his expectant wife and his mother as waitresses, he started with eighteen seats in 1995 and added fourteen more a year later. He soon moved to a red house up the street, where he put on a kitchen addition, has a full liquor license and seats 50 in two country-rustic dining rooms. Jason was only 20 when he opened, and has never been to Italy. "That amazes all my customers," he concedes.

The obscure, hard-to-pronounce ("zay son-yay") name is Venetian dialect for "these dreams" and this, for Jason, is the fulfillment of a dream. Although his original had more distinctive character, some of the remarkable floor-to-ceiling murals of the Tuscan countryside, painted by a friend who lives in West Africa, have been relocated wall-by-wall to the new location, which looks like an Italian farmhouse.

The large open kitchen yields a succession of tasty treats. For starters, how about the house-baked bruschetta topped with wild mushrooms, honey-dijon glazed quail on a bed of wilted chard, or chicken livers sautéed with garlic and marsala? Four pasta dishes can be ordered as appetizers or main courses. The main event could be grilled swordfish on herbed orzo, grilled duck with orange glaze and juniper berries, wood-grilled veal chop with a porcini demi-glace, or pan-seared medallions of antelope with a thyme-madeira sauce. A couple of exotic salads are recommended to follow the main course.

Most desserts, like everything else, are made here by this one-man show. Expect raspberry or blackberry crème brûlée, apple crisp, chocolate-espresso cake with chocolate ganache or poached pears.

(914) 373-7755. Entrées, $18 to $21.75. Dinner, Wednesday-Sunday from 6.

Bois d'arc, 29 West Market St., Red Hook.

James Jennings, a CIA grad from eastern Texas, and a couple of CIA-trained assistants oversee the kitchen of this intimate, snazzy restaurant, whose French name signifies the curve of a hunter's bow. They added a side patio for seasonal use, but most of the dining takes place in a subdued storefront space with gray walls, white-clothed tables and black chairs. About the only splashes of color come from the flowers painted on a mural above the bar at the far end.

Plenty of color emanates from the dinner menu, which changes weekly. Short but sweet, it carries a Southern accent. Expect distinctive dishes like homemade hedgehog mushroom ravioli, roasted monkfish with braised collard greens, pan-seared pork tenderloin with jalapeño demi-glace, and black angus filet mignon wrapped in bacon with fried zucchini. Appetizers range widely from Southern fried frog's legs and truffle poached oysters to Maine lobster shepherd's pie with crispy mashed potatoes. Jim's favorite East Texas pulled pork barbecue is often available. Desserts include shortcake with fresh fruit, a changing cheesecake, homemade ice cream served in a tuile and fallen chocolate soufflé cake.

In 1998, Jim expanded with a new and bigger, similarly styled Bois d'arc across the Hudson in Woodstock. It took over a 200-year-old stone farmhouse formerly occupied by New World Home Cooking, which moved to Saugerties.

(914) 758-5992. Entrées, $18.95 to $23.95. Dinner, 5:30 to 9:30. Closed Tuesday and Wednesday in winter.

A Touch of France

Le Canard Enchaîne, 278 Fair St., Kingston.

Chamonix in the French Alps was home for chef Jean-Jacques Carquillat, who trained in Paris and New York before marrying the daughter of Catskills restaurateurs and launching his own ever-so-French bistro in uptown Kingston. "Welcome to the South of France," proclaimed their opening menu. "Delicious," advised one local connoisseur when asked what she thought of the low-key newcomer. A Kingston reviewer rated it the area's best restaurant.

Jean-Jacques and his wife, Jennifer Madden, employed two side-by-side storefront rooms to create a bistro that looks as if it belongs on the main street of Avignon. They expanded with a jazz room, Le Privé, and opened the Lounge Bar, a plush room featuring single-malt whiskeys and food from Le Canard's kitchen. Local folks come in for homemade croissants and café au lait, served as it is in France in "a big bowl," Jean notes. Lunch could be a sampling from more than a dozen salads or a sandwich, perhaps grilled cajun chicken with watercress on a baguette.

The namesake duck is the specialty at dinner at Le Canard, varying from grilled with orange-fennel sauce on braised endives to roasted with grilled sweet potatoes. Other entrées include grilled salmon in a bordelaise sauce, seared Chilean sea bass with a saffron-tomato coulis, beef bourguignonne, provençal lamb shank and grilled ribeye steak maître-d with french fries.

Start with mussels meunière, tuna tartare on a Granny Smith and corn salad, or fricassee of escargots with wild mushrooms flamed in cognac. Finish with crème brûlée, tarte tatin or another of the specialty fruit tarts.

(914) 339-2003. Entrées, $14 to $23. Lunch and dinner daily, 11 to 10.

Trio from Tivoli

Santa Fe, 52 Broadway, Tivoli.
Margaritas are a claim to fame of this restaurant in a colorful burnished plum building at the only intersection in the riverside hamlet of Tivoli. It's long been held in high regard by aficionados of serious Mexican fare. So much so that owner David Weiss, who has traveled extensively in Mexico and knows its cuisine well, has expanded from 25 seats to 150 in three dining areas on the main floor and another upstairs. The decor is colorful: woven rugs adorn the salmon-colored walls and the ceiling has been painted blue. Votive candles flicker in brandy snifters.

Margaritas come by the glass or pitcher and in flavors from peach to raspberry to cuervo to blue curaçao, served up with gusto from the ornate bar. Although Santa Fe started with strictly authentic Mexican food made from scratch, as its reputation grew, David added "eclectic Southwestern fare" and an emphasis on grilling.

Now you'll find the tried-and-true Mexican standbys supplemented by an appetizer of sundried-tomato and Coach Farm goat-cheese quesadilla or a shrimp chimichanga, rolled up like a spring roll and served with a homemade ginger broth. Among entrées, the Oaxacan taco is a corn tortilla with grilled chicken, cheddar, cilantro and homemade molé made with thirteen kinds of dried chiles. The Baja shrimp burrito comes with spinach, grilled onions, tomatoes and cheddar cheese. The grilled pork tenderloin is marinated in Dos Equis dark beer and served with mango salsa. The grilled strip steak might come with a chipotle pepper and goat cheese sauce. The vegetarian stew pairs Santa Fe black beans with melted Wisconsin cheddar. Dessert could be homemade flan, ginger crème brûlée or key lime pie.

(914) 757-4100. Entrées, $8.95 to $15.95. Dinner, Tuesday-Sunday 5 to 10. Closed in January.

Max's Memphis Barbecue, Route 9, Red Hook.
Flush with the success of his Santa Fe restaurant in Tivoli, David Weiss turned his attention southward. On the south side of Red Hook he rebuilt and expanded an old ice-cream shop into a yellow, pillared structure with a country Greek Revival look. Inside is a temple to smoked meats and barbecue.

There's no better barbecue hereabouts than the pulled pork, which turns up in chili and sandwiches as well as a platter with barbecued baked beans and corn. But barbecue is only a smokescreen for some serious, wide-ranging fare, both traditional and in the new Southern style. Almost every item is rubbed with a blend of secret spices and slow-smoked over hickory wood in a semi-open kitchen.

You can start with Tennessee smoked wings, portobello barbecue chili or Gulf shrimp with horseradish barbecue sauce. Move on to smoked chicken, pork ribs or combination thereof. Or try the curried crab cakes, smoked brook trout, grilled portobello mushrooms on cheese grits, a thick black angus steak, grilled vegetable salad or a veggie sampler of five side dishes. The peach cobbler with praline ice cream and the bourbon pecan mousse add dimension to Southern desserts.

All this good, robust eating transpires in a lively warren of rooms and lofts, including a three-story high central space with a protruding bar and an enormous sculpture of Max the griffin flying overhead. It's some temple.

(914) 758-6297. Entrées, $8.95 to $17.95. Dinner, Tuesday-Sunday 5 to 11.

Cafe Pongo, 69 Broadway, Tivoli.
This began as the Tivoli Bread Co., an offshoot of the well-known Santa Fe restaurant up the street. When the bakery expanded into a cafe, co-owner Valerie Nehez sold her share of Santa Fe to David Weiss and concentrated her efforts here.

Bakers start at 3 a.m., making up to ten kinds of organic breads from scratch as well as interesting pastries, everything from chocolate-espresso torte to cranberry-walnut tea bread to focaccia incorporating goat's-milk ricotta. The cafe serves breakfast fare both ordinary (granola and scones) and exotic (salmon benedict, huevos rancheros) for weekend brunch.

The kitchen comes into its own at night, when the fare ranges from healthful to indulgent, with plenty of it. Upon being seated, you're served a basket of homemade breads and three accompaniments: infused olive oil, a vegan chipotle sauce and shaved cheese. There are a few appetizers like curried vegetable samosas, goat cheese croustades and a salad of warm blue cheese, walnuts and caramelized onions, but perhaps you had better go easy. Ahead are entrées like Thai green curry shrimp, chicken breast stuffed with wild mushroom boursin and seared filet mignon with melted blue cheese. Or Pongo pastas: perhaps pesto with artichoke hearts, marinated chicken and shaved parmesan, or pan-seared penne and greens with feta and shrimp. Or "steam pots" served in pewter pots: the house-smoked fillet of salmon, served Thai style with coconut milk, lemongrass and garlic over angel-hair pasta, or Moroccan-style lamb with couscous in a wine-cinnamon-cumin broth.

Desserts from the bakery follow suit, but only the seriously hungry have room. One of us sat at the bar/counter and lunched on a tarragon chicken salad sandwich served on a hefty baguette with roasted rosemary potatoes that proved to be a meal and a half. The coffee comes in bottomless white mugs, there's a full license and you may sit, as we did, next to Valerie's dog Pongo leashed at the bar. The casual, convivial place has a decidedly hip (or hippie) air. The day's baguettes are available for $2 to go.

(914) 757-4403. Entrées, $13 to $17. Lunch-brunch, Friday-Sunday 9 to 3. Dinner, Tuesday-Sunday from 5:30.

Offbeat Gourmet

The Texas Taco, Route 22, Patterson.
Rosemary Jamison, who hails from Texas, began selling tacos in front of the Plaza Hotel in Manhattan in 1968 "before anyone even knew what they were," she says with a laugh. Within a week she had lines down the block. Moving to Patterson in 1971, she proceeded to fill her small house with flea-market objects and now not an inch is left uncovered and barely a blade of grass outside, either. Even the curbs, paving stones and driveways are painted in wild colors to match the exterior of the house.

Cooking from her old New York cart that's ensconced in what must have been a dining room off the kitchen, she serves tacos, burritos, tostadas, chili, guacamole and fiesta pups and that's it. "Very simple, and I don't have to do a lot of ordering," she explains. With a rhinestone on her front tooth and long green hair ("I change it to fit my mood") at our visit, Rosemary is someone hard to miss.

Tiny dining rooms are filled with small tables, with hundreds of business cards

Rosemary Jamison at The Texas Taco.

displayed under their glass tops. Old toys, Marilyn Monroe collectibles, posters, jewelry – there's so much to look at you can't begin to take it all in. The bathroom is unique – Rosemary thinks it gives one a feeling of being in an aquarium, with a huge shark on the ceiling. On the front lawn are a bunch of pink flamingo statuettes and the most motley collection of lawn chairs we ever saw. Even Rosemary's pickup truck is decorated to the max with stickers and jewelry. The Patterson flea-market people understand her tastes and bring to her door things they know she'll buy. Now an icon in the area, she lives in the cellar and rarely goes out except to cater parties. "I have no family," she volunteers, "so this is my life."

Her place sure has character. We think her tacos are pretty darned good, too.

(914) 878-9665. Prices, $1.15 to $2.50. Open daily, 11:30 to 9.

Dining and Lodging

Le Chambord, 2075 Route 52, Hopewell Junction 12533.

Here, thanks to the eighteen-hour days of versatile innkeeper Roy Benich, is a distinguished restaurant, a shop and an inn and conference center focused on a pillared, glistening white Georgian Colonial mansion with dark green shutters and an ornate statue on the front patio. The dining rooms are posh, the guest rooms quite European, and romance permeates every nook and cranny. "New Yorkers love this," says Roy, who was previously at the city's Tavern on the Green. "They're only an hour from Midtown but way out in the country."

First things first. The contemporary French food overseen by executive chef Leonard Mott is superb, from the duck pâté and green salad with all kinds of julienned vegetables that began our dinners to the almond pastry shell filled with whipped cream and luscious fresh raspberries that was the crowning touch.

A complimentary plate of small canapés (two like an egg salad and four of salmon mousse with golden caviar) and a small loaf of sourdough bread came with drinks. For appetizers, expect such exotica as Hudson Valley camembert in puff pastry with celery root, almond and apple slaw or lobster raviolis with sturgeon caviar sauce. Among entrées ranging from sautéed sweetbreads to tournedos rossini, the veal chop sautéed with diced onions and a touch of paprika proved a standout. One of us tried the tasting menu, which changes weekly. It brought mesquite-smoked flank steak carpaccio with corn relish, sea scallops in puff pastry with ginger and oregano, medallions of pork in calvados sauce, steamed salmon with carrots, and breast of chicken with broccoli and fennel, plus a trio of chocolate desserts and excellent decaf coffee.

All this was served with polish in one of the two intimate dining rooms, where the tables for two were so large that we had to slide our chairs and place settings closer together to avoid shouting. Lighting is fairly bright from a crystal chandelier as well as candles, plus the lights illuminating each work in a collection of art worth quite a bundle, we were told. The bound wine list, complete with table of contents, starts in the high teens and rises rapidly to $2,200. Roy sold for $4,100 an 1891 port from Portugal, one of the oldest available in the world and one of more than 30 vintage ports he had obtained on trips to Portugal and Madeira and displays proudly on a hallway credenza. Our more modest Parducci chardonnay was poured into champagne flute glasses.

Rack of lamb for two is highly recommended; it might be encrusted with pistachios or topped with a coating of kiwi, grapefruit, honey and cumin, and served with a tarragon sauce. The fish course represents "a new creation every night," says Roy, and the sauce that accompanies the roast duck is ever-changing – plum one night, tangerine and vodka the next – "to keep things exciting." Desserts range from chocolate mousse and tulipe aux framboises to soufflés and crêpes suzette.

Upstairs on the second and third floors are nine spacious and newly refurbished guest rooms, each with private bath, television and telephone. They're furnished in different periods with European and American antiques.

Out back in a pillared Georgian Colonial structure that Roy had built and named Tara Hall are sixteen large guest rooms with sitting areas and what he calls a "Gone with the Wind" theme. Imported tapestries adorn the sofas and chairs, the queensize beds include canopies and four-posters, and toiletries await on faux-marble vanities in the large bathrooms. The mahogany furniture includes a European-style desk and a full-length, free-standing mirror in each room. An outdoor terrace with a sitting area goes off the fireplaced lobby.

Ensconced in front of Le Chambord is **Rajko's,** the innkeeper's suave gourmet and gift shop (see Gourmet Treats).

Guests are served a complimentary continental breakfast (fruit, juices, and croissants and scones baked by the inn's two pastry chefs) in the main restaurant. Downstairs in the cozy Marine Bar at night, exotic coffees and cordials are offered in front of the fireplace.

(914) 221-1941. Twenty-five rooms with private baths. Doubles, $135.
Entrées, $19.95 to $29.95. Lunch, Monday-Friday 11:30 to 2:30. Dinner, Monday-Saturday 6 to 10, Sunday 3 to 9.

Belvedere Mansion, Route 9, Box 785, Rhinebeck 12572.

Erected in 1900 on a hilltop overlooking the Hudson, this Greek Revival mansion is named for its beautiful view. Most recently a fasting spa, it took on quite a different life in 1995 as an elegant restaurant and an expanding inn.

The restaurant on the main floor gets consistently good reviews under auspices of owners Nikola and Patricia Rebraca, who had run Panarella's restaurant on Manhattan's West Side since 1979. Here Patricia is executive chef, teaming with chef Patricia Panarella to provide contemporary regional cuisine. They seat 60 diners in three high Victorian dining rooms of the chandelier, fireplace and gilt-framed painting variety. Forty-five more can be accommodated at tables beneath umbrellas on a spacious side deck in season. There's also an unusual but romantic table for two or four in a little tea room at the head of the stairway landing.

It's an elegant, formal setting for food that is not at all intimidating. The short

Hilltop Belvedere Mansion is named for its beautiful view of mountains and river.

dinner menu is straightforward and quite affordable. Appetizers vary from a napoleon of salmon carpaccio with corn and scallion pancakes to ravioli of Coach Farm goat cheese and duck confit with saffron cream. Entrées could be sesame-encrusted yellowfin tuna with baby bok choy with ginger marin, grilled pork medallions on creamy mascarpone polenta and New Zealand rack of lamb with a crimini mushroom and potato lasagna. Expect surprises like pan-seared Alaskan cod served over ratatouille or sautéed ocean perch over a purple peruvian potato with fennel and blood orange reduction. Homemade desserts include chocolate truffle cake with mango crème anglaise, raspberry swirl cheesecake with berry coulis and a trio of sorbets.

Upstairs are five guest rooms of mansion proportions, appointed with the Gilded Age in mind. The rear Roosevelt Room with an English Tudor canopy bed is masculine and mysterious in chocolate brown with gold trim. "There are a lot of pictures to get crooked around here," Patricia noted as she straightened a couple while showing us around. All rooms have private baths with abundant marble, ceiling fans and matching French Empire queen beds and mirrored armoires. The Astor and Lafayette in front offer fireplaces and river views.

Behind and to the side of the mansion is a lineup of ten rooms with separate entrances in a carriage house. Euphemistically called cottages, they're decorated differently with as much pizzazz as their simplicity and space would allow (a hand-painted bureau here, a wicker chair there). Six have king beds and four "cozies" each have a double bed tucked away in an alcove, a bathroom and not much more. They're perfectly serviceable, but not exactly the kind of place where you'd want to hang out and, at any rate, most have no places to sit (except for colorfully painted wood chairs out front).

More accommodations emerged in 1999 in a renovated lodge in the Adirondack style beyond the carriage house. Ten rooms here are dressed in Ralph Lauren and Laura Ashley country style. All have bathrooms with slate floors and walls (even the showers), and some have whirlpool tubs. Lighting is low, the chairs cane and the feeling rather Oriental – Nikola calls it "very Zen like." Rooms open off a wraparound cedar porch shared by guests.

A country breakfast is served in the dining room or on the terrace. It generally includes a choice of omelets with Coach Farm goat cheese and oven-dried tomatoes, walnut-crusted french toast or Hudson Valley pear pancakes.

The ten-acre property includes a rear pool with cabanas, a tennis court and a pond with a gazebo. At a recent visit, an elaborate French garden was being planted and a trellised glass conservatory furnished with lounges was ready beside. Next on the agenda was a paneled library/common room off the bar.

(914) 889-8000. Fax (914) 889-8811. Twenty-five rooms with private baths. Doubles, $225 to $275 in mansion, $175 in lodge, $95 to $150 in cottages. Two-night minimum on weekends.

Entrées, $18 to $26. Dinner, Wednesday-Sunday 5:30 to 9:30.

Beekman Arms, 4 Mill St. (Route 9), Rhinebeck 12572.

Dating from 1766, America's oldest continuously operating inn now has been brought up to date, from the new American cuisine emanating from its restaurant leased to celebrity New York chef Larry Forgione to its Delamater Courtyard rooms with color TV, air-conditioning and working fireplaces. In fact, from the outside, as you gaze upon the striking, contemporary greenhouse restaurant at the side of the main entrance, you might think history is deceiving.

But you can have your history and eat it, too, in the dark and beamed, low-ceilinged Tap Room, the Pewter Room and the Wine Cellar Room, with wooden tables and many private booths, all lit by candles, even at midday. Or you can feel more contemporary in the greenhouse room facing the center of town, which can be opened to the outside on nice days.

The restaurant, **The Beekman 1776 Tavern,** reopened to unprecedented fanfare after it was leased to Forgione, owner of An American Place in Manhattan, who was familiar with the area as an early CIA graduate. Charles LaForge Jr., the inn's owner since 1958, "wanted to pull back and this was the perfect match," said the manager – "America's oldest inn and An American Place's country restaurant." Forgione, who has opened a third restaurant in Miami and seldom is in the kitchen here, regularly updates a menu that incorporates American classics and regional ingredients. A chef from Argentina, Tony Nogales, executes his commands.

The solid, American-to-the-max menu is not quite as trendy now as in the beginning. It lists such appetizers as marinated forest mushrooms with warm Coach Farm goat cheese polenta, a local camembert crisp with field greens and gooseberry chutney, and crispy fried squid with tarragon mayonnaise.

Typical main courses are cedar-planked Atlantic salmon atop a creamy corn pudding, Eastern yellowfin tuna garnished with bok choy and steamed sticky rice, honey-glazed Adirondack duck on a stone-ground corn cake, and Colorado leg of lamb with mint pesto. Those with lower aspirations can try glazed country-style meatloaf, Pennsylvania Dutch free-range turkey pot pie, pizza of the day or a burger on a fresh sesame bun.

Desserts include old-fashioned double-chocolate pudding, individual farm-stand fruit crisp, homemade ice cream and sorbet of the day, and something endearingly called a campfire s'mores ice-cream sandwich, a throwback to one's youth but with *homemade* marshmallows and graham crackers.

Obviously, much of the menu implies excitement, many of the accompaniments are interesting and unusual, and the prices are far lower than they would be in Manhattan. But the food critics' raves seem to exceed ordinary customers' reality. The local food community has mixed reactions and some find the welcome less than warm.

Elsewhere in the main inn, history is evident. We marveled over the glass-enclosed replica of an old tavern in the far main-floor parlor, an incredible table-top display complete with miniature glasses and liquor bottles behind the bar and the most intricate little chairs and bar stools we ever saw. The specialty foods of Larry Forgione's American Spoon Foods line are featured in the Beekman Country Store off the lobby.

The thirteen guest rooms upstairs have been remodeled and redecorated with folk art accents lately, but remain dark and historic, as you'd expect from their 18th-century heritage. More luxurious and spiffy are those in the Delamater complex a long block up the street from the main inn. The gingerbread-trimmed 1844 Delamater House, one of the few early examples of American Gothic residences still in existence, offers a B&B experience. Television sets are hidden in the armoires of its six rooms, sherry awaits in decanters, and front and rear porches are great for relaxing. Behind it are top-of-the-line rooms in the cathedral-ceilinged Carriage House and five other guest houses scattered around the perimeter of the Delamater Courtyard. Each holds four to eight rooms, about half with working fireplaces. Guests here take continental breakfast in a side building with a gift shop and tables overlooking the courtyard lawn.

(914) 876-7077 or (800) 361-6517. Delamater House (914) 876-7080. Fifty-seven rooms and two suites with private baths. Doubles, $80 to $120 in inn; $85 to $150 in Delamater complex.

Entrées, $15.95 to $23.95. Lunch daily, 11:30 to 3. Dinner, 5:30 to 9 or 9:30. Sunday, brunch 10 to 2, dinner 3:30 to 9.

Lodging

Inn at the Falls, 50 Red Oaks Mill Road, Poughkeepsie 12603.

Hard to find but worth the effort is this elegant bed-and-breakfast hotel beside a picturesque stream in a tranquil section of suburban Poughkeepsie.

Owners Arnold and Barbara Sheer, who previously ran a nearby motor inn, liked to visit New England inns and B&Bs, "but we didn't like bathrooms down the hall or sharing the house with its owners," Arnold explained. So they decided to create in their hometown a combination of what they felt were the best features of a hotel and a B&B.

An unusual architectural scheme, a Boston decorator and $3 million produced a curving, two-story, residential-style building following the path of the stream. It has 36 rooms and suites, beautifully decorated in seven themes from English country to oriental to contemporary. A California artist did the striking paintings that enhance the rooms. Our suite had a comfy sitting room with extra-high ceilings, good reading lights, a dining table and kitchen sink with wet bar, plus two TV sets, three telephones and a canopied kingsize bed. It also had one of the biggest bathrooms we've seen, with an oversize tub and a huge walk-in shower. Floor-to-ceiling mirrors, bottles of toiletries and a marble-topped sink added to the imposing effect.

The marble floors of the lobby lead to a large living room with a soaring ceiling, a gigantic chandelier, plush sitting areas and a wall of windows onto the stream.

Breakfast room at Inn at the Falls looks out onto passing stream.

Here, cocktails are available at night and a complimentary continental breakfast is waiting in the morning (you also can have it sent to your room). French doors open to a terrace, where chairs and tables are put out in summer.

The Sheers pamper guests with nightly turndown service and chocolate mints on the pillow. They even provide cards with explicit written directions to each of their favorite restaurants.

(914) 462-5770 or (800) 344-1466. Fax (914) 462-5943. Twenty-two rooms and fourteen suites with private baths. Doubles, $150 to $155. Suites, $160 to $185.

Bykenhulle House, 21 Bykenhulle Road, Hopewell Junction 12533.

A fifteen-room Georgian manor house built in 1841 for a Dutch silversmith was opened as a B&B in 1990 by Florence Beausoleil. Listed on the National Register and located on six acres off an exurban residential street not far from Le Chambord, the house has seven fireplaces and double living rooms that are decorated with imported crystal chandeliers. A new chandeliered ballroom in the Greek Revival style with parquet floors and fourteen doors is used for weddings, and a few B&B guests have been known to dance there at night.

We were particularly impressed with the plant-filled side sunroom with a marble floor, outfitted in chintz and wicker and yielding a view of the patio and vast lawn. Beyond the 20-by-40-foot swimming pool, a stone path edged with thyme leads through Florence's perennial gardens to a fountain and gazebo. Guests enjoy viewing a rare buffalo farm nearby.

On the second floor are three large bedrooms, two with fireplaces and all with private baths. Four-poster beds and antique furniture are the rule. The third floor has two large bedrooms with sitting areas and whirlpool baths.

A full country breakfast is served on fine china in the formal dining room, the table set with crystal candelabra. The innkeeper prepares things like cheese frittata, french toast, eggs benedict, apple pancakes and other recipes from her studies at the Culinary Institute.

(914) 221-4182 or 227-6805. Five rooms with private baths. Doubles, $125 to $145.

The Mansakenning Carriage House, 29 Ackert Hook Road, Rhinebeck 12572. A gourmet breakfast – delivered to one's room in a basket – is a high point for many guests at this rural but plush B&B. "We used to serve breakfast in the main house," said owner Michelle Dremann. "But we found that our guests didn't really enjoy making small talk with strangers in the morning."

Many of the celebrity and high-powered business clientele view her hideaway as a place for escape and romance. "They cherish their privacy and independence," says Michelle, "so they have everything they need in their rooms."

The point was confirmed after a Country Living magazine article in 1999 pictured the chef delivering breakfast in a basket to the carriage house. "You won't believe how many people phoned to say they couldn't wait to have that breakfast experience for themselves," Michelle relates.

The treat arrives with the local newspaper in a hefty basket at the decadent hour of 9:30. Guests, most still in their robes, take it at a table in their room or on a balcony. The fresh orange juice is in a chilled glass flask and the homemade croissants, scones, mini-bagels and rugelach are in a heated cookie tin. The exotic fruit is a work of art surrounding the main dish, in our case diminutive slices of french toast stuffed with pecans and cream cheese, garnished with edible flowers and so good alone we passed on the side of peach-apricot sauce. The menu, printed daily, might yield cheese blintzes, specialty quiches, or buckwheat crêpes filled with fruit or smoked salmon. The inn's recipes have been included in a couple of inn cookbooks.

Michelle started in 1990 with two rooms and a suite in the main 1895 Colonial house that actually was the carriage house for a larger estate listed on the National Register and hidden in the woods some distance away. She now has four more suites, a husband and a child, and a full-time staff to assist.

The seven romantic hideaways here range from a small bedroom with a hall bath in the twelve-room main house to a sumptuous suite fashioned from four horse stalls in the former Stable. Five suites have fireplaces, three have whirlpool tubs and four have private balconies or decks.

A Philadelphia artist painted the remarkable stencil designs in each room, and Michelle decorated each to the hilt. The queen or kingsize beds are dressed with Ralph Lauren linens and down comforters. Satellite TV/VCRs, private-line telephones, Caswell-Massey toiletries, terry robes and a basket of extra towels are the norm. A coffeemaker, a decanter of sherry and a refrigerator stocked with complimentary beverages are in each room. The small Library common room on the main floor of the Stable is stocked with books and more than 200 videos.

The largest accommodation is the adjacent Country Covert Suite. The corner fireplace is positioned to face the kingsize bed, and the jacuzzi is enclosed in wainscoting that matches the bedroom ceiling. A bird's nest is hand-painted under a sheer half canopy above the Victorian trundle bed in a sitting room in one of the former horse stalls. The bedroom desk is next to a built-in ladder and a grain feeder from the original hayloft.

A wall in the Stable's upstairs hallway is a garden delight of hand-painted flowers, birds, butterflies, a squirrel on a wheelbarrow and even a ladybug tucked in a blossom. Guests in the Huntsman's Hideaway find trompe-l'oeil books painted on the fireplace mantle and remarkable hand-painted walls that look like wallpaper in the bathroom. At the other end of the hayloft is the sunny Fox Den with kingsize canopy bed, fireplace, jacuzzi and private deck.

Most in demand in the main house is the original, light and airy Manaskenning Suite with a kingsize bed beneath a beamed cathedral ceiling and eleven windows on three sides. Two casual chairs face the fireplace. French doors open onto a narrow wraparound balcony.

Guests rarely venture forth from their quarters into the huge living room with game tables that go begging in the main house, where the family occupies the first and third floors. They may walk around the five acres of wooded grounds, relax on hammocks or Adirondack chairs, play badminton or ogle the oversize koi in the fish pond.

(914) 876-3500. Fax (914) 876-6179. www.mchrhinebeck.com. Two rooms and five suites with private baths. Doubles, $125 and $250 weekends. Suites, $295 to $375 weekends, $195 to $250 midweek. Main house reserved for family Sunday-Thursday. By reservation only. Two-night minimum on weekends.

Veranda House, 82 Montgomery St., Rhinebeck 12572.

This attractive 1845 Federal house started as a farmhouse and once was an Episcopal church parsonage. Ward and Linda Stanley of Philadelphia, who bought the place to run as a B&B, offer four air-conditioned guest rooms with telephones and private baths. Three have a variety of queensize beds, from four-poster Shaker with lacy canopy to antique brass, and one has old-fashioned wood twin beds convertible to king. Two bedrooms, one downstairs in what had been a dining room and the other above, are architecturally notable for their bay windows attached to a five-sided bay.

The Stanleys have outfitted the common areas with rather modern furniture from their Philadelphia home. The living room opens onto a breakfast room as well as a TV room/library. The original parquet floors and nice glassware are on display throughout. Ward, who recently retired from a university job teaching the history of architecture and design, hosts lively wine and cheese hours for weekend guests on the wicker-filled front veranda or on a new terrace off the dining room. In his "retirement," he has become a B&B consultant and has taught courses on how to open a B&B at Westchester Community College.

Linda serves a full breakfast, starting with a fruit plate and a homemade pastry, perhaps sour-cream coffeecake. Orange-yogurt pancakes, sweet and savory crêpes – ham and mushroom paired with ones filled with jam – or eggs Veranda (her own elaborate version of eggs benedict with portobello mushrooms) could be the main course. Apple or pecan strudel might follow. Linda says she gave out the recipe several times in the first month for her sausage and tomato tart, made with tomatoes from their garden.

(914) 876-4133. www.verandahouse.com. Four rooms with private baths. Doubles, $95 to $130 weekends, $75 to $100 midweek. Two-night minimum most weekends.

Olde Rhinebeck Inn, 37 Wurtemburg Road, Rhinebeck 12572.

This rambling, low-slung farmhouse began in 1738 as one room. Fittingly it's the dining area, where Jonna Paolella – proud to have been designated at age 28 as the youngest owner-innkeeper in America – serves up fruit smoothies and lavish breakfasts as up-to-date as today.

Open to her kitchen, the dining room is the heart of the house. It's where she begins tours of a structure that oozes history in almost every inch between wide-plank floors and rough, hand-hewn beamed ceilings.

The dining room focuses on a long trestle table she crafted of stained white oak salvaged from Jimmy Cagney's barn in nearby Stannardsville. The chair seats were upholstered in fabric from an old church. An old pig barn on the property furnished the wood for the kitchen cabinets, and the counter tops are made of wood from a carriage barn across the street. The stone floor of a sunken TV/family room off the kitchen came from a nearby gristmill. The woodwork in the living room is patched and weathered and shows its age (1745) and National Register status.

"I'd never even been in an historic house this old," said Jonna, before she saw it in 1998 as the fulfillment of her dream conceived two decades earlier as the daughter of an innkeeper in Brooklyn. "Why, here you can sleep in a place built before Mozart was born."

Her guests sleep in three bedrooms that convey creature comforts amidst antiquity. The floors creak in the Ryefield Suite as you step out of the rare queensize bed, from which six inches had to be cut from the legs for the elaborate carved-wood canopy to fit beneath the chestnut ceiling beams. The queen bed angled in the corner of the light and airy Spirited Dove Room wouldn't fit going up the steep, narrow stairway. "So we blew open the side wall of the room – hence the balcony," says Jonna, referring to the appealing hideaway overlooking a fish pond on the pastoral property.

Each bedroom comes with satellite TV, CD player, terrycloth robes, stocked guest refrigerator and fresh flowers. The Spirited Dove adds a whirlpool tub, while the Deer Hill incorporates a separate sitting area and a private covered porch.

Each also is equipped with a table for breakfast, but most guests prefer to eat communally between 9 and 9:30 in the dining room. The meal starts with a choice of juices or fruit smoothies and an elaborate fruit platter. The main event could be baked french pear pancakes with sides of potatoes and eggs and a maple-pumpkin-walnut mini-loaf. Other possibilities include fluffy German pancakes and sweet-potato frittatas layered with spinach, three cheeses and tomatoes.

Welcome amenities might be fruit, fudge made with goat's milk, cookies and assorted pastries. Entertainment is provided out back by Jonna's two pygmy goats. Feedings take place twice a day, and the goats respond with the makings for goat cheese.

*(914) 871-1745. Fax (914) 876-8809. **Two rooms and one suite with private baths. Doubles, $275 to $295 weekends, $225 midweek; $175 to $195 midweek, off-season.***

Wine Tastings

Millbrook Vineyards & Winery, Wing Road off Route 57, Millbrook.

The Hudson Valley's first winery dedicated exclusively to the production of vinifera, Millbrook occupies 130 remote, hilly acres, somewhere in the back of beyond. It's blessed with dramatic views of vine-covered hillsides, three ponds, a picnic area and an unparalleled vista toward the Catskill Mountains. Owner John Dyson, former New York agriculture and commerce commissioner, converted a former dairy barn into the winery.

He and winemaker John Graziano produce 14,000 cases of fine wine a year, including award-winning chardonnays, pinot noirs, cabernet sauvignons and merlots (most in the $15.99 to $25.99 range) that some find as spectacular as the setting. Everything is state of the art, from the manmade ponds that help moderate temperatures to a patented "goblet" trellis system that lets pinot noir grapes get more sun and air for better ripening. Dyson, who also has purchased two California vineyards, grows and experiments with about 25 European grape varieties, more than anyone in the East. By example he has proved two claims: that the Hudson Valley can produce world-class viniferas, and that grapes provide a better return for farmers than cows, hay or corn.

You can follow his interesting story during a twenty-minute winery tour. Sample the results in a small sales room holding literature and a tasting counter barely big enough for two. A fine olive oil from Dyson's Italian estate also is on sale here. In summer, a changing local restaurateur operates the winery's outdoor **Vineyard Grill,** usually offering a lunch menu of salads and grilled items from noon to 3. The grill is also open on concert evenings (the winery hosts about six concerts each summer).

(914) 677-8383 or (800) 662-9463. Open daily, noon to 5.

Clinton Vineyards, Schultzville Road, Clinton Corners.

With Millbrook and Cascade Mountain, this is the third component of the scenic (and tasty) Dutchess Wine Trail.

Owner-winemaker Ben Feder patterns his in the tradition of small European estate vineyards. His specialty is a crisp, fruity seyval blanc, which he likens to a sancerre or a Loire Valley muscadet. Clinton was the first in the Hudson valley to produce seyval naturel, a rare domestic champagne fermented in the bottle in the classic methode champenoise. In good years, it produces a limited number of Johannesburg riesling wines in the spatlese style. Visitors sample wines in the tasting room and view the champagne cellars and winemaking facility.

(914) 266-5372. Open Friday-Monday, 11 to 5, or by appointment.

Benmarl Vineyards, 156 Highland Ave., Marlborough-on-Hudson.

Touted as "the mother vineyard" of New York State, this is particularly interesting for its seasonal **Benmarl Bistro,** a rakish cafe that has served some extraordinary lunches over the years, depending on circumstances and chefs, most from the Culinary Institute. Sit inside or out at a table with a grand view of the Hudson as you sip a bottle of seyval blanc.

Another distinction for the winery, founded in 1957 by illustrator/artist Mark Miller, is that it also represents (and sells) wines from "offspring" wineries, including two from Long Island and five from the Finger Lakes. On hand are nearly 35 varieties, from blush to cabernet. The winery operation seems to have been upstaged lately by its Gallery in a Vineyard, now the world headquarters for the Museum for the Preservation of Illustrative Art. It displays octogenarian Miller's collection of art and works by his contemporaries.

(914) 236-4265. Open daily, noon to 5. Tour and tasting, $5. Bistro open seasonally, Friday-Sunday 11:30 to 3:30.

Gourmet Treats

The Corner Bakery, 10 Charles Colman Blvd., Pawling, is one of the new breed of bakeries, featured in a New York Times magazine article and described by Redbook magazine in 1993 as one of the five finest bakeries in America. Shannon McKinney and Brian Doyle, who studied with Swiss dean of pastry Albert Kumin, expanded a small bakery into McKinney & Doyle Fine Foods Cafe and a large takeout-food operation. Using all natural ingredients, they bake exquisite cakes, pastries and pies (how about eggnog chiffon?), Irish soda bread that was written up in Food & Wine magazine, gingerbread houses and stollen. We can vouch for their blueberry muffins and a scone, which we enjoyed with a latte from the espresso bar. They also bottle their own dijon herb dressing, English mint sauce and preserves made on site by Shannon's mother, and offer a large selection of soups, salads, appetizers and entrées to go. Open daily from 7 to 5.

At **Adams Fairacre Farms,** 195 Dutchess Tpke. (Route 44), Poughkeepsie, you'll find a farm market like few others – really a one-stop supermarket sprawl of produce, gourmet foods and garden items. The produce section is bigger than many a grocery store, dwarfing even the Adams grocery section. Besides a gift shop and The Chocolate Goose for chocolates and ice creams, there is a Pastry Garden bake shop, where the aromas fairly overwhelm. Fresh rabbit was $2.99 a pound at the Country Butcher shop when we were there. The country deli and cheese shop offers all kinds of interesting goodies. Ralph Adams and company run a somewhat smaller branch along Route 9W just north of the Kingston-Rhinecliff bridge.

Rajko's at Le Chambord, 2075 Route 52, Hopewell Junction, billed as the Hudson Valley's "most unique gift shop," is a must stop in the area. It features a variety of Le Chambord's gourmet food products, from balsamic vinegar with capers to chocolate-covered raisins, plus a line of handmade gourmet pastas, including lobster fettuccine. Also part of the repertoire are exquisite porcelain and ceramics, handmade jewelry from Greece, stunning Italian silk neckties designed by innkeeper Roy Benich, hand-painted fused glass and island imports.

In Hyde Park, **The Uncommon Caffé,** Route 9, is the place to stop for espresso and cappuccino, specialty drinks and light fare, served inside or on an outdoor patio. The retail shop sells coffees and teas, gourmet accessories and country gifts. Nearby is the **Eveready Diner,** Route 9, a gleaming 10,000-square-foot tribute to yesteryear, serving everything from breakfast to diner classics. The **Hyde Park Brewing Co.,** 514 Albany Post Road, offers four brews plus a restaurant with an interesting menu that includes Asian vegetable salad with grilled chicken and wok-seared salmon fillet to go with.

New additions have helped Rhinebeck enhance its reputation as a mecca for food lovers. In 1999, **Bread Alone,** an offshoot of a bakery based across the Hudson in Boiceville, opened a retail store and café with a Tuscan country look at 43-45 East Market St. The organic breads, pastries, soups, sandwiches and coffees are highly rated. Up the street at 64 East Market is **Kitchen & Home,** where Arlene Chairamonte has stocked two floors of an old house to the ceilings with high-tech kitchen ware, gadgets, cookbooks, oils and vinegars, ceramics, birdhouses and much more. Down the street at 15 East Market, at the rear of the Book Corner, is **Country Touch.** James and Kelli Ellithorpe took over his late parents' bookstore and, to distinguish themselves from encroaching superstores, started sharing their homemade fudge and candies as well as related gifts. "Homemade candy is an art that not many people can do," says candymaker James, who employs his grandmother's recipes. Chocolate addicts are in heaven. Items of interest to cooks and hostesses are among the home/life/gifts at **Habitu.**

Well worth a side trip is the **Hammertown Barn,** an antiques store plus much more at 4027 Route 199 in Pine Plains, N.Y. Owner Joan Osofsky's expanding sideline is gourmet foods and dishware. We reveled in all the preserves and salsas, the hand-painted pottery, suave placemats and latest cookbooks. The old Gatehouse in front is furnished like a house and everything is for sale. On weekends, its working kitchen is opened for tastings of soups (perhaps mixed bean or potato-leek), salad dressings and mulling juices. Joan's husband Sid, a principal in the nearby Ronnybrook Dairy that the New York Times called "the Dom Perignon of Dairy," may offer samples of some of his ice creams. We tasted his yummy green apple and pumpkin flavors.

Gourmet Producers

McEnroe Organic, Route 22/44, between Millerton and Amenia.

The area's only certified organic produce market, this is also the biggest, with an almost overwhelming selection. The farm plants 6,000 heads of exotic let-tuces a week from March through October, selling them off at about $1 a head. Here is a paradise of produce: mesclun, coriander, garlic, walla walla onions, leeks, fingerling potatoes. A garlic festival was on when we were there. Pies, breads, jellies and vinegars are among the sidelines.

(518) 789-4191. Open daily, 8 to 5, May-December.

Coach Farm, Mill Hill Road off Route 82, Pine Plains. (518) 398-5325.

America's premier producer of goat cheese, this is the brainchild of Miles and Lillian Cahn, who gave America the classic Coach leather handbags from their New York City factory. In 1984, the Cahns imported a French cheesemaker and a Californian who owned the nation's largest goat herd to their 700-acre farm in the remote town of Gallatin. Within a few years, they had 1,000 goats, 40 employees and a goat cheese "that is the equal of any French chèvre sold in this country," according to the New York Times. They are the largest American producer, "though that doesn't mean much," Miles quips. The music of Bach plays during milking, from 3 to 7 daily, and the milk from each goat yields about one pound of cheese a day. Coach goat cheese comes plain or with herbs or pepper, and the farm also produces yogurt and Yo-Goat, a natural yogurt drink with no preservatives or sugar added. The farm shop is open occasionally in summer, and tours of the milking parlor during the milking may be arranged. Since he wasn't selling cheese on the premises at the time, Miles directed us to the nearby General Store in Ancramdale, where we bought Coach Farm yogurt and peppered chèvre.

Ronnybrook Farm Dairy, Ancramdale, (518) 398-6455.

A family farm that has overcome the ups and downs of the dairy business, this produces dairy products in demand at the area's finest restaurants, and you can't spend any time in the valley without coming across the name Ronnybrook. The Osofsky family has revived the old-fashioned glass bottle to showcase its now-famous milk, which it delivers to grocery stores across the region. There's little to see at the 1,000-acre farm, other than more than 100 award-winning Holsteins, but you can seek out its exotic ice creams at Peck's in Pine Plains or at the McEnroe Organic farm stand near Amenia (see above). The ice creams are available at Ronnybrook retail outlets in New York's Chelsea Market and Grand Central Station.

Keuka Lake provides backdrop for wines on Bluff Point.

Finger Lakes

The Pleasures of the Grape

Anyone who has indulged in the pleasures of the grape in the California wine country yearns to return, especially when the harvest is at its height. But Easterners no longer have to go out West. Closer to home, the Finger Lakes region of upstate New York embraces a cluster of vineyards and wineries that produce wines of international distinction.

The New York Times headlined an article posted later at many a local winery: "Sorry, France. Too Bad, California. Some New York Wines Outshine Even Yours." At last count, 49 wineries were located in an area about the size of Connecticut. It is a landscape of rolling hills, lakes and vineyard vistas that are not only the equal in terms of scenery of most in California but often exceed them because of their proximity to water.

The Finger Lakes wineries range from venerable Widmer's, which attracts hundreds of tourists on busy days, to tiny Shalestone Vineyards, a new winery with an underground cellar and a tasting room marked by a shale sign and the words, "Red is all we do." Most are clustered along the hillsides rising sharply from the southern ends of Cayuga, Seneca and Keuka lakes.

The wine boom has spawned related ventures, far beyond the winery visits that beckon more than one million tourists annually to the Finger Lakes, most in the late summer and fall.

Foremost, of course, is the sale of grapes – pick-your-own, or available by the basket or in juice for wine. Grape pie is a staple on traditional dessert menus. Fire hydrants are painted purple in Naples for the annual Grape Festival in September.

Good restaurants, most featuring Finger Lakes wines, have emerged, particularly in the Ithaca area. So have a handful of inns and a multitude of B&Bs.

Also emerging lately is a cottage food industry, which is at roughly the same stage of development as the wine scene was twenty years ago. Particularly noteworthy is the local cheese industry. Ithaca was the site for the first annual meeting of the American Cheese Society, and the Ithaca Journal reported the Finger Lakes were "becoming known as the wine and cheese region of the country." Ithaca's Farmers' Market is known across the country as a model of the genre.

These days, a tour of the Finger Lakes wine country is much more than a one-day affair, and involves far more than simply touring a winery or two. On a leisurely trip, all the senses are at once heightened and lulled as you sample wines and indigenous foods on a sun-bathed deck overlooking one of the Finger Lakes, particularly in autumn when the grapes are being harvested and the hillsides are ablaze in color.

Tippling Through the Wineries

Canandaigua Wine Co. is the biggest, Widmer's the most picturesque and Bully Hill Vineyards the most controversial of the larger Finger Lakes wineries.

But others are more interesting for visitors with an interest in winemaking and an appreciation for finer wines, especially those who seek personalized, informal tours that follow the dictates not of the leader but of the led.

For orientation purposes, start at one of the larger wineries, whose guided tours offer a comprehensive if perfunctory overview of the winemaking process followed by a quick short course on the proper way to taste wines and a commercialized pitch to purchase your favorites on the way out. Then head for the smaller wineries, where the tours are intimate, the conversations spirited, the tastings more varied and the guide may be the winemaker or the owner. The tastings are usually free, although some wineries charge $1 or more. Since they tend to be clustered at the southern ends of three lakes, you can visit the wineries along one lake each day. Locally available brochures group them under the Cayuga and Seneca Lake wine trails and the Keuka Lake Winery Route.

The traditional Finger Lakes specialty has been white vinifera wines, especially rieslings. Lately, red wines are coming of age.

Because the wineries are so central to the Finger Lakes and their appeal is so special, we begin this chapter with a guide to some of the best or most interesting.

Dr. Konstantin Frank/Vinifera Wine Cellars, 9749 Middle Road, Hammondsport.

This is where the "new" Finger Lakes wine tradition was launched in 1962. Dr. Frank was the first to plant European vinifera grapes successfully in the Finger Lakes. His son Willy and grandson Fred continue the tradition. The Frank wines have been served at the White House and have consistently outscored French wines in blind tastings.

The low-key tasting room along an unpaved side road is the place to go for world-class pinot noir and cabernet sauvignon. "We could spend a quarter of a million dollars and make this a very attractive tourist destination," says Willy. "We prefer instead to make the best wines that can be made from our grapes." They produce 10,000 to 14,000 cases a year, exporting internationally to countries as far away as Japan.

Willy also has opened **Chateau Frank** in the cellar of the Frank home for the

Visitors to Glenora Wine Cellars enjoy lunch on new restaurant deck overlooking Seneca Lake.

making of methode-champenoise sparkling wines, including a flagship brut in the French style that sells for about $17.95.

(607) 868-4884 or (800) 320-0735. Daily, 9 to 5, Sunday noon to 5.

Hermann J. Wiemer Vineyard, Route 14, Dundee.

Hermann Wiemer, whose family has grown grapes and made wine for more than three centuries along the Mosel River in Germany, ranks as today's icon among Finger Lakes vintners.

Wiemer, then the winemaker for the legendary Walter Taylor, acquired an abandoned soybean farm on a slope on the west side of Seneca Lake in 1973 and began planting viniferas as well as the traditional hybrid grapes. Fired by Taylor six years later as disloyal to the hybrid cause, Wiemer set up his own winery and never looked back. His soaring barn winery, renovated to state-of-the-art condition, is low-key and very serious, as befits a producer of award-winning chardonnays and rieslings that command top dollar

Wiemer established a nursery that has become one of the country's most important sources for top-quality grapevines, a sideline that in its way dwarfs his vineyard and winery. He produces about 12,000 cases of wine annually, samples of which can be tasted in a rather forbidding tasting room where the solo visitor senses that the staff has other priorities. In its annual pick of the world's finest wines, Wine Spectator gave Wiemer's semi-dry riesling ($10) the top rating. There are self-guided tours. Private tours may be arranged by appointment.

(607) 243-7971. Monday-Friday 10 to 5, year-round; also Saturday 10 to 5 and Sunday 11 to 5, April-November.

Glenora Wine Cellars, 5435 Route 14, Dundee.

Among medium-size Finger Lakes wineries, this is a pace-setter with a commanding view from the west side of Seneca Lake. Glenora has been winning awards since it opened in 1977 as the first winery along Seneca. Its Johannesburg riesling was rated the best in America two years in a row, and its reserve chardonnay was served at President Bush's inauguration. Glenora long ago abandoned variety in order to concentrate on premium white viniferas and French-American varietals, plus premium sparkling wines. Wine Spectator magazine ranks it among the world's 70 top producers of fine wines.

Glenora's merger with the smaller Finger Lakes Wine Cellars of Branchport doubled output to 60,000 cases a year. A large, two-story addition has expanded the production facility as well as the upstairs tasting area and added an impressive new showroom. The expansion continued in 1999 with a new building housing a restaurant, inn and conference center with a stupendous view (see below).

After viewing a video presentation, visitors sample up to five wines. Questioners who linger may get to try a few others, as is the case at most smaller wineries. Glenora offers a line of table wines ($5.99), but we always pick up a few of the dry rieslings ($7.99), which we think are about the best anywhere. Also great are the brut and blanc de blanc and the merlot. Ever-enterprising, Glenora sponsors food and wine festivals and occasional Sunday afternoon concerts on its lawn.

(607) 243-5511 or (800) 243-5513. Daily, 10 to 8 in July and August, 10 to 6 in June, September and October; 10 to 5 (Sunday noon to 5), rest of year.

Wagner Vineyards, 9322 Route 414, Lodi.

This is another favorite among the larger estate wineries, thanks both to its fortuitous location on the eastern slope overlooking Seneca Lake and to the myriad endeavors of owner Bill Wagner, a dairy farmer-turned grape grower-turned winemaker. He started in 1979 with eight wines and now offers more than 30 wines and champagnes, as well as six beers from the new Wagner Valley Brewing Co.'s microbrewery adjacent. One of his most appealing endeavors is the large Ginny Lee Cafe (see below), but he's no doubt proudest that the winery has been ranked among the world's top 70 by Wine Spectator.

Bill Wagner differs from some in that he grows all his grapes ("my philosophy is that good wine is made out in the vineyards, which makes winemakers shudder, but I like that full-time control over the grapes," says its owner). It also differs in the amount of research ("more than the rest of the wineries put together") and the proportion of red wines (at one point nearly 50-50). He claimed another first in 1999, opening an off-premise farm winery store and cheese shop called the Channel Marker 225 Gourmet Wine Shop in Clayton in the Thousand Islands area.

He and his staff here host hundreds of visitors on busy weekends in the octagonal building he designed himself, as well as Friday night musical bashes on the deck of the microbrewery in summer. After tours of the winery, visitors are offered a tasting of wines and then browse through a large and busy shop. The limited-release chardonnays and pinot noirs have been much honored; ditto for a couple of dessert ice wines. We came home with a good gewürztraminer for $7.99.

(607) 582-6450. Monday-Thursday 10 to 8:30, Friday-Sunday 10 to 4:30, June-August; daily 10 to 4:30, May and September-October and weekends rest of year; Monday-Friday 11:30 to 2:30, November-April.

Lamoreaux Landing Wine Cellars, 9224 Route 414, Lodi.

In its construction stage, passersby thought this striking structure atop a hill commanding a panoramic view of Seneca Lake was to be a cathedral. It turned out to be a temple – a temple glorifying some of the best wines in the Finger Lakes

Lamoreaux Landing Wine Cellars occupies neo-Greek Revival barn above Seneca Lake.

region. Owner Mark Wagner's "neo-Greek Revival barn" houses perhaps the region's most exciting new winery. California architect Bruce Corson, a friend whose father was president of Cornell University, designed a four-level masterpiece of open spaces, oak floors, floor-to-ceiling windows and cream-colored walls hung with changing artworks.

The elegant showroom provides a perfect backdrop for the tasting of premium viniferas, including a 1998 gewürtzraminer and a 1997 merlot that won gold medals in prestigious wine competitions. Mark, a distant cousin of Bill Wagner of the adjacent Wagner Vineyards, had been growing classic vinifera grapes on his 130 lakeside acres for other wineries before opening his own winery in 1992. His early rieslings won a total of 30 medals in the first four years. The 1990 blanc de noir was Wine Spectator's highest rated sparkling wine in New York. We savored the barrel-fermented chardonnay ($12) and cabernet franc ($14). At our latest visit, Lamoreaux had been judged the best winery at the 1999 Mid-Atlantic Wine Festival, which cited its 1995 brut, a 1996 chardonney and 1997 merlot, and was preparing for a Tuscan winemaker's dinner.

Mark explains that some of his wines may not be at their best as stand-alone tasting wines, "but I drink wines with food so those are the kind I'm producing here." He plans to remain small and aim for the ultra-premium market. The first of two wings on either side of the slender building was added in 1996 for increased production space. Plans call eventually for a concert pavilion with a hillside view of the lake.

(607) 582-6011. Monday-Saturday 10 to 5, Sunday noon to 5.

Standing Stone Vineyards, 9934 Route 14, Valois.

Who'd expect a year-old winery open only on weekends to win the Governor's Cup (best of show) at the 1995 New York Wine and Food Classic? With a red wine, no less? The best-in-state award for its ruby red cabernet franc put Standing Stone quickly on the connoisseur's map.

Owners Tom Macinski, a chemical engineer with IBM, and his wife Marti, a litigation lawyer, commute on weekends from Binghamton to their home and vineyard along the eastern shore of Seneca Lake. Even before their winery opened in 1994, their first gewürtztraminer had won a gold medal at the New York State Fair and their riesling and dry vidal also had won awards. The part-time winemakers won awards for every wine they produced in their first two harvests, and have been reaping more honors ever since for products that are quickly sold out.

The winery is in a restored barn and the tasting room is in an old chicken coop enhanced by a covered outdoor deck. The Macinskis have increased their output from 800 cases to 7,000, still operating basically weekends but hiring a winemaker. Their stylish chardonnay, riesling, merlot and pinot noir offerings are priced from $10.50 to $17.99.

In 1999, they teamed up with Ithaca restaurateur Daño Hutnik to add another deck and open a Viennese-style heuriger serving light foods and wines overlooking a little pond and the lake (see below).

(607) 582-6051 or (800) 803-7135. Monday, Thursday, Friday and Sunday, noon to 5, Saturday 10 to 6; Friday-Sunday in winter.

Knapp Vineyards Winery, 2770 County Road 128, Romulus.

A vaguely California air pervades this winery, a growing family operation on 100 acres of a former chicken farm above Cayuga Lake. There's a large, airy tasting room with a California-like veranda, but the prize addition is the restaurant fashioned from a storeroom at the rear of the winery (see below).

Winery owners Doug and Suzie Knapp say theirs is one of the few wineries producing "methode-champenoise" champagne. It also is one of the growing number doing red viniferas, including pinot noir and cabernet sauvignon. Total production is 10,000 cases a year. The late-harvest riesling is a gold-medal winner. Recently released was a velvety ruby port, fortified with brandy from the Knapp still. The new grappa had won a gold medal and, aging slowly in oak, a cognac-style brandy was released. In 1999, an addition substantially expanded the size of the tasting room and shop.

(607) 869-9271 or (800) 869-9271. Monday-Saturday 10 to 5:30, Sunday 11:30 to 5:30, March-December; weekends only in January and February.

King Ferry Winery, 658 Lake Road, King Ferry.

Peter and Tacie Saltonstall (he's a grandson of the Boston Saltonstalls) release 7,000 cases of their award-winning Treleaven wines at their small winery on the former Treleaven farm along the east shore of Cayuga Lake. Aged in oak casks in the French tradition, the chardonnays are highly rated, selling for $11.99 a bottle (the reserve is $16.99 and the vintner's reserve, $29.95). The rieslings and merlots are other good offerings, and the winery's melange blends merlot and pinot noir. An innkeeper-friend tried to buy a case of the first release of merlot, but it already had sold out.

(315) 364-5100 or (800) 439-5271. Monday-Saturday 10 to 5, Sunday noon to 5, May-December. Also weekends, February-April.

Special Winery Treats

The Inn at Glenora Wine Cellars and Veraisons Restaurant, 5435 Route 14, Dundee 14837.

This inn with 30 upscale guest rooms, a restaurant and a conference center opened in 1999 in a $5 million building straddling a hillside overlooking Seneca Lake, behind and beneath the winery. The view of the lake and vine-covered hillsides here is arguably the most spectacular of any in the Finger Lakes.

The inn, still manifesting its newness at our early visit, will – like a good wine – mature with age. The ambitious restaurant already is a class act.

Winery principal Gene Pierce sensed the need for an upscale hostelry and restaurant along the lake. "We're right at the stage where the Napa Valley was in 1977 when we started," he said, noting the growth from one winery on Seneca (Glenora) to 26, with more popping up every year. "There's suddenly all this synergy to support a destination inn and conference center."

He designed the low-slung, spread-out board and batten building as a country hotel "to fit in with the architecture of upstate farm country" and to blend into the vineyard. Rooms go off an interior corridor on two floors. Each has a private balcony or patio with a view over vineyards to the lake. The interior incorporates Stickley mission furniture, an armoire containing an entertainment center and refrigerator, a bureau, a table and two hard-back chairs. Two Adirondack chairs provided more seating on the balcony. Our room was one of ten with a king bed and a corner fireplace, plus a spacious bath with whirlpool tub, separate shower and pedestal sink. Others have two queen beds, but no whirlpool tub nor fireplace. Each room comes with a coffeemaker, hair dryer and a chilled bottle of our favorite Glenora riesling.

At one end of the sprawling building is a lobby and a 150-seat restaurant, a knockout of a space with vaulted ceiling, white walls with wood trim and well-spaced tables decked out in green and beige. In season, the prime attraction is the spacious rear deck, where we were fortunate enough to book a table with an unencumbered lake view. Dinner began with an amusé, tapenade with crackers, to accompany a $13 Glenora chardonnay, selected from a list of Glenora wines plus those from "our neighbors along Seneca Lake." A loaf of bread sliced on a board and a choice of excellent salads (one bearing grapes, toasted pinenuts and shaved ricotta on baby greens) came next. Main courses were excellent Montauk scallops served with a corn salsa and herbed risotto cake and succulent medallions of grilled Chilean sea bass, sauced with herbed pinot blanc and served with roasted Israeli couscous. Dessert was a flavorful port-poached pear and ice cream.

Executive chef Jeffrey Bates, who had managed Glenora's former Wine Garden Cafe, returned to his home area from Long Island to open the restaurant and manage the inn. His deft touch in the kitchen turns out appetizers like a polenta sandwich of herbed asiago over greens and a napoleon of eggplant, roasted red peppers and peppercorn chèvre with a tomato coulis. Entrées range from chargrilled bison ribs to shredded Soba duck, from pancetta chicken to stuffed rack of lamb, each with a different accompaniment.

At breakfast, we were impressed with the Veraisons poached eggs, topped with crabmeat and hollandaise sauce and served over herbed risotto cakes. Super-sounding salads, interesting sandwiches (smoked salmon, blackened catfish) and several wine boards of shrimp or cheeses are featured at lunch.

(607) 243-9500 or (800) 243-5513. Thirty rooms with private baths. May-October: doubles, $110 to $225 weekends, $100 to $215 midweek. Rest of year: doubles $100 to $175.

Entrées, $14 to $27. Breakfast daily, 7 to 10. Lunch, 11:30 to 3. Dinner, 5 to 9.

Knapp Vineyards Restaurant, 2770 County Road 128, Romulus.

The Knapp family launched one of the earliest and best of the Finger Lakes winery restaurants at the rear of their winery. An interior dining room opens onto a trellised outdoor terrace where vines grow above, herb and flower gardens bloom beyond, vineyards spread out on three sides, you can see or hear wild turkeys and

Vines grow over trellised dining terrace outside restaurant at Knapp Vineyards.

pheasants, and bluebirds fly all around. It's a delightful setting for some inspired meals. Recently, Suzie Knapp returned from a winter trip to Thailand and incorporated the occasional Thai accent into the menu and tall teak Thai carvings into the dining room. Chefs Chris Lego and Al Miller change the menus every six weeks to take advantage of local ingredients.

The dinner menu produces a choice of six entrées as small plates or main courses. They include maple-glazed salmon fillet atop lime scallion and red pepper couscous, tuna steak kabobs, pan-seared duck breast over a bed of mixed greens, capers and roasted red peppers and grilled butterflied beef tenderloin stuffed with stilton. Starters could be Tuscan bean or mulligatawny soups, crab cakes with chipotle tartar sauce and citrus shrimp salad. Desserts vary from cold lemon soufflé to kahlua crème brûlée. Strawberry riesling sorbet with fresh fruit was a special at our latest visit.

Lunchtime brings similar treats at lower prices ($6.95 to $8.95). You might try a grilled portobello sandwich, curried chicken salad, grilled sirloin with chipotle mayo, or the "big salad" of greens, three cheeses, salami, capicola, kalamata olives, local tomatoes and an egg from Knapp's Rhode Island Reds.

(607) 869-9481 or (800) 869-9271. Entrées, $16.95 to $19.95. Lunch daily, 11 to 4; dinner, Thursday-Sunday 5:30 to 8:30. Closed January-March.

Ginny Lee Cafe, Wagner Vineyards, 9322 Route 414, Lodi.

With its reasonably priced wines and charming setting (a panoramic view of its vineyards and Seneca Lake), the Ginny Lee has long been a treat. The expansive deck has been enclosed to better weather the elements and to extend the season. Now there's a vast interior space with cathedral ceiling, white walls and white garden-type furniture. A section of the outdoor deck remains. Although the fare has been scaled down from its original heights, the menu has been broadened and Wagner's new microbrewery offers a Friday night pub menu.

Wagner wines and Aurora grape juice by the bottle, half carafe and glass are available at winery prices at the cafe, which was the first at a Finger Lakes winery and was named for the owner's then-infant granddaughter.

You can order anything from a burger to a grilled chicken sandwich to a flank steak salad to creative pizzas conceived by executive chef William Cornelius, a self-styled pizza snob who formerly was managing chef at the famed Pierce's 1894 Restaurant in Elmira Heights. Or you can make lunch an event with an appetizer like crabmeat rangoons with hoisin-red wine sauce and a light entrée of shrimp scampi, fillet of salmon with cabernet shallot butter or cashew coconut chicken. At various visits we've enjoyed a Greek salad, shrimp salad on a croissant, a seafood and cheese pizza, and a fruit and cheese platter with French bread. We won't soon forget the fuzzy navel peach pie, the raspberry praline tulipe and the strong cinnamon-flavored coffee, which after lunch with a bottle of wine was the only way we managed to make it through the afternoon.

(607) 582-6574. Entrées, $8.95 to $14. Cafe, Monday-Thursday 10 to 8:30, Friday-Sunday 10 to 4:30, June-August; daily, 10 to 4:30, May, September and October, and Monday-Friday 11:30 to 2:30, weekends 10 to 4:30, rest of year. Pub, Friday 8 to 11, June-August.

The Bistro at Red Newt Cellars, 3675 Tichenor Road, Hector.

Caterer Deb Whiting and her husband Dave, the winemaker, opened this winery with spacious dining room and covered deck in 1999 in renovated space that once housed the Wickham Winery. Dave had proved his winemaking mettle for a decade at Standing Stone and other Finger Lakes wineries before going on his own. Deb ran the upscale Seneca Savory catering service in nearby Burdett before launching the bistro. On their days off, the versatile couple teach ballroom dancing.

Early reports were that the innovative food was terrific, as presented in the white-linened dining room with a view of the Seneca Lake valley (but not the lake itself). The changing menus are brief and to the point. Salmon wraps, baked chèvre and a spinach and arugula salad are among starters all day. Lunchtime might yield a chicken and portobello sandwich on focaccia, an open-face prosciutto sandwich with grilled tomatoes and provolone, or a red pepper stuffed with basmati rice, zucchini, onion and capers and sauced with marinara on a bed of wilted spinach and black beans. The dinner menu adds entrées like grilled shrimp on a bed of zucchini and red peppers, seared duck breast in a blueberry port sauce, pork tenderloin grilled in riesling-soaked corn husks with a cherry relish, and pan-seared beef tenderloin with currants, leeks and mushrooms in a port wine sauce. Desserts include a chocolate-covered cherry cheesecake and a lemon mousse and blueberry napoleon.

The winery is named for the Eastern red spotted newt, which the Whitings consider one of nature's more beautiful but obscure creatures. Their spacious tasting room also is a gallery showcasing local art.

(607) 546-4100. Entrées, $14.95 to $18.95. Lunch, Thursday-Sunday 11 to 4. Dinner, Thursday-Sunday 4 to 8.

Sheldrake Point Vineyard & Cafe, 7448 County Road 153, Ovid.

Near a point jutting into Cayuga Lake, this newly built winery bottled its first blend in 1998 with plans to plant 75 acres of grapes. An opening feature was a part-time cafe and tasting bar, offering creative fare at the side of the wine showroom and outside under a canopy and umbrellas. Two principals who know their food, chef Doug Leach and partner Chuck Tauck, offer lunch and tapas five days a week as well as dinners on weekends.

The crowd was standing-room-only the Saturday afternoon we stopped by. They were awaiting tapas like roast duck confit over potato roesti, sautéed wild mushrooms en croûte and Caribbean scallops with gingered coconut and pineapple salsa over sweet potato lattice, a Santa Fe chicken salad plate and sandwiches like Alsacian French dip, albacore tuna on a croissant and grilled vegetable focaccia.

Dinner fare changes each night. The choices when we were there were grilled swordfish with pesto cream sauce, broiled grouper with citrus beurre blanc, veal marsala and beef medallions au poivre.

(607) 532-9401. Entrées, $15.95. Wednesday and Thursday 11 to 2, Friday and Saturday 11 to 9, Sunday 11 to 6. Closed November-March.

Daño's on Seneca, 9934 Route 414, Valois.

Leading Ithaca restaurateur Daño Hutnik teamed up with the folks at Standing Stone Vineyards in 1999 to open a novel, Viennese-style pub called a heuriger on a covered deck outside the winery. Daño, a former Czech ballet dancer who admits to a bit of gypsy wanderlust, said this was the next best thing to his dream of moving to the Napa Valley. He likens it to a wine bar outside Vienna, where "an afternoon of food and wine at the heuriger is an important family event."

Here he offers an enticing selection of breads and spreads, salads, charcuterie and rotisserie items, as well as luscious sweets. Terrines, bratwurst, cold poached salmon, roast pork, chicken, wiener schnitzel – you name it and Daño may have it in his deli case. Snack on liptauer cheese, the Austrian house specialty, spread over hunter's or fishermen's bread, or perhaps Hungarian goulash or a fruit strudel. Standing Stone bottles Heuriger wines specially for the venture.

(800) 803-7135. Saturday and Sunday noon to 6, June-October.

Dining

The Best of the Best

Madeline's, 215 The Commons, corner North Aurora and East State Streets, Ithaca.

The main floor of the old Rothschild's department store is unrecognizable in its latest transformation. The manager of the family-owned Thai Cuisine restaurant (see below) went off on his own in 1997, opening the stylish Madeline's at a prime downtown corner. Sunit ("call me Lex") Chutintaranond and his fiancée, Phoebe Ullberg, started with a patisserie named for a favorite character from French children's literature. The establishment has since expanded into the city's handsomest restaurant. Slick and urbane, it would appear to be more at home in Manhattan than in upstate Ithaca. The look is modern-minimalist Asian, colorful and vaguely art deco, with a bar and tables spaced well apart on several levels.

Gregarious Lex, the head chef, oversees Pacific Rim fusion fare that dazzles in flavor and execution. "We call it East meets West," he says. In his newly expanded kitchen, "we can do anything." Changing the menu every couple of months, he might pair French and Japanese or Italian and Asian. For dinner, he could serve shrimp in a roasted chile and coconut milk sauce over green tea rice or sear sea bass with a black bean sauce and Korean chile butter. He might roast his pork shank with a black tea citrus crust, and finish the New York sirloin with a port and three-peppercorn sauce. Accompaniments could be Asian soybeans, steamed baby

Well-stocked bar adjoins dining room at Madeline's restaurant.

bok choy, garlic-sesame bean sprouts, spinach ohitashi and chilled steamed napa cabbage.

Starters are as simple as chilled Asian soybeans in the pod and as complex as poke, the Hawaiian seafood preparation, served sashimi-style and seasoned with seaweed, chiles, onions and such. Asian shrimp cakes are offered with pickled cucumber and ground roasted peanuts. The house-baked focaccia with caramelized onions and calamata olives is to die for. Ditto for the desserts, which fill sixteen feet of display cases in the restaurant. Pastry chef Gail Brisson prepares up to 20 patisserie-style treats a night from a repertoire of more than 50. We've heard their praises sung across the city.

The lunch menu is as interesting as the dinner. The bar features more than 80 single-malt scotches as well as rare cognacs, grappas and small-batch bourbons.

Given the quality and ambiance, the prices throughout are so low as not to be believed.

(607) 277-2253. Entrées. $12.95 to $16.95. Lunch, Monday-Saturday 11:30 to 3. Dinner nightly, 5 to 10 or 11.

Rosalie's Cucina, 841 West Genesee St., Skaneateles.

A plaque on the wall in the rear foyer says this was "built with great love for my sister" and, after listing the architectural credits, adds "with way too much money." Both the love and the money are manifest in the chic Tuscan-style restaurant, wine cellar and bakery – a testament to the late Rosalie Romano from Phil Romano, the restaurant impresario who started the Fuddrucker's chain.

It seems that Phil, who grew up in nearby Auburn and lives in Texas, still summers on Skaneateles Lake and "wanted a nice place to eat," in the words of co-owner Gary Robinson. "He'd been all over Italy, so he built this the way he wanted it for himself."

His reported investment of more than $1.5 million includes a stylish 120-seat restaurant backing up to a designer's dream of an open kitchen, a downstairs wine cellar and an upstairs Romano Room for family reunions and private parties, a bakery, an outdoor bocce court, a small vineyard for show, and an elaborate herb layout and vegetable garden for real.

The result: The hottest culinary establishment in the Finger Lakes. Without advertising, no press kit and not even a listing in Skaneateles or Finger Lakes promotional materials several years after opening, the place was mobbed nightly, and up to two-hour waits were the norm on weekends. The bocce court, the wine cellar and a delightful Mediterranean-style courtyard – all holding areas for the waiting crowds, who are given breads, olives and cheese –get quite a workout.

Inside the salmon-colored building identified by a sign so small we missed it on the first pass is a dark and spacious dining area understated in white and black. Black chairs flank well-spaced tables covered with white butcher paper over white cloths. A few columns break up the expanse. The white walls are enlivened with hundreds of splashy autographs of customers, who pay $25 each to charity to enshrine their name and the date for posterity. Most of the color comes from the open kitchen at the end of the room, where cooks work amid hanging ropes of garlic, arrangements of bounty and chickens roasting on the rotisserie.

The menu changes daily. The specialty is prime meats, as in aged New York strip steak and grilled veal loin chop. The slow-roasted pork with oregano and garlic and the lamb loin with white wine and garlic are done according to family recipes. So are the scampi alla Rosalie (with artichokes and garlic butter) and the farfalle con pollo (chicken with pancetta, asiago cream, red onions and peas). Prices have escalated since the early days, although the pasta, risotto and chicken dishes remain in the teens. Portions are large and value is received.

Antipasti include carpaccio, pizza margarita, cannelloni with ground meat and ricotta, steamed mussels and grilled portobello mushrooms. Of the insalata, the one with arugula, prosciutto, reggiano and lemon is special.

The homemade desserts vary daily. The pastries and breads come from **Crustellini's,** the bakery at the rear of the establishment, where several varieties of sensational "hand-made breads" are for sale daily from 9 a.m.

Rosalie came in most nights to be hostess before passing on to her eternal reward. The staff continues her legacy in this cucina that love built.

(315) 685-2200. Entrées, $17.95 to $29. Dinner nightly, 5 to 9 or 10.

Daño's on Cayuga, 113 South Cayuga St., Ithaca.

Daño Hutnik had quite a background before opening a small downtown-Ithaca restaurant that quickly became one of the area's best. Born in the Ukraine, he grew up in Czechoslovakia and was a ballet dancer for fifteen years in Vienna before embarking on a restaurant career in New York and San Francisco. A classified ad in the New York Times led him in 1990 to Ithaca and this old space that he and his wife, artist Karen Gilman, transformed into a chic French-style bistro in peach and blue-gray. There's seating for 44 at white-linened tables topped with white paper against a backdrop of her artworks on the walls and a spotlit alcove showcasing her fabulous desserts at one visit, his showy bottled preserves, chanterelles and pickles the next.

Chef Daño (pronounced Dan-yo) changes his menu of contemporary central European, French and northern Italian fare seasonally. Those in the know go for such specialties as oxtail stew with black and green olives or veal sausage with braised red cabbage and spaetzle. One autumn night we sampled an appetizer of melted raclette cheese with boiled potatoes, cornichons and pearl onions, the classic version and enough for two, and the house terrine of chicken, pork, duck, veal "and everything – a little cut here, a little there," according to the chef.

Flowers and pastries are displayed in niche at Daño's on Cayuga.

Among main courses we were delighted by the sautéed chicken breast with artichoke hearts and smoked mozzarella, served with incredibly good polenta sticks, and the linguini with shrimp, peas and scallions. Other tempters included sautéed sea scallops served in a basil-butter sauce with a corn cake, haddock basquaise on a bed of garlic-mashed potatoes and sautéed veal flank steak with green onion sauce and mushroom-fennel risotto. We liked the Hermann J. Wiemer dry riesling, at the time the only Finger Lakes choice on an excellent little wine list specializing in imported wines and rarely seen Californias. Crème brûlée and a bittersweet-chocolate gâteau with raspberry sauce were worthy endings to one of our better meals in a long time. The occasion was made more enjoyable as congenial chef Daño, table-hopping at night's end, proved to be quite the talker and philosopher.

Ever looking to keep busy, in 1999 he opened Daño's on Seneca, a seasonal weekend adjunct at Standing Stone Vineyards (see above).

(607) 277-8942. Entrées, $13.95 to $21.95. Dinner, Tuesday-Saturday 5:30 to 9:30 or 10.

Pangea, 120 Third St., Ithaca.

Talented young chef Paul Andrews took over the striking Italian trattoria known as Tre Stelle in 1998, did some refurbishing and changed the theme to modern American. The sleek dining room, with a mix of art and artifacts on the walls, is light and airy. Colorful mismatched vinyl covers accent the white-clothed tables. A wraparound terrace provides sylvan courtyard dining beside vine-covered walls on three sides.

The seasonal menu favors local products and is categorized under small, medium, large, side and sweet plates. The bold-flavored dishes begin with starters like grilled squid with roasted chiles and togarashi-dusted scallops with grapefruit and greens. Medium plates might be grilled shrimp with avocado and papaya, grilled onion and watercress salad with feta and chickpeas, and grilled quail with warm sweet potato salad, stir-fried scallions, honey and soy glaze. Among large plates, consider pan-seared cod with paprika butter, grilled salmon with ginger-braised

Plants thrive in dining room at Renée's Bistro.

lentils, wilted spinach and saffron beurre blanc, and crispy duck breast with tamarind glaze.

Formerly for pizzas, the wood oven is now used for roasting rack of lamb with rosemary-coriander sauce. It also produces a chocolate lava cake that is Pangea's signature dessert. Other sweets include coconut brûlée and lemon cream napoleon.

(607) 273-8515. Entrées, $15.75 to $18.50. Dinner, Wednesday-Sunday 5:30 to 10 or 11.

Renée's Bistro, 202 East Falls St., Ithaca.

This appealing American bistro was opened by Renée Senne, who had been sous chef at L'Auberge du Cochon Rouge and chef at the Greystone Inn upon her return to Ithaca from studying at La Varenne in France and teaching in New York.

Ficus trees and hanging plants thrive in the airy dining room and a small bar, both with a wall of windows across the front. It was in the former that we enjoyed a fine spring lunch: an excellent cream of onion soup, a slice of French bread topped with fresh mozzarella, sundried tomatoes and basil, and a special of fettuccine with grilled shrimp and garlic-cream sauce.

Alas, lunch has fallen victim to the restaurant's success, as Renée decided to concentrate on dinner. "Now we do more refined French cuisine, but with a neighborhood feel," says she. "I don't want anyone to feel intimidated." Dining is at tables dressed in white linens topped with butcher paper. Innovative seafood preparations are highlighted on a short menu supplemented by myriad specials. You might find broiled salmon served with yellow pepper coulis, smoked potatoes and scallion mashed potatoes; game hen braised with garlic and served with tomato risotto; grilled duck breast and confit with caramelized orange sauce, or grilled delmonico steak with morel demi-glace and dartois of potatoes, onions and smoked gouda cheese.

Renée's repertoire includes such starters as a buckwheat crêpe yielding mushrooms and gruyère, a terrine of fresh and smoked salmon, polenta with artichoke hearts and chèvre, and shrimp cakes served with roasted-pepper sauce. How we'd like to graze through a couple of those, a salad of new potatoes served warm with chèvre on baby greens, and one of the pasta dishes, perhaps squid ink linguini with sautéed calamari.

The owner's background as a pastry chef shows in the desserts. They run from mille-feuille to vacherin with roasted strawberries to peach shortcake, and include lots of ices and granités.

(607) 272-0656. Entrées, $16 to $23.50. Dinner, Monday-Saturday 5:30 to 10.

John Thomas Steakhouse, 1152 Danby Road (Route 96B), Ithaca.

For some years, a restaurant has been ensconced in this farmhouse on a hillside overlooking the Cayuga Lake valley about a mile south of the Ithaca College campus. A kitchen fire closed the long-popular L'Auberge du Cochon Rouge, a French restaurant of renown, in 1994. When owner Walter Wiggins rebuilt, he surprised almost everyone by turning the country-French landmark into a New York-style steakhouse. He also surprised local skeptics, some of whom were persuaded that this was even better than its predecessor. The beef is prime and the prices lofty, since everything is à la carte.

The restaurant's original French theme had run its course and its traditionally masculine decor lent itself to the steakhouse concept, explained manager Mike Kelly, who had overseen a similar venture in Roslyn, Long Island. The interior of the farmhouse remains basically the same, although the inner Red Room was enlarged following the fire. The upstairs L'Auberge Lounge retains links with the past.

Former L'Auberge sous chef William Peterson stayed on as chef. The predictable menu ranges from ribeye to T-bone steak. The specialty is porterhouse steak, $47 for two. There are grilled or blackened tuna, broiled swordfish or salmon, shrimp scampi, jumbo lobster, a vegetarian platter and chicken pommery for non-beef eaters. Salads, vegetables and the usual side orders cost extra. Appetizers include smoked trout, baked deviled crab, shrimp cocktail and clams casino. Desserts range from crème brûlée and puff pastry with Italian cream and blueberries to assorted ice creams and triple berry strudel.

L'Auberge's acclaimed wine cellar, destroyed in the fire, was being rebuilt.

(607) 273-3464. Entrées, $16.95 to $27.95. Dinner nightly, 5:30 to 10 or 11.

Seasons Restaurant, 108 North Franklin St., Watkins Glen.

The dining situation in up-and-coming Watkins Glen improved markedly with the opening of this with-it establishment in the historic Watkins Hotel. Young chef-owner Brud Holland and his wife Shari got their start nearby at the Glen Mountain Market before opening Seneca Valley Kitchens in Glenora, producer of specialty foods and a vegan food line called Salama della Terra for national distribution.

"This is more up our alley," Brud said as he prepared dinner the night we visited and told of plans to restore sixteen guest rooms upstairs in the abandoned hotel. Scheduled to be done in phases starting in 2000, the rooms would be priced at $125 to $175 a night in summer.

On the ground floor of the 1891 structure, the Hollands lightened up the dark space formerly occupied by the Town House restaurant. Two dining rooms are elegant in cream and beige, with lighting from wall sconces and votive candles on heavily linened tables set with delicate stemware. Across the center hallway is the Kendall Club, a Victorian bar and lounge featuring grilled pizzas baked on stone hearth bricks in a special oven. Among choices are the Chesapeake with blue crab and the Goat Hill Farmer with goat cheese.

Creativity reigns in the dining room, where both food and presentation are highly regarded. Specialty breads and a house salad are included with the main course. Typical choices are vermouth-braised salmon served on herbed red potato wedges with spinach-chive butter, pan-seared lump crab cakes served on cheese risotto with roasted garlic mayo, roasted veal tenderloin with romano cheese, and grilled New York strip steak with caramelized red onions and balsamic vinegar sauce. Pasta options could be hand-rolled gnocchi with braised shallots and romano cheese or gemelli with alderwood-smoked salmon and baby tomatoes.

At our visit, Brud was obviously into crab, topping his grilled beef tenderloin with a blue crab gratin and featuring a crab cake over mixed greens dressed with orange pommery mustard as an appetizer. Another starter was barbecued pork loin served on gingered coleslaw. Typical desserts are crème brûlée, chocolate-cherry cheesecake and mint ice-cream cake.

(607) 535-4619. Entrées, $14.95 to $21.95. Dinner nightly, 5:30 to 9:30. Closed Tuesday and Wednesday in winter.

Spinnakers, 4375 West Lake Road, Geneva.
A more superb lakeside location – with a stylish, shaded dining terrace to match – is hard to envision. This new restaurant, occupying a gently sloping spit of land jutting into Seneca Lake, was beautifully transformed from the old Geneva Rod & Gun Club. The spacious interior dining areas and bar are nicely nautical, but the terrace just inches from the lakeshore is breathtaking. Pots of petunias topped every table at our visit.

Chef-owner Matthew Wooster's eclectic, seafood-oriented menu features Finger Lakes products and is fairly inspired for a large "view" restaurant. For appetizers, you might find Thai curry mussels, alligator tempura with Creole mustard dipping sauce, crab cakes with cajun rémoulade sauce and grilled portobello mushroom slices served over baby greens with roasted red peppers and balsamic vinaigrette.

Main courses could be pecan-crusted salmon drizzled with a honey-amaretto glaze and served over whipped yams, grilled sesame yellowfin tuna with wasabi cream, mahi-mahi marinated in coconut milk and rum and paired with a jìcama-mango slaw, and grilled chile-marinated pork tenderloin with a five-spice apple chutney. Even the angus ribeye steak is a cut above, placed atop a bed of fried leeks, topped with caramelized onions and accompanied by roasted garlic and asiago mashed potatoes. All the time we lived in this area we never thought we'd see a menu proclaiming a "Finger Lakes penne:" chicken, sea scallops, sundried tomato and shiitake mushrooms in a light asiago cream sauce. All dinners come with a roasted garlic bulb, breads and salad with homemade dressings that include kiwi vinaigrette and creamy roasted garlic along with the ubiquitous thousand island.

Desserts like cheesecake and decadence pie sound more pedestrian than the rest of the fare, but we expect that to change as well.

(315) 781-5323. Entrées, $12.95 to $19.95. Lunch, Tuesday-Sunday 11:30 to 2. Dinner, Tuesday-Sunday 5 to 9 or 10.

More Dining Choices

The Heights Cafe & Grill, 903 Hanshaw Road, Ithaca.
Ensconced next to Talbots in the Community Corners shopping plaza in tony Cayuga Heights, this storefront operation is plainer than plain. Black upholstered

chairs are at mottled gray tables, each topped with a votive candle in a little flower pot. A few paintings on the white walls above gray wainscoting, dim lighting from wall sconces and a couple of ceiling fans, and that's it for decor.

Chef-owners James and Heidi Larounis are known for good American fare with Mediterranean flair. The early bargain prices have given way an upscaling of the menu with more expensive ingredients. Typical dinner entrées now are cedar-planked halibut fillet with roasted lobster vinaigrette, caramelized salmon fillet with a European-Thai cucumber salad, roasted lacquered duckling with a sundried currant balsamic glaze, pommery-crusted beef tenderloin with oyster mushroom jus, and herbed veal chop with roasted shallot zinfandel sauce. Also available are brick-oven pizzas and assertive pastas like grilled chicken pesto "ala" Greque, Mediterranean seafood stew and ziti California style. Everything comes with choice of Greek or caesar salad.

Starters could be tomato-basil bruschetta, taramasalata (a caviar dip) with baked pita chips, and carpaccio of portobello mushroom with a grilled octopus salad. Desserts range from baklava to crème brûlée.

The wine list, mainly from the Finger Lakes and California, is affordably priced.
(607) 257-4144. Entrées, $15.95 to $26. Lunch, Monday-Saturday 11 to 3. Dinner, Monday-Saturday 5 to 9 or 10.

Thai Cuisine, 501 South Meadow St., Ithaca.
The best Thai food in New York State – that's the opinion of many knowledgeable Thai-food lovers. It's served up in a serene, white and pink linened, L-shaped dining room and a new front solarium in a commercial plaza by a Thai family of cooks and a mainly American staff out front. With the departure of Lex Chutintaranond to his new Madeline's restaurant downtown, this is now owned and run by his younger brother, Noi. As one staffer explained it, nothing has really changed: "They learned from the same mother, and she's still in the kitchen."

A large choice of starters at dinner includes a couple of exotic soups, spring rolls, skewered pork and yum talay, a salad of shrimp, clams, scallops, mussels, Bermuda onions, mint leaves and ground chile peppers on mixed greens. There are six rice and noodle dishes, including pad Thai.

You'll have a hard time choosing among such entrées (all served with jasmine rice) as panang neur, sliced beef simmered in panang sauce with sweet basil and pineapple, served with a side of pickled cauliflower, and gaeng goong, shrimp simmered in Thai green curry with coconut milk, sliced eggplant, bamboo shoots, baby corn, fresh chile peppers and kaffir lime. The selection is enormous. Nothing is over $13.95, except for a few of "Mom's favorites."

Sunday brunch is the Thai equivalent of a dim sum meal, offering more than 30 exotic little plates for $1.95 each. Thai Cuisine has a fairly good wine list and, of course, Thai beer.
(607) 273-2031. Entrées, $8.50 to $19.95. Dinner nightly except Tuesday, 5 to 9:30 or 10. Saturday lunch, 11:30 to 2:30. Sunday brunch, 11:30 to 2.

Just a Taste, 116 North Aurora St., Ithaca.
This is billed as Central New York's largest wine and tapas bar. Originally opened by Lex Chutintaranond of Thai Cuisine, it has since been sold it to one of the cooks, Jennifer Irwin, and Stan Walton. They have made it better than ever with a carousel of treats that change daily, sometimes twice a day.

Sleek in gray, black and white with black lacquered chairs, the downtown establishment also has a small outdoor courtyard in the rear.

More than 50 wines are offered by the glass – in two sizes – or by the "flight," a sampling of 1½ ounces in a particular category, say five chardonnays for $7.50 or six local wines for $7.75. There are also Spanish, Italian and sherry flights, as well as a "Big Red" flight of heavy reds, three for $4.75. Assorted beers are available from a beer bar.

We know folks who like to order a couple of flights and a selection of international tapas and while the night away here. We had to settle for a quick lunch, sharing a spicy breaded oyster served on a bed of spinach, a chicken teriyaki kabob with an array of vegetables, and a pizza of smoked salmon and brie (the most expensive item at $5.95). The last was great; the other two were marred by the missing house sauce (so spicy when we finally got it that one of us wished we hadn't) and no semblance of an "array" of vegetables. Cappuccino and a terrific pineapple cheesecake made up for the lapses.

The dinner hour brings tapas in appetizer and larger sizes, as well as several pastas and entrées. Expect tapas like flatbread with roasted squash and goat cheese, portobello and fennel pie over baby greens, and salmon gravlax tostada with cannellini hummus, cucumber-citrus relish and tobiko caviar. You can order treats like crispy fried quail legs with Chinese sausage in oyster sauce and spicy Mexican chicken on basmati rice in either tapa or larger sizes. Or try the penne with wild mushrooms, onions and romano or the grilled ribeye with fried russet potatoes, blue castello cheese and demi-glace.

For dessert, regulars demand more than "just a taste" of Jennifer's signature chocolate soufflé.

(607) 277-9463. Tapas, $3.50 to $7.25. Entrées, $8 to 14. Lunch/brunch daily, 11:30 to 3:30; dinner, 5:30 to 10 or 11.

A Landmark for Vegetarians

Moosewood Restaurant, 215 North Cayuga St., Ithaca.

Once small and plain, this establishment on the lower level of the quirky Dewitt shopping mall is known to vegetarians around the country because of the *Moosewood Cookbook,* written by a former owner of the co-op operation, which had nineteen owners last we knew. Now there are six cookbooks associated with the enterprise. All are for sale along with other Moosewood memorabilia in the new Moosewood Bar and Cafe, which opens off the entry and features juices, coffees and a full bar.

Expansion and remodeling have produced a lighter look in blond pine, with yellow-sponged walls and wooden banquettes all around. The covered sidewalk cafe out front is pleasant and obviously popular in season.

Original and natural-food cuisine is featured, although purists are skeptical. ("Beware," warned a printed vegan and vegetarian guide to the area. "This well-known vegetarian restaurant is no longer vegetarian and has virtually no vegan courses" – a charge disputed by the restaurant, which says it always has at least one soup and one entrée that are dairy-less.)

"We're lazy about changing prices," one owner told us, and indeed they are quite modest. Tofu burgers, pasta primavera and Hungarian vegetable soup are frequent choices – the menu changes with each meal to take advantage of what's

Sherry and Charles Rosemann continue to expand The Rose Inn.

fresh. Pitas, frittatas, Caribbean stew, a mushroom-cheese strudel, a plate of Middle Eastern salads, cauliflower-pea curry and flounder rollatini are regulars. The blackboard menu lists an imaginative selection of casseroles, curries, ragoûts, salads and luscious homemade desserts like strawberry cream pie, lemon-glazed gingerbread, peach trifle and a pear poached in wine with whipped cream. We liked the sound of tagine, a Moroccan vegetable stew simmered with lemon and saffron on couscous, at one visit. Also tempting was a Chesapeake platter – baked catfish with old Bay seasoning, salt potatoes and stewed corn and tomatoes. The pasta al calvofiore with cauliflower and Italian cheeses and the Japanese braised eggplant appealed to others. The food varies, depending on which of the rotating chefs is in the kitchen.

Fish is offered Thursday through Sunday, and Sunday nights are devoted to varying ethnic or regional cuisines.

(607) 273-9610. Entrées, $10 to $11.50. Lunch, Monday-Saturday 11:30 to 2; light cafe menu, 2 to 4. Dinner nightly, 5:30 to 8:30 or 9, summer 6 to 9 or 9:30.

Dining and Lodging

The Rose Inn, 813 Auburn Road (Route 34), Box 6576, Ithaca 14851.

Charles Rosemann, who had moved to Ithaca to manage the Cornell University hotel school's Statler Inn, gave it up to join his wife Sherry full-time in running the inn she started. Their large and classic Italianate mansion, known locally as "The House with the Circular Staircase," was built around 1850 on twenty acres in the hilly countryside ten miles north of Ithaca.

Working constantly to improve and expand the guest quarters, they now offer twelve rooms with private baths, plus ten glamorous suites with fireplaces and whirlpool tubs. A 1999 addition produced the newest suites, plus a large gathering room and a new entry in the front foyer so guests don't have to arrive through the kitchen. Also available for guests' enjoyment are fine dining, a jazz club and more casual restaurant in the carriage house, outdoor terraces, a rose garden and formal gardens focusing on an open-air chapel – the last designed by their son for his wedding.

In a short time, the Rosemanns built the Rose Inn into New York State's only four-diamond, four-star country inn, as rated by AAA and Mobil, and one of the nation's ten best inns, according to Uncle Ben's.

Rooms are individually decorated by Sherry, and those in the most recent two-story addition at the side capture the classic flavor of the rest of the house. All are luxurious, with everything from lace curtains, ceiling fans and fresh flowers to telephones, luggage racks, terry robes, Vitabath and other amenities. In two, the bathroom fixtures (including a stretch-out tub) are from the Eastman House in Rochester. Folk art and antiques abound. Our rear suite came with a sunken whirlpool tub in a garden-like space filled with plants off the bedroom, a majestic kingsize bed and antique furnishings in the bedroom, a large closet and a modern bathroom. Even the smallest room is no slouch, with beautiful wall coverings and borders coordinated with the bedspread and the bathroom, an Empire desk and a plaster bust of King Tut on the wall. At nightly turndown, a candle is apt to be lit beside the bed, the towels replenished, your toiletries neatly lined up on the bath vanity and your clothing hung in the closet. A thank-you note bids "Sweet Dreams."

Breakfast is an event worthy of the rest of the inn experience. Rose mats are on the polished wood tables, as are white baskets filled with seasonal flowers. The juice glasses sport the Rosemann crest. Because fifteen varieties of apples are picked from their apple orchard, homemade cider is often poured. Also on the table are Sherry's homemade jams and preserves – maybe black currant/red raspberry, mirabelle plum or gooseberry/red currant. Local fruit is served from early June to mid-September (we loved the raspberries), often with the Rosemanns' own crème fraîche. There's always a choice of two main dishes. One day it might be a custard french toast with bananas foster and a smoked salmon and dill quiche; the next, eggs sardou and Charles's extra-special puffy Black Forest apple pancake, which we can testify is absolutely yummy. The coffee is his own blend of beans, including Kona from Hawaii.

The Rose Inn sets an elegant dinner table as well. The traditional prix-fixe meals in the main house gave way in 2000 to dinner six nights a week in the hunt-themed Carriage House restaurant at the side of the property. It's open to the public as well as inn guests.

New chef Robert Gedman, British-born and European-trained, came to the inn from the Four Seasons Hotel in Houston, Tex. The à la carte menu offers eight entrées from grilled ostrich loin to brandy-flambéed lobster tail. Live music is played weekends from 7:30 to 11:30.

(607) 533-7905. Fax (607) 533-7908. www.roseinn.com. Ten rooms and twelve suites with private baths. August, October and weekends Easter through Thanksgiving: doubles, $145 to $200; suites, $260 to $320. Rest of year: doubles, $115 to $175; suites, $230 to $290. Two-night minimum most weekends.

Entrées, $21.95 to $29.95. Dinner by reservation, Tuesday-Saturday 6 to 9:30, Valentine's Day to Thanksgiving.

Morgan-Samuels Inn, 2920 Smith Road, Canandaigua 14424.

Actor Judson Morgan, not J.P. Morgan as was first thought, built this rambling stone mansion in 1810, and eventually it became the home of industrialist Howard Samuels, who ran unsuccessfully for governor of New York a couple of decades

John and Julie Sullivan serve sumptuous breakfasts on terrace at Morgan-Samuels Inn.

ago. The house was acquired in 1989 by Julie and John Sullivan, who left jobs in nearby Geneseo to convert it into a very special inn. They named it the J.P. Morgan House, but later learned they were in error and, honest and perfectionist as they are, they renamed it the Morgan-Samuels. Remotely situated on 46 rural acres and run ever so personally by the Sullivans, it offers one of the more peaceful, utterly relaxing situations we know of.

One fastidious innkeeper of our acquaintance said she had the best breakfast ever here. Ours certainly was a triumph, and so pretty we wished we'd brought along a camera for a color photograph, although this was an instance where a photo could not do it justice.

The meal – for some the highlight of a stay at this sophisticated and enchanting B&B – is taken in the beamed dining room, in a glass-enclosed breakfast-tea room with potbelly stove or outside on the rear patio. John is in charge of cooking – he and eleven-year-old son Jonathan make an early-morning run to the supermarket to pick out the perfect fruit for the first course. We counted 26 varieties on the exquisitely put-together silver platter, including local Irondequoit melon, mango, two kinds of grapes, papaya, persimmon, figs, kiwis and prunes sautéed in lemon sauce. Gilding the lily was half a baked grapefruit with port wine and brown sugar. Preceding the platter was fresh orange juice served in delicate etched glasses. Following were huge and delicious carrot muffins and a choice of buckwheat pancakes with blackberries, blueberries or pecans (or all three), scrambled eggs with herbs, french toast or a double-cheese omelet. The last was one of the best breakfast treats we've had. It looked like a pizza with slices of tomato, scallions, red peppers, jalapeño peppers, mushrooms, herbs and parsley. Monterey jack, mozzarella, parmesan and blue cheeses were on top. Spicy sausage patties and sunflower-seed toast accompanied this breakfast worthy of a Morgan, as did hazelnut coffee.

The Sullivans join their guests for snacks and beverages in the late afternoon, which helps break the ice so "everybody is friends when they get together for breakfast the next morning," says Julie. The treats range from John's homemade sauces on chicken wings and piegogi (tenderloin sautéed in a Korean sauce) to cheese and crackers. They accompany hot or iced tea, cider or sparkling grape juice from local vineyards.

John will prepare dinners by advance reservation for eight or more guests ($55 each). Guests bring their own wine and enjoy togetherness in the dining room or the enclosed garden porch, or privacy in five separate dining areas. The birds were chirping, the fountains trickling and classical music playing as we dined by candlelight with fine silver and china on the porch. Our meal, which John assured was typical, produced a procession of whitefish with horseradish sauce, pasta shells in a hot Bahamian sauce, garlic bread, a fabulous chilled peach soup and a mixed salad bearing everything from strawberries and apples to beets, snow peas and artichoke hearts, dressed with raspberry vinaigrette studded with bacon and capers. The main course was filet mignon with a sherry-herb sauce, accompanied by green beans, mushrooms, cauliflower, potatoes, and broccoli and cheese. Dutch apple pie with ice cream ended a spectacular meal. "I cook the way I like to cook," says John, who has no formal training. He certainly cooks the way we like to eat, although we would have had to be super-human to finish it all.

Although food is obviously a passion here, the five guest rooms and a suite and the common areas are hardly afterthoughts. All eleven rooms in the house come with fireplaces. The Morgan Suite is lavish with early 18th-century French furniture, a kingsize bed, an over-length loveseat in front of the TV and a double whirlpool tub in a corner of the bathroom. An outside fountain sounds like a babbling brook beneath Evy's Chamber, a Victorian fantasy with a rosewood queensize bed, sitting area and balcony. The Antique Rose Room has french doors onto a balcony, a floral carpet and one of the first kingsize beds ever made. Our room on the third floor, small but exquisitely done, featured an interesting Gothic window beneath a cathedral ceiling and a kingsize bed awash with fourteen pillows. All rooms are air-conditioned and equipped with reproduction radios and tape cassettes.

Soft music is piped throughout the house and across the grounds, and candles glow in the common rooms. Besides the aforementioned garden porch where we like to relax, there are a well-furnished living room, an intimate Victorian library with a TV, and fine oil paintings all around. Outside are no fewer than four landscaped patios (one with a trickling fountain and another with a lily pond and waterfall), a tennis court and gardens. Ducks and chickens and a heifer and sometimes a horse roam around in the distance. You could easily imagine you were at a house party in the country with *the* J.P. Morgan et al.

(716) 394-9232. Fax (716) 394-8044. www.morgansamuelsinn.com. Five rooms and one suite with private baths. Mid-May through November: Doubles, $139 to $199; suite, $255. Rest of year: doubles, $109 to $179; suite, $195. Two-night minimum weekends and mid-May to mid-November.

Dinner for house guests by reservation, Thursday-Sunday at 7 or 7:30.

Geneva on the Lake, 1001 Lochland Road (Route 14), Geneva 14456.

If you want to pretend you are in a villa on an Italian lake, stay a night or two at this onetime monastery, now a small European-style resort hotel beside Seneca Lake.

Geneva on the Lake resort accommodates guests in Italian-style villa.

Built in 1910 as a replica of the Lancellotti Villa in Frascati outside Rome, with marble fireplaces and symmetrical gardens, the original Byron M. Nester estate was the home from 1949 to 1974 of Capuchin monks, who added a chapel, dormitory and dining room. Ithaca developer Norbert Schickel of Ithaca turned it first into apartments and then into a resort with 30 rooms and suites in 1981.

The Schickel family sold in 1995 to Alfred and Aminy Audi of Syracuse, who had saved the ailing Stickley furniture company and put it in an expansion mode. The Audis kept a low profile, but financed a much-needed refurbishing and upgrading designed to produce "the crown jewel of all resorts."

Aminy Audi makes the decorating decisions, employing the vast Stickley collection of furnishings, accessories and art objects. "She has the vision," says general manager Bill Schickel, who personally oversees every detail. Accommodations range widely from six studio suites with fold-down murphy beds to two-bedroom suites with fireplaced living rooms to two-story townhouses. The bigger ones like the Landmark one-bedroom suite with kitchen and elegant living room in which we stayed are comfortable and luxurious in an understated way. Others are more showy. The new Whirlpool Suite in the monastery's former sanctuary is a knockout with cathedral ceiling and a bright red whirlpool tub, big enough for four, in a mirrored alcove off a living room furnished in Stickley Hepplewhite. The premier Classic Suite, with fireplaces in both living room and master bedroom, is 1,100 square feet of luxury, furnished in Stickley Chippendale. The Loft Suite appears more modern in Stickley mission oak. It offers a kingsize bed, a living room with a fifteen-foot ceiling and a balcony sitting area with a view of lake and gardens. Half the suites are two bedrooms, and most come with full kitchens and large living rooms. Some of the apartment vestiges (like mailboxes in the entries) inevitably remained, although under the new ownership, one suspected, not for long. Now the emphasis is on amenities, with robes, irons and boards, and down feather pillows. Complimentary wine is in the refrigerator, a bowl of fruit on the table, and chocolates are at bedside after nightly turndown service. A small, redecorated parlor is the only inside gathering area for guests, since individual living rooms suffice for most.

The verdant, private setting is spectacular. Manicured grounds outlined in privet and dotted with marble statues stretch to the 70-foot-long swimming pool on a bluff at lake's edge. A trail leads down to the lake, where guests may swim, fish or use a paddleboat, or board the inn's new fifteen-seat pontoon boat for a late-afternoon tour of the lake. An impressive colonnade pavilion provides a lovely shaded area for breakfast, lunch or cocktails on the rear terrace.

Guests are treated on Friday nights to a tasting of New York State wines and cheeses in the pavilion. Marion Schickel, widow of the resort's founder, has hosted the event every weekend for seventeen years.

A light continental breakfast of fresh juice and croissants is included in the rates. A full country breakfast is available for $11.50. We can attest that the scrambled eggs with cream cheese and the shirred eggs with Canadian bacon are excellent.

Candlelight dinners with live music are offered to guests and the public nightly in the intimate and romantic Lancellotti Dining Room that could well be in Rome. It's the former foyer with carved wood ceilings, marble mantle and tapestries. A 17th-century Mexican tin-crafted mirror and Italian chandeliered sconces are among its treasures. Its nine tables are supplemented by five more in an adjacent Garden Room.

The ambiance is quite festive as a singer and a pianist or a cellist entertain throughout the meal. The pricey, set menu varies by the night of the week, early in the week prix-fixe and weekends à la carte. Diners partake of appetizers like dilled jumbo shrimp cocktail (the recipe featured in Bon Appétit magazine), and entrées like veal scampi diane, mesquite-grilled filet mignon chasseur and cold-water rock lobster thermidor. Chef Korey Goodman's signature dishes rarely change. We've enjoyed his chicken Jacqueline in port wine and heavy cream with sliced apples and toasted almonds, and a special sherried shrimp dejonghe, both with crisp beans and mixed rice, followed by pumpkin cheesecake and a grand marnier mousse. Another occasion produced a tasty special of poached salmon with salsa and rack of lamb dijonnaise, teamed with excellent spinach salads with warm bacon dressing. Bananas foster and strawberries romanoff finished a memorable meal.

Locals shocked by the dinner prices are quite smitten with summer lunches on the Colonnade terrace. Options range from a vegetarian delight to a ham sandwich to a seafood salad. We liked the garlicky and chunky vegetable gazpacho with a curried chicken and avocado plate and the carrot-ginger soup with a curried chicken in pita sandwich, followed by a cheesecake with blueberries and a delectable frozen grand-marnier coupe.

(315) 789-7190 or (800) 343-6382. Fax (315) 789-0322. www.genevaonthelake.com. Six rooms and 24 suites with private baths. Summer-fall: weekends, doubles, $210 to $230, suites $295 to $730; midweek, doubles $189 to $207, suites $266 to $657. Rest of year: weekends, doubles $153 to $202, suites $215 to $642; midweek, doubles $138 to $182, suites, $194 to $578.

Prix-fixe, $44.50; entrées, $26.50 to $45. Lunch in summer, Monday-Saturday noon to 2. Dinner, Sunday-Thursday 6 to 9, Friday-Saturday 7 to 9:30.

Lodging

Hanshaw House B&B, 15 Sapsucker Woods Road, Ithaca 14850.

She loves country inns, decorating and entertaining, so the wife of an Ithaca College dean put it all together in a sumptuous country B&B. Helen Scoones, who used to work for a decorator, did the decorating herself in this 1830 farmhouse with a second-story addition and a new rear wing for the couple's living quarters.

Furnished with flair and an eye to the comforts of home, Hanshaw House offers four air-conditioned guest quarters, all with private baths and two with sitting areas. We lucked into the second-floor suite, with a queensize feather bed, down comforter and pillows, English country antique furnishings, a modern bath and plenty of space to spread out. We didn't need all that space, however, for we had the run of the house – a classy living room outfitted in chintz and wicker with dhurries all over, a side room with TV, and a lovely yard backing up to a small pond and woods full of deer, woodchucks and other wildlife.

Always upgrading her rooms, Helen showed the newly tiled bathroom, the floral sheets and the new curtains in a main-floor bedroom that she decorated in "MacKenzie-esque style," a reference to the colorful pottery from the nearby MacKenzie-Childs studio.

Gardens are now on view on both sides from the refurbished television room. Beyond it in the new wing is "my pièce de résistance," a formal dining room with a crystal chandelier, oriental rugs on pegged floors and french doors opening onto the rear patio and gardens

Helen greets guests with iced lemon tea or mulled cider and cookies in the afternoon. Early-risers are pampered with a choice of exotic coffees, perhaps taken at a table in the country kitchen as Helen prepares a gourmet breakfast. Ours included fresh orange juice, an orange-banana yogurt frappe and Swedish pancakes puffed in the oven with peaches and crème fraîche. Other main courses could be quiche, frittata with homemade popovers, baked french toast with caramel sauce, baked eggs and heart-shaped waffles.

Breakfast is served in the new dining room on blue and white china. The table is set with crocheted lace mats and field flowers in colorful MacKenzie-Childs pottery. The candles are dressed with MacKenzie-Childs lamp shades and the glasses are hand-painted with rosebuds. They epitomize the interesting touches that abound at Hanshaw House.

(607) 257-1437 or (800) 257-1437. Fax (607) 266-8866. www.wordpro.com/ hanshawhouse. Four rooms with private baths. April-December: doubles, $90 to $125 weekends, $77 to $105 midweek. Rest of year, $72 to $84 weekends, $68 to $78 midweek. Two-night minimum weekends in season.

Buttermilk Falls B&B, 110 East Buttermilk Falls Road, Ithaca 14850.

A huge painting of the Buttermilk Falls gorge graces the stairway landing at this attractive, white brick 1825 house, which is the closest private building to Buttermilk Falls. Margie Rumsey came to the home of her late husband's grandfather as a bride in 1948. The couple ran it as a tourist home until they had children. When their youngest son graduated from Cornell in 1983, she reopened it as a B&B and has been improving it ever since.

Now all six guest rooms have private baths, though some are down the hall, and some retain a homey look (built-in cupboards like those one of us grew up with). But good art of Finger Lakes scenes, oriental rugs and early American antiques enhance each room. The luxurious downstairs bedroom in which we stayed has a kingsize bed, wood-burning fireplace and a double jacuzzi surrounded by plants in the corner, from which we could glimpse Buttermilk Falls through the window beyond a hedge.

Classical music plays throughout the public rooms. These include a parlor with games like chess and checkers and collections from Margie's world travels, a plant-filled dining room notable for a long cherry table flanked by twelve different styles of windsor chairs made by her son Ed, a large kitchen and a comfortable screened porch with a garden in one corner.

Breakfast is an event, starting perhaps with a frozen orange concoction that includes a whole banana and is spiced with fresh ginger. Margie invites guests to build "a cereal sundae" with a variety of fruit and nut toppings on her hot whole-grain cereal. Next might come a cheese soufflé with a hot local salsa, served with yogurt to cool it down. "I never serve muffins; everyone else has them," says she. Instead she features toasted sourdough-rye bread or popovers, with intense peach-ginger, raspberry and rhubarb-raspberry jams that we found sensational. Guests in the dining room barter with those on the porch – and vice-versa – for exchanges on jams, seconds and what not, with loquacious Margie encouraging it all as she cooks up a storm on her AGA stove in the kitchen in the midst of all the fun.

A rear carriage house includes a simple two-room cottage good for families. It's not far from the large maple tree up which the hostess sometimes climbs in good weather to sleep out in an open-air tree house.

(607) 272-6767. Fax (607) 273-3947. Six rooms with private baths. Doubles, $85 to $145; jacuzzi room, $150 to $250. No credit cards.

The Federal House, 175 Ludlowville Road, Lansing 14882.

Antiques collector Diane Carroll closed her former Decker Pond Inn south of Ithaca and reopened north of town in the rural mill hamlet of Ludlowville. Here, instead of a pond, she has Salmon Creek Falls within earshot, plus a park-like setting. Diane has fashioned a great side yard, complete with prolific flower gardens, a gazebo and a white garden swing beneath a trellis canopy. There's an expansive wicker-filled side porch from which to take it all in.

The interior of the gracious 1815 house was stripped to its original woodwork and floors before Diane decorated it elegantly in the Federal style. Candles flicker by day in the handsome living room and at breakfast in the formal dining room.

Any cook would covet Diane's enormous country kitchen that stretches across the back of the house and includes a center island and a dining area. Here she prepares lavish breakfasts for guests. One day it might be fresh orange juice, an apple-banana crisp with sour cream sauce, banana bran muffins and stuffed french toast with cream cheese and peach marmalade with sautéed peaches on top. The next day could bring cantaloupe with lime-yogurt sauce and fresh mint, blueberry muffins and oven-baked eggs with vegetables. Individual vegetable soufflés are served with steamed asparagus and broiled tomatoes on the side.

Upstairs in the rear of the house is the Seward Suite, named for William Seward of nearby Auburn, secretary of state under Abraham Lincoln. He courted his future wife in this, her uncle's summer house. The accommodation of choice comes with a sitting room with gas fireplace, TV and a day bed, and a large and airy high-ceilinged bedroom decked out in wicker with a queen bed, plush carpeting and spiffy white and green decor. Also with air-conditioning and private baths are two more bedrooms reached by a steep rear staircase. Each is decorated with flair and appointed with antiques. The front Lincoln Suite has a queensize canopied four-poster bed, gas fireplace and TV.

Diane sells antiques and gifts in her little Blueberry Muffin Gift Corner at the side entrance. Every guest leaves with a tiny loaf of banana bread, wrapped with a blue ribbon.

(607) 533-7362 or (800) 533-7362. Fax (607) 533-7899. Two rooms and two suites with private baths. Doubles, $90 to $95 weekends, $75 to $85 midweek. Suites, $125 to $150 weekends, $100 to $115 midweek.

Hobbit Hollow Farm, 3061 West Lake Road, Skaneateles 13152.

This substantial, 100-year-old Colonial Revival on a 320-acre hillside horse farm overlooking Skaneateles Lake offers the grandest new accommodations in the Finger Lakes.

Michael and Noreen Falcone, who live lakeside across the street, bought the property to save it from development. They totally rebuilt the original farmhouse and spared no expense in furnishing it in the style of an elegant country house. Forty horses are boarded and roam the pastures.

Guests enter the side door of what looks to be two complete houses joined by a hallway wing in the middle. In the reception foyer is a stunning mural of the house and its setting. On one side of the foyer are a cozy library with TV and a lemon-yellow dining room where breakfast is served at a table for eight. On the other side are two sumptuous living rooms, each open to the other. At the far end of the house, facing the lake, is a nifty porch furnished with chairs so comfortable that "we had to wake up one gentleman there," reported innkeeper Richard Fynn in his British accent.

Upstairs, widely separated from each other because of the layout of the house, are five guest rooms of varying size. Standard are triple-sheeted beds with high-thread-count Italian linens, heavy draperies puddled to the floor, MacKenzie-Childs accessories, telephones, terry robes and hair dryers. The smallest room, basically for overflow, is barely big enough for a double bed tucked in its bay window and has a bath across the hall. Another, with an 18th-century Italian queen bed, has a bath with shower and soaking tub.

The other rooms are substantially larger. The Chanticleer, done in French country style, offers a queensize pencil-post bed and a huge bath with a large soaking tub. The front-corner Lake View room is aptly named. It comes with a carved oak queen poster bed, a double armoire, gas fireplace, thick oriental rugs, a marble-encased double whirlpool tub and a glass-enclosed, walk-in shower. The Master bedroom occupies the other front corner and is even more grand, with a majestic kingsize poster bed facing a gas fireplace, two plump silk-covered chairs, a double whirlpool tub, and a large screened porch furnished in wicker. Relax there with a view of the lake and you may never want to leave.

But leave you must, if only for the wine and cheese offered every evening around 6. Chocolate truffles arrive when the beds are turned down. In the morning, breakfast is served amidst sterling, Waterford and Wedgwood. The main course could be a puffed ham and cheese omelet, blueberry pancakes, belgian waffles or cinnamon-roll french toast stuffed with seasonal fruit.

(315) 685-2791. Fax (315) 685-3426. Five rooms with private baths. Doubles, $120 to $270, May-December; $100 to $250, rest of year.

The Red House Country Inn, 4586 Picnic Area Road, Burdett 14818.

Innkeepers Joan Martin and Sandy Schmanke and their guests are the only humans in this preserve in the Finger Lakes National Forest, full of birds and wildlife. Leaving careers in Rochester, they opened their charming B&B inn in an 1844 farmhouse. Three dogs, two cats, a goat and a horse are part of the entourage.

Five upstairs bedrooms, all lovingly furnished with antiques in a quaint country style, share four baths, two up and two down, nicely outfitted with perfumes, powders and soaps. Guests sip sherry by the fireplace in the old-fashioned parlor and sometimes play board games. A stunning scene of the area, hand-stitched with 60 kinds of material by a guest from Canada, graces the wall of the main dining room. Country items are offered in the good little gift shop. There are a kitchen for making drinks or snacks and a wicker-filled front veranda to relax on, as well as berries to be picked and miles of trails awaiting in the forest.

And, for her 50th birthday, Sandy treated herself and guests to a great new swimming pool, flanked by a patio and cabana where guests can lounge and cook on the barbecue. The last is a good thing, as it's a bit of a trek into Watkins Glen or Ithaca for dinner.

In the off-season from November through April, for an astonishingly low $20 a head, the owners will prepare country dinners for house guests with advance notice. Ours started with a great composed spinach salad and homemade rolls. The main course was a whole roasted chicken with a rice and pecan stuffing, green beans with mushrooms and delightful pattypan squash. Banana-cream pie capped a meal that was nicely paced and graciously served. Other entrée possibilities might be duck garnished with fresh raspberries in vodka and accompanied by wild rice, or poached salmon steaks with dill sauce on the side. A frequent guest brings saffron to put in the rice pilafs and paellas. Meals often begin with Red House chowder, which has a potato and leek base and adds cream and fresh vegetables. Warden tarts made with local warden grapes, butter-pecan-rum cake, chocolate-chestnut cake with kahlua-butter cream, and fruit pies and tarts are among desserts.

Breakfast, served in the main dining room with its pressed-oak chairs and lace cloths or in a smaller adjunct to the side, always includes juice and a fruit course, which in our case was a dish of peaches, blueberries and raspberries, garnished with mint from the owners' garden. Butter scones with black currants, pecan popovers, banana pancakes and cottage french toast are some of the goodies. We were quite happy with scrambled eggs, ham and toast.

"Our raspberries are as big as most strawberries," says Sandy. We know. She led us up the road to her favorite haunts to pick blueberries and black raspberries, and then directed us to a pick-your-own raspberry patch. We enjoyed assorted berries from the Finger Lakes for days afterward.

(607) 546-8566 or 546-4105. www.fingerlakes.net/redhouse. Five rooms with shared baths. Doubles, $69 to $89. Two-night minimum weekends.

Gourmet Treats

There's a growing regional awareness of what one booster calls the "foods of the Finger Lakes," a reference to the diversity of locally produced foods, from goat cheese to exotic produce. Having returned from California, where he had spent ten years in the food business, a restaurant manager in Ithaca contended that "some of the foods being produced here are as good if not better than their more publicized California counterparts."

A national model, the **Ithaca Farmers' Market** is a joy for fresh produce, local crafts and odds and ends (free kittens, bluegrass music, hand-stenciled shirts and such). Fresh egg rolls or falafel sandwiches washed down with homemade raspberry juice are one local innkeeper's Saturday lunch of choice. The market operates at Steamboat Landing off Route 13 north of downtown on Saturdays from 9 to 1, April-December.

Another market is **The Windmill,** the first rural farm and craft market in New York State and now with more than 240 vendors. Likened to the Pennsylvania farm markets (Mennonite foods are available), it's off Route 14 between Penn Yan and Dundee. Wineries are among the booths that operate Saturdays from 8 to 4:30, May-December.

Ludgate Farms, 1552 Hanshaw Road, Ithaca, is where you can get an idea of the variety and magnitude of the local food phenomenon. It is a produce stand without peer, as well as a purveyor of fresh herbs (eight kinds of mint; seven kinds of thyme), edible flowers for garnishes, wild game and a potpourri of specialty items. Linda Ludgate and her brother Michael started two decades ago with a card table along the road, selling produce from their father's fields. Today, the stand is an enclosed store open 365 days a year from 9 to 9. Local restaurateurs shop here for hard-to-find foods, exotic lettuces and rare vegetables.

Now You're Cooking at 116 Ithaca Commons carries unusual aprons, many regional and other cookbooks, dishes painted with colorful fruits and vegetables, fine flatware and napkins. Along with classic cookware are hard-to-find gadgets and an enormous collection of cookie cutters.

North Side Wine & Spirits boasts the largest selection of Finger Lakes wines in the world. It may be an idle boast, although the owner says he checked around. The selection is mind-boggling and nicely priced. The toughest part is finding the place, which actually is on the south side of town in the Ithaca Shopping Plaza off Elmira Road (Route 13), where the sign calls it Discount Beverage Center. The cognoscenti follow the advice of wine writer David Sparrow at the new **Sparrow's Fine Wines,** 511 North Meadow St.

The Brous and Mehaffey families have cornered a good share of the specialty-foods market in Ithaca since they bought **Collegetown Bagels** at 413 College Ave. in 1981. A downtown branch and **CTB Appetizers,** a gourmet deli and production kitchen in Triphammer Mall, followed. They purchased the **Ithaca Bakery** at 400 North Meadow St. to create a flagship store with the best of all their operations in a single location. Here is a gourmet paradise, where we've often found the makings for a fabulous picnic or a dinner at home. We have a tough time deciding between salads and roasted chicken items, but that's nothing compared to our dilemma in front of the pastry counter.

Paradise for Food Shoppers

A supermarket for gourmets? You bet, in Ithaca. College students take their parents to the all-new **Wegmans,** a grand superstore (as opposed to a mere superstore) at 500 South Meadow St. This is an incredible outgrowth of the Wegmans markets we frequented years ago when we lived in Rochester, its headquarters. The new Wegmans in Ithaca, and to a lesser extent the one in Canandaigua, are heaven on earth for food lovers. This even has a demonstration kitchen and a school of culinary arts, presided over by an executive chef who now makes Ithaca his home after working around the country. The Market Cafe and coffee bar at the entry set the stage for the wonders to come. We enjoyed a latte as we watched sushi chefs rolling their treats, ogled breads and French pastries that are putting some local bakeries out of business, visited the wokery (one huge table of just Chinese prepared food) and the Mediterranean snack bar, and pondered the choices at the gourmet salad bar, not to mention all the pizzas and pastas. With choices like these to eat here or to go, who'd ever cook at home? But if you want to, Wegmans will oblige. The 30 checkout counters at the front await.

Ithaca, 500 South Meadow St., (607) 277-5800.
Canandaigua, 345 Eastern Blvd. (716) 394-4820.

In Watkins Glen, **Sullivan's** at 309 North Franklin St. is the place for homemade fudge, hand-dipped chocolates and butter crunch. Head for the **Glen Mountain Market** at 200 North Franklin for fine sandwiches ($3.95 to $5.95). The Blues Brother is turkey breast with sliced apples and blue cheese on homemade bread. Vegetarians will find a good selection of salads and sandwiches as well as a tofu burger. You can eat at one of the market's picnic tables.

A new house on a hilltop just north of Penn Yan has become a food destination for some. **Miller's Essenhaus Restaurant & Bakery** at 1300 Route 14A offers wholesome foods and breads, prepared by local Mennonites. Sandwiches, Amish stew and country platters are featured at lunch in the $2.50 to $5.95 range. The dinner menu varies from a church supper ham loaf to grilled New York strip steak. The bakery alone is worth a stop. Open Monday-Saturday 7 a.m. to 9 p.m.

Gilded Age Gardens

Sonnenberg Gardens, 151 Charlotte St.. Canandaigua.

Restored in 1973 after 40 years of neglect, the Victorian gardens are recognized by the Smithsonian as some of the most magnificent ever created in America. The 50-acre estate around their 40-room summer home was planned at the turn of the century by Mary Clark Thompson, who traveled the world to create nine formal gardens, an arboretum, a greenhouse complex and more as a memorial to her banker husband. We were quite taken by the Japanese hill garden and tea house, the Pansy Garden in which even the bird bath is shaped like a pansy, and a rock garden with streams, waterfalls and pools fed by geysers and springs. Marvelous, too, are all the accompanying statues, gazebos, belvederes, arbors, a temple of Diana, a sitting Buddha and even a Roman bath. The mansion, a testament to the extravagances of the Gilded Age, has its own delights, among them the Lavender & Old Lace gift shop. In summer, Sonnenberg usually offers a casual luncheon restaurant and a wine-tasting room on the grounds. The annual Festival of Lights decorates the mansion and illuminates the gardens, extending the season from Thanksgiving to New Year's.

(716) 394-4922. Gardens and museum open daily, 9:30 to 5:30, mid-May to mid-October, also nightly in holiday season, 4:30 to 9:30. Adults, $8.

Canandaigua has two special shops of interest to gourmets. **Renaissance – the Goodie II Shoppe at 56 South Main St.** stocks all the socially correct gifts, from jewelry to porcelain dolls, Port Merion china and lovely Christmas ornaments. Cookbooks (we picked up Linda McCarthy's for a vegetarian son) and nifty paper plates and napkins abound. At **Cat's in the Kitchen,** 367 West Ave.,

Laurel Wemett has collected, from tag sales and auctions, all the things our mothers and grandmothers used in the kitchen. She specializes in the Depression era to the 1960s, and it's fun to check the old canisters, cookie jars, china, pots and pans and more. New items are mixed in.

Skaneateles has become a mecca for shoppers lately, and the shops backing up to Skaneateles Lake are manifestly upscale. **Rhubarb** at 59 East Genesee is a small but select kitchen and garden shop, where everything from gadgets and gourmet foods to espresso makers is chosen with great taste and nicely displayed. **Pomodoro,** our favorite gift shop here for many years, occupies a ramble of rooms in a house at 61 East Genesee St. Cookbooks, a few specialty foods, dishes and placemats are among the wares. Friendship pays, says owner Kay DiNardo, for her **Vermont Green Mountain Specialty Co.** at 50 East Genesee is the only retailer to whom Albert Kumin sells his famed Green Mountain Chocolate Co. candies. His luscious chocolates vie for attention with Green Mountain coffees and Vermont specialty foods at this most unlikely place for a Vermont shop.

Color This Fanciful

MacKenzie-Childs Ltd., 3260 State Route 90, Aurora.

You may have seen the fanciful hand-painted china of the studio in fine gift shops and department stores across the country. Be advised that their design and production studio is in the area – a wonderful estate called Highbanks on 55 acres above Cayuga Lake, a couple of miles north of Aurora. Until lately, two rooms of great fantasy in the Victorian home of Victoria and Richard MacKenzie-Childs showed their furniture, china, painted floor rugs and trimmings, all noted for their intricate stripes, dots, checkerboards, fish and pastoral landscapes. In 1996, the shops were merged into an old barn relocated to the grounds. Seconds are available, but command high prices. Artisans sometimes lead enlightening, hour-long tours of the studios by reservation, but they were canceled while the studios were undergoing major expansion in 1999 and their future was in doubt.

Eclectic food comes from the three-story **Canteen at MacKenzie-Childs,** its colorful ceiling filled with pieces of "Happy Accidents." The menu is rather whimsical, in the spirit of the china. Visitors may have a late breakfast of a coddled egg with toast sticks or a crumpet. Ploughman's lunch (incorporating a tin of sardines – something we've never seen at an English pub), croque monsieur, moroccan egg sandwich, waldorf salad and a french fry jumble are among lunchtime choices. Wash it down with a cup of french chocolate, along with bread pudding or floating island. Picnicking beside a pond on the beautiful grounds is also an option.

(315) 364-7123. Shop and canteen, Monday-Saturday 10 to 5, shop also Sunday noon to 5.

Niagara-on-the-Lake
Wine, Orchards and Shaw

We first met Niagara-on-the-Lake in the late 1960s when it was Sleepy Hollow, as Canadians sometimes called it.

With a set of parents in tow, we had driven to Ontario from our home in Rochester, N.Y., so a visiting father could see "The Devil's Disciple" by one of his favorite playwrights, George Bernard Shaw. After a matinee performance at the Court House Theatre, we browsed through the few shops worth browsing, ate dinner at the quaint Oban Inn and headed home under a full moon. It was the historic night when man first landed on the moon, and that extra-terrestrial feat remained etched in our consciousness long after the Niagara outing had been forgotten.

Now, many moons later, we regard Niagara-on-the-Lake much more favorably. This Sleepy Hollow has awakened, spread its wings and come of age. The opening in 1973 of the Shaw Festival Theater sparked a renaissance in culture and tourism on a scale perhaps unmatched in eastern North America.

It was quite a change for this charming, tree-lined town located where the Niagara River meets Lake Ontario. The first capital of what was called Upper Canada, it played a pivotal role in the War of 1812 – still called "the war" in local circles today. But the capital was moved to safer ground in Toronto and business languished as the Welland Canal bypassed Niagara to the west.

Spared the onslaught that an economic boom can wreak, Niagara's Old Town was an architectural treasury of early buildings awaiting revival. The homegrown Shaw Festival provided that impetus, attracting visitors who demanded good lodging, good food and good shopping.

Geography has afforded the area natural advantages that won it recent acclaim as Canada's prettiest town. Old military reserves and farmlands provide a greenbelt around the Old Town. The Niagara River Parkway cuts through 35 miles of some of the most picturesque parklands and scenery you'll ever see. The Niagara fruit belt yields an abundance of fresh fruits and vegetables. And wineries flourish in what Canadians call "the Napa of the North." The marriage of local produce and wines has inspired the development of a regional cuisine of its own.

We're always struck by the British ties of so many innkeepers and restaurateurs in this most English of Canadian towns, which traces its roots to the United Empire Loyalists who fled to Canada during and after the American Revolution. Many an inn and restaurant goes all-out for afternoon tea, a daily ritual here.

Niagara's burgeoning success now threatens its appeal, however. Crowds of visitors choke the Old Town in summer to the extent that residents avoid downtown for weeks on end. An entrepreneur has acquired all the town's largest hotels and is attracting a clientele that has, old-timers feel, more money than taste.

Yet there are no chain stores or hotels, beyond a large Crabtree & Evelyn branch that seems very much at home and a newer Dansk outlet that doesn't. There is only one traffic light (at the edge of town). A clock tower in the middle of Queen Street is the dominant landmark of a downtown swathed in flowers.

Come along and see why Niagara-on-the-Lake is such a choice getaway for the gourmet.

Dining room at On the Twenty Restaurant & Wine Bar looks onto wooded ravine.

Dining

The Best of the Best

On the Twenty Restaurant & Wine Bar, 3836 Main St., Jordan.

Ontario's first full-service winery restaurant draws food lovers from miles around. Housed in the old Jordan Winery dating to 1870, the restaurant has an elegant country air and food to match.

"You can't imagine what it's like for a cook to come into an area like this," said executive chef Michael Olson, who trained in Toronto and Ottawa restaurants. Upon arrival at the ambitious food and catering venture launched in 1993 by the owners of the adjacent Cave Spring Cellars, Michael took off on his mountain bike to scout out local purveyors. His forays turned up growers who provide him with everything from mesclun to mushrooms. With Angelo Pavan, Cave Spring's winemaker, he set about matching wines and foods for adventuresome palates. He bottles his own vinegars and preserves, and bakes the incredible breads that accompany every meal.

His ambitious lunch menu would serve as dinner almost anywhere else in terms of content and price (entrées, $17 to $22). You·could start with a cucumber ricotta torte with smoked salmon and Pelee Island caviar or watercress salad with goat cheese truffles. The dozen main courses range from a mushroom-brie strata with roasted peppers and eggplant to duck confit on risolee potatoes with braised greens and caramelized shallots.

At dinner, our party of four was impressed with both the tastes and presentations. A bruschetta of toasted sourdough bread with herbed tomatoes barely made it around the table, so good was each morsel. Among other starters, the Hamilton Mountain mushroom bisque with chardonnay cream and sourdough croutons was a work of art and the salad of roasted sweet bell peppers on greens with baked olives and feta cheese was sensational. The pan-fried chicken livers with sour cherries atop greens and toasted pumpkin seeds was an interesting if not wholly successful combination, and the chilled cucumber soup with smoked trout and chives turned out a bit bland. For main courses, we were delighted with the Pacific halibut with sweet-corn salsa, grilled trout with golden plum and mint salsa, roast lamb with red and black currants, and fresh spaghettini with roast chicken, leeks and apricots in a riesling-olive oil sauce. Each plate came with chef Michael's trademark decoration, squiggles of puréed beets blended with yogurt, as well as simple steamed vegetables.

The night's desserts included blueberry/sour-cream cake with maple hard sauce, chocolate-espresso torte with caramelized orange glaze and cardamom cream, and a selection of standard ice-cream flavors. We passed in favor of a sample of Cave Spring's riesling icewine, which winemaker Angelo correctly described as "dessert in a glass" – a heavenly ending to a most pleasing meal.

Dining is at white-linened tables in a couple of airy rooms with sponged pale gold walls, floors and columns of travertine marble, striking art works and floor-to-ceiling windows onto a garden terrace atop the ravine shielding Twenty Mile Creek from view below. More rooms, including a spacious knock-out upstairs, are pressed into service for functions and overflow. Cave Spring wines are featured at little markup. The restaurant has a full liquor license and carries the best of other local winery offerings.

(905) 562-7313. Entrées, $25 to $30. Lunch daily, 11:30 to 3. Dinner, 5 to 10. Closed Mondays, January-May.

Hillebrand's Vineyard Cafe, Highway 55, Niagara-on-the-Lake.

Big money went into the new restaurant at Hillebrand Estates Winery, and it shows. Interesting architectural lines delineate the handsome, high-ceilinged establishment on two levels. A wall of windows opens onto the barrel-aging cellar along one side, while taller windows in back yield views of the vineyards. Cushioned wood chairs are at well-spaced, white-linened tables, each topped with a different potted herb. A few dramatic artworks and the odd ficus tree add color. Canvas umbrellas top the tables seating 80 more on the sunny outside patio.

Prominent chef Antonio de Luca was lured from Toronto to oversee the kitchen. Menus neatly bound with grapevines detail some exotic fare. To start, a changing array of breads arrives in a grapevine basket with a daily spread – at our lunch, an unusual black bean concoction to soothe an assertive olive focaccia, cornbread with peppers and fennel-seed bread. One of us sampled the day's cold cucumber soup, "garnished" with an awkward-to-handle hunk of smoked salmon, and the salad of arugula and radicchio with a confit of tomatoes, smoked scallops and dill. The other was impressed with the penne pasta tossed with caramelized vidalia onions, smoked chicken and roasted garlic with a spicy tomato sauce. At $10.50, it was the least expensive among main courses priced up to $21.95 for a sampling of Niagara's regional specialties. The highly touted mango and cardamom crème brûlée with fresh berries lacked the traditional crust and any hint of mango or cardamom.

Dinner fare is similarly elaborate. You might start with a terrine of lobster, smoked salmon and king crab with sweet pea salad or seared foie gras on toasted polenta with berry glaze. Main courses range from pan-seared Muskoka lake pickerel with wilted greens and cucumber noodles to local lamb loin wrapped in basil and spinach with a roasted garlic flan. A trio of seasonal sorbets with almond biscotti makes a worthy ending.

Dining room at Hillebrand's Vineyard Cafe looks onto umbrellaed patio and vineyard.

Besides turning up in some of the sauces, Hillebrand wines make up the entire wine list, nicely varied (particularly among whites).

(905) 468-7123 or (800) 582-8412. Entrées, $19.95 to $32.95. Lunch daily, 11:30 to 5. Dinner, 5 to 11.

Vineland Estates Winery Restaurant, 3620 Moyer Road, Vineland.

Ontario finally allowed wineries to open on Sundays, accept credit cards and serve food on the premises. Vineland Estates, which with its hilly country setting is the area's most picturesque winery, was the first to oblige. It enclosed the porch of its original 1845 estate house and opened a bistro-style restaurant. The side deck was later expanded to seat 100 under cover and outside, where on a clear day you can discern Lake Ontario and the Toronto skyline through the grapevines.

A subsequent major kitchen expansion allowed the winery to offer lunch and dinner year-round. Another deck was added, the original enclosed and the tasting room moved to make way for the expanding restaurant operation. Talented chef Mark Picone was the icing on the cake, pioneering a distinctive regional cuisine. Every morning, he bakes his own sourdough bread and baguettes and makes his own pastas and gelatos. What local farmers can grow dictates the dishes he creates. He obtains Asian pears not from Japan but from grower Hank Saito down the road, and pays homage to his suppliers on the menu.

The fare has become far more ambitious than in the early bistro days, when we lingered over platters of cheeses and pâtés for lunch and, more recently, a supper of bruschetta, caesar salad with Canadian bacon and a platter of smoked salmon.

Nowadays, about the only bistro fare is a Sterling salmon burger for lunch. The seared foie gras, steamed lobster and peameal bacon sandwich on toasted egg loaf with tomato-vanilla marmalade raises the bar. So does the Solstice Farm custard of garlic confit with summer sprouts and peppered flatbread. The soup could be chilled berry with mint, riesling and lemon-drained yogurt; the salad, pan-roasted Peck Farm quail on a lacy potato cake with a honey-sage vinaigrette. With choices like these, the entrée list, good as it is, may be superfluous.

Save that for dinner, when the chef obliges with treats like Atlantic turbot fillet in a crust of tarragon-almond matzo, sweetbreads rolled in cornmeal and herbs on "Sno White whipped potatoes with a confit of Niagara tender fruit," and Red Deer loin chop, "twice cooked with apple skreech and fire," served with dried cherry dumplings. Sit outside at a beige-clothed table, sip a fine wine and watch the sunset paint a changing palette across the western sky.

Though the food and service are urbane and the interior dining areas stylish, the setting could not be more bucolic. If you linger, you may want to stay the night. The little stucco cottage down the driveway is a B&B called **Wine 'n Recline.** It harbors a fully equipped kitchen, living room, bathroom and sleeping accommodations for four. There's a TV set for contact with the outside world. You can barbecue on the deck, and the refrigerator is stocked with a bottle of wine as well as the fixings for the next day's breakfast.

(905) 562-7088 or (888) 846-3526. Entrées, $25 to $40. Lunch daily, 11 to 3. Dinner, 5 to 9. B&B, $150.

Wellington Court Restaurant, 11 Wellington St., St. Catharines.
A small brick house at the edge of downtown St. Catharines has become a dining destination for folks from Niagara-on-the-Lake. Credit chef Erik Peacock and his mother, Claudia, the owner, for what some consider the best small restaurant between Buffalo and Toronto, one that's known for personality and value.

Two intimate dining rooms are sleek in black and white and accented with colorful art. Mirrors make the place appear larger.

The short menu is supplemented by nightly specials that are really special, including at our visit a truffle-crusted salmon fillet sauced with asparagus butter and a rack of baby venison with a walnut crust. The regular entrées range from roasted sea bass scented with citrus on a fava bean and wild mushroom ragoût to grilled calves liver with a shallot and sherry butter sauce. A ballotine of capon might be stuffed with Indian mashed potatoes and rest on a carrot and saffron jus. Cappellini could be tossed with white truffle butter, romano and shrimp. Orrechiette could yield smoked chicken, charred onions and asiago cheese.

The treats begin with things like a goat cheese and ricotta flan, homemade pâté with pear compote and dried fruit bread crisps, and lemon blini with wilted red onion, crème fraîche and wasabi flying fish roe. Almond sponge cake with raspberry compote, lemon mascarpone in phyllo pastry, and crème brûlée with amaretto and peaches are some heavenly sounding desserts.

A select wine list is rich in Niagaras and boutique imports.

(905) 682-5518. Entrées, $18 to $28. Lunch, Tuesday-Saturday 11:30 to 2:30. Dinner, Tuesday-Saturday 5 to 9:30.

Other Dining Choices

The Queenston Heights Restaurant, Queenston Heights Park, 14276 Niagara Pkwy, Queenston.
Operated by the Niagara Parks Commission, this restaurant is a cut above – in

culinary aspiration, as well as in location, commanding a panoramic view down the Niagara River toward Lake Ontario.

The menu mixes traditional with contemporary regional cuisine. One of us made a wonderful lunch of two appetizers: a tomato and eggplant salad, served on a black octagonal plate brightened by corn kernels and colorful bits of peppers, and smoked-salmon carpaccio, garnished with shavings of romano cheese, herbs and tiny purple edible flowers. The other enjoyed smoked turkey with cranberry mayonnaise on a whole-wheat croissant. From the dessert cart we picked a super chocolate-strawberry charlotte with curls of chocolate and savored both it and the afternoon sunshine on the capacious outdoor terrace.

The lunch menu still offers creative appetizers and focaccia sandwiches, as well as substantial entrées, such as baked arctic char with golden pineapple salsa and sesame couscous and baked free-range chicken with creamy shiitake mushrooms and wild rice pilaf.

At night, you might be tempted by main courses like garlic and ginger sea scallops and tiger prawns with banana-mango-curried cream sauce or grilled veal chop with caramelized onions and melted plum tomatoes on penne arrabbiata. The pesto-crusted rack of lamb comes with minted sweet pepper jelly and a vegetable ragoût. One of the interesting starters is cedar-smoked salmon and potato pancakes with baby greens, capers and red onions. Desserts might be profiteroles with mint-chocolate chip ice cream, cabernet poached bosc pear in a brandy-snap basket, and mascarpone semifreddo with raspberry coulis.

The extensive wine list is strong on Niagara whites and reds.

The formal main dining room is Tudor in feeling with a high timbered ceiling, armchairs at well-spaced tables and a painting of Niagara Falls above a huge stone fireplace. The view down the length of the river, while sitting at a table by the expansive windows, gives one the sense of being on an airplane.

(905) 262-4274 or (877) 642-7275. Entrées, $19.95 to $25.95. Lunch daily, 11:30 or noon to 3, summer Saturdays from 11. Dinner nightly, 5 to 9, summer Saturdays to 10. Sunday brunch, 11 to 3. Closed mid-January to late March.

Shaw Cafe & Wine Bar, 92 Queen St., Niagara-on-the-Lake.

You can't miss this striking circular restaurant jutting onto the downtown sidewalk, part of a new Victorian shopping complex built by local hotelier Si Wai Lai, who knows and likes good food. It juts onto the downtown sidewalk, is flanked by flowers and statuary, fountains and dining terraces, looks like something out of modern-day Italy and is mobbed by tourists at lunch time.

The interior is unexpectedly trendy, for little old Niagara-on-the-Lake: a prominent pizza oven, an open kitchen, a deli case loaded with sophisticated offerings, a dessert and gelato counter, an upstairs loft area with paneled wine bar overlooking the scene and dining tables all around, inside and out.

The Lithuanian chef says he starts with continental cuisine and adds Eastern European flavors and local produce. But for the crowds waiting for tables, we would gladly have paused for lunch from an enticing all-day menu: perhaps a smoked salmon plate, a vegetarian club sandwich, fettuccine with smoked chicken or a smoked trout pizza. The "showcase" yields a choice of four salads and sandwiches for $11.50. Desserts include sorbets and ice cremes, crêpes and fresh fruit strudel. Espressos and lattes, wines and beers round out the offerings.

(905) 468-4772. Entrées, $14.85 to $21.95. Open daily, 10 to 9, weekends to midnight.

Fans Court, 135 Queen St., Niagara-on-the-Lake.

"We serve gourmet Chinese food only – no chow mein," proclaims the sign at the door. In the opinion of local gourmands, this unpretentious Chinese restaurant is one of the town's better places to eat.

There's a pleasant outdoor patio for dining in front. Inside are a couple of nondescript rooms, where tables are set simply with silverware and chopsticks atop peach cloths. Oriental art and music provided a soothing backdrop as we nursed an Inniskillin brae blanc from a short list featuring Canadian wines and Chinese beers.

The menu advised that "sharing is one of the biggest enjoyments of a Chinese meal." Yet orders were not served in typical, help-yourself Chinese fashion, but rather on small dinner plates that made sharing difficult.

For starters, we chose deep-fried wontons and an intriguing-sounding radish and pork soup that arrived without much evidence of radish. For main courses, the shrimp and scallops in a phoenix (crisp noodle) nest and double-cooked pork tenderloin were fine. But we were astounded that steamed rice *(rice!)* cost extra, as did tea – the first time we have encountered this in a Chinese restaurant. For that matter, there were no Chinese noodles and plum sauce to nibble on, as in most Chinese restaurants, and the service, while correct, was icy.

(905) 468-4511. Entrées, $9 to $16.80. Lunch daily, noon to 2:30. Dinner, 4:30 to 9 or 10.

The Epicurean, 84 Queen St., Niagara-on-the-Lake.

Select your choices from the lengthy display case here to eat in a colorful blue and buttercup yellow dining room or take out back to the shaded patio. Soups could be Mexican chicken or gazpacho, or you might order chicken and feta pie or seafood quiche. Sandwiches range from tuna to seafood and avocado or egg-plant with roasted peppers and chèvre. We sampled a medley of three salads ($7.50), served with homemade bread, and cleared our own table afterward on the patio.

The Epicurean also prepares "pampered picnics" ($11.95 to $12.95), packed in a hamper with utensils and wineglasses. Salads and desserts accompany a choice of poached salmon, sliced filet mignon or grilled chicken with lime and ginger.

You'll find a selection of specialty foods and culinary books in an adjoining storefront called **Kitchen Accents.**

(905) 468-3408. Daily, 9 a.m. to 11:30 p.m.

Dining and Lodging

The Prince of Wales Hotel, 6 Picton St., Niagara-on-the-Lake L0S 1J0.

This fashionable old-timer has been reborn in a studied effort to create a "five-diamond hotel that will both inspire and awe every guest." We don't know about the inspiration, for the guest rooms were either occupied or under renovation at our visit, but the awe was everywhere else apparent. Here is the ultimate showcase for the taste, energy and money of Niagara's ubiquitous hotelier, Si Wai Lai. In 1966 at age 16, she fled mainland China by swimming for 36 hours to Hong Kong and now is equally fearless as she buys up much of Niagara-on-the-Lake.

Si Wai moved to Canada in 1980 and started as a desk clerk at the Niagara Falls Sheraton. She slowly acquired small properties, using her own resources and, it's reported, those of her twin brother Jimmy Lai, a Hong Kong clothing magnate

Escabèche in Prince of Wales Hotel offers opulent setting for dining.

and publisher. Niagara-on-the-Lake first took notice when she brought the quirky and quaint Pillar and Post out of bankruptcy in 1994, pouring $12 million into renovations and a new wing for additional rooms and a European health spa. She also acquired The Buttery restaurant and opened the casual Shaw's Cafe & Wine Bar in a Queen Street retail complex she built called Shaw's Corner. In 1996, she purchased the larger and more conference-oriented Queen's Landing Inn for the highest price per room ever paid for a Canadian hotel, and outdid that in 1997 with the purchase of the family-run Prince of Wales Hotel for $24 million, an even higher price per room. In 1999, she exercised her option to buy the venerable Oban Inn.

As is her style, Si Wai's mark is everywhere evident at The Prince of Wales, which she closed for eight months and $25 million worth of renovations in 1999. She gutted the interior and bought new furnishings with such abandon that some were still in storage a year later. The result is opulent Victorian, in the high British or continental style – as opposed to trophy hotels of the Trump and Helmsley era.

The riches begin in the lobby, where the wallpaper is embossed gold to match the carved molding, a stained-glass mural is back-lit and Italian statues preside here and there. The former bar was converted into a drawing room. Here the wall sconces match three glittering crystal chandeliers and afternoon tea is served on a 24-carat gold china service for $28 per person. The tiled indoor pool with spa is flanked by murals of princes of Wales watching over any swimmers who can get through all the frou-frou – not that anyone was swimming at our July visit.

The 108 guest rooms ramble through a square block of buildings behind a meandering brick facade that looks more residential than commercial. Quite comfortable and tasteful under the previous family ownership, they were deemed tired. Their exaggerated luxury now matches the public spaces, our guide advised, and reflects the apparent Si Wai credo that too much is not enough. They come in

23 color schemes and all have Italian marble baths. Plush fabrics, velour bathrobes, towel warmers and hair dryers are standard.

The hotel's restaurants spread across three rooms with thick carpeting, white linens, and sparkling crystal and china. One is a Cigar Room. Beyond is Churchill's Lounge, a huge mahogany space with the look of a gentleman's library and quite a stash of wines and champagnes offered by the glass.

Formerly Royals, the main restaurant has been renamed **Escabèche** (for a popular marinated fish dish in southern France). Lee Parsons moved from England and a three-star Michelin restaurant in Oxfordshire to become executive chef. He "fell in love with Canada and Si Wai can be quite persuasive," we were advised. The contemporary French cuisine is simple yet distinguished. The service is polished, as in "domed."

The appetizers here are priced like dinner entrées elsewhere – the soup ("chilled essence of pressed tomatoes") for $16, the rest from $22 for tuna tartare to $27 for lobster and mango salad. Main courses range from herb-crusted fillet of Atlantic cod "en meurette" to roasted lamb with a garlic-shallot purée and niçoise jus. Standouts on the opening menu were roasted sea bass with seared scallops and sauce vierge, and grain-fed chicken with asparagus, leeks and morels. Typical desserts are seasonal fruit mille-feuille with light grand marnier cream and a dark chocolate dome with orange-flavored crème brûlée.

Similar dinner fare at less heart-arresting prices ($16 to $22) is offered in Churchill Lounge. A short sandwich and quiche menu ($12) is offered for lunch in the Drawing Room.

(905) 468-3246 or (888) 669-5566. Fax (905) 468-5521. Ninety-one rooms and seventeen suites. May-October: doubles, $425 to $645; suites, $745 to $845. Rest of year: doubles, $275 to $495 weekends, $175 to $395 midweek; suites, $595 to $695 weekends, $495 to $595 midweek.

Entrées, $28 to $43. Lunch daily, 11 to 2. Tea, 2 to 5. Dinner, 5 to 9. Sunday brunch, 11 to 2:30.

Queen's Landing Inn and Conference Resort, 155 Byron St., Niagara-on-the-Lake L0S 1J0.

New in 1990, this three-story, Georgian-inspired hotel backing up to the Niagara River has matured under Si Wai Lai's aegis. She brought it back to life after two previous owners had failed, making it Niagara's first four-diamond establishment for both dining and lodging.

The rear of the brick hotel looks across the busy Niagara-on-the-Lake Sailing Club marina onto the Niagara River, but inside all is placid and sumptuous. Si Wai's major renovation included a two-story entrance foyer with a marble floor and a stained-glass ceiling. There are large mirrors, reproduction antique furniture and flowers everywhere (one bouquet alone contained 120 long-stemmed roses, a Si Wai trademark). A couple of shiny elevators take guests to their rooms, which have plush furnishings, minibars, and tiled and marble bathrooms, some with whirlpool tubs. Three dozen rooms offer gas fireplaces.

The lower floors, built into the side of a slope, offer a restaurant and lounge, business center, twenty conference rooms, a health facility and a light, airy area with a large indoor swimming pool, a whirlpool and a lap pool.

Most noticeably improved is the dining situation. The Bacchus Lounge bar menu is considered good value and its outdoor dining terrace positively idyllic, if you

Curved ceiling and columns grace Tiara dining room at Queen's Landing.

aren't distracted by the giant statue of David clad only in a fig leaf. The pillared **Tiara** restaurant is a majestic oval of soaring windows onto the sailing club beneath a curving ceiling accented with stained glass. On two levels, it is spacious and serene in cream and mauve, with tables well separated.

Executive chef Stephen Treadwell, known for strong flavors and complex cooking, is credited with some of the best food in town. Four of us sampled the night's eight-course tasting menu ($85), paired with appropriate wines (the steward's recommendations from the all-Niagara wine list can rapidly run up the tab). The four-hour feast, from foie gras terrine through the signature "symphony of desserts," proved exceptional.

The regular menu might start with Asian-spiced mussels in ancho chile cream, green curry tempura soft-shell crab and a thin-crust pizza with artichoke and smoked gruyère. Our tasting menu yielded two of the main courses, Szechuan-crusted sea scallops with a carrot emulsion and charred yellowfin tuna with chili gazpacho and vodka-lime goat cheese. Other treats were sesame grilled quail with Niagara peach preserve and mustard greens, a feature on the lunch menu, and pan-roasted veal loin with chanterelles, zucchini blossoms and truffle essence. A plate of imported cheeses with oven-dried fruit and date-walnut bread followed the veal course.

The dessert sampling indicated that any of the pastry chef's choices would suffice. We'd happily settle for the trio of three intense fruit sorbets served in macadamia nut petals.

(905) 468-2195 or (888) 669-5566. Fax (905) 468-2227. One hundred thirty-seven rooms and five suites. May-October: doubles, $360 to $450 weekends, $220 to $310 midweek; suites, $525 to $695 weekends, $385 to $695 midweek. Rest of year: doubles, $165 to $285 weekends, $99 to $159 midweek; suites, $250 to $595 weekends, $184 to $595 midweek.

Entrées, $24 to $36. Lunch daily, noon to 2. Dinner nightly, 5 to 10; 6 to 9 in off-season.

The Pillar and Post, 48 John St., Box 1011, Niagara-on-the-Lake L0S 1J0. This campus-like hostelry with 123 guest quarters, a variety of dining rooms, a glamorous spa and health center and a gift shop dates to the 1890s when it began life as a canning factory. The building was converted in 1970 into a restaurant, inn and crafts center to launch Niagara's inn boom. Vastly expanded to ramble across a square block, it was the first of Si Wai Lai's major acquisitions here and the first to which she devoted her considerable resources.

She enlarged and opened up the formerly cramped lobby, reconfigured the gift shop area into a fancy dining room, and glamorized the Vintages Wine Bar and Lounge with a wine mural (said to be the largest hand-painted mural in Canada) and a huge, gently curving oak bar. The lower level of the new wing holds an indoor pool flanked by stuffed Florida palm trees, the One Hundred Fountain spa with lion's heads spewing water, an outdoor hot spring pool and waterfall surrounded by tiers of lush begonias, a state-of-the-art health club and seven treatment salons, each individually themed to represent an exotic country. You might think you were in the Roman baths, not Niagara.

Si Wai's 32 new rooms and suites followed suit, hinting of things to come at her more recent hostelries. She picked all the furnishings and fabrics, from the pink and raspberry colors of Suite 251 to the hand-painted wash basin from Spain in No. 247. Kingsize four-poster and crown canopy beds, sumptuous sitting areas, antiques, rich woods and dark colors prevail. Twenty-seven rooms have whirlpool tubs, and a total of 82 have fireplaces. Most are turned into themselves in a cozy and dark way that may appeal more in winter than in summer.

Guests partake of complimentary hors d'oeuvres in the evening. An extensive breakfast buffet is available in the morning, as is a full menu.

The renovated **Carriages** restaurant is elegant and formal in one section, less so in the beamed and pillared **Cannery** areas and in the lounge. Si Wai was proud to have hosted for dinner here 26 members of the prestigious Club des Chefs des Chefs, the international association of chefs to reigning royalty and heads of state during its annual meeting in Toronto. Under less regal circumstances, the dinner menu is contemporary and regional, from an appetizer called a smoked scallop daiquiri to a main course of basil-crusted roasted black sea bass. Cappuccino-cinnamon mousse and chocolate-cherry kirsch pâté are typical desserts. The extensive wine list is strong on Niagara vintages.

An interesting, less expensive all-day menu is offered in the **Vintages Wine Bar and Lounge.**

(905) 468-2123 or (800) 669-5566. Fax (905) 468-3551. One hundred thirteen rooms and ten suites. May-October: doubles, $360 to $425 weekends, $220 to $285 midweek; suites, $450 to $695 weekends, $310 to $695 midweek. Rest of year: doubles, $165 to $285 weekends, $99 to $159 midweek; suites, $250 to $595 weekends, $184 to $595 midweek.

Entrées, $23 to $33. Lunch daily, noon to 2:30. Tea, 3 to 5:30. Dinner, 5 to 9, winter 6 to 8, lounge to midnight.

Gate House Hotel, 142 Queen St., Niagara-on-the-Lake L0S 1J0. This sleek, mirrored hotel in black and white was the first glitzy hotel in Niagara-on-the-Lake. It emerged in 1988 from the simple, old Gate House Inn – tastefully on the outside, contemporary Italian and showy on the inside. Managed by Tullio Calvello, it's the town's only major player without the involvement of "that Chinese woman," as some refer to Si Wai Lai

Expansive windows bring outside in at Ristorante Giardino in Gate House Hotel.

A marble entry leads to the reception desk, where guests are directed to the two-tiered dining room (until lately considered the fanciest in town) or upstairs to ten guest rooms on the second floor. We were shown a very modern, deluxe room done in teal and black with two double beds, German and Italian furnishings, and a bathroom with double sinks, a bidet and Auberge toiletries. Rooms have TVs and all the usual amenities in high-tech European style. A continental breakfast is included.

The hotel's **Ristorante Giardino** is the gem of the operation. Huge windows in the ultra-chic dining room look onto the gardens and lawns (and passersby look in as well). Generally well-spaced tables are set with black-edged service plates, white napkins rolled up in black paper rings, pink carnations in heavy crystal vases, votive candles and two long-stemmed wine glasses at each place. All the plates and water glasses are octagonal. Masses of flowers brighten the room's dividers, and good art hangs on the walls here and in the halls.

The modern Italian fare is on the expensive side. Dinner possibilities range from a soup of artichoke purée with slivered gorgonzola to an appetizer of braised rabbit tenderloin salad drizzled with barrel-aged balsamic vinegar to homemade squid-ink pasta layered between lobster and spinach. Main courses could be seared monkfish in saffron cream sauce or a trio of lamb Giardino style.

Not wishing to break the bank, we settled for lunch, which – as is often the case at high-end establishments – is a better value. A plate of crusty Italian bread arrived along with two glasses of the house Inniskillin wine (brae blanc and brae rouge). One of us started with an intensely flavored and silken shrimp bisque, followed by a rolled pasta with spinach and ricotta cheese. The other sampled a trio of pastas: spaghetti with pancetta and parmesan-cream sauce, tagliatelle sautéed with salmon and chives and a house specialty, eggplant Giardino, baked with mozzarella, basil and tomato sauce.

Dessert was a thin slice of carrot cake with vanilla ice cream and fresh strawberries – imported from California, which seemed strange, given all the fresh peaches, pears and plums in season at the time around Niagara. Good cappuccino and coffee finished a memorable repast. The extensive wine list is especially strong on Niagara and Italian vintages.

(905) 468-3263. Fax (905) 468-7400. Ten rooms with private baths. Doubles, $175 to $210 May-October, $145 to $180 rest of year.
Entrées, $23.50 to $32. Lunch daily, noon to 2:30. Dinner nightly, 5 to 9. No lunch in off-season. Closed January and February.

The Oban Inn, 160 Front St., Box 94, Niagara-on-the-Lake L0S 1J0.

This Niagara icon faces Lake Ontario across a strip of golf course. It's been around since 1824 and looks it. Which is quite remarkable, given that it was destroyed by fire on Christmas Day 1992 and was rebuilt to its original specifications for reopening the following November.

A favorite of traditionalists, it was the latest to be acquired by Si Wai Lai. She assumed ownership in November 1999 and pledged to keep it much as it is – despite a sharp increase in room rates and her obvious proclivity for upgrades.

In the main inn, nineteen rooms go off narrow corridors adorned with a multitude of ornate paintings. Those in front looking toward the lake are larger and have queen or twin beds, antique furnishings, gas fireplaces and plush armchairs or a loveseat facing a TV set. A second-story balcony, outfitted with tables, chairs and many plants, goes off the rooms at the back of the inn and is available to all house guests. Vivid wallpapers, terrycloth robes, a clock-radio and a phone in each room are the rule. Guests enjoy a library/sitting room upstairs with TV, gas fireplace and lots of books and games.

Besides rooms in the main house, the inn offers three that are highly prized in the adjacent Oban House. One is a suite with a queen bedroom, a loft with twin beds, a full kitchen, sunroom and living room.

The waiters and bartenders are in tartan plaids in the formal dining rooms and the ever-so-British **Shaw's Corner** piano bar full of festival memorabilia. The place is abuzz day and night, for the bar is a popular gathering place and the inn is considered the quintessential Niagara experience.

Until Si Wai's takeover, the same was no longer true for the dining situation – the service in particular having slipped over the years, according to local consensus. The traditional dinner fare includes such English specialties as dover sole with sorrel-dill butter and prime rib with Yorkshire pudding and horseradish among entrées. Starters include potted shrimp (blended with spices and butter and served with toast points) and deep-fried camembert with English crackers and homemade red-pepper jelly. Desserts run from a signature meringue chantilly and hot fudge sundae to English trifle and fruit cobbler "with ice cream or pouring cream."

Steak and kidney pie, fried salmon fish cakes, and cold pork pie with piccalilli relish are included on the lunch menu. These and other English specialties are featured on the lounge menu in winter.

(905) 468-2165 or (888) 669-5566. Fax (905) 468-4165. Twenty-one rooms and one suite with private baths. April-October: doubles, $295 to $360 weekends, $220 to $285 midweek; suite, $385 weekends, $310 midweek. Rest of year: doubles, $165 to $205 weekends, $99 to $139 midweek; suite, $230 weekends, $164 midweek.
Entrées, $18.40 to $28.50. Lunch daily, 11:30 to 3; tea, Sunday-Friday 3 to 4:30; dinner nightly, 5 to 9.

Horse and carriage arrive for Christmas festivities at Lakewinds.

Lodging

Besides the larger inns and hotels, Niagara-on-the-Lake had more than 250 B&Bs at last count – double the number only three years earlier and increasing every year. By zoning ordinance, most offer three or fewer guest rooms.

Lakewinds, 328 Queen St., Box 1483, Niagara-on-the-Lake L0S 1J0.

Pristine white with dark green trim, this substantial Victorian manor sits amidst an acre of trees and gardens facing Lake Ontario across the golf-course fairways. Besides a scenic residential location, it offers Niagara-on-the-Lake's most elegant B&B accommodations and culinary treats, and was the setting for a country-inn scene in the Bette Midler movie, "That Old Feeling."

You'd never suspect that "the house was falling down," as owner Jane Locke put it, when she and her husband Stephen from nearby Hamilton bought it in 1994 with the idea of turning the front section into a B&B. "We were trying to make a silk purse out of a sow's ear."

The main floor is devoted to a formal living/dining room in which the Lockes serve breakfasts to remember, an ample games room for billiards or cards, and an airy solarium that becomes a working greenhouse in the winter to produce the seedlings for the lavish flower, vegetable and herb gardens that grace the grounds. The solarium opens onto a back-yard swimming pool much enjoyed by guests.

The second floor holds four guest quarters, three with queensize beds and one with a king. All have private baths. The Venetian suite with double whirlpool tub and separate shower is so named for all the silver and glass and the hand-painted mirrored furniture. Others bear furnishings appropriate to their names: Florentine, Singapore and the Algonquin, in which we found the most comfortable of beds and a guest diary whose entries embellished on three themes: sumptuous surroundings, delicious breakfasts and personable hosts.

The transformation to silk purse culminated in the conversion of the third floor into two king-bedded suites. A large handcrafted angel watches over Heaven, a secluded hideaway with loveseat and window seat offering a bird's-eye view of the lake and golf course, a stereo system, and bath with a jacuzzi tub and an antique marble-top vanity. French country decor enhances the cathedral-ceilinged Sans Souci, with a fireside sitting area, TV, balcony and a double jacuzzi with separate shower.

Guests are welcomed with tea, and help themselves to mixers in a bar area off the solarium. The Lockes, whose family quarters are in the rear of the house, often mingle with guests and provide turndown service at night.

The highlight is the morning repast, a communal sit-down affair at 9 o'clock. Ours began with apple-cassis juice, cantaloupe harboring port and berries, and five varieties of breads, from orange-date muffins to muesli baguettes to croissants. The main event was a melt-in-your-mouth leek and sage quiche with roasted red pepper coulis, teamed with a crostini bearing sautéed mushrooms, pesto, tomato and goat cheese. On tap the next morning was honeydew melon marinated in lime and gin, followed by orange-cointreau french toast. Crêpes, often incorporating asparagus or smoked salmon, are a specialty. Five of Jane's recipes are included in the Canadian edition of the *Rise and Dine* inn cookbook. Lakewinds was filmed to appear as one of the best B&Bs in North America on the Food Network in 2000.

Jane, who was preparing a batch of rhubarb-ginger jam at our arrival, challenges herself by inviting top local chefs for dinner. She attributes her cooking talents to training in a private yacht club and corporate travels around the world with her husband, Stephen, who now devotes full time to Lakewinds and heads the local B&B Association. Both love to entertain, and treat their guests royally.

(905) 468-1888. Fax (905) 468-1061. www.lakewinds.niagara.com. Three rooms and three suites with private baths. Weekends, mid-April to mid-December: doubles, $195; suites, $215 to $235. Midweek and other weekends: doubles, $165; suites, $180 to $195. Two-night minimum weekends. Closed mid-December through New Year's.

The Vintner's Inn, 3845 Main St., Jordan L0R 1L0.

Plush accommodations join the Cave Spring Cellars winery, restaurant and shopping equation with this expanding inn across the street, fashioned from an old sugar warehouse. Helen Young, wife of winery owner Leonard Pennachetti, offers sixteen suites with sitting areas, gas fireplaces, TVs, whirlpool tubs and kingsize or two double beds. Eight are double-deckers with powder rooms and sitting areas downstairs and loft bedrooms and baths up. The skylit Deluxe Loft adds a wet bar, refrigerator and a down seated-settee so deep you can barely get up. Three garden suites on the lower floor offer columned sleeping alcoves and bathrooms with heated floors, plus large windows facing demonstration gardens. The deluxe garden suite opens through french doors onto a private garden.

Handsomely decorated in restful Mediterranean tones, each suite contains a colorful painting (for sale) by local artist Jane Kewin, whose works adorn the restaurant. You'd never guess that some of the furnishings took on new life after resting in Buffalo junk shops. Helen mixed refurbished castoffs with antiques, chintz fabrics and old marble vanities to create "an eclectic country look," simple but stylish.

Although the kind of place that you might not want to venture forth from your

Brockamour Manor is known for showy gardens as well as elaborate breakfasts.

room, you can gather by the fireplace in the soaring, fashionably furnished lobby on the second floor. A lavish continental breakfast is complimentary at the inn's companion On the Twenty restaurant across the street. The variety of fruits and pastries on the buffet was sufficient to forego the more elaborate breakfast for $8.

In 1999, the inn readied two more suites with a connecting garden in a nearby house renamed the Winemaker's Cottage.

(905) 562-5336 or (800) 701-8074. Fax (905) 562-0009. Eighteen suites with private baths. May-October: $250 to $325 weekends, $219 to $295 midweek. Rest of year: $210 to $275 weekends, $169 to $225 midweek. Two-night minimum weekends.

Brockamour Manor, 433 King St., Box 402, Niagara-on-the-Lake L0S 1J0.

Elaborate breakfasts have proven to be "our best advertising," says Thea Wisch, the chief cook and bottle washer as well as innkeeper with her husband Uwe. The outgoing couple of German background had operated a farm B&B north of London, Ont., before purchasing this 1812 Georgian mansion in 1997 to run as a deluxe B&B. They named it for British general Sir Isaac Brock, the administrator of Upper Canada, who was killed in the American attack on Queenston Heights in the War of 1812, and for his inconsolable fiancée, Sophia Shaw, who remained true to her love and never married. (A headless mannequin in a white gown stands behind the reception desk at the foot of the stairs. The Wisches call her Sophie, "the house ghost.")

Overnight guests gather for breakfast in a double parlor that has been turned into formal dining areas. The home-baked croissants come out of the oven at 9 o'clock sharp, when the feast begins with juices, homemade peach or blueberry yogurt and seasonal fruits. Potatoes play starring roles. The main course at our visit was stuffed potato with Canadian bacon, red peppers, cheese, chives and sour cream. The previous day produced smoked salmon with eggs benedict and German potato cake; the following day, shrimp cakes with eggs and bacon and potato croquettes. "Our guests don't need lunch," Thea stresses.

They sleep it off, perhaps, in six bedrooms with fireplaces and most with whirlpool tubs. Among them are a couple of small rooms with queen beds in the former servants' quarters, One claims the first bathroom in town – with clawfoot tub and separate shower. Sir Isaac's master chamber comes with a kingsize sleigh bed, big wing chair and chaise lounge, French country decor and a showy glass bathroom. Lady Sophia's suite has an English country look, a queen bed in the corner, wicker chairs beside the fireplace and a new bath with heated floor and double whirlpool tub. The huge third-floor Loft above the servants' quarters holds two kingsize beds (good for families or "ladies' night out," says Uwe), a TV/VCR and a step-up bath with double whirlpool.

Outside, wide verandas overlook spectacular gardens, where sitting areas are scattered beside a pond and waterfall. The summer flowers and hanging baskets are as much a show as the breakfasts. Talented Thea turns some of the flowers into swags and dried arrangements in her Brockamour Creations studio.

(905) 468-5527. Fax (905) 468-5071. Six rooms with private baths. Doubles, $120 to $190 weekends, $110 to $175 midweek.

Shannaleigh, 184 Queen St., Box 1357, Niagara-on-the-Lake L0s 1J0.

Fine architectural details grace this 1910 Tudor mansion on a substantial property with a one-acre garden. Consider leaded windows, tiger oak doors, mahogany fireplaces mantels and paneling, and three kinds of intricate moldings in the dining room. They're quite a backdrop for the museum-quality Native Art paintings displayed throughout by owners Carol and John Holmes, who show them for his brother, a Toronto art dealer. They make the large living room into a low-key gallery, where plush seating abounds and the house TV is hidden in an armoire. The gardens outside make the large side screened porch furnished in wicker seem like an open-air solarium.

Understated luxury prevails in the five upstairs guest rooms, reached by a sweeping staircase flanked by barley twist spindles. A kingsize carved mahogany canopy bed is the focal point of the master bedroom, decorated in English country style. It has a settee beside the fireplace. French provincial is the theme in the other front corner bedroom, with a queensize brass bed, wicker sun porch and a bathroom with its original cast-iron soaking tub and rain-head shower. Three attractive, slightly smaller rooms are in back. The bedrooms bear the names of her nieces, but Carol told her daughter she would name the inn for her. "Well, of course, Mother," was the reply.

The formal dining room with wine-colored walls, leaded windows and leather banquette and the adjacent sun porch are the settings for three-course breakfasts. "I cook and John schmoozes," says Carol. The repast begins with fruit and yogurt. Next might come a sweet pepper frittata or a cheese soufflé with grilled tomatoes and herbed potatoes. Lemon-yogurt waffles or blintzes and raspberries might follow.

(905) 468-2630. Fax (905) 468-1254. Five rooms with private baths. Doubles, $145 to $180 weekends, late April through December; $135 to $170 midweek and weekends rest of year. Two-night minimum weekends.

Robson-Grieve House, 100 John St., Box 431, Niagara-on-the-Lake L0S 1J0.

Tranquility and privacy away from the hubbub are among the hallmarks of this B&B in an updated early Canadian Loyalist house across from the Common and the historic Butlers Barracks and adjacent to a thirteen-acre walled estate. A fine collection of Canadian art and low-fat, heart-smart breakfasts are other features.

Gloria and Jim Grieve turn over the front portion of their handsome house to overnight guests in three bedrooms "fitted out according to how we like to travel," says Gloria. One has twin Shaker poster beds and wicker chairs. Another with two club chairs has the lowest queensize iron bed we ever saw, although the hostess maintains it is normal height. She dresses it with mounds of pillows. The premier accommodation is over the garage, a secluded space with queensize iron sleigh bed, sitting area and a window seat and a writing desk in the dormers.

The front of the main floor has a small guest library with a TV that's rarely turned on and an elegant dining room where breakfast is served at 9. Gloria offers local fruit, homemade granola and yogurt, plus a main dish like crust-less quiche or a cheese and tomato "pizza" on an English muffin. A guest favorite is low-fat lemon polenta pancakes with heart-smart orange sauce.

The shady grounds feature a pleasant terrace and an Inuit (Eskimo) stone sculpture called "Our Inukshuk" that directs guests to the doorway.

(905) 468-5581 or (888) 608-8783. Three rooms with private baths. Doubles, $135 to $150.

The Stable, 243 Mississauga St., Niagara-on-the-Lake L0S 1J0.

"Proprietor and bon vivant" is how the brochure for this neat, three-room B&B describes its owner and inspiration, Roy W. Clark. Business teacher and management consultant are other titles for the personable and energetic Roy, whose favorite sideline is his B&B. "I opened on a whim," says he. "Everyone else in town – the lord mayor, the Chamber of Commerce president – has one, so why not me?"

His is a private residence converted from an 1887 carriage house and stable. The large, open living room, library and dining area reflects Roy's tastes: contemporary yet historic, "eclectic, you might say." Three sofas are grouped as sectionals near the wood-burning stove and upright Mason & Risch piano. The rear windows look onto a shady, secluded back lawn harboring a swimming pool.

The antique dining room set was a wedding gift from his grandparents to his parents in 1936. "I remember playing under the table as a child," he says. Now it's the setting for a breakfast to remember, the fare posted daily on a printed menu. Cheese soufflé was the main dish the day we were there. Fresh fruit cocktail, homemade muffins and breads, Florida red grapefruit, assorted cereals, preserves and "homemade sweet salsa – otherwise known as chili sauce" – accompanied.

The laundry room doubles as a hospitality center, with a refrigerator, microwave and such available for guests. The former stable was converted into a game room and cozy lounge.

Upstairs are three guest rooms with private baths and TVs. Shaw's Corner holds some of the playwright's memorabilia and a kingsize bed. The other two rooms have queen beds, and the China Room revives memories of Roy's travels in Asia.

(905) 468-4140 or (800) 335-6877. Fax (905) 468-3113. Three rooms with private baths. Doubles, $114 to $119.

Cranberry House, 169 Gate St., Niagara-on-the-Lake, L0S 1J0.

Building from the ground up allows would-be innkeepers the opportunity to create the kind of B&B in which they like to stay. That's what Justin Venhuizen, an IBM early-retiree, and wife Fran did in 1995. Buying a small vacant lot from the owner of an adjacent residence, they built a cheery Queen Anne-style home that feels new but looks as if it's been there forever. The 75-year-old corkscrew willow in the rear garden enhances the impression.

The requisite wraparound porch, the front of the house and the upstairs are the domain of overnight guests. Three guest rooms are named after Justin's mother, the couple's daughter and their first grandchild. Nicole's has a queen poster bed and a whirlpool tub and separate shower. Cornelia's reflects Justin's mother's Dutch background with Delft blue tones and a queen poster bed. Granddaughter Jessica's, done in country pine, has a double bed with hand-sewn quilt, a white wrought iron daybed, a gas wood stove and an antique doll carriage in which the Seven Dwarfs reside.

Breakfast is served on the porch or in a garden dining room with a notable hand-stenciled ceiling. Fran employs 30 recipes, including strata, asparagus quiche, strawberry-stuffed french toast and cottage cakes (small pancakes made with cottage cheese). Sherry and port are offered later in the day.

Guests also enjoy a parlor and a basement entertainment room with TV, fireplace, dart board and pool table.

The Venhuizens also host periodic seminars for aspiring innkeepers.

(905) 468-4966. Fax (905) 468-8108. Three rooms with private baths. Doubles, $120 to $140.

Touring the Wineries

Geographically, one would not think of Canada as a wine-producing country. The Niagara Peninsula has changed that perception in a big way.

Shortly after New York's Finger Lakes region started proving that European viniferas could be grown in the Eastern climate, Niagara scrapped acres of concord and niagara grapes in favor of chardonnays, rieslings and pinot noirs. Today, vineyards are everywhere around Niagara-on-the-Lake, interspersed among more orchards of diverse fruit trees than we've ever seen in close proximity. Both are the area's distinguishing features, yielding mile after mile of beauty and bounty.

Vineyards proliferated in recent years to the point where Niagara-on-the-Lake boasted a Group of Seven, borrowing a well-known name from the Canadian art world. That since has become a group of twelve, and still another was in the works for 2000.

The grape-growing region is wedged between Lake Ontario to the north, the Niagara River to the east and the picturesque Niagara Escarpment to the south. The escarpment – a long, tiered ridge shaped something like a bench – separates the flatlands along Lakes Erie and Ontario. (The land along the seat of the bench is considered the most fertile, giving rise to the local phenomenon of "the Bench," whose growers put down the flatlands below as "the Swamp.") The escarpment is responsible for making this such a prolific fruit belt, both in terms of the rich minerals eroded into its soil and the micro-climate created by its sheltering effect and the moderating influence of Lake Ontario.

Its location near the 43rd-degree latitude places Niagara in the same position as such wine-growing regions as northern California, southern France and northern Italy. Some increasingly acclaimed wines, particularly rieslings, are the result. "For an area our size," says Cave Spring Cellars winemaker Angelo Pavan, "we probably win more awards in international competitions than any other region in the world."

The Niagara region also has become the world's leading maker of icewine (eiswein), a rare, sweet, almost chewy dessert wine whose minuscule production formerly was centered in Germany and Austria. Riesling and vidal grapes for icewine are left to freeze on the vine and are pressed frozen in winter to yield a wine that will age for ten or fifteen years. The limited supply fetches $30 to $50 or more a half bottle, and one wine writer predicted icewine could become "as Canadian as ice hockey."

Connoisseurs enjoy following the scenic, marked Wine Route, spending a day touring the wineries in the flatlands around Niagara-on-the-Lake and another day touring those along the Bench.

Inniskillin Wines Inc., Line 3 Road off Niagara Parkway, Niagara-on-the-Lake.

In 1975, Inniskillin was granted the first Ontario wine license since 1929 and became Ontario's first cottage winery, specializing in viniferas. Karl Kaiser, winemaker who learned the art in Austria as a monk, and Donald Ziraldo, promoter, are co-founders of what many consider to be Canada's finest winery, seller of more than 150,000 cases annually, nearly half from its own 120 acres of vineyards. In 1999, co-founder Ziraldo was profiled as one of the top 25 Canadian CEOs of the century in a National Post magazine article for his leadership in the Canadian wine industry.

Visitors may take a twenty-station self-guided tour or a 45-minute guided tour and taste wines in a 1920s barn (said to have been inspired by Frank Lloyd Wright), the ground floor of which has been transformed into a retail store and tasting area. A menu at the door shows that Inniskillin's cabernet sauvignon reserve was served at former Prime Minister Mulroney's 1993 dinner for Mikhail Gorbachev. The 1997 icewine made by Karl Kaiser from vidal grapes won a record three gold medals in a row, culminating in the Civart Award of Excellence at Vinexpo in France. In 1999, Inniskillin produced Canada's first VQA sparkling icewine. Otherwise, it continues to concentrate on premium viniferas, particularly pinot noir, here and at its newer winery in the Okanagan Valley of British Columbia.

Tastings are featured at a nominal fee based on the retail price of the wine. Older vintages are periodically available to taste, as are the internationally known icewines.

(905) 468-3554 or (888) 466-4754. Tours daily at 10:30 and 2:30, May-October, also weekends rest of year. Wine boutique and visitor center open daily, 10 to 6, May-October, to 5 rest of year.

Hillebrand Estates Winery, Highway 55, Niagara-on-the-Lake.

Billed as Canada's most award-winning winery and top producer of premium Vintners Quality Alliance (VQA) wines, this is the nation's largest estate winery, producing more than 300,000 cases a year and running more than 100 retail stores across Ontario.

The frequent tours here are said to be the most lively and informative of any Niagara winery. Indeed, it was the first winery to give regular tours year-round and they last an hour or longer.

A welcome center and gallery provides directions to the expanding complex, which includes a 110-seat restaurant and a vineyard concert series on three summer weekends. Complimentary tastings are offered in the large retail boutique, which looks like a wine store and purveys a selection of regional gourmet foods, Hillebrand's Vineyard Cafe specialties and wine-related items. The superb Collector's Choice chardonnay and cabernet-merlot (both $13.95) bear the labels of some of Canada's famed Group of Seven artists. We coveted the poster of their labels, but left empty-handed because they sell faster than they can be produced.

(905) 468-7123 or (800) 582-8412. Tours daily on the hour, 10 to 6. Showroom daily, 10 to 6.

Château des Charmes, 1025 York Road, Niagara-on-the-Lake.

This was touted by a Finger Lakes winemaker as Niagara's "best of the bunch" and owner Paul Bosc Sr., the French-born patriarch, has been dubbed the "Baron Philippe Rothschild of Ontario." The winery is known for estate chardonnays, aged in oak barrels imported from France for $550 each. Its brut sparkling wine is widely considered to be Canada's best, and its recent cabernet and merlot releases are quite good. The winery was Canada's first to experiment with the French barrels. Its 60-acre vineyard was the first in Canada planted entirely with European vinifera vines.

Another 85 acres have been planted lately around a rather pretentious, $6 million French château built in 1994 seemingly in the middle of nowhere beneath the St. David's Bench. The stone mansion houses the winery, a champagne cellar, a banquet facility and a showroom and reception area. A $2 ticket gets you a video presentation, a tour, a visit to the underground cellars and a tasting of three wines. The place does catering and special events, including a luncheon prepared by seven top Canadian chefs for the 1995 meeting of the international Club des Chefs des Chefs. You might stumble onto one of the periodic Taste of Niagara lunches, featuring visiting chefs, under the tent. With a facility like this and the Bosc family's avowed desire to "marry food and wine," one would not be surprised to find a full-fledged vineyard restaurant here someday.

(905) 262-4219. Tours daily on the hour, 11 to 4. Showroom daily, 10 to 9.

Konzelmann Estate Winery, 1096 Lakeshore Road, Niagara-on-the-Lake.

Wines in the German style are made here by Herbert Konzelmann, the fourth generation involved in a family winery founded in Germany in 1893. Rows and rows of grapes, all labeled, grow primly on 40 acres along the shores of Lake Ontario, which has particularly beneficial effects for the vineyard.

The winery bottled its first harvest in 1986, has won more than 180 medals in national and international competitions since, and now produces 40,000 cases a year of 29 different wines. The dry riesling is especially good, as is the gewürztraminer. Konzelmann's vidal icewine won the grand gold award at the VinItaly competition in 1993 and again in 1999 at an international competition in Brussels. A couple of pinot noirs, a cabernet/merlot and a gamay noir attest to Niagara's success with red wines as well.

The 1998 riesling icewine was dedicated to Matthias Konzelman, whose young life was cut short after a courageous battle with leukemia. He had returned from studying in Germany to join his parents as winemaker.

(905) 935-2866. Tours by reservation, May-September, free daily tour at 2. Boutique, Monday-Saturday 10 to 6, Sunday noon to 5:30, April-December; Monday-Saturday 10 to 5, rest of year.

Spacious deck at Vineland Estates Winery Restaurant yields view of Lake Ontario in distance.

Vineland Estates, 3620 Moyer Road, Vineland.

This expanding winery is Niagara's most picturesque – situated in the rolling countryside along the Bench, with a view of Lake Ontario to the northwest. Lots of trees and hills make for a pleasant break from the sameness of the flatlands scenery below (follow Route 81 and the Niagara Winery Route along the Bench and you may think you're in the upper vales of California's Napa Valley).

German wine grower Hermann Weis wanted to prove to skeptical Canadian growers that his riesling grapes could be cultivated so far north, so he established a vineyard of his own here. Today, his original 45 acres produce 12,000 cases annually of mostly riesling and some chardonnay. New owner John Howard, a Hamilton wine connoisseur, acquired 50 more acres, planting cabernet, merlot and pinot noir vines and doubled production to 25,000 cases. He vastly expanded the restaurant in the original 1845 estate house and restored a rear carriage house with soaring windows and Napa-style views for craft shows, themed wine dinners and private functions. One of Ontario's last log-construction heritage barns was converted in 1999 into a beauty of a wine shop and tasting room.

In the planning stage was a culinary center with a 50-room hotel, where Vineland's chef as well as others would give cooking classes as part of the owner's oft-stated desire to showcase the new Canadian cuisine.

Vineland's premium dry rieslings are decisive proof that Niagara rieslings are "better than anything outside the Rhine-Mosel axis itself," one writer proclaimed. Brothers Allan and Brian Schmid, the winemakers, are also known for gewürztraminers, pinot noirs and icewines.

(905) 562-708 or (888) 846-3526. Tours daily at 1 and 3, June-October. Showroom daily, 10 to 9 in season, to 5:30 rest of year.

Henry of Pelham Family Estate Winery, 1469 Pelham Road, St. Catharines.
Here is a small but growing winery with quite a history. Located in the heart of

the Bench, the hilly 80-acre vineyard has been owned by a single family since Henry Smith planted the first grapes in 1794. Some 190 years later, Paul Speck Sr. ripped out the original vines and replanted with French hybrids and viniferas. In 1993, when his quickly successful winery had reached his goal of producing 20,000 cases, its founder died and the business was left to his sons' care.

Since then, Paul Jr., Matthew and Daniel Speck increased annual production to 45,000 cases. Their chardonnays, rieslings and icewines are considered some of the best in Canada. The brothers have experienced success with red wines, too At the prestigious Cuvée 1999 awards in Niagara-on-the-Lake, the winery's 1997 baco noir was named the best red hybrid, while its cabernet-merlot was honored as top red wine over-all.

We sampled a variety from the house Loyalist cabernet-foch ($8.95) to an elegant reserve chardonnay ($13.65) in the stone basement of a stone inn and tollgate built in 1842 by Henry Smith, the brothers' great-great grandfather, who licensed the inn under the name Henry of Pelham. The building houses a wine boutique, tour center and a gallery of Canadian art collected by the brothers' parents. The Specks also were renovating an old barn on the property to house new wine-tasting facilities and special events, such as their popular Shakespeare in the Vineyard series.

(905) 684-8423. Tours daily at 11:30, 1:30 and 3:30, May-December. Showroom daily, 10 to 6, to 5 in winter.

Cave Spring Cellars, 3836 Main St., Jordan.

Serious, prize-winning wines from vinifera grapes are the specialty of this boutique winery on the Bench, housed in a lineup of buildings that comprised the defunct Jordan Winery, Ontario's oldest winemaking facility. The small wine-tasting and sales room is as stylish as the owner's On the Twenty restaurant at the other end of the complex.

Chardonnays and rieslings are featured here, the elegant and oaky chardonnay reserve selling for $19.95 and the smooth, award-winning riesling icewine commanding $44.95 a half bottle. The venture headed by Leonard Pennachetti also produces rosé, cabernet, merlot, gamay and pinot noir varietals among its 15,000 cases annually in an effort to put Cave Spring in the vanguard of small North American wineries. The bone-dry riesling reserve is winemaker Angelo Pavan's favorite.

The Cave Spring enterprise has inspired more than a dozen one-of-a-kind shops (from clothing to Inuit and Canadian native art to gardening to antiques) leased to the owners in its buildings along both sides of Jordan's Main Street. They help make Jordan a special destination.

(905) 562-3581. Tours, weekends at 11 and 3, weekdays at 11, May-October. Showroom, Monday-Saturday 10 to 6, Sunday 11 to 6, to 5 November-April.

Other wineries worth a visit:

Reif Winery, Niagara Parkway, Niagara-on-the-Lake, the closest to town and river, opened in 1983 and is known for wines in the German style. All North American grapes were uprooted in favor of European vinifera and premium French hybrids on the 135-acre estate behind the winery. Klaus W. Reif, descendant of a winemaking family in Germany, selects only the best 40 percent of the harvest for his own wines, selling the rest to other wineries. The dry riesling and gewürztraminer are standouts here. The winery stages functions in conjunction with the Grand Victorian B&B next door. Tours daily at 1:30, May-September. Showroom, daily 10 to 6, to 5 in winter.

Marynissen Estates, Concession 1 off Line 3, Niagara-on-the-Lake, specializes in red wines. Winemaker John Marynissen, a Dutch immigrant who started planting vinifera grapes in 1974, won amateur winemaking competitions for years before his daughters convinced him to open an estate winery in 1991. His wines were judged by local winemakers as the "Best Red" two years in a row at Cuvée 1996 and 1997. Among leading Marynissen wines are cabernet franc, cabernet sauvignon, pinot noir, gamay and petit syrah. Showroom daily, 10 to 6, to 5 in winter.

Sunnybrook Farm Estate Winery, 1425 Lakeshore Road, Niagara-on-the-Lake, produces wines made from fruit grown in Gerald Goertz's orchards. Fruit wines tend to be sweeter than grape wines because of a higher sugar content, but among his two dozen varieties Gerald ranks his Empire apple and Damson plum wines up there with the best. He finds his Bosc Pear wine an excellent match with cheeses, and "more civilized than the fruit itself – no peel to deal with." Showroom open Monday-Saturday 10 to 6, Sunday to 5, May-October; daily 10 to 5, November-December; Wednesday-Sunday 10 to 5, rest of year.

Peller Estates Winery was under construction along John Street, near the Niagara Parkway, for opening in spring 2001. John Peller, head of the company that owns Hillebrand Estates Winery and Andrés Wines Ltd. in Grimsby, planned to concentrate on small lots of high-end wines. His 40-acre vineyard focuses on chardonnay and three premium reds, cabernet franc, sauvignon and merlot, as well as Cristalle, a methode-champenois champagne flavored with a touch of icewine. Annual production was set for 15,000 cases a year. In addition, the winery will feature a formal, white-linen restaurant offering lunch and dinner. John said the goal would be to marry the European dining tradition with the Niagara regional cuisine. Dinner entrées were expected to be in the $30 to $35 range.

Fruit Stands

In harvest season, the fruit fairly drops off the trees, evidence of how prolific the Niagara Peninsula orchards are. They represent 90 percent of the fruit raised in Ontario, and Niagara is a major fruit bowl for much of Canada. Country markets, some of them run by local Mennonites, stand chock-a-block between orchards along every road. Prices naturally are lower the farther you get from the Queen Elizabeth Way and population centers. Some of the best are around Niagara-on-the-Lake.

Harvest Barn Country Market, Highway 55 at East-West Line, is a large country market selling everything from fresh produce to home-baked breads, pies, cornish pasties, and steak and kidney pies; two of the last made a good dinner back home. We also made a picnic lunch out of the fantastic salad bar (priced by the pound, supermarket style), with ever-so-fresh ingredients set out on ice in about 50 separate dishes.

Kurtz Orchards Country Market, Niagara Parkway at East-West Line, is the biggest and most commercial market, but don't be fazed by the tour buses out front. Jean and Ed Kurtz started more than 25 years ago with one table under an umbrella and maintain the family touch. There are varieties of jams, maple syrups, honeys and plum butter with crackers for sampling, many specialty foods, baked goods like almond-raisin bread (a local specialty with marzipan in the middle) and huge cookies, drinks like cherry cider and peach nectar, and salad and sundae bars.

Rempel's Farm Market, 75 Queen St., is the downtown retail outgrowth of the Rempel family's 50-acre farm at 1651 Lakeshore Road. The farm specializes now in growing roses, but Debbie Rempel's Queen Street outlet is favored by those in the know for seasonal fruit, baked goods, maple syrup and the like. Her bakery produces great strudels, cappuccino nanaimo bars and raspberry squares. We took home a rempelberry pie ($4.99) baked with raspberries, blackberries, rhubarb and apples, and a sample of Mennonite platz. Frozen yogurts (even a rempelberry), made with their own fruits, are in demand in summer.

Gourmet Treats

Angie Strauss, 125 Queen St., has become the town's best-known shopping destination for with-it visitors, thanks to the artist's watercolors and her vibrant floral designs. They're on everything from high-fashion sweatshirts in the $50 range to gifts, cards, wine labels and kitchen accessories, among them placemats, coasters, bibs and oven mitts. We acquired a couple of refrigerator magnets and a large print at a fraction of the cost of one of her lovely originals ($2,000), and thus qualified for a pair of free sweat pants at the **Angie Strauss Fashion Outlet** store at 183 Victoria St., where discontinued patterns are sold. Angie's is quite a story – previously a potter, she disabled her left elbow in a roller-skating accident and started dabbling in watercolors with her good right arm, painting the flowers that husband Hartley brought her each week. People admired her paintings, asked to buy them and the rest, since the early 1980s, is history. All the designs are Angie's, created in the studio and stunning gardens behind her house at 178 Victoria St. But the copies and products are the work of 25 Mennonite women whom Angie employs around town. Ever the entrepreneur, she rents a one-of-a-kind studio apartment known as **Victoria Cottage** (468-2570) for $130 a night in the coach house her husband built next to their home.

Imagine an entire downtown store in a prime corner location devoted to jams. **Greaves Jams & Marmalades,** 55 Queen St., looks just as it must have more than 50 years ago. This is where the Greaves family retails its jams, marmalades and preserves. Bins of jams, shelves of jams, boysenberry, peach, raspberry, red and black currant – you name it, they have it, and they use no pectin, preservatives or coloring. We picked up six mini-jars for $6.30, as well as some special mustards (these they don't make).

Niagara is known for its fudge. **Maple Leaf Fudge** at 114 Queen St. is where you can choose from many kinds, made with "real butter," including chocolate-ginger studded with chunks of fresh ginger.

The **Niagara Home Bakery** at 66 Queen St., the oldest surviving business in town, operates as it did nearly a century ago. The bread is still baked in an old stone oven and the Easter chocolate is made by hand. Scones, tea biscuits, bridies, almond tarts, sausage rolls, quiches and more are for sale.

Taylors at 69 Queen is the place to stock up for an old-fashioned picnic. You could get a submarine for $3.95, but why not try a schnitzel on a bun or a cornish pastie? Sandwiches come on a choice of breads or "balm" cakes, which are large rolls. Have a date square or an Empire biscuit for dessert, or one of the more than 50 flavors of ice cream, including Laurentian vanilla.

Yes, Niagara keeps up with the times. **Monika's Coffees,** a coffee and pastry shop at 126 Queen St., sells espresso, cappuccino, caffe mocha and caffe latte, along with strudels, muffins, broccoli-cheese puffs, spinach pies and – a new one for us – smoked-salmon cheesecake.

L'Esprit Provence, 106C Queen St., is a haven of food, kitchen gadgets, cuisine posters, pottery, serving bowls and much more from the South of France. It now has a thriving catalog and website operation.

The facade of **The Shaw Shop** "doesn't exactly shout shop," conceded the manager, which may be why we missed it the first time around. With a location at 79 Queen St. next to the Royal George Theatre, the Shaw Festival's memorabilia shop features books, festival posters, music, gifts and ShawWear.

Savor Niagara

Niagara Presents, 4000 Jordan Road, Jordan Station.

Billed as "the best of Niagara specialty foods," this fledgling enterprise showcases the local jams, vinegars, chutneys and the like produced by a co-operative network of women. They're available individually or combined in lovely gift baskets in the $20 to $80 range. Many of the products, like peach champagne jelly, inferno red pepper jelly and pumpkin butter, may be opened for sampling before you buy. Occupying the front of a commercial food-processing facility, the community-sponsored venture includes a retail showroom as well as a kitchen that can be rented for the making of preserves, with equipment and staff available to help.

Dozens of products are marketed under the label, the number growing as more people join the co-op, originally designed to help low-income and immigrant women establish home-based businesses. In its first appearance at the annual Canadian Fine Food Show in Toronto, Niagara Presents won a remarkable four of the sixteen awards. We left with four bottles of special basil vinegar (there were twelve varieties of basil vinegar alone) for Christmas gifts.

(905) 562-1907. Open daily, 10 to 6.

Gourmet Theater

Shaw Festival, 10 Queen's Parade, Box 774, Niagara-on-the-Lake L0S 1J0.

No report on Niagara-on-the-Lake would be complete without mention of the Shaw Festival. Twelve productions of George Bernard Shaw and his contemporaries are staged in three theaters from late March through November. Artistic director Christopher Newton and one of the world's largest permanent ensembles of actors explore classic plays in a modern way for contemporary audiences. The 861-seat Festival Theater, built in 1973, contains the larger epic works. The 345-seat Court House Theater presents smaller Shaw works and the more intimate American and European dramas of the period. The 353-seat Royal George Theater houses musicals and perhaps an Agatha Christie mystery.

(905) 468-2172 or (800) 511-7429. Performances, Tuesday-Sunday at noon, 2 and 8. Tickets, $15 to $70.

Saratoga Springs

The Summer Place to Be

The party's really hopping these days in that grand dowager of American resorts, Saratoga Springs. The small town that mineral springs, horse racing and society summers made famous had nearly died in the 1950s and 1960s. It re-emerged slowly in the 1970s and now is back on track, as it were, with a five-and-a-half-week racing season that extends through Labor Day, live performances almost nightly in July and August at the Saratoga Performing Arts Center, and a summer social scene that brings back the good old days. Little wonder that Saratoga proclaims itself "the summer place to be."

A culinary renaissance has added dimension to what U.S. News and World Report termed "the August delirium of Saratoga, for generations America's symbol of high living." A single square block below Broadway around Phila Street held the new Palmetto's and Putnam Street markets, the restaurant lineup of Four Seasons Cafe, 43 Phila Street, Hattie's and Beverly's Specialty Foods, plus Ben & Jerry's, not to mention a tavern and a sports bar.

The result is a uniquely Saratoga spirit and panache, one that gives it an odd parochialism as if encased in its own cocoon with a north-south focus on Albany and New York, oblivious to points east and west.

The romance of the old Saratoga was evident in its grand, long-gone hotels with their sprawling porches along Broadway, the wide main street. Herbert A. Chesbrough, longtime executive director of the SPAC, which was instrumental in the city's rejuvenation, says "the romance of the new Saratoga is in the small cafes, unusual restaurants and the boutiques that have opened in some of the community's oldest buildings."

Food has become a big – and expensive – business in Saratoga, and some restaurants stay open in August until 3 a.m. to accommodate the after-the-concert or after-the-race crowds. In fact, scoffs one restaurateur, "even the clothing stores sell food. Everything and anything becomes a restaurant for two months." In a bit of local hyperbole, she claims the town has more restaurants and bars per capita than any other in the United States.

Most of the year, Saratoga is "very low key," says Linda G. Toohey, former Daily Saratogian publisher who became executive vice president of the local Chamber of Commerce. "We think we're the best-kept secret in the world."

The pace picks up in late June with racing at the Saratoga Raceway harness track, the Freihofer's Jazz Festival and performances by the Miami City Ballet and the New York City Ballet at SPAC, and the opening of the party season that culminates in socialite Marylou Whitney's grand entrance in a horse-drawn carriage at her annual ball.

Come August, the crowds converge for the height of Saratoga's storied racing season, the Saratoga Chamber Music Festival and the Philadelphia Orchestra series at SPAC. Prices double and even triple, but many are the people who are willing to pay them.

Where else would a Holiday Inn switch from a rack rate of $86 to $109 for most of the year to a base of $209 to $469 in August?

That's Saratoga for you, a curious anomaly of a world-class resort with a shiny gold sheen and a hand out for the big bucks. Especially in season.

Sophie Parker prepares plate for dinner at Chez Sophie Bistro.

Dining

The Best of the Best

Chez Sophie Bistro, 2853 Route 9, Malta Ridge.

Long considered the Saratoga area's finest restaurant, Chez Sophie is back on track after a decade's absence. Sophie and Joseph Parker turned up south of town in a sleek stainless steel diner that once housed Sam's Place, and her fans could not have been happier.

Flawless French fare and a seasonal schedule had been Sophie's trademarks over the years, starting in 1969 in the rural restaurant that was an addition to their home north of town in Hadley, then in an elegant Saratoga townhouse and eventually back at the Hadley retreat. That ultimately closed, and Sophie took a break for a few years as she sought a more urban, year-round venue.

Assisted by their son Paul, who moved from Long Island to help manage, the Parkers bought the diner in 1995, did some renovation and rechristened it a bistro. Some bistro. This has black booths and banquettes, white tablecloths and lacy cafe curtains on the windows, through which the setting sun casts colorful streaks of light. The bar holds some of Joseph's fantastic wire sculptures, produced in his Hadley gallery. His sketches serve as menu covers.

Sophie has discarded her traditional prix-fixe format in favor of à la carte. "The menu is basic, but we always have specialties such as salmon, lamb, duckling, and different appetizers and desserts," said she, happily at work in the kitchen, where she's most at home. Born of Polish parents in northern France, she cooks in the classic French style. "I don't even think of it as French," she demurs. "I just think of it as good food."

That translates to appetizers like mussels billi-bi, house-cured smoked salmon, goat cheese in puff pastry and, when available, a dynamite rabbit pâté with prunes and armagnac and a coulis of blueberries, an odd combination that tastes simply wonderful. Main courses vary from fillet of sole in lobster sauce to a trio of grilled quail to roasted veal loin chop to steak au poivre. Dessert could be a light crème caramel, rich chocolate mousse, fresh lemon cheese pie or our old favorite, vacherin, a meringue filled with vanilla ice cream and served with raspberry purée and chocolate sauce.

While his wife is in the kitchen, husband Joseph makes sure folks in the front of the house are well looked after. Paul helps wait on tables and oversees the all-French wine list, a delightful compendium of affordable and unusual vintages.

(518) 583-3538. Entrées, $19 to $29. Dinner, Tuesday-Sunday from 5:30, nightly in August. Closed January to mid-February.

43 Phila Bistro, 43 Phila St.

Winner of top culinary honors in downtown Saratoga is this suave American cafe-bistro run by Michael Lenza, an ex-South Jersey chef who cooked locally at Sperry's before launching his own venture in 1993. "I might as well own a place if I'm working so hard," he figured.

Sixteen-hour days have paid off for Michael, who spent eight months gutting and remodeling a former cafe. He and chef John Winnek earn rave reviews for their contemporary fare served with finesse. His wife Patricia oversees the 90-seat dining room, lovely in peach and terra cotta. The bar and banquettes are custom-made of bird's-eye and tiger's-eye maple. Caricatures of local businessmen brighten one wall. Tables, most of the deuces rather close together, are covered with white linens topped with paper mats bearing the 43 Phila logo (a curious but attractive touch that we far prefer to glass). Atop each are fresh flowers, a lucite pepper grinder and a bottle of red wine – a different label at each table.

Arriving almost as we were seated for dinner was a dish of assorted spicy olives marinated in olive oil – the oil useful for soaking the accompanying bread from Rock Hill Bakery, an area institution. Featured among starters is a Maryland crab martini, jumbo lump crabmeat served with citron vodka, lettuce and an olive in a chilled martini glass. Others are a sampler of three soups, panzanella bread salad and, in our case, a smooth chicken-liver pâté served with crostini and cornichons, a terrific trio of smoked seafood (with capers in a little carrot floret and roasted red-pepper crème fraîche) and an enormous pizzetta on Italian bruschetta, a meal in itself.

Had we eaten more than a sliver of the pizzetta we never would have made it through the main courses, a choice of up to a dozen ranging from roasted Chilean sea bass with a tapenade crust to grilled lamb chops with mint pesto and lingonberry jelly. The Tuscan chicken pasta with roasted peppers, olives and white beans was a lusty autumn dish; ditto for the jerk chargrilled swordfish with papaya-lobster salsa and a Thai red curry sauce. A bottle of our favorite Hogue Cellars fumé blanc accompanied from a varied, well-chosen wine list.

The pastry chef is known for distinctive desserts, including an acclaimed 43 Phila chocolate cake soaked in kahlua and covered with a brandied chocolate ganache, deep-dish peach crumble pie, and white chocolate raspberry tart. We settled for a dish of plum-port sorbet, a refreshing ending to an uncommonly good meal.

(518) 584-2720. Entrées, $21 to $36. Lunch daily, 11:30 to 3. Dinner nightly, 6 to 10 or 11. Closed Sunday in off-season.

Artworks are backdrop for diners at 43 Phila Bistro.

Chianti, Il Ristorante, 208 South Broadway.

A former fast-food eatery was the hottest restaurant in town – according to both its ebullient Italian chef-owner and his growing following. Chianti is lovingly tended by David Zecchini from Rome, whose grandparents run a restaurant there, and his wife Maria.

David, who claims to have been the youngest maitre-d' in California at age 22, went on to open La Fontana, a highly rated restaurant in Newport Beach. He sold it at age 29 to move to Maria's hometown, where he transformed a Long John Silver's seafood franchise into a place of earth tones and Mediterranean beauty. "I built this restaurant piece by piece," he said. He made the handsome tabletops with Italian tiles, hand-painted the ceiling a burnt sienna color, and installed an open kitchen with a shiny copper effect at the rear. He also created the prototype for the colorful new service plates custom-made for the restaurant. Close-together tables seat 70 inside and an additional 40 on the front patio.

David's labor of love includes a passion for food. His is creative, robust and considered good value. Among antipasti are bruschetta topped with garlic and tomato, carpaccio marinated in truffle oil and topped with gorgonzola, fried calamari with spicy marinara sauce, and grilled scampi tossed with wild greens. Can't decide? Consider the chef's-choice antipasto sampler, $13.95 for two.

Two risottos, one with porcini mushrooms and the other with crab and scampi, come highly recommended. So do pastas like tagliatelle in a light porcini mushroom-cognac sauce and capellini with scampi in a lobster grappa sauce.

Favorite main courses are scampi marinated with mint in a balsamic-lemon sauce, chicken with artichokes in a lemon-wine sauce, braised pork loin in a port wine sauce, veal saltimbocca and filet mignon with a wild mushroom sauce.

Desserts range from lemon or orange sorbet to profiteroles, tiramisu and a light lemon tort finished with pinenuts and powdered sugar.

The predominantly Italian wine list starts in the low twenties and includes a number in the triple digits.

Chianti dining area reflects versatile talents of chef-owner David Zecchini.

David is apt to break into song as he works in the kitchen. It's the friendly, neighborhood kind of a place where the patrons join in. Go with friends and leave with more.

(518) 580-0025. Entrées, $14.95 to $19.95. Dinner nightly, from 5:30. Closed Monday in off-season.

Sperry's, 30 Caroline St.
Only in Saratoga could what "looks like a gin mill" (a local booster's words) pass itself off as a good restaurant. Everyone we talk with, from top chefs to hotel desk clerks, mentions Sperry's among their favorites.

It's certainly not for the speakeasy-look decor – peek through the window and you might not venture inside. A long bar with a black and white linoleum floor takes up about half the space. At either end of the room are dark old booths and tables covered with blue and white checked cloths. On one side is a small dining addition, similarly outfitted and used for overflow. Beyond is an enclosed (and heated) patio for outdoor seating in season.

Chef-owner Eldridge Qua is known for consistently good food – with Asian and Louisiana accents – at reasonable prices. The menu rarely changes, but the preparations and lengthy list of specials do.

For lunch, one of us enjoyed a great grilled duck-breast salad with citrus vinaigrette and the other a cup of potato-leek soup with an enormous open-face dill-havarti-tomato sandwich, served with a side salad. Service on a slow day, unfortunately, was so leisurely as to be interminable. We had to go to the bar to request – and later to pay – the bill.

At night, when we assume service is better, the menu ranges widely from jambalaya to steak au poivre. Fillet of sole sautéed with malt vinegar, an extra-garlicky shrimp scampi, and rack of New Zealand lamb with a garlic-rosemary demi-glace were among choices at our latest visit. The day's pasta was sautéed rock shrimp, escarole, snow peas and roasted red peppers over linguini. The wasabi dinner was baked jumbo shrimp wrapped in bacon with Japanese horseradish, served over rice with Thai sauce. The salad du jour produced beer-battered catfish over mesclun greens with spicy salsa and a New Orleans rémoulade dressing.

Appetizers like escargots, a smooth chicken liver pâté, wasabi shrimp and grilled portobello mushrooms with chèvre and garlic toast are better than run-of-the-gin-mill offerings. Desserts include tortes, cheesecakes, seasonal fruit tarts, crème caramel, and lemon and chocolate mousses.

The wine list is reasonably priced, a further attraction for locals who gravitate here when outsiders take over their other favorites.

(518) 584-9618. Entrées, $14.95 to $21.95. Lunch daily except Sunday in season, 11:30 to 3. Dinner nightly, 5:30 to 10 or 11.

Longfellows Inn and Restaurant, 500 Union Ave.
The famed Caunterbury restaurant complex has given way to this well-regarded restaurant with a new inn adjacent (see below).

The principals are Steve and Yvonne Sullivan, owners of the Olde Bryan Inn restaurant downtown. Here, on the far outskirts of town, they gave two 1915 dairy barns a facelift and toned down the Caunterbury's eye-popping Disneyesque theme to create a pleasing Federal-style steakhouse and grill.

It's still quite an eyeful, this grand barn of a space with an amazing variety of venues for dining. There are dining rooms on several levels behind the façades of "village houses" set around what had been an interior lagoon. One room has a wooden footbridge crossing a pond full of goldfish. Other rooms are smaller and more standard. The tavern and wine cellar with a fireplace is favored in winter. All told, the place seats 425 – if there's a wait, check out the enormous upstairs cocktail lounge with its lighted ficus tree.

The food used to be secondary to the atmosphere, but that situation has changed. A mesquite grill produces a variety of steaks and other items, perhaps swordfish steak with melon-lime salsa, bourbon-glazed salmon fillet, walnut encrusted breast of chicken with a dried cranberry and honey-balsamic glaze, and twin pork chops with an Asian plum and ginger sauce. Slow-roasted prime rib is a specialty. Other possibilities include shrimp stuffed with lobster and mandarin oranges, served with a tarragon beurre blanc, and pistachio-encrusted rack of New Zealand lamb.

The menu also offers a quartet of pastas, salads and appetizers from a lobster and asparagus tart to mesquite-grilled Southwestern chicken strudel. Cheesecake, triple chocolate terrine, apple-walnut pie and crème brûlée might be on tap for dessert.

(518) 587-0108. Entrées, $14.95 to $21.95. Dinner, 4 to 11, Sunday 2 to 10.

One for the Season

Siro's, 168 Lincoln Ave.
Imagine a fancy restaurant next to the race track, open a mere five weeks a year (for the racing season) and considered an institution. Only in Saratoga could such a place survive. Siro's has not only survived since the 1930s but thrived.

Siro's occupies a little white house that sports blue awnings and canopies. There's a tent at the side for jazz, a prominent bar inside the front entry and a couple of dining rooms dressed in white linens with white candles standing tall.

Expect to spend upwards of $200 (or more) for dinner for two with wine. The menu changes nightly, but the contents are always inventive, the product acclaimed and the delivery polished.

High-rollers like to start with exotic hors d'oeuvres, perhaps stir-fried manila clams with garlic, ginger and Chinese black beans or seared Hudson Valley foie gras with smoked onion relish, a corn pancake and red currant glacé. The lobster tortilla with corn relish and peppered guacamole is a menu staple. So is a service of Beluga caviar, $90 for 42 grams.

Then it's on to a "first course,' say tea-smoked muscovy duck with lo mein noodles, Asian vegetables and ginger-black bean dressing; fusilli with house-smoked salmon, tomatoes and cream; local beefsteak tomato salad with fresh mozzarella, or Siro's romaine salad with anchovy, reggiano shards and caesar dressing. Typically, the dozen or so main courses run from a signature crusty baked fluke with caramelized banana and tropical salsa or roasted Bresse-style chicken breast with lobster mousse, bacon-leek flan and sauce nantua to roasted rack of lamb with rosemary jus and garlic bread pudding. Roasted loin of Arctic caribou with natural game jus and a grilled vegetable shepherd's pie stood out on a recent menu.

Longtime executive chef Ken Maceachron's cooking background in Hawaii is often evident.

(518) 584-4030. Entrées, $26 to $44. Dinner nightly, 6 to 11, late July to Labor Day.

Gourmet for the Soul

Hattie's, 45 Phila St., Saratoga Springs.

After 55 years as Hattie's Chicken Shack, this well-known institution changed hands, shortened its name and raised its culinary aspirations. Hattie Austin, who was then still doing the baking at age 93, sold in 1993 to Christel Baker, then a 33-year-old Wall Street investment banker. "We're old friends," explained Christel. "Our families go way back."

Personable Christel, who was making apple butter in the kitchen at our first visit, has gradually broadened the emphasis from soul food to southern home cooking to "bayou" cuisine with a distinct New Orleans bite. She kept the homey, cozy, checkered-tablecloth decor, but added a brick patio surrounded by a southern-style garden "just like one I saw in New Orleans" out back. She expanded the hours, added po'boys for lunch and live blues in season, offered the traditional side dishes à la carte and won a liquor license, featuring southern drinks like mint juleps (with mint picked from her garden). She also offers specialties through her **Hattie's General Store,** based on the premises and featuring mail-order chutneys, pies and free-range pork and pasture-raised aged beef from her 110-acre farm near the Vermont border.

In 1999, Christel and her husband, Colin McLean, a Montreal-born actor, covered the patio with a tent draped in fabric and christened it their patio bar. It's a dramatic spot in which while away a summer evening.

The whole enterprise is decidedly with-it and upbeat, the ambiance appealing and the food spirited. Typical starters are Louisiana-style crab cakes, rum and coconut shrimp, chicken wings and warm portobello carpaccio, a Hattie's original. At night, you can order Hattie's famous southern fried chicken, pan-fried cornmeal catfish or barbecued spare ribs. Each comes with a green salad, homemade biscuits

Christel and Colin McLean relax in new canopied courtyard patio bar at Hattie's.

and a choice of two sides (perhaps collard greens and candied yams). Bayou and New Orleans specialties include creole jambalaya, low-country crab cakes and red snapper provençal. Four of the southern side dishes with a salad and biscuits make a vegetarian sampler. Christel urges patrons to mix and match appetizers, soups and salads for a light meal.

Breakfast in season features beignets and café au lait. Try an oyster po'boy for lunch, or the fried chicken or barbecued spare ribs if you will. Finish with the apple cobbler or sweet-potato pie.

(518) 584-4790. Entrées, $11.95 to $16.95. Dinner, Wednesday-Sunday, 5 to 10. Open daily in race season, breakfast 8 to 11:30, lunch 11:30 to 5, dinner, 5 to 10, patio bar to 3 a.m.

More Dining Choices

Maestro's, 371 Broadway.

This storefront space on the ground floor of the landmark Adelphi Hotel building has been home to several restaurants. The latest and best is this, run by chef Joseph DeVivo Jr., a Saratoga native who offers new Italian cuisine with American and French accents.

Up to 36 diners can be accommodated at white-clothed tables inside, with fourteen more seats on the sidewalk out front. A few musical instruments and colorful paintings provide color, and an oversize mirror along a side wall makes the intimate space seem bigger.

Defining maestro as "master of an art," Joe prepares three meals a day in season. The short dinner menu might offer homemade crabmeat ravioli with tomato-basil cream, chicken stuffed with prosciutto and fresh mozzarella, veal osso buco and pan-seared beef tenderloin encrusted in dried juniper berries. A small house salad accompanies the entrées, but a classic caesar and a mesclun slad with grilled portobello mushroom, roasted red peppers and goat cheese are also available.

A crab cake with red pepper hollandaise sauce is the signature starter. Other options are a smoked duet of salmon and tuna, served with red onion, lemon aioli and capers, and cornflake-encrusted baked brie with a chardonnay-raspberry glaze.

Banana-cinnamon pancakes and Texas-style french toast with maple-sweetened strawberries are specialties for summer breakfast. Pastas, polentas and interesting sandwiches and salads are offered at lunch.

(518) 580-0312. Entrées, $15.50 to $17.50. Breakfast in summer, 8 to 11. Lunch daily, 11:30 to 4. Dinner, 5 to 10. Closed Monday in off-season.

Beverly's Specialty Foods, 47 Phila St.

A Coca-Cola cooler may be the most noticeable decorative feature of this small cafe and catering service that serves up some of the more assertive food in town. There's space for about a dozen tables that are filled day and night plus, of course, the ubiquitous Saratoga restaurant patio for outdoor dining. Otherwise the interior is plain-June mundane, from gray walls to pink pressed-tin ceiling.

Stop in for breakfast – anything from cinnamon buns and croissants to omelets, Irish oatmeal, french toast, belgian waffles made with homemade baguettes and Beverly's own pancakes with a touch of wheat germ.

Sandwiches, salads and specials like salmon cakes with dill-hollandaise and New Mexican chili with green peppers are featured at lunch. We enjoyed a fall vegetable soup with a Greek salad and a salad platter bringing a choice of three (pasta with tuna and pesto, curried chicken, and sesame snow peas, very good but very niggardly for $6.95). The sandwiches looked to be much more filling.

Bailey's Irish Cream cheesecake, chocolate-chambord torteand apple-bourbon cake with bourbon sauce are among the desserts, which Beverly prepares for customers here and at other restaurants. Her scones are considered the best in town.

Son Michael Bowman, who joined the venture from New York, was planning to open in 2000 for supper (entrées, $10.95 to $18.95) and offer beer and wine.

(518) 583-2755. Lunch entrées, $6.95 to $9.95. Breakfast and lunch daily, 7 to 3.

A Sweet Homecoming

Mrs. London's, 464 Broadway.

The pastries made famous by Michael and Wendy London came back in style in 1997 to the town in which they got their start two decades earlier on Phila Street.

The Londons acquired a more prominent storefront location along Broadway to purvey their Rock Hill Bakehouse breads and pastries in what Michael likened to a French patisserie and espresso bar. A larger retail area than before, a stylish cafe setting in the Neo-Classical style of New York of the 1820s, and a pastry and demonstration kitchen occupy the main floor. A bakery is planned eventually in the basement. The unusual cafe decor showcases Federal period pieces and the Londons' collection of early American silk embroideries. The kitchen is a showcase for Michael and Wendy, who were happy to get back to baking, and is a teaching facility for their licensees. The onetime Skidmore College professor-turned-world-class-baker revives memories of such Mrs. London's favorites as

Wendy and Michael London prepare Rock Hill Bakehouse breads at home in Greenwich.

lemon tarts and chocolate whiskey cake as rich as fudge, with bitter chocolate curls on top.

In the decade since their Phila Street bake shop closed, the Londons had concentrated on baking fabulous sourdough and natural grain breads at their Federal farmhouse outside Greenwich, producing a ton of bread a day for delivery to fine stores and restaurants around the East. They also had licensed fourteen bakers to produce Rock Hill breads across the country, and now produce Rock Hill reserve breads from a unique, enormous wood-fired oven made of volcanic rock in a new bakehouse addition in Greenwich.

The Saratoga operation offers espresso, teas and light sandwiches as well as their trademark pastries.

(518) 692-2943. Open daily in summer, 7 to 6; Wednesday-Sunday, rest of year.

Wine Bar Plus

The Wine Bar, 417 Broadway.

A shared interest in wine and travel prompted Judith Evans and her daughter Melissa to open this wine and tapas bar in 1999. "We thought it was something Saratoga would enjoy," explained Melissa. "There was a niche here." They opened after the season in October and immediately struck a chord with locals.

The Evanses gutted a former hair salon to produce one of Broadway's most beautiful buildings, inside and out. The contemporary interior in grays and mauves is elegant and stylish – a cross between New York and San Francisco, in Melissa's words. Tables flank a long granite bar, and a glass-enclosed room with a humidor serves as a smoking lounge.

More than 50 wines by the glass are offered. They may be upstaged by the food, as prepared by Susan Fairgrieve, a chef from northern California. Her opening menu offered three exotic cheeses, a cheese sampler and a terrine of chicken liver pâté, plus tapas and desserts.

You could make a satisfying meal of "small plates" like a salad of local greens, Bartlett pears, blue cheese and pinenuts; a wild mushroom croustade, seared sea scallops wrapped in smoked salmon with chive nage, and pepper-crusted beef carpaccio. Herb-roasted prawns with spaghettini and vermouth cream and beef tenderloin with truffled potatoes and cognac reduction serve heartier appetites.

Desserts include warm blueberry cobbler with vanilla ice cream, tarte tatin with lavender crème anglaise and vanilla bean rice pudding with zinfandel poached pear and cinnamon caramel sauce.

(518) 584-8777. Small plates, $6 to $14. Open Wednesday-Sunday, 5 to midnight.

Lodging

The Batcheller Mansion Inn, 20 Circular St., Saratoga Springs 12866.

Saratoga's most spectacular, conspicuous and architecturally fanciful landmark is now an urbane city inn. Built in 1873 and patterned after a Bavarian castle, the 28-room edifice sports Moorish minarets and turrets and reflects what has been variously called flamboyant French Renaissance and High Victorian Gothic styles. It had been condemned and abandoned as a rooming house when a bachelor attorney bought it for $25,000 in 1972 and started a restoration that culminated in its conversion two decades later into one of the grandest B&Bs of all.

Guests enter through arched mahogany front doors. Off one side of the hall is a living room with gilt-edged mirrors and an enormous crystal chandelier. Off the other side is a mahogany-paneled library with plump red velvet sofas beside the fireplace and towering ficus trees by the tall windows in the bay. The dining room is large enough to hold a long table for twelve and four side tables for two. The dream of a kitchen is a breathtaking space, long and narrow and 26 feet high – contemporary and stark white except for an extravagant display of colorful culinary artworks and three soaring arched windows that bring the outdoors in.

All nine guest rooms on the second and third floors come with private baths, queen or kingsize beds, fancy wallpapers and coordinated fabrics, oriental rugs atop thick carpeting, writing desks, television sets, telephones, mini-refrigerators, monogrammed bathrobes, thick towels and Haversham & Holt toiletries. Some have gas fireplaces. They vary widely in size from two small front rooms with hall baths to the enormous third-floor Diamond Jim Brady Room, outfitted with a billiards table in the middle, a kingsize iron canopy bed, a sitting area and a huge bathroom with an oversize jacuzzi, large stall shower and mirrored wall.

On weekdays, an elaborate continental breakfast is set out buffet style on the kitchen counters, It includes fresh fruit (perhaps melon wrapped in prosciutto), cheeses, cereals and homemade granola as well as homemade muffins, scones and croissants. On weekends, a full breakfast is cooked to order – a choice of eggs one day and pancakes or french toast the next.

(518) 584-7012 or (800) 616-7012. Fax (518) 581-7746. Nine rooms with private baths. Doubles, weekends $160 to $265, midweek $125 to $210. Racing, $250 to $395. Two-night minimum most weekends, four nights racing weekends.

The Westchester House, 102 Lincoln Ave., Box 944, Saratoga Springs 12866.

One of Saratoga's oldest guest houses, this Queen Anne Victorian structure has been taking in guests for more than 100 years. But never so lovingly as in the nearly fifteen years since Bob and Stephanie Melvin of Washington, D.C., realized a dream by restoring the abandoned house into an elegant yet welcoming B&B in which guests' comfort is paramount.

Dining room is stylish setting for breakfast at The Westchester House.

All seven guest rooms have handsomely tiled private baths, telephones and king or queensize beds except for one with two three-quarter beds. Each is attractively furnished to the period. On the chest of drawers you'll find fresh flowers and chocolates embossed with the raised Westchester House logo. Handsome woodwork, blue tiles, two elaborate fireplaces and distinctive wainscoting are all original. The Melvins collect antiques, which are scattered throughout the house, along with "old" and modern art.

Guests gather on a wraparound porch overlooking old-fashioned gardens for tea and cookies or wine and cheese. The side and rear gardens contain six distinct sitting areas, where guests also can relax. Or they can enjoy two main-floor parlors, one with a great suede sofa and a grand piano (upon which Stephanie practices, when no guests are around, for her performances as an opera singer).

The Melvins serve a continental breakfast stylishly amid fine linens, china, crystal mugs and stemmed glasses in the dining room or on the porch. Juice, fresh fruit salad, baked goods from the nearby Bread Basket and sometimes cheese are the fare, enhanced by Stephanie's homemade peach butter and apple preserves. After breakfast, Bob snaps photos of guests, which are forwarded to their homes with a thank-you note to remind them of their stay.

(518) 587-7613 or (800) 581-7613. www.westchesterhousebandb.com. Seven rooms with private baths. Doubles, $95 to $175. Racing, $200 to $290. Off-season, $85 to $135. Closed December and January. Two-night minimum weekends.

Saratoga Arms, 495-497 Broadway, Saratoga Springs 12866.
Saratoga's most versatile innkeepers have turned their attention to the small concierge hotel they opened in 1998. Noel and Kathleen Smith restored a downtown hotel built in 1873 by Gideon Putnam's grandson, transforming what had become a derelict rooming house into a place of charm and beauty. "It was horribly

neglected but never abused," said Kathy. "We found the original chandeliers, fireplaces and woodwork beneath layers of subsequent renovations."

The Smiths, who moved from their original B&B into quarters in the hotel, keep the front entrance locked to ensure privacy for guests. A wraparound front porch outfitted in wicker overlooks the Broadway scene.

The main floor holds a formal sitting room with a prized black floral carpet and not one but two dining rooms. "We have a lot of guests to feed for breakfast," Kathy points out.

A modern elevator takes guests to fourteen rooms on the second and third floors. All have tiled baths (some with whirlpool tubs, others with clawfoot tubs), telephones and TVs. Six have restored gas fireplaces. Beds are king, queen or twin-size. Each room has at least one fine piece – an armoire here, a full mirror there – along with antique and reproduction furnishings and the splashy décor that is Kathy's trademark.

Quarters differ in style and size. A third-floor room with kingsize poster bed is decorated in black and white French toile, from wallpaper and draperies to bed coverings and shower curtain. Another with two queen beds is colorful in moss green and lavender florals and adds a small sitting room just big enough for two chairs. A colorful wooden piece serves as a headboard above the king bed in another room. Light from tall windows lends a bright and airy look to each high-ceilinged room. Expect to find coordinated fabrics, hand-painted dressers, and custom-made Kleenex boxes and wastebaskets hand-painted by a local artist.

Two premier rooms are situated on the walkout lower level, opening onto a sunken front terrace. Each with a fireplace and cool ceramic tile floors, they come with two-person jacuzzi tubs and separate showers. One has a small kitchenette and, with a separate outside entrance, is like a maisonette apartment.

Aforementioned artist has inscribed a local quote or factoid onto a tile at eye-level in each shower bath. The most notable carries the blessing of Marylou Whitney, "the Queen of Saratoga," with a crown slightly askew. The inscriptions make for good ice-breakers as guests swap secrets at the breakfast table in the morning.

Breakfast is a hearty affair. Noel handles the cooking while Kathy converses with guests. The fare was vegetable or cream cheese and herbed omelets the day of our visit. Irish scones often accompany.

(518) 584-1775. Fax (518) 581-4064. www.broadwaysaratoga.com. Sixteen rooms with private baths. Doubles, $150 to $250, May-October; $275 to $450, racing; $125 to $225, rest of year.

The Mansion, 801 Route 29, Box 77, Rock City Falls 12863.

About seven miles west of Saratoga in an old mill town is a 23-room Venetian, villa-style mansion that has been carefully turned into a fine Victorian B&B. Built as a summer home in 1866 by self-made industrialist George West, known as the Paper Bag King for his invention of the folded paper bag, the imposing white Victorian house with cupola on top was acquired in 1999 by Louise Brown, a specialist in early childhood education from Schenectady, and Lori Dutcher, a practicing attorney. They share their house with guests who luxuriate in grand parlors, four bedrooms and a suite amid priceless Victoriana, and enjoy a swimming pool and four acres of landscaped grounds across from the mills. Off the central hall with its deep green rug and an unsigned Tiffany chandelier is a double parlor with recessed pocket doors and an old hand pump organ. One parlor is furnished in Empire furniture and the other in Eastlake.

Upstairs is a small, plant-filled alcove, where you can sit on bentwood rockers and admire the river and falls across the road, plus four spacious guest rooms, all with queen beds, private baths and the original inside shutters. Armoires, wing chairs and puffy comforters are among the furnishings. A selection of hard candies is in each room, as are fresh flowers and plants that attest to Louise's green thumb and eye for arranging. The main-floor guest suite in which we happily spread out has a queen bedroom and a sitting room with a Victorian couch from Saratoga's old Grand Union Hotel, parquet floors and marble fireplaces.

Classical music from Louise's extensive collection of tapes plays in the front library, a fascinating room so full of coffee-table books and magazines that one of us could hardly be pried away for breakfast.

The weekend's gourmet feast quickly tempered any reluctance. A bowl of exotic fruits centered by an alstroemeria blossom was followed by fresh orange or grapefruit juice. Next came a platter with a variety of delectable breads, including lemon-poppyseed and banana-nut. The main course was a vegetable omelet with a slice of ham, although yours might be a strata or baked french toast with blueberry topping. Chocolate-almond coffee was poured throughout at a long, linen-covered table topped with votive candles and fresh pastel roses from a florist. A flame flickered from an Aladdin's lamp in front of the mirror on the fireplace mantel.

Breakfast is continental-plus on weekdays. In season, it may be offered on a side porch with outdoor bistro furniture or in a gazebo on the side yard. Afternoons bring homemade cookies and pastries, offered with Saratoga spring water.

The house is full of striking details, among them the six fireplaces with massive mantelpieces, brass and copper chandeliers with Waterford glass shades, etched-glass doors, parquet floors of three woods, and Currier and Ives prints. Brass doorknobs detailed with classical heads – including a dog with one paw outstretched – greet you at the front door.

(518) 885-1607. Fax (518) 885-6753. www.thesaratogamansion.com. Four rooms and one suite with private baths. Doubles, $95; suite $120. Racing: doubles, $165 to $185; suite $210. Children over 14. No smoking.

Saratoga Bed & Breakfast, 434 Church St., Saratoga Springs 12866.

Some of Saratoga's most luxurious B&B accommodations are offered by Noel and Kathleen Smith and eldest daughter Amy in their 1850 House. The four sumptuous suites there are a far cry from the simpler 1860 farmhouse in which they got their start as Saratoga's first B&B across the street, or their basic motel that gives them an unusually broad range of accommodations and prices.

Let Kathy lead a tour of the brick Federal structure whose modest facade belies its plush interior. First comes the President Grant Suite, named for her husband's distant cousin (who died not far from here), which harbors a partial-canopy kingsize bed and beautiful oriental rugs. Next is the Roberts Room, done up in 1920s masculine style. Beyond is the McKinley Room, where one of the accessories is an Irish cradle from which Kathy first saw the world, her mother having brought it from Ireland. To the rear and upstairs is the Irish Cottage Suite, very quiet and private with two queensize beds and two curved loveseats facing the TV and fireplace. The Waverly Sweet Violets fabrics match the curtains and wallpaper; even the clawfoot tub is painted violet. All the suites have gas fireplaces, splashy coordinated fabrics, walnut and mahogany antique furniture, glistening hardwood floors, TVs and bottles of Saratoga water. There are a main-floor sitting room and an enclosed side porch, where breakfast is served in the summer.

The four lodgings in the Smiths' farmhouse vary from a couple of small rooms with double beds and maple and oak furniture to two larger rooms with fireplaces, wicker furniture and queensize beds topped by colorful quilts made by local church women. All have private baths.

Breakfast is an event, staged on the porch in season and in the farmhouse in winter. With her parents now at their new Saratoga Arms, Amy handles the cooking chores. The fare might be blueberry-walnut pancakes one day and cream-cheese omelets with bacon the next. Juice, fresh fruit and corn muffins or toast accompany.

(518) 584-0920 or (800) 584-0920. www.saratogabandb.com. Four rooms and four suites with private baths. May-October: doubles, $65 to $95; suites, $120 to $145. Racing: doubles, $85 to $145; suites, $160 to $225. Rest of year: doubles, $65 to $95; suites, $110 to $135.

Longfellows Inn and Restaurant, 500 Union Ave., Saratoga Springs 12866.

Situated on knoll east of town is this pair of elaborate tan dairy barns with bright red roofs built in 1915 as part of a 1,000-acre dairy farm. One barn has long been a restaurant. In 1998, the second – previously used for storage for the restaurant – was converted by owners Steve and Yvonne Sullivan into a stylish eighteen-room inn with a Saratoga theme and creature comforts.

Each room comes with a kingsize or two queen beds, TV and bath with jetted tub and separate glass-enclosed shower. Bath amenities include Caswell-Massey toiletries, hair dryers and antique mirrors. The decorative theme is country Shaker with hints of Victorian Saratoga, as in the tasseled window shades. Vivid hunter green and beige wallpaper borders run atop the wainscoting beneath walls accented with Saratoga photos, each room reflecting a different variation on a local horse theme. Windows in all rooms yield views of the distant Adirondacks.

Original beams are used to good advantage beneath the vaulted ceilings of the eight second-floor loft suites. These have sitting areas with sofa and chair, wet bars and TV here as well as upstairs in the kingsize loft bedroom, which have skylights over the beds.

Interesting local photos from the George S. Bolster Collection, benefiting the Historical Society of Saratoga County, enhance the inn's corridors and are for sale.

Guests are welcomed with baskets containing a pair of the locally ubiquitous blue bottles of Saratoga water and a box of Saratoga Sweets chocolates.

A deluxe continental breakfast – with pastries baked by the restaurant's pastry chef – is put out with fruits and cereals in the Rose Room of the restaurant.

(518) 587-0108. Fax (518) 587-6649. Seventeen rooms and one two-bedroom suite with private baths. May-October: doubles $115 to $145, suite $295; racing: doubles $245 to $275, suite $495; rest of year, doubles $95 to $115, suite $295.

The May West Inn, 142 Lake Ave., Saratoga Springs 12866.

Mae West is featured in all her glory at this new B&B. That's not all. The front parlor holds a billiards table, and the side lawn a swimming pool with a curving slide, statuary and a hot tub. And food and drink are hardly after-thoughts.

Such is the fantasyland created by Eloise and Bruce Palmisano, transplanted

New Jerseyites. They didn't want a horse theme for the substantial 1913 residence they converted into a B&B in 1998. They also didn't like the idea of people "sitting around on the couch sipping tea – a Saratoga B&B should be more lively than that." So the Palmisanos put the billiards table in the W.C. Fields Room front and center, beside the richly paneled entry hall and adjacent to the side parlor full of plush velvet furniture and ornate carved burl woodwork. The butler's pantry off the dining room holds a cappuccino machine that gets a workout day and night. The pool and hot tub also have their devotees.

Eloise went through 12,000 yards of fabric as she decorated five upstairs guest rooms to the hilt. All the bed covers, shams and window treatments are hand-done and double layered. The opulent Diamond Lil, also known as the purple room for its deep purple satin draperies puddled to the purple-carpeted floor, comes with a kingsize bed and a balcony overlooking the pool. The Fightn' Jack Room is masculine in showy purple, gold and green. It has a wrought-iron bed with a long wooden bench at its foot, and a bathroom with a stained-glass window and one of the B&B's two whirlpool tubs. Twinkling lights are draped around the lavender and lace canopy of the kingsize bed in the light and airy Peaches Room. The rear Angels Room contains a kingsize poster bed plus two twin beds for traveling families. The Tillie Room, richly dressed in eggplant colors against a white backdrop, holds a fainting couch from Bruce's childhood. Sticklers for Mae West detail, the Palmisanos embossed the insignia from her mink coat on all the guest towels. There are Mae West robes and essential oils for aromatherapy in every room, plus Saratoga water of lemon-lime essence. Standard are TVs, phones and mini-refrigerators. Chocolates are placed on the pillows at turndown.

The chandeliered dining room is the setting for a sumptuous breakfast of fresh orange juice, fruits and the local Oscar's smoked meats. The main course might be eggs benedict, praline pancakes or grand-marnier french toast.

During racing season, there's a complimentary open bar for guests. Bruce mixes a mean martini to accompany his wife's artichoke and crab dip.

(518) 583-2990 or (800) 959-6722. Five rooms with private baths. Doubles, $250 in summer, $325 in racing, $89 in off-season.

A Hotel in the Park

Gideon Putnam Hotel and Conference Center, 24 Gideon Putnam Road, Saratoga Springs 12866.

Deep in the heart of the Saratoga Spa State Park, the huge, red-brick and white-columned Gideon Putnam Hotel – its front outdoor cafe almost walled in by colorful hanging plants and window boxes – looks as if it's been there forever. It's owned by the state, operated by a new concessionaire and on its way up. About $5 million invested in the hotel in recent years has produced new and renovated bathrooms, better air-conditioning and heating, and new carpeting and lighting.

Each of the 132 guest quarters has at least a glimpse of part of the 1,500-acre park. Rooms are furnished in Colonial reproductions and wicker in rose or blue color schemes. Because two double beds didn't fit well, most rooms have one queensize and an extra-long twin bed. All have enormous closets, television sets and telephones. Guests who spend the season usually snap up the eighteen parlor and porch suites. The latter come with large screened porches furnished in bamboo overlooking a forest.

The Sunday buffet brunch ($18.95 each, $21.95 with unlimited bloody marys, mimosas or margaritas) draws mobs of people. We know traditionalists who come here regularly for lunch, savoring the quiet and majestic setting, the sensitive refurbishing and the restored murals in the main Georgian Room, the modestly updated menu and service by "real" waitresses. Nachos supreme, taco and chicken caesar salads, vegetarian melts and grilled reubens are the fare, and old-timers lament the passing of such standbys as welsh rarebit and chicken pot pie.

At night, the menu takes on international overtones. Expect the (for the Gideon) unexpected: sautéed shrimp and scallops provençal, grilled duck breast with raspberry glaze and smoked duck couscous, veal saltimbocca, and pork T-bone steak with apple-cranberry chutney. The **Saratoga Grill** offers more casual fare.

The canopied **Cafe in the Park** outside the front portico is particularly popular before and after events at the nearby Saratoga Performing Arts Center.

(518) 584-3000 or (800) 732-1560. Fax (518) 584-1354. One hundred ten rooms and 22 suites with private baths. Rates EP. Mid-April to late July and Labor Day to mid-November: doubles, $139 to $159; suites, $185 to $205. Racing: doubles, $265 to $299; suites, $445 to $480. Rest of year: doubles $99 to $119; suites, $135 to $175. Two-night minimum weekends in season.

Entrées, $20.95 to $24.95. Lunch daily, 11:30 to 2. Dinner, 6 to 9 or 10.

Gourmet Treats

Two exceptional specialty-food markets opened about the same time within a block of each other near Phila Street's Restaurant Row. Sisters Cathy Hamilton and Gloria Griskowitz converted an old beer warehouse into a wondrous emporium named the Putnam Street Market Place. Upscale in the fashion of Dean & DeLuca, it moved in 2000 to a more visible location at 433 Broadway, calling itself the **Putnam Market**. You'll find a juice bar, delectable sandwiches, salads and prepared entrées to go, baked goods, imported chocolates, a butcher shop, gift baskets and even an "olive tasting bar."

As purposely old-fashioned as Putnam Market is au courant, **Palmetto's Market** at 42 Phila St. occupies another old warehouse that dispenses good vibes along with steaks, seafood, baked goods, deli items, coffee, meats from Oscar's Smoke House, antiques and more. Owner Peter Marquis even carries groceries to your car.

If you're into gourmet pizzas, check out **Bruno's,** a transformed 1950s roadhouse full of character and good aromas – not to mention pizzas, pastas, burgers and salads – at 237 Union Ave. Closer to downtown, the new generation of owners at **D'Andrea's** offers deep-dish pizzas, stuffed breads (one is chicken cacciatore, $4.25 a loaf), and hot and cold focaccia sandwiches in a colorful old paint store at 33 Caroline St.

Worth a side trip is **Sutton's Country Store and Cafe,** Lake George Road (Route 9), Glens Falls, a favorite gourmet shop hereabouts. It has an abundant selection of gourmet foods, Crabtree & Evelyn bath items, handmade chocolates (even a chocolate sheep with a white-chocolate bow), delectable baked goods, zillions of cookbooks, a line of Adirondack coffee cups that look as though they're made of birch bark, and all kinds of fine gifts and accessories. Hearty, homemade food is served in the large, contemporary cafe at down-to-earth prices. We sometimes take out a couple of Sutton's hefty deli sandwiches ($3.95 to $5.95) for a picnic. Breakfast, 7 to 11:30 (noon on Sunday); lunch, 11:30 to 3; Friday dinner, 5 to 8.

Food products are among attributes of monastery at New Skete.

A Gourmet Excursion

New Skete, 343 Ash Grove Road, Cambridge 12816.

The smoked chicken we noticed years ago on many area menus prompted us to ask where it came from. "The monks at New Skete," we were told.

We learned that the monastery east of Cambridge near the Vermont border has a gift shop, and on our next trip – with cooler and ice in the trunk – we set out to find it. At the traffic light in Cambridge, take Main Street east, which becomes Route 67 after it crosses Route 313. First, you come to the Nuns of New Skete sign on the left. In their gift shop you will find a varied assortment, from the bakery products from New Skete Kitchens to dried flower arrangements to religious icons. Continue east another five miles until you see the monks' distinctive sign of white with a red cross. Up and up a road you go until 1,500 feet up, you finally arrive at what looks to be a Russian Orthodox Monastery ("we are really American but with Russian roots," a spokesman explains).

We were there on a Sunday morning when services, open to the public, were just ending. The only sounds we could hear were the birds and the mixed choir of monks and nuns singing. The monks are known for breeding German shepherds – a story told in their books called *How to Be Your Dog's Best Friend* and *The Art of Raising a Puppy.*

They also smoke bacon and hams, make many flavors of cheddar-cheese spread, and sell maple syrup and acclaimed cheesecakes made by the nuns. The cheesecakes appear on the tables of some first-rate restaurants, in flavors of amaretto and cream, raspberry ripple, kahlua, pumpkin and more.

We departed with a few pounds of chicken, smoked over apple and hickory wood, and some delicious horseradish-cheese spread that we served at a gathering soon after. The memories of an utterly peaceful place linger still.

(518) 677-3928. Fax (518) 677-3810. Gift shop open Tuesday-Friday 8:30 to 4, Saturday 10 to 4, Sunday varying hours between community functions.

The Breakfast Tradition

Breakfast is a Saratoga tradition, from the buffet at the Saratoga Race Course thoroughbred track to Sunday brunch at the Gideon Putnam Hotel. On the porch outside the historic clubhouse at the track, watch the horses take their morning exercise as you sip the Saratoga Sunrise – a concoction of vodka, orange and cranberry juices, and a slice of melon – and pick your way through a selection of à la carte breakfast items. Breakfast is served from 7 to 9:30 every racing day.

The Bread Basket at 65 Spring St. is where many innkeepers in town obtain their breakfast breads. Proprietor Joan Tallman bakes daily "from scratch – no mixes used" in a basement bakery beneath her retail showroom. There's also a front room with help-yourself coffee, tables and chairs, and a new addition for more retail and eating space. Besides at least 30 varieties of breads, Joan offers muffins, walnut sticky buns, coffee cakes, apple-raspberry and peach pies, coconut-apricot dessert bars, raspberry mousse brownies, assorted cookies and a triple-layer chocolate cheesecake that's to die for. There's an off-price bin for "yesterday's temptations." Plus – would you believe? – dog biscuits.

Wonderful coffees and pastries are featured at **Uncommon Grounds,** 402 Broadway, a long cavern of a room with bags of coffee beans inside the entrance and more than 40 bulk coffees and teas. Pick out a cranberry-orange muffin or a slice of English toffee cheesecake or peanut-butter-mousse pie to go with a café au lait or iced latte. Enjoy with the day's newspapers at one of the many tables.

Coffee and Cabaret

Caffé Lena, 47 Phila St., (518) 583-0022, is a coffeehouse par excellence. The first of its type in the country, it was run from 1960 until her death in 1989 by Lena Spencer, and friends have continued the tradition since. Her legacy remains in the small upstairs room full of atmosphere as patrons enjoy the music along with good coffees, teas and homemade pastries (no alcohol served). Many are the name folk and cabaret singers who have entertained here. Open Thursday-Sunday evenings.

Taking the Cure

The Lincoln Mineral Baths, Saratoga Spa State Park.

The Lincoln Bathhouse – built in 1930 as the largest of its kind in the world – is a good place in which to relax after over-indulging in Saratoga's good life. Stress and pain float away as you sink into a deep tub of hot, bubbly, beige mineral water in a private room, $16 for twenty minutes, followed by a half-hour's nap while wrapped in hot sheets. For $30 more, a massage therapist will massage you from head to toe. Other wrap, facial and spa treatments are available by appointment. This and the other two architecturally grand mineral baths that drew thousands to Saratoga in years past for the cure are being upgraded by the concessionaire that runs the Gideon Putnam Hotel.

(518) 583-2880. July and August: daily 9 to 4, Saturday to 4:30. June and September: Wednesday-Monday 9 to 4. Rest of year: Wednesday-Sunday 9 to 4. Mineral baths are offered without appointments.

Downtown and Mount Royal are on view from Altitude 747 restaurant atop Place Ville Marie.

Montreal

A Tale of Two Cities

What can one say that hasn't already been said about Montreal, that changing, cosmopolitan slice of the continent just north of the Canadian border?

It's the city and the heritage in which one of us was raised, and it's been a home away from home ever since. But it's very different from the Montreal we once knew, the French-Canadian majority having asserted itself to give the city and the province in which it is located a singular, strong sense of place.

More than any other, Montreal is a city of duality. Which side one sees depends on the eye of the beholder.

The reigning duality is, of course, the "French fact." After Paris, Montreal is the world's second largest French-speaking city, and Canadian bilingualism translates in Quebec into French, down to the street names, store signs and restaurant menus.

Its English heritage has given parts of Montreal a British character. The mix of British and French in North America makes Montreal unique – solid, sedate and sophisticated but also surging, swinging and sensual.

We do not aspire here to give a definitive guide to Montreal, which has been well defined since it hosted two international extravaganzas, the Expo 67 World's Fair and the 1976 Summer Olympics. Instead, we share our personal observations of a city that always surprises our friends as being so near, yet so far – never more than a six-hour drive or an hour's flight from where we've lived but a world apart from the one most Americans know.

As a destination for fine dining for every taste and pocketbook, Montreal takes a back seat to no city in North America. Haute cuisine competes side by side with more casual fare in thousands of cafes and bistros. Although Montreal claims the densest concentration of French restaurants in North America, its ethnic enclaves span the spectrum of the world's cuisines. There's also a sampling of the hearty regional Quebeçois fare.

To the casual visitor along the main streets, all Montreal appears to be one vast emporium of food and drink, from boucherie to bistro. There are four principal concentrations of restaurants: for urban sophisticates, the downtown hotels and the Crescent-Mountain street area off Sherbrooke Street West; for tourists, the charming mix of haute and honky-tonk that is Old Montreal; for the young and young at heart, the swinging Left Bank bistro row along lower St. Laurent Boulevard and St. Denis Street, and for the real thing, the chic spots in the Plateau Mont-Royal and Outremont, where many of the savvy, affluent French-Montrealers go.

Be advised: you don't need to know French (almost everyone can speak some English). But it certainly helps – if only to read visitor brochures, signs and menus. In the mysteries of translation, "essence de col-vert en surprise" in the Sheraton Centre Hotel dining room becomes "duckling consommé."

Be advised also that prices in Montreal, as elsewhere, run the gamut from bargain to rip-off (liquor and wine prices are unduly high). When the currency exchange rate is in Americans' favor, as it has been in recent years, food items can be cheap – American money may stretch 40 to 50 percent farther than the Canadian prices quoted here. Some of that difference may be negated by Canada's wide-ranging Goods and Services Tax, however.

Finally, be advised to look beyond the Basilica-Wax Museum-calèche on Mount Royal tourist circuit of the Montreal of yore. Look beyond the glittering skyscrapers, shiny shopping concourses, the underground city and subways that are the monuments of new Montreal.

Savor the spirit and style of the real Montreal, the joie de vivre that makes it so special. Especially when it comes to culinary pleasures.

Dining

Most restaurants offer several-course, table-d'hôte meals that are good values compared with the à-la-carte prices if ordered separately. On Montreal menus, "entrées" are appetizers, "pâtes" are pastas and "plats" are main courses. The barbecued chicken you'll find at a host of places is some of the best in the world, and the brochetteries offer marvelous meals on a skewer.

The Best of the Best

Toqué! 3842 St. Denis St.

There's near universal agreement as to Montreal's foremost restaurant. Its chef-owner, Normand Laprise from eastern Quebec, established a following at the former Citrus restaurant on St. Lawrence Boulevard. He and his former sous chef, Christine Lamarche, opened Toqué! in the heart of the St. Denis Street restaurant row in 1993. In 1996, he was the first Montrealer invited to cook at the James Beard Foundation in New York, where he later was consulting chef for a large (and, through no fault of his own, short-lived) restaurant called Cena. Now back full-time in Montreal, he is hailed by the North American food press as the hottest chef in town. And his restaurant is the highest-rated not only in Montreal but in all of Quebec province. Even the AAA dining evaluators, seldom in the vanguard of things culinary, rank it up there with the four-diamond standbys that some consider has-beens.

Chef Normand Laprise and partner Christine Lamarche welcome diners at Toqué!

The quality and presentation of food are foremost to Normand, who is known for his imaginative approach and devotion to product. Indeed, at one late-afternoon visit, he was shopping at the fish market, and would send that night's dinner menu to the computer at 5:55.

Toqué! is suave, stylish and serious – all the more so following a couple of renovations and expansions. It closed for a month in 1996 for a total renovation that replaced the open kitchen beside the front entry with a bigger one in the basement (the floor had to be lowered two feet). The freed-up space on the main floor added ten more seats but, more importantly, a more spacious feeling in two rear dining areas separated by a wall upholstered in red velvet. The banquette serving close-together tables has been relegated to the bistro section up front.

In 1999, Toqué! expanded into space formerly occupied by a Vietnamese restaurant and created a more serene, non-smoking dining room with gray velvet walls, maroon chairs and nicely spaced tables dressed in white. An extra kitchen for baked goods and a glass-enclosed showplace of a wine cellar also resulted.

The name – a play on the name for a chef's hat – means crazy or nuts when it takes on the accent, advised Christine, the engaging and omniscient hostess. We didn't know whether it referred to the spirit or the food, but our initial lunch was one of the nuttier we'd had – pricey, oddball and not at all what we had expected having perused the dinner menu a few weeks earlier. Discontinuing lunch service to concentrate on dinner in a more spacious and refined setting has helped establish Toqué! as one of Canada's best restaurants.

The short menu, available in English as well as French, changes nightly. Ours detailed a tantalizing choice of six first courses and six main courses. Those really out for a meal to remember can select a five-course dégustation menu ($68, with wine $105). It yields two seafood courses, a choice of main courses (at our visit, roasted haunch of venison or saddle of lamb), a cheese platter and selection of desserts. For $78, Normand also will prepare a dégustation menu of five courses with foie gras "pour les aventuriers."

As we were seated, the waiter suggested a kir royale and a champagne as well as "the chef's proposal" – a poached Pearl Bay (B.C.) oyster with clementines and tarragon. It proved a worthy if pricey ($3) little indulgence. A custom-made wooden bread cart laden with breads and rolls (including a stellar olive and feta cheese bread) arrived at the table and stayed there, except when it was quietly replenished after we ran short on butter. Appetizers were a tasty arctic char tartare with avocado and chives, ginger-marinated parsley root and taro chips, and a sensational rare yellowfin tuna tempura with pickled yellow beets, sevruga caviar, two spears of seemingly extraneous asparagus, and an almond and Cortland apple compote. Although we had not ordered the dégustatation menu, the chef sent out a taste of shrimp tempura with yellow beets and russet apples, as well as a sample of his seared scallops with risotto, fried leeks, pomegranates and truffle sauce.

Among main courses, Jerusalem artichokes, cauliflower purée and wilted wild daisy leaves might accompany the roasted halibut. The roasted venison could be paired with sautéed lobster mushrooms, "Mr. Daignault's organic carrots" and wilted pak choi. We tried the sweetbreads, grilled simply with apple juice flavored with cinnamon and paired with gnocchi stuffed with wild mushrooms, sautéed Japanese artichokes and parsley root. Equally good was "Mr. Leroux's barbarie duck" roasted with licorice and caramelized kumquats, fanned in slices around the plate and accompanied by a polenta with duck confit and dried fruits, wilted field mix and artichoke hearts. The duck was pronounced the best ever by a Toronto relative. He was so smitten that he ordered a cheese plate when we were too sated for dessert.

Dessert could have been a caramelized fig tart with lemon-thyme ice milk, chocolate mille-feuille with pineapple sorbet, or warm molten chocolate cake with red wine reduction, spices and berries. Like the rest of the meal, the presentations of those we saw were as dazzling as the ingredients. Seamless service was provided team style by an ever-changing cast of waiters in black pants and natty colored dress shirts. They didn't miss a beat.

(514) 499-2084. Entrées, $25 to $32. Dinner, Monday-Saturday 6 to 11.

Le Passe-Partout, 3857 Decarie Blvd.

Call this a bakery, a restaurant, an art gallery. It's a classic Parisian-style neighborhood establishment of the old school, lovingly tended by ex-New Yorker James MacGuire, the chef and baker par excellence, and his French-Canadian wife, Suzanne Baron-Lafrenière, the art enthusiast and printmaker.

After closing for a couple of years when the rent tripled on their simple, unsigned Monkland Avenue quarters that had packed in serious gourmands, the couple resurfaced in larger quarters (now signed) with a bakery of note, a small and serene dining room, and an art gallery downstairs. The name reflects the link, Suzanne explains. Passe-partout means both the soft brush with which bakers remove excess flour from dough and the cardboard matte used to frame artworks on paper.

The bakery tends to upstage the restaurant in its new incarnation (a loyal patron and newspaper columnist called its bread the best in America, noting travelers from all over make it their last stop on their way home). Although famous for his breads, his compatriots consider James one of the top chefs in the city. "I'm here at the bakery anyway," he says, "so I might as well be cooking in the kitchen."

And cook he does, as attested by a sensational lunch we ate a few years ago. The meal is basically table d'hôte, $21.50 for three courses with two or three choices

Artworks and flowers enhance dining experience at Le Passe-Partout.

changing daily, although there are a few à-la-carte options. A suave carrot soup and an ethereal mussel soup were auspicious starters. Three kinds of perfect breads from the adjacent bakery accompanied, inspiring us to return the next day to buy a loaf to take home. One of us concluded with smoked salmon (a generous portion) accompanied by a savory cucumber salad ($10.50), while the other continued on the table d'hôte journey with poulet basquaise, a boneless chicken with tomatoes, peppers and delicate white rice. That route led to the dessert du jour, a fabulous dense almond cake with homemade vanilla ice cream incorporating vanilla from Madagascar. We passed on the proffered cheese tray, including "two imported specially for us," but munched on a sampling of sugar-coated almonds, bite-sized maple sugar candies and chocolate orange rinds that came with the coffee. With a glass each of the house white wine (Suzanne opens a fresh bottle and pours "whatever we think goes well with the food"), the luncheon tab came to a rather memorable $70, including tax and tip.

Parisian prices and style extend to the bakery counter and deli, which you pass both on entering and leaving the dining room. Suzanne notes it specializes in the two items that go well with bread – cheeses and pâtés, both of which they have in abundance. A couple of each and a loaf of bread to go and, voilà, another $30 charge to the good life.

White damask linens and bud vases of red roses dignify the eleven tables in the romantic peach-colored, high-ceilinged dining room. There are artworks on the walls and a showy spray of gladioli at the entry. The fare changes daily and provides what James says is a choice between simple and complex. While regional food (cooked meals from the baker's oven) is featured at lunch, dinner gets more sophisticated with individual preparations. Start, perhaps, with cream of celery soup, a terrine of duck or a special of raviolis of sweetbreads with asparagus and mushrooms. Main courses could be supreme of red snapper with eggplant caviar, tomato concasse and fresh basil, and saddle of lamb with moutarde de meaux and haricots verts. Refresh with a perfect little salad or a plate of unpasteurized French cheeses. Finish with chocolate mousse, floating island, puff pastry with Italian plums or homemade orange-banana sorbet or grand marnier ice cream.

"We're not à la mode to appeal to the critics and the twenty-somethings in their BMWs," says Suzanne of their restaurant's low profile locally. But the seasoned food cognoscenti – and, increasingly, the North American media – are in the know.

(514) 487-7750 or (877) 487-7750. Entrées, $28.50. Lunch, Tuesday-Friday 11:30 to 2. Dinner, Thursday-Saturday 6:30 to 9:30.

La Chronique, 99 Laurier Ave. West.

A small pumpkin or gourd on each table typified the season on our recent visit to this inspired bistro that's considered one of Montreal's finest. Belgian-born chef-owner Marc de Canck, who trained at Michelin restaurants in his native land, moved to Quebec and worked at our old favorite, Hovey Manor in North Hatley, before opening his own place in 1994.

Behind an unassuming storefront facade that you might well pass by lies an intimate interior suave in beige and black, with double layers of white cloths on the tables, gray patterned banquettes, and black and white art photos on the walls. Marc calls his "fine fusion cuisine," a blend of French, Asian and Latin American in particular, and presents it in the trendy architectural style. He shares some of his secrets in a fancy new French cookbook, titled simply *La Chronique.*

The lunch menu is table-d'hôte for two courses, the price ($13 to $27) varying according to the choice of main course, with substantial surcharges for about half the appetizers. Our party of four sampled each of the appetizers included in the tab: a subtle cream of asparagus soup, a coarse pâté with green salad and tasty coulis, a terrific mesclun salad dressed with the chef's signature vinaigrette and a dumpling of fresh tuna. Each was quite satisfactory, but the main courses were far more impressive. The succulent fillet of vivaneau (a variation of the snapper family) arrived atop a julienne of vegetables. Also architectural were the "conjugaison" of sweetbreads wrapped in smoked salmon with miso sauce, resting on a tempura (nest) of straw potatoes. The duet of barbarie duck and shrimp won over the resident skeptic, who sliced the duck breast like steak and called it the best he ever tasted. His spouse found her less exotic (and less costly) order of seafood fettuccine a model of its genre. Served in paper coffee filters in spring-form pans were bread slices and toasted melbas, so good we asked for seconds.

La Chronique was full and the pace leisurely, to put it kindly – the clock on the wall opposite registered 4:50 (unchanged since the opening day, the waitress advised. "It either relaxes people or makes them panic.") We ended a wonderful lunch by polishing off a sampling of three good sorbets (coconut, mango and strawberry) before continuing on our rounds, leaving our guests to relax and savor "the best lunch ever" as they finished their wine.

Nearly half the lunch standouts turn upon the dinner menu, which is à la carte. Among them are the sensational sweetbreads and the duet of duck and shrimp, as well as medallions of grilled tuna, venison with cabernet sauce and waterzooï, the famous dish of Belgian comfort food: a pot-au-feu of chicken and root vegetables supplemented here with market items such as steamed mussels. You might start with a traditional South of France fish soup garnished with croutons, rouille and

La Chronique dining room is suave in beige and black.

saffron or an unusual yam soup with bocconcini cheese and coriander. Other starters include a sashimi of salmon, foie gras and duck confit in phyllo dough with tomato chutney, and a parfait of ossetra caviar.

Finish with a trio of crème brûlées (anise, chocolate and coffee), chocolate marquise or the chef's signature pecan tart flambéed in Jack Daniel's bourbon.

(514) 271-3095. Entrées, $18 to $26. Lunch, Tuesday-Friday 11:30 to 2:30. Dinner, Tuesday-Saturday 6 to 10.

Jongleux Café, 3434 St. Denis St.

The elusive, baby-faced chef in his early 30s is the wunderkind of Montreal chefs. Who else has two leading, separately owned restaurants bearing his name? Nicolas Jongleux, who trained in France with renowned chefs Georges Blanc and Alain Chapel, settled into his own place on the Plateau Mont-Royal in 1999 after wowing downtown diners at Les Caprices de Nicolas and later Opus II at the Omni/ Westin hotel.

Here, in a split-level space that earlier made headlines as Alumette, he is finally an owner as well as the chef. The décor is country sophisticated: orange and deep blue upstairs, light green and blue down near the kitchen, and mainly windows in the mid-level reception area. Tables are dressed with white linens and antique china from Nicolas's family's business in France.

The food is foremost. Lunch is table d'hôte, two courses varying from $19 to $22 with a choice of four main dishes. Ours began with a "teaser" from the chef, a complimentary treat that changes with the meal. This day it was an exquisite poached quail egg on a baby potato with tomato confit and balsamic dressing. Excellent French bread preceded the appetizers. One was a fabulous cappuccino soup of jerusalem artichokes with gnocchi made of guinea hen (the cappuccino label turned out to be self-explanatory upon its frothy arrival). The other was a salad of marinated herring and yellow organic beets with a fouetté of caviar.

Main courses were roasted salmon en croûte de vermicelles, with a sauce of tomato and paprika, and arctic char topped with a teepee of chives, sauced with beurre-blanc and teamed with yellow tomatoes, asparagus and snow peas. Desserts were a warm chocolate torte with cocoa crisps and pistachio ice cream, and a paillasson of bourbon, vanilla, pineapple and rosemary with spiced rum ice cream.

This is obviously a refuge for the serious dinner, according to co-owner Patricia Hovington. Nicolas, whose sensitivity to product reflects his upbringing in a small town in Burgundy, "spends almost more time at the market than here." A typical dinner might offer the starters that we experienced at lunch, plus braised endive with prosciutto, pan-fried rabbit livers and pinenuts in a port-caramel sauce, and a salmon and caviar potato crêpe inspired by mentor Georges Blanc. Main courses could be "the salmon" (steamed smoked salmon with sautéed peanuts and soy, buttered spinach with celery salt and parsley sauce), "the chicken" (smoked breast of farm-raised chicken with winter potato stew, beer gravy and chestnuts) and "the venison" (roasted buck in a coffee crust with crispy polenta and prunes marinated in wine).

Nicolas credits his dessert touch to his training with Alain Chapel. Night-time offerings include an acclaimed chocolate soufflé with a dollop of burnt-coffee ice cream, warm pumpkin pie with maple syrup ice cream and a classic Lyons gaufrette (a waffle-like cookie) with a puré of chestnuts and an ice milk preserve.

(514) 841-8080. Entrées, $19 to $29. Lunch, Monday-Friday noon to 2:30. Dinner, Monday-Saturday 6 to 11.

Les Caprices de Nicolas, 2072 Drummond St.

The chef is in his late 20s, and les caprices reflect the whims of the ingredients and cooking style. William Frachot, scion of five generations of restaurateurs in Dijon, arrived in Montreal in 1996. He started at Toqué! and quickly became sous chef here under Nicolas Jongleux, who left to open his eponymous restaurant (see above). The tradition of exciting French haute cuisine in a stunning yet refined setting continues.

Located on the ground level of a downtown rowhouse, the welcoming restaurant seats 50 at large tables spaced well apart – a rare attribute in Montreal – in a garden atrium, an intimate library/salon and a serene dining lounge with an antique marble and oak bar. In fact, the ambiance was so appealing and the menu so enticing that when we dropped by to check it out, we decided on the spot to stay for lunch (since discontinued, but indicative of the restaurant's style as overseen by co-owner Daniel Medalsy, genial host and the business half of the team).

The seats of choice are beside a trickling fountain in the garden courtyard, an idyllic space soaring three stories to a skylight, with vines hanging down the sides.

You might start with a chilled sweet corn flan with a marinated salad of sugar peas and dried apricots, lemongrass-marinated scallops with basil in coconut milk sauce, roasted quail with oyster mushrooms or alder-smoked crispy sweetbreads with maple vinegar-beet root salad. Duck foie gras is offered "caprice du moment."

Main dishes at our latest visit included roasted snapper with clam chowder jus, roasted magret breast with sweet and sour elderberry sauce, sautéed rabbit with licorice jus, strip loin of Alberta beef with hazelnut oil vinaigrette, and braised lamb shank with a tatin of goat cheese and caramelized endive.

Few can resist the cheese board, considered the city's best. But save room for the sweets – those we sampled may be surpassed by the latest repertoire. How about clove-spiced upside-down peach cake, frozen coffee dacquoise with cinnamon chantilly cream and kirsch-marinated cherries or a sampling of chocolates called Varhona Grand Crus? Perfect café filtre follows.

Curving bar flanks contemporary dining room at Mediterraneo.

Upon departure, check out the shelves in the front window displaying flavored oils, herbs, dried morels, antique teacups and such. They're caprices reflecting attention to detail in a place that cares.

(514) 282-9790. Entrées, $27 to $35. Dinner nightly, 6 to 10.

Mediterraneo, 3500 St. Lawrence Blvd.

Commanding a rare corner space along the Main (as English-speaking Montrealers call St. Lawrence Boulevard) near Sherbrooke Street, this hot newcomer has differentiated itself as a California-style grill and wine bar with a plush, urbane look. Floor-to-ceiling windows look out onto the streets, and the interior is a sea of well-spaced tables in blue and white. A serpentine bar running the length of one side echoes the curves in the ceiling, a huge white disc designed to resemble a space ship.

Chef Claude Pelletier, acknowledged as one of Montreal's best, serves beautifully presented, imaginative fare that changes every two weeks. The logo and menu covers convey a beachy theme, and seafood takes top billing. The descriptions read more like those in Los Angeles or New York, which is a refreshing change for Montrealers. Expect lightly grilled tuna with a lemon confit vinaigrette, striped bass steamed in an oriental broth, pan-seared scallops with grilled bok choy and grilled swordfish with braised oxtail jus and red wine reduction. Sweetbreads are served with white asparagus and lobster fricassee in a tartlet along with crispy eggplant. Among meats are grilled veal chop with a fondue of black olives and herbs, pecan-crusted rack of lamb and a trio of duck: foie gras on creamy polenta, sliced magret and confit cassoulet. Saddle of rabbit, mignonette of venison and guinea fowl stuffed with foie gras are other choices, each with different accompaniments, from a barbecued root vegetable quartet to wild mushroom-mashed potatoes to spaghetti squash timbale.

Start with sashimi tuna, warm-crusted goat cheese atop a stack of roasted peppers and sautéed spinach, or crispy ravioli of braised rabbit with spinach, mushrooms, sweet and sour shiitakes and golden raisins. Finish with crème brûlée, assorted sorbets, mint soufflé with candied oranges or a caramelized banana split consisting of vanilla and chocolate ice creams, diced fruits, peanut brittle and two sauces. The Grand Finale sampler is a two-foot-long platter serving two to four. The food is considered as fabulous as the presentation.

The extensive California-Australian-Italian wine list starts at $29. A number of grappas are offered.

(514) 844-0027. Entrées, $23.75 to $29.75. Dinner nightly, 6 to midnight.

Globe, 3455 St. Lawrence Blvd.

"Cuisine du monde" is featured at this beauty of a place in the midst of the hottest restaurant block along The Main. Originally housed in the second-floor loft of a warehouse, it moved downstairs for better visibility and a more urbane setting of white-clothed tables spaced nicely apart, stunning red brocade fabric chairs and walls in varying shades of gray. Accents include a twelve-foot-high banana tree in the rear and brightly striped red and green banquettes along a wall of the side lounge.

Co-owner Matteo Yacoub, who opened this as an adjunct to his first love, Buona Notte, up the street, leaves the cooking here to hotshot young chef David McMillan. The Globe's reach may be global (appetizers like beef sashimi, chilled soba noodle salad and Italian prosciutto with apple-pear salad). But its new emphasis is more local. A recent autumn menu also listed Bar Harbor fried clam strips with cayenne aioli, hot Eastern Townships goat cheese with tomato confit and chive-crushed yellow flesh potatoes, and "a dozen large count Canadian oysters."

More substantial dishes range widely from sautéed skate wing with caramelized lemon-caper sauce and roasted Fundy salmon with chive emulsion to braised local rabbit tournedos, roast duck breast with sesame-ginger jus, and roast veal loin with porcini jus. Besides a couple of angus steaks there's apt to be a vegetarian grilled portobello mushroom steak. The menu states what the detail makes obvious: "We purchase organic produce, free-range meats and fowl from local farmers."

The pastry chef is as market-oriented as the chef, whose appetizer specials are categorized under "daily market search appetizers." Desserts might be basil-banana cake with rum and roasted bananas, bittersweet hot chocolate torte with vanilla ice cream, almond-raspberry cake with raspberry compote and sorbet, a fresh fruit ratatouille and lemon curd gratin with homemade cookies, and lavender crème brûlée with lemon-rind wafers.

(514) 284-3823. Entrées, $21 to $35. Dinner nightly, 6 to 11 or midnight.

Two for the Show

Quelli della Notte, 6834 St. Lawrence Blvd.

This is a showplace of a restaurant, worthy of the revolving searchlights that pointed the way for the 2,500 invitees who turned out for its 1996 premiere. Thanks to a tip from one who was there, we first visited two weeks later without benefit of a precise address and before it even had a sign out front. There was no mistaking the building, its facade trimmed in bronze, in the heart of Little Italy. But it did take three tries before we got the right entrance – a circular aluminum affair that opens like a revolving door into a tube-like red velvet vestibule. It has a velvet door that in turn revolves into a two-story space bespeaking its multi-million-dollar renovation price tag.

The establishment seems larger than its 120 seats, partly because dining takes

Feather topiaries and circular wall lights are part of dining show at Quelli della Notte.

place on the main level in two distinct areas separated by a two-story space open to a sunken lounge. All is plush as can be in pale yellows and reds accented with aluminum railings and sculptures. Large circular glass lights on the walls with mirrors in the middle serve as art, as do stylish grappa bottles in a couple of mounted displays. The well-spaced tables are topped with white linens, heavy cutlery and feather topiaries and flanked by suave brown Bertoni leather chairs from Italy. Mod lights hang from the ceiling over the lounge, where heart-shaped blue velvet stools face a curving redwood bar.

A sushi bar at the rear serves up some fabulous treats. The glamorous downstairs bar was Montreal's first cigar lounge, complete with Cuban cigars, and the rest rooms are more mod than any we've seen. The kitchen is a beauty, too. One section has bouquets of impeccably fresh herbs, each in its little pot of water.

Salvatore Donato, the host and manager, heads a team of five owners who came from local Italian hot spots. Against the trends toward California and fusion fare, Salvatore said, "we're going back to our roots." That means regional Italian fare, featuring a guest chef from each of Italy's twenty regions every two months, and a menu del mercato of seasonal specialties obtained from the famed Jean Talon Market nearby. These and the sushi offerings are in addition to the regular menu, a not overwhelming compilation of contemporary Italian treats that earn high ratings from reviewers.

Primi plates yield sophisticated pastas and risottos, among them an acclaimed ravoli of porcini mushrooms. Secondi range from grilled swordfish and grilled veal livers marinated in herbs and wine to scampi in rosé wine sauce and carré of caribou with mushrooms and port wine. Antipasti might be beef carpaccio with parmigiano reggiano, polenta with wild mushrooms, lightly cooked salmon topped with green peppercorns, and grilled pork slices on a bed of pumpernickel croutons spread with mascarpone and goat cheese and topped with blueberries. Desserts range from feuilleté de chocolat to assorted glacés and sorbets. The bill comes with dessert biscotti, imported Italian candies and a complimentary liqueur.

The breads and pastas are house-made, olive oils are imported from Umbria and the cappuccino is about the best we've tasted. Two sommeliers help with the wine list, which is heavily oriented to the regions of Italy. France is almost ignored.

(514) 271-3929. Entrées, $19.75 to $39.75. Lunch, Tuesday-Friday noon to 3. Dinner, Tuesday-Saturday 5:30 to midnight, Sunday to 11.

Le Latini, 1130 Jeanne Mance St.

From a modest beginning in 1979, Moreno de Marchi and two partners have built quite a culinary establishment. They transformed an unremarkable townhouse into what has been described as a medieval town square in mid-festival, adding a two-story glass atrium and an incredible wine cellar below.

Ebullient Moreno gave us a tour of the large and festive establishment, which is indescribably handsome with pillars, arches, untold kinds of custom-made chairs (he changes them every year) and damask-covered tables, each with a bottle of Manciuti extra-virgin olive oil as a centerpiece. We were mighty impressed by the dining rooms up and down with views from soaring windows, the canopied dining patio, the three fireplaces, the entry facing extensive antipasto counters and display shelves for fruits, cheeses and more. To say nothing of the 85,000-bottle wine cellar, with a table for sixteen set with seven glasses at each place for a wine-tasting dinner (the all-Italian cellar is one of the biggest of its kind in North America, with prices starting in the thirties). Not to mention the gleaming kitchen, where seven chefs man the stations at every meal "and they all can do everything." A stickler for detail, Moreno imports bread from his hometown in Italy – "I'm crazy, they say."

As for the food, he showed his computer, which itemized 154 hors d'oeuvres, 231 pasta dishes, 121 beef and veal dishes and 99 fish entrées at the time ("more now," he said at a recent visit). He changes 75 items on the menu twice daily. Appetizers range from brodino with tortellini or capelli d'angelo to grilled shrimp with citron linguini; pastas from penne all'arrabiata to a specialty porcini risotto and tagliolini with mushrooms and truffles, and "plats résistances" from veal piccata to filet mignon with morels. The three-course table-d'hôte dinner offers six choices, priced from $27.50 to $36.75 for the likes of scampi and veal chop.

Unlike most Montreal restaurants, Le Latini posts no reviews at the entry – except for one in French, which is accompanied by Moreno's typewritten reply in French. It seems he disagreed with what was said. But the Montreal Gazette reviewer hailed its "spectacular makeover and superb food," and an Outremont restaurateur praised this as a knockout place, which it certainly is.

(514) 861-3166. Entrées, $24 to $43.75. Lunch, Monday-Friday 11:30 to 3. Dinner, Monday-Saturday 5 to 11:45.

The Best of Old Montreal

Bonaparte, 443 St. Francois Xavier St.

A dining-room addition and a talented chef have restored Bonaparte to its position of pre-eminence in the shadow of famed Notre Dame Basilica in the Old City. Add the stylish new 30-room auberge opened on the upper floors in 1999. The result is a destination for gourmands.

Illuminated orchids floating in glass bowls are dramatic focal points for tables at Bonaparte.

The new dining room, in what had been a bakery, doubles the size of a restaurant whose fortunes rise and fall with the chef du moment. Here, a miniature statue of Napoleon stands guard on the fireplace mantel amid potted plants and rich mahogany details. The two-level original room is dark and intimate. Pinpoint lights illuminate orchids floating dramatically in glass bowls on the white-clothed tables. Seats of choice are a handful up a few steps by the front windows, whose occupants watch horse-drawn buggies pass by and fancy themselves in gay Paree. Others popular tables are in a small, glass-enclosed atrium terrace in the rear.

The setting is an elegant foil for chef Gerard Fort's take on classic French cuisine. Reviewers rave about the menu dégustation ($52.50), a six-course parade of nicely paced, flawless delights starting with an aromatic lobster bisque flavored with ginger and saffron and ending in a "symphony" of homemade desserts. Standouts are the mushroom raviolis perfumed with a delicate sage sauce and a fish course of shrimp and scallops. Three choices are offered for main course: roasted duck flavored with maple syrup and blueberries, veal filet sauced with morel mushrooms and cream, and filet mignon laced with five peppercorns and cognac. Desserts include mandarin-orange crème brûlée and a towering triumph of chocolate and hazelnut called Palais Royal.

Many of these treats also are available à la carte. That option gives access to a couple of house specialties, beef tartare, served with fried potatoes, and poached lobster in vanilla sauce. Other possibilities are tuna steak flavored with raspberry vinegar and mushrooms, roast haunch of rabbit with dijon mustard, and filet of wild boar with onion compote and pasta. Value-seekers are served by table-d'hôte menus. They offer five choices for appetizer, main course and dessert, $12.95 to $17.95 for lunch and $21.95 to $25.95 for dinner.

(514) 844-4368. Entrées, $18.50 to $28.50. Lunch, Monday-Friday noon to 2:30. Dinner nightly, 5:30 to 10:30.

Patrons enjoy dinner on front porch at Claude Postel.

Claude Postel, 443 St. Vincent St.

This elegant restaurant is not widely known, but three of the city's leading restaurateurs tipped us off to its existence. It's owned by Claude Postel, a chef from Chartres, who helped turn Bonaparte into the best restaurant in Old Montreal.

Here he makes the rounds to describe for early patrons the day's selections before he gets too busy in the kitchen. He'll likely recommend the salmon and scallops from his own smokehouse, the salad of mesclun and smoked duck, the lamb's lettuce and goat cheese seasoned with truffle-flavored oil, the vegetable tartare, and the terrine of venison and foie gras for starters. Main courses on the all-day menu range from Atlantic salmon on parsley sauce to rack of lamb. The emphasis is on seafood (rack of monkfish from the Grenadine Islands, porgy fillet with tapenade, oriental sea-perch fillet, dover sole meunière or lobster grilled with chives). You'll also find seasonal treats like magret of barbary duck with pears and cinnamon, bison tournedos with wild berries, and roast caribou sauced with cranberries and blueberries. Two découverte menus incorporating favorite dishes in five courses are available for two at $59 each. The pastry cart is known for its lemon-meringue tart and chocolate-hazelnut cream cake. Traditionalists opt for the showy crêpes suzette or liqueured soufflés.

Full of history, the structure was built in 1861 as the Hotel Richelieu, in which actress Sarah Bernhardt once stayed. It served as a morgue before it was transformed by Claude Postel.

Dining is in two masculine-looking rooms with dark wainscoting, high beamed ceilings, wrought-iron light fixtures, deep-set windows with fresh flowers on each sill, and flowers in gleaming copper planters. A canopied porch adds dressy tables above the sidewalk in summer.

(514) 875-5067. Entrées, $24 to $35. Lunch, Monday-Friday 11:30 to 2:30. Dinner nightly, 5:30 to 11.

Les Remparts, 97 Commune St. East.

This newcomer in the basement of Auberge du Vieux Porte is a charming hideaway. Literally. The entrance from the hotel is an antique spiral staircase descending from the lobby into the heart of the dining room (there's a small entrance from the street, as well). The stone-walled room contains the cornerstone of a rampart, discovered when the basement was excavated to make the ceiling higher. Dating from the days when Montreal was a fortified city, it is now cordoned off like a museum piece from the well-spaced, white-clothed tables seating 50 amidst a comforting backdrop of barn beams, copper pipes, upholstered chairs and low-lit oil lamps with delicate fabric shades.

In the kitchen is the youngest of the city's wunder-chefs, Jannick Bouchard. Originally from the Lac St. Jean area, he moved to Montreal in 1989 to train with two of the city's top chefs, Normand Leprise of Toqué! (then at Citrus) and James McGuire at Le Passe-Partout. He left the latter in 1997 to take over his own kitchen here at the ripe young age of 25.

His menu is à la carte and short but select – in the idiom of those in the vanguard of the new Quebec cuisine. Expect the freshest and best ingredients, as in "Mr. J.R. Paquin's garden salad," duly credited as the menu's lead-off item. Ditto for the shellfish terrine, a changing panoply enhanced by fine herbs and served with a mussel broth and lemongrass. And the bundle of zucchini stuffed with goat cheese, hazelnuts, lentils and shallots and sauced with fresh thyme.

Ask Jannick what he recommends. "I come here to eat and have this," he says, pointing to appetizers of tortellini of braised lamb shank with melted foie gras and assiette of yellowfin tuna served with endive and apple salad and fennel vinaigrette. For the main course, he cites his scallops and saffron risotto served with a spinach and horseradish sauce and the seasonal tenderloin of boar with a confit of shallots in a wild mushroom and cranberry sauce. Other options include semi-smoked escalope of salmon with a light butter sauce of beer and coriander, striped bass with an oyster and vermouth sauce, and breast of pheasant and breaded leg with a mango sauce.

The treats continue with a Valrhona chocolate torte, a puff pastry of strawberries and rhubarb with mint glacé, a "soupe" of fruits and banana genoise with blueberry ice cream, and apple beignets with a coulis of cassis and vanilla ice cream. The wine list is choice and expensive, with a supplemental reserve list.

(514) 392-1649. Entrées, $26.95 to $34.95. Lunch, Monday-Friday 11:30 to 2:30. Dinner nightly, 6 to 11.

The Best Bistros

Laloux, 250 Pine St. East.

A high-ceilinged storefront formally done up in striking black and pale yellow and an inspired, reasonably priced menu recommend this classic bistro, considered tops in the city for food and style. It's run by chef André Besson, who trained with Paul Bocuse and proclaims his membership in the Academie Culinaire de France.

The decor is modern Parisian bistro, simple and stark: bare floors, white linens, black banquettes, hanging globe lamps and a wall of mirrors – not even flowers to intrude on the prevailing black and white theme.

The cuisine is nouvelle and the chef's reach far ranging. With the menu comes a little bowl of assertive chicken-liver mousse to spread on homemade bread crisps. Changing three-course, table-d'hôte dinners are priced from $23.75 for fillet of doré with nouilles and riesling to $25 for sweetbreads with truffles and port wine. Friends sampled both items at our latest visit and found them wonderful. Ordered à la carte, the dozen main courses visit ranged from veal-stuffed agnolotti with parmesan crème and pesto to lamb filet with a pepper, aubergine and thyme cake. Other choices were grilled salmon on pesto with crispy vegetables, fillet of yellow pike with caramelized sweet peppers and zucchini, veal medallions with sage and white wine, and filet mignon in coriander, shallot and cahors wine sauce.

Appetizers run from soup du jour (seafood, at our visit) and a dynamite French onion soup to a service of fresh hot foie gras with sauternes and grapes. The crab ravioli with orange sauce, the crab en papillote with lime and coconut, and the shrimp and poultry tempura with mangoes and mint intrigued. Salads might be papaya and watercress, mesclun and grapefruit, or "toute verte" (all green).

Desserts are delectable: genoise with pralines, chocolate and crème anglaise; an acclaimed chocolate mousse topped with coconut, ginger and chocolate shavings; candied pear on grand-marnier ice cream, and praline crêpes. André suggests the grand dessert, a selection of three and "better to share." He's also proud of his platter of assorted French cheeses.

Many wines are available by the glass. The wine list is comprehensive and rather pricey.

(514) 287-9127. Entrées, $11.95 to $21.50. Lunch, Monday-Friday noon to 2:30. Dinner nightly, 6 to 10:30.

Le Club des Pins, 156 Laurier Ave. West.
The South of France is the theme at this cheery little bistro painted in rich tones of burnt sienna and sunflower yellow. The floor is polished chestnut, and the full-length front windows open in summer to the outdoors. A stunning, hand-stenciled design of fish and vegetables accents one of the walls. Another wall is a most unusual, changing trompe-l'oeil mural that looks to be a street scene right out of Provence. "I change and add every year," owner Danielle Matte explains. "This is my house and I like to change it." She acquired the unusual yellow, red-orange, blue and green waxed fabric tablecloths in France, and chef Martin Picard hews to the theme with a short menu of specialties from Provence in summer and southwest France in winter.

The menu is table d'hôte, with an interesting selection of starters that come with. In a city that goes wild over foie gras, the star among appetizers is a "hamburger" of thick-sliced foie gras with honey and lavender, set atop a thick round of toasted baguette. It's the only item that carries a surcharge, unless you add foie gras to the soupe à la citrouille and raviolis au parmesan or start with an amuse-bouche of foie gras, $2 a piece. Otherwise go for the mousse of sweetbreads, the confit of duck, the roulé of salmon cru or the escargots, all included in the tab.

For the main course, how about the salmon with end-of-summer ratatouillle, a lamb shank confit, a pot au feu of duck or beef tartare with dauphine potatoes?

Dessert could be a lemon tart topped by fluffy meringue, tarte-tatin, chocolate fondant, creamy vanilla crème brûlée or assorted sorbets.

The wine list, nicely priced in the twenties and thirties, is oriented to the South of France, with an emphasis on young vintages ready to drink without aging.

(514) 272-9484. Table d'hôte, $24 to $29. Lunch, Thursday and Friday 11:30 to 2. Dinner nightly, 6 to 10:30.

L'Express, 3927 St. Denis St.

No sign identifies this chic bistro, only the name discreetly inscribed in white tiles on the front sidewalk. But L'Express, as authentic a French bistro as they get, is generally packed day and night with Montreal's trend-setters, media types and restaurateurs. Everybody who's anybody seems to turn up to see and be seen – a phenomenon enhanced by the squeezed-together tables and the mirrors on the walls.

Bistro interior glitters at L'Express.

So we were rather surprised to have the place completely to ourselves for a weekday continental breakfast of cafe au lait, flaky croissants and a couple of slices of grilled brioche. With jam and cheese on the side, the bill came to a rather continental $10-plus, but, hey, isn't this the good life in Montreal?

The waitress was chatty, the white paper tablecloths rolled out like gift wrap and printed with Perrier bottles, and the no-smoking signs appreciated in a city that has too few non-smoking dining rooms. The fare is simple and ever so French. The only egg dish at breakfast was basic egg with sausage or ham. No one comes to be dazzled by the food, although it is reputed to be quite good.

They come for the ambiance, the conviviality and a short menu of well-turned-out bistro standards, all available à la carte. The menu strikes the adventurous as somewhat old-hat, as in appetizers of soupe paysanne, jellied egg, celeriac rémoulade and quiche du jour. But reviewers consider the chicken-liver mousse with pistachios the city's best. Ditto for the terrine of duck foie gras (at $21.50 the most expensive item on the menu, except for the three caviars).

More substantial dishes start with a cold roast beef sandwich, served with legendary fries that set the standards to which others aspire. Pickled duck salad, fillet of doré amandine, grilled salmon on a bed of spinach, pot au feu, pan-fried veal livers with tarragon, steak tartare, roast lamb with rosemary and grain-fed chicken in mustard sauce are among the standbys. Specials are simply inserted in the plastic-covered menus diner style, as in "six oysters."

Desserts include a floating island that our waitress called "the bombe," chocolate mousse cake, raspberry charlotte and a couple of "frozen logs" made of pear and raspberry sorbets or black cherry and chocolate ice creams with crème anglaise.

The wine list is extensive, and the selection of eaux de vie exceptional.

(514) 845-5333. Entrées, $10.85 to $17.35. Open daily, 8 a.m. to 1 or 2 a.m.

Le Persil Fou, 4669 St. Denis St.

This "adorable" little prize, as headlined over a French newspaper review, is typical of many a neighborhood bistro in Montreal, but enough of a cut above in food, style and price to make it a destination. We have fond memories of the place when it was Citron-Lime, with a bit of California flair. Now it's even better and truly French with a chef from Alsace and two caring owners, Pierre Gauthier and France Grenier, he mostly in the back of the house and his wife up front.

The shoestring decor reflects her artistic touch. Fabric swagged along a rod dresses the top of a fieldstone wall, vines twist around the bar, and masses of artificial flowers turn up in unexpected places. Why not, with a name that means "crazy parsley." Pierre says it stands for freshness, and for affordable cuisine de marché.

Affordable it certainly is, with the printed menu listing four pastas for $8.25 to $13.25 (for smoked salmon) and five main dishes from $10.95 (for supreme of chicken with "sauce confuse") to $20.90 for loin of lamb with goat cheese. The choices are few but the variations multiple, in that you can order à la carte and add side dishes (the menu suggests artichokes with the goat-cheese pasta and hearts of palm with the vegetarian pasta). Six more "folies du chef" are available nightly à la carte or table d'hôte. The latter go from $21.95 for salmon à la mangue to $25.10 for osso buco, and include soup or salad and beverage. Fancier appetizers cost extra, as do desserts like chocolate praline, crème brûlée and tiramisu.

(514) 284-3130. Entrées, $10.95 to $21.95. Dinner nightly, 5:30 to 10 or 11.

Gastronomic Landmarks

Chez la Mère Michel, 1209 Guy St.

For more than three decades we've been directing friends heading for Montreal to this welcoming downtown restaurant we first visited during the summer of Expo 67, shortly after it opened. None has been disappointed, nor have we on subsequent trips.

Inside a typical Montreal graystone townhouse are three small dining rooms, plus a massive downstairs wine cellar and a skylit courtyard that's exceptionally pleasant for dining year-round.

Decor is elegantly rustic: high ceilings with dark beams and stuccoed arches, shiny hardwood floors, stained-glass windows, walls of showy fabric above mottled gray and copper pots here, there and everywhere. White lace over bright red linens and arrangements of roses and lilies grace the tables. Candles inside graters cast fascinating shadows. Brilliant enamel paintings add to an already colorful scene.

The crowning glory is the atrium courtyard, lovely with banquettes and high-back chairs, antique tables, a Delft-tiled fireplace and a sixteen-foot enamel mural.

Seasonal and contemporary specialties enhance the traditional fare from the kitchen of Micheline Delbuquet. She bestowed her childhood nickname Michel on her "little house" in the city and her French Riviera restaurant background on her cuisine, which has become lighter and more refined over the years.

Over the years, we've enjoyed as appetizers a light and fluffy sweet onion pie, a pâté en croûte with pistachios, baked pheasant and mushrooms au gratin, and asparagus and sweetbreads in puff pastry.

Each of the dozen or so entrées comes with garnishes and vegetables – purées of celery root and carrot on one visit, brussels sprouts and carrots with rosettes of potatoes, whipped and then sautéed on another. At dinner, many dishes are finished tableside and served on piping-hot plates. The veal kidneys flamed in armagnac, which we've always recommended, are as good as when we first had them here in the 1960s. We've also liked sweetbreads with wild mushrooms en croûte, noisettes of lamb with tarragon sauce, the specialty lobster soufflé nantua and, at a recent fall visit, a tender caribou steak with sauce poivrade.

Micheline Delbuquet at Chez la Mère Michele.

At lunch, when a three-course meal runs from $14.50 to $17.50, we've enjoyed a wonderful vegetable terrine that was a mosaic of colors, a tender noisette of beef with bordelaise sauce, chicken with coconut sauce and an interesting special of skate fish.

Such desserts as a smashing strawberry napoleon, grand-marnier soufflé, fresh fruits with kirsch and black-currant sorbet are refreshing endings. The chocolate delice with grand marnier, kiwi and raspberry sauce is a work of art. So is a whole poached pear, its cavity filled with black-currant sorbet and served atop an almond tuile.

The wine list is handsome and extensive, as you'd guess when you look at the wine cellar. Micheline's husband René ranks it among the four or five best in the city. His was the city's first to offer a trio of wines from three new Quebec vineyards. We sampled a couple and found them surprisingly good.

Micheline and René, a widely traveled photographer, are caring hosts. They've had only two chefs over the years, and the staff welcomes returning customers by name. The cozy French provincial ambiance, consistently fine food and value combine to make La Mère Michel a good bet for visitors in this city where more trendy establishments can be pricey, pretentious and perhaps short-lived.

(514) 934-0473. Entrées. $23 to $30.50. Lunch, Tuesday-Friday 11:30 to 2. Dinner, Monday-Saturday 5:30 to 10:30.

Les Halles, 1450 Crescent St.

Following the departure of its longtime chef and one of the original partners, Les Halles has slipped a trifle since the lofty years when it was considered the best restaurant in Montreal. In the mid-1990s it remodeled and repositioned itself and, among traditionalists and big spenders, still ranks right up there.

The two-story lineup of rooms is patterned after the old market in Paris. After two inquiries and a 45-minute wait for a table following our arrival for an 8:45 dinner reservation, we were seated in one of two main-floor dining rooms, not far from the working boucherie/charcuterie/pâtisserie that is a focal point with its colorful awnings. The rooms are small and bright, and the tables so close together that a friend claims you can eavesdrop and hear everything going on in Montreal, if you understand French.

The oversize menu is extensive, expensive (appetizers from $13.50 to $17.50 and even the three-course table-d'hôte is $35 to $47) and somewhat intimidating.

So was our waiter, who rattled off the daily specials at some length from memory until the female half of our party interrupted to ask the price of the duck. "Twenty-eight dollars," he could barely let out through his clenched lips, affronted by both the question and its source. He condensed the rest of his recital and departed. We were left wanting to know more about the specials, which are reputed to be the high points of the kitchen, and their prices, which are usually quite a bit more than dishes on the regular menu.

For appetizers, one of us settled for the cold assortment of cochonouilles and terrines from the menu, a lunch-size plate of salamis and three pâtés from the boucherie. The other tried a special appetizer, St. Peter's fish – an entrée-size portion of rather boring European white fish in a superior sorrel sauce and garnished with green beans (later priced on our bill at $14).

For main courses, we had sliced guinea hen with red cabbage, artfully arranged in a swirl with carrots, beans and turnips, and sweetbreads in a raspberry-vinegar sauce with the same vegetables plus cauliflower. Both were sensational.

With our meal we had the least expensive bottle we could find on the lengthy wine list, $29 for a smooth Château Mondetour bordeaux. Prices are mainly in the three figures and we noticed that the wines of those more selective than we were poured in extra-large balloon glasses. (We all got the same white Les Halles bags on departure. We had thought they were doggie bags, but they contained an apple and an orange to go.)

Desserts are fairly classic French. We shared a plate of homemade sorbets – orange, raspberry and pear, served with kiwi, tangerine, fresh mint and a red sauce notable for its herbs, including rosemary.

After dinner, we looked upstairs at three other dining rooms, which were more formal and quiet, lacking the market flavor. There we happened to bump into owner Jacques Landurier, who was making the rounds to talk with regulars. He recommended that next time we try the $69 menu gastronomique, which includes two substantial appetizers, a sorbet, a small main course, dessert, coffee and sweets. Unlike many such feasts, longtime chef Dominique Crevoisier ensures that each person at the table has a different dish for each course and that most of his specialties are presented. And we wouldn't have to ask the price.

(514) 844-2328. Entrées, $25 to $35. Lunch, Tuesday-Friday 11:45 to 2:30. Dinner, Monday-Saturday 6 to 11.

Les Chenêts, 2075 Bishop St.
This relative old-timer, with an awesome wine cellar and a collection of copper that's out of this world, also is one of the coziest, warmest restaurants we've seen. It's doubly so on a wintry Yuletide afternoon, when the copper pots and pans that cover every available bit of wall space reflect the glow of candles and even the Christmas tree behind the reception table is trimmed mostly in copper.

Chef-owner Michel Gillet, a Frenchman who opened the restaurant in 1973 after a stint at Le Chambord in Westport, Conn., employs one person full-time just to keep all that copper gleaming. Copper service plates top the white-linened tables in two dining rooms, and there's a mix of semi-circular banquettes and chairs upholstered in velvet.

Wine connoisseurs marvel at two weighty tomes of wine selections mounted on a bookstand behind the reception table. They list 2,800 choices representing some 46,000 bottles at prices up to $15,000 for an 1890 Château Lafite-

Rothschild. The pricier bottles are too old to drink, our waiter advised; instead, they are sold as collector's items. He led us upstairs (yes, up) to the wine cellar on the second floor, where he hoisted himself to the top shelf to retrieve the 1890 Lafite, which, we must say, looked much like any other. Michel, who's partial to white wines himself, also has an outstanding collection of cognacs – more than a hundred kinds, we're told.

His menu is quite traditional, but the preparation is innovative. The soup du jour might be a delicate cream of watercress swirled with crème fraîche and centered with croutons. The seafood feuilleté comes in puff pastry shaped like a little fish; the terrine of rabbit is enhanced by anisette. House specialties are fish with two sauces (salmon with beurre blanc and halibut with hollandaise and a dollop of caviar, the two separated by a purée of broccoli over slivered carrots) and pheasant with morels (accompanied by a pastry barque filled with beans, carrots and potato sticks).

Main courses vary from chicken in wine sauce to filet mignon with goose liver. The best bet may be the lunch menu gastronomique, five courses with choice of beef filet or saddle of rabbit for $35. That includes such desserts as grand-marnier parfait, pears hélène and raspberry-mousse cake. The evening menu gastronomique is $350 for two, wine included. Or perhaps you'd be interested in the nine-course menu for six, $5,500, wine included.

Although this is considered a place for a splurge, you also can find good value. The $14.50, three-choice lunch special is one of the city's best bargains.

(514) 844-1842. Entrées, $22.50 to $32. Lunch, Monday-Friday noon to 3. Dinner nightly, 5 to 11.

Paris-Match

Fouquet's, 2180 Mountain St.

In many Montreal restaurants, you can feel as though you are in France. But in the new outpost of Fouquet's, you are transported right to the Champs Elysée, where its parent restaurant has been wowing tourists for more than a century.

With its framed pictures of celebrities (both at the Paris venue and here) on the pretty yellow walls, its burgundy velvet chairs, its little lamps on the tables, its stunning murals of Paris, its maze of seating on various levels, Fouquet's is elegant and comforting. The Limoges china bears the restaurant's name, and bottles of champagne are on ice with sparkling champagne glasses alongside on a table at the entrance (the Paris original reputedly serves more champagne than does the neighboring Elysée Palace with its state functions). The all-male staff, some from France, is solicitous, especially if you are big spenders.

We aren't, so we dropped in for a Saturday lunch when Fouquet's is not particularly busy (and when most serious Montreal restaurants are closed). The lunch menu is not quite as breathtakingly expensive as at night, especially if you stick to appetizers, salads, pastas or pizzas (one from Harry's bar comes with tomatoes, eggplant and parma ham). The soupe de poissons, unfortunately served only lukewarm, was rich and thick with puréed seafood. Its garlicky rouille was thickened with potato and was delicious spread on baguette slices. The salade niçoise had all the right ingredients, and the salade frisée was a nice blend of curly endive, lardons and a poached egg. With a glass of wine and a foamy cappuccino, we got out for a not unreasonable $50.

The dinner hour brings starters like seafood salad with candied tomatoes and green beans with truffle oil, snails grand-mère and salmon crêpes in a light lemon sauce. Dover sole meunière, broiled lobster with pan juices and "petit" vegetables, noisette of salt meadow Rimouski lamb with parsely, roast partridge and sweetbreads with herb purée are some of the main dishes. You could finish off (or be finished off) with sabayon, mango and green lime sorbet, or crêpes suzette.

Four prix-fixe menus range from $42.50 to $75.50. For the last you get foie gras sautéed with grapes, seafood salad, a choice of the fish of the day or the lamb, dessert and coffee. The wine list is mostly French and très expensive.

(514) 284-2132. Entrées, $22.75 to $36.75. Open daily, noon to 1 a.m.

Worldly Exotica

Mondexo, 400 Laurier Ave. West.

Here's a cafe/lounge/restaurant that must be seen to be believed. You can tell from the entry. Just past the palm trees is a magazine stand and coffee bar that opens into a cafe with individual CD players at each seat for those who wish to imbibe or eat with their choice of music.

Head up the stairs to the second-floor lounge, a dark and jungly space with custom-made chairs incorporating zebra skins, reptiles coiled around the columns and individual TVs housed in oval affairs that we thought looked like explorers' helmets and our informant likened to eggs. This is the place for light meals, coffee and dessert, afternoon tea and drinks, with live jazz on weekends.

Continue on to the third-floor dining room, a drop-dead scene resembling an African village. There are a three-dimensional mural of tribesmen along one wall, a desert-colored floor, napkins bearing jungle animals folded wildly on the tables with miniature palm trees beside, a fountain in the center, and a pair of large stained-glass eyes peering out from either side of the wine bar.

The menu is quite extensive and exotic (the place opened as Exotica and only the name has changed). The usual French suspects are trendied up with all the latest ingredients. How about grilled ostrich with fried plantains or alligator braised in red wine perfumed with lemongrass? Pan-fried stingray wing is served in a red and green curry and caper vinaigrette. Rack of lamb comes with a caramelized port sauce and coconut. The veal is stuffed with litchis and onions.

(514) 273-5015. Entrées, $16.95 to $31.95. Open daily, from 9 a.m.

Great Values

Le Poissons Rouge, 1201 Rachel St. East.

This corner storefront facing Lafontaine Park is a find – both for food and ambiance. Not to mention the bottom-line tab, since it's one of the few in the Plateau Mont-Royal area that encourage patrons to bring their own wine.

The most astonishing surprise of all is the man behind the stove, Pascal Gellé, one of the famed "Group of Six" chefs who launched the new Quebec cuisine in the 1980s. Former owner of Montreal's much-acclaimed La Chamade and later of Bagatelle (both now defunct), he resurfaced here in 1999 after a few years of wanderlust. "This is easier to run and the rent is much lower," he advised.

It has to be a labor of love. Pascal and "two and one-half" assistants in the kitchen and a host/manager and servers out front represent a rather high staff-to-patron ratio for a 30-seat gourmet restaurant whose tables turn at most twice an evening. The menu is both table d'hôte ($25 for three courses) and à la carte. As in the past, fish is the specialty, including signature main courses like shark au poivre and noisettes of skate au beurre, plus perhaps dore with saffron cream, grouper with beer sauce and arctic char with rhubarb. Our party of three can vouch for Pascal's appetizers of mussels au lait du coco, a mussel and zucchini gratin glazed with crayfish bisque and a chicory salad adorned with croutons topped with warm goat cheese. The usual good French bread – you really can't get bad French bread in Montreal – was great for mopping up the sauces.

Two main courses of quenelles Val de Loire, a Gellé trademark, were light and airy and in a delicious sauce, but were served with a bland rice that did nothing much for the quenelles. Also exquisite was a duo of sweetbreads and smoked salmon, an early combination turning up increasingly now in Montreal restaurants.

For dessert, we enjoyed Pascal's ethereal "gâteau des crêpes" (layers of crêpes and hazelnut mousse), a heavenly chestnut ice cream over a hot chocolate sauce, and a gratin of fruits that included figs and pears.

These treats and more, plus your own bottle of wine, can be enjoyed in a convivial and colorful room with rag-painted orange and yellow walls, green bistro lights hanging from the ceiling and an abundance of plants. Green runners and orange napkins top the pine tables, which look to have been handcrafted in Quebec but actually came from Ikea.

(514) 522-4876. Entrées, $15.75. Dinner nightly, 5:30 to 11. BYOB.

Première Rue, 355 St. Paul St. West.

If you peruse the menu posted in the window of this little storefront at the western edge of Old Montreal, you won't know what to make of the prices. The table-d'hôte is in the low teens for three courses. That must be for lunch, you think. Perhaps it is. But it's almost the same for dinner.

This new, little-known establishment is packed at noon with business people from the nearby Financial District. The financial types are less in evidence at night, when the twenty-table dining room is given over to regulars and visitors who stumble across the place and are taken by the charm. The interior is a mix of stone, dark blue and yellow walls. Ladder-back chairs face small tables covered with brown butcher paper over white cloths.

The menu is chalked in French on a large blackboard on one wall. There are modest surcharges for some appetizers, such as escargots, smoked salmon or goat cheese salad. A choice of a modest salad, celeriac rémoulade or soup du jour, perhaps cauliflower with a dollop of beet purée for color, come with. So do desserts, a bit more lavish: among them, pear crêpes with raspberry sauce, profiteroles, and blackberries in crème anglaise.

The main dishes are classic French and executed to perfection. Among the choices at our visit were fillet of tilapia andalouse, seafood in puff pastry prepared Gaspé style, sweetbreads dijonnaise, rabbit with two mustards, tagine of lamb Madras style and entrecôte of beef with blue cheese sauce. Appropriate starches and vegetables accompany. Even the wine choices are posted on the blackboard. They're humanely priced, about a dozen in the $20 to $30 range at our visit.

How can you afford *not* to eat here?

(514) 285-0022. Table-d'hôte, $11 to $15.25. Lunch, Tuesday-Friday noon to 2:30. Dinner, Thursday-Saturday 6 to 10.

Hotel Dining

Société Café, Loews Hotel Vogue, 1415 Mountain St.

Fine Eurasian cuisine has given this stunning, split-level space a reputation as the city's top hotel dining room. Executive chef Lionel Godron from Provence calls it "cuisine actuelle, a step up from nouvelle." Aptly named, the café is imbued with what one reviewer calls terminal fashionableness. The action seems to unfold around a chrome-topped bar in the center of the dining room. The speckled faux marble tables set with white runners are spaced on different levels around the room. There's lots of stainless steel and gray with accents of reds and yellows.

The menus are short and quite reasonably priced, given the setting. And the beautifully presented food is as tasty as it looks. At dinner, you might start with a fricassee of wild mushrooms in puff pastry with cream of mascarpone and foie gras, or artichoke risotto garnished with truffles and roasted quail. The seven main courses vary from tournedos of sea bass with wasabi butter to New York steak with roquefort sauce. Among desserts are frozen sabayon with pecans and maple tuile, a chocolate pear with vanilla mascarpone, and carrot and pineapple cake with coffee crème anglaise.

A three-course table-d'hôte menu ($39) offers three choices for appetizer and main course. The dessert at our visit was frozen pear soufflé with peppered chocolate sauce and orange lace.

(514) 987-8168. Entrées, $21.25 to $28. Open daily, 7 a.m. to 10 p.m.

The Ritz-Carlton, 1228 Sherbrooke St. West.

In a city that becomes more French every year, the Ritz is a tradition to be treasured. It is a nostalgic reminder of the days when Sherbrooke Street West was a bastion of English institutions and tastes.

Its restaurants have been favorites of anglo-Montrealers for years. One of us remembers having the businessman's lunch in the Ritz Café for about $3.95 for three courses back in the late 1950s. It was there she was introduced to such unfamiliar dishes (because her mother certainly never cooked them) as calves brains in black butter.

The main restaurant is known as the **Café de Paris** in winter and the **Ritz Garden** in summer. The latter in particular, utterly charming, has been the scene of family celebrations. Tables on a covered terrace on two sides of a courtyard look out over an oasis of lawns, flowers and a duck pond. Here, Sunday brunch is an event, as it should be for $42.50.

The extensive dinner menu offers an entire page of caviars, including two dégustation options. For appetizers, chef Gerard Bahon mixes the classic and the trendy: venison consommé or fresh duck foie gras with an apple beignet, shrimp cocktail or goat cheese and portobello mushroom ravioli with braised radicchio and arugula coulis. Silver cloches are raised in unison to reveal the main courses, perhaps dover sole with dill butter sauce, grilled Charlevoix veal chop with honey-cranberry sauce or filet mignon of Alberta beef. Sample some Canadian Oka cheese for dessert with a glass of vintage port, or try some of the marvelous French pastries.

A martini hour in the Grand Prix piano bar offers a selection of seventeen kinds of martinis with complimentary snacks, more substantial hors d'oeuvres and piano

Ritz Garden is a traditional favorite for outdoor dining at the Ritz-Carlton.

music. Served in oversize martini glasses, they vary from Russian with vodka, cointreau and lemon to Greek with ouzo and a black olive.

(514) 842-4212. Entrées, $28.50 to $42.50. Lunch daily, noon to 2:30. Dinner, 6 to 10; Sunday brunch, 11:30 to 2. Jackets required for dinner.

Restaurant Zen, 1050 Sherbrooke St. West.

The first North American venture for the Zen restaurant chain, originating in Hong Kong and London, operates in the depths of the Hotel Omni Montreal. The two-tier, circular space is dramatic in white and black, with red and yellow accents. It has a curved bar, an elliptical pit in the center and raised tables bearing stunning oriental floral service plates all around. Chopsticks and soup spoons are ready for exotic fare.

The lengthy menu makes for fascinating reading. You'll want to peruse the entire epistle, unless you opt for "the Zen experience" – three special pages detailing 45 signature dishes from all the Zen restaurants. It's an incredible bargain for $27, and you can choose as many items as you like. The menu reflects chefs from China, Thailand, Malaya and Indonesia as well as Montreal.

The regular table-d'hôte offerings run from lemon chicken and sesame orange beef to sautéed shrimp in black pepper sauce with crispy spinach.

(514) 499-0801. Table d'hôte, $13.14. Lunch daily, 11:30 to 3. Dinner, 5:30 to 11.

Lodging

Of the multitude of choices, we suggest a few with special appeal:

The Ritz-Carlton, 1228 Sherbrooke St. West, Montreal H3G 1H6.

Splendidly posh and comfortable in the Old World sense, Montreal's oldest hotel (1912, and the original Ritz, as envisioned by Cesar Ritz), is still favored by many knowledgeable travelers over the more glitzy newcomers. "The grand dame of Sherbrooke Street" is the city's symbol of elegance and service. It has 230 high-ceilinged guest rooms and suites, a lobby that is refreshingly clubby and old-line Montreal, and noted restaurants.

Renovated and grandly updated over the years, the hotel has preserved much of its cherished interior even as all rooms have been redone. Lately, it has added an exercise room to keep up with the times and each guest room comes with three telephones. Twenty rooms contain fireplaces and many have original moldings, embossed ceilings and chandeliers.

Afternoon tea from 3:30 to 5 is a must, offered seasonally in the Ritz Garden or beside the fireplace in the gold-trimmed Palm Court amid crystal chandeliers, marble floors and palm trees. More than a dozen loose-leaf teas are offered (Imperial Gunpowder, Scottish Brteakfast and Spiced Orange are some). "English Traditon" finds your tea presented with tea sandwiches, scones with devonshire cream, petits fours and sweets ($15.75), while the "Royal Tea" adds a glass of champagne and a bowl of strawberries.

(514) 842-4212 or (800) 426-3135. Fax (514) 842-3383. One hundred eight-five rooms and 45 suites. Doubles, $215 to $425. Suites, $395 to $700.

Hotel Omni Montreal, 1050 Sherbrooke St. West, Montreal H3A 2R6.

If the Ritz is Montreal's grand, understated hotel, the Omni is arguably its most sumptuous high-rise.

Built by the Four Seasons chain for the Summer Olympics in 1976 and until recently known as the Westin Mont-Royal, it was acquired by the Omni chain in 1999 and was undergoing what were described as major renovations a year later. It has 300 large, tastefully appointed rooms and suites with kingsize or two twin beds, an indoor-outdoor pool, saunas and a full-service health club. Each guest room has a stocked minibar, most have sitting areas with sofas, and the bathrooms offer bidets, hair dryers and terrycloth robes.

The hotel's showy Mediterranean restaurant called **Opus II** is very visible with its skylit, glass-enclosed bistro adjunct beside the sidewalks along Sherbrooke and Peel streets. Those in the know head downstairs to Zen for a more authentic dining experience (see above).

(514) 284-1110. Fax (514) 845-3025. Two hundred seventy-one rooms and 29 suites with private baths. Doubles, $225 to $240.

Hotel Inter-Continental Montreal, 360 St. Antoine St. West, Montreal H2Y 3X4.

In the heart of the Financial District and close to Old Montreal is this 26-story hotel, which opened in 1991. A towering atrium connects the hotel with the World Trade Center and hotel function rooms, as well as shops and restaurants in an underground complex.

The lobby is full of rich wood paneling and potted palms. Rooms with kingsize or two double beds are as up-to-date as can be, with in-room coffee makers, mini-fridges, irons and hair dryers. Bathrobes are provided in the marble bathrooms, each with tub and separate shower. Fifteen suites situated in the hotel's corner turret offer panoramic views of the city. The hotel's club level is a private floor with 39 rooms and an exclusive lounge, where complimentary continental breakfasts, cocktails and hors d'oeuvres are served.

Guests take advantage of a fitness center with sauna, exercise room and indoor pool.

The plush main dining room, **Restaurant Les Continents,** with big windows looking onto St. Antoine Street, offers a contemporary menu ranging from grilled fillet of salmon with a prune compote to sliced ostrich filet flavored with spice caramel and cranberry chutney. It was the setting for a month-long oyster festival when we were there.

(514) 987-9900 or (800) 361-3600. Fax (514) 847-8550. 334 rooms and 23 suites with private baths. Doubles, $149 to $330.

Loews Hotel Vogue, 1425 Mountain St., Montreal H3G 1Z3.

This boutique-style downtown hotel, opened in 1991 as an independent but lately acquired by Loews, is the ultimate in luxury. It's geared toward the business traveler (with a fax machine in every room), but tourists will find it an exceptional place to stay, too.

Each guest room has a kingsize or a canopied queensize bed, dressed in duvet comforters and pillows and European linens. They're stylishly decorated in soft greens, creams and pinks. Each marble bathroom has a remote-controlled TV facing the whirlpool bath and a separate shower. The suites, in deep jewel tones, are decorated in late Empire style by internationally renowned Stanley J. Friedman.

Of course, there are a 24-hour concierge, room service and turndown service, and a workout room with exercise equipment is on the ninth floor. The **Opera Bar** in the intimate and stylish lobby atrium is the place for afternoon tea and desserts for post-theater snacking.

Hotel Vogue's location is terrific, just off St. Catherine Street and across from Ogilvy's, our favorite department store.

(514) 285-5555 or (800) 465-6654. Fax (514) 849-8903. One hundred twenty-six rooms and sixteen suites with private baths. Doubles, $265 to $399.

L'Hôtel de la Montagne, 1430 Mountain St., Montreal H3G 1Z5.

Backing up to Ogilvy's, an historic enclave of anglo merchandising, this apartment building-turned-hotel represents another part of the diverse spectrum that is Montreal. It caters to business people, couples and singles, many of them French. Welcoming guests in the lobby is a prominent nude sculpture with stained-glass butterfly wings, perched atop a gurgling fountain. Rooms on nineteen floors are decorated in five styles. They contain original art, plush seating, bathrobes and fruit baskets, and beds are turned down nightly at sundown.

That's when the action really picks up in **Le Lutecia,** the hotel's Greco-Roman-Victorian dining room bedecked in palms, sofas and table lamps. We know English Montrealers who take their maiden aunts here for lunch, despite (or because of?) hotelier Bernard Ragueneau's claim that his restaurant is "a place for intrigue." So is the rooftop cafe and outdoor swimming pool, where some of the lithesome sunbathers go topless.

A tunnel from the hotel leads to a multi-level ramble of disco and drink, plants and people called **Thursday's,** part of an evolving enterprise that includes a club called **Crocodile.**

(514) 288-5656 or (800) 361-6262. Fax (514) 288-9658. One hundred thirty-eight rooms and suites with private baths. Doubles, $145 to $155. Suites, $205 to $225.

Inns and B&Bs

Auberge Bonaparte, 447 St. Francois Xavier St.

An outgrowth of the restaurant Bonaparte, this 31-room inn emerged with great style in 1999 in the shadow of Notre Dame Basilica in Old Montreal. Owner Louis Ladouceur teamed up with B&B impresarios Daniel Soucy and Michael Banks from neighboring Les Passants du Sans Soucy (see below), who helped design and manage the place.

You'd never guess that the four floors above the restaurant had been a rundown apartment and rooming house. The owner gutted the interior and dressed up the 1886 facade, graced with granite and wrought-iron trim work in front and brick in back. It's now the place of choice for those seeking prime yet historic accommodations at reasonable rates in the heart of Montreal.

Bonapart guest room looks onto basilica courtyard.

A variety of rooms, each rather different, go off central corridors notable for their walls of French yellow and floors covered with showy oriental runners. The shiny maple floors in the rooms are left bare. Expect to find TVs hidden in armoires, tiled bathrooms with pedestal sinks and double showers or whirlpool tubs, a single cushioned chair, closets with automatic lights that turn on when the doors are opened, and – blessed wonder in today's cocooned urban society – windows that open (the air conditioning shuts off automatically). Rooms we saw had antique iron sleigh beds in queen or king sizes, dressed in colorful fabrics. Eight others have one double bed and more basic bathrooms. Private balconies are attributes in two, one of them a suite. The latter encompasses a living room with sofabed, a queen bedroom and a bath with double jacuzzi.

A complimentary full breakfast, prepared in the Sans Soucy style, is served in the Bonaparte restaurant.

(514) 844-1448. Fax (514) 844-0272. Thirty rooms and one suite with private baths. Doubles, $145 to $195. Suite, $325.

Les Passants du Sans Soucy, 171 St. Paul St. West, Old Montreal, H2Y 1Z5.

The first real B&B in Montreal, located at the quieter western edge of Old Montreal, is as authentic as all get-out. Daniel Soucy, a French-speaking Quebecker, and partner Michael Banks from Ontario offer eight bedrooms and a suite on three floors of an old fur-trading warehouse dating to 1773.

Each has the requisite beamed ceilings, brick and stucco walls and European ambiance you'd expect, as well as all the comforts of home and then some. All rooms have private baths (four with whirlpool tubs), bedside telephones and TVs ensconced in armoires made by a Quebec craftsman and painted a distressed green. Beds (most of them queensize) are made up in the European fashion, with pillows showing. The wood floors are left bare, but colorful bed covers, draperies and, in some rooms, paisley sofas add warmth. Petunias brighten the window boxes facing the street, and we loved the colorful Parisian glass sconces in varied colors in the halls and bedrooms. They're a pricey $500 a pair, and Michael says he has sold quite a few. A ground-floor suite contains a living room with sofabed, a queen bed in the rear bedroom and a marble bath with jacuzzi.

You enter through a lobby also serving as a gallery showcasing Quebec art and crafts. To the rear is an open, skylit living room with a fireplace and a dining area, where Michael serves a breakfast cooked to order by Dan. A choice of seven kinds of juices, flaky croissants (some with chocolate filling), feta-spinach and ham and cheese omelets, bottled mineral water and cafe au lait served in big bowls made ours a breakfast to remember.

(514) 842-2634. Fax (514) 842-2912. Eight rooms and one suite with private baths. Doubles, $105 to $140. Suite, $175.

La Maison Pierre du Calvet, 405 Bonsecours St., Old Montreal H2Y 3C3.

Montreal's oldest private house (1725) open to the public is this charmer, which had four years as a restaurant under its belt before adding a B&B in 1995. The sense of history is palpable in the residence of Calvet, a wealthy merchant and patriot, located in the heart of Old Montreal across the street from the historic Notre-Dame-de-Bonsecours Chapel. Behind the Breton-style facade of thick stone walls, French windows and heavy chimneys lies a complex of nine baronial guest quarters.

The accommodations are large, luxurious and decidedly masculine except for the 18th-century costumes on a hook here and an old pram in a corner there. Otherwise they're all fieldstone walls, rich walnut paneling, dark wood floors and high, step-up queensize canopy beds with oversize bedding made up in the European style. Expect gas fireplaces, Canadian art and tapestries on the walls, a mix of sturdy Quebec antiques and apparent hand-me-downs, and, in at least two cases, carved bed headboards fashioned from church pews. Lord & Mayfair toiletries enhance the marble bathrooms.

Resident innkeeper Martin Ortiz from New Mexico prepares a hearty breakfast of fruit, croissants, and bacon and eggs for guests to take in an appealing plant-filled solarium with three talkative parrots or outside in a tiny garden courtyard.

Guests also may join the public for dinner by candlelight in the plush main-floor restaurant of the same name, an elegant, living-room-like affair with leather sofas grouped around a fireplace in the center and tables around the perimeter. Classic French cuisine is offered à la carte (five choices from $26 to $33) or table d'hôte (three courses from $30 to $40), nightly 5 to 11.

(514) 282-1725. Fax (514) 282-0456. Nine rooms and suites with private baths. Doubles, $195 to $225, May-September; $165 to $195 rest of year.

Auberge du Vieux-Port, 97 De la Commune East, Old Montreal H2Y 1J1.

Dan Soucy and Michael Banks always wanted to have an inn on the waterfront in Old Montreal, but satisfied themselves with Les Passant du Sans Soucy (see above) in the interim. Their chance came in 1996, when they gutted a five-story leather factory and created a deluxe 27-room auberge facing the St. Lawrence River. They sold in 1999 to their partners, Greek brothers Costa and Tony Antonoupoulos, after helping win a Montreal design award for the stunning architectural restoration.

Nearly half the rooms in this urbane small European-style hotel have kingsize brass beds; the rest are queens or two doubles. All but four come with single or double jacuzzis in the bathrooms. Each has a TV and a minibar in the armoire, Canadian pine doors and handsome maple floors "with as many knots as we could find," in the words of a manager. Hair dryers and irons are among the amenities.

Guests have a choice of bagels with cream cheese, omelets or waffles with all the trimmings for breakfast. Downstairs is Les Remparts, a hidden French restaurant serving some of the best food in the city. Upstairs is a rooftop terrace yielding a great view of the river. The promotion calls a light meal with wine here "the height of romance."

(514) 876-0081 or (888) 660-7678. Fax (514) 876-8923. Twenty-seven rooms with private baths. Doubles, $190 to $260, April-October; $135 to $180, rest of year.

Gourmet Treats

More than any place we know, all Montreal seems passionate about food. In a city where there is a bakery or charcuterie or cafe issuing forth delectable aromas at almost every corner, we can do no more than cite a few favorites.

Le Faubourg Ste.-Catherine, 1600 St. Catherine St. West. This is the ultimate food hall, a block-long stretch of stalls, markets and eateries on two floors, with some of the eating areas on floors suspended between. The $40 million renovation of a downtown block is a frenchified version of Boston's Faneuil Hall Marketplace. You can find places like Le Hamburger, Crêpes Maison, Le Wok, La Creole, Pasta Villa, Istanbul Express and Sushi Plus. After scouting the choices, we settled on a filling (but mediocre) lunch of steak teriyaki with salad and rice for $3.99.

If you find Le Faubourg rather dizzying, cross Guy Street to our favorite Montreal store, **Ogilvy's,** the born-again department store, spiffed up with boutiques and specialty shops (including Crabtree & Evelyn, Lalique, Christofle and Godiva). In the basement are a small kitchen shop offering jams and relishes, a pâtisserie and the sprightly Café Romy, which dispenses quiche, sandwiches, salads and such.

Another good food court is on the lower level of **Les Cours Mont-Royal,** 1455 Peel St., near St. Catherine. At our visit, it looked like most of working Montreal was here for lunch, but we wandered around and found **Cafémania,** a little out of the main stream, where we had delicious panini, Italian grilled sandwiches. Great cookies, soups and all kinds of fancy coffees are offered here. **La Boutique du Terroir** is a shop full of Quebec products like fiddlehead ketchup and silkweed vinaigrette, and, of course, the ubiquitous maple sugar candies. There are interesting crafts as well. **Guy et Dodo** is a full-service popular restaurant in this complex; you could make a good lunch of lobster bisque and salade niçoise.

Self-described as "the Disney World of Gastronomie" is **Marché Mövenpick** at 1 Place Ville. An offshoot of the Swiss original, it's an enormous, cafeteria-style restaurant based on a festive, open Mediterranean market concept. After you are shown to a table, you take a tray to food stations throughout the "market" and pay as you leave – probably with some flowers, baked goods or pottery, which are displayed to good advantage at the front of the market.

Rooftop cafe at L'Hotel de la Montagne   Food hall at Le Faubourge Ste.-Catherine

There is probably not a Montrealer who hasn't at some time in his or her life had a smoked meat sandwich at **Bens Delicatessen,** 990 Maisonneuve Blvd. West. Although it has expanded and now has a liquor license, it hasn't changed much since one of us, who attended nearby McGill University in the 1950s, would stop in late at night after parties to sit with other students under dreadful fluorescent lights that made faces green and nosh on the inch-high smoked-meat creation (now $3.95). Bens has lost some of its lustre lately, left behind by **Schwartz's Hebrew Delicatessen** at 3895 St. Lawrence Blvd., a favorite of the younger generation. Here you share communal tables to enjoy the kitchen's trademark stack of spicy smoked meat sandwiched between rye bread. The recipes, from Romanian Jewish emigrés, are a family secret.

Two huge indoor/outdoor markets in Montreal, **Jean Talon Market** in the East End and **Atwater Market** on the southwest edge of downtown, are well worth a visit. Jean Talon is bigger and has more produce stands and Italian items; Atwater more indoor shops and butchers. We are more familiar with the Atwater Market, and frequently fill our cooler with things like stuffed quail or boned rabbit, and exotic cheeses and olives, as well as the most impeccable of vegetables, to take home to Connecticut for a dinner to remind us of "La Belle Province."

Les Paradis du Gourmet

The really suave food emporium du moment is **Le Marché Westmount Square** at St. Catherine Street West and Greene Avenue in uppercrust Westmount. Starting as an underground retail complex in the 1960s, it has evolved into a first-rate market and food court. The freshest produce, baked goods, seafood (including sushi) and ready-to-heat take-out items, from delectable looking pizzas to vegetarian tortes, are offered by several vendors. Pick out your treats and find a table in one of the little alcoves, or take something out for a picnic or dinner.

Across the street at 1250 Greene Ave. is **Les 5 Saisons,** an anglicized version of the original at 1180 Bernard Ave. West in Outremont. We've shopped both, but are partial to the Outremont store for exotic vegetables, fresh salmon pies, pastas, beautiful steaks and seafood, a salad bar with hot soups and café filtre, a charcuterie with fantastic pâtés, and a pastry shop with adorable animals made out of marzipan. Here is the ultimate gourmet paradise.

Or so it seems until you find **Patisserie de Gascogne**. There are four, but the most accessible is at 4825 Sherbrooke St. West (a newer, non-anglicized version is at 237 Laurier Ave. West in Outremont). From platters loaded with delectable little tea sandwiches, to the fanciest ice-cream desserts we have seen, this is a treasure. Brioche, croissants, an incredible selection of cheeses (some made with raw milk), quiches with all kinds of fillings, pâtés, mini-pizzas, pastries – no wonder Westmount's elite love this place. There are a coffee bar and a few little tables where you could have one of the made-up sandwiches or a fancy dessert and a cafe au lait. We took home one of the vacuum-packed dinners for two – poached salmon in a citrus sauce with rice – and it was about the best salmon dish we have ever had. And all we had to do was stick it in the microwave.

Healthful Gourmet

Optimum, 630 Sherbrooke St. East at Union, is billed as Montreal's largest all-natural supermarket and department store. It's full of a wondrous variety of natural foods, a takeout counter, vitamins, minerals, healthware appliances, juicers and such – the biggest selection we've seen in Canada.

Also of interest to those into healthful eating is the local chain called **Le Commensal,** specializing in "gastronomie végétarienne." We were surprised by the number of lunchers lined up at the cafeteria-style buffet on the second floor of the sleek downtown outlet, a glass-enclosed solarium running for nearly a block at 1204 McGill College St. From couscous to vegetable pizzas to ginger tofu, the midday spread has something for everyone. It's open daily from 11 to 10.

Gourmet Chic

For the authentic French experience, tour the shops along Laurier Street in Outremont. Before you get there, you can smell the coffees at **Cafe GVH (Gerard Van Houtte)** at 1042 Laurier, a large grocery store specializing in coffees, health foods, gourmet items and cookware; it also has a bakery and a cafe. The tiny smoked-salmon rolls and kiwi cakes are delicious. There are GVH cafes all over Montreal. **Anjou Quebec** at 1025 is about the most authentic charcuterie/ boucherie we've seen, a paradise of terrines, wild mushrooms, exotic fruits and more. The tiny haricots verts are flown in from France. **La Maison d'Emile** at 1073 is an excellent kitchen and bath shop. **La Pâtisserie Belge** at 1075 has display cases full of pastries, and the windows are full of exotic breads at **Au Pain Dore** at 1145, one of a local chain. An overpowering aroma of Belgian chocolates emanates from **Daskalides** at 377 Laurier, a high-ceilinged space that is as much a treat to the eyes as it is to the nose. Newest in a local chain of five, the chocolatier also offers coffees. Be sure to check out **Patisserie de Gascogne** at 237 Laurier, newest in the chain (see above). Across Park Avenue on Laurier is **La Petite Ardoise,** a contemporary boutique gourmande with fabulous-looking desserts, salads and sandwiches, recently expanded with a café.

Burlington's Church Street Marketplace is a smorgasbord of carts and cafes.

Burlington

A Culinary Sense of Place

Few areas exude such strong feelings of pride and place as Vermont, and nowhere are these more pronounced than in Burlington, the state's Queen City, poised along a slope above Lake Champlain. From a university town that once had little more than college hangouts and greasy spoons, Burlington has blossomed into the culinary mecca of northern New England.

A dozen restaurants of distinction have opened in the last decade in the city, as well as south along the lake toward Shelburne. "They seem to spring up every other day here," reports the manager of one of the better ones, the Daily Planet. "This town is ripe."

At the edge of downtown Burlington, one short block of Church Street one finds a lineup of side-by-side eateries that run the gamut from Tex-Mex to vegetarian and multi-Asian.

The main shopping area, the Church Street Marketplace pedestrian mall, is a smorgasbord of carts and cafes dispensing everything from chicken wings to chimichangas. Coffee à la Carte pours espressos and lattes as long as the temperature does not fall below 20 degrees.

Ben & Jerry, the gurus of fancy ice cream, got their start in Burlington in 1978. Since 1979, the New England Culinary Institute in nearby Montpelier has focused attention on regional cuisine, and moved closer to the action when it opened restaurants in the Inn at Essex outside Burlington and, most recently, on Church Street itself.

In Shelburne, the Webb family's Shelburne Museum is renowned as a remarkable "collection of collections" of Americana. Another part of the Webb family operates Shelburne Farms, which is known for its farm programs and cheddar cheeses, and has received national recognition for its majestic Inn at Shelburne Farms. The area claims the Lake Champlain Chocolates factory, New England's largest cheese and wine outlet, the Harrington ham company headquarters and a showplace bakery, plus countless gourmet food shops and growers or producers of Vermont-made products.

Almost every restaurant in the Burlington area offers al fresco dining in season, and tables spill onto sidewalks and decks at every turn. This is a casual, outdoors city, where people go for interesting food with a Vermont-made theme.

Dining

The Best of the Best

Cafe Shelburne, Route 7, Shelburne.

This prize among small provincial French restaurants has been going strong since 1969, but never better than under chef-owner Patrick Grangien, who trained with Paul Bocuse and came to Vermont as part of the much-ballyhooed but short-lived Gerard's Haute Cuisine enterprise in Fairfax.

Talk about happy circumstance: after twenty years, owners André and Daniele Ducrot offered the cafe for sale in 1988, Patrick was available, and he and his wife Christine bought it and moved in upstairs. They built on a tradition of inspired French food and good value.

The copper bar and the dining areas with their black bentwood chairs and white-linened tables topped with tiny lamps retain much of the original ambiance. Patrick covered and screened the rear patio, a beauty with lattice ceiling and grapevines all around. It's a good choice for dinner on a pleasant evening.

Patrick calls his cuisine "more bistro style than nouvelle." Seafood is his forte (he won the National Seafood Challenge in 1988 and was elected best seafood chef of the year). His prize-winning fillet of lotte on a bed of spinach and mushrooms in a shrimp coulis is a fixture on the menu. Try his herb-crusted salmon served with a seafood ragoût, lasagna St. Jacques layered with sea scallops, spinach and cheddar cheese, or the panache of assorted steamed seafood with champagne-chervil sauce. Other entrées might be duck breast served with a duck risotto and a white wine sauce, filet of lamb with a red wine sauce, filet mignon with green peppercorns and a creamy port wine sauce and, a staple on the menu here, steak tartare, seasoned at tableside.

Soups are a specialty, and all of the night's four offerings are usually winners. Typical are chilled pea garnished with prosciutto ham, creamy mussel perfumed with saffron, lobster bisque and the two vichyssoises – creamy leek and potato and cold asparagus soups served in the same bowl. Tempting appetizers include a warm salmon mousse with a chive and shiitake mushroom sauce, a baked tomato filled with garlicky mussels and vegetables, and escargots with prosciutto, mushrooms, almonds and croutons.

Crème brûlée is the favorite dessert. Others include warm chocolate cake soufflé, raspberry mousse, profiteroles, assorted fruit sorbets and a trio of chocolate ice creams – semi-sweet, white and cacao.

Chef-owner Patrick Grangien at entrance to Cafe Shelburne.

The heavily French wine list, priced from the twenties to the triple digits, harbors considerable variety. Quite a few wines are available by the half bottle.

(802) 985-3939. Entrées, $18 to $22. Dinner, Tuesday-Saturday 6 to 9:30, also Sunday from Labor Day to mid-October.

Pauline's Cafe & Restaurant, 1834 Shelburne Road, South Burlington.

One of the earliest of the Burlington area's fine restaurants, this unlikely-looking roadside place has been expanded under the ownership of local restaurant impresario Robert Fuller.

The original downstairs dining room is now an attractive, clubby cafe paneled in cherry and oak. A side addition adds bigger windows for those who like things light and airy. The original upstairs lounge is now a ramble of small, elegant dining rooms. All is serene in sponged yellows and reds. The walls are hung with handsome artworks, heavy draperies obscure the view from the windows of busy Route 7, and the nicely spaced tables are topped with small oil lamps and, at our spring visit, vases of tulips. Outside is a hidden brick patio enveloped in evergreens and a latticed pergola decked out with small international flags and tiny white lights.

These are versatile settings for some of the area's best food. Both the cafe and dinner menus are offered in the cafe and on the patio, which makes for unusual range and variety.

With the cafe menu you can make a mighty good meal of appetizers and light entrées like fettuccine with smoked salmon, seafood mixed grill with a tangy Thai vinaigrette, maple mustard pork medallions, chicken with Shelburne Farms cheddar-cream sauce and grilled flank steak.

The changing dinner menu is the kind upon which everything appeals. You might start with roasted garlic soup or a sauté of wild mushrooms and move on to soft-shell crabs meunière, grilled yellowfin tuna with saffron aioli, grilled duck breast with citrus and green peppercorn sauce, or herb-roasted rack of lamb with goat cheese medallions.

Our spring dinner began with remarkably good appetizers of morels and local fiddleheads in a rich madeira sauce and a sprightly dish of shrimp and scallops with ginger, garnished with snow peas and cherry tomatoes. A basket of oh-so-good steaming popovers and so-so bread accompanied, as did salads with zippy cream dressings and homemade croutons.

The entrées were superior: three strips of lamb wrapped around goat cheese, and a thick filet mignon, served with spring vegetables and boiled new potatoes. The glasses bearing the house Père Patriarche white wine, generous and good, were whisked away for the proper globes when it came time for a Rutherford Hill merlot. A honey-chocolate mousse from Pauline's acclaimed assortment of desserts (Bon Appétit magazine requested the recipe for the bananas foster) and a special coffee with cointreau and apricot brandy ended a fine meal.

(802) 862-1081. Entrees, $15.95 to $22.50; cafe, $9.95 to $13.95. Lunch daily, 11:30 to 2. Dinner, 5 to 9:30.

Isabel's on the Waterfront, 112 Lake St., Burlington.

This cafe with a canopied terrace, not far from Lake Champlain, is one of a kind. Started as a catering business and cooking school, it began serving lunch and brunch, and now also offers dinners with great panache. About 50 diners can be seated in the high-ceilinged room, and perhaps 50 more on the outdoor terrace with a view of the lake. (Those who want to get closer to the lake can do so at **Whitecaps,** Isabel's ultra-casual bar and grill at the Community Boathouse.)

Isabel's is the happy brainchild of Beverly Watson, who ran a catering service out of her home for nine years before moving in 1987 to the Waterfront Place complex of offices fashioned from an old lumber yard. Isabel is her middle name, and good food her raison d'être.

The spaciousness of the main room surprises the first-time visitor, as do the well-spaced, cloth-covered tables and the bouquets of field flowers. In the rear is a short blackboard menu, a self-service counter upon which samples of the lunch-time offerings are displayed on show plates (which makes the choice really difficult), and an open kitchen.

The blackboard menu changes daily, but you can be assured that everything is good. We enjoyed a piquant platter of shrimp and snow peas oriental with egg fettuccine, plus a build-your-own salad with the biggest fresh croutons ever and a choice of four dressings. We also were enticed by the Mexican pizza, a luscious-looking pan-fried pork with maple-mustard sauce, a wild mushroom and lobster alfredo, an omelet with olives, onions and artichokes, and a grilled turkey sandwich with cheddar and apples.

On another occasion we were too late for the lunch spread but were served from a light grill menu, outside on the terrace. The grilled chicken sandwich with mango chutney and the chilled blueberry soup and sausage quiche were quite satisfactory.

At night, the menu changes often and the price of main courses includes soup or salad. Among the possibilities might be orange-sesame glazed salmon with a creamy ginger sauce, smoked-cheddar baked scallops, Caribbean chicken with

Canopied terrace offers outdoor dining at Isabel's on the Waterfront.

mango chutney, sautéed lamb with basil-walnut pesto and chive polenta, and filet of beef with a mustard-thyme sauce. Starters could be Maine crab cakes with sweet tomato salsa, chèvre-stuffed polenta, sweet and sour shrimp with Vietnamese vegetable wonton cups, and baked brie topped with almonds and homemade cranberry-apple chutney, served with seasonal fruit.

For weekend brunch, try the banana and walnut pancakes, the broccoli benedict or "Old MacDonald Goes to France," a croissant topped with two poached eggs, sausage patties, mushrooms, brie and hollandaise.

(802) 865-2522. Entrées, $10.95 to $19.95. Lunch, Monday-Friday 11 to 2. Dinner, Tuesday-Sunday 5:30 to 9. Saturday and Sunday brunch, 10:30 to 2.

Smokejacks, 156 Church St., Burlington.
"Bold American food" is the billing for this innovative restaurant opened in 1997 by chef-owner Leslie Meyers. She and executive chef Maura O'Sullivan share a fondness for smoked foods, robust tastes, a martini bar and an extensive cheese tasting menu. The pair smoke their own salmon, duck, turkey, mushrooms and more in the restaurant's smoker in the basement. They even smoke peanuts in the shell for munchies at the bar.

Their fare lives up to its billing for boldness, starting with the focaccia and sourdough breads served with sweet butter. At lunch, the maple-cured smoked salmon with pickled red onions and horseradish cream made a fine appetizer. A crispy gruyère cheese risotto square, served with sautéed spinach, was an assertive main course. The star of the show was a grilled wild mushroom bruschetta, emboldened with roasted garlic and served on sautéed greens. A lemon curd upside-down cake with strawberries and whipped cream and white chocolate bread pudding with a rhubarb and sour cream compote and toasted almonds were memorable desserts. A watery cappuccino was the only disappointment.

The dinner menu is categorized by small plates (incorporating many of the lunch dishes) and main courses. Typical of the former are seared yellowfin tuna, smoked mushroom quesadilla and a "big bold burger," served with Cabot cheddar on onion focaccia with bacon-roasted potatoes. Main dishes include seared

Atlantic salmon with red chile sauce, pan-roasted monkfish in a spicy lobster-tomato broth, smoked Long Island duck breast with pineapple chutney and grilled black angus ribeye steak with zinfandel sauce.

Signature items on the interesting Sunday brunch menu are smoked turkey hash with scrambled eggs, smoked ham and cheddar grits and brioche french toast with apple-wood smoked bacon.

The menu includes an entire page of exotic cheeses (most from Vermont), each served with dried apricots, candied hazelnuts and crostini. They are recommended as a sampler with a glass of wine or beer, as an appetizer or as a savory ending to a meal.

All these bold tastes are served up in a long, narrow storefront room painted silver gray, from floors to ceiling. Exposed ducts, candle chandeliers over the bar, tiny purple hanging lights and splashy artworks provide accents.

(802) 658-1119. Entrées, $14.95 to $19.95. Lunch, Monday-Saturday 11:30 to 4:30. Dinner, Monday-Saturday 4:30 to 9:30 or 10:30. Sunday, brunch 10:30 to 3:30, dinner, 3:30 to 9.

Five Spice Cafe, 175 Church St., Burlington.

This spicy little prize occupies two floors of a former counter-culture restaurant at the edge of downtown. Since 1985, chef-owner Jerry Weinberg has won a host of followers for his multi-Asian menu of unusual, tantalizing dishes from Thailand, Vietnam, Indonesia, China and Burma.

We had the upstairs dining room almost to ourselves for a weekday lunch, but our waitress said it would be packed that night.

Our meal began with a bowl of hot and sour soup that was extra hot and a house sampler of appetizers, among them smoked shrimp, Siu Mai dumplings, Hunan noodles, Szechuan escargots and spicy cucumbers. The less adventurous among us passed up the Thai red snapper in black bean sauce for a blackboard special of mock duck stir-fry in peanut sauce (the vegetarian dish really does taste like duck, just as, we were assured, the mock abalone really tastes like abalone). Sated though we were, we simply had to share the ginger-tangerine cheesecake.

Chef Weinberg's wizardry in the downstairs kitchen is apparent on a chatty, wide-ranging dinner menu that boasts that some of the items and spices have been imitated locally but never matched. Main courses range from spicy Hunan noodles and Chinese chicken curry to Thai red snapper and a trio of shrimp dishes, one an eye-opener called Thai fire shrimp ("until this dish, we had a three-star heat rating. Now we have four.")

A drunken chocolate mousse laced with liqueurs and a blackout cake drenched with triple sec are among favored desserts. The aforementioned ginger-tangerine cheesecake won Jerry a first prize somewhere, and the ginger-honeydew sorbet is extra-appealing. A dessert sampler teams the chocolate mousse with three other sweets.

Oil lamps flicker on each table even at noon. Beige cloths and flowers in green vases comprise the decor. Above the serving sideboard is a collection of Five Spice T-shirts emblazoned with fire-breathing dragons and the saying, "Some Like It Hot." Yes, indeed.

(802) 864-4045. Entrées, $7.95 to $15.95. Lunch daily, 11:30 to 2:30. Dinner nightly, from 5. Dim Sum brunch, Sunday 11 to 3.

Leunig's Bistro, 115 Church St., Burlington.

The garage doors go up in the summer to open this European-style bistro and cafe to the sidewalk. The high-ceilinged interior is pretty in peach with black trim. In season, much of the action spills onto the sidewalks along the front and side. People pack the tables day and night, sipping drinks and espresso and savoring the appetizers and desserts, but increasingly they also come for full meals.

New owner Robert Fuller, who also owns Pauline's Café & Restaurant in Shelburne, has kept the bistro as popular as ever. He aimed for a Parisian look and ambiance to give credence to Leunig's slogan as "the soul of Europe in the heart of Burlington." The fare is international with a French accent, as in soup au pistou, onion soup gratinée, duck cassoulet salad and grilled quail salad. Other possibilities on the varied menu range from grilled chive polenta, fried calamari with spicy chipotle aioli and grilled asparagus topped with Vermont chèvre to mussels Tuscan style, Portuguese chicken and a number of pasta dishes.

Dinner entrées such as sesame-crusted salmon fillet, sliced duck with ginger chutney, veal forestière and steak au poivre are highly rated by serious eaters.

Among homemade desserts are French tarts, fresh fruit crisps and crème brûlée.

(802) 863-3759. Entrées, $14.50 to $18.50. Breakfast, Monday-Friday 7 to 11. Lunch, 11:30 to 3. Dinner, 5 to 10. Weekend brunch, 9 to 3:30, dinner, 5 to 10.

Opaline, One Lawson Lane, Burlington.

This tasty little secret originated as an elegant Victorian bar hidden away at the rear of an office building. Former owners converted it into a continental restaurant called the Iron Wolf. In 1998, Steven Perei Jr. took over after stints as maître-d' and sommelier at leading restaurants in Burlington, Nantucket and Naples, Fla. He turned it into a bistro and wine bar like those he cherished in the south of France. The handful of tables has been filled since by word of mouth.

Lest the bistro terminology mislead: this is more like a convivial, intimate club, in feeling as well as in decor. The handsome bar facing the kitchen is flanked by formal, white-clothed tables on three sides amid much dark wood paneling and etched-glass windows.

Opaline takes its inspiration from the turn-of-the-century art nouveau movement popularized by Oscar Wilde, Vincent Van Gogh and Toulouse Lautrec. Chef Denis Chauvin specializes in the fare of his native France.

The short menu lists such starters as traditional onion soup, a classic caesar salad, escargots in puff pastry and rosettes of marinated salmon. Typical main courses are mixed seafood in champagne sauce and puff pastry, poached fillet of redfish with ginger-garlic sauce, grilled chicken in maple-mustard sauce and rack of lamb with brown garlic sauce. The cassoulet and the roasted duck opaline (crisp leg and sliced breast, with a red wine saucer) come highly recommended.

The wines are mostly rustic French varietals. Dessert could be sorbet, crème caramel, chocolate mousse or soufflé glacé.

Linger over an after-dinner drink, and you'll know why this place has such a loyal and protective following. They want to keep it for themselves.

(802) 660-8875. Entrées, $14 to $24. Dinner by reservation, Tuesday-Saturday 6 to 9.

The Daily Planet, 15 Center St., Burlington.

Creative food at down-to-earth prices is the forte of this quirky place, advertised in the alternative press as an "inner city playground."

The name reflects its "global fare – ethnic and eclectic," in the words of the staff. Casual, innovative and a favorite local watering hole among knowledgeable noshers, it has a large bar with a pressed-tin ceiling, a solarium filled with cactus and jade plants plus a jukebox, and a lofty, sun-splashed dining room where the pipes are exposed, the walls are covered with works of local artists, and the oilcloth table coverings at noon are changed to white linens at night.

The chefs, many trained at the Culinary Institute of America or the California Culinary Academy, are known for turning out some of the most imaginative fare in town. For lunch, how about a tropical shrimp salad, Marrakech chicken over almond couscous, a grilled mushroom sandwich, a Korean vegetable pancake or a sundried tomato tapenade with flatbread? The warm stellar salad encircles a slab of goat cheese with small mounds of spaghetti squash, spinach, roasted red peppers and toasted walnuts.

At night, the Daily Planet sparkles with appetizers and light entrées like smoked-salmon flatbread pizza, seared sea scallops with a sesame Asian vegetable slaw, and corn cakes with black-bean and chipotle salsa and cilantro crème fraîche. Entrées might include Greek seafood pasta, potato-crusted salmon, grilled Yucatan-style pork and roast chicken stuffed with goat cheese. When was the last time you saw rack of lamb for $19.50, rubbed with garlic and served with curried ratatouille, mint-coriander chutney and a salad of honeyed lentils and roasted shallots, no less? Have you even heard of pork vindaloo, an Indian hot and sour pork loin sautéed with tomatoes and chickpeas and served with a scallion flatbread?

Desserts intrigue as well. Some are pear-blueberry pie, white-chocolate/apricot cheesecake, Southern nut cake with bourbon crème anglaise, fresh plum ice cream, and baked apples with figs and cranberries.

As you might expect, the wine list, though small, is well-chosen and offers some incredible steals.

(802) 862-9647. Entrées, $9.95 to $18.50. Lunch, Monday-Friday 11:30 to 3. Dinner nightly, 5 to 10 or 11. Saturday and Sunday brunch, 11 to 3.

More Dining Choices

NECI Commons, 25 Church St., Burlington.

The New England Culinary Institute's education and outreach program now reaches into downtown Burlington. The large culinary center opening onto the Church Street Marketplace has been likened to "an interactive dining experience, where chefs interact with students who interact with the patrons, who interact with the food that comes beautifully plated without extraneous frou-frou," in the words of one reviewer.

There's a lot going on here, from the sidewalk cafe out front to the deli cases full of sophisticated exotica inside and, in back, dining areas and kitchens staffed by professionals and students. An events list is full of tastings, cooking demonstrations and continuing education classes, from summer salads to "Encore Provence."

Plenty of good, creative food is available at affordable prices. You can order light (a sampling of soups – perhaps carrot and ginger, Asian vegetable, and tomato and fennel – and a mini-pizza). Or you can be more ambitious with, say, an appetizer of crab cakes with black bean/corn relish and red pepper coulis, plus and a main dish of blackened Chilean sea bass over wilted spinach, or barbecued meatloaf.

Rotisserie specials change daily, from duck à l'orange to leg of lamb. So do such culinary classics as bouillabaisse and coq au vin.

Come here for a smoked salmon club sandwich or a turkey BLT, a warm bread and chicken salad or grilled free-range Quebec chicken. Finish with the chef's dessert sampler for two: mocha mousse torte, vanilla bean crème brûlée and a trio of sorbets. You won't leave hungry or unimpressed.

(802) 862-6324. Entrées, $10.95 to $14.95. Light fare, daily 7:30 to midnight. Lunch, 11:30 to 2. Dinner, 5:30 to 9:30.

Sweet Tomatoes Trattoria, 83 Church St., Burlington.

Borrowing a page from their smash-success restaurant of the same name in Lebanon, N.H., Robert Meyers and James Reiman opened a carbon copy here and, more recently, in downtown Rutland.

From Burlington's first wood-fired brick oven come zesty pizzas like the namesake sweet tomato pie, a combination of tomato, basil, mozzarella and olive oil ($9). From the rest of the open kitchen that runs along the side of the surprisingly large downstairs space emerge earthy pastas, grills and entrées at wallet-pleasing prices. Offering range from grilled Atlantic salmon to chicken saltimbocca and veal piccata. For a quick dinner, we were quite impressed with the cavateppi with spit-roasted chicken. Less impressive was a special of linguini infused with olive oil and mushrooms, rather bland and desperately in need of more pecorino romano cheese. The waitress sprinkled the container of cheese less than liberally and guarded it as if with her life until we finally asked for (and received) our own container-full to rescue the dish. A huge salad topped with romano, a basket of bread for dipping in the house olive oil and a $14 bottle of Orvieto accompanied.

The stark decor in white and black is offset by brick arches and stone walls with a neon strip over the kitchen. It's a convivial and noisy setting for what Robert calls "strictly ethnic Italian cooking, as prepared in a home kitchen." The sidewalk cafe in front is an even busier setting in summer. We were amazed to see all the people waiting for tables for a late lunch here on an August weekday.

(802) 660-9533. Entrées, $9 to $14. Lunch, Monday-Saturday 11:30 to 2; late lunch, 2 to 4; dinner, 5 to 9:30 or 10, Sunday to 9.

Village Pump House Restaurant, On the Green, Shelburne.

The hand-written menu changes frequently at this much-loved but not widely known restaurant. Thirty-five diners can be seated in two intimate dining rooms and an enclosed porch.

Assisted by his sister in the prep department, chef David Webster prepares some exciting fare. The menu is categorized into dinners, including choice of soup and a green salad, and suppers, with salad only. One night's dinner offerings were Thai shrimp sautéed with scallions and ginger, baked halibut with mustard and herbed bread crumbs, veal chop sautéed with Greek olives, and sautéed loin of lamb finished with port and shallots. Four "suppers" produced crab cakes, baked polenta, pork tenderloin with dried cherry chutney and broiled New York sirloin.

Start with vegetable potstickers, smoked trout cheesecake or mushrooms stuffed with sausage and parmesan. Finish with a raspberry-peach crisp, chocolate-hazelnut meringue tart, maple crème caramel or cream-cheese crêpes with apricot sauce.

Decor is country simple, with a stress on the simple, according to David. Most of the assorted oak and maple chairs came from his parents' barn.

David's partner, host-bartender David Miner, is responsible for the large beer list. It's as lengthy as the wine list, and includes seven on draft.

(802) 985-3728. Entrées, $15.25 to $23.50. Dinner, Tuesday-Saturday from 5:30.

Sài-Gòn Cafe, 133 Bank St., Burlington.

This authentic, highly rated establishment is run by Phi Doane, who had married an American soldier in Vietnam. Here she connected two houses by enclosing the driveway between them and offers several dining areas with the look of a Victorian residence, a Vietnamese market and a lounge.

The extensive menu is a little pricier than most Vietnamese restaurants of our acquaintance., Start, perhaps, with the steamed imperial rolls, which another restaurateur touts as the freshest ever. Your salad might be layers of shrimp, cucumber, carrots, onion and mint leaves, topped with peanuts and shrimp chips. Pho Ha Noi, a traditional soup, is served in three sizes; the extra large is a meal in itself. There are several other regional soups; one is asparagus and crabmeat topped with cilantro and scallions.

The entrée list details beef, pork, chicken, seafood and vegetarian items. We like the sound of the grilled chicken with lemongrass, served with lettuce, cucumber, cilantro, mint and rice noodles. Rice paper, to make little packets of the dish, is served upon request. Under special entrées is hu tieu xao, rice noodles stir-fried with vegetables in an oyster sauce, with choice of pork, shrimp or chicken.

(802) 863-5637. Entrées, $8.50 to $12.95. Lunch, Monday-Saturday 11 to 3. Dinner, 5:30 to 9:30 or 10.

Mona's, 3 Main St., Burlington.

The best thing about this relative newcomer in the restored Cornerstone Building at the foot of Main Street may be the view – if you know about it. We apparently entered through the wrong door of the showy, copper-ceilinged bar beside the semi-open kitchen, asked for an outdoor table and were seated by ourselves on a side patio, with only a glimpse of the lake across the rusting roof of an industrial shed. Only after lunch did we find where the views and the action were – upstairs in three Mediterranean-style dining rooms and a jaunty outdoor balcony stretching across the rear of the building, yielding a wide-angle view of Lake Champlain.

That setting would have been enough to compensate for what we found to be the unexpectedly mediocre food, given the reputation of its owner, Manon O'Connor, and her late husband Art, who earned their spurs uptown at the Bourbon Street Grill. The signature Vermont cheddar and ale soup turned out to be rather tasteless, and the spinach salad had the strangest dressing we ever tasted (the waitress noticed our uneaten plate, and took the salad off the bill). The specialty flatbread pizza topped with calamari and roasted garlic was quite good, however.

At dinner, entrées are numerous and range widely, reportedly to better success lately. The seared yellowfin tuna steak on a bed of gingered vegetables and fettuccine, the salmon fillet roasted in a crust of pecans, whole-grain mustard and maple syrup, and the grilled New York strip steak come highly recommended. The something-for-everyone menu contains three vegetarian dishes, one vegan, and recommends a different wine for each entrée.

Salmon cakes and skewered Asian beef are favorite starters. Desserts run to profiteroles, key lime pie, bread pudding and cappuccino chocolate mousse. Some

Dinner is served with a view of Lake Champlain on veranda at The Inn at Shelburne Farms.

of the specialty foods from the smaller Bourbon Street Grill are for sale here, among them Big Art's Jazz Sauce for chicken wings, caesar salad dressing and a fire sauce for those who like things extra-hot.

(802) 658-6662. Entrées, $13.95 to $19.95. Lunch daily, 11:30 to 3; dinner, 5 to 11 or midnight. Sunday, brunch 11:30 to 3, dinner 5 to 10..

Dining and Lodging

The Inn at Shelburne Farms, Shelburne 05482.

It's hard to imagine a more elegant inn, albeit in an old-school way, or a more spectacular setting than the summer mansion built by Dr. William Seward Webb and his wife, Lila Vanderbilt Webb, high on a promontory surrounded on three sides by Lake Champlain.

Their 1,400-acre Shelburne Farms agricultural estate was planned by Frederick Law Olmsted, the landscape architect who designed New York's Central Park. The focal point is their incomparable summer home, a lakeside landmark completed in 1899 for $10 million and converted in 1987 into an inn and restaurant of distinction.

The rambling, towered and turreted, Queen Anne-style mansion has 24 bedrooms and suites, seventeen with private baths. It retains the original furnishings, although Old Deerfield Fabrics created for the inn a Shelburne House line of fabrics and wall coverings reproduced from original designs dating to the turn of the century.

Most guest rooms on the second and third floors are awesome in size, some with three windows onto the water and non-working fireplaces. Each is done in its own style, but four-poster beds, armoires, settees, lavishly carved chairs, writing tables and such barely begin to fill the space. Fresh flowers adorn the bathrooms, mostly original and some with skylights. Guests' names are on the doors and bowls of fruit in the rooms upon arrival.

For their spaciousness and aura of royalty, we would choose to stay in Lila Webb's south corner sitting room with its twin pencil-post beds and a fine view of forests and lake from mullioned windows, or Dr. Webb's room with William Morris wallpaper setting off a massive double bed, a two-story bathroom and spiral stairs up to his valet's quarters (now the White Room full of wicker and containing one of the inn's few queensize beds). Other choices would be the Overlook bedroom in between, or the Rose Room with a canopy bed, silk moiré wallpaper and a view of sunsets over mountains and lake that defies description. Although they represent good value, most would not happy in some of the smaller rooms with shared baths and hard-to-climb-in double beds up against the wall.

The main floor is a living museum reflecting the graciousness of another era. There are porches full of wicker, a library with 6,000 volumes, several sitting rooms (one for afternoon tea and pastries), a dark and masculine game room harboring an 1886 billiards table, and a formal dining room in which breakfast and dinner are served. Telephones in the guest rooms, TV sets on request and a tennis court are among the few concessions to modernity.

Meals are quiet and formal at twelve well-spaced tables dressed with white linens and Villeroy & Boch china in the spacious Marble Room, quite stunning with black and white tiled floors and walls covered in red silk damask fabric. Favored in summer are outdoor tables on the adjacent veranda with views of Lake Champlain. The public may join house guests by reservation.

Executive chef David Hugo grew up on a farm in nearby Colchester. A Culinary Institute of America graduate, he had worked for restaurants in San Francisco before returning in 1998 to head the kitchen here. He incorporates produce from the farm's organic gardens and uses local purveyors in keeping with the Shelburne Farms mission of sustaining local agriculture.

Dinner begins with complimentary canapés, perhaps truffle mousse or salami with Shelburne Farms cheddar. Then there could be a choice of vichyssoise with chives and cheddar croutons, a Maine crab and leek tartlet in a rye flour shell with local mizuna greens, or goat cheese ravioli in a smoked ham consommé with broccoli rabe. Salads could be miskell tomato with Vermont chèvre and grilled spring onions, or grilled asparagus, radishes and local greens with a lemon-herb vinaigrette.

For main courses, how about grilled scallops, prawns and mussels with a saffron linguini and roasted tomato sauce, roasted Vermont free-range chicken with yukon gold potato and artichoke ragu, or roasted rack of lamb with a sundried tomato crust and caramelized garlic demi-glace?

Desserts vary from assorted fruit sorbets and seasonal fruit cobblers to a compote of berries with champagne sabayon and a chocolate mousse torte with hazelnut ganache, cherry amaretto, white peach brandy and raspberry sauces.

Breakfast for overnight guests is à la carte. Unusual items include Vermont oatmeal and dried cherry pancakes with Shelburne Farms syrup and mascarpone cheese, french toast with strawberry-rhubarb compote and crème fraîche, and grilled flatbread with raspberry sauce, sweet Vermont chèvre and roasted mango.

Guests can walk the grounds, enjoy the superb gardens, swim at a small beach, play croquet on a manicured lawn and hike up Lone Tree Hill for a 360-degree view of the lake and mountains, says Alec Webb, president of Shelburne Farms and great-grandson of the original owners. The quiet and sense of privacy are overwhelming.

The Inn at Essex is home of two New England Culinary Institute restaurants.

The house was opened as an inn "to preserve the structure and generate revenues," adds Alec, who spent summers in the house as a teenager before his father bequeathed it to a non-profit foundation. "It's an appropriate use since it was basically a guest house originally."

(802) 985-8498. Fax (803) 985-1233. Twenty-four rooms, seventeen with private baths. Doubles, $95 to $350, EP. Two-night minimum on weekends. No smoking. Open mid-May to mid-October.

Entrées, $18 to $26. Dinner nightly by reservation, 5:30 to 9:30; Sunday brunch, 8 to 1.

The Inn at Essex, 70 Essex Way, Essex Junction 05452.

"We have a chef for every room," says innkeeper Jim Lamberti of this elegant small country hotel that emerged in the midst of a large field on the commercial outskirts of Essex Junction.

That's because Jim and his wife Judy, who built the inn with the help of Hawk Mountain Corp., approached the New England Culinary Institute for advice on a leasee for their planned food and beverage operation at the very time NECI was seeking a teaching kitchen in the Burlington area. NECI decided to run the inn's two restaurants with faculty and students. The Lambertis devoted their personal touch to the inn, from inspiration to decor to training of the exceptionally welcoming staff.

Now owned by the Lambertis in partnership with Eurowest Inns of California and other investors, the inn has overcome early challenges. It opened as the recession hit, its original developer went bankrupt and the out-of-the-way location made the task of filling its 97 rooms daunting, to say the least. The economy bounced back, funding was restructured and the first part of the planned Route 289 circumferential highway opened with an exit near the inn. A designer factory outlet center emerged across the highway interchange, and the Lambertis began to talk of expansion.

The white, three-story main structure is one of several built around what Jim likens to a New England village green. Furnishings and wallpapers in each room are different, and decor varies from Shaker to Queen Anne, from canopy to pencil-post to brass beds. Each room has a sitting area with comfortable upholstered chairs, a TV hidden in the armoire and a modern bath. Thirty have working fireplaces.

An attractive outdoor swimming pool beckons beneath a large fountain/rock sculpture chiseled on the property by a Vermont artist.

At one end of the main inn are two restaurants: the formal, 50-seat **Butler's** with a Georgian look in pale green and lavender, upholstered Queen Anne chairs, heavy white china and windows swagged in chintz, and the more casual **Tavern,** where woven mats on bare tables, dark green wainscoting and small lamps with gilt shades create a Vermont country setting. There's considerable creativity in the enormous professional kitchen, thanks to fifteen teaching chefs and a hundred student assistants.

The Tavern was where we had a fine Christmastime lunch: sundried-tomato fettuccine with scallops and a wedge of pheasant pie with a salad of mixed greens, among entrées from $6.75 to $7.95. Although the portions were small and the service slow, we saw signs of inspiration, on the menu as well as in a dessert of chocolate medallions with mousseline and blueberries in a pool of raspberry-swirled crème fraîche, presented like a work of art. Two pieces of biscotti came with the bill, a very reasonable tab.

Dinner in Butler's, NECI's temple to haute American cuisine, is a study in trendy food prepared and served by second-year students. A specified four-course prix-fixe dinner is available for $33. The rest of the menu is à la carte and changes daily.

A pre-wedding party added festivity the summer night we dined. Piano music emanated from the lounge as one of us made a meal of three starters: a subtle duck and chicken liver pâté garnished with shredded beets and wild mushrooms, pan-seared scallops with potato-garlic coulis and a salad of organic greens with a cilantro-lime dressing. The other enjoyed an entrée of crispy-skin salmon with wilted greens, tomatoes and risotto. A complimentary canapé of mushroom duxelles in pastry preceded, and a scoop of honeydew melon sorbet appeared between courses. From the delectable looking desserts on display at the entry we shared the trio of sorbets – mango/passion-fruit, strawberry daiquiri and peach champagne – spilling from a cookie cone, and splurged for an eau de vie for a bargain $5. Four little pastries and candies accompanied the bill, $77 for a highly satisfactory experience.

Thirty deluxe rooms opened in 1999 in a new building called The Manor. Designed for longer-stay guests, these range from studios to one- and two-bedroom suites. They include kitchens and fireplaces and many have whirlpool tubs.

(802) 878-1100 or (800) 727-4295. Fax (802) 878-0063. Ninety-two rooms and 28 suites with private baths. Doubles, $175 to $235. Suites, $209 to $499. No smoking.

Butler's, entrées, $17 to $21. Lunch, Monday-Saturday 11:30 to 2; dinner nightly, 6 to 9:30 or 10. Sunday brunch buffet, $10 to 2. The Tavern, lunch and dinner daily, 11:30 to 11.

Lodging

The Willard Street Inn, 349 South Willard St., Burlington 05401.

Enter the handsome cherry-paneled foyer of this 1881 brick mansion in the city's Hill Section to reach Burlington's first historic, B&B-style inn. Beverly Watson, the restaurateur who runs Isabel's on the Waterfront, and husband Gordon bought the property that had been a retirement home in 1996 and became resident innkeepers. The house was in beautiful shape, Beverly said, needing only some fresh paint and wallpaper. A mere three weeks transpired between closing the purchase and opening in time for fall foliage and the first guests.

Fourteen guest rooms on three floors are furnished in traditional style with period antiques and reproductions, plus TVs and phones. Starting with a majority of shared baths, the Watsons continued to refine and improve to the point where all now are private. Rooms vary widely, from a large first-floor bedroom with kingsize bed, armoire and floral wallpaper to second-floor corner bedrooms with handsome ornamental fireplaces and small, plain rooms on the third floor. One of the last, the Tower Room, is among Beverly's favorites. Beyond the simple bedroom with a queen bed and country decor is a wicker sitting area in the turret, with a smashing view of Lake Champlain in the distance. Settle here and you might never want to leave.

There are other attractions, however. Guests share a high-ceilinged living room, a formal dining room and an inviting, plant-filled rear solarium with a marble floor. It's furnished with six tables for breakfast as well a plush sitting area. From here a marble exterior staircase descends to the elaborate English gardens in back. They were featured in the 1999 benefit garden tour for the Flynn Theater for the Performing Arts.

Afternoon tea is offered in the solarium. Breakfasts have become more elaborate as staff trained at Isabel's experiment with the fare. Homemade peanut-butter apricot granola with fresh fruit and yogurt is a staple. You might find homemade corned beef hash with poached eggs and hollandaise sauce and whole wheat pancakes with spiced peaches one day. The next day's choices could be cranberry-pecan bread pudding with vanilla custard sauce and an unusual spinach, pear, gorgonzola and sausage omelet garnished with edible flowers.

(802) 651-8710 or (800) 577-8712. Fax (802) 651-8714. Fourteen rooms with private baths. Doubles, $115 to $225.

Heart of the Village Inn, 5347 Shelburne Road, Box 953, Shelburne 05482.

An understated Queen Anne Victorian, built by a local merchant in 1886, is now the centerpiece of a thriving B&B operation. Shelburne resident Bobbe Maynes, formerly Vermont's commissioner of tourism, knew what the market wanted when she opened the B&B in 1997. She and two partners provide comfortable accommodations and a welcoming, on-site presence.

They renovated what had always been a private home into a five-room B&B, with plenty of main-floor common space. A rear carriage barn that had been full of antiques was restored to make four more spacious, quieter accommodations away from the busy road.

The main house has two living rooms, a wraparound porch and a large dining room where four tables are set for breakfast, available from 8 to 10 o'clock. The sideboard is laden with muffins, fresh fruit, juices and granola. From the kitchen comes the day's main dish, perhaps maple toast cups holding a baked egg, garnished with dill and hollandaise sauce, or baked puff pancakes with Vermont maple syrup.

The second floor of the house, listed on the National Register, holds five bedrooms. They range in size from the front Van Vliet master bedroom with king bed, armoire, bath in a former closet and sink in the room to a small rear room with the largest bath.

More deluxe quarters are available in the carriage house. The king-bedded Bostwick is housed in an old horse stall in which you can see where the horses chewed around the windows. It is also notable for its original dark bead board barn walls. Upstairs is the spacious Webb, with queen bed and a two-person whirlpool tub.

(802) 985-2800. Fax (802) 985-2870. Nine rooms with private baths. Doubles, $95 to $195.

The Inn at Charlotte, 32 State Park Road, Charlotte 05445.

Located just off Route 7 near the foot of Mount Philo south of town, this B&B started as a boutique in an old schoolhouse with the owner's living quarters behind. You'd never know it today, such is the transformation into a rambling, contemporary, chalet-style house with six guest rooms, all with private baths. Most also have private entrances via sliding doors onto a tiered rear garden around a swimming pool and tennis court. We're partial to the two rooms at the far end, one with a kingsize bed and full bath and the other with twin four-posters and a closet-size shower. Another favorite is a detached cottage with twin beds. A thermos of Vermont spring water is in every bedroom.

Besides the pool, tennis court and garden area, guests enjoy a large and comfortable living room and a dining room in which owner Letty Ellinger, a caterer, serves dinner to guests by reservation (she was making delectable-smelling Chinese egg rolls at our visit). A typical $25 prix-fixe meal might involve oriental soup or green salad, chicken teriyaki or New York strip sirloin (grilled outside on the barbecue), a homemade pie, a glass of wine and gourmet coffee. A $30 tab gets you a full Asian dinner with several appetizers, three main dishes with rice, and choice of dessert.

Letty serves a full breakfast in the morning, perhaps ham and eggs, quiche, french toast or blueberry pancakes.

(802) 425-2934 or (800) 425-2934. Six rooms with private baths. Doubles, $85 to $105.

Thomas Mott Homestead, Blue Rock Road, Alburg 05440.

This lakeside prize at the top of the Champlain Islands north of Burlington is one of our favorite, down-to-earth B&Bs anywhere. Ex-California wine distributor Pat Schallert transformed an 1838 farmhouse into a homey B&B with five spacious guest rooms and a secluded lakeside location with panoramic water and mountain views that won't quit. Three porches invite lounging, the fireplaced living room is stocked with books and magazines, and a massive collection of cookbooks and wine books flanks the stairway.

Each of the five guest rooms with private baths is furnished with antiques and quilts from different states. The queen-bedded Carrie's Room could not be more colorful with hooked rugs, pillows and quilts, even on the walls. Laura's Room has two queen beds, and the downstairs Corner Suite in which we stayed offers a queen bed, day bed, cathedral ceiling and large walk-in closet.

The ultimate is Ransom's Rest, nestled beneath a cathedral ceiling with a queen bed, Shaker pegs, two comfy chairs in front of an angled fireplace and a balcony onto the lake, affording a view to Mount Mansfield and Camel's Hump. Between the moonlight and the fire, it's heaven on earth, guests say. (It's also booked so far ahead that we've never managed to snag it for a night.)

A hearty breakfast is served amid much camaraderie in the kitchen open to the dining room. The french toast stuffed with cream cheese and five kinds of nuts, served with warm maple syrup, and the crab omelet proved stellar during our visit.

Other special touches that make this place a winner: chocolates from the local Shoreline Chocolates put out at turndown, a help-yourself stash of at least ten varieties of Ben & Jerry's ice cream in the refrigerator, a lakeside gazebo and boating dock, a barnyard pen where Pat raises quail and a patch of what he calls "stealing" raspberries. We were surprised they were still producing in late September and gladly would have picked a few quarts to take home – but that would have been stealing!

(802) 796-3736 or (800) 348-0843. Fax (802) 796-3736. www.thomas-mott-bb.com. Five rooms with private baths. Doubles, $79 to $105.

Gourmet Destinations

Shelburne Museum, Route 7, Shelburne.

The incredible collections of Electra Havemeyer Webb, wife of a Vanderbilt heir, became the Shelburne Museum in 1947, and the resulting 37 exhibit buildings spread across a 45-acre heritage park fascinate young and old. The almost overwhelming display of Americana, unrivaled in New England, spans three centuries and a multitude of interests. People into things culinary will enjoy the kitchens in four restored homes, each with large open hearths full of gadgets that our ancestors used. The Weed House has a remarkable collection of pewter and glass, and the dining-room tables in the side-wheeler Ticonderoga are set with Syracuse china. A free shuttle tram transports visitors from the new visitor center to the far ends of the grounds every fifteen minutes.

(802) 985-3346. Open daily 9 to 5, mid-May to mid-October; rest of year, guided tours, daily at 1. Adults, $17.50; second consecutive day free.

Shelburne Farms, 102 Harbor Road, Shelburne.

The 1,400-acre agricultural estate of Dr. William Seward Webb and Lila Vanderbilt Webb has been opened to the public lately as a working farm. Blessed with one of the more spectacular lakeside-mountain settings in the Northeast, Shelburne Farms combines an active dairy and cheese-making operation, a children's farmyard, walking trails, a bakery, a market garden, furniture-making and other leased enterprises in a working-farm setting that has a Camelot-like quality. These are included as part of the day pass admission.

Additionally, guided tours leave every 90 minutes from the Visitor Center after a multi-media slide introduction. Visitors board an open-air wagon to view the enormous Farm Barn, the Dairy Barn, the formal gardens and the Shelburne House, where they stop to tour a few of the public rooms. You may see grazing along the way the choice herd of Brown Swiss cows, descended from stock raised for cheese making in Switzerland. Their Shelburne Farms farmhouse cheddar (the extra-sharp is one of the best cheddars we have ever tasted) is sold in the welcome center and farm store, where a fine shop also stocks other Vermont farm products and crafts and is open daily year-round.

Tea tours are scheduled two to three afternoons a week for those with a special interest in the Shelburne House inn and gardens. Following tours, which include all public areas and some of the upstairs bedrooms, tea is served in the library or on the South Porch.

(802) 985-8686. Day pass, adults $5. Guided tours daily at 9:30, 11, 12:30, 2 and 3:30, mid-May to mid-October. $5. Tea tours at inn, Tuesday and Thursday at 2:30 by reservation (985-8442), adults $15.

Gourmet Treats

In Burlington, **Lake Champlain Chocolates** at 750 Pine St. produces some of the best chocolates in the Northeast. It's an outgrowth of Jim Lampman's original Ice House restaurant, where partner Richard Spurgeon was the baker and produced truffles that generated such demand that they branched into the chocolate enterprise in 1983. The relocated and expanded production area adjoins a showroom that smells like chocolate heaven. Production starts with Belgian chocolate but the addition of Vermont heavy cream and sweet butter and intense natural flavoring puts their creations "on a par with the best in the world," according to Cuisine magazine. Among the latest treats are "Vermints," and factory seconds are offered at 40 percent off. A sampling is available downtown at 61 Church St., where a couple of guys making chocolate-covered strawberries attracted quite a crowd of passersby at our latest visit.

"Custom-built coffees" are the trademark of **Speeder & Earl's,** a high-tech, high-ceilinged space in black and white at 412 Pine St. Its boutique roastery and coffee bar are located here, while a small Speeder's coffee bar is situated downtown on the Church Street Marketplace. You'll find rare coffee roasts that are served plain, with foam and/or with flavored syrups. What are custom-built coffees? The menu answers: "Simply put, if you want hazelnut Italian syrup in a nonfat latte, with nonfat whipped cream topping, sprinkled with mint-flavored sugar, don't be shy. Just ask." Ask also for teas, Italian sodas, biscotti and pastries. It seems enough people asked that owners Gordon and Jeannie Blankenburg opened a 50-seat restaurant and espresso bar purveying their Speeder's premium blend in the Copley Square Hotel in Boston.

The best breads in town come from **Klinger's Bread Company**, headquartered at 10 Farrell St. in South Burlington and with a small downtown sidewalk outlet at Church and College streets. Designed to resemble a European village courtyard, complete with murals and a tiled roof, the bakery's Disneyesque display area dispenses countless varieties of breads, sandwiches and salads. There's even a retail wine cellar. Big windows open onto the bakery area launched in 1993 by Judy Klingebiel, who learned the trade as accountant to master baker Michael London of Rock Hill Bakehouse near Saratoga Springs, N.Y. At last count, Klinger's twenty-plus varieties ranged from jalapeño cheddar to chocolate cherry to Jewish rye, some made only on certain days and best reserved in advance.

Desserts and pastries that turn up at the best parties in town come from **Mirabelles,** 198 Main St., a terrific bakery and deli created by Alison Fox and Andrew Silva and named for the golden plums grown on the Continent, where both had worked. Sandwiches are inspired, perhaps black forest ham and brie, artichoke pesto with vegetables or goat cheese with Mediterranean tapenade and vegetables, served on homemade wheat, sourdough, honey oat breads or a baguette. The ploughman's lunch is a sampling of cheeses, breads, fruits and a sweet. Finish with a raspberry butter tart, chocolate-raspberry mousse cake or a slice of cappuccino-truffle cake.

Another good spot for breakfast or lunch is **Penny Cluse Cafe,** housed in the quarters where Ben & Jerry's got its start at 169 Cherry St. Charles Reeves and Holly Cluse offer an extensive variety of tempting creations. Come here for huevos rancheros, breakfast burritos, tofu scramble, polenta and eggs or sourdough french toast. Grilled flank steak on a grilled baguette is a lunchtime favorite.

Bennington Potters North, a multi-level emporium at 127 College St. in downtown Burlington, carries everything from the popular Vermont pottery to aprons to egg cups. Housed in an old warehouse restored with taste, it's enormous, and so is the selection.

Enterprises of particular interest among the national chains along the Church Street Marketplace include a **Lindt of Switzerland** factory store and **Kiss the Cook,** a good kitchen store that teams up with NECI Commons for cooking demonstrations. **Liquid Energy Cafe** is a deluxe juice bar (try a vegetable tonic) and a gourmet soup kitchen in a high-energy, TV and Internet setting.

The **Cheese Outlet/Fresh Market** at 400 Pine St. has evolved into a gourmet emporium with a café, bakery, a section of local produce, a specialty deli featuring good-looking salads, an olive bar and a case of all kinds of pasta, some with interesting fillings, where you can take as much or as little as you want. It remains northern New England's largest cheese and wine warehouse, with an excellent selection of pâtés and cheeses, quiches and cheesecakes at bargain prices.

Shelburne is home to the **Shelburne Country Store,** opposite the village green. It still sells penny candy but now also offers an upscale assortment of country things, accessories, kitchenware, homemade fudge and specialty foods, including its own line of chowders and finnan haddie. All kinds of mustards and sauces are opened for tasting.

"The world's best ham sandwich" is advertised at **Harrington's of Vermont,** Route 7, next to Cafe Shelburne. Headquartered in nearby Richmond, this has a cafe as well as everything for the kitchen from cookbooks to Cuisinarts. It sells a panoply of gourmet foods, including every kind of cracker imaginable. The cob-smoked ham, turkey and pheasant are famous, and you also can find delicious country sausage, Canadian bacon, air-dried beef and smoked salmon.

Woodstock and Hanover
Quintessential New England

Woodstock, which has been called one of America's prettiest towns by National Geographic, is the quintessential New England village. Across the New Hampshire state line is Hanover, a quintessential New England college town.

Put them together and you have an extraordinary destination area for those who seek the real New England, relatively unspoiled, even if highly sophisticated. Happily, both towns have escaped the commercial trappings that so often accompany tourism. The Rockefeller interests have enhanced much of Woodstock, even burying the utility wires in the center underground for a picture-perfect Currier and Ives look. Dartmouth College sets the character for Hanover. Both towns exude an aura of culture and class.

The attraction of the area is epitomized by historic Woodstock, where America's first ski tow was installed in 1934, propelling it into a winter sports mecca called "the St. Moritz of the East – without the Ritz." There's still no Ritz, although the Woodstock Inn and Resort built in 1969 by Rockefeller interests and the Twin Farms luxury hideaway that emerged in 1993 could qualify.

The Rockefeller connection with Woodstock began in 1934 when Laurance Rockefeller married Mary Billings French, the granddaughter of railroad magnate Frederick Billings. Now the town's largest landowner and employer, until recently he lived about two months of the year in the mansion north of town that was once the home of conservationist George Perkins Marsh, the 19th-century ambassador and a founder of the Smithsonian. The Rockefellers are preserving the family heritage – and that of Vermont – in their Billings Farm & Museum with its thousands of 19th-century farm implements. Their home and 550 acres of surrounding gardens and woodlands have been given to the National Park Service for preservation as the new Marsh-Billings National Historical Park, the first to focus on conservation history and the changing nature of land stewardship in America.

A generation ago, chowders, boiled dinners and pumpkin pies were the fare served at the White Cupboard Inn – which closed in 1967 – and at the old Woodstock Inn, which was razed to make way for the new. "Had a patron requested chocolate mousse he probably would have been told that the pharmacy didn't carry those but they did have maple sugar candies shaped like Indians," a local magazine once wrote.

Today, the Woodstock and Hanover region abounds with restaurants and inns appealing to diverse tastes.

Dining

The Best of the Best

Barnard Inn Restaurant, Route 12, Barnard, Vt.

Its red-brick facade accented by four white pillars and surrounded by mighty trees, the Barnard Inn is a handsome, two-story structure dating to 1796. It really is out in the country, ten miles north of Woodstock almost at the "back of beyond."

All is elegant and historic in Barnard Inn's main dining room.

But its fans consider the distance a trifle to be put up with for a meal at a restaurant they tout as one of the best in Vermont.

The Barnard has held that lofty status since 1975, so Marie-France and Philip Filipovic from Quebec knew they had a lot to live up to when they purchased it in 1994. They came with high credentials. Self-taught Yugoslav chef Philip, who started as a waiter in Montreal's Ritz-Carlton Hotel, and his wife owned a four-star restaurant called simply Marie Philip in the Laurentian resort town of St. Sauveur. The Quebec government rated it the best in the province.

Moving to Vermont for "quality of life," Marie said, they took over a going concern and began adding their imprimatur. They hung their favorite paintings, put down oriental rugs, added more French wines to an already choice cellar and started smoking their own salmon. We, who enjoyed several great meals here previously, were pleased to find that the new Barnard Inn was equal to, if not better than, the old.

A fire blazes in the hearth in the biggest of four small dining rooms in the elegant, late-Colonial inn. Dusky rose cloths, gold-rimmed china, candles in hurricane chimneys and sparkling wine globes dress the well-spaced tables. The only lighting is from the candles and the wall sconces.

The menu is à la carte, with both the specialty roast duck and rack of lamb going for $21 at our latest visit. The crisp roasted duck, done as in the past, is a sure winner. Phillip has added more chicken dishes (one is stuffed with small vegetables and served with pickled ginger and turmeric sauce). A five-course tasting menu ($35) represents exceptional value.

Choosing the latter, we began with a couple of complimentary hors d'oeuvres: tastes of prosciutto and melon and a cherry tomato stuffed with French boncoccini cheese. Next came the house-smoked salmon, a signature presentation shaped like a rose and served with endive, and a zucchini blossom bearing lobster and shrimp mousse over lemongrass beurre blanc. Crusty sourdough bread and perfect green salads preceded the main courses, noisettes of Green Mountain lamb wrapped in spinach mousse and tenderloin of rabbit with wild mushrooms. Everything was beautifully presented on dramatic square plates and garnished with flowers. Snap peas, baby squash, beets and potato gaufrette accompanied.

A plate of four cheeses arrived bearing one of the Barnard's decorative trademarks, in this case a swan carved from an apple, with a clove for its eye. (The house potatoes are shaped and coated to look like a pear, with a clove at the bottom and a pear stem on top.) Dessert was a perfect crème brûlée laced with orange and ginger, and an assortment of remarkable sorbets (chocolate, papaya, peach and raspberry) looking like an artist's palette. The bill came in a lacquered box with two truffles on a doily.

Lingering over coffee and eau de vie in the cozy bar, we felt mesmerized by the setting as well as by the exceptional meal.

(802) 234-9961. Entrées, $21 to $27. Dinner, Tuesday-Sunday from 6. Also closed Sunday in winter.

Hemingway's, Route 4, Sherburne, Vt.

The restored, 19th-century Asa Briggs farmhouse has been earning culinary accolades since Linda and Ted Fondulas moved over from Annabelle's in Stockbridge in the early 1980s.

Antiques, locally crafted furniture, fresh flowers from Linda's gardens and original oil paintings, watercolors and sculpture enhance the decor in each of three dining rooms. A European feeling is effected in the formal, peach-colored dining room with dark upholstered chairs and sparkling chandeliers. A fire is often blazing in the hearth in the smaller garden room done up in white and pink with brick floors, pierced lamps on the walls and ivy adorning the windows. Most unusual is a charming, secluded wine cellar with stone walls, hand-crocheted tablecloths and elaborate candlesticks.

These are diverse settings for ever-changing, new American fare that made Hemingway's the first four-star, four-diamond restaurant in northern New England. An added accolade came a few years later when Food & Wine magazine ranked it among the top 25 restaurants in America. Hemingway's also is known for its monthly food and wine tastings featuring wine experts as guest speakers. The Fondulases stock more than 175 wine selections, at prices from $18 to $200.

Dinner is prix-fixe, available in three formats: $55 for three courses, plus hors d'oeuvres, bread, coffee and confection; $75 for four selected courses from the regular prix-fixe menu, each served with a glass of selected wine, champagne or port, and $45 for a four-course vegetarian menu.

About six choices are available in each category for the main option. For starters you might find yellowfin tuna tartare with a crispy sushi rice cake, pan-seared sea scallops with lemongrass broth, confit of duck strudel with currants and hazelnuts, and a "plantation soup" of lobster, crab and mussels. The main course could be halibut and lobster with fettuccine, fillet of salmon with chanterelles and corn sauce, or pan-roasted pork with double-cured prosciutto and cherries.

Typical of desserts are piña colada bavarian, black and white chocolate sandwich with pistachio sauce, gingered lime sorbet with a phyllo nest and mango, fallen soufflé of goat cheese with lavender honey and almonds, or "local anything," says Linda, whose husband oversees the kitchen.

(802) 422-3886. Prix fixe, $45 to $75. Dinner, Wednesday-Sunday 6 to 10. Closed mid-April to mid-May, and early November.

The Prince and the Pauper, 24 Elm St., Woodstock, Vt.

Walk up the brick walkway alongside one of the area's oldest buildings, open the green door, pass the pubby bar and enter the L-shaped dining room. You're in what is considered to be the best restaurant in Woodstock proper.

Oil lanterns cast shadows on beamed ceilings and pink-clothed tables are surrounded by Hitchcock chairs or tucked away in high, dark wood booths, the ultimate in privacy. Antique prints decorate the white walls, one of which has a shelf of old books.

Chef-owner Chris Balcer calls his cuisine "creative contemporary" with French, continental and international accents. The prix-fixe menu ($36, for appetizer, salad and main course) changes frequently. The pasta of the day could be raviolis filled with smoked ham and Vermont goat cheese; the soup, charred carrot garnished with crème fraîche. Other appetizers could be house-smoked rainbow trout with raifort sauce and Thai mussels steamed in coconut milk, curry, garlic and ginger.

Entrées at our last visit included broiled mahi-mahi with pineapple-mango salsa, roast duckling with a sauce of kiwi and Meyers's rum, and the house specialty, boneless rack of New Zealand lamb with cabernet demi-glace.

Spend some time reviewing the interesting wine list (strong on California chardonnays and cabernets), priced from the high teens to more than $100. But save room for dessert – maybe a fabulous raspberry tart with white chocolate mousse served with raspberry-cabernet wine sauce, cappuccino cheesecake, or a homemade sorbet like Jack Daniels-chocolate chip. Finish with espresso or an international coffee.

A bistro menu is available in the elegant bar. It offers half a dozen entrées, ranging from grilled farm-raised rainbow trout to grilled black angus strip steak. Also offered here are six kinds of hearth-baked pizzas for $12.

In the off-season, the Prince offers a series of wine-tasting dinners called Tour de France. The in-depth study of the wines of France, region by region, is conducted by wine director Dan Morgan in tandem with the chef.

(802) 457-1818. Prix-fixe, $36. Bistro menu, $15 to $19. Dinner nightly, 6 to 9 or 9:30.

La Poule à Dents, Main Street, Norwich, Vt.

Texas chef Barry Snyder gave up an innkeeping stint at the Parker House in nearby Quechee to open his own restaurant. When the former Carpenter Street Restaurant became available in 1990, he jumped at the chance to take over. Knowing diners have been applauding his fare and sense of culinary adventure ever since.

A Culinary Institute of America graduate, Barry cooks in the classic French style and changes his short, contemporary menu every few weeks. He's known for his monthly wine theme dinners and, at a recent visit, had just completed a series of Taste of the City dinners, based on adaptations of his solitary dining forays at some of New York's finest restaurants. After which he concluded, "The quality of food we present here is equal to that of New York City. It's just that our presentations are not as complicated."

Dinner is prix-fixe, $39 for three courses plus a substantial complimentary hors d'oeuvre – a half-portion of, say, smoked salmon with caramelized onion salad. Appetizer choices range from cream of chestnut soup with chive blossoms to a warmed black currant pâté sandwich with toasted fig bread and caramelized onion jam.

Typical main courses include citrus-rubbed halibut with lemon sabayon sauce, potato-encrusted trout with caper sauce, and grilled fennel-encrusted pork loin with mushroom-marsala sauce. Another could be seafood risotto with shrimp, lobster, niçoise olives and tomatoes

With typical bravado, Barry calls the restaurant's dessert tarts the best around. But you might want to order a chocolate mousse tower with pistachio cream and nut brittle, a strawberry napoleon with lemon curd and chantilly, or pear and ginger sorbet with raspberry purée in an almond tuile. A little tray of hand-dipped or molded chocolates arrives with coffee.

All this is served in three dining rooms. A handsome oak bar flanks a more casual, post and beam, café-style dining area with high-back, windsor-style chairs. Two smaller dining rooms are more formal, the Burgundy Room outfitted in floral wallpaper and the Bordeaux hung with royal purple swags and jabots. The latter harbors a couple of romantic recessed alcoves. The tables are set with crystal from Judot, Villeroy & Boch china and three forks at each place, face down.

We got a taste of Barry's work a few years ago at lunch, which since has been discontinued. Three of us enjoyed various soups – a velvety purée of butternut squash with dill chantilly, an intense wild-mushroom broth with porcini and shiitakes, and the winner, a hearty zuppa di pasta e fagioli. Among main dishes that gave a hint of dinner preparations were breaded salmon anglaise with herb vinaigrette and estockificada, a bouillabaisse of shrimp, scallops and mahi-mahi on a plate with saffron sauce and a bowl of broth topped by garlic toast on the side.

Oh yes, the French name? Loosely translated, Barry says, it means "as scarce as hen's teeth." It's his way of noting that the best things in life, at least in terms of food and wine, are rare indeed.

(802) 649-2922. Prix-fixe, $39. Dinner nightly, from 6.

Simon Pearce Restaurant, The Mill, Quechee, Vt.

Irish glassblower Simon Pearce's intriguing mill complex includes a restaurant serving Irish and regional Vermont specialties in a smashing setting beside the Ottauquechee River. We think the spacious enclosed terrace with retractable full-length windows almost over the waterfall is great for an open-air lunch or dinner year-round, and the Pennsylvania friends to whom we recommended the restaurant liked it so much they took relatives back the next day. Countless others have been directed here and, captivated by the magic of a special place, now make it a point to stop for a meal whenever they're in the vicinity.

The interior dining areas, vastly expanded since its opening, reflect the exquisite taste of the entire complex. Sturdy ash chairs are at well-spaced wood tables dressed with small woven mats by day and white linens at night. The heavy glassware and the deep brown and white china are made by Simon Pearce and his family at the mill. Plants, dried flowers in baskets and antique quilts lend a soft counterpoint to the brick walls, bare floors and expansive windows.

The chefs train at Ballymaloe in Ireland, and they import flour from Ireland to make their great Irish soda bread and Ballymaloe brown bread. They change the menu periodically, but there are usually specialties like shepherd's pie and beef and Guinness stew (which we tried at lunch – for $9.25, a generous serving of fork-tender beef and vegetables, plus a small side salad of julienned vegetables). We also liked a pasta salad heaped with vegetables and a superior basil-parmesan dressing. One of us nearly always orders the mouth-watering smoked salmon

Arched windows give diners view of waterfall outside Simon Pearce Restaurant.

with raifort sauce. For dessert, the walnut meringue with strawberry sauce and whipped cream is the crowning glory. A menu fixture, it's crisp and crunchy, and melts in the mouth. Irish apple cake, profiteroles and white chocolate mousse cake with raspberry sauce are other possibilities.

Candlelight dinners might start with a warm shrimp and artichoke salad with roasted peppers and feta, marinated grilled chicken with a spicy peanut sauce or grilled portobello mushrooms with shaved parmesan, fennel and watercress. Entrées range from Maine salmon baked in phyllo with roasted shiitake mushrooms and spinach, served with Vermont chèvre cream and balsamic syrup, to herb-roasted leg of lamb with sweet garlic jus. Other choices might be horseradish-crusted cod with crispy leeks, chile-cured grilled pork tenderloin with corn and black bean salsa, and Tuscan grilled sirloin steak with rosemary and arugula.

The wine list, printed on the menus, is short but choice. It's supplemented by a longer list priced from the high teens up. Naturally, you can get beers and ales from the British Isles.

(802) 295-1470. Entrées, $18.50 to $25. Lunch daily, 11:30 to 2:45. Dinner nightly by reservation, 6 to 9.

More Dining Choices

Sweet Tomatoes Trattoria, 1 Court St., Lebanon, N.H.

Pizzas from a wood-burning oven, pastas, and entrées from a wood and charcoal grill at wallet-pleasing prices. These are the hallmarks of a sleek but casual, New Yorkish place that quickly became the dining sensation of the Upper Valley, despite an unlikely location fronting the green in oft-overlooked Lebanon.

Occupying the key front-corner space of a new downtown commercial complex, this is the brainchild of James Reiman, who was formerly at the Prince and the

Pauper and opened Spooner's in Woodstock, and Robert Meyers, a builder whose experience was pivotal in putting the space together. And it's quite a space. Seats for 100 are at tables placed well apart under mod California spotlights, their neon-like rims echoing the neon encircling the exposed metal grid beneath a high black ceiling. Tall windows, a black and white tiled floor, a few indoor trees, a mural along one wall, a tin mobile and plants hanging on pillars complete the minimalist decor.

Excitement is provided by the totally open kitchen, where the owners sometimes join the cooks at the grills, wood-burning oven and work counters amidst garlic ropes hanging from on high. Theirs is what Robert calls "strictly ethnic Italian cooking, priced for the times." You'll find pastas like linguini with shrimp and sweet peas or fusilli with chicken and artichoke hearts, and pizzas from the namesake sweet tomato pie to one with fresh clams.

Entrées include grilled chicken with herbs, skewers of marinated lamb, rainbow trout stuffed with bay shrimp and crabmeat, and, our choice, grilled swordfish with basil pesto, served with a side salad of red potatoes, peas, leeks and garlic.

We thoroughly enjoyed the cavatappi with roasted chicken, plum tomatoes and arugula, a memorable concoction served with two slices of herbed sourdough bread and cheese sprinkled liberally from a hand grater. The enormous clam pizza, its thin crackly crust weighted down with clams and mozzarella, proved too much to eat at one sitting. We had to forego the delectable desserts, which included chocolate-espresso cake, cannolis and dacquoise.

Success here led the partners to open carbon copies in downtown Burlington and Rutland, Vt.

(603) 448-1711. Entrées, $7.95 to $14.95. Dinner nightly, 5 to 9 or 9:30.

Monsoon, 18 Centarra Pkwy., Lebanon, N.H.
This modern Asian bistro and satay bar is a sight to behold. Opened in 1998 in the new Centarra Marketplace opposite the Dartmouth Hitchcock Medical Center, it is a sleek and dramatic space with twenty-foot-high ceilings, bamboo columns, potted tropical plants, lots of metal and glass, bright red walls, black tables and a fountain at the door. Not to mention curving gray screens pretending to be clouds and a timed lighting system that simulates the sky during a monsoon to convey the atmosphere of Southeast Asia. The 144-seat restaurant looks as if it cost far more than the $500,000 specified in a design article in Nation's Restaurant News.

Co-owners Robert Meyers and Jim Reiman of Sweet Tomatoes Trattoria sought a spectacular Asian industrial look for their newest – and, Robert claims, last – restaurant prototype. They now advertise "unforgettable tastes from opposite ends of the world." As opposed to Italian trattoria, this is really Asian bistro – right down to the spare tables set with chopsticks standing tall in copper vases and the place settings wrapped in copper tubing used as napkin rings.

Asian cooks are among those manning the large, angular kitchen open to full view to both dining room and part of the side bar/lounge. Their fare spans the spectrum of Asian cuisines, although is light on Japanese. Dinner begins with complimentary shrimp chips and a small platter of spicy bean sprouts and boiled peanuts. Expect appetizers like Thai hot and sour soup, potstickers with sesame-soy-ginger dipping sauce, wok-seared littleneck clams with black bean sauce and Thai basil, and warm duck salad on cabbage and greens with orange hoisin dressing.

Popular main dishes are Monsoon "big bowls," noodles and broth topped with a choice of grilled items. Otherwise, look for peppercorn-crusted yellowfin tuna

Monsoon features spectacular modern Asian bistro look.

Greg Premru Photography

with wasabi, wood-grilled Chilean sea bass with sweet yellow chile-shallot marmalade, spicy Thailand squid with ginger and garlic, crispy wok-braised half duck, lemongrass chicken with red chiles and lime leaves, and grilled Korean barbecued pork ribs with sweet chili marinade.

Desserts vary from mango sorbet and rainbow chiffon to mandarin chocolate mousse and key lime pie.

(603) 643-9227. Entrées, $9.95 to $14.95. Dinner nightly, 5 to 9 or 9:30.

Cafe Buon Gustaio, 72 South Main St., Hanover, N.H.

New management runs this engaging Italian bistro, transforming a once-decrepit eatery into a picture-pretty room of intimate tables outfitted with white linens, carafes of alstroemeria and votive candles. A bottle of extra-virgin olive oil is on every table, ready to pour into a saucer for dipping the crusty Tuscan bread. Candles flicker in the wall sconces, and tiny white lights twinkle on the beams in the adjacent bar.

The restaurant generally lives up to its name, which means "good eats," although reports have been mixed lately. The menu, printed nightly but not all that much changed over the years, is categorized by appetizers, salads, pastas, pizzettas and entrées.

You might start with crostini of oak-smoked salmon and mascarpone, buckwheat polenta with lamb and rosemary sausage or Maine crab cakes with scallion curry cream sauce. Pizzettas could include sundried tomatoes with roasted peppers and brie or grilled chicken with cilantro pesto and button mushrooms.

Expect pasta dishes like black pepper lasagna of lobster, mushrooms and three cheeses in tomato cream sauce; farfalle with chicken and spinach in fontina cream sauce, and four-cheese ravioli with smoked ham, mushrooms, tomatoes and asiago. Typical entrées are seared yellowfin tuna with lemon-shallot vinaigrette and baby greens, sautéed veal medallions with porcini-marsala cream sauce and asparagus, and grilled lamb loin with madeira-peppercorn sauce.

Desserts include toffee-lime tart, napoleons and chocolate lover's cake topped with chocolate-dipped strawberries.

(603) 643-5711. Entrées, $20 to $22. Dinner, Tuesday-Saturday 5:30 to 9 or 9:30.

Dining and Lodging

The Jackson House Inn, 37 Old Route 4 West, Woodstock, VT 05091.

Fabulous appetizers with complimentary champagne. Superior dinners. Extravagant breakfasts. Flawless and friendly service. We didn't think a B&B could get much better than this. But new owners Juan and Gloria Florin, former Argentineans by way of Connecticut, had ambitious plans for the three-story Victorian house on four acres of beautiful grounds west of the village. Taking over in 1997, they turned the B&B into an inn – adding four luxury suites, an acclaimed dining room open to the public, and a higher level of service.

The prize of the operation now is the restaurant, worthy of a four-diamond rating by AAA. A new rear addition holds a pleasant bar, the kitchen and a dining room with cathedral ceiling and big windows onto four acres of gardens. Nicely spaced tables are flanked by chairs handcrafted by Charles Shackleton, a local furniture maker. The focal point is a soaring, see-through open-hearth fireplace of Pennsylvania granite. A stone mason laid it slab by slab, a laborious process that took three weeks and appears so natural one wonders how it's held together.

Young executive chef Andrew Turner, who trained in California and France, prepares new American cuisine. Dinner is prix-fixe ($49), with several choices for each of three courses. The chef's tasting menu ($58, or $78 with wine pairings) adds a second appetizer, a palate-cleansing mango-lime sorbet and a plate of cheeses with fig walnut toast before dessert.

A typical autumn dinner might start with a potato, leek and roasted garlic soup with Maine crabmeat or roasted quail stuffed with tart apples and wrapped in brioche. Main courses range from steamed Atlantic salmon to breast of Vermont free-range chicken roulade.

Dinner actually begins in the elegant living room and library, where complimentary champagne and wine accompany an elaborate buffet of hors d'oeuvres. One occasion produced California rolls, curried grilled chicken with diced green apple on a chickpea flour crisp and prosciutto-wrapped black mission figs. The latest yielded a remarkable seared salmon and frisée salad atop a wafer, alsatian-style onion tarts, and phyllo-wrapped brandade and root vegetable mash.

Later, the tasting dinner in the candlelit dining room opened with appetizers of pan-seared diver scallops with belgian endive and parsnip purée, and pheasant confit and wild mushroom crepinette with a young field green salad. The main course, designed to showcase a masterful 1996 echezeaux from Labouré-Roi in Burgundy, was slow-braised short ribs of beef with an oxtail croquette. The riches were topped off by a dense chocolate-almond truffle cake with bittersweet chocolate sauce and a glass of vintage port.

Open-hearth granite fireplace is focal point of dining room at The Jackson House Inn.

Fortunately, we had only to toddle off to Clara's Corner in another new wing, where more chocolates awaited on the pillows. It's one of four large rooms there with corner gas fireplaces, sitting areas and modern bathrooms with whirlpool or message therapy tubs, separate showers and cherry floors. We were enveloped in the lap of comfort, but for lack of a TV (the house satellite TV in the basement offers more than 200 channels and three lounge chairs for watching) or good lights placed appropriately for reading (could that be why several couples were reading in the main-floor living room and library in the late afternoon)? The queensize Sheraton poster bed was topped with red and gold Anichini fabrics and a sheeted duvet. Antique pots and vases graced the shelves, and an array of antique pillboxes topped a lace doily on a side table. There were fresh flowers, assorted fruits for nibbling and replacement towels at turndown. The staff even produced a new toothbrush for the one that had been forgotten.

Each of the new suites is different, as are rooms in the original inn, where decor varies from French Empire to British Oriental to old New England. Each is eclectically furnished with such things as antique brass lamps on either side of the bathroom mirror, a marble-topped bedside table, an 1860 sleigh bed, an 1840 English mahogany pedestal desk, a prized Casablanca ceiling fan, Chinese carved rugs, handmade afghans coordinated to each room's colors, bamboo and cane furniture, a blanket box made of tiger maple, an antique three-drawer sideboard with its faded original green paint and much more.

Most choice are two third-floor beauties, considered suites because they're about twice the size of many other rooms, which are admittedly small. Both have queensize cherry sleigh beds, gas fireplaces, Italian marble baths and french doors onto a rear deck overlooking an English garden. At an earlier visit, we found plenty of room in the Francesca suite to spread out on an upholstered sofa, a wing chair and, on the rear deck beyond, two lounge chairs. The mirrored bathroom was so sparkling it looked as if we were the first ever to use it.

The treats continue in the morning. The buffet might be laden with homemade granola, spiced pear yogurt and an array of sliced fruit, from pineapple to kiwi to cantaloupe. Juices, scones, croissants and muffins come next. The main course in one case was a scrambled egg and country sausage tart with goat cheese. Others could be ricotta pancakes, brioche french toast or – one we'll never forget – poached eggs on dill biscuits with poached salmon and hollandaise sauce.

After all this, settle into a deep wing chair in the library or retire to a lounge chair around the pond in the remarkably landscaped back yard for a morning nap. Or work it off in a small spa located on the lower level. It includes exercise equipment and a steam room.

(802) 457-2065 or (800) 448-1890. Fax (802) 457-9290. www.jacksonhouse.com. Nine rooms and six suites with private baths. Doubles, $180 to $240. Suites, $260 to $340.

Prix-fixe, $42. Dinner by reservation, nightly except Wednesday and some Tuesdays, 6 to 9.

Home Hill Country Inn & Restaurant, River Road, Plainfield, N.H. 03781.
There is something about the undulating Connecticut River area south of West Lebanon that reminds some of France. That reminder drew Frenchman Roger Nicolas from California to open this imposing white brick Federal house as an inn and restaurant in 1983. And it prompted fellow countryman Stephane du Roure and his American wife Victoria to take over the establishment in 1996.

"When I saw this for the first time," said Stephane, "I thought I was in Europe." He and his wife were having dinner at Home Hill during a visit to her family's vacation home in nearby Cornish. One thing led to another, and they decided to buy the place.

The similarities in background are striking: Their predecessor, from Brittany, had come here from California. Stephane, from Provence, also came from California, where he had run patisseries in San Diego. The difference is Victoria, an aspiring cook from Boston who had trained at the Ritz Escoffier in Paris and apprenticed with celebrity chef Bradley Ogden in California. She added not only culinary expertise but also a woman's touch to an inn that needed it. The couple redecorated five guest rooms upstairs and added three more rooms in a carriage house. They also serve dinners of distinction to the public. "We're still two years from having this the way we want it," Stephane apologized at our visit. We could tell then, however, that here was one of New England's outstanding country inns and restaurants nearing the apex.

Home Hill is quiet, refined and polished. It was so quiet that we slept far past our planned awakening in a suite with two blazing gas fireplaces and a living room as big as the bedroom. And, as the maitre-d' advised, people come here to get away "so there are no TVs or telephones anywhere to disturb them." Otherwise, there are all the comforts of a well-endowed home in five upstairs guest rooms furnished with antiques in rather formal country French style. The queensize beds are triple-sheeted and dressed with fabric crown canopies that coordinate with

Elegant appointments dignify dining rooms at Home Hill Country Inn & Restaurant.

the window treatments. Oriental rugs grace the hardwood floors. One bathroom still contains an original toilet and a bidet. Out back in the carriage house are two more rooms and a suite, each due in 2000 for an upgrade along with the addition of three new rooms with fireplaces. A seasonal cottage with queen bed and white wicker sitting room is situated behind the swimming pool. The 25-acre property also includes a tennis court, bocce court, putting green and restored gardens, as well as a corral for the owners' two horses. A small outbuilding was being transformed into a guest reception area and a country store. It specializes in handmade dishes like the monogrammed chargers custom-designed for the inn by a Frenchman in Moustier Ste.-Marie.

"Our dream is to be known for our food," affirmed Stephane at the end of a property tour. The du Roures were renovating and reconfiguring the inn's spacious kitchen, the better for Victoria to prepare upwards of 75 dinners on busy nights for those for whom Home Hill has become a thoroughly engaging gastronomic destination.

The fare is contemporary French with California accents and reflects Victoria's determination to offer nothing but the best, even having fish sent overnight from France for her classic bouillabaisse. Stephan is "my palate," she says. "His family is really into food." He responds that her cooking is better than theirs, especially her sauces.

Dinner is prix-fixe, $49 for three courses, served in three elegant but comfortable dining rooms. Ours began with a couple of complimentary canapés with drinks – caramelized fennel and tapenade with fromage blanc, on toasted bread slices. One appetizer was chilled belon oysters interestingly counterpointed with warm savoy cabbage, periwinkles and littleneck clams. Another was delicious house-made raviolis of artichokes, goat cheese and aromatic vegetables. Seared foie gras enriched a salad of baby arugula with braised fennel and warm grapes poached in olive oil.

A dollop of homemade green apple sorbet prepared the palate for the main courses, which ranged from imported French royal sea bream cooked in a salt crust to roasted squab stuffed with foie gras mousse. We were well satisfied with the house cassoulet of duck and rabbit confit, braised lamb leg, country sausage and white beans, and veal osso buco braised with apricots, onions and white wine.

After sampling a couple of French and local cheeses as we finished a bottle of côtes du rhone from a pricey, predominantly French wine list, we adjourned to the library/lounge for dessert and espresso. The former was a masterful tarte tatin with crème fraîche. Instead of brandy, Stephane suggested Glenmorangie single-malt scotch aged in port wood. For a Frenchman to recommend that over cognac, he said, it has to be very good. It was. So is Home Hill.

(603) 675-6165. Fax (603) 675-5220. www.homehillinn.com. Ten rooms and three suites with private baths. Doubles, $150 to $195. Suites, $195 and $245. Closed two weeks in early November and late March.

Prix-fixe, $49. Dinner, Wednesday-Sunday from 6.

Woodstock Inn and Resort, 14 The Green, Woodstock, Vt. 05091.

Sitting majestically back from the village green, the three-story, Vermont-white Woodstock Inn built by Rockresorts in 1969 replaces an older inn that was torn down. A ten-foot-high stone fireplace warms the lobby, where in chilly weather guests congregate on sofas in front of the always-burning fire. Later renovations and additions created a number of other cozy sitting areas, including an inviting library for card-playing and a rear wicker room where afternoon tea and cookies are served to the melodies of a grand piano.

The 144 luxurious guest quarters are among the most comfortable in which we have stayed, with peppy color schemes, handmade quilts on the beds, upholstered chairs, TV sets, three-way reading lights, and large bathrooms and closets. Nightly turndown service brings chocolates and fresh, fluffy towels. Paintings and photographs of local scenes decorate the walls. The latest addition is the Tavern Wing, designed as three attached townhouses. It features 34 deluxe rooms with built-in bookcases and desks, fine cabinetwork, mini-refrigerators, safes and double marble vanities in the bathrooms. Twenty-three have fireplaces, and three have sitting-room porches overlooking the putting green.

Besides an eighteen-hole golf course, ten tennis courts, an outdoor pool and an indoor sports center, hundreds of acres of forests managed by the inn are available to guests for hiking, horseback riding and cross-country skiing. The woods also contain troves of fiddlehead ferns, morels and wild leeks, which the chef incorporates into his menus in season.

The glamorous main dining room is characterized by pillars, graceful curves and large windows onto a spacious outdoor terrace overlooking the pool, putting green and gardens. Vases of lavish flower arrangements, wineglasses and the inn's own monogrammed, green-rimmed china sparkle on crisp white linens. Off each side of the main room are smaller, more intimate dining areas.

The dinner menu is short but select, and gets high marks under executive chef Thomas Guay, who added a special "chef's hotline" and a participatory "chef for a day" program. Dinner entrées range from oven-roasted Chilean sea bass with smoked tomato-tarragon coulis to veal wellington with Hudson Valley foie gras.

Seasonal specialties include an appetizer of Green Mountain fiddlehead terrine, entrées of sautéed veal with Vermont cheddar cheese and fresh morels and roast loin of pork glazed in maple syrup with apple-prune stuffing, as well as a dessert of flambéed pineapple with maple syrup.

The Sunday buffet brunch, a good value at $23.95, is enormously popular.

You can dine well and quite reasonably in the **Eagle Cafe,** transformed from the old coffee shop and more attractive than most in both decor and fare. At lunch, we've enjoyed interesting salads – chef's, grilled steak, chilled bouillabaisse and seared tuna with wild rice – and, most recently, the smoked chicken and green onion quesadillas and a grilled chicken sandwich with melted jack cheese, roasted peppers and herbed mayonnaise on toasted focaccia, accompanied by assertively seasoned fries. The varied dinner menu repeats some of the lunch offerings and adds entrées from chicken satay to black angus strip steak.

Linger with an after-dinner drink in the sophisticated **Richardson's Tavern,** as urbane a night spot as you'll find in Vermont.

(802) 457-1100 or (800) 448-7900. Fax (802) 457-6699. One hundred thirty-seven rooms and seven suites with private baths. Doubles, $165 to $312, EP. Suites, $325 to $535, EP. Add $59 per person for MAP.

Entrées, $20.95 to $25.95. Lunch, 11:30 to 2. Dinner, 6 to 9. Sunday brunch, 10 to 1.

The Hanover Inn, Main Street, Box 151, Hanover, N.H. 03755.

As its advertising claims, this venerable inn is really "an elegant small hotel." Facing the Dartmouth College green, the five-story, 19th-century brick structure contains 92 Colonial-style rooms decorated with period furniture, handmade lampshades and eiderdown comforters. Hand-tied quilts, coordinating window treatments and Crabtree & Evelyn bath amenities are the norm.

The older East Wing has been remodeled to make the rooms larger and more comfortable, like those of the West Wing. An expanded lobby and a new front entrance are the latest in a continuing series of renovations.

Veteran executive chef Michael Gray, whose credentials include the old Rarities in Cambridge and Seasons in Boston, oversees a menu of contemporary American cuisine, described as "simply prepared but with adventurous twists."

Dining is in the elegant Daniel Webster Room or the more intimate **Zins Winebistro,** a warm and mellow wine bar and bistro transformed in 1998 from the rather New Yorkish-looking former Ivy Grill. The two-level grill has interesting angles, curves, arches and alcoves to go with a new menu of "wine-friendly food."

The Zins menu changes weekly, even daily. A chilly autumn day's appealed enough to entice us in for lunch, even though we had been alerted by previous visitors that the menu reads better than it delivers. Alas, they were right. The staff was in training and had to depart for answers to every question, which did not help matters. We asked for bread – and bread we eventually got, two slices that looked like Wonderbread (a waiter later advised that he had gone AWOL to scrounge up some rolls from the neighboring Daniel Webster Room but they had run out). From the cup of "white bean soup with vegetables" that tasted like lukewarm water with a few beans in it to "Sunja's vegetable roll" that was burnt to a crisp, one meal was a travesty. The other was marginally better, the lobster and crab ravioli at least tasting of seafood but upstaged by the tasty julienned vegetables in the middle. For dinner, the menu offers an interesting selection of "apps and salads," dinner plates, pastas, flatbreads and burgers. The food *has* to be better than what we experienced, and we certainly expected better based on previous visits to the grill. You can order wines by the glass or flight.

More formal meals are served in the gracious, gray and white **Daniel Webster Room,** a vast space in the Georgian style with potted palms, brass chandeliers, and changing food and wine displays at the entry. While Zins is designed for a younger crowd, this is the dining venue of choice for Dartmouth alums of a certain age, although again the menu tells a different story. Typical among dinner entrées are pan-seared yellowfin tuna with scallion roesti, grilled sweetbreads with lemon vinaigrette, braised rabbit leg and macadamia-crusted loin with truffled pappardelle, and roast venison loin with merlot sauce.

In season, meals from both restaurants are available on a shady outdoor terrace overlooking the Dartmouth green. Canvas umbrellas, planters and tiny white lights in the trees make it a most engaging spot.

(603) 643-4300 or (800) 443-7024. Fax (603) 646-3744. Ninety-two rooms and junior suites with private baths. Doubles, $237 to $247. Suites, $287 to $297.

Daniel Webster Room, entrées, $19 to $26. Lunch, Monday-Friday 11:30 to 1:30; dinner, Tuesday-Saturday 6 to 9; Sunday, brunch 11 to 1:30.

Zins, entrées, $11.50 to $16.95. Open Monday-Saturday 11:30 to 10, Sunday 1:30 to 10.

Twin Farms, Barnard, Vt. 05031.

The secluded farm once owned by writers Sinclair Lewis and Dorothy Thompson is now the crème de la crème of small, luxury country hotels, ranked among the finest in the world. One of a kind, it offers six suites and eight cottages, superb dining and a full-time staff of 30 to pamper 28 guests.

The tab? A cool $800 to $1,500 a night for two, including meals, drinks and recreational activities, but not tax or service charge. The clientele? A moneyed international crowd that likes to travel. Twin Farms is deluxe, of course, but understated and not at all ostentatious – not nearly as drop-dead showy as one might expect. "The idea is you're a guest at somebody's country estate for the weekend," says Beverley Matthews, innkeeper with her husband Shaun, both of whom are British and arrived here with impeccable resort-management credentials.

The idea evolved after the Twigg-Smith family of Honolulu acquired the estate's main Sonnenberg Haus and ski area as a vacation home in 1974. In 1989, Laila and Thurston Twigg-Smith acquired the other half of Twin Farms, returning the estate to its original 235 acres. Son Thurston (Koke) Twigg-Smith Jr. and his wife Andrea, twenty-year residents of Barnard, managed the development phase of Twin Farms. Andrea and Ibby Jenkins of Woodstock, Koke's sister, assisted with the interior design and product selection.

Their resources and taste show throughout the property, from the electronically operated gates at the entrance to the fully equipped fitness center and separate Japanese furo soaking tub beneath a pond-side pub reached by a covered bridge. In the main house, three living rooms, each bigger than the last, unfold as the innkeepers welcome their guests. One with a vaulted ceiling opens onto a neat little library loft and soaring windows gazing onto a 30-mile view toward Mount Ascutney. Decor is elegantly rustic and utterly comfortable.

Upstairs are four bedrooms bearing some of the Twin Farms trademarks: plump kingsize feather beds, tiled fireplaces, comfortable sitting areas, fabulous folk art and contemporary paintings, TV/VCR/stereos, tea trays with a coffee press and Kona coffees from the family-owned corporation, twin sinks in the bathrooms,

Vaulted ceiling, chandeliers and fireplaces enhance dining room at Twin Farms.

baskets of all-natural toiletries, and unbleached and undyed cotton towels. They impart a feeling of elegant antiquity, but come with every convenience of the perfect home away from home.

Less antiquity and even more convenience are found in the stone and wood guest cottages, each with at least one fireplace, a screened porch or terrace, a twig-sided carport and its own private place in the landscape. The Perch, for instance, is situated above a small stream and beaver pond. It harbors luxuriant seating around the fireplace, a desk, a dining area, a refrigerator with ice-maker, a bed recessed in an alcove and shielded by a hand-carved arch of wooden roping, a wicker-filled porch where a wood sculpture of a shark hangs overhead, and a bathroom with a copper tub the size of a small pool and a separate shower stall, both with windows to the outdoors. The soaring Treehouse is furnished in Adirondack twig, while the Orchard Cottage is striking in Japanese contemporary. The Moroccan theme in the Meadow Cottage imparts the feeling of being in a desert king's traveling palace.

Good food and drink (from well-stocked, help-yourself bars) are among Twin Farms strong points. Guests meet at 7 o'clock for cocktails in a changing venue – perhaps the wine cellar, one of the living rooms or, the night before our first visit, in the Studio, the largest cottage. A set, four-course dinner is served at 8 in a baronial dining hall with vaulted ceiling and fieldstone fireplaces at either end. Tables for two are flanked by luxurious bent hickory and Guatemalan leather chairs. Although the hefty 32-page, four-color book that serves as the inn's brochure initially noted that guests "are often inspired to dress for dinner," the reality is that more casual attire is encouraged.

The talented chef is Neil Wigglesworth, who came from The Point on Saranac Lake in the Adirondacks, a smaller but similarly grand inn that has been somewhat upstaged by Twin Farms. A typical dinner might start with medallions of lobster with avocado relish and angel-hair pasta, followed by warm red cabbage salad with slices of smoked chicken. The main course could be hardwood-grilled Atlantic salmon with crayfish tarragon essence and a compote of baby fennel, or veal mignon with timbales of wild rice and xeres sauce. For dessert? Perhaps fresh figs with beummes de venese ice cream and peach-caramel sauce, or a chilled soufflé of lime and Bergamot, with dark chocolate tinged almond tuiles. Local and imported cheeses, and a glass of aged port might round out the evening.

A visit to the glittering professional kitchen is instructive – and Neil says he likes to have guests in to "talk and dabble." We enjoyed seeing the three patterns of Wedgwood china (one each for breakfast, lunch and dinner), the pantry wall of table linens in every color and material (there were about 25 sets of placemats and it was like being inside a well-stocked linen shop), the Fiestaware used exclusively for picnics, the fine sterling-silver pieces, the pottery from Miranda Thomas and the glassware from Simon Pearce.

Breakfast is continental if taken in the guest rooms and cooked to order in the dining room from a small menu – raspberry pancakes or eggs benedict with lobster the day we visited. The property is a registered natural organic farm, and Neil and his kitchen staff of five make their own oils, vinegars, breads and preserves, some from the raspberry bushes planted by Dorothy Thompson 60 years earlier.

Lunch is a movable feast, depending on the day and guests' inclinations. It could be a sit-down meal in the dining room, a picnic of lobster and champagne anywhere, or a barbecue beside the inn's seven-acre trout pond or at its own ski area, where there's never a lineup for the pomalift. Afternoon tea is a presentation worthy of the Ritz, complete, perhaps, with little edible gold leaves on one of the five kinds of tea pastries.

The creekside pub, incidentally, is nearly a museum piece with its collection of beer bottles from around the world. Beer-bottle caps cover the light shades over the billiards table, outline the mirror and sconces above the fireplace, and cover the candlesticks on the mantel. Even a pub chair is dressed in beer caps – a dramatic piece of pop art from the Twigg-Smiths' renowned art collection. Such are some of the delights and surprises encountered by guests at Twin Farms.

Now the top inn in the country as rated by Zagat and two-time winner of the grand award by Andrew Harper's Hideaway Report, Twin Farms is opening a sister property in California. In 1999, it bought the Timberhill Ranch, a fifteen-room country inn at Cazadero, near the Pacific Ocean in Sonoma County. The Matthewses, managing directors for both properties, expect to reopen Timberhill in late 2001 after two years of upgrades in the Twin Farms style.

(802) 234-9999 or (800) 894-6327. Fax (802) 234-9990. Six suites and eight cottages with private baths. Suites, $800 and $950. Cottages, $1,150 and $1,500. All-inclusive, except for 15 percent service charge and 8 percent state tax. Two-night minimum on weekends, three nights on holidays.

Lodging

The Maple Leaf Inn, Route 12, Box 273, Barnard, Vt. 05031.

Guests are showered with hospitality at this four-diamond-rated inn built from scratch by Texans Gary and Janet Robison. They couldn't find the perfect old

New England inn in their search among existing buildings. So they built it – a brand new, meant-to-look-old Victorian structure with the requisite gingerbread and gazebo – in a clearing amid sixteen acres of maples and birches in tiny Barnard.

Crackers with a mango-chutney cheese spread or a homemade Texas chili cheese log – incorporating pecans grown in her yard by Gary's aunt and sent as "a CARE package from home" – are served arriving guests on the wraparound front porch with its corner gazebo and Tennessee oak rockers, or inside in the library or fireplaced parlor. Light suppers of soup, bread, salad and dessert are served by request in winter. Two chocolates are placed at bedside at nightly turndown. A small bottle of maple syrup, a packet of wildflower seeds or a personalized maple leaf wood Christmas ornament is hung on the doorknob with a thank-you note for being their guests. And effervescent Janet is apt to send you on your way with a farewell package of pumpkin bread or muffins for midday sustenance. Between arrival and departure, guests are cosseted with unusual warmth and creature comforts, the latter the result of "being able to build what we wanted from the ground up," in Gary's words.

Most of the seven luxurious bedrooms are positioned to have windows on three sides. All have kingsize beds, modern baths (four with whirlpool tubs and two with two-person soaking tubs), sitting areas with swivel club chairs, TV/VCRs secreted in the armoires, ceiling fans and closets. Five have wood-burning fireplaces with antique mantels. Janet spent a week in each room doing the remarkable hand stenciling. She stenciled an elaborate winter village over the fireplace and around the doors and windows in the Winter Haven room in which we stayed. Birds are the stenciling theme in the Spring Hollow Room; foliage the theme in Autumn Woods.

The Robisons' attention to detail continues throughout, from the maple leaf engraved in the window of the front door to the "pasta-hair angels" that Janet fashioned from angel-hair pasta and placed atop bud vases as centerpieces in the dining room. The love stamps that she needlepointed and framed on the dining-room walls were anniversary gifts to Gary and, by extension, to their guests, who take breakfast by candlelight at individual tables near the fireplace.

And what a breakfast! Ours began with buttermilk scones garnished with flowers. The accompanying orange and cranberry-apple butters were shaped like maple leaves, and the preserves were presented in leaf dishes. The fruit course was sautéed bananas with Ben & Jerry's ice cream, an adaptation of bananas foster at Brennan's in New Orleans. The main event was stuffed french toast with peach preserves and cream cheese, garnished with nasturtiums. A savory favorite is a dijon egg puff sprinkled with Italian cheese and confetti bell peppers.

The Robisons' two newest rooms on the third floor carry lower price tags, so getaway couples on tighter budgets may also enjoy the hosts' abundant hospitality.

(802) 234-5342 or (800) 516-2753. Fax (802) 234-6456. www.mapleleafinn.com. Seven rooms with private baths. Doubles, $115 to $190. Two-night minimum holidays and foliage season.

Ardmore Inn, 23 Pleasant St., Woodstock, Vt. 05091.

The guest book at this newish B&B is full of raves about the breakfasts prepared by resident innkeepers hired for their cooking talents. Served at an English mahogany banquet table inlaid with rosewood and seating ten in a formal dining room, the main dish might be pumpkin pancakes, stuffed french toast or vegetable frittata. The masterpiece is the "Woodstock Sunrise," flatbread bearing baked spiced eggs, Vermont cheddar, smoked apple sausage and asparagus with béarnaise sauce. It's designed to look like a sunrise.

In the afternoon, tea biscuits and cheesecake are offered with tea and cider on the rear screened veranda, richly furnished in wicker and oriental rugs.

The guests' raves also cite the hospitality dispensed by Bill Gallagher, owner of the impressive white Georgian Greek Revival house that for years was the home of the well-known F.H. Gillingham family. Bill bought the house with its distinguished palladian windows as "a nice place for my aunts and me" when he retires from Our Lady of Snows church across the street. He called it Ardmore, which means "Great House" in the Irish tradition.

In his booming baritone voice, the ebullient priest likes to point out prized features of the house, including the etched glass in the solid mahogany front door, the circular moldings around the original light fixtures on the ceilings and the recessed pocket windows screened with Irish lace curtains in the living room. The five bedrooms, all with small private baths, are painted in light pastel colors. "That's my grandmother's bed," says Bill of the carved black walnut headboard in the mint-green front bedroom, which is accented with Waverly fabrics and hand-hooked area rugs. "My father was in the marble business," so the bathroom floors are enhanced with marble. The biggest bedroom is in the rear. Called Tarma, Irish for sanctuary, it lives up to its name with a kingsize bed, a loveseat facing a marble coffee table and guardian angels as night lights. The inn's own toiletries are placed in little white baskets.

Lately, Bill added a couple of fireplaces and a jacuzzi to his room repertoire.

(802) 457-3887 or (800) 497-9652. Fax (802) 457-9006. www.ardmoreinn.com. Five rooms with private baths. Doubles, $110 to $175.

The Trumbull House, 40 Etna Road, Hanover, NH 03755.

Lights in the windows welcome guests year-round to this rambling white Colonial house built in 1919 on a hillside four miles east of Hanover. Hilary Pridgen operates it "with the able assistance" of her five children, aged 8 to 19. "The whole family is involved." Her eldest son receives guests and carries their bags, a younger son lights the fireplaces, and her 8-year-old daughter helps with breakfast."

The family, who originally occupied the front of the house, live in the attached barn at the rear. Their guests have the run of the front, including an enormous living room with oriental rugs and several seating areas and tables for breakfast overflow. Breakfast is served whenever the guests want it, in the dining room at a table for six or in the living room. They are offered a choice of entrées, following a fruit course of perhaps honeydew melon with prosciutto or pineapple with cinnamon. "Fat and puffy omelets" are Hilary's specialty, although her menu also includes raisin bread french toast, Mexican eggs with salsa and scrambled eggs with smoked salmon.

Upstairs are four guest rooms and a suite. All have TV/VCRs, telephones, sitting areas with good reading lights, plush carpeting and king or queensize beds with feather comforters and all-cotton sheets. Spacious and extra-comfortable, the rooms are named for the prevailing colors of their décor. Two offer sofabeds for extra occupants and two others add window seats. A second-floor suite has a living room with a queen sofabed and a window seat, a king bedroom with two club chairs, an enormous bathroom with jacuzzi tub, double vanity and separate water closet, plus a second bathroom with a shower.

Behind the house are sixteen acres containing a trout-stocked swimming pond, hiking and cross-country ski trails, and a paved basketball half-court.

(603) 643-2370 or (800) 651-5141. Four rooms and one suite with private baths. Doubles, $125 to $200. Suite, $250.

Gourmet Treats

Alice's Bakery & Café, Main Street at Elm, Norwich, Vt.

What began as a mid-life switch into a wholesale baking business has blossomed into an upscale French bakery, patisserie, boulangerie and charcuterie that's a culinary mecca for the Upper Valley. Alice Kacherian Trent left New York and began baking breads for a single wholesale customer, the Hanover Consumer Co-op. Six years later, she went retail, opening this elegant, country-modern store in a commercial complex in the heart of Norwich. She imported a baker from France to bake her breads in an authentic French bread oven relocated from Strasbourg. The four-ton oven, which has two stone decks and holds a hundred loaves, is the heart of the production facility a few miles away. Alice spends her time at the retail shop, where her classic sourdough baguettes and soft pistolet rolls are stuffed with a selection of cheeses, meats, imported tuna or smoked salmon for delectable sandwiches ($6.25). Regulars from as far as Woodstock sit on custom-made iron chairs with bronze ribbon seats at a counter of Italian granite facing the rear wall of glass and linger over cappuccino. They often purchase some of the French cheeses, the homemade pâtés, the dessert pastries (the hazelnut dacquoise caught our eye) and the assorted prepared foods to go, from Moroccan chicken with peppers to seven-vegetable slaw. The take-out menu prepared for the week by Maria Hall, who had been sous chef at the late great D'Artagnan restaurant nearby, is often sold out in a day. "Everything is select," says outspoken Alice, a perfectionist who knows good food and gets what she wants. "We're doing this more for love than money," adds her husband Walter. Her customers are the happier for it.

(802) 649-2846. Open Tuesday-Thursday 9:30 to 5:30, Friday to 6, Saturday to 3.

The Woodstock area also has a good bakery as well as an excellent farm market. **Pane Salute,** an Italian bakery at 61 Central St., specializes in Tuscan-style artisan breads. Owners Caleb and Deirdre Barber also offer an espresso bar, sandwiches, light lunch specials and prix-fixe dinners on weekends.

Not the usual transient farmers' market, the **Woodstock Farmers Market,** west of the village, is a permanent fixture where you can find not only fruits and vegetables, but "Famous" deli sandwiches, Vermont food products, baked goods, seafood – all the "right" things are here.

Woodstock is chock full of elegant stores – just stroll along Central or Elm streets. The most fun shop of all is **F.H. Gillingham & Co.** at 16 Elm, a general store owned by the same family for more than a century and reputed to have been a favorite of Robert Frost's. It's now run by Jireh Swift Billings, great-grandson of the founder. His is a sophisticated and varied emporium, with everything from spa dessert sauces produced in nearby Norwich to trapunto aprons (embroidered with blue jays, rabbits or squirrels). Fresh fruits (even baskets of lichee nuts) and vegetables, wines, cooking equipment, Blue Willow dinnerware, dozens of mustards, cloudberry preserves from Scandinavia, Black Jewel American sturgeon caviar – you want to cook with it? They probably have it.

Next door is **The Village Butcher** with wines, a deli and gourmet items. Across the street is **Bentleys Coffee Bar and Florist Shop,** which has lovely flowers and twelve flavors of cappuccino, which you can drink at little marble tables amid the plants. **Aubergine,** a good kitchenware shop, is a few doors away. You'll probably find a thermos of the day's coffee flavor to sample, as well as a whole lineup of jams, relishes and salsas to try on various crackers. We particularly like the majolica pottery here. **The Chocolate Cow** offers coffees along with assorted candies.

The historic **Taftsville Country Store,** an 1840 landmark in tiny Taftsville, has the requisite general store and post office in back. Up front are all kinds of upscale Vermont foodstuffs, including jams, chutneys, mustards, wines and maple syrups from South Woodstock. The selection of cheeses is exceptional, and the cheddars are cut to order off 38-pound wheels.

The old mill built in Quechee has been turned into a nationally known glass-blowing center and shop known as **Simon Pearce.** Simon Pearce, the Irish glassmaker, moved here in 1981. It's worth a visit just to see how space is used in his tremendous mill, but it's also fascinating to watch the glass blowers by the fiery furnaces on the ground floor (the main production facility has been relocated to nearby Windsor). You can see the water roar over the dam outside from a floor-to-ceiling window on the second floor, and you can buy the handsome glass pieces (and seconds that are a bit more gently priced), as well as pottery and woolens from Ireland. The table settings are to be admired. Shop is open daily, 9 to 9.

Classy Co-ops

Hanover Consumer Cooperative Society, Hanover and Lebanon, N.H.

To our minds, the area's best supermarkets are off the tourist-path and run by this member-owned co-op. The Hanover original at 45 South Park St., long favored by the Dartmouth and medical intelligentsia, is notable for its automotive service center as well as its enormous selection of prepared foods cooked daily in its kitchens. We picked up the makings here for a grand dinner for our weekend hosts at a nearby lake.

In 1998, the co-op opened a huge new store in the Centerra Marketplace off Route 120 between Hanover and Lebanon. This is the ne plus ultra, a state-of-the-art establishment that emulates some of the co-op supermarkets found in the Pacific Northwest. Here you'll find bulk foods, fresh fish and meats, local produce, wines, a sampling station, a café, more than 200 cheeses, and the largest selection of ethnic and imported foods in northern New England. And, nice touch, the store even has a map and alphabetized directory. You'll need it to negotiate your way around.

Hanover: (603) 343-2667. 45 South Park St. Open daily, 8 to 8.
Lebanon: (603) 643-4889. 12 Centarra Pkwy. Open daily, 7 a.m. to 9 p.m.

Pristine white facade of venerable Equinox resort hotel is symbolic of Southern Vermont.

Southern Vermont
Old Inns, New Style

As verdant as the Green Mountains and as New England as they come. That's the area of Southern Vermont slicing from Dover to Dorset, names that have an English ring to them, but that are the heart of old New England – or is it old New England, new style?

The fairly broad area embraces such storybook Vermont towns as Wilmington, Newfane and Manchester. It ranges from unspoiled Dorset, a hamlet almost too quaint for words, to changing West Dover, where condominiums and resorts thrive in the shadow of Mount Snow ski area.

This is a land of mountains and lakes, ski and summer resorts and, because of its fortuitous location for four-season enjoyment within weekend commuting distance of major metropolitan areas, a center for fine inns and restaurants.

Some of the East's leading inns were established here before people elsewhere even thought of the idea. In an era in which new inns and B&Bs seem to be popping up everywhere, most of those featured here have been around a while, the better to have established themselves in the vanguard of lodging and culinary success.

The food here is far more than Vermont cheddar cheese and maple syrup, as adventuresome diners have known for the last 25 years or so. Many of the area's better dining rooms are found in its inns. Several country restaurants are dining destinations as well.

Dining and Lodging

The Inn at Sawmill Farm, Route 100, Box 367, West Dover 05356.

For a country inn, the Inn at Sawmill Farm has long been one of the more sophisticated. Owned by architect Rodney Williams, his interior-decorator wife Ione, daughter Bobbie Dee and son Brill, who is the talented chef, it is the epitome of country elegance and a member of the prestigious Relais & Châteaux.

Admiring the old barn and farmhouse during ski expeditions to Mount Snow, the elder Williamses bought the property in 1967 and spent the next few years turning it into a decorator's dream.

The rates here are MAP and such that, for many, this is a special-occasion destination: up to $495 for suites with fireplaces in four buildings called cottages. However, the indulgences lavished in any of the twenty accommodations are considerable – queen and kingsize beds, comfortable upholstered chairs with good reading lights, little gold boxes of Lake Champlain Chocolates, plus terrific dinners, incredible breakfasts, even afternoon tea with nut bread and ginger cookies by the fire in the living room. Not to mention a splashy decor of color-coordinated fabric and chintz that nearly overwhelms in one inn room with busy pictures on the walls, but proves more restful in the outlying Spring House and Cider House. The ten outlying rooms come with fireplaces and five sport new whirlpool tubs and separate showers.

The large brick fireplace in the cathedral-ceilinged living room, festooned with copper pots and utensils, is the focal point for guests who gather on chintz-covered sofas and wing chairs and read magazines that are spread out on a gigantic copper table. Other groupings are near the huge windows, through which you get a view of Mount Snow. Upstairs in a loft room are more sofas, an entire wall of books and the lone television set in the inn, which does not seem often to be in use. Anyway, the guest rooms are so cheery that you may not want to leave such private, comfortable surroundings, although in season the pool, tennis court and two trout ponds beckon.

The three attractive dining areas display the owners' collection of folk art. One, off the living room, has a cathedral ceiling, with large wrought-iron chandeliers and Queen Anne-style chairs contrasting delightfully with barnwood and fabric walls. We like best the Greenhouse Room in back, with its indoor garden and rose-papered and beamed ceiling.

You can pop into the cozy bar between the dining rooms for a drink before dinner; crackers and cheese are set out then. The dining rooms at night are dim and romantic: tables are set with heavy silver, candles in pierced-silver lamp shades, napkins in silver napkin rings, fresh flowers and delicate, pink-edged floral china.

Quite a selection of appetizers and entrées awaits, warranting the National Restaurant Association's selection of Brill as Vermont's top chef in 1999. Look for starters like sautéed foie gras with a caramelized onion tart or Scottish smoked salmon with ossetra caviar, onion brioche and a quail egg. The dozen or so entrées range from Indonesian curried chicken breasts to lobster savannah, roasted poussin stuffed with foie gras and grilled veal chop with rosemary sauce.

Guests are served canapés and a basket of hot rolls and crisp homemade melba toast. That will hold you while you choose from Brill's remarkable and quite costly wine compendium (selected annually by Wine Spectator as winner of its grand award, ranking it as one of the 82 best in the world). The house wine is French, bottled specially for the inn, and the côtes du rhône rouge we tried has been acclaimed better than many a châteauneuf du pape. Prices rise steeply, with only a few in the high teens and twenties. Those with a special interest can descend to the wine cellars, where more than 1,200 selections and 32,000 bottles reside. Brill says he does this "more as a hobby than a business," but manages to sell $4,000 to $6,000 worth of wine a week.

For an autumn dinner, we liked an appetizer of thinly sliced raw sirloin with a shallot and mustard sauce and the salads of baby field greens topped with blue cheese. Rabbit chasseur and sautéed sweetbreads were hearty dishes, and the garnish of french-fried parsley on the sweetbreads was both unusual and delicious. Creamed salsify and onion with sautéed cucumber, celery root purée, squash

Main dining room at The Inn at Sawmill Farm is country elegant.

stuffed with pinenuts and maple syrup, and wild mushroom or spinach and tomato timbales might accompany the entrées.

Game specialties include pheasant, partridge and venison with a foie-gras sauce.

Dessert lovers will appreciate whiskey cake with grand marnier sauce, fresh strawberry tart, bananas romanoff, and ice cream with chocolate-buttermilk sauce.

Breakfast lovers will be in their glory in the sun-drenched greenhouse, watching chickadees at the bird feeders and choosing from all kinds of fruits, oatmeal and fancy egg dishes (eggs buckingham is a wonderful mix of eggs, sautéed red and green peppers, onions and bacon seasoned with dijon mustard and worcestershire sauce, placed on an English muffin and topped with Vermont cheddar cheese and baked). Scrambled eggs might come with golden caviar, and poached eggs with grilled trout. Don't pass up the homemade tomato juice. Thick and spicy, it also serves as a base for the inn's peppy bloody marys.

(802) 464-8131 or (800) 493-1133. Fax (802) 464-1130. Ten rooms and ten suites with private baths. Rates, MAP. Doubles, $360 to $395; suites, $420 to $470. Add $25 surcharge during foliage, Thanksgiving and Christmas. Closed April to mid-May.

Entrées, $27 to $35. Dinner nightly by reservation, 6 to 9.

The Equinox, Route 7A, Manchester Village 05254.

In a class by itself is the grand old Equinox, a resort hotel dating to 1769 and renovated to the tune of $20 million in 1985 and again in 1992 for another $12 million. The finishing touches were applied by a partnership whose majority owner is Guinness, the beer company that owns the noted Gleneagles Hotel in Scotland. The Equinox was closed for three months in 1992 to correct shortcomings in the previous renovation. This one, which really made a difference, involved all the hotel's 141 guest rooms and eleven suites, a new lobby, a vastly expanded Marsh Tavern and the formal Colonnade dining room.

The classic, columned white facade now embraces a world of lush comfort, starting with a dramatic, two-story lobby with a view of Mount Equinox, converted from what had been nine guest rooms. All bedrooms have been winterized, equipped with modern baths, TVs and telephones, and dressed in light pine furniture, new carpeting, and coordinated bedspreads and draperies. Rooms come in five sizes (standard, superior, deluxe, premium and suite), and anything smaller than deluxe could be a letdown.

The former lobby gave way to the **Marsh Tavern,** attractive in deep tones of dark green, red and black. The tavern is four times as big as before with a handsome bar and well-spaced tables flanked by windsor and wing chairs and loveseats. We found it too bright one winter's night with lights right over our heads, although the hostess said that was a new one on her – most folks thought the place too dark. We also found the dinner menu rather pricey and lacking in depth, given that it was the only restaurant open in the hotel that evening. Witness a caesar salad with a few baby shrimp for $8, a simple mesclun salad for $5.50, a good lamb stew with potato gratin for $15 (it was called shepherd's pie but wasn't) and a small roasted cornish game hen for $19. With a shared cranberry-walnut torte and a bottle of Hawk's Crest cabernet, a simple supper for two turned into something of an extravagance for $80. Our reaction, we should point out, does not seem to be shared by a loyal clientele, who sing the plaudits of the tavern and its food starting at $8.75 for a burger and steak fries. A trio plays here most nights after 9:30.

The barrel-vaulted ceiling in the enormous **Colonnade** dining room was stenciled by hand by a latter-day Michelangelo who lay on his back on scaffolding for days on end. It's suitably formal for those who like to dress for dinner and splurge for the likes of salmon wellington, pan-seared duck breast au poivre or roasted veal rack and shrimp with a lobster risotto. The short menu details such appetizers as lobster and roasted red pepper bisque, a terrine of lobster with charred sweetbreads, and chèvre and spinach ravioli with a sweet corn and tomato stew. Desserts might be frozen key lime semifreddo with raspberries, and a chocolate-covered strawberry bombe with white chocolate anglaise.

Work off the calories at the Equinox Spa in an adjacent building, which contains a pool, steam rooms, an exercise room with Nautilus equipment, massage therapy, aerobics programs, the works. The challenging Gleneagles Golf Course has been improved as well, and we're told there's no better setting for a summer lunch than the seasonal **Dormy Grill** on the veranda at the clubhouse, where the evening lobster fest and cookout also is a draw Friday-Sunday from 5:30 to 8:30 in summer.

You can learn to handle and free-fly a hawk along the scenic trails under auspices of The British School of Falconry, or learn off-road driving techniques at the Land Rover Driving School and Shop.

If you really want to splurge, settle into one of the suites in the Equinox's nearby **Charles Orvis Inn,** the famed fisherman-innkeeper's former home and inn renovated in 1995 for $2.8 million. From the fly-fishing gear framed in the "lift" to the game room with not one but two billiards tables next to the cozy Tying Room Bar, it takes club-like luxury to new heights. The three sumptuous one-bedroom and six two-bedroom suites come with king or queen beds, stereos and TVs in armoires in both bedroom and living room, gas fireplaces, marble bathrooms, full cherry-paneled kitchens, and rich colors and furnishings in the English style. Charles Orvis "would have approved," according to its elaborate brochure.

Until now, "stately" was the word that came to mind every time we visited this

Expanded dining room at Windham Hill Inn looks onto lawns and pond.

imposing presence. Now it's "extravagant." The golfers and conventioneers who most frequent the Equinox seem to agree.

(802) 362-4700 or (800) 362-4747. Fax (802) 362-4861. One hundred eighty-three rooms, suites and townhouse accommodations with private baths. Rates EP: Doubles, $179 to $329; suites and townhouses, $389 to $589. Orvis suites, $589 to $899. Add $60 per person for MAP, $80 per person for full AP.

Marsh Tavern: Entrées, $15 to $21. Lunch, Monday-Saturday noon to 2:30; dinner nightly, 6 to 9:30.

Colonnade: Entrées, $22 to $25. Dinner, Tuesday-Saturday at peak periods, 6 to 9:30, jackets requested; weekends only in off-season; Sunday brunch, 11:30 to 2:30. Dormy Grill: Lunch daily, 11:30 to 4, late-May to mid-October.

Windham Hill Inn, West Townshend 05359.

Gourmet dining is part of the appeal of this elegant but remote inn on a hill overlooking the West River Valley. Once here, you tend to stay here, which is why innkeepers Grigs and Pat Markham go out of their way to make their guests' stays so comfortable and satisfying.

Five-course dinners of distinction are served nightly to guests and, increasingly, the public, as the innkeepers capitalize on their expanded dining room and on the talents of chef Cameron Howard, who studied at the French Culinary Institute in New York and trained there with celebrity chef Daniel Boulud. Guests gather for drinks and hors d'oeuvres in a bar off the parlor. Then they adjourn to a dining room dressed in pale pink, with oriental scatter rugs, upholstered chairs at well-spaced tables, and views onto lawns and Frog Pond.

Dinner is prix-fixe ($40), with up to four choices for each course. Summer starters might be saffron mussel bisque, smoked salmon en croûte, orange fettuccine with grilled portobello and sherry-ginger sauce, and Vermont quail with lingonberry-amaretto sauce. A salad of mesclun greens and French nut bread come next. Typical main courses are pinenut-crusted fillet of red snapper with rhubarb-pineapple sauce, tamarind-glazed breast of duck with lemon confit, and grilled black angus beef tenderloin with a rosemary-pancetta-red wine sauce.

Refreshing desserts include lavender flan, apricot-ginger mousse cake, berries in meringue and blue moon sorbet..

The wine list, with prices starting in the mid-teens, has been honored by Wine Spectator. Grigs is as proud of his wine selection as Pat is of the accommodations, which have been expanded and upgraded since we stayed here a few years back.

All 21 air-conditioned rooms have private baths, telephones and a stuffed animal from the local Mary Meyer factory store on the bed. Sixteen have fireplaces or Vermont Casting stoves. They're furnished with a panache that merited a six-page photo spread in Country Decorating magazine. We've always been partial to the five rooms fashioned from nooks and alcoves in the White Barn annex, particularly the two sharing a large deck overlooking the mountains and the renovated Taft Room with fireplace, bay window and floor-to-ceiling bookshelves. Even these have been upstaged by three deluxe rooms carved out of the former owners' quarters in the south wing. These come with kingsize beds, two armchairs in front of the fireplace, and jacuzzis or free-standing soaking tubs. Since our stay in the Tree House (so named because it gives the feeling of being up in the trees), it has gained a Vermont Castings stove and an idyllic deck from which to enjoy the view.

The most lavish accommodations are three new extra-spacious rooms in the third-floor loft of the barn. Each has a king bed, fireplace and private deck facing the mountains. Two have double soaking tubs and the other a double jacuzzi. The one in the middle has a winding staircase up to the cupola with a window seat and a 360-degree view.

The Markhams pamper guests with gourmet touches, from complimentary juices and Perrier in baskets in each room to candy dishes at bedside and Mother Myrick's chocolates on the pillows at nightly turndown, when small votive candles are lit.

Besides a new bar room off the living room, common areas include another sitting room and a rear game room with windows on three sides. Outside are a heated gunite swimming pool and clay tennis court, as well as 160 acres of woods and trails.

Full breakfasts are served amid a background of taped chamber music, antique silver and crystal: fresh orange juice in champagne flutes, a buffet spread of granola, breakfast pastries and fresh fruits, and a main dish like lemon pancakes with blueberry syrup or scrambled eggs with chives and sausages.

(802) 874-4080 or (800) 944-4080. Fax (802) 874-4702. Twenty-one rooms with private baths. Doubles, $270 to $395 MAP; $50 surcharge during foliage and Christmas week. Two-night minimum most weekends. Children over 12. Closed week before Christmas.

Prix-fixe, $40. Dinner nightly by reservation, 6 to 8:30.

Deerhill Inn & Restaurant, Valley View Road, Box 136, West Dover 05356.

The former owners of Two Tannery Road Restaurant spent seven years traveling and catching their breath before deciding "it was time to be grown up and responsible again." Michael and Linda Anelli purchased this inn on a hillside overlooking the Mount Snow valley and injected it with the warmth and style that had made Two Tannery such a hit.

The restaurant is the star here, thanks to Michael's cooking talents and Linda's passion for art and flowers. Both turn up in abundance in two dining rooms decorated in the country garden style. There's a lot to look at, from a garden mural and floral paintings to ivy and tiny white lights twined all around.

Award-winning Waverly Room opens onto deck and rear lawn at Deerhill Inn & Restaurant.

The Anellis grow much of their produce, butcher their meat and hand-select the fish for freshness. The fare is contemporary continental-American. Our leisurely dinner began with potato and leek soup and a signature portobello mushroom stuffed with lobster and crab, a couple of tasty treats at either end of the appetizer spectrum. Other choices include escargot bruschetta with tomato-garlic sauce, shrimp K-Paul with spicy cajun fish sauce and andouille sausage, and grilled vegetable tortilla topped with guacamole and salsa.

A good mixed salad preceded the main course, a choice of about a dozen ranging from sliced grilled chicken breast with apple and sweet onion relish to black peppered sirloin steak. The sliced grilled leg of lamb with a wedge of saga bleu cheese and the five-layer veal with roasted red pepper sauce were exceptional. A $25 Forest Glen merlot accompanied from what Linda called "our NAFTA wine list," all North and South American from Chile to Virginia to Oregon. Winner of Wine Spectator awards, it is pleasantly priced in the teens and twenties. Desserts were a refreshing lemon mousse parfait and peanut-butter/banana ice cream in a decorated pastry shell.

The culinary treats continued at breakfast, available from a full menu. Juice and strawberries with cantaloupe, garnished with a pansy, preceded a poached egg in one case, a mushroom and cheese omelet with homefries in the other.

Overnight, we stayed in one of three front rooms off a long, full-length balcony built by Michael and equipped with wicker rockers to take in the view. Each bath here has a whirlpool tub. The queen canopy bed was outfitted with fancy sheets and pillows – "one of my things," explained Linda, who switches to flannel sheets in winter. Two armchairs flanked the fireplace, a pastoral mural graced one wall, and bowls of fruit and candy were at hand. Behind was a swimming pool (since relocated to higher ground for a commanding view across the valley) and prolific cutting gardens that furnish the bouquets for guest rooms and restaurant tables.

Others of the inn's fifteen guest rooms and suites, all with bright and cheery decor, can best be described as eclectic. The Waverly room, named for its decor and winner of Country Inns magazine's annual Room of the Year award in 1996, has a king bed with a picket-fence headboard and a deck facing the rear gardens. Two rear rooms with vaulted ceilings and kingsize beds open onto private decks. In a room with an oriental theme, a fan is displayed on the wall and the queen bed has a canopy of mosquito netting.

Common areas include a couple of fireplaced living rooms, their walls hung with a veritable gallery of local art for sale, a comfy library with TV, and a small bar called The Snug.

(802) 464-3100 or (800) 993-3379. Fax (802) 464-5474. www.deerhill.com. Thirteen rooms and two suites with private baths. Weekends: doubles, $120 to $195; suites, $245. Midweek: doubles $105 to $175, suites $225. Add $40 to $50 for holiday periods and $75 to $80 for MAP.

Entrées, $18.50 to $28. Dinner nightly except Tuesday, 6 to 9:30.

The Reluctant Panther, West Road, Box 678, Manchester Village 05254.
Creature comforts. Fine food. Urbane atmosphere. Intimate setting.

Innkeepers Robert and Maye Bachofen have made the most of these attributes, parlaying the venerable Reluctant Panther into one of the fine small inns of the Northeast since they took over in 1988.

Creature comforts they provide aplenty in twelve rooms in the main inn, striking for its lavender facade with yellow trim, and in four suites in the stark-white Mary Porter House next door. All rooms have air conditioning, TVs and telephones. Twelve come with fireplaces, five have porches or decks and all have king or queensize beds. During our tenure in the Seminary Suite we were enveloped in comfort, although we wished we could open some of the windows on all sides to let in that fresh Vermont air and we rued the lack of good reading lights in the places we wanted to read, namely the sofa and the armchair. The bathroom was deluxe, though not quite as showy as the one we'd observed earlier in the Mark Skinner Suite downstairs. That has a double whirlpool tub in the center of one of the largest bathrooms we've seen, with a fireplace opposite, two pedestal sinks and a separate shower. "If you ever find another room like this, you tell me," Maye said proudly. She found one herself, creating an even larger Pond View Suite lately in a third building. A wide deck with three sets of french doors opening onto it, a living room with a huge fireplace also open to the kingsize bedroom, and a marble bathroom with another fireplace and a double jacuzzi are fit for the most self-indulgent. Sparkly Maye, who hails from Peru, has redecorated most of the rooms in a mix of styles, each with splashy wallpapers, fabrics and window treatments, and goose down comforters on the beds.

Guests find a half-bottle of wine in their room upon arrival. That's a mere preliminary to what's to come in the attractive dining room, crisply dressed in white linens and fine china, and harboring a plant-filled solarium at one end. Robert, who is Swiss and has an extensive background in the food and beverage business, usually does the cooking. The menu changes daily and the contemporary fare is so highly regarded that fully two-thirds of the diners, on average, are from outside the inn.

The room was full and pleasantly vibrant the Monday night we were there. An amuse-gueule – lobster salad in a hollowed-out cucumber slice – preceded our appetizers, an excellent terrine of pheasant with sundried-cherry chutney and an assertive caesar salad topped with three grilled shrimp. Main courses range widely from yellowfin tuna with a lemon-cognac butter glaze and steamed salmon with sage on an olive tapenade to emincée of Swiss veal sautéed with mushrooms, and grilled flank steak marinated in whiskey and maple syrup. We enjoyed the medallions of New Zealand venison with green peppercorns and Beefeater gin

and, one of Robert's favorites, the fricassee of Vermont rabbit with local chanterelles and pearl onions – good but rather rich and more than we could eat. An array of new potatoes, sautéed baby carrots, broccoli and zucchini accompanied. Among the delectable desserts were a fan of berries in sparkling wine around apricot sherbet and plums baked in a light cointreau custard. Maye oversees a dining room in which the ambiance is sophisticated and the service friendly but flawless. She and Robert have put together an exceptional, and quite reasonable, wine list.

The couple serve breakfast at round marble tables topped with floral mats in a fireplaced breakfast room. At our visit, fresh orange juice, a baked apple stuffed with nuts and raisins, and corn muffins preceded a plate of blueberry pancakes

Dining area at Reluctant Panther.

topped with powdered sugar and garnished with blueberries, blackberries and raspberries.

We left feeling well fed and well taken care of. The New Yorkers who make up much of the inn's clientele consider the experience quite a bargain.

(802) 362-2568 or (800) 822-2331. Fax (802) 362-2586. www.reluctantpanther.com. Twenty-one rooms and suites with private baths. Rates, MAP: doubles, $218 to $375; suites, $278 to $575. Midweek in winter, B&B: doubles, $110 to $180; suites, $220 to $325. Two-night minimum most weekends.

Entrées, $19.95 to $25.95. Dinner nightly from 6; weekends only in winter. Closed Tuesday-Wednesday in off-season.

The Four Columns Inn, 230 West St. on the Common, Box 278, Newfane 05345.

This inn has gained vibrant new life and enhanced its dining reputation as a culinary landmark in Southern Vermont. Pam and Gorty Baldwin, New Yorkers who moved here for a lifestyle change, have reconfigured the inn's entry, refurbished the dining room, expanded the rear lounge, added creature comforts and opened several new guest rooms that are the ultimate in luxury.

Through it all, chef Gregory Parks has led the inn to a fourth AAA diamond for dining and has been invited to prepare a dinner for the James Beard Foundation in New York. Starting here more than twenty years ago as sous chef under René Chardain, then the famed chef-owner, he enjoys free rein in the kitchen, where he turns out inventive regional cuisine.

The dining room is in a white building behind the white clapboard 1832 structure containing guest rooms and the four Greek Revival columns that give the inn its name. With beamed ceilings and a huge fireplace, the redecorated dining room has been simplified with new window treatments, pristine white table linens, shaded oil lamps and new stemware. The look is quite sophisticated to match the cuisine. The new look starts in the charming lounge behind a new entry foyer. The lounge has been expanded into one long room opening onto a new side deck with umbrellaed tables overlooking gardens and a spacious trout pond. Inside the bar area are the inn's only TV set and a stunning impressionistic mural of 1850s Newfane progressing through the seasons.

The dinner menu is supplemented by blackboard specials. "Greg's an artist," said his mentor, "so the menu is constantly changing."

Starters are exotic: perhaps yellowfin tuna tartare with American sturgeon caviar and wasabi cream served with a miso tapenade, smoked salmon mousse with assorted smoked fish on pumpernickel croutons and spicy Vermont quail with greens, goat cheese and smoked bacon. A novel warm clam salad with fresh herbs and tomatoes enticed on a recent summer menu. The soup, "composed and priced daily," could be leek and onion with herbed biscuits or potato and spinach with shrimp and green-chile salsa.

International and ethnic flavors influence many of the main courses these days. The chef teams assorted seafood with Chinese black beans, bok choy and a Thai lemongrass broth. Chilean sea bass is marinated in red miso, soy and ginger. Crispy sweetbreads and shrimp are paired with porcini mushrooms and artichoke hearts. A sweet and sour dipping sauce accompanies the grilled black angus steak with portobello mushrooms.

The dessert repertoire here has long been famous. Typical are banana-rum cheesecake, chocolate truffle torte with chocolate-bourbon cream, white chocolate mousse with lemon cream sauce, and homemade sorbets and ice creams. You can stop in the lounge to enjoy one from the cart, even if you haven't dined at the inn.

Afterward, enjoy sweet dreams in one of the fifteen guest rooms on the property. Most deluxe are two created from office space above the main inn's foyer and new stairway. With vaulted ceilings, they offer see-through fireplaces between bedroom and large tiled baths, complete with two-person whirlpool tubs and separate showers. The one in front, Suite 15, has an iron canopy bed, pale yellow walls accented with red-orange, club chairs in the bedroom and a chaise lounge in the bath. Even more dramatic is Suite 12 in back with skylit bath. It adds a sitting alcove and a rear balcony overlooking the trout pond.

Other rooms have been upgraded and gas fireplaces have been added in five, bringing the total to nine. Most have king or queensize beds. All are decorated colorfully with hooked rugs, handmade afghans and quilts. Suite 3, with a four-poster bed, comes with a jacuzzi for two in a marble bathroom that's larger than the bedroom. Suite 18 is newly equipped with a gas fireplace, kingsize sleigh bed and a free-standing soaking tub in a corner near the bathroom. Another favorite is the third-floor hideaway, with trim of old wood and Laura Ashley fabrics in shades of deep rusts. It has a canopied bed set into an alcove, plush beige carpeting and a sitting room with a private porch overlooking the Newfane green.

The longtime breakfast cook prepares a healthful country breakfast. The buffet table contains fresh orange juice, ample fruit, yogurt, homemade granola, hot oatmeal in winter and an assortment of homemade muffins, scones and croissants. The Baldwins added a choice of an egg dish or french toast in the winter, and were planning to offer a full country breakfast year-round.

New innkeepers Stacy and David Hiler at entry to Three Mountain Inn.

The 150-acre property also has a swimming pool, hiking trails, lovely gardens and spacious lawns on which to relax in country-auberge style.

(802) 365-7713 or (800) 787-6633. Fax (802) 365-0022. Eleven rooms and four suites with private baths. Doubles, $110 to $145; suites, $175 to $240. Foliage and holidays: doubles, $140 to $195; suites, $225 to $270. Pets accepted.

Entrées, $20 to $26. Dinner nightly except Tuesday, 6 to 9.

Three Mountain Inn, Route 30, Jamaica 05343.

This venerable 1790s inn looks its age, but took on new life – in more ways than one – in mid-1999. David and Stacy Hiler celebrated the inn's purchase by Stacy giving birth to their first-born, a son. "It was a close race," she said. "We signed the papers at 4:30 and were at the hospital by midnight."

The inn is as much a tale about people as about an aging hostelry in need of new life. The Hilers are joined in the venture by his mother, Heide Bredfeldt, and his stepfather, Bill Oates, well-known inn consultants, who were getting a first-hand taste of what they had been telling prospective innkeepers for years. Vermont native David Hiler had spent ten years in California, where he became the youngest manager in the Hard Rock Café organization. He and his Louisiana-born wife returned to Brattleboro to join the Oates & Bredfeldt consulting business before buying an inn. They found their choice nearby in the Three Mountain Inn, for which coincidentally Bill Oates had arranged the sale to outgoing innkeepers Charles and Elaine Murray two decades earlier.

The Hilers, who live on site, hired a chef to upgrade the dining situation and were adding the first of three luxury units in outlying buildings at our visit. William Hollinger, who trained and taught at the New England Culinary Institute, returned to Vermont from Florida to join the inn as chef. In two cozy fireplaced dining rooms, he offers upscale continental fare with regional Indian and Southeastern accents.

His opening menu gave a choice of soups: white bean and pancetta and a vegetarian Vermont cheddar ale, served with a homemade pretzel from the inn's beehive oven. Appetizers were baked mussels with almonds and garlic, served in a sizzling pan, and a rustic galantine of pheasant garnished with quail eggs, pistachios and truffles. For main courses, Will offered trout en croûte with scallop mousse and shiitake mushrooms, and stuffed his veal with lump crabmeat and St. André cheese. Later options included sautéed sea scallops with truffles and lobster-ginger sauce, striped bass spiced with North African sauce, roasted poussin stuffed with pancetta and wild mushrooms, and grilled beef tenderloin with whole-grain mustard sauce. The signature dessert – pronounced so even before opening – was chocolate silk torte with vanilla poached pears and a crisp cookie crust.

Before or after-dinner drinks are offered in an atmospheric pub with wide-plank pine walls and floors. Common rooms include a large living room with an original Dutch oven fireplace and a library that doubles as a conference room. Oates & Bredfeldt planned to use the inn for training workshops and internships.

For 2000, the Hilers upgraded a number of rooms and now have fireplaces in nine. The seven accommodations in the main house vary from a corner room with private balcony and kingsize four-poster bed in shades of green and rose in the new "Wing Up" above a stable to a couple of simple, cozy rooms. Architect Rodney Williams of the nearby Inn at Sawmill Farm designed the new wing with his trademark barnwood and beamed-ceiling touches, as well as a rear honeymoon cottage. The Hilers built a new cottage on that site with whirlpool tub, gas fireplace, TV/VCR/stereo system, queen poster bed and heated floor and billed it as "true luxury." They planned two more luxury units in a rustic building formerly used as a conference center. Next door in the Robinson House are seven more guest rooms, one notable for a square bathtub and another that the previous owner decorated around a lovely patterned rug. A small living room with a wood stove connects with a bedroom to form the Jamaica Suite. Guests enjoy a large deck out back. An inviting swimming pool is a favorite backyard gathering spot in the summer.

Pecan waffles, french toast, local sausage and eggs, homemade biscuits and blueberry muffins are typical fare at breakfast.

(802) 874-4140 or (800) 532-9399. Fax (802) 874-4745. Thirteen rooms, one suite and one cottage with private baths. Doubles, $115 to $165, suite, $165, cottage, $250. Foliage and holidays: doubles, $125 to $180; suite, $190; cottage, $295.

Entrées, $25 to $35. Dinner, Tuesday-Sunday 6 to 8:30.

The Red Shutter Inn, Route 9, Box 636, Wilmington 05363.

This hostelry nicely blends the old and new: a main Colonial house and adjacent carriage house dating to 1894, a homey restaurant, and contemporary guest rooms and amenities.

The blend was achieved by owners Renée and Tad Lyon, who previously were in the restaurant business in Baltimore. They offer five rooms in the main house with queen or kingsize beds and private baths. The burgundy showing through a crocheted white bedspread is repeated in the wallpaper in one of the handsomely decorated rooms. We like best the rear two-room Joseph Courtmanche Suite with fireplaced sitting room with TV, vaulted ceiling and bay window, its bedroom with a queensize brass bed and full-length windows opening onto a private deck.

Also impressive are the four rooms in the reborn carriage house, especially the fireplaced Molly Stark Suite with queensize brass bed, sitting room with loveseat and armchair, and a bathroom with two-person jacuzzi beneath a skylight. A vintage radio here is juxtaposed beside a new color TV.

Comfortable as the accommodations are, it is dining for which the Red Shutter is best known, thanks to chef Graham Gill from London, who trained in Europe in the French style and whose food we sampled when he was at the Doveberry Inn. Working alone in the inn's small kitchen, he has so enhanced the restaurant's reputation that, despite Renée's background as a commercial chef, the Lyons were not about to change. The pine-paneled main dining room is appropriately Vermonty with shelves of books, cane-back chairs, cloth mats and candlelight. Tables in the narrow back room sport floral cloths, and there's a canopied dining deck in front.

The blackboard menu lists entrées from baked scrod to rack of lamb richelieu. Among the dozen possibilities might be horseradish-crusted salmon with lemon butter, native trout topped with dill pesto, stuffed pork chop with walnuts and apples and Long Island duck with raspberry sauce. Accompaniments one night we were there were broccoli with cheese sauce, oven-roasted potatoes and butternut squash (so good that a guest from Texas phoned afterward for the recipe).

Appetizers might be escargots with wild mushrooms, three-fish pâté with lemon-dill sauce and artichoke ravioli in pesto sauce. Homey desserts include apple crisp and maple-pecan pie, both with ice cream, and berry cobblers. Tad has expanded the wine list, most in the $18 to $28 price range. There's a small honor bar off the cozy living room.

Inn guests partake of a hearty breakfast cooked by Renée, perhaps western omelet with bacon or blueberry pancakes with sausage.

(802) 464-3768 or (800) 845-7548. Seven rooms and two suites with private baths. Fall-spring: doubles, $120 to $175; suites, $205 to $210. Summer: doubles, $110 to $120; suites, $150.

Entrées, $18.50 to $24.50. Dinner nightly except Tuesday, 6 to 8:30, mid-May to mid-October; daily in winter; Wednesday-Saturday rest of year.

Doveberry Inn, Route 100, West Dover 05356.

Glowingly described by a fellow innkeeper as "a diamond in the rough, like us," this small inn has a pleasant restaurant and eight comfortable guest rooms. Michael Fayette, the young chef-owner who trained at Paul Smith's College in New York and 21 Federal in Nantucket, and wife Christine, the baker, offer acclaimed northern Italian fare. They also added a wine bar in the common room, and attract the public for dessert and cappuccino as well as dinner in the evening.

They seat 30 guests in a two-part, beamed dining room with mint green walls and swag curtains. The tables are covered with Christine's mother's handmade quilt overcloths that change with the seasons. The menu changes weekly. Typical starters might be garlic and corn soup, pan-seared scallops tossed with roasted peppers and pinenuts atop homemade spinach pasta, grilled shrimp with tomato-chive risotto and the evening's bruschetta. A salad of field greens is included with the main course. Choices range from sautéed chicken served over a hash cake with orange-tapenade sauce to wood-grilled veal chop with wild mushrooms. Rare grilled tuna over roasted garlic risotto, pinenut-crusted salmon over spaghettini, shrimp and scallops tossed with penne in a light pink sambucca sauce, and roasted duck topped with apples, figs and pistachios are among the possibilities. Christine might prepare mascarpone cheesecake, a plum napoleon or frozen tiramisu with bittersweet chocolate for dessert.

Overnight guests order a complimentary breakfast from a full menu. Choices range from belgian waffles to eggs benedict with a crab cake.

Some of the renovated inn's guest rooms, all with private baths and TV/VCRs, convey a contemporary air. A few have skylights and one luxury room adds a kingsize bed, a private deck and a sitting area. The spacious East Room had a queensize and a double bed, and a basket of apples at our fall visit. A typical smaller double has two cat pillows on the chairs, floral curtains matching the wallpaper (which also covers the ceiling) and a bathroom with copper in the sink and shower.

Overstuffed dark blue sofas and armchairs are grouped around the open brick hearth that warms the large common room. Tea and cookies are served here in the afternoon.

(802) 464-5652 or (800) 722-3204. Fax (802) 464-6229. www.doveberryinn.com. Eight rooms with private baths. Fall-spring: doubles, $115 to $145 weekends, $110 to $125 midweek. Summer: doubles, $100 to $115 weekends, $95 to $100 midweek. Two-night minimum weekends.

Entrées, $18.50 to $28.50. Dinner nightly except Tuesday, 6 to 9.

Dining

Chantecleer, Route 7, Manchester Center.

Ask anyone to name the best restaurants in the Manchester area and the Chantecleer traditionally heads the list – absolutely tops, says an innkeeper whose taste we respect. One of Swiss chef Michel Baumann's strengths is consistency, ever since he opened his contemporary-style restaurant in an old dairy barn north of town in 1981. The rough wood beams and barn siding remain, but fresh flowers, oil lamps, good art, hanging quilts, shelves of bric-a-brac, and navy and white china atop white-over-blue calico tablecloths lend elegance to the rusticity. A pig tureen decorates the massive fireplace.

The contemporary continental menu has Swiss and American touches. Except for staples like rack of lamb, it changes bi-weekly.

Our party of four sampled a number of offerings, starting with a classic baked onion soup, penne with smoked salmon, potato pancakes with sautéed crabmeat and a heavenly lime-butter sauce, and bundnerfleisch, the Swiss air-dried beef, fanned out in little coronets with pearl onions, cornichons and melba rounds. Artichokes stuffed with crabmeat and a terrine of eggplant and roasted peppers with goat-cheese mousse are other favorites among appetizers. Caesar salad is prepared tableside for two.

Entrées range from wiener schnitzel to a mixed grill of rack of lamb, venison medallions and veal chipolata sausages glazed with a port wine raspberry coulis. We savored the specialty rack of lamb roasted with fine herbs, veal sweetbreads morel, sautéed quail stuffed with duxelles and the night's special of boneless local pheasant, served with smoked bacon and grapes. Fabulous roësti potatoes upstaged the other accompaniments, purée of winter squash, snow peas and strands of celery.

Grand marnier layer cake, bananas foster, Swiss tobler chocolate mousse and trifle were memorable endings to a rich, expensive meal. A number of Swiss wines are included on the reasonably priced wine list. Yodeling may be heard on tape as background music.

Michel has added another restaurant to his entourage that earlier included **The**

Window tables overlook Bromley Brook outside Mistral's at Toll Gate.

Little Rooster Cafe in Manchester Center (see Gourmet Treats). Taking over the old Park Bench Cafe just down Route 7A from the Rooster, he and partners opened **Jasper's,** a casual establishment offering a mix of international fare for lunch and dinner.

(802) 362-1616. Entrées, $25 to $33. Dinner by reservation, nightly except Tuesday from 6.

Mistral's at Toll Gate, Tollgate Road, Manchester Center.
The old Toll Gate Lodge was a classic French restaurant of the old school, one of Vermont's original Travel-Holiday award winners with a tuxedoed staff and lofty prices. Brown with bright blue trim and looking a bit like grandmother's cottage out in the woods, it was reborn by young chef-owners Dana and Cheryl Markey, who live upstairs and have given it a personal, less formal touch. Both local, they met as teenagers at the Sirloin Saloon and worked their way through area restaurants before buying the Toll Gate in 1988.

Although the two dining rooms seating 80 are country pretty with dark woods, lace curtains, blue and white linens, and gold-edged white china, it is the views through picture windows looking onto the trickling flume of Bromley Brook that are compelling. After dark, when the brook and woods, accented in summer by purple petunias and brilliant impatiens, are illuminated, the setting is magical.

The menu offers a choice of about ten starters and a dozen entrées, most classic French with some nouvelle and northern Italian touches. Tempting starters include French onion soup gratinée, crab cakes grenobloise, escargots bourguignonne en croûte and venison ragoût.

Main courses range from breast of chicken provençal to grilled filet mignon with roquefort ravioli. Homemade bread and house salad with a choice of dressings accompany. The options could be grilled tuna with ginger cream sauce, sautéed Newfane trout stuffed with scallop mousse, crispy sweetbreads dijonnaise, and tournedos of veal with morels. The specialty châteaubriand béarnaise and rack of lamb rosemary may be ordered for two.

The signature dessert is coupe mistral (coffee ice cream rolled in hazelnuts with hot fudge sauce and frangelico). Others include a complex chocolate godiva cake, praline cheesecake, and assorted fruit sorbets.

While Dana is in the kitchen, Cheryl oversees the front of the house and a growing wine list, honored recently by Wine Spectator.

(802) 362-1779 or (800) 279-1779. Entrées, $20 to $28. Dinner nightly except Wednesday, from 6.

Bistro Henry, Routes 11 & 30, Manchester Center.

We first met chef-owners Henry and Dina Bronson at Dina's, the fine contemporary American dining room they ran at the Inn at Willow Pond north of town. The Bronsons and the inn parted ways, and it took the couple a year to find another suitable place.

Enter Bistro Henry, née Dina's, serving "a slice of Paris" in the center portion of a hillside motel. Once past the motel facade, you're in for a dining treat. The Bronsons' 64-seat establishment looks like the country bistros they enjoyed while living in France – "not rustic, but not Parisian – contemporary Mediterranean," in Henry's words. Assorted toys and puzzles remain the centerpieces at each table. Patrons use them to pass the time and trade with (or help) their neighbors.

The centerpieces indicate that this is a restaurant that doesn't take itself too seriously. Yet Henry's food sparkles with authenticity. Recent examples were grilled rare tuna niçoise, Moroccan grilled chicken with couscous, merlot-braised lamb shank, steak frites and grilled veal chop with pinot noir sauce. The menu was supplemented by tempting specials, among them soft-shell crab sauté, red snapper with orange-basil butter, wild Alaskan salmon with champagne beurre blanc, and risotto with Wellfleet littleneck clams and white wine.

Start with a classic onion soup gratinée or escargots or more innovative pork kabobs Seville style, or grilled vidalia onion with three-mushroom hash. Finish with one of Dina's great desserts, perhaps her ever-famous fruit crisp, gâteau diablo, a praline custard tart with caramel sauce, or lemon sorbet. She sells them retail and wholesale as Dina's Vermont Baking Company.

The wine list merits a Wine Spectator award.

(802) 362-4982. Entrées, $15 to $25. Dinner. Tuesday-Sunday from 5.

Two Tannery Road, 2 Tannery Road, West Dover.

The first frame house in the town of Dover has quite a history. Built in the late 1700s and moved "stick by stick" from Marlborough, Mass., it was the summer home in the early 1900s of President Theodore Roosevelt's son and daughter-in-law, and the president is said to have visited. In the early 1940s it was moved again to its present location, the site of a former sawmill and tannery. It became the first lodge for nearby Mount Snow and finally a restaurant in 1982.

Along the way it also has been transformed into a place of considerable attractiveness, especially the main Garden Room with its vaulted ceiling. It's a many-windowed space so filled with plants and so open that you almost don't know where the inside ends and the outside begins. A wall of windows looks onto the Garden Room from the Fireplace Room, which along with two smaller interior dining rooms has beamed ceilings, barnwood walls and wide-plank floors dotted with oriental-patterned rugs. Charming stenciling and folk art are everywhere. A pleasant lounge contains part of the original bar from the Waldorf-Astoria. A light tavern menu is offered here Friday-Sunday from 6 to 9.

Longtime chef Brian Reynolds stayed on when Karen and Steve Steinfeldt took ownership. Dinners start with a hot or cold soup du jour (hot cauliflower and cold cucumber with dill the night we were there) and more than a dozen appetizers. The country pâté, escargots alsacienne, grilled cajun steak tips and Acadian pepper shrimp are popular. We enjoyed duck livers with onions in a terrific sauce.

Sixteen entrées plus nightly specials range from three chicken dishes to filet mignon with a tarragon-shallot-balsamic vinegar sauce. Veal is a specialty, so we tried veal granonico in a basil sauce as well as grilled New Mexican chicken with chiles, herbs and special salsa, accompanied by a goodly array of vegetables – broccoli, carrots, parsley and new potatoes in one case, rice pilaf in the other. Shrimp lyonnaise or Singapore style, roast duckling and grilled lamb medallions with onions and lingonberries are frequent choices on the changing menu.

A four-layer grand marnier cake with strawberries testified to the kitchen's prowess with desserts. They include a renowned mud pie, frozen black and white mousse with raspberry sauce, apple crêpes and homemade peanut-butter ice cream.

Colombian-blend coffee and espresso end a pleasant meal. And if the dining room is a wondrous garden retreat with rabbits running around the lawn in summer, think how lovely it must be when the lawn is covered with snow in winter.

(802) 464-2707. Entrées, $20 to $26.50. Dinner nightly except Monday, 6 to 9:30 or 10.

Le Petit Chef, Route 100, Wilmington.

Although the renovated 1850 Cutler Homestead looks tiny from the outside, it is surprisingly roomy inside, with three dining rooms and an inviting lounge. The chef is Betty Hillman, whose mother Libby is the noted cookbook author and food writer. Betty studied in France for a year and her menu is rather classic with contemporary accents.

Signature starters include a tomato and goat cheese tart, roulade of smoked salmon with salmon caviar, and ragoût of escargots and shiitake mushrooms. Recent tempters were a lobster and guacamole salad with crisp wontons, and grilled sea scallops on a branch of rosemary with a medley of vegetables.

Among entrées, you might find fillet of salmon baked in a horseradish crust on a bed of mashed potatoes, a crab cake with confetti shrimp on a julienne of vegetables bordered by a Mexican corn sauce, and spicy Cuban grilled shrimp with mango salsa. Others are free-range chicken roasted with garlic and lemon-grass, sliced rare moulard duck with a crisp spring roll and red onion marmalade, and beef tournedos with merlot sauce and morel mushrooms on a pastry crouton.

Homemade lemon sorbet and ice creams, fruit tarts, apple cake, crunchy meringue and chocolate torte are among desserts.

The dining rooms are notable for grapevine wreaths on the walls, oriental rugs on the floors, and cabinets filled with antique china and glass. Tables are topped with white linens, handsome and heavy white china and cutlery, and oil lamps.

(802) 464-8437. Entrées, $22 to $30. Dinner nightly except Tuesday, 6 to 9:30 or 10.

T.J. Buckley's, 132 Elliot St., Brattleboro.

"Uptown dining" along a side street in Brattleboro is how chef-owner Michael Fuller bills this choice little black, red and silver diner with tables for up to twenty lucky patrons. The setting is charming; the food, creative and highly regarded. The city slicker from Cleveland, who came to Vermont two decades ago to ski and to apprentice with René Chardain at the Four Columns in Newfane, does everything here himself, except for some of the prep work, the desserts and serving.

He usually offers four entrées a night at a fixed price of $25, which he's quick to point out includes rolls, vegetables and a zippy salad of four lettuces, endive, radicchio and marinated peppers dressed with the house vinaigrette. At a recent visit, Michael was preparing a neat-sounding shrimp and clam dish with a purée of roasted plum tomatoes and dill oil with shaved fennel and slices of reggiano, to be served with polenta. Other choices were poached Norwegian salmon topped with a purée of Maine rock shrimp and coriander, roasted guinea hen, and grilled beef tenderloin with portobello mushrooms and red wine sauce.

Typical appetizers include an elaborate country pâté of veal and pork garnished with all kinds of fruit, a smoked trout tart with chèvre and a four-cheese tart that resembles a pizza. For dessert, look for a lime-macadamia tart that's very tart, a chocolate-hazelnut torte and a trio of sorbets: kiwi, blood orange and pineapple. Only beers and wines are served, the latter priced from $20 to $58.

Red roses grace the linen-covered tables in wintertime, and other flowers the rest of the year. They add a touch of elegance to this tiny charmer.

(802) 257-4922. Prix-fixe, $25. Dinner, Wednesday-Sunday 6 to 10. No credit cards.

Artistic Gourmet

The Artist's Palate Cafe, West Road, Manchester.

Halfway up a mountain, this seasonal cafe at the Southern Vermont Art Center is a great place for lunch with a view of the sculpture garden as well as birch trees, valleys and hills.

Dine inside or on the outdoor terrace on ice-cream parlor chairs. The changing menu depends on the season's concessionaire. It seems to change every year, but generally is one of the area's better restaurants. At one visit, the menu, attached to an artist's palette, offered choices like crab and asparagus melt over a toasted English muffin, warm ham and cheese croissant, seafood caesar salad (with smoked shrimp and scallops), poached salmon and vermicelli, and a burger topped with Vermont cheddar. We remember a fantastic tomato-orange soup and a good chicken salad with snow peas. Dessert could be a crispy apple tart or melon with berries.

(802) 362-5223. Entrées, $7 to $9.50. Lunch, Tuesday-Saturday 11:30 to 3, Sunday noon to 3, June to early October.

Lodging

Cornucopia of Dorset, Route 30, Dorset 05251.

One of the more inviting and elegant B&Bs anywhere is offered by John and Trish Reddoch, ex-Californians who moved east when they found themselves empty-nesters and wanted to run a B&B. They took over from the original owners in late 1999 and kept everything basically the same. "We'll do a minor improvement or two," said John, "but there's not a lot of room for that."

A onetime manager for the late Magic Pan Crêperie chain, he pledged that Cornucopia's traditional culinary forte would continue. "We're using the same menus and recipes," he said.

Cornucopia lives up to its name, offering an abundance of warmth, comfort and personality. It has only four guest rooms and a cottage suite, but what accommodations they are! All air-conditioned and with large, modern baths, they contain king or queensize poster or canopy beds, all afluff with down comforters or colorful quilts and pillows and merino wool mattress pads. All but one have fireplaces. Upholstered chairs flank three-way reading lamps. Terrycloth robes, bowls of fruit, freshly baked cookies, telephones, CD players and Crabtree & Evelyn toiletries are the norm. Check out the walls in the rear Dorset Hill Room; they are painted in two kinds of white stripes that look like wallpaper. We found the Mother Myrick Room particularly comfortable with a kingsize bed against a wall of shelves containing books and photos. The rear cottage with cathedral-ceilinged living room, fireplace, eat-in kitchen, loft bedroom and a sun deck is a private retreat.

Complementary champagne is served at check-in (wines and champagnes are available for purchase as well). Help-yourself coffee, tea and hot chocolate are at hand 24 hours a day, although a wake-up tray of coffee or tea arrives outside your door in the morning. Upon your return from dinner, you'll find your bedroom lights dimmed, an oil lamp or scented candle flickering, and candy – perhaps a Lindt truffle or a slice of yummy buttercrunch from our favorite Mother Myrick's Confectionery – on the pillow of a bed turned down ever so artistically.

Delightful as the guest quarters are, they are nearly overshadowed by the common rooms. The entire first floor of the house is turned over to guests. The cozy front library has bare oak floors, a leather chair with hassock and a backgammon table. It offers a fireplace, as does the living room with its inviting loveseats. The large dining room is centered by a family-style table on a huge oriental rug. It opens into a contemporary sunroom with comfy seating, where we would gladly while away the hours. More than 50 movies are available for the VCR here. Outside are Adirondack chairs and rockers on Dorset's obligatory marble patio, this one canopied and looking across colorful gardens.

The Reddochs pamper their guests with everything from scrapbooks displaying mounted restaurant menus to lavish breakfasts, the menu for which is detailed on a personalized card left in your room the night before. The meal starts with fresh orange juice and a fruit course, at one visit a colorful dish of honeydew melon topped with raspberries, strawberries, kiwi and banana slices, and French vanilla yogurt. A winter day brought warm spiced applesauce topped with granola, toasted almonds and crème fraîche. Berry and pecan muffins follow. The pièce de résistance was a baked croissant à l'orange with crème fraîche at one visit, a baked ham and egg cup with Vermont cheddar served with a petite croissant at another. The baked raspberry pancakes were so good that we asked for the recipe.

You won't leave the table hungry or the Cornucopia unimpressed.

(802) 867-5751 or (800) 566-5751. Fax (802) 867-5753. www.cornucopiaofdorset.com. Four rooms and one cottage with private baths. Doubles, $135 to $175 weekends and foliage, $125 to $150 midweek. Cottage suite, $255 weekends, $210 midweek.

The Inn at Ormsby Hill, Route 7A, Manchester Village 05254.

Chris and Ted Sprague, who turned the dining room at their Maine inn into a destination for gourmands, now lend their considerable innkeeping talents to this expanded B&B backing up to Robert Todd Lincoln's Hildene estate.

Chris, who cooked six nights a week in Maine, found she could not keep up the pace. "The change has rejuvenated me," she advised after they acquired the Ormsby Hill in her native Vermont. "I'm able to do more creative breakfasts here, and we've reached a level of elegance that would have been impossible in Maine."

The elegance comes in five new luxury rooms they added in an unfinished wing of this sprawling manor house long owned by Edward Isham, an Illinois state legislator and senior partner in a Chicago law firm with Abraham Lincoln's son, whom he entertained here. Each has a gas fireplace, whirlpool tub and handsome decor. Rooms come with interesting angles – "we don't like squares," says Chris – and novel touches, a see-through fireplace between the bedroom and corner jacuzzi in one, a jacuzzi accessed through cupboard doors in another, and shuttered doors that open to reveal fireplaces in a couple more.

The main house already offered five comfortable guest rooms, all with fireplaces and two-person whirlpool baths and separate showers. All contain king or queen canopy or four-poster beds, plush armchairs, antique chests, artworks and oriental rugs. We stayed in the main-floor library room, beamed and dark with well-stocked bookshelves and a wood-burning fireplace. Some are partial to the Spragues' new Tower suite, a three-level affair located in the tower section of the inn. There's a writing desk in the foyer, which leads to a raised bedroom with fireplace, sitting area and a tiger maple queensize canopy bed. The top level has a tiled bathroom with an oversize whirlpool tub in the corner and an oversize shower that doubles as a steam shower for two.

The best part may be the common rooms and the culinary treats. The main foyer leads to a front parlor furnished with antiques. From here one looks to the rear through a spacious library with fireplace into a conservatory dining room extending 40 feet back. At first glance, the total depth, in what is a strikingly wide house, is breathtaking. So is the view across the terrace, back yard, gardens and Hildene property to mountains through the many-paned windows.

Breakfast is usually a lavish buffet, taken in the conservatory or on the outdoor terrace. The sideboard holds three kinds of cereal including homemade granola (which inspired the new Ormsby Hill cereal in a bag being distributed nationally by a subsidiary of Kellogg), a bowl of assorted fruit, a basket of English muffins and two kinds of pastries (perhaps espresso or chocolate coffee cake and blueberry-lemon pound cake). The main dish could be cheese strata, blueberry bread pudding, leek-bacon-gorgonzola polenta or wild mushroom risotto. Dessert is the icing on the cake, so to speak: perhaps peach or apple-cranberry crisp with vanilla ice cream.

From welcoming madeleines and almond crescents upon arrival to a doggy bag of white-chocolate pound cake to take on your way, food is the star at this winning B&B. Surely it contributed to the AAA's new four-diamond rating for 2000.

(802) 362-1163 or (800) 670-2841. Fax (802) 362-5176. Ten rooms and suites with private baths. Doubles, $235 to $275 weekends, $175 to $215 midweek. Foliage and holidays: $295 to $335.

1811 House, Route 7A, Manchester Village 05254.

Bowls of popcorn and no fewer than 65 single-malt scotches – the biggest selection in Vermont, they say – are available in the intimate pub of this elegant B&B full of antiques, oriental rugs and charm. The pub (open nightly from 5:30 to 8) is where owners Marnie and Bruce Duff offer McEwan's ale on draught or one of their rare scotches, $4.50 to $20 a shot or three for $10 for a wee dram of

Conservatory dining room at The Inn at Ormsby Hill is setting for creative breakfasts.

each, if you're into testing. Although it's supposed to be a reproduction of an early American tavern, it looks like a Scottish pub with its McDuff tartan seats and horse brasses, and a McDuff coat of arms above the polished wood bar. A warming fireplace, a regulation dart board and Waterford glasses add to the charm.

Nearby are the elegant yet comfortable parlor and library. Each has a fireplace, dark wood paneling, fine paintings and porcelains, and stenciled flowers of the British Isles (the thistle, shamrock, rose and daffodil). Decanters of port and sherry await guests. Downstairs is a game room with a ping-pong and a regulation billiards table.

The eleven guest quarters in the nationally registered Federal house are air-conditioned and, except for two with double beds, are quite spacious. Three have fireplaces, including a corner main-floor suite with a sitting room and kingsize canopy four-poster bed. The fabrics in the draperies and bedspreads are exceptionally tasteful.

The bedroom of Mary Lincoln Isham (Abraham Lincoln's granddaughter, who lived here for a short time) contains a marble enclosure for the bathtub that she had put in. The Robinson Room with kingsize canopy bed offers a private porch overlooking the grounds, pond and mountains.

An addition in a rear cottage has produced three deluxe rooms with kingsize beds and fireplaces. The largest takes up the entire second floor. It has a vaulted ceiling, and two oversize leather chairs facing the fireplace.

In the big kitchen with a commercial stove, Marnie Duff whips up hearty English breakfasts, perhaps including fresh scones, fried tomatoes, eggs any style or special french toast soaked overnight with pecans. The Sunday specialty is eggs benedict.

Guests partake in the dining room or pub amid Villeroy & Boch china and the family sterling.

(802) 362-1811 or (800) 432-1811. Thirteen rooms and one suite with private baths. Doubles, $120 to $230; suite, $230. Two-night minimum stay weekends, holidays and foliage. Children over 16. No smoking.

Light Fare

The Little Rooster Cafe, Route 7A south of Manchester Center, started as an offshoot of the Chantecleer restaurant, and the chef continues the tradition. For breakfast, the Rooster tops an English muffin with poached eggs, Canadian bacon, creamed spinach and smoked salmon in a light mustard sauce. The french toast triple-decker, layered with smoked ham and pineapple, is served with raspberry butter. For lunch ($6.50 to $8.95), we've enjoyed the crab cake baguette, the leg of lamb sandwich and the grilled tuna niçoise salad. There's a wine list, plus the usual coffees. Open daily except Wednesday, 7:30 to 3.

Across the street is **The Buttery Restaurant** at the Jelly Mill, on the second floor of a fun, four-story collection of shops selling gourmet foods and kitchenware, among other things. It purveys many sandwiches, including smoked salmon on a toasted croissant with capers. The Buttery special is ham, cheese, artichoke hearts and hollandaise on toasted rye. Snacks like nachos, soups, salads and specials such as a tomato, bacon and cheddar quiche are offered, and you can end with neapolitan mousse torte or amaretto bread pudding. Open daily, 9 to 4; weekend brunch, 10 to 1.

More exotic sandwiches and salads are available at **The Village Fare Cafe & Bakery,** Union Street, Manchester Village. Guests at the nearby Equinox resort take a break from high living to lunch on a tuna rollup, a roast beef and boursin sandwich, or quiche of the day in the $6 to $7 range. You can get soup and half a sandwich or a choice of four deli salads with a side of bread. The pastries change daily, but they always include the biggest muffins you ever saw. Stop in the morning for espresso and the pita eggwich (scrambled eggs, peppers, onions and diced tomatoes with provolone). Or come in the afternoon for coffee and a fancy dessert. Open Tuesday-Saturday 6:30 to 4 (to 6 in season), Sunday 7:30 to 4.

Up for Breakfast, Main Street, Manchester Center, is just what its name says: upstairs above a storefront, and open for breakfast only. Although reports on the food lately have been mixed, you'll find pain perdu, cajun frittata, huevos rancheros and belgian waffles in the $5 to $7.25 range. We chose "one of each" – one eggs benedict and one eggs argyle (with smoked salmon). These proved hearty, as did the heavy Irish scone, both dishes garnished with chunks of pineapple and watermelon. Only after we'd eaten did we see the blackboard menu around the side, listing some rather exotic specials like rainbow trout with eggs and mango-cranberry-nutmeg pancakes. Open weekdays 6 to noon, weekends 7 to 1.

For a break from high prices, check out the new **Lion's Share Bakery and Coffee Roasters** at Center Hill and Elm Streets in Manchester Center. The place is up to date, but the prices are from yesteryear. Stuffed croissants are in the $2.50 range and sandwiches, $4 to $5.50. There's nothing particularly exotic, but a cranberry-almond scone ($1.35) and a cafe latte ($1.50) proved a worthy mid-morning break at about half the tab charged by competitors.

Gourmet Treats

Long known for its high-fashion designer outlets, Manchester Center is branching out lately with factory stores of food interest. Besides the predictable **Mikasa, Dansk** and **Harrington Hams, Godiva Chocolatier** and **Baccarat** caught our eye recently.

Peltier's Market on the Green in Dorset has been the center of Dorset life since the early 1800s. A true country store with all the staples, it also caters to the upscale. You might pick up a sandwich from the refrigerator – perhaps smoked salmon or avocado, cheese and tomato. Caviar, good wines, Vermont products like cheese from Shelburne Farms, Peltier's own pancake mix and flavored horseradish spreads, exotic vegetables and prime meats can be found here. So can worms and night crawlers, close by the pesto and sundried tomatoes in the chilled produce case.

Billed as "a true factory store," **Adams Gourmet Woodware** on Route 30 just south of Dorset has a fine selection of cheeseboards, spice racks, butcher blocks, and the like made of native hardwoods. On the second floor, seconds are sold at substantial savings. There's a smell and sound of woodworking in the air, and you can see some of the action through a factory-viewing window.

"Not your average...we cater to all cuisines," advertises the new **Flat Road Diner,** 709-A Depot St. (Routes 11/30), Manchester Center. A handbill cites truck and trailer parking, and gives directions off the ramp from the Route 7 bypass. But many customers seem to be outlet shoppers, feasting on breakfast specialties like crab benedict, cilantro breakfast burrito and Japanese scrambled eggs with tofu. Not your usual truck stop fare are offerings like beefalo burger, portobello sandwich with goat cheese, cobb salad and croque monsieur. You can stop for a beer and a burger at the counter, enjoy a full dinner with a bottle of wine, or just check out the hub-cap collection. Open daily for breakfast and lunch, 6 to 6, dinner Wednesday-Saturday 5:30 to 9:30.

Mozzarella and More

For superior fresh mozzarella, drop into **Al Ducci's Italian Pantry,** Elm Street, Manchester Center, and meet Al Scheps, who has been making his own since he was eight years old. The name of the little Italian grocery is a takeoff on Balducci's in Manhattan. "We have a lot of fun here," says Al, who jokes back and forth with customers. A one-pound ball of mozzarella is $4.99 and, as Al suggests, it is delicious cut into cubes and mixed with ripe tomatoes, red onions, fruity olive oil, balsamic vinegar and cubes of homemade Italian bread, all of which he sells. Good sandwiches ($4.50 to $6.50) are also made with the bread; you can have additions like grated carrots, sundried tomatoes and roasted peppers. Homemade sausage, cannoli and sfogliatelle (a flaky pastry with ricotta cheese) are other goodies. Open daily, 7:30 to 6, Sunday 9 to 6.

In the Mount Snow valley, **Taddingers,** Route 100 at the Haystack Access Road, is an expansive country store with seven unusual shops under one roof. We especially liked the Vermont specialty-foods section, with quite an array from horseradish jam to hot sauces and bread mixes, the Wilcox Ice Cream parlor and the Nature Room, full of more kinds of birdhouses than we thought existed.

Café Tannery, Route 100, West Dover, took over the space formerly occupied by Julie's Café and any number of predecessors. An offshoot of the acclaimed Two Tannery Road Restaurant, it's one of the few places offering lunch in the area. There's a deck in front by the road, an enclosed deck in back beside a stream and a couple of dining areas. You can order interesting appetizers all day, wraps and burgers at lunchtime and entrées from cajun catfish to bangkok chicken to Kentucky bourbon steak for dinner. Open Wednesday-Sunday, 11 to 9 or 10.

Wilmington is home to **Bean Head's,** an espresso bar and bagelry that serves soups and sandwiches as well as gourmet coffees and pastries. Two good gift shops here are **For All Occasions** and **The Incurable Romantic.**

A gaggle of wooden Canada geese on the roof identifies the woodworking showroom of **John McLeod Ltd.** along Route 9 west of Wilmington. The Scotsman produces fabulous bowls, spoons, chopping boards and such. Adjacent is **The Eclectic Eye,** with specialty foods and gourmet jewelry (spatula and teapot pins) among its gift items.

Fine produce, fruit, plants, fresh pies and more are featured at **Dutton Farm Stands,** a fixture along Route 30 in Newfane and with an expanded second location along Routes 11/30 in Manchester Center. Wendy and Paul Dutton grow the produce on their 105-acre Newfane farm and apples on a 30-acre orchard in Brattleboro. In melon season they offer slices of many kinds to sample – an instructive touch, and refreshing, too.

Gourmet Sweets

Mother Myrick's Confectionery, Route 7A, Manchester Center.

Here is paradise for anyone with a sweet tooth. Jacki Baker and Ron Mancini have operated Mother Myrick's (named for a famous midwife) since 1977. Their chocolates and candy are known across the East.

It's fun to watch the confections being made. Using old-fashioned equipment wherever possible (like a two-foot cream beater from the 1940s for fondant), they make a myriad of chocolates, truffles, fudge, apricots hand-dipped in dark chocolate, fancy molds and their most popular candy, buttercrunch, rolled in roasted almonds and cashews, $18.95 a pound and worth every penny.

The best fudge sauce we have tasted (even better than mom's) comes out of the kitchen here. Several flavors of ice cream changing by the season (Irish coffee and bittersweet-pumpkin at a fall visit), stollen, pies, cookies and much more are for sale. The couple's scones are a hot item; the coffee-hazelnut-chocolate chip is delicious. Stop by for sour cream-chocolate chunk coffee cake and superior cappuccino in the morning or anytime for a myrtle (their kind of turtle) or a piece of blueberry-raspberry pie or Vermont maple cheesecake with fresh berries.

These are served to go or to enjoy in the charmingly art-deco cafe or outside on the front deck. They also are available by mail-order

(802) 362-1560 or (888) 669-7425. Open daily 10 to 6, summer and peak periods to 10.

Blantyre, a replica of a Tudor-style castle in Scotland, symbolizes the good life in the Berkshires.

The Tri-State Berkshires

A Tradition of High Tastes

Country inns may seem more historic in Vermont, but they have reached their pinnacle in the Berkshires, an area whose name is inseparably linked in the national perception with country inns and summer tradition.

That may be a result of Norman Rockwell's depiction of the Red Lion Inn and Main Street in Stockbridge, a scene that has come to epitomize the essence of New England for anyone west of the Hudson River.

Indeed, when friends from Switzerland visited us one foliage season and asked to "see" New England in a day, we headed off to the Berkshires and Stockbridge so they could sense what New England is all about. They shot two rolls of color film before departing for Texas.

Had their visit been in the summer, we would have taken them to Tanglewood in Lenox, where the elaborate picnics complete with tablecloths and candelabra on the lawns beside the Music Shed are as delightful a tradition in which to partake (and observe) as the Boston Symphony Orchestra is to hear.

The inns in the Berkshires are keeping up with the times, both in quality and in numbers. And although the area has had good restaurants longer than most resort regions, thanks to its early and traditional status as a destination for summer visitors, new restaurants pop up every year.

As with the inns, the dining situation reflects the sophisticated tastes and often the prices of a noted resort and cultural area close to metropolitan centers.

But there also are rural, rustic charms to be discovered amid the luxury of Lenox or Lakeville and the sophistication of Stockbridge or Salisbury. Seek them out as well, to savor the total Berkshire experience.

Dining and Lodging

The Berkshires are such a popular destination that three-night (and even four-night) stays are the minimum for weekends in summer and foliage season at many inns. Restaurant hours generally vary from daily in summer and foliage to part-time the rest of the year.

The Old Inn on the Green and Gedney Farm, Route 57, New Marlboro, Mass. 01230.

Bradford Wagstaff bought this abandoned 1760 inn on the old Hartford-Albany stage route in 1973 and took ten years to get it back into shape. The result was initially a six-room B&B and a dining room of distinction. He later opened eleven luxurious rooms and suites in a great Normandy-style barn called Gedney Farm down the road and added a sculpture park and farm gallery. In 1999, he bought a house beside the green and restored it to create five top-of-the-line guest rooms furnished in high Colonial style.

In the main inn, Brad's wife, Leslie Miller, a baker who used to supply area restaurants, and chef Kristofer Rowe oversee gourmet dinners served totally by candlelight in as historic a setting as can be conceived. About 50 people are seated in the tavern room, a formal parlor or at the harvest table in the dining room. In each, the original wainscoting, stenciling, antiques and windows draped in velvet are shown to advantage. Pamela Hardcastle's unique handmade wreaths using branches and bark are fascinating, the large mural of cows grazing on the New Marlboro green is wonderful to see, and it's easy to imagine yourself transported back a couple of centuries for the evening.

Where the inn traditionally served only prix-fixe dinners on weekends, it now offers à-la-carte menus the rest of the week in the tavern or on the canopied outdoor terrace in summer. Its culinary claim to fame continues to be the Saturday prix-fixe dinners ($55): a set menu each month with three choices among appetizers, entrées and desserts. Arranged three months in advance for mailing to 2,000 regulars, the quarterly menu makes for delicious reading and is guaranteed to make you think about getting yourself to New Marlboro pronto.

Chèvre and almond puff-pastry sticks accompany drinks, served in delicate stemmed glasses. From a mushroom and herb soup that is the essence of mushroom to the final cappuccino with shredded chocolate on top, things go from great to greater. We can't say enough for both the food and the experience. A recent summer meal began with a choice of fried heirloom tomatoes with roasted fennel sauce, local blue cheese and organic mustard greens; lobster and shrimp salad with mango salsa, toasted pinenuts and frisée, or smoked salmon roulade with smoked trout mousse, roasted pepper-horseradish cream and farm greens. The main dish options were roasted yellowtail snapper with savory broth, wheatberry salad and steamed watercress; farm-raised pheasant breast with apricot-fig jus, sautéed ruby chard and charred asparagus, and a trio of lamb with rosemary glace, truffled potato purée and baby vegetable ragoût. Dessert was bittersweet chocolate sorbet in toasted almond cups with coffee sauce, blueberry and nectarine croustade with crème fraîche, or a tasting of French cheeses.

Besides Leslie's breads and desserts, the couple's specialties are lamb and veal raised on their Willow Creek Farm. Brad's wine list is extensive and expensive, with most bottles $30 and up.

Mural of scene outside graces dining room at The Old Inn on the Green.

The candlelit bar area and rear terrace are popular for casual dining. The terrace/fireside à-la-carte menu is short but appealing. Typical appetizers are Asian grilled shrimp, wild mushroom feuilletée, duck leg confit and herb-crusted oysters. Expect entrées like roasted Chilean sea bass, farm-raised poussin and herb-roasted veal loin.

Upstairs in the inn are six guest rooms, two with private baths, authentically furnished with old armoires, hooked rugs and crewel bedspreads. The second-floor veranda across the front of the inn is a serene spot from which to view the passing scene. A generous continental breakfast – including fresh fruits, cereals, pastries, coffeecake, croissants and homemade preserves – is served on the terrace or in the tavern.

The Gedney Farm restoration is a sight to behold. Beneath the barn's soaring, 30-foot ceiling is a lineup of six guest rooms and six two-level suites, their second floors fashioned from the old hayloft and reached by private staircases. Most have fireplaced sitting rooms. The modern baths are outfitted with Neutrogena amenities; some have deep, two-person whirlpool tubs under glass ceilings open to the roof structure. Leslie has decorated each room with panache in styles from French provincial to Moroccan. Oriental and kilim rugs are on the floors, woven or fabric coverlets are on the beds, and Pamela Hardcastle's exotic wreaths adorn the walls.

And now, crowning glory, comes the restored 1821 Thayer House, which had been owned for 40 years by the late sister of editor Ben Bradlee. Brad Wagstaff bought it and renovated it "from stem to stern," creating "our nicest rooms – more blue-bloody than Gedney." It's a luxurious refuge with a parlor, a fireplaced den, a library and an outdoor pool. A mural of the village green as it appeared in the 19th century graces the foyer. The five guest rooms have fireplaces, baths with marble vanities, bidets, double whirlpool tubs (except for one with a double footed tub) and separate showers. The premier accommodations are on the main floor: a corner room with two queen beds and a private porch onto the pool area, and a rear room with a kingsize bed and sitting area. Upstairs are three more rooms with queen sleigh beds.

(413) 229-3131 or (800) 286-3139. Fax (413) 229-8236. Nineteen rooms with private baths and four with shared baths. Doubles, $135 to $175 in inn, $185 to $285 at Gedney Farm, $300 to $350 in Thayer House.

Dinner by reservation, prix-fixe $55, Saturday 6 to 9:30. À la carte, $21 to $29, Sunday-Friday 5:30 or 6 to 9:30. Closed Tuesday, also Monday-Wednesday in winter.

Aubergine, Intersection of Routes 22 and 23, Box 387, Hillsdale, N.Y. 12529. This classic country inn is the worthy successor to the famed L'Hostellerie Bressane, a culinary landmark since 1971. When French chef-owner Jean Morel and his wife Madeleine decided in 1995 to retire, they approached David and Stacy Lawson to uphold their tradition. David, a native Minnesotan who had trained in London in the French tradition with Albert Roux, had earned his spurs in the Berkshires as executive chef at the Old Inn on the Green and at Blantyre. There was only one remaining step – a restaurant he could call his own. He found it in this rosy brick inn, built in 1783 by a Revolutionary War soldier in the Dutch Colonial style, across the Massachusetts/New York state line at the crossroads of Hillsdale. "I learned this was a thriving corner at the gateway to the Berkshires," says David. "And it certainly was a going concern."

With a change in name to the easier-to-pronounce Aubergine (French for eggplant) and some dramatic changes in the entry, the establishment barely skipped a beat. The lightened-up foyer now focuses on a stunning display (at our late summer visit) of huge sunflowers in a vase, and eggplants, runner beans and squashes on a table. The walls of the men's room are still papered with wine labels and the four smallish, fireplaced dining rooms retain a quaint, somewhat dated look. The fare continues to reflect the French tradition, but the menu is in English and blends contemporary nuances and techniques that quickly earned it a four-diamond AAA rating as a destination restaurant. Smoker dinners for cigar aficionados, wine tastings and cooking classes are among special events.

Three accomplished cooks assist David in the kitchen, while wife Stacy and three of L'Hostellerie's senior wait captains oversee the dining rooms. The silver forks and spoons are set upside down in the European style beside Villeroy & Boch service plates on tables spaced decently apart. Fresh flowers, pretty wallpapers and curtains, and ladder-back or round-back velvet chairs in a plum color convey French country charm. A few tables are set up for overflow in the lounge with its copper bar, where we were seated.

Dinner begins with a complimentary amusé, perhaps a slice of rich country pâté, served on a crouton with cornichons, or triangles of duck confit and scallions wrapped in an Algerian feuille-de-bric. Among starters are a classic caesar salad garnished with crispy fried onions and what has become a signature dish: three Maine scallop cakes with shiitake mushrooms, scallions and bean sprouts, dressed with a warm ponzu vinaigrette. Sautéed Hudson Valley duck foie gras with cracked Szechuan peppers and slow-roasted plums with eau de vie and thyme was a recent treat. Soups (perhaps creamy mushroom bisque with croutons or onion with madeira and cognac) are served from a silver tureen at tableside.

Typical main courses range from panko-crusted tournedos of Atlantic salmon with Thai sweet and sour ginger sauce to skillet-seared sirloin steak with black

Chef-owner David Lawson examines stock in wine cellar at Aubergine.

olive tapenade, caramelized onions and a rich red wine sauce. Two specialties are roasted loin and confit leg of local rabbit with sautéed apples, potato galette and grainy mustard sauce, flan, green lentils, mushrooms and bacon lardons, and roasted breast of squab with honey-vinegar jus and creamy Minnesota wild rice.

The most special desserts here have always been the soufflés, hot or cold, and we'll never forget the frozen coffee soufflé with kirsch, ringed by figs and candied chestnuts. David continues to offer grand marnier and hazelnut soufflés, "as much for theater as anything else." He prefers a classic tarte tatin with calvados-caramel sauce, pumpkin crème brûlée or what he calls a Roux Brothers' lemon tart "in the style of my mentors."

To the distinguished, mostly French wine cellar he inherited, David has added a number of American offerings at fair prices. Rare wines command up to $400 and fine ports up to $200, but a quite decent muscadet and beaujolais can be had for about $20, the same for our favorite Millbrook chardonnay from the Hudson Valley.

Aubergine offers two plain but comfortable guest rooms, each with queen bed and private hall bath, on the second floor. On the third are two more luxurious bedrooms with private baths. One is done in soft lavenders with a queensize bed and one is in coral shades with twins. Continental breakfast (an artfully arranged fruit plate, muffins and scones, and strong French coffee) is available for $10 each. The price is a bit of a deterrent. But, David explains, this is not an inn: "we're adamantly a restaurant with rooms."

(518) 325-3412. Fax (518) 325-7089. Four rooms with private baths. Doubles, $95 and $120.

Entrées, $22.50 to $32. Dinner, Wednesday-Sunday 5:30 to 10.

Blantyre, 16 Blantyre Road, Lenox, Mass. 01240.

Past a gatekeeper and up a long, curving driveway in the midst of 85 country acres appears the castle of your dreams. In fact, the 1902 Tudor-style brick manor built as a summer cottage for a millionaire in the turpentine business as an authentic replica of the Hall of Blantyre in Scotland used to be called a castle. It's full of hand-carved wood ornamentation, high-beamed ceilings, crystal chandeliers and spacious public rooms, plus turrets, gargoyles and carved friezes – just as in the English country-house hotels that innkeeper Roderick Anderson, speaking with a trace of a Scottish accent, seeks to emulate. And emulate it does rather well, as attested by membership in the prestigious Relais & Châteaux group.

Faithfully restored by owner Jane Fitzpatrick of the Red Lion Inn in nearby Stockbridge, Blantyre houses guests in eight elegant rooms and suites in the mansion, twelve more contemporary quarters in a distant carriage house and three scattered about the property in small cottages.

The public rooms and guest rooms are so luxurious in a castle kind of way as to defy description – take our word or that of those who pay up to $685 a night for the Paterson Suite with a fireplaced living room (complete with a crystal chandelier over a lace-covered table in the middle of the room), two bathrooms and a large bedroom with a kingsize four-poster bed. A typical bathroom has a scale, a wooden valet, heated towel racks, embroidered curtains and more toiletries than one ever hoped to see. With hand-painted tiles and marble floors in the bathrooms, newly renovated rooms in the carriage house have balconies or decks and wet bars. Some have lofts or sitting rooms, and all are near the pool.

A continental breakfast of croissants and muffins is served in Blantyre's sunny conservatory. Tables topped with mustard jars full of flowers are set beside windows overlooking gnarled trees and golf-course-like lawns. Additional breakfast items can be ordered for a charge.

Country-house cuisine, lately lightened up in style and made more contemporary by chef Michael Roller, is available to house guests and the public in the formal dining room or two smaller rooms. The tables are set with different themes, the china and crystal changing frequently as Jane Fitzpatrick adds to the collection. Investing in its kitchen, Blantyre added a barbecue for grilling purposes and new and adventurous dishes for what chef Michael considers a savvy clientele with high expectations. Dinner is prix-fixe, $75 for three courses with many choices.

A typical dinner starts with a "surprise," perhaps foie gras or veal sweetbreads with sauternes and carrot sauce. Just a couple of bites to whet the appetite for what's to come – perhaps chilled sweet corn soup with Maine lobster timbale and scallion coulis, a salad of grilled rabbit and roasted summer fruits with frisée, or pan-seared Hudson Valley foie gras with chive polenta, tart cherries and arugula. Main courses could include seared turbot and sea scallops with wilted greens and lemon verbena sauce, roast orange-scented squab with smoked tomato ravioli and cardamom jus, and grilled wild Texas antelope with tarragon sauce.

For dessert, how about bitter Swiss chocolate cake with sour orange compote and blackberry sorbet, white chocolate mousse and plum roulade with ginger-lime sauce, or lemon meringue tart with blueberry compote and passion-fruit coulis? The wine list is strong on California chardonnays and cabernets and French regionals, priced into the triple digits. After dinner, guests like to adjourn to the Music Room for coffee and cordials, Blantyre having the atmosphere of a convivial country house.

Elegant main dining room is set for dinner at Wheatleigh.

Lunch on the terrace ($34 for any two courses and $42 for three courses) is a sybaritic indulgence. Walk it off around the gorgeous property. Play tennis on one of four Har-Tru courts or croquet on the only bent-grass tournament lawn in Massachusetts. The oversize guest book in the entry hall is full of superlatives written by happy patrons. The consensus: "Perfect. We'll be back."

(413) 637-3556 (November-April, 298-3806). Fax (413) 637-4282. Twelve rooms, eight suites and three cottages with private baths. Doubles, $310 to $485. Suites and cottages, $435 to $685. Closed early November to early May.

Prix-fixe, $75. Lunch in July and August, Tuesday-Sunday 12:30 to 1:45. Dinner by reservation, nightly in summer and foliage season, 6 to 9; otherwise, Tuesday-Sunday. Jackets and ties required.

Wheatleigh, Hawthorne Road, Lenox, Mass. 01240.

When he arrived at Wheatleigh as general manager, François Thomas from Paris was so impressed with the inn's executive chef, Peter Platt, that he took him to Paris the next spring to demonstrate American cooking – "the first time that's ever happened back there," he said.

The suave young Frenchman, who had managed a four-star hotel in Bordeaux, was not so impressed with Wheatleigh's accommodations, which tended to be dark, overbearing and cold. That situation changed following a total refurbishing of all seventeen rooms and the addition of two suites. The lodgings are now light and elegant in a sophisticated European style that is appropriate for the extravagant Italian palazzo built in 1893 as a wedding gift for the Countess de Heredia.

Like the French châteaux, says François, the pride of Wheatleigh is its main-floor restaurant. It includes a handsome chandeliered dining room and a large and glamorous glass-enclosed portico. Their round tables are set with white linens, service plates in three patterns, delicate wine glasses and vases of fresh flowers. Three tile murals from England, each weighing 500 pounds, dress the walls of the dining room and acquire a luminescent quality in the candlelight. The portico, pristine in white, is positively idyllic and is now used year-round.

Chef Peter, a 1980 Williams College history graduate, trained at the Cordon Bleu in London and worked under Jasper White and Lydia Shire at the Parker House in Boston before joining Wheatleigh in 1986. Lean and lanky, he's articulate and as down-to-earth as his food aspirations and prices are lofty. He oversees a cooking staff of fourteen, some of whose foreign backgrounds impart an international flavor to what he calls "new French classic cuisine."

Dinner here is serious business. Three four-course tasting menus are prepared each evening – regular (with three choices per course), low-fat and vegetarian, each prix-fixe for $75. You can pick and choose between them. Or the entire table may sample treats from a special, six-course dégustation menu of the night's treats for $95 per.

One recent night's offering opened with a choice of seared medallion of Hudson Valley foie gras with raspberry vinegar sauce, game consommé with roasted breast of squab, or roquefort cheese soufflé with a beet salad and hazelnut vinaigrette. One of the fish courses teamed Scottish salmon and black truffles wrapped in puff pastry with foie gras sauce. The main course could have been grilled veal loin and braised veal shank with sage sauce, roasted saddle of wild Texas antelope with chanterelles, or rack of lamb persille. Desserts included a tropical parfait terrine with a melange of caramelized blood oranges and berries, a glazed chocolate praline and lemon mousse with blackberry coulis, and a thin apple tart served with cinnamon and vanilla ice creams.

Owners Susan and Linwood Simon have doubled the size of the wine list, with a number available in half-bottles. "At the high end," says Linwood, "our wines become very reasonable. If you're of a mind to drink Château Lafite, this is the place to do it."

François was of a mind to make the wines more affordable, adding some in the $30 range – a price point that previously was out of the question. For overnighters, he also added Evian water and bowls of fruit in guest rooms upon arrival, and chocolates at nightly turndown. Also new was a series of cooking classes and food theme weekends. One of the first featured truffles – for a cool $1,450 a couple.

The latest redecorating and refurbishing has vastly upgraded most guest rooms. To enhance the classical Renaissance architecture, the style is a light European look in muted, not-quite colors with a mix of English and French antiques. Bathrooms were redone in imported English limestone or Italian marble, with silver-plated fixtures from England and Bulgari toiletries from Italy. Heavy fabric canopies have been removed in favor of French-designed bedspreads of imported silk. More comfortable seating has been added.

The most exotic is the new Aviary Suite, an unusual two-story affair joined by an outside spiral staircase enclosed in glass. Upstairs are a kingsize bedroom with big windows onto a garden, dark chestnut ceiling and pale brick walls. Adjoining is an expansive "wet room" with an open shower, one of Wheatleigh's original deep soaking tubs and a separate water closet. The sitting room on the main floor is surrounded by glass and opens onto a terrace. Also new is the main-floor Terrace Suite, formed by enclosing part of a portico that matches the dining

Mayflower Inn dining room is appointed in English country-house style.

portico. It has a king bed with fabric headboard and two oversize loveseats in the portico enclosed in glass, bronze and brick, but no lights anywhere to read by. "No one has mentioned that before," our guide advised.

Of the other guest rooms, six are huge, six are medium size and three, frankly, small. Nine have fireplaces and some have terraces or balconies. Susan's aim was to be "true to the period of the house and its architectural style" (it took her five years to find the right pattern of English axminster for the carpeting in the halls). The period can be austere, but finishing touches have been added since the arrival of François. Each room now has a TV/VCR and – a first in our experience – a portable telephone for those who want to be in touch wherever they are. Terrycloth robes, slippers, hair dryers and umbrellas are in the closets. On the walls are large and splashy canvases by painter Daniel Cohen

A portion of the basement has been transformed into a state-of-the-art fitness room with computerized equipment that tallies how you're doing as you watch the overhead TV. Adjacent is a massage room with a masseur on call.

Outside are the joys of a 22-acre property within walking distance of Tanglewood, a tennis court and a heated swimming pool hidden away in a glade.

(413) 637-0610. Fax (413) 637-4507. Seventeen rooms and two suites with private baths. Rates, EP: Doubles, $325 to $585; suites, $585 and $725. Tanglewood and foliage weekends: doubles, $425 to $745; suites, $745 and $975.

Prix-fixe, $75. Lunch in summer, Monday-Saturday noon to 1:30. Dinner nightly by reservation, 5 to 9. Sunday brunch, 9:30 to 1.

Mayflower Inn, Route 47, Washington, Conn. 06793.

"Stately" is the word to describe this renovated and expanded inn, as styled by owners Robert and Adriana Mnuchin of New York and general manager John Trevenen. They took a venerable inn, once owned by The Gunnery school and hidden away on 28 wooded acres, and – with a Midas touch – renovated and expanded it in into one of the premier English-style country hotels in America.

No expense was spared in producing accommodations that are the ultimate in comfort and good taste. Fifteen rooms are upstairs on the second and third floors of the main inn. Ten more are in two guest houses astride a hill beyond.

Fine British, French and American antiques and accessories, prized artworks and elegant touches of whimsy – like the four ancient trunks stashed in a corner of the second-floor hallway – dignify public and private rooms alike. Opening off the lobby, an intimate parlor with plush leather sofas leads into the ever-so-British gentleman's library. Across the back of the inn are three handsome dining rooms and along one side is an English-style piano bar.

Chef John Moran is known for high-caliber regional country cuisine. He changes the menus daily. For dinner, expect starters like house-smoked salmon with crisp lavasch and tomato-caper relish, a Jonah crab spring roll with Thai mango salsa and cucumber salad, and country-style venison pâté with chicory and pear vinaigrette. Main courses might be pan-seared Chilean sea bass with roasted garlic-tomato sauce, oven-roasted free-range chicken with cranberry chutney, and grilled veal chop with a sautéed garlic potato cake. Desserts vary from the simple (honey-roasted pear with apricots and gingersnap) to the exotic (lemon custard chiffon with cranberries and whipped cream, baked alaska with mixed nuts and caramel center, and warm chocolate pudding cake with orange milk chocolate ice cream). The perennial house favorite is the plate of Mayflower cookies, a tasty assortment including perhaps macaroons, thick butter shortbreads and chocolate chip with cocoa. Wine Spectator has honored the expensive wine list.

The setting for meals is exceptional, especially the outdoor terrace with its view of manicured lawns and imported specimen trees.

Each guest room is a sight to behold and some are the ultimate in glamour. We like Room 24 with a kingsize canopied four-poster featherbed awash in pillows, embroidered Frette linens and a chenille throw. An angled loveseat faces the fireplace and oversize wicker rockers await on the balcony. Books and magazines are spread out on the coffee table, the armoire contains a TV and there's a walk-in closet. The paneled bathroom, larger than most bedrooms, has marble floors, a double vanity opposite a glistening tub, a separate w.c. area and a walk-in shower big enough for an army. Even all that didn't prepare us for a second-floor corner suite with a spacious living room straight out of Country Life magazine, a dining-conference room, two bathrooms, a bedroom with a kingsize canopied four-poster, and a porch overlooking the sylvan scene. The rear balconies and decks off the rooms in the two guest houses face the woods and are particularly private.

Across from the entrance to the main inn, a magnificent tiered rose garden tiptoes up a hill to a heated swimming pool and a tennis court. On the inn's lower level is a state-of-the-art fitness center. Such amenities, along with a pampering staff of 85, contributed to the inn's speedy elevation to the ranks of Relais & Châteaux, the prestigious international hotel group whose clientele appreciates the finest.

(860) 868-9466. Fax (860) 868-1497. Seventeen rooms and eight suites with private baths. Doubles, $390 to $550, EP. Suites, $590 to $1,200. Two-night minimum weekends. Entrées, $18.50 to $36. Lunch daily, noon to 2. Dinner nightly, 6 to 9.

The Birches Inn, 233 West Shore Road, New Preston, Conn. 06777.
Young French chef Frederic Faveau has elevated the dining experience at this renovated inn to unprecedented heights. Lured by the opportunity, he and his wife,

Window table at The Birches Inn yields view of Lake Waramaug.

Karen Hamilton, who handles the front of the house and the guest rooms, moved here from Litchfield's West Street Grill.

The spacious dining room, painted coral with eucalyptus green trim, seats 70 at well-spaced tables draped in white over floral undercloths. Big windows look down the lawn toward Lake Waramaug. "The view is beautiful and so is the food," says Frederic, not immodestly. He and two assistants do all the cooking for dinner, and Frederic, who lives on the property, is back in the kitchen to prepare breakfast in the morning.

Frederic's food, which we experienced at the West Street Grill, has earned rave reviews. His short menu might list seven entrées. Their simple descriptions – grilled Atlantic salmon, grilled chicken, grilled pork loin and grilled leg of lamb, each with different accompaniments – do not do justice to the subtleties of taste and complexities of presentation.

Appetizers are lighter and more green oriented than the norm: soups, salads, red beet tartare and roasted garlic custard. An exception is the house mesquite-smoked salmon with a corn blini, scallion crème fraîche, red tobiko and smoked tomato vinaigrette. The herbed potato galette with a ragoût of wild mushrooms, watercress and cognac reduction is a specialty.

The dessert tray reflects Frederic's French heritage: fresh berry tart with almond paste, chocolate marquise with candied orange and a specialty plum clafouti from Burgundy. The wine list is select and fairly priced, and a number are available by the glass.

Under general manager Nancy Conant, the guest rooms and the inn experience are much improved as well. The inn's second floor has been renovated and reconfigured to produce five handsome guest rooms. The lake-view Room 7, the largest, has a king bed, two armchairs, an impressive armoire, TV, telephone and hand-painted bureau. Its bathroom with a double vanity comes with the terry robes, hair dryer and Caswell-Massey toiletries common to all. Most coveted are three rooms in the Lake House. They're smaller but share an extended deck beside the water, and the views are spectacular. "You can almost fish from the porch," Frederic said wistfully as he led a tour. One has a king bed with a brass headboard, a loveseat, a wicker rocker and the inn's only jacuzzi. The other two have queen beds.

Guests enjoy breakfast in the main inn in a sunny room overlooking the front deck. In the French style, it's a meal to remember. Frederic makes his own saucisson, which he hangs for eight weeks, and bakes his croissants, scones and brioches. They and a fresh fruit salad precede the main event, perhaps poached eggs with arugula and a potato pancake.

Wine and cheese are put out in the afternoon in a small parlor with a fireplace.

(860) 868-1735 or (888) 590-7945. Fax (860) 868-1815. Eight rooms with private baths. May-October: doubles, $225 to $300 weekends, $125 to $225 midweek. Rest of year: doubles, $150 to $225 weekends, $95 to $150 midweek. Two-night minimum weekends in season.

Entrées, $18 to $21. Dinner, Wednesday-Monday 5:30 to 9, May-October; Thursday-Monday, rest of year. Closed January-February.

The Lakeview Inn, 107 North Shore Road, New Preston, Conn. 06777.

This successor to the Inn on Lake Waramaug opened in 1998 with surprisingly little fanfare, considering its pedigree. It's owned and overseen by Doug and Dorothy Cann Hamilton, he the head of a New York investment firm and she the founder/owner of the French Culinary Institute in New York. They have a summer house across the street and bought the expansive inn property, razed some of the old chalet-style buildings, and grandly restored the main inn and restaurant to appeal to sophisticated New Yorkers.

The inn maintains a low profile, at least locally. On the late Friday afternoon we were there as the place was being readied for dinner, no one was around to receive visitors, give a tour or offer more than perfunctory answers to questions. We left after a self-guided look around with the inn's understated brochure, a menu and word that further information had to come from the management in New York.

Physically, the centerpiece of the restaurant is a handsome lounge with a horseshoe-shaped bar in the center. André Soltner, founder of Restaurant Lutèce and current master chef for the Institute, donated a small French zinc bar for the restaurant's opening. The Hamiltons built the rest of the large bar around it to match. Reached via the lounge are two attractive white dining rooms on enclosed porches. The larger has a skylit vaulted ceiling and big windows onto an outdoor deck with a glimpse of the lake. The tables are well spaced, set with white linens and fine glassware, and flanked by Hitchcock chairs.

The chef de cuisine is William Lopata Jr., executive chef at the Restaurant at National Hall in Westport between celebrity owners. He coordinates with the inn's executive chef, Alain Sailhac of the Institute, for regional American cuisine with classic French influences.

The menus change seasonally and are as understated as the rest of the place. The straightforward preparations show little sign of innovation and are relatively unembellished to enhance the natural flavors. Dinner starters vary from the

Airy dining room at The Lakeview Inn opens onto spacious outdoor deck.

predictable country pâté and smoked salmon with traditional accompaniments to wine-steamed mussels with saffron cream, fennel, garlic and herbs, and a fricassee of wild mushrooms and lobster with sautéed spinach and tarragon curry cream.

Main courses could be sautéed trout amandine, broiled flounder with mustard cream, roasted free-range chicken, slow-braised lamb shank and grilled black angus sirloin steak. Expect desserts like frozen lemon soufflé, pumpkin pie tart with streusel topping, and apple pie with cheddar cheese crust and homemade vanilla ice cream.

The lunch menu ($10.50 to $15) offers some of the dinner items as well as smoked salmon frittata, a cobb salad with roasted chicken and a grilled black angus burger with house-made fries.

Despite a handful of glowing reviews, the local consensus was that the Lakeview's restaurant is not as good as it ought to be.

Upstairs are five refurbished guest quarters, some quite sumptuous. The largest Scandinavian Suite is furnished in Scandinavian contemporary blue and white with a kingsize country-pine poster bed, separate sitting room, large bathroom with shower and a wet bar/kitchen area. The Burgundian Suite offers a queensize wrought-iron poster bed and a full bath with clawfoot soaking tub and shower. The light and lacy Victorian Room contrasts with the rich reds surrounding the double bed in the Red Room. All have featherbeds, fine linens, sound systems and cable TV. Continental breakfast is included in the rates.

(860) 868-1000. Fax (860) 868-2595. Three rooms and two suites with private baths. May-October: doubles, $225 to $275; suites, $300 and $350. Rest of year: doubles, $175 to $225; suites, $250 and $300. Two-night minimum weekends.

Entrées, $19 to $27. Lunch daily except Tuesday, noon to 3. Dinner nightly except Tuesday, 5 to 9, weekends 5:30 to 10.

The Red Lion Inn, Main Street, Stockbridge, Mass. 01262.

As far as one of our relatives from Montreal is concerned, there is only one place to stay and eat when he's on business or pleasure in the Berkshires. It's the Red Lion, the quintessential New England inn that is a mecca for visitors from near and far.

For more than two centuries, it has dominated Stockbridge's Main Street, its guests rocking on the wide front porch or sipping cocktails in the parlor. Antique furniture and china fill the public rooms, and the Pink Kitty gift shop is just the ticket for selective browsers. The 110 rooms and suites in the rambling inn and seven nearby guest houses are furnished in period decor. All have telephones and air-conditioning, 80 have private baths and most have color TV. The Red Lion also rents a two-bedroom apartment called **Meadowlark,** part of sculptor Daniel Chester French's summer studio at Chesterwood, for $350 a night, May-October.

Dining is formal in the Red Lion's bright and spacious main dining room, where new takes on regional favorites are featured on a contemporary American menu. Entrées run the gamut from roast turkey with the trimmings and prime rib with a popover to – don't these sound au courant? – crispy rice paper-wrapped sea scallops with foraged mushrooms, salsify and truffle cream, and roasted rack of lamb with cumin chickpea pie and ragoût of eggplant and tomato. The menu has been updated in every category, but traditionalists can still start with an enhanced shrimp cocktail and finish with Indian pudding for a meal out of yesteryear.

More intimate dining takes place in the dark-paneled **Widow Bingham Tavern,** everyone's idea of what a Colonial pub should look like. In season, the shady outdoor courtyard lined with spectacular impatiens is a colorful and cool retreat for a drink, lunch or dinner. The same menu is served inside and out. A smaller menu is available downstairs in the **Lion's Den,** which offers entertainment at night.

For lunch ($8.25 to $14.75), you can order almost anything from burgers and chicken pot pie to crispy New England crab and corn cakes with mustard sauce and – a real novelty at a recent autumn visit – a sweet-potato and grilled date salad with smoked cured ham and local goat cheese. Why they even offer a grilled tempeh sandwich with roasted eggplant and olive tapenade on multi-grain bread. The aforementioned relative always gets the caesar salad, which he says is terrific.

(413) 298-5545. Fax (413) 298-5130. Eighty-four rooms and 26 suites, most with private baths. Rates, EP. Mid-April to late October: doubles, $115 to $175; suites, $185 to $450. Rest of year: doubles, $97 to $140; suites, $175 to $375. Two-night minimum weekends June-October.

Entrées, $19 to $29. Lunch daily, 11:30 to 2:30. Dinner nightly, 6 to 9 (5:30 to 9:30 in summer), jackets required; Sunday, noon to 9.

Dining

The Best of the Best

West Street Grill, 43 West St., Litchfield, Conn.

Two of the best meals we've ever had were served at this jaunty establishment, which, we think, offers the most exciting food in Connecticut. It's the subject of universal adulation from food reviewers and is the perfect foil for the Litchfield Hills trendoids who make this their own at lunch and dinner seven days a week. The two dining rooms were full the winter Saturday we lunched here, and the manager rattled off the names of half a dozen celebrities who had reserved for that evening.

Lunch began with a rich butternut-squash and pumpkin bisque and the signature grilled peasant bread with parmesan aioli that was absolutely divine. Main dishes were salmon cakes with curried French lentils and a special of grilled smoked-pork tenderloin with spicy Christmas limas. Among the highly touted desserts, we succumbed to an ethereal crème brûlée and a key lime tart that was really tart.

With two generous glasses of wine, the bill for lunch for two came to a rather New Yorkish $60.

That was nothing, however, compared to the special tasting dinner that Irish owner James O'Shea presented to showcase his summer menu. The meal began with beet-green soup, grilled peasant bread with parmesan aioli and roasted tomato and goat cheese, corn cakes with crème fraîche and chives, roasted beet and goat cheese napoleons with a composed salad, and nori-wrapped salmon with marinated daikon, cucumbers and seaweed. A passion-fruit sorbet followed. By then we felt that we had already dined well, but no, on came the entrées: tasting portions of pan-seared halibut with a beet pappardelle, spicy shrimp cake with ragoût of black beans and corn, grilled ginger chicken with polenta and ginger chips, and grilled leg

Dining room at West Street Grill.

of lamb with a ragoût of lentils, spicy curried vegetables and fried greens, including flat-leaf spinach.

A little bit here, a little there, and next we knew came a parade of desserts: a plum tart in a pastry so tender as not to be believed, a frozen passion-fruit soufflé, a hazelnut torte with caramel ice cream and a sampling of sorbets (raspberry, white peach and blackberry). How could we be anything but convinced, if ever there was a question, of West Street's incredible culinary prowess?

The talented chefs de cuisine come and go, moving on to open their own restaurants. But James orchestrates both the menu and the style. Recent dinner entrées included wood-grilled salmon fillet with green herb oil, quince-stuffed pork loin with port wine reduction, and "super slow roasted osso buco with intense pan gravy."

The long, narrow dining room is sleek in black and white, with a row of low booths up the middle, tables and mirrors on either side, and a back room with trompe-l'oeil curtains on the walls. Lavish floral arrangements and artworks add splashes of color.

Lately, James and partner Charles Kafferman closed Grappa, their outlying Italian restaurant in Litchfield Commons. Charles and a partner, Prasad Chirnumula, who has five Tandoori restaurants in Fairfield and Westchester counties, reopened it as a pan-Asian eatery called **Saffron.**

(860) 567-3885. Entrées, $19 to $27. Lunch daily, 11:30 to 3, weekends to 3:30 or 4. Dinner nightly, 5 to 9 or 10. Shorter hours and closed some Tuesdays in winter.

Church Street Cafe, 69 Church St., Lenox, Mass.

This is the casual, creative kind of American bistro to which we return time and again for an interesting meal in Lenox. Co-owners Linda Forman and Clayton Hambrick, once Ethel Kennedy's chef, specialize in light, fresh cafe food, served inside by ficus trees and eclectic paintings and outside in season on a canopied deck.

The kitchen has lately been tripled in size, the better to produce the blackboard specials that supplement the seasonal menus. Clayton once worked at a creole restaurant in Washington, a background that shows in his Louisiana gumbo and a special of blackened redfish. But expect innovative international twists. Dinners might start with spicy Gulf Coast catfish cakes with creole rémoulade sauce and corn salsa, an Asian grilled beef salad with lemongrass vinaigrette or a smoked salmon and Maine crabmeat tart with cucumber and dilled mascarpone. Summer entrées include pan-roasted halibut with a corn and tomato sauce, grilled Jamaican jerk chicken with black beans and chunky Caribbean salsa, and southern spice-rubbed pork tenderloin with sweet potato fries and barbecued beans. One of the pasta dishes might incorporate garlic-roasted shrimp and vegetables with Thai noodles and a peanut-curry dressing. The Provençal vegetable bouillabaisse employs many vegetables, saffron broth, roasted pepper rouille and Mediterranean couscous.

A recent lunch included a super black bean tostada and the Church Street salad, a colorful array of greens, goat cheese, chickpeas, eggs and red pepper, with zippy balsamic vinaigrette dressing. The whole wheat-sunflower seed rolls were so good that we accepted seconds.

For dessert, try the chilled cranberry soufflé topped with whipped cream, if it's available. Frozen rum-raisin mousse, white-chocolate crème brûlée and bitter-sweet chocolate-espresso torte with vanilla crème anglaise are other possibilities. The house wine is Georges Duboeuf. Two dozen other wines are priced in the teens and twenties.

There are fresh flowers on the white-linened tables and white pottery with colorful pink and blue flowers in three dining areas. Track lights illuminate colorful artworks on the walls at night.

(413) 637-2745. Entrées, $18.50 to $26.95. Lunch, Monday-Saturday 11 to 2. Dinner nightly, 5:30 to 9. Sunday brunch in summer and fall. Closed Sunday and Monday in off-season.

John Andrew's, Route 23, South Egremont, Mass.

"Innovative and spectacular" are words that area chefs and innkeepers employ when describing this culinary star fashioned by Dan and Susan Smith. The Smiths met in Florida while he was cooking at the Ritz-Carlton in Naples. She wanted to return to her native Berkshires and named their restaurant after her grandfather, John Andrew Bianchi.

The sponged walls are a romantic burnt red, the ceiling green and the striking chairs that came from the Copacabana in New York have been reupholstered and repainted green. Metal wall sconces and a tiled fireplace add warmth. At night, the walls "positively glow – like copper," says Susan. The enclosed rear porch, mod in cane and chrome, overlooks an outdoor dining deck.

Chef Dan favors Northern Italian and Mediterranean cuisine on his straightforward menu, which changes seasonally and represents good value.

Sponged walls and tiled fireplace add warmth to John Andrew's.

Favorite starters include tuna and salmon tartare with a salad of pea tendrils, crispy oysters with baby greens and anchovy-mustard vinaigrette, and foie gras and sweetbreads with pear fritter, fig and thyme jam and sherry-vinegar sauce. The homemade pastas might pair fettuccine with wild mushrooms and pinenuts, or ravioli of goat cheese with arugula.

Main courses range from sautéed pistachio-coated skate with port wine and sherry vinegar sauce to grilled chipotle-marinated strip steak. The sautéed duck breast and crisp confit might come with a balsamic and maple glaze, the grilled pork loin with tamarind and green peppercorns.

Desserts include plum crisp with vanilla ice cream, fresh berry lemon tart, chocolate torte with white chocolate chip ice cream and caramelized apple tart with cider crème anglaise. The lengthy boutique wine list, heavily American, is priced from $18 to $90.

The Smiths and several partners also run the casual **Union Bar & Grill** (see below) in Great Barrington.

(413) 528-3469. Entrées, $17 to $24. Dinner nightly except Wednesday, 5 to 10. Sunday brunch, 11:30 to 3.

La Bruschetta, 1 Harris St., West Stockbridge, Mass.

Steven and Catherine Taub – both young alumni of Wheatleigh and Blantyre, where he last was executive chef and she the pastry chef – opened their own winner of a place in 1992. Sticklers for making almost everything from scratch, they offer contemporary and traditional Italian cuisine at down-to-earth prices to an appreciative clientele.

The short but complex menu is strong on pastas, perhaps straw and hay with a sauté of rock shrimp and asparagus, rigatoni with roasted chicken and braised escarole, and cioppino over linguini.

Main courses could be pan-roasted rainbow trout with orange butter and pinenuts, pan-roasted pork tenderloin with a wild mushroom-marsala sauce, and grilled New York strip steak with shallot glaze, grilled peppers, garlic mashed potatoes and housemade ketchup. Osso buco and grilled rib chop are veal possibilities. The sausage sampler yields a spicy garlic sausage, Gunter's veal brat and a mushroom sausage, served with garlic whipped potatoes and rappini.

The namesake bruschetta might come with chèvre, grilled radicchio and black and green olive tapenade. Other starters include chilled poached shrimp with mango-basil salsa, mussels Livorno style, and a salad of baby spinach and frisée with leg of confit duck and oven-roasted grapes.

By all means save room for one of Catherine's incredible desserts, perhaps chocolate-hazelnut cake, a rich chocolate-orange crème with caramel-liqueur sauce, or assorted gelati. The Taubs have fun with their wine list, which is layered in sheets with "our latest finds" on top.

The decor in two small rooms consists of white linens, upholstered rattan chairs, glass vases full of fresh flowers and sheer French curtains draped over the windows. Two big wine globes are part of every setting.

(413) 232-7141. Entrées, $18.95 to $24.95. Dinner nightly except Wednesday, 6 to 8:30 or 9, Sunday 5:30 to 8:30.

The Old Mill, Route 23, South Egremont, Mass.

In the charming and oft-overlooked hamlet of South Egremont, the Old Mill (which really is an old gristmill and blacksmith shop) has been impressing diners since 1978. The atmosphere is a cross between a simple Colonial tavern and a European wayside inn, warm and friendly, yet highly sophisticated.

The large, L-shaped main dining room has wide-planked and stenciled floors, beamed ceilings, pewter cutlery and bottles of olive oil as centerpieces on the nicely spaced tables, and a collection of old mincing tools on the cream-colored walls. Reflections of candles sparkle in the small-paned windows. An addition to a sunken rear dining room provides large windows onto Hubbard Brook.

Owner Terry Moore – a Brit who trained as a chef on the Cunard Line ships – adds a few nightly specials to supplement the ten entrées on the seasonal menu. Appetizers and smaller portions of some of the entrées turn up on the bar menu ($8.50 to $16), available in both bar and dining room except on Saturdays.

The black-bean soup is a treat – hot and thick with pieces of spicy sausage. Other starters might be country-style pâté with peasant toast and cornichons, a lobster spring roll with soy-oyster drizzle, and a Merrimac smoked fish plate with horseradish sauce. Three kinds of rolls are served in a handsome basket. The salad is a mixture of greens, tomatoes and sliced mushrooms..

Of the entrées, which always include the freshest of fish, we have enjoyed broiled red snapper, sesame-crusted mahi-mahi and baked bluefish with ginger and scallions. Veal piccata with a lemony sauce was sensational, and calves liver with sweet onions and apple-smoked bacon superior. Other possibilities might include double-thick pork chop au poivre with apple-ginger relish and roasted moulard duck with cranberry-cabernet sauce.

Of the desserts, we think the mocha torte and the meringue glacé with cointreau

Artifacts decorate walls of beamed dining room at The Old Mill.

and strawberries are most heavenly. Others include profiteroles au chocolat, apricot charlotte and flourless chocolate cake.

The interesting wine list, reasonably priced, is split in origin between California and France, with nods to Italy and Australia. There's a cozy parlor bar for drinks while you wait for a table, a not unlikely occurrence since reservations are not taken for less than five.

The Old Mill's 65 seats may turn over four times on busy nights. No wonder the guest book at the entry is full of praise for food, hospitality and ambiance.

(413) 528-1421. Entrées, $17 to $24. Dinner, Tuesday-Sunday from 5.

Castle Street Café, 10 Castle St., Great Barrington, Mass.

The locals cheered when Michael Ballon, who used to cook at the Williamsville Inn in West Stockbridge, returned to the Berkshires to open his own cafe after several years at upscale restaurants in New York City.

Other restaurants had not had much luck in this space beside the Mahaiwe Theatre, but Michael succeeded first with his bistro, especially on nights the theater was busy, and more recently as well with the new Celestial Bar adjacent, featuring live music on weekends. Artworks are hung on the brick walls of the long narrow room with white-linened tables and windsor chairs. Michael puts out goodies like pâté and cheese at the bar at the rear. The wine bar dispenses a number of select choices by the glass from a selection cited by Wine Spectator.

With appetizers like grilled shiitake mushrooms with garlic and herbs, fried shrimp dumplings, an olive sampler with focaccia, and a mesclun and goat-cheese salad and entrées like a Castle burger with straw potatoes or eggplant roulade stuffed with three cheeses, there is something for every vegetarian and carnivore. Other main courses include pistachio-crusted trout with ginger and orange sauce, grilled cornish game hen, and rack of lamb with garlic and rosemary sauce.

The dessert list is headed by the world's best chocolate-mousse cake, as determined by the late New York Newsday. Others include apple crisp with vanilla ice cream and frozen lemon soufflé.

A bar menu ($5 to $12) offers light fare, from an eggplant napoleon to meatloaf with mashed potatoes. Michael makes a point of buying from Berkshire farmers and purveyors, whom he acknowledges on the back of his menu.

(413) 528-5244. Entrées, $16 to $22. Dinner nightly except Tuesday, 5 to 9:30 or 10:30.

Bistro Zinc, 56 Church St., Lenox, Mass.

The beautiful bar is a big deal at this stylish new bar and bistro.

Made of ribbon-stripe mahogany and topped with polished zinc, it curves gracefully for 30 feet along the side of the rear cocktail lounge. Windows behind interrupt here and there to let in light, and three rows of bar shelves are backlit to illuminate bottles from Zinc's extensive liquor inventory. The room itself is cheerful with lemon yellow walls above rich wood wainscoting between a floor of rock maple and a silver ceiling of stamped tin. The custom-made bar stools and chairs with reddish leather cushions are distinctive for the circular holes in their backs – part of the Zinc logo signed Zn, the chemical symbol for zinc. Everything is done with style, from the unique, rectangular matchboxes in the bar's amber blue ashtrays to the china bearing a small Zinc logo, from the wall full of fine framed photographs by the co-owner's wife to the restroom doors made of lettered wood wine crates. Not to mention the sophisticated little "bar book," a 36-page, four-color giveaway that itemizes with photos much of the beverage stock.

Credit Lenox architect Frank Macioge with the stunning design for Zinc, both for the bar as well as the bistro in front. Credit Judith Gordon Macioge, a partner in the Mary Stuart Collections shop across the street, with the spectacular floral arrangements in the foyer and restrooms (one at our November visit was a lavish display of yellow roses and bittersweet, an unlikely combination that worked). Credit their son Jason and a friend of the family, Charles Schultz, for the vision that led to Zinc's opening in 1999. Jason had worked in Canadian restaurants during and after college and wanted to open his own back home. Charles, who is in real estate and has a farm in France, bought the building that now houses Zinc. They leave the cooking to chef Rob Ferris, who returned to the Berkshires after cooking with Lydia Shire at Biba in Boston.

French authenticity and nuances are everywhere evident. The mustard on the tables is Dijon, and water is poured from antique glass bottles inscribed in French with the date 1895. The menu is so authentic as to be a bit ho-hum, as real French bistro menus tend to be. The food, though rather minimal in portion, is not at all ho-hum. We lunched in the bar on a lovely French onion soup gruyère, a salad of goat cheese, arugula and roasted tomato, and a special entrée of cumin-crusted lamb with couscous. The salad was mostly goat cheese, and cried out for bread upon which it could be spread (the bread was doled out as sparingly as the few leaves of arugula and a single tiny roasted tomato). The lamb was sensational, fanned around couscous that never before tasted so delectable. A not-so-classic tarte tatin was nonetheless delicious, paired with vanilla ice cream drizzled with caramel sauce. The bill was presented in a Zinc folder with a postcard.

The bar seats 50 at tables and stools, the same number as can be served in the mirrored front dining room, full of cherry trim, mirrors, mosaic tiled floors and white-clothed tables squeezed together in the convivial bistro style. The abbreviated

Walls of mirrors and windows convey bistro look in front dining room at Bistro Zinc.

menu we sampled at lunch is similar but much expanded at night. Expect appetizers like a charcuterie plate, rabbit pâté, Vietnamese pork spring rolls, roasted quail stuffed with apricot and braised greens in puff pastry, and salads, one of frisée with pancetta and a poached egg. Typical entrées are oven-roasted salmon with mousseline sauce, wood-roasted free-range chicken, steak frites, and grilled lamb loin with wild mushrooms. Desserts at our visit were vanilla crème brûlée, profiterole with mocha ice cream, something called "birthday cake" and a platter of petits fours, lemon tart and cookies.

The all-French wine list is priced in the twenties (a house carafe goes for $18), although there's a large selection from the reserve cellar. The bar book touts American single-barrel bourbons and single-malt scotches from Scotland. "There were a lot of high-end restaurants but no bars in town," said Jason. "We tried to fill a niche, and so far it's gone over very well."

(413) 637-8800. Entrées, $17 to $21. Lunch, Wednesday-Monday 11:30 to 3. Dinner, Wednesday-Monday 5:30 to 10.

The Cannery, 85 Main St., Canaan, Conn.
The most prolific flowers and herbs spill forth from window boxes outside this downtown storefront – quite a surprise, since the boxes face north and would appear to be shaded all day. Surprises also emanate from the kitchen of the small American bistro, which retains the name of its predecessor in which canning jars were the theme.

Chef-owner William O'Meara lightened up the formerly homey decor with pale yellow walls bearing gold stars. A paneled divider with a windowed arch separates the small front dining room and the rear bar. White cloths, votive candles and fresh flowers in tall, thin glass vases dress the tables and a handful of booths.

Bill's imaginative contemporary American fare is highly regarded across the tri-state Berkshires. A basket of Italian and sourdough breads with a tasty spread of eggplant caponata arrives with the menu. At our fall visit, we were tempted by starters like pan-seared scallops with lemon-thyme butter, garlicky steamed cockles in tomato broth, sautéed calamari tossed with pesto and greens, and a warm goat cheese and arugula salad with herb croutons.

Main courses ranged from pan-roasted monkfish with soy-ginger butter and udon noodles to lamb loin chops with arugula oil and potato cake. Especially appealing were the spice-rubbed salmon with fennel, the braised rabbit with oven-roasted tomato sauce and polenta, and the duck breast with lentil salad and root vegetables. Desserts included apple brown betty with calvados crème anglaise, chocolate mousse terrine with raspberry sauce and pear-almond tart with caramel sauce. Except for a few pricier tokens for connoisseurs, the choice wine list is priced in the teens and twenties.

(860) 824-7333. Entrées, $18 to $24. Dinner nightly except Tuesday, 5 to 9 or 10. Sunday brunch, 11 to 2.

West Main at Pocket Knife Square, 8 Holley Place, Lakeville, Conn.
The highly rated little West Main Café up and moved at the turn of the millennium from an intimate house in Sharon to a vacant restaurant in Lakeville. "We'd been looking for larger quarters for some time," said co-owner Susan Miller. "This was a place just waiting for someone to move in."

Indeed, the lower floor of the imposing red brick mill-type structure that formerly was the Holley Manufacturing Co. knife factory had been beautifully transformed in the 1980s into a restaurant called Holley Place. Its 40-foot-long serpentine bar of mahogany, etched-glass doors and interior skylit atrium remained intact. Susan undertook a refurbishing to "infuse this great old historic building with funky stuff, cool lighting and more of an upbeat New York look." There are two dining areas – casual with paper table covers and crayons in the bar and more formal with an Asian theme in the atrium room, whose walls of huge honey-colored stones are set off with aqua blue accents. An outdoor terrace is open in summer.

Hotshot chef Matthew Fahrner, who earned his spurs at Litchfield's West Street Grill, continues to make the kitchen sing, as he has since he and Susan left the late Bee Brook restaurant in Washington Depot to open their own place. The entire team from Sharon moved into the relocated quarters, where Susan is in partnership with Bill Harris, who owned the former Harris Foods specialty store in Salisbury. Their boutique wine list is really select, and about half are priced in the twenties.

As in earlier venues, Matt proved to be a master of innovation and assertive flavors. Our latest lunch began with an appetizer of his signature crisp vegetable rolls served with sweet-pea shoots and pickled cucumber salad, all bursting with intense tastes. One of us went on to an appetizer of lightly fried oysters served with garlic, mustard and anchovy mayonnaise. The other had an entrée of Asian chicken salad, piled high in the architectural style on a Japanese tray with spicy peanuts and crisp wontons. We dipped rosemary and black olive breads in olive oil, and finished with a fabulous banana napoleon that literally melted in the mouth.

The fusion menu changes monthly, and many of the lunchtime treats show up for dinner. Expect appetizers like a smoked salmon and brie quesadilla with mango-chile salsa, sesame shrimp toast with mandarin-ginger sauce, and carpaccio of portobello with collard greens. For main courses, how about tempura-style catfish with mirin-ginger sauce, bok choy and sweet potato matchsticks; chevrè-stuffed free-range chicken with shiitake crisps and butternut squash risotto, or grilled New York strip steak with cracked pepper, scallion and gorgonzola sauce?

Cool off with one of Susan's refreshing desserts, perhaps hot and cold chocolate

Antique furnishings are for sale in upstairs dining room at Charlotte.

torte with berry coulis, ginger crème brûlée or sorbet with pomegranates. The tastes will linger in your memory.

(860) 435-1450. Entrées, $17.50 to $20.95. Lunch, Wednesday-Monday noon to 3. Dinner, Wednesday-Monday 5:30 to 9 or 10. Also closed Wednesday in off-season.

Charlotte, Main Street (Route 44), Lakeville, Conn.

Antiques. Innovative cuisine. An atmospheric wine bar.

These are the hallmarks of an unusual establishment opened by two culinary enthusiasts who met at the New England Culinary Institute and talked of launching a restaurant together. They named it for the owner's black labrador retriever.

No ordinary restaurant, theirs. It's very contemporary, yet ensconced in a handsome white house dating to 1775. James Simpson, the proprietor-sommelier, worked for a large wine importer in Boston. His focus is on the main-floor wine bar offering cheeses, exotic light fare and flights of wine (there's also a living room where customers wait for tables or play backgammon). Aspen-trained chef Charles Norman heads the kitchen, sending innovative plates upstairs to a spacious dining room where all the tables and chairs are different and the furnishings are for sale. They are provided by Hammertown Barn, the great country furnishings store across the New York line in Pine Plains. Diners can purchase the mostly one-of-a-kind antique tables and decorative accents that Hammertown owner Joan Osofsky turns up from England and France.

Chef Charlie, a Montana native, apprenticed with George Mahaffey at the four-star Little Nell in Aspen before moving to a neighboring four-star hotel, the Sardy House, where he was executive chef. He returned east to be best man at Jamey's wedding to the former Dana Osofsky. There he met (and soon married) the bride's cousin. He brought to Charlotte several Southwest dishes imparting a cosmopolitan flair that he describes as "new world bistro."

Consider such starters as Southwest caesar salad enlivened with red peppers, jicama, roasted corn and chipotle dressing; a salad of duck confit and quinoa tossed with matchstick apples, morels and leaf lettuces; a terrine of foie gras with pistachio, leeks and pomegranate syrup. Most unusual is the beet carpaccio: thinly sliced roasted beets and matzoh-encrusted herbed goat cheese drizzled with clove oil and twenty-year-old balsamico.

Main courses vary from grilled Atlantic salmon on lemongrass mashed potatoes with a carrot-ginger emulsion and wasabi pesto to roasted duck breast and leg confit served with penne pasta, peas, carrots and haricots verts in a mushroom sherry cream. Charlie touts the potato and swiss chard lasagna, served with basil pesto and red pepper coulis. We liked the sound of roasted squab on a ragoût of sweetbreads, apricots, oyster mushrooms and walnuts.

Dessert could be warm chocolate cake with raspberry coulis and Ronnybrook mint-chocolate lace ice cream, poached bartlett pear stuffed with eucalyptus honey and goat cheese, or peach crisp with Ronnybrook toasted hazelnut ice cream.

Downstairs, the wine bar menu offers a changing selection of lighter fare, from Thai-steamed mussels to cassoulet to Irish lamb stew. A favorite in both venues is the house-smoked salmon with a trio of tasters: ossetra caviar, shaved fennel salad and "tartare" on rye crisps with honey crème fraîche and potato galette. The wine list typically offers more than 80 selections, focusing on varieties from the Rhone Valley as well as their domestic counterparts.

(860) 435-3551. Entrées, $17 to $28. Dinner nightly except Wednesday, 5:30 to 10. Sunday brunch, 11:30 to 2:30.

More Dining Choices

Cafe Lucia, 90 Church St., Lenox, Mass.

Authentic northern Italian cuisine is served by Jim Lucie at this serious little cafe, which has evolved from its days as an art gallery with a cafe. Jim opened up the kitchen so patrons could glimpse the culinary proceedings and replaced the artworks with family photos on the exposed brick walls. A spiral staircase remains the focal point of the main dining room. Especially popular in season are the expansive outdoor cafe and garden bar, their tables topped with umbrellas.

An antipasto table with the day's offerings is showcased at the entry. Fans praise the carpaccio with arugula and shaved reggiano, pastas like imported linguini with shrimp in a seafood velouté, and such entrées as pepper and parsley-crusted tuna over sautéed spinach, paillard of chicken with Italian salsa, braised chicken and sausage Roman style, veal saltimbocca and a signature osso buco with risotto, so good that it draws New Yorkers back annually.

Desserts include fresh fruit tarts, flourless chocolate torte and gelatos. Those desserts, a fine port or brandy, and cappuccino can be taken on warm evenings on the flower-bedecked patio. A few Californias augment the basically Italian wine list.

(413) 637-2640. Entrées, $17 to $30. Dinner nightly from 5:30. Closed Sunday and Monday in winter.

Spigalina, 80 Main St., Lenox.

Fresh out of the Culinary Institute of America, Lina Aliberti got a job as garde manger at Wheatleigh and awaited the day when she could open her own restaurant in the house her father had bought in the center of Lenox and leased out for commercial purposes. That day came in 1997 when the main floor was transformed into a Mediterranean-style bistro and bar focusing on a large center fireplace with a Count Rumford oven. Forty-two diners can be seated at well spaced tables inside, with an equal number on the front porch that quickly became a popular gathering spot to sit and watch the passing parade. The tables are covered with cloths portraying colorful blue and yellow Provençal-style plates.

The restaurant is a play on the chef's name (she originally called it Semolina, but had to drop it for trademark purposes). The new name means wheat stalk in Italian and Spanish. The menu is Mediterranean in spirit: pan-seared lemon sole with Moroccan preserved lemons over smashed artichokes and potatoes, bourride (a Provençal seafood stew) over homemade pappardelle, pan-seared duck breast with confit leg and a port wine-plum reduction, and sautéed veal medallions over wild mushroom raviolis.

Expect starters like roasted garlic soup with polenta croutons, wild mushroom and spinach tartlet with field greens, a Mediterranean antipasto that spans many countries, and portobello mushroom strata layered with potatoes, ratatouille, asparagus and caramelized red onions. Desserts vary from the predictable tiramisu to the unexpected Greek spiced honey almond-walnut nest with orange-raisin compote.

(413) 637-4455. Entrées, $17.50 to $22. Dinner, 5 to 9. Closed Tuesday, also Wednesday in off-season.

Union Bar & Grill, 293 Main St., Great Barrington, Mass.

This casual dining hot spot is run by Dan and Susan Smith of John Andrew's restaurant in South Egremont and three partners. Taking over a storefront space that had been a French restaurant, they fashioned what Susan called a light industrial look in silver, black, yellow and red, with a bar along one side and dining areas along the other. The name reflects a union of partners as well as the fusion cuisine bearing the unmistakable influence of Dan Smith.

The all-day menu is perfect for those who like to mix and match. Many like to start with the signature basket of baked and grilled house-made breads with a tapenade of kalamata olives, sundried tomatoes, and roasted peppers and garlic. Others go for the crabmeat and vegetable summer roll with wasabi and soy, the steamed mussels with sake and spicy lime sauce or the beef carpaccio with sliced artichoke, daikon sprouts, shaved parmesan and black truffle oil.

Among salads and sandwiches are spinach with Asian pear and pinenuts, grilled flank steak with smoked gouda on flatbread and grilled Cuban (pork, chicken, onion, avocado, manchego and dijon mustard). Four with-it versions of pizza and pasta are offered. "After 5" choices for dinner include plantain-wrapped salmon with tarragon cream and salmon roe sauce and roasted chicken with porcini butter. A cassoulet of duck with chestnuts and house-made sausage, and grilled shrimp and tempura of shrimp in a Thai coconut-curry sauce indicate the kitchen's range.

(413) 528-8226. Entrées, $14.95 to $19.95. Open daily except Wednesday, 11:30 to 11.

Bizen, 17 Railroad St., Great Barrington, Mass..

This true Japanese restaurant and sushi bar opened to such acclaim that it doubled in size three years later. It's the inspiration as well as the handiwork of Michael Marcus, a Berkshires potter who apprenticed in Japan, where he became enamored not only of its ancient pottery style but of its cuisine. "I am obsessed by quality," says Michael, and it shows.

Two "chef-associates," Hideo Kikuchi and Hideo Furakawa, head a cooking staff of five. Some work at the large marble and cherry sushi bar in the original space, which holds two Japanese-looking dining rooms of modest proportions. Others man the robata charcoal grill in the new section added in 1999. Here are elegant tutaimi areas and a crisp and contemporary sake lounge visible from the street. It looks as if it would be more at home in San Francisco, say, than in Tokyo, but dispenses an ambitious selection of estate sakes from ancient Japanese microbreweries.

The fare is authentic Japanese, served on the museum-quality pottery made by Michael in a multi-chambered, wood-fired climbing kiln at his celebrated Joyous Spring Pottery in nearby Monterey. The dramatic fire- and ash-detailed bowls and platters showcase the food because, in artist Michael's words, "eating is a form of theater."

The extensive menu, somewhat intimidating to the uninitiated, produces what the cognoscenti call "a real Japanese gourmet experience."

In the robata bar and sake lounge, choose grilled items to snack on, perhaps grilled corn, jalapeño kabob or grilled baby abalone with choice of sauces. Squid, cod roe, tiger shrimp and cherrystone clams are some. Of course, there's a great selection of sushi by the piece, rolls (the Bizen combines lobster and avocado) and combinations (a sushi dinner for $20.95). Dishes from the charcoal grill, with miso soup or salad and rice, might be Canadian sea scallops on fried sweet potatoes or unjyu, Asian grilled river eel. Noodles, tempuras and many appetizers like spring rolls and grilled Japanese yellowtail cheek teriyaki are available.

You might start with a deluxe seafood soup and end with blackberry sorbet or ginger ice cream.

(413) 528-4343. Entrées, $13.95 to $17.95. Lunch daily, noon to 2:30, weekends to 3. Dinner, 5 to 9:30 or 10.

Oliva, 18 East Shore Road (Route 45), New Preston, Conn.

Chef Riad Aamar, who had carried on the tradition of Doc's up the street, moved into his own ground-level café of many incarnations to immediate acclaim. People love his Mediterranean cuisine, broadened from the inimitable Doc's northern Italian original. They cherish the grotto-like setting, snug with stone walls, bleached barnwood and a huge, warming fireplace for chilly evenings. In summer, folks spill out from the 30-seat interior onto tables on a jaunty, flower-bedecked front terrace, which doubles the capacity.

Here, in an even smaller kitchen than at Doc's, Riad and his team produce dynamite pizzas, super appetizers and a smattering of robust pastas and entrées. Among the latter are linguini with garlicky shrimp and mushrooms, seared striped bass with olives and sundried tomato pesto over greens, and Moroccan lamb shank with rosemary, prunes, and almonds.

The menu is printed daily. You might start with the house antipasto (roasted vegetables and mixed cheeses), seared sea scallops over greens or grilled grape leaves stuffed with goat cheese, sundried tomatoes and basil. Most choose one of the new-wave pizzas, perhaps the artichoke with prosciutto and olives or the portobello with spinach and sundried tomatoes. Pizzas, served in small and large sizes, like the appetizers can be ordered "assaggi" style (a sampler of any two).

Canopied front terrace doubles dining capacity of Oliva in season.

Desserts could be a caramelized pear marzipan tart, coffee-espresso ice cream or hazelnut biscotti.

(860) 868-1787. Entrées, $12.75 to $25.75. Lunch, Thursday-Sunday noon to 2:30. Dinner, Wednesday-Sunday 5 to 9. BYOB.

Once Upon a Time

Once Upon a Table, 36 Main St., Stockbridge, Mass..

Hidden at the side of the Mews is this little culinary treasure, which has been packing in the cognoscenti for French comfort food without pretense and at reasonable prices.

Christian Urbain, a chef from France, and his wife Lynne, a Culinary Institute of America graduate, opened the plain-Jane, 30-seat eatery in 1997. They impressed one and all with a repertoire of appetizers like a Maine crab cake with horseradish cream sauce, chicken liver pâté laced with peppercorns and apricot brandy, and a portobello, goat cheese and red pepper roulade. A classic coq au vin vied for attention with such main courses as horseradish-crusted rainbow trout with a fennel fish velouté, seared Maine salmon with carrot-coriander sauce and navarin of lamb with a white bean stew.

We made a terrific lunch of the white bean minestrone, the pot pie of escargots topped with a beehive of puff pastry and the succulent Prince Edward Island mussels, steamed in a broth of garlic and shallots that proved so addictive that one of us sopped up every last drop with the wonderful French bread. Although desserts like apple-cranberry tart and flourless chocolate decadence were offered, we like almost everyone there sampled the signature profiteroles, a massive plateful of four with a choice of ice creams and generous chocolate sauce.

The tables in the tiny place often turned three times for lunch and at least twice most evenings for dinner. "We broke a record serving 157 lunches one Memorial Day holiday," Lynne recalled. Except for wait staff and an occasional dishwasher, they did everything themselves. And therein lay the rub. They sharply cut back their hours and finally put the business up for sale, to the dismay of the loyal following devoted to an endearingly personal place. They quickly sold to Nicholas Caplan and Alan O'Brient of Bistro Zampano's in Lenox. As this edition went to press, Nicholas was on site training with Christian. He pledged to continue the French tradition and to increase the hours.

(413) 298-3870. Entrées, $14.95 to $19.50. Lunch, Thursday-Monday 11 to 3. Dinner, Friday-Sunday from 5.

Offbeat Gourmet

Helsinki Tea Company Cafe and Bistro, 284 Main St., Great Barrington, Mass.

Owner Deborah McDowell's mother was from Helsinki, which accounts for the name and some of the theme at this colorful establishment hidden behind a shopping arcade, beside a parking lot and across from a movie theater. But the exotic treats that emanate from a pint-size kitchen are more international, and all kinds of local foodies seem to have discovered the place.

Live jazz on Thursday evenings and the fact that tea cups and pots are for sale indicate that this is not your ordinary cafe. The interesting food, the combination of teas and wines, and the laid-back service prove it.

Seated for lunch in the back dining room at one of the burgundy velvet booths (more comfortable than the usual), the table topped with a cloth like our grandmothers had, we enjoyed listening to music from the '40s on tape, with teapots on ledges all around us. One of us liked Emma's Hymyilla, a chef's salad of sorts – greens topped with ham, chicken, swiss and havarti cheeses, broccoli, a boiled egg and olives, and tamari-basil dressing. The other lucked out with Anni's Smörgasbord, "little bites from the land of the midnight sun." Marinated herring, a generous serving of gravlax, cucumber-dill salad, havarti, smoked gouda and finlandia swiss cheeses, shredded beets and cherry tomatoes were some of the bites, and we also loved our side order of mango-chipotle coleslaw. Soups of the day included Tuscan vegetable and chilled fruit, and every table was served a high metal contraption containing ryevita and French bread. We split an ethereal lemon tart with berry compote and whipped cream. Service was lethargic and, while we had heard that Helsinki was quite reasonable, our lunch tab totaled nearly $40.

At dinner time, appetizers go global: tempeh fries with honey-dijon sauce, spiced shrimp with a chipotle-lime dip, cossack salad and wild Alaskan salmon. Entrées run from vegetarian chili to Swedish ribs (honey-orange barbecue, served with Swedish baked beans, coleslaw and home-baked corn bread). Also available are a meatloaf made with tofu (a tad pricey at $15, we thought), seafood frittata and the "Mad Russian," potato latkes with gravlax, caviar and sour cream.

Changing desserts might be a strawberry-lemon-hazelnut torte, coffee meringue with chocolate mousse, or a vanilla and chocolate checkerboard cake. Helsinki has a beer and wine license.

(413) 528-3394. Entrées, $15 to $17. Open daily, 11 to 10.

Bagels or Beer

Allentuck's New York Delicatessen, 148 Main St., Great Barrington, Mass.

Josh Allentuck's new establishment is the real thing, reminding regulars of delis in The Bronx. The typical standard New York deli selection features two dozen sandwiches and up to three dozen salads. Soups, prepared entrées, bagels and pastries are available for here or to go. A sign advised: "Yes, we have bialys." Our favorite David Glass desserts were displayed next to Streit's Passover matzos. Amid the bounty, we settled for a chicken salad sandwich on whole wheat with a pickle, plain and simple.

(413) 528-4500. Open Monday-Wednesday 10 to 6, Thursday to 7, Friday and Saturday to 8, Sunday 9 to 3.

The Pub & Restaurant, Route 44, Norfolk, Conn.

International cuisine and beers are offered here by a former owner of the famed Stonehenge restaurant in Ridgefield, Conn. David Davis created what he called "an English-style pub with good food in a relaxed setting." The menu varies from seven kinds of burgers to grilled chicken, flank steak and dinner specials like poached salmon, moussaka, poached chicken Chinese style, New Age salad with gravlax, and fettuccine with roasted garlic, peppers, radicchio and snow peas. Of special interest is the list of 160 beers from across the world. David says it's the most extensive selection in Connecticut and, he reports, he's tried them all.

(860) 542-5716. Entrées, $12.50 to $15.95. Lunch, 11:30 to 5; dinner, 5 to 9 or 10. Closed Monday.

Lodging

Cliffwood Inn, 25 Cliffwood St., Lenox, Mass. 01240.

Joy and Scottie Farrelly walked in the door of this gorgeous Belle Époque mansion built in 1904 in the Stanford White style for a former ambassador to France and said, "this is it." The Ralston Purina Co. executive and his wife had been looking for a retirement activity and a place to house the furnishings they had collected while living in Montreal, Brussels, Paris and Italy. Cliffwood was the perfect find.

Seven luxurious guest rooms (all with private baths and six with fireplaces, one of them in the bathroom) are beautifully furnished with the fruits of the Farrellys' travels. Each is named for one of their ancestors, and a scrapbook describing the particular ancestor is on the bed – an illustrious lot they were. Joy had a bookcase and hutch designed and built in Vermont to fill a space in the second-floor hall and to pick up the pattern of the rounded windows nearby. It holds books from sixteen different countries. A gaily painted lunch pail is a decorative accent in one room; Joy has done folk-art boxes for Kleenex in the others. The Farrellys also are dealers in Eldred Wheeler 18th-Century American furniture and 24 of the prized pieces are in the rooms (and for sale). Notable at a recent visit were the queensize canopy Sheraton field bed and side tables in the Nathanial Foote room, enlarged by removing a wall between two rooms and sporting two wing chairs in front of the fireplace.

Guests gather in the magnificent living room, foyer and dining room, much as they would as house guests in a mansion. A full-length back porch overlooks a lap swimming pool with hammocks nearby. And, for those who want their swimming exercise year-round, the Farrellys have installed a counter-current pool and spa in a new cedar-walled enclosure underneath the porch. Wine and hors d'oeuvres – things like marinated olives, cheeses and a hot artichoke dip – are served in the late afternoon. "Dinners in a party atmosphere" are offered occasionally in the spring. "Sharing our house is a great way to keep busy and have fun," Joy explains.

Former ambassador's Belle Epoch mansion accommodates guests at Cliffwood Inn.

A copious buffet-style continental breakfast in the elegant dining room brings homemade breads and muffins, Joy's granola for which she shares the recipe, and a special hot fruit compote with nuts and crème fraîche. Wonderful popovers emanate from her prized AGA cooker.

(413) 637-3330 or (800) 789-3331. Fax (413) 637-0221. www.cliffwood.com. Seven rooms with private baths. Mid-May through October: doubles, $127 to $240. Rest of year: $87 to $155. Three or four-night minimum stay Tanglewood weekends. Three-night minimum some other weekends. Two-night minimum midweek in season.

Applegate Bed & Breakfast, 279 West Park St., RR 1, Box 576, Lee, Mass. 01238.

A pillared porte cochere hints of Tara at this majestic, sparkling white Georgian Colonial, built by a New York surgeon in the 1920s as a weekend retreat. Surrounding it are six tranquil acres bearing venerable apple trees, towering pines, flower gardens and a beckoning swimming pool.

Inside are elegant common rooms, six guest rooms with private baths and an effervescent welcome by Gloria and Len Friedman, she a retired educator and psychotherapist and he a retired computer executive. The Friedmans purchased Applegate in 1999, moving from their home in New York City.

Off a lovely entry foyer are a fireplaced dining room, where three tables are each set for breakfast for four, and a large living room equipped with a grand piano and evolving art shows by local artists. To the side of the living room is a sun porch, recently enclosed for use as a reading and TV room. Off the dining room is a screened back porch facing the pool and gardens.

A carved staircase leads to the four main guest rooms, one the master suite with a kingsize poster bed, family photos on the mantel above the working fireplace, a sitting area with a sofabed and two chairs, and a great steam shower. The other rooms are slightly less grand in scale, holding queensize beds. A couple sport new gas fireplaces. One has Shaker-style pine furniture, another a walnut sleigh bed and a third an antique white iron bed and white and blue wicker furnishings. Two newer rooms are situated in a far wing of the house. One is a sunny corner space swathed in pale lavenders and greens with a tiger-maple four-poster, a sitting area and the best view of the grounds. The other is a smaller room done up in Victorian style with an antique bed and matching marble-topped dresser. A rear carriage house has been renovated into a two-bedroom, condo-style apartment, available for $300 a night, three-night minimum.

Godiva chocolates and decanters of brandy are in each room. The Friedmans offer wine and cheese "like a house party" in the early evening. The continental-plus breakfast, including cereal and yogurt, is served amid stemware and Wedgwood china. "I love to cook," says Gloria, who was experimenting with more substantial offerings at our recent visit.

Outside in the side woods, the Friedmans discovered a long-hidden pocket garden, which they have been uncovering. "It must have been fabulous," she says. "It could have been a botanical garden."

Having run out of ways to improve Applegate, the owners have taken to wallpapering the closets. And Len tends to the rose gardens.

(413) 243-4451 or (800) 691-9012. Fax (413) 243-9832. www.applegateinn.com. Six rooms with private baths. June-October: doubles, $145 to $245 weekends, $100 to $190 midweek. Rest of year: $100 to $190 weekends, $95 to $175 midweek. Three-night minimum summer and holiday weekends, two-night weekend minimum in June, September and October.

Devonfield, 85 Stockbridge Road, Lee, Mass. 01238. –

The former summer home of George Westinghouse Jr. is now a comfortable, traditional New England-style B&B run with fun and flair by Ben and Sally Schenck, old friends who surprised us when they turned up as innkeepers. They purchased it in 1994 from Gerhard Schmid, former chef-owner of the Gateways Inn in Lenox, who had shared his family's home with overnight guests in a low-key B&B known as Haus Andreas.

Theirs is a handsome Federal mansion dating to the late 1700s, looking across 40 pastoral acres toward Beartown State Forest. Manicured lawns surround a tennis court and a swimming pool flanked by a showy flower garden designed by a house guest.

The Schencks have gradually upgraded the accommodations, which had been outfitted in European florals and traditional furnishings. Do not expect yet a "decorated" inn with canopy beds and fancy window treatments. The emphasis here is on relaxed comfort, spacious bedrooms and common rooms, and warm hospitality.

The ten guest lodgings, all with private baths, include six rooms with queen or king beds, one with a canopy and two with fireplaces. Two more are suites with sitting areas and TVs, one with a fireplace. Top of the line are a couple of apartment-size areas that were the personal quarters of the former innkeepers and a set of parents. The third-floor "penthouse" holds a modern living room, a king bed facing a skylight under the eaves, and a skylit jacuzzi with a shower. A poolside guest house comes with a kingsize bedroom, an open living room with a pullout sofa facing a corner fireplace, a kitchenette and dining area, a jacuzzi tub in the bathroom and pleasant patios beckoning on two sides.

The main house includes a large living room and library, a cozy television room, a guest pantry off an enormous dining room and a great side porch, with enough wicker furniture to seat everyone in the house and then some. This is the setting for festive weekend breakfasts in summer, starring cooked-to-order omelets featuring such add-ins as goat cheese and grilled vegetables. Otherwise, breakfast is taken at individual tables in the dining room. Guests help themselves to a buffet of fruit, granola, yogurt, muffins and such before a hot dish of scrambled eggs or blueberry pancakes is served.

(413) 243-3298 or (800) 664-0880. Fax (413) 243-1360. www.devonfield.com. Six rooms and four suites with private baths. June-October: weekends, doubles $165 to $200, suites $205 to $275; midweek, doubles $110 to $145, suites $155 to $190. Rest of year: weekends, doubles $105 to $140, suites $150 to $190; midweek, doubles $70 to $105, suites, $120 to $155. Three-night minimum summer weekends.

Historic Merrell Inn, 1565 Pleasant St. (Route 102), South Lee, Mass. 01260.

History buffs particularly like this elegantly restored inn, one of the first properties in the Berkshires to be listed in the National Register of Historic Places.

Saved early in the century by Mabel Choate of Naumkeag in Stockbridge, the 1800 building a mile east of Stockbridge was acquired by Faith and Charles Reynolds of Rochester, N.Y., who carefully created nine guest rooms on three floors in 1981 and undertook a complete redecoration a dozen years later.

All with private baths and some with fireplaces, many bedrooms are furnished with canopy or four-poster queensize beds and antiques the couple have collected over the years. They have been upscaled lately with cable TV, telephones, Gilbert & Soames toiletries, tiled floors in the bathrooms, comfy sitting areas, fancy window treatments, and color-coordinated linens and towels. The owners even ignored the period to furnish a couple of bedrooms in fancy Victorian style, based upon customer requests. An air of luxury is created by decorator fabrics and oriental rugs throughout as well as by prized possessions like an 1800 grandfather's clock. A new Riverview Suite, located in a separate wing in back, has a spacious kingsize bedroom, a fireplace and a porch overlooking the Housatonic River beneath Beartown Mountain.

Guests register in the old tavern room at the birdcage bar, the only surviving circular Colonial bar still intact. It also serves as a guest parlor and sitting room.

The old keeping room with a beehive oven is where Faith serves breakfast of the guest's choice, remarkably cooked to order by Chuck in what he calls the world's smallest kitchen. The room is a beauty, with handmade Bennington pottery, well-aged woodwork and a fireplace of Count Rumford design. The fare might be a mushroom and cheese omelet, blueberry-walnut pancakes or french toast with raspberry syrup, garnished with parsley and johnny jump-ups from the inn's garden. Chuck also painted the incredible murals in the front hall, and built the screened gazebo down by the river in the deep back yard.

(413) 243-1794 or (800) 243-1794. Fax (413) 243-2669. www.merrell-inn.com. Eight rooms and one suite with private baths. Summer and fall and some holiday weekends: doubles, $155 to $165 weekends, $105 to $115 midweek; suite, $225 weekends, $135 midweek. Winter and spring: doubles, weekends $95 to $115, midweek $75 to $105; suite, $145 weekends, $125 midweek.

The Inn at Stockbridge, Route 7, Box 618, Stockbridge, MA 01262

A lovely pillared, Georgian-style mansion on twelve acres bordering the Massachusetts Turnpike has been upgraded by new owners Alice and Len Schiller. Originally from New Jersey, the Schillers have made the main house even more comfortable and added four junior suites in a new Cottage House.

An expansive living room and adjacent library are where guests meet over complimentary wine and cheese. The table in the elegant dining room is set for sixteen, with eight more seats available in a smaller room beyond. Breakfast is by candlelight from 9 to 9:30, starting perhaps with juice and a fresh fruit plate, orange-cranberry compote or baked pears. The main course could be baked eggs with havarti and dill, sausage soufflé, portobello mushroom strata, lemon cottage-cheese pancakes or vanilla french toast. Orange-blueberry bread, apple crisp or apricot cheese bread could accompany.

The Schillers have upgraded the eight original bedrooms, each with telephone and CD players and one with TV/VCR. All but two have kingsize beds (the queen-bedded "Petite Room" with bath adjacent, rents for $115 to $135 a night). There are fans over the bed in the Madame Butterfly Room, with original headboards and oriental accents, and vintage rose wallpaper and two posh chairs in the Rose Room. The main-floor Terrace Room overlooking a reflecting pond and swimming pool features a private deck and a circular whirlpool tub in the skylit bathroom. The toiletries bear the inn's private label.

The Schillers built the Cottage House to add four spacious rooms they call junior suites. Each has a gas fireplace and TV/VCR. Two add large whirlpool tubs. A giraffe sculpture occupies a corner of the room aptly named Out of Africa, and three black masks grace the wall. An interesting wall hanging of five golf clubs linked horizontally by leather cords is a focal point in the St. Andrews Room, also notable for a high, plump fishnet canopy bed. The largest Provence Room has windows on three sides and is decorated in mauve and white toile florals.

For 2001, the Schillers were planning another building to house four top-of-the-line suites.

(413) 298-3337. Fax (413) 298-3406. Twelve rooms with private baths. Mid-June through October, doubles $200 to $260 weekends, $185 to $230 midweek. Rest of year: doubles, $160 to $215 weekends, $150 to $185 midweek.

The Inn at Richmond, 802 State Road (Route 41), Richmond, Mass. 01254.

Sumptuous breakfasts, elegant accommodations with modern amenities and a secluded country setting are hallmarks of this stylish B&B. In their restored 18th-century farmhouse, Jerri and Dan Buehler offer three guest rooms and three suites, each with king or queen bed, modern bath, thick carpeting, cable TV and telephones. The largest is the front Federal Suite with king poster bed, a sitting room, and a clawfoot tub and shower. An ornate iron queen bed dignifies the Victorian Suite. An unusual louvered headboard graces the queen bed in the Nantucket Retreat. Accommodations in a rear carriage house and a cottage are more like mini-apartments and are rented mainly by the week.

What seems to be every Copenhagen plate ever issued joins books and games on the shelves of the comfy library. Other common rooms are a small parlor, a garden room looking onto a reflecting pool and a greenhouse.

The breakfast menu, posted on the sideboard in the six-table dining room, conveys the day's treats. At our visit, the meal began with choice of three juices, granola and yogurt, cranberry-lemon and banana-yogurt breads, old-fashioned rice pudding and a compote of nectarines, pineapple and plums. The main course was sesame-cornmeal pancakes with wild blueberry-lemon sauce. Other main dishes could be frittatas, stratas and maple-walnut french toast. Port and sherry are complimentary in the evenings.

The rear of the 27-acre property is a breeding and training farm for Morgan

Huge stone fireplace is feature of living room at Manor House.

horses. The location is utterly rural and requires a bit of a trek for dinner, although Lenox is just over the mountain and West Stockbridge not far down the road.

(413) 698-2566. Fax (413) 698-2100. Three rooms and five suites with private baths. Memorial Day through October: doubles, $135 to $185; suites, $175 to $250. Rest of year: doubles, $110 to $145; suites, $135 to $195.

Manor House, Maple Avenue, Box 447, Norfolk, Conn. 06058.

One of the grander estates in a town of many is an elegant Victorian B&B run by Diane and Henry Tremblay, self-styled "corporate graduates" from the Hartford insurance world. Theirs is a 24-room, Tudor-style manor home built on five acres in 1898 by Charles Spofford, architect of London's subway system and the son of Abraham Lincoln's Librarian of Congress.

The nine guest quarters on the second and third floors come with private baths, one with a double jacuzzi and another with a double soaking tub. All are furnished to the period with fine antiques, French armoires and antique sleigh, spindle, canopy or four-poster beds covered with duvet comforters. The Lincoln Room contains a fainting couch and a carved walnut bed that belonged to Diane's great-grandmother. The Spofford Room boasts a kingsize canopy bed, a fireplaced sitting area and a balcony. Always upgrading, the Tremblays recently added a gas fireplace to the king-bedded Victorian Room, which has the double jacuzzi beneath a skylight.

The Chalet Suite offers an antique French queen bed and adjoining sitting room with a gas stove. The sitting room can become a bedroom with twin beds.

The original Tiffany and leaded-glass windows, cherry paneling and stone fireplaces enhance the main floor. Guests spread out in a baronial living room with a gigantic stone fireplace and a view onto the back gardens, a small library, a sun porch with a wood stove, a little bar area with stereo and TV, and two dining rooms, where the Tiffany windows represent fish on one side and fowl on the other.

In the afternoons, Diane puts out popcorn, cheese and crackers, and serves tea from her collection of teapots. In the morning, the good coffee is laced with cinnamon. The Tremblays cook a couple of breakfast entrées each day, among them scrambled eggs, blueberry pancakes, french toast stuffed with raspberries, orange waffles with honey and maple syrup, and poached eggs with a sauce of lemon, butter and chives on muffins. The honey comes from their beehives and the herbs from their garden.

(860) 542-5690. Eight rooms and one suite with private bath. Doubles, $135 to $225. www.manorhouse-norfolk.com. Two-night minimum stay weekends.

Gourmet Treats

This entire area is a hotbed of culinary activity, with Great Barrington increasingly the focal point. Its railroad station is the site of a farmers' market Saturday mornings in season.

Focus on Great Barrington

Guido's Fresh Marketplace, established in 1979 along Route 7 at the Pittsfield-Lenox line, is a fascinating complex of small food markets. It now has a branch at 760 South Main St. (Route 7) in Great Barrington, to which we'd gladly repair to turn marketing chores into fun. There were samples of crenshaw melons at the entry at a recent visit, and a wondrous assortment of exotic produce. Pasta Prima dispenses eight varieties of homemade pasta and many zippy sauces. A seafood wholesaler and butcher showcase their wares. But we always head to our favorite gourmet takeout emporium, **The Market Place Kitchen,** which moved its retail store here. It's fun to browse, but you'll likely be tempted to take home some of their terrific breads (the olive bread is sensational), salads (perhaps lo mein with shiitake mushrooms), quiches, dinner entrées like Thai-basil chicken and moussaka, and desserts. We couldn't resist picking up a special of lamb rolled with pinenuts and spinach, new potatoes with dill and grilled vegetables for a fancy dinner at home.

Owner John Campanale didn't realize it at the time, but he came to "smoked fish heaven" when he moved his **Merrimac Smoked Fish** wholesale and retail operation from eastern Massachusetts to 955 South Main St., Great Barrington. Seafood is smoked on the premises, resulting in superior Scotch-style Atlantic salmon, Idaho rainbow trout, mussels, bluefish, catfish and sea scallops, among others. Smoked fish is popular for takeout (we enjoyed the salmon at a Tanglewood picnic) and turns up on many a local restaurant menu. It also complements the H&H Bagels, imported from New York City. Olives, Greek olive oil, smoked sturgeon from California and some interesting sauces made by a local caterer are other offerings.

Main and Railroad streets in Great Barrington have been the happening retail sites lately in the Berkshires. Billing itself as "Provence in the Berkshires," **Mistral's** offers a fine selection of kitchenware along with perfumes and bed and bath accessories. **T.P. Saddle Blanket,** the most colorful store we've been in recently, stocks hot sauces along with rugged mountain and western apparel and furnishings.

The funky **Berkshire Coffee Roasting Co.** at 286 Main St. offers all the right coffees, teas, fresh juice, muffins and croissants at a handful of tables or to go. Adjacent is **Baba Louie's Sourdough Pizza Co.,** where the wood-fired oven produces organic and San Francisco sourdough pizzas. Breakfast is served all day at **Martin's Restaurant,** an L-shaped storefront at 49 Railroad St., where former

Waldorf-Astoria chef Martin Lewis whips up incredible omelets along with luncheon salads and sandwiches.

Locke, Stock and Barrel, just north of Great Barrington at 265 Stockbridge Road (Route 7), is more than a large gourmet store with a nifty name. Sophisticated as all get-out, it supplies a great selection of English cheeses, salsas and a remarkably extensive supply of preserves, conserves and jellies from all over the world (as in apricot jam from Lebanon). Owners Pat and Locke Larkin must have a lot of fun finding the dozens of hot sauces (oink ointment is a barbecue sauce), the hundreds of olive oils, the exotic cheeses and hams, rice from Thailand, the glazed violets, the chutneys, the nutmeg syrup – you get the picture. Locke sells granola made from his own recipes, too. At our latest visit, we came out with a couple of good bargains from his eclectic wine selection.

Lenox's Little Luxuries

In Lenox, **Mary Stuart Collections,** 81 Church St., carries fine china and glass, exquisite accessories for bed and bath, hand-woven rugs, imported needlepoint designs, potpourris and fragrances, adorable things for babies, beautifully smocked dresses for little girls and hand-painted stools. The owners know their food and steered us to Bistro Zinc, run by the son of one across the street.

Bev's Homemade Ice Cream, 38 Housatonic St., is the place to head for an ice-cream fix. Ex-Californian Beverly Mazursky opened this establishment after graduating from the Culinary Institute of America in 1989. She and sons Dan and Jeff make all the wonderful flavors in two machines behind the counter. They're known for their raspberry-chocolate chip and their margarita sorbet, served in sugar cones. You can order gelatos, frappes, smoothies, sherbet coolers and even a banana split, as well as espresso, cappuccino and cafe latte. Soups and sandwiches are available except in summer, when their popular Jamaican patties (different kinds of Caribbean breads with such fillings as beef, mixed veggies and broccoli-cheese) are about the only things that get in the way of the ice cream.

At **Suchèle Bakers,** 31 Housatonic St., the breads of the day might be sourdough, anadama, beer rye, toasted sunflower or white potato. We picked out some oatmeal-raisin lace cookies from the pastry case, full of sticky buns and absolutely gorgeous tarts, cakes and fruit pies, including peach and plum.

Seldom have we seen so many kitchen resources, so enticingly displayed, as at **Different Drummer's Kitchen,** on the north side of Lenox at 374 Pittsfield Road (Route 7). Everything you could ever want for kitchen or dining room is here, from the best cookware to gadgets galore. If we were getting married today, this is where we would register. Since we've been married more than a few years, there isn't much we need (but how we'd love a new set of pots). We did come away with a little gizmo for making gyozas (Joyce Chen, and it really works) and a practical thing for peeling garlic cloves, a tube that you put the garlic into, roll it and the skin comes right off.

Two for Tea

Harney & Sons, 23 Brook St., Salisbury, Conn.
Master blender John Harney, former innkeeper at the White Hart Inn here, sells exotic teas by the bag or tin at his packing factory with a new tasting room. All the

Michael, John and Paul Harney are set for tea in tasting room at Harney & Sons.

teas – ordered through a catalog by discriminating customers and purveyed to Williams-Sonoma and Ritz-Carlton hotels across the country – can be sampled here. Loose teas, flavored iced teas and tea bags, as well as accessories like solid black walnut tea chests, thermometers and permanent tea filters, even a "tea-shirt" are on display. So are preserves, mixes for scones and lots of information about tea, including the Harneys' book on tea-leaf reading. John is a genial host as he shows novices the proper way to taste tea in his expanded tea-tasting room. He makes it more fun to sample teas than we could have imagined. And the teas come in an amazing variety of flavors and hues. After sampling three or four, meticulously timed by little timers to just the right flavor and served in small handle-less white cups, we left with some Indian spice tea and some wonderful (and expensive) Japanese green tea. At our close-to-Christmas visit, local folks kept coming in for a stash of holiday tea, spiced with citrus, almond, clove and cinnamon. All the teas in the catalog are rated for smokiness, added flavors, body, aroma and astringency.

(860) 435-5044 or (800) 832-8463. Open daily 10 to 5, Sunday 11 to 4.

Chaiwalla, 1 Main St., Salisbury, Conn.

Tea lovers like Chaiwalla (which means teamaker in Sanskrit) and flock in for owner Mary O'Brien's pots of rare tea. They sit at gate-leg tables with mismatched chairs in her dining room and a three-seat counter facing the open kitchen. Mary serves morning fare ("offered whenever it is 'morning' for you"), tiffin (midday fare) and tea. A stunning selection of perfectly brewed teas, using local spring water, is served in clear glass pots on warmers and poured into clear glass mugs. You also may try Chaiwalla's own granola, eggs en cocotte, fruit-filled french toast, perhaps a soup like corn chowder or tomato-kale, pot stickers or a sandwich like "scholar's delight," roast beef with watercress and homemade herb mayonnaise. At teatime, Scottish shortbread, crumpets and scones with lemon curd are among the goodies. When we stopped in, plum kuchen and three-berry cobbler were a couple of the desserts.

(860) 435-9758. Open daily, 10 to 6.

Connecticut's Cornucopia

In Connecticut, Lakeville is the home of **April 56 Extreme Cookery,** which carries gourmet foods, Junior League cookbooks and original gifts; we liked the ceramic pie plates with lids topped with berries and apples. At **Riga Mt. Coffee Roasters,** you can sample the Internet on computers as well as many kinds of coffee, pastries and panini sandwiches.

Head to Salisbury for **Habitant,** a small but complete kitchen store ensconced in a house at 10 Library St. Everything from crab cakes to baba ghanoush to four-cheese lasagna and wonderful salads is available in another little house called **Harvest Bakery & Prepared Foods,** a bakery and deli at 10 Academy St. The San Francisco sourdough, baguettes, peasant bread and other baked goods are much in demand in the area. There are a handful of tables upon which to partake.

Two of the best gourmet food shops anywhere thrive in tiny Washington Depot. The long established **Pantry** off Titus Road, in the center of town, is a winning specialty shop and café. Tables are set amidst high-tech shelves displaying condiments, kitchenware and table settings. Owners Michael and Nancy Ackerman dole out an extensive repertoire of innovative soups, salads, sandwiches, entrées and desserts, as well as wine and beer, for here or to go. At our latest visit the chef offered a special muffaletta sandwich, as well as Asian chicken and Thai snap pea salads, a Greek pasta and the best-looking pecan tarts and petits fours we ever saw.

Just north of town on Route 45 is **Jack's,** an incredible new venture advertising "market, bakery, pizza, pasta and juice bar." That barely scratches the surface. Restaurateurs Reggie Young and Robert Margolis of the nearby G.W. Tavern offer the most exotic produce and fruits, seafood, meats and pastries in northern Connecticut. From Petrossian caviar and salmon roe to pattypan squash and mini brussels sprouts, they have it all. Not to mention a juice bar where a sign asks: "Have you had your wheatgrass today?" From a terrific choice of prepared foods to go, we settled on cod cakes with cucumber-dill sauce, sautéed bok choy with roasted garlic and caramelized onions, and roasted root vegetables with fennel for a memorable dinner at home.

Two Northwest Connecticut wineries are of interest to visitors. **Hopkins Vineyard** in New Preston is the largest producer of estate bottled wines in Connecticut. Bill and Judy Hopkins produce a superior seyval blanc, which has won many awards, among nine varieties from their twenty acres of French-American hybrid grapes. Recently they expected their new cabernet franc plantings to develop into one of their signature wines. The rustic red barn provides a self-guided tour, an attractive showroom and tasting area, and the country-sophisticated Hayloft Wine Bar upstairs, where you can order a cheese and pâté board and wines by the glass. The gift shop sells wine-related items like baskets, grapevine wreaths, stemware and handmade linen towels. Outside, you can picnic with a bottle of chardonnay or Vineyard reserve white and bask in the view of Lake Waramaug below. The winery is open daily from 10 to 5, Sunday 11 to 5, May-December; Wednesday-Sunday in March and April, Friday-Sunday rest of year.

Haight Vineyards and Winery near Litchfield, the first farm winery in New England's biggest wine-producing state, is Connecticut's largest. The Haight family take pride in their covertside white and red award-winners as well as their chardonnay and riesling labels. There's an informative vineyard walk and guided tours are available in the Tudor-style winery, which is open daily 10:30 to 5.

Rural pond with swan and geese is an attraction at Stonehenge inn and restaurant.

Ridgefield

An Enclave of Elegant Eateries

For its size, no town in Connecticut – perhaps even in all New England – enjoys the reputation that Ridgefield has for fine dining. "Some people think that Ridgefield was put on the map by our restaurant," claims the brochure for Stonehenge. The same could be said by a couple of other restaurants after the rural charm of Ridgefield was discovered by New Yorkers in the post-war era.

For three decades or so, Stonehenge, the Inn at Ridgefield and The Elms had things pretty much to themselves. In recent years, more first-rate restaurants have sprouted in Ridgefield and just to the west across the New York State line.

That there is such a concentration of great establishments in one small area does not surprise the restaurateurs. "It's like opening a fine shoe store," said one. "You don't want to be the only good store around."

Lately, the early emphasis on haute has been superseded by a proliferation of bistros and cafes that specialize in everything from Southwest fare to bagels. "This town has really taken to gourmet takeout," says Lynelle Faircloth of the Ridgefield General Store, whose cafe caters to the luncheon crowd as well as the takeout trend.

That trend was noted by the folks from Hay Day, the Westport-based, country-chic farm market, who opened a market with an extensive takeout section, a coffee bar and a cafe in Ridgefield in 1991. Successful beyond expectations, it served as a prototype two years later for the expanded Westport operation.

The Hay Day concept was tailor-made for Ridgefield. This is, after all, a town where a sidewalk vendor dispenses gourmet hot dogs and a store called Bone Jour advertises gourmet treats for pets.

The burgeoning of the restaurant business extends to lodging, with a fine B&B next to the Inn at Ridgefield, upgraded and expanded accommodations at Stonehenge and The Elms, and a private B&B suite with a 30-mile view.

But food remains foremost in Ridgefield, an enclave of creative cuisine.

Dining

The Best of the Best

Elms Restaurant & Tavern, 500 Main St., Ridgefield.

They were high-school sweethearts at Ridgefield High, Class of 1976. Twenty years later, they returned to take over the restaurant in Ridgefield's oldest (1799) operating inn.

It was a happy homecoming for Brendan and Cris Walsh. The pioneer in new American cuisine had got his start "flipping crêpes" at Stonehenge and was a waiter at The Elms and the nearby Le Château while attending the Culinary Institute of America. At age 26 after working in the California kitchen of Jeremiah Tower, he made a national name as opening chef at Arizona 206 in New York City. Three Long Island restaurants of his own and three children later, he got a phone call from his old boss, Robert Scala, of The Elms: "I'm retiring. Do you want the restaurant?" It was a godsend, recalls Cris. "All our family was still here." They negotiated to take over the restaurant operation, added a more casual tavern concept and launched a new, flag-waving cooking style.

Brendan, the master of innovative Southwestern cooking who helped create the trend of small plates called "grazing," took inspiration from 18th-century food associated with New England. He elevated stews, roasts, spoonbreads and puddings to new culinary heights and quick acclaim in the national media (Esquire magazine named The Elms one of the ten best restaurants of 1996). His renowned "food of the moment" now is refreshingly familiar, its presentation new and exciting.

For starters, consider the signature shepherd's pie, masterfully done here with lobster, peas and chive mashed potatoes. Macoun apples enhance the curried apple and buttercup squash soup, with a crème swirl on top. Braised lamb, celery root and goat cheese embellish the corn cake, and the smoked magret duck comes with grilled fig and mixed grain salad. Among main courses, the tasty skillet-roasted organic chicken might be accented with a sausage made of its leg and paired with sweet-potato spoonbread, creamed collards and truffle whipped potatoes. The Connecticut seafood stew is a melange of lobster, mussels, shrimp, sole and scallops in a tomato, fennel and leek broth. The grilled Montauk swordfish with mango relish is as good as swordfish gets. Other seasonal favorites are maple-thyme grilled loin of venison with buttered brandy glaze and, a Thursday special, pheasant with apple sausage.

Desserts are new twists on traditional themes. The apple pandowdy with granny

Chef-owner Brendan Walsh and wife Cris in dining room at the Elms.

smith apples is teamed with Tahitian vanilla yogurt. The pumpkin mousse comes with cranberry granité and cinnamon cookies, and the pear-ginger charlotte with a spiced wine glaze.

A more casual tavern menu is offered for lunch and dinner in the handsomely refurbished, Tudor-look tavern. Atmospheric as all get-out, it has a beamed ceiling, sturdy dark wood tables seating 30, a neat birdcage bar with four seats, a big fireplace with a roaring fire in season and windows onto a covered, stone-floored deck with a cottage garden in one direction and a park in the other. Here you can order "one-dish meals" like bangers and mash, bowtie pasta with vegetable ragoût and goat cheese pesto, citrus-spiced hangar steak with potato cake and wilted spinach or an alderwood smoked-salmon sandwich that an admiring local chef says is to die for.

Cris Walsh, an interior decorator and graphic artist, stenciled the four small dining rooms in 18th-century patterns, painted the walls white with "lantern-glow yellow" trim, cloaked the well-spaced tables in white over 18th-century fabric, and added simple Colonial plaid curtains for the windows. It's a stylish, updated setting for food that's the last word in New England dining.

(203) 438-9206. Entrées, $21 to $28. Dinner by reservation, Wednesday-Sunday 5 to 9 or 10. Tavern, $8.95 to $14.95, Wednesday-Sunday 11:30 to 9 or 10.

Stonehenge, Route 7, Ridgefield.

The famed Swiss chef Albert Stockli of Restaurant Associates in New York put Stonehenge on the culinary map back in the 1960s. Since his death, owner Douglas Seville has survived changing dining habits and a disastrous fire, adding a variety of settings for dining as well as upgrading and expanding the overnight accommodations.

Rebuilt following a 1988 fire, the restaurant could not be more sophisticated in a country way. Slightly smaller than the original early 19th-century, Colonial white edifice upon which it is modeled, it has a new side entrance and a layout that gives almost every table a view of the property's tranquil pond. The main dining room is light and airy in a peachy coral, green and white color scheme. Fresh flowers and small lamps are on the widely spaced tables flanked by upholstered Chippendale-style chairs. Handsome swagged draperies frame the large end window onto the pond, and french doors open into an enclosed Terrace Room adding 60 seats for overflow on the former flagstone cocktail terrace. More masculine is the cozy tavern in hunter green, where English sporting prints cover the walls and the sconces are made from hunting horns.

The ambiance is sheer luxury, but not pretentious. "Stonehenge has left no stone unturned," a fellow restaurateur pointed out, no pun intended. "Everything is perfection."

The chefs cook in the classic continental style with nouvelle accents. Stonehenge's famed beer-batter shrimp, a mainstay for 30 years, has been retired from service. So have the complimentary canapés that traditionally helped justify the expense of an extravagant meal.

Generous drinks are served in pretty, long-stemmed goblets. The half American, half French wine list is short and somewhat pricey, mostly in the $30 to $60 range. A page of rare vintages is priced from $150 to $2,000, for a magnum of 1970 Château Petrus Pomerol.

Among dinner appetizers, we found the snails baked with hazelnut and garlic butter and the mushroom crêpes with a mornay sauce and gruyère cheese out of this world. Although the menu changes, keep an eye out for the house-smoked fish, perhaps smoked and marinated salmon with ginger and dilled cucumber yogurt salad. The terrines are terrific, and a recent offering was a lobster medallion with a warm artichoke heart, poached egg and coral vinaigrette.

The short list of entrées ranges from sautéed organic chicken breast with roasted garlic jus to lobster "of the evening, out of the shell." Specialties include dover sole meunière and roast rack of lamb with tarte niçoise, an artfully created pastry basket, complete with handle and holding diced tomatoes, zucchini and other vegetables. We can vouch for the veal scaloppine with truffle sauce and savoy cheese and the tournedo of seared salmon with ginger-chive beurre blanc.

Desserts look luscious. House favorites are the three versions of soufflés (chocolate, praline and grand marnier), tarte tatin, and warm chocolate cake with white chocolate ice cream. Ours was a strawberry tart with an abundance of fresh berries on a shortcake crust and topped with a shiny glaze. We're also partial to the ginger crème brûlée. Requests for Stonehenge's chocolate recipes arrive almost weekly from across the country. Such is the stature of an extraordinary establishment.

(203) 438-6511. Entrées, $18 to $34. Dinner nightly except Monday, 6 to 9. Sunday, brunch noon to 2:30, dinner 4 to 8.

Auberge Maxime, Ridgefield Road, North Salem, N.Y.
The charming white Normandy-style house at the intersection of Routes 116 and 121 is named for Westchester chef Maxime Ribera, who opened it in 1977 and sold a couple of years later to Bernard Le Bris, who arrived in this country from France in 1976. Bernard, a practitioner of contemporary French cuisine, is thoroughly at home in this picture-perfect French provincial restaurant, which now has an herb and vegetable garden that strolling diners like to inspect. "We

Heidi and Bernard Le Bris in dining room at Auberge Maxime.

have the ambiance of a real French auberge," says Bernard, who was negotiating with the town in hopes of offering four or five bedrooms for overnight guests.

Tables in the 45-seat main-floor dining room are booked far in advance on weekends. A pleasant new room in the walkout lower level takes care of overflow. It looks out onto a patio where lunch and cocktails are served beside tranquil gardens, fields and hillsides.

You enter through a small lounge graced with a mass of fresh and silk flowers, and panels of etched glass depicting a bevy of ducks over the bar. The rectangular dining room has a mirrored rear wall that makes it seem larger. Chairs upholstered in a striped fabric, chintz draperies, dark paneling, candles in tall silver candlesticks, custom-designed white china from France bearing the restaurant's logo, and gleaming table settings present an elegant country flair. Carved ducks hand-painted by a woman from Sherman, Conn., grace each table and are available for purchase ($125 each).

Dinners are à la carte during the week and prix-fixe ($58) for three courses on Saturday nights. A three-course table-d'hôte meal for $29.99 is offered on weeknights.

Duck is the specialty of the house, served in six versions from traditional l'orange to roasted with a medley of cherries (tart, bing, rainier), or green peppercorns or sundried blueberries. Pressed duck à la Tour d'Argent is available with 48 hours' notice.

The six other entrées on a seasonal menu might include roast fillet of bass with herb sauce, grilled chicken with morels, and veal marsala with fennel seed and garlic jus.

Meals begin with appetizers like ragoût of escargots and chanterelles, smoked salmon with blinis and cucumber-lime salad, grilled lamb sausage with a wild mushroom crêpe, and foie gras terrine with onion marmalade. A salad of mesclun might be served with root vegetables.

Chef Bernard offers nightly specials – soft-shell crabs with saffron, baby pheasant with wild mushrooms and a heavenly sounding blueberry soufflé one spring evening we visited. Although soufflés are the specialty, other worthy desserts include banana mousse crêpe with walnut and rum ice cream and cappuccino-apple bread pudding with Belgian chocolate sauce.

The wine list, strong on champagnes, runs from $30 to $1,000 and is notable for its grid chart signifying the year. The chef makes his own vinegars and cherries in vodka and gives small bottles to regular customers at Christmas. He also will prepare a dégustation menu for two or more. It's priced at $75 for eight small courses and includes "foie gras, lobster and all that fancy stuff," says Bernard.

Some lunch patrons like to start with the special house cocktail, a glass of champagne with passion-fruit liqueur, a dash of campari and a scoop of sorbet. The lunch menu is the same as the dinner, at about two-thirds the price. If you opt for a three-course lunch here, you'd better consider it your main meal. So live it up with one of those marvelous soufflés.

(914) 669-5450. Entrées, $23 to $29. Lunch, noon to 3. Dinner, 6 to 9. Closed Wednesday.

Chez Noüe, 3 Big Shop Lane, Ridgefield.
The decor is whimsical. The service is without pretension. And the food is somewhat offbeat and represents good value.

Such is this worthy successor to Le Coq Hardi and later Sam's Grill, unfortunate victims of changing culinary times. After the demise of Sam's, the former cave-like space returned to its French roots under brothers Christian and Jehan deNoüe, early emigrés from France where their father's roots trace back to 900 A.D. and their mother was a Cabot (their uncle was Henry Cabot Lodge, ambassador to France). With the departure of Christian to the West, Jehan is maintaining the tradition of a clubby place, much favored by New Yorkers.

Pale yellow walls alternate with whitewashed fieldstone beneath a beamed ceiling, creating a country French setting. Brocade floral banquettes and bleached cane-seated chairs flank close-together tables dressed in white over blue linens. Shelves display copper pans and bottles of vinegar. High stools are at faux marble tables in the airy bar in front.

You won't find swordfish or tuna on the country French menu here "because everybody else has them," Jehan says. Instead, chef Jacky Desjardins goes for the classical: a stew of the day (perhaps rabbit or vol-au-vent), duck cassoulet, charcuterie plate or beef bourguignonne. With the exception of a few salads and sandwiches at lunch and more substantial entrées at dinner, the menus for both meals are similar.

Start with (or make a meal of) wild mushroom and chèvre strudel, mussels marinière, ratatouille baked with grated cheese or salade niçoise. The main course could be pan-seared sole with seafood-saffron cream sauce, baked salmon pesto, roast duck breast and baked leg confit finished with dried cherries and black currants, or herb-crusted rack of lamb.

Desserts vary from chocolate mousse, fruit crêpes and crème brûlée to pear-walnut tart and apple-cinnamon bread pudding with hard rum sauce.

Jehan deNoüe uses sword to open champagne bottle in Napoleonic tradition at Chez Noüe

Jehan also chooses French and California wines that are "off the beaten path" with an eye to value. Most are priced in the teens and twenties. "I'd rather sell them than have them collect dust," he says.

He also likes to have fun. He opens champagne bottles in the Napoleonic tradition with a saber, pulling out a hefty sword and popping a cork fifteen feet.

(203) 894-8522. Entrées, $16.95 to $24.95. Lunch, Monday-Saturday 11:30 to 2. Dinner nightly, 6 to 10.

The Inn at Ridgefield, 20 West Lane (Route 35), Ridgefield.

Masses of azaleas and rhododendron in spring brighten the canopied entrance to this elegant restaurant founded in 1947, the same year as Stonehenge. The entrance is lined with the sides of wine crates from across the world. Inside are a small cocktail lounge, three fireplaced dining rooms and a piano bar where a pianist entertains. There's a lovely summer garden cafe, where lunch and dinner are served on the side lawn.

The main dining room, with the grand piano at the entrance, is our favorite. Some tables have window views of surrounding lawns and all focus on a huge spotlit painting of Monte Carlo. The upholstered chairs are comfortable, tables are well spaced, and the eye-catching pewter service plates are emblazoned with a picture of the inn.

Longtime owner Henry Prieger is back following a twelve-year hiatus at the Roger Sherman Inn in New Canaan. The oversize dinner menu is continental as ever, lately scaled down a bit in scope and bearing a few contemporary touches.

His chefs pepper the inn's traditional dishes like dover sole meunière and filet of beef wellington with such surprises as corn-crusted halibut with tomato and basil concasse and medallions of venison with mushrooms, chestnuts and lingonberries. Chicken Toulouse-Lautrec with truffle sauce, roasted duckling with black currants and citrus, and steak au poivre are other standbys. The appetizers are even more classic: chilled vichyssoise, duck pâté with cumberland sauce, marinated Norwegian herring, avocado with crabmeat à la russe, and escargots with chanterelles en croûte.

Dessert could be raspberry mousse cake, chocolate or grand marnier soufflé, crêpes suzette or a trio of sorbets.

The lunch menu has a smattering of the dinner items, priced from $9.75 to $23. Recent offerings included omelet du jour, broiled Florida red snapper, lobster and seafood salad, wiener schnitzel, and blinis à la Reine. The tuxedoed staff outnumbered the customers at our two latest midday visits.

(203) 438-8282. Entrées, $17.50 to $34. Lunch, Monday-Saturday noon to 2. Dinner nightly, 6 to 9:30 or 10:30, jackets required. Sunday, brunch noon to 3, dinner 3 to 8.

Le Château, Route 35 at Route 123, South Salem, N.Y.

Drive through the gate and up the winding, dogwood-lined road to the baronial stone mansion built by J. Pierpont Morgan on a hilltop in 1907 for his former minister and you'll get one of the most majestic views of any restaurant – a sylvan panorama across the northern Westchester valley. The entry hall is paneled in rare chestnut, hand-hewn and held together by butterfly pieces. Dining is in high-ceilinged rooms, a couple facing onto the garden patio and all with expansive views. No wonder Le Château does such a lively wedding and function business.

Despite the numbers, dining is correct and quiet. It's well regarded locally, a credit to Joseph Jaffré, son-in-law of the original owners who came here from Le Coq au Vin in New York in 1974, and his longtime staff. The fabulous arrays of appetizers and desserts, on display buffet-style on either side of the entry foyer, make the most diet-conscious succumb.

Window table at Le Château.

Chef Claude Moreau has imparted more colorful and dramatic presentations to the continental fare, which received a rare excellent rating from the New York Times. The menu is of manageable size. Entrées prices start, as most locally do, with a basic chicken dish (here, roasted free-range with a wild mushroom sauce) and rise rapidly with more exotic ingredients. The ubiquitous baked Chilean sea bass is enhanced with caviar beurre blanc to command a $29 price tag. The top-priced sautéed lobster is served with a truffle and shiitake sauce on a bed of spinach. The filet of beef gets a sauce of port wine, foie gras and truffles.

Appetizers bear Manhattan prices. Those with the wherewithal are rewarded with fine renditions of lump crabmeat in phyllo with champagne sauce, grilled jumbo shrimp with toasted almonds and raspberry vinaigrette, and lightly poached duck foie gras with toast points and a truffle aspic.

Desserts include grand marnier soufflé and a creamy chocolate-kahlua terrine. The wine list is choice and rather expensive, although the price-conscious can find a few in the $20s.

It's idyllic in summer to have cocktails on the lawn, enclosed by gray stone walls as in a castle. And it's great any time to tarry at the bar, its windows offering the best view around.

(914) 533-6631. Entrées, $19 to $34. Dinner, Tuesday-Friday 5:30 to 9:30; Saturday 6 to 9:30, Sunday 2 to 9. Jackets required.

More Dining Choices

Biscotti, 3 Big Shop Lane, Ridgefield.

A 19th-century blacksmith shop is home to this small but ambitious Italian eatery where chef Silvia Bianco-Anthony lends authenticity and heart to a thriving operation run by her husband, Corwyn.

Glass cases and counters display some of the day's offerings, including wonderful panini, salads and luscious desserts. We picked up an oversize chunky chicken salad platter ($8.95), tasty and filling, for a quick lunch on the run, after considering the fajita omelet and ogling the array of three-berry and pear-cranberry tarts that beckoned near the entry.

Takeout is not the preferred route at this "true" food emporium. Silvia believes cooking is "an act of love, meant to be shared with others." In Italy there are "gathering places," she said. "I wanted to establish this as a gathering place." She expanded into an adjacent space, doubling the size of the dining room. A light country bistro look was produced, with white-clothed tables, wide-plank floors, dark wood beam and stuccoed walls dressed with plants and grapevines. There's courtyard dining under a trellis in season.

Corwyn, a wine connoisseur, acquired a Cruvinet to keep wines "on tap," allowing fourteen varieties to be served by the glass.

Silvia describes her cuisine as provincial Italian with a French accent. Her sauces are based on wine or cream rather than on tomatoes or olive oil. The food is "home style, rustic, honest." The unusually extensive dinner menu harbors a dozen antipasti, fourteen pasta and ten entrée choices. Among the latter are fillet of arctic char served over risotto with sautéed spinach and a fruit and tomato salsa, seafood risotto, medallions of pork with mozzarella in a tomato-wine sauce and grilled sirloin with a shallot-port wine sauce.

Sautéed smoked mozzarella, several versions of wild mushrooms, bruschetta, grilled polenta and crab cakes are featured among antipasti. Many opt for a sampling platter, $10.95 for two.

A special low-fat menu adds treats like chicken and asparagus salad, tomato seafood risotto and poached fillet of tilapia in a tomato broth. Lately, Silvia started offering "Super Mom" prepackaged frozen dinners for family meals for mothers too busy to cook. She also was working on a cookbook, "The Inspired Cucina," to spread the gospel.

(203) 431-3637. Entrées, $15.95 to $19.95. Lunch, Monday-Saturday 11:30 to 3. Dinner, Monday-Saturday 5:30 to 9:30 or 10. Sunday, brunch 9 to 3, dinner 5 to 9. Closed Monday in winter.

Thirty Three & 1/3, 125 Danbury Road, Ridgefield.

Everything comes up threes in this jaunty storefront known for innovative American cuisine. Culinary Institute of America-trained chef Arthur Michaelsen, his sister Nancy Burke, the hostess, and their mother (Josephine Connelly, who

Cheery dining room at Thirty Three & 1/3 is reflected in mirrors.

we're told arranges the flowers) took this approach because each has a one-third interest.

Fashioned from a storefront pizzeria in a shopping plaza, the place is fresh and fun, from decor to food. The family gutted the kitchen and produced a long and narrow dining room behind the front bar. A few paintings and murals brighten white walls above mottled gray vinyl wainscoting, and much of the scene is reflected in big mirrors. A mural of Art, Nancy and one of their chefs running across the countryside, food in hand, starts at the kitchen door and sets the theme.

From the kitchen comes a variety of treats, all with prices ending in 33. The dinner menu offers more than a dozen entrées from a sauté of sweet and hot Italian sausage in tomato-parmesan cream over farfalle to grilled filet mignon topped with gorgonzola and a black pepper-burgundy wine sauce. The pecan-crusted brook trout might come with a mango purée, the pan-seared yellowfin tuna on a roasted rice cake with a roasted shiitake and corn salsa, the cornmeal-crusted swordfish on a warm black bean ragoût with cilantro aioli, and the hoisin-glazed chicken breast on wasabi mashed potatoes with pineapple and mandarin orange relish and steamed snow peas.

Expect starters like smoked salmon tartare on toasted German pumpernickel, grilled beef and scallion rolls with sesame-ginger sauce, and cornmeal-crusted calamari over baby greens tossed with a chili-lime dressing and fried wonton strips.

Desserts are predictable, from chocolate-chip cheesecake to crème brûlée.

Despite the stylish digs, this is a community hangout kind of a place, where you can order a hamburger for dinner and cobb salad or a crab cake sandwich for lunch. There's a lively happy hour in the bar up front.

(203) 438-3904. Entrées, $15.33 to $23.33. Lunch, Monday-Saturday 11:30 to 4. Dinner, Monday-Saturday from 5.

Gail's Station House, 378 Main St., Ridgefield.

One of the endearing and enduring places in Ridgefield is this offshoot of Gail's Station House in nearby West Redding. Original partners Gail Dudek and Nancy Broughton converted the old Brunetti's Market into a lively, casual arena for good, basic food at affordable prices. They sold recently to John Finnegan, their original chef, and his wife Patty, who expanded the dinner hours and offerings.

Gail's is known for its baked goods, and all the baking is done downstairs. It's also known for its breakfasts, featuring a variety of pancakes and omelets in the $3.75 to $5.95 range (for corn and cheddar pancake). The skillet specials are something else: Texas Pink combines red-skinned hash browns, jalapeño peppers, and scrambled eggs topped with salsa and sour cream with a wedge of pink grapefruit; Leo's brings scrambled eggs, smoked salmon, scallions, red potatoes and a bagel with cream cheese.

At lunchtime, burgers are featured in a range of sizes and accessories. Sandwiches, salads, veggie casseroles and blackboard specials go for $4.25 to $7.95.

The changing dinner menu lists appetizers and light fare like jalapeño-cheddar crab cakes, goat cheese and green chile chimichanga, and oriental chicken salad. Main courses could be rainforest stir-fry (vegetables and tropical nuts over brown rice), lemon sole, chicken enchiladas, veal ragoût and New Zealand lamb. New York-style cheese cake, fruit pies, and freshly baked cookies are good desserts.

The ambiance is a mix of baked-goods displays, a counter with stools, and mismatched chairs at tables dressed up with floral cloths under glass. Assorted hats decorate one wall. A small rear dining room (once the market's store room) is perked up with a huge window and floral wallpaper above the wainscoting. Three layers of linoleum were removed to expose the original wood floors.

The establishment conveys a 1960s feel as "a home away from home," a frequent customer volunteered. "It's a Cheers kind of place." It also keeps up with the times. Gail's was hosting a wine and cigar dinner at a recent visit.

(203) 438-9775. Entrées, $9.95 to $18.95. Breakfast daily, 8 to 3. Lunch, 11:30 to 3. Dinner, 5:30 to 9:30, Sunday to 8.

Ridgefield General Store Cafe, 103 Danbury Road, Ridgefield.

In the basement of a marvelous country store in Copps Hill Common is this cafe, decorated in English tearoom style by store owner Lynelle Faircloth, an interior designer. Although the whole store is her bailiwick, the cafe with its demonstration kitchen is her pride and joy. In it her staff serves everything from creative lunches and Sunday brunch to formal English tea.

The blackboard lists soups, salads, sandwiches and quiches, to eat at one of the 36 seats or to take out. Everything's made fresh on the premises and is oh-so-good, from deep-dish chicken pie and Texas cornbread casserole to desserts like double chocolate fudge cake, pumpkin-spice cheesecake and fresh fruit tarts. The smoked turkey, apple and melted brie on oat bread is her most popular sandwich, Lynelle says, although she seems to devise a new twist for the menu every day and lately has added a number of seafood and vegetarian items.

The British tea involves three courses – scones and sandwiches, crumpets and sweets. It comes on doilies atop Portuguese floral pottery, the presentation being done with as much flair here as the food.

(203) 438-1740. Entrées, $6.95 to $9. Lunch, Monday-Saturday 11:30 to 3. British tea, Wednesday-Saturday 3 to 5. Sunday brunch, 10 to 3.

Southwest Cafe, 109 Danbury Road, Copps Hill Common, Ridgefield. A simple cafe with black and white tile floors and nine tables is where Barbara Nevins dishes up lunch and dinner and lots of takeout orders. Barbara, who used to live in Taos, N.M., is known for her green chile sauce. It's the base for a hearty green chile stew of carrots, celery and new potatoes, topped with melted cheese and served with a warm flour tortilla. Barbara also employs the sauce in many of the dinner dishes, such as cheese, chicken, seafood or beef enchiladas (the last layered New Mexican style and topped with a fried egg), chicken or beef chimichangas, chalupas, shrimp tostadas, quesadillas and huevos rancheros. It's not often you find huevos on both lunch and dinner menus, or Colorado tostadas with chicken or shredded beef and New Mexican red chile sauce, for that matter.

Much the same menu is available at lunch, as are sandwiches and salads, varying from chicken and artichoke to shrimp and vegetables. Southwest dishes include a bowl of green chili and green chile chicken, vegetable or beef stew. Start with tortilla soup and end with Mexican flan, strawberry cobbler or kahlua-pecan pie. Mexican beers and Spanish wines are featured.

(203) 431-3398. Entrées, $8.95 to $14.95. Lunch daily, 11 to 4. Dinner nightly, 4 to 9:30 or 10.

Bagels or Pizzas Plus

Steve's Bagels, 463 Main St., Ridgefield. Ex-Vermont restaurateur Steven Grover saw a need for a good bagel shop in his new hometown. He went to New York and "tasted all the bagels in Manhattan. When I found the ones I liked, they said to cut the sugar and increase the malt. So I did." The rest is history. Steve's bagels took the town by storm, and he quickly had to expand, both in space and offerings.

The bagels are the foundation, upon which his friendly crew builds sandwiches. They range from $4.25 to $6.75 (for smoked salmon, cream cheese and onions) and include tuna, hummus, turkey, chicken salad and roast beef with watercress and horseradish. Or you can have said sandwiches on Steve's caraway rye or whole wheat breads. There are vegetarian sandwiches (lentil burger, sundried tomatoes with brie, hummus with cucumbers and sprouts) as well. Accompany with one of the soups, the daily vegetarian (perhaps Armenian barley and yogurt), chicken and beef or sweet potato and kielbasa.

Steve's CIA-trained baker is also the chef, overseeing production of wonderful pastries, oversize cookies, pecan squares, blueberry crumble cake and the like. The deli case displays salads to go. There are tables at which to eat in this spare but spiffy place, or you may take out.

Is there life after bagels? "We toyed with the idea of gourmet pizzas in the evenings," said Steve, "to fill out the other side of the day." They eventually decided to stress espresso and cappuccino instead.

(203) 438-6506. Open daily, 6 to 3.

Piccolo, 24 Prospect St., Ridgefield. Jazz accompanies pizzas, pastas and creative entrées at this stylish newcomer that swings to a different beat. What other pizzeria has an a professional saxophonist as owner, an accomplished chef in the kitchen and offers live jazz four nights a week?

Matthew Criscuolo, who between jazz gigs runs Wilton Pizza & Pasta in nearby Wilton, acceded to customer demand with this popular offshoot in a downtown Ridgefield shopping plaza. The pizza oven is front and center in the kitchen, but the musical instruments hanging on the dining area walls set a novel tone. Recorded jazz plays during the day, and visiting jazz combos entertain Tuesday-Thursday and Sunday evenings from 6:30 to 9:30.

The pizzas and pastas are first-rate, but the panini, wraps and salads at lunch and the chicken, veal and seafood dishes for dinner set this place apart. So do the week's dinner specials, perhaps a cream of sweet potato soup or an appetizer of grilled sea scallops and cherry tomatoes on skewers, served over coleslaw and finished with a cilantro vinaigrette. The main-course choices are what you'd expect from the trendiest restaurants. How about pan-seared red snapper with artichoke hearts and haricots verts in a mirepoix broth served with wilted greens and finished with red bell pepper essence? Or dried fruit-stuffed pork tenderloin served over caramelized radicchio and roasted new potatoes and finished with bacon-sherry vinaigrette? Or pan-seared chicken breast crusted with macadamia nuts, served over wilted watercress and finished with lemongrass coconut emulsion and herb oils? Specials like these are available every night but Wednesday, the chef's day off.

(203) 438-8200. Entrées, $11.95 to $16.95. Open daily, 11 to 10, Sunday noon to 10. BYOB.

Offbeat Gourmet

Chez Lenard, Main Street, Ridgefield.

We can't give you a proper address for this operation, which he officially calls "Les Delices Culinaires de la Voiture," but it's usually near the corner of Prospect Street. Anywhere else but in Ridgefield it would be merely a hot dog cart, but this one has chutzpah, or we should say its pusher, young Chad Cohen, who changes his hats with the seasons, has. He and wife Kirsten bought the long-running business in 1999 from founder Michael Soetbeer, who opted to retire.

Year-round on even the chilliest days, the "voiture" dispenses le hot dog, le hot dog supreme, le hot dog choucroute alsacienne, le hot dog garniture Suisse (topped with cheese fondue), and le hot dog façon Mexicain, $1.50 to $3.50.

Chad and Kirsten, who also run a catering business, claim "the first gourmet hot dog rolls in the world," made for them at Martin's Bakery with semolina flour and potato water. We thought le hot dog supreme with the works ($2.25) was the best we'd ever had. Beverages to go with these elegant hot dogs are cold sodas Americaines and Pellegrino with lime (de rigeur in the area). For dessert, Chad offers candies – "for the kids." His wife was about to have their first child, but expected to be out with baby in tow the following spring.

Open year-round, daily 11 to 4, sometimes later and sometimes closed Monday.

Lodging

Stonehenge, Route 7, Box 667, Ridgefield 06877.

Instead of a country inn, this is now a fine inn in the country, stresses owner Douglas Seville of the "new" Stonehenge, southwestern Connecticut's grand old inn. He was showing some of the sixteen redecorated guest rooms – six in the inn, six in the Guest Cottage and the rest in a large new outbuilding called the Guest House – and a grand job has been done indeed.

Fashioned in 1947 from a country farmhouse into an English inn by a World War II veteran who had been stationed on the Salisbury Plain near the ancient monument of the same name, Stonehenge has been synonymous with fine food for many years. Since the guest rooms were refurnished and more were added in 1984, it has been a place for country getaways as well.

Each room has its own style, from the corner Windsor Room in the inn with a bookcase, antique dresser, wing chairs and ornamental fireplace to the spacious bridal suite with large living room and kitchenette in the Guest House. The two master bedrooms and two suites can sleep four, and are particularly sumptuous and comfortable. All rooms have private baths, air-conditioning, telephones and TV.

Trays containing continental breakfast and USA Today are delivered to the rooms each morning. In season, guests like to take them to the pond to watch the antics of the geese, ducks and swans. Guests also enjoy a cozy, fireplaced parlor in the main inn, full of the latest magazines and books.

(203) 438-6511. Fax (203) 438-2478. Fourteen rooms and two suites with private baths. Doubles, $120 to $160; suites, $200.

The Elms, 500 Main St., Ridgefield 06877.

At Ridgefield's oldest operating inn, parts of the original 1760 structure look appropriately ancient, although the restaurant has been dramatically updated by new owners Brendan and Cris Walsh. The adjacent inn, totally refurbished in 1983, is up to date and continues under the thumb of the Scala family

Thirteen rooms and three suites are located on three floors of the inn. They are spacious, carpeted and outfitted with television and telephones; many of the bathrooms have dressing areas. Antique furnishings, a few four-poster beds and striking wallpapers add a feeling of tradition and luxury.

Two rooms and two suites above the restaurant in the original inn are redecorated but retain their historic look, even to sloping floors. Two have stenciled bluebirds on the walls.

"The annex had reached the point where we either had to knock it down or build it up," said innkeeper Violet Scala, who decided on the latter and is justifiably proud of the results.

A continental breakfast with croissants is served in guests' rooms.

(203) 438-2541. Fifteen rooms and four suites with private baths. Doubles, $135 to $175. Suites, $170 to $200.

West Lane Inn, 22 West Lane, Ridgefield 06877.

Beside the Inn at Ridgefield restaurant, this quiet inn is much favored by corporate types moving into the area or visiting on business. Innkeeper Maureen Mayer has decorated the comfortable rooms in the early 1800s home in soft colors. Two have working fireplaces. All have two queensize or one queen bed, upholstered wing chairs and/or sofas, private baths, telephones and TVs. The sheets are 100 percent cotton and there are scales in the bathrooms.

Fourteen rooms are in the main inn; six more are out back in a converted garage named "The Cottage on the Hill." Each of the latter has a kitchenette and a private rear balcony looking onto emerald-green lawns. Three suites have been fashioned

Early 1800s residence now houses West Lane Inn in Ridgefield.

from the former home of innkeeper Maureen Mayer, hidden behind green plantings and a redwood fence between the inn and the restaurant.

Off the inn's rich, oak-paneled lobby is a cheery breakfast room for a complimentary continental breakfast. A full breakfast is available from a menu. You can choose to have it in summer on the wide front porch with its inviting wicker furniture.

(203) 438-7323. Fax (203) 438-7325. Twenty rooms with private baths. Doubles, $115 to $185.

Gourmet Treats

Hay Day, The Country Farm Market, 21 Governor St., Ridgefield. Hidden behind Main Street in the old Grand Central supermarket is this branch of the Westport-based market par excellence. When it opened in 1991, it was the biggest and most diverse of the Hay Days with a "real marketplace atmosphere," in the words of a principal. The 10,000-square-foot facility became the model for a 1993 relocation and expansion of the original Westport store, which started as a farm stand. It's a food lover's paradise of produce, bakery, fish store, butcher shop, gourmet shelf items and a deli to end all delis, plus a wine shop, a coffee-espresso bar and a small pastry cafe. Best of all for noshers: you can sample your way through the store, tasting perhaps a spicy corn chowder and an addictive chunky clam and bacon dip at the deli, exotic cheeses at the cheese shop, hot mulled cider and Connecticut macoun apples, and French vanilla coffee at the door. Hay Day conducts cooking classes, publishes a monthly newspaper chock full of recipes and food tips that formed the nucleus of the wonderful *Hay Day Country Market Cookbook,* and does an extensive mail-order business. Open daily, 8 to 8, Sunday to 7.

The Ridgefield General Store in Copps Hill Common, 103 Danbury Road, is a nifty contemporary place full of all kinds of gourmet goodies, from exotic vinegars and its own line of jellies to good-looking china and cooking paraphernalia. Owner Lynelle Faircloth calls hers "a mini-department store" with fifteen departments stocking antiques and "gifts for all reasons." A large area of children's toys and a great selection of paper items from cards and wrapping to invitations are attractions.

Sweet Pierre's, 3 Danbury Road, is what every chocolate store should look like. The cottage is dressed inside with French toile window treatments and enveloped outside in tiny white lights. Owner Janice Mazzamaro makes fudge in the rear kitchen and imports European chocolates for her display cases. She named it for her late brother, who loved to cook. He'd surely love her sweets.

Complete Kitchen is a good kitchen shop at 410 Main St., with a companion store in Greenwich. Cooking classes are scheduled here in a demonstration kitchen in the rear.

Some think the best ice cream around is served at **Mr. Shane's Homemade Parlour Ice Cream,** 409 Main St. Energetic John Ghitman bought the former branch of Dr. Mike's, a well-known Bethel operation, where he learned how to make ice cream. Now he serves up dozens of flavors, from a rich chocolate ("very powerful," says John) to spiced apple, pumpkin and eggnog. We can vouch for his pralines 'n cream, as well as his new caramel swirl ice cream "that's been flying out the door." John also offers frappes (milkshakes, to those not familiar with the Massachusetts variety), brown cows (root beer with two scoops of ice cream) and frozen yogurt he doctors up from Columbo.

On the lower level in the front of the same building is **Bongo and Capacci Pasta,** producer of gourmet pastas – all natural, without preservatives. The place is open limited afternoon hours on Friday, Saturday and sometimes Sunday. Featured when we were there were two raviolis: pumpkin with apples, figs and mascarpone, and sweet potato with sage, caramelized shallots and goat cheese.

Consider the Cook, Route 35, Cross River, N.Y., is an excellent kitchen shop in the interesting Yellow Monkey Village shopping complex west of Ridgefield. Quimper plates, fabulous table settings and all the latest gourmet foodstuffs are among the offerings. The village also contains **Happiness Is...Bakery Café,** which speaks for itself. You can eat at tables here or take out.

A Destination for Cooks

The Silo, 44 Upland Road (off Route 202), New Milford.

No report on culinary affairs in this section of Connecticut would be complete without mention of the fabulous cookery shop and cooking instruction classes offered by Ruth and Skitch Henderson. In former stables and dairy barns are displayed everything from oversize Mexican pottery planters in shapes of rams and hens to a sizable collection of cookbooks interspersed among cooking equipment and jars and bottles of the most wonderful jams, sauces and herbs. The Gallery features changing exhibitions of Connecticut artists and craftspersons. Well-known cooking teachers give classes here; chefs from area restaurants do as well. There are two-week seminars and interesting one-session courses – for example, "Make Ahead Holiday Desserts," "Healthy Cooking for Busy People," "Two in a Tuscan Kitchen" and "My First Dinner Party" (ages 8 and up). The 200-acre Hunt Hill Farm, set among rolling hills and flower gardens where kittens tumble around and horses and cows are pastured nearby, is a destination in itself.

(860) 355-0300 or (800) 353-7456. Open daily, 10 to 5.

Seagull and sailboat are part of typical scene viewed from restaurant along Connecticut shore.

Southeastern Connecticut
Down the River and Along the Shore

For reasons not entirely evident, many of Connecticut's better restaurants have clustered through the years along the lower Connecticut River and the shore of Long Island Sound.

Perhaps it is the natural affinity of restaurants for water locations. Perhaps it is the reputation for the good life that accompanies people of affluence with demanding palates and high tastes. Perhaps it is the busy but low-key resort status of the shore, summer home to thousands of inland Connecticut and Massachusetts residents.

Some of Southern New England's top innkeepers and restaurateurs put the area on the dining map in the 1970s. Several fine French restaurants followed, and in recent years, more inns of distinction and restaurants have joined the scene.

"We've found this area full of people with discriminating tastes," says Bob Nelson, a New Jersey corporate dropout who has given new life to the old Bee and Thistle Inn in Old Lyme.

Except for Mystic, the Connecticut shore has been discovered relatively lately by most travelers.

The area this chapter covers has no large cities. Rather, it harbors quaint villages like Chester and Stonington, affluent enclaves like Essex and Old Lyme, and resort areas like Mystic and Old Saybrook. It also claims the growing Foxwoods and Mohegan Sun resort casinos, two of the largest and most profitable in the world for the Indian tribes that own them.

Because this is our home territory, we cover our favorites in a broad sweep down the lower Connecticut River and along the shore of Long Island Sound.

Dining room decor is country French at Restaurant du Village.

Dining

The Best of the Best

Restaurant du Village, 59 Main St., Chester.

Of all the Southern New England restaurants in which we've dined, we think this is the most like what you would find in a French village. Its blue wood facade – with specially grown ivy geraniums spilling out of window boxes and the bottom half of the large windows curtained in an almost sheer white fabric – is smack on the main street of tiny Chester. One enters by walking up a brick path attractively bordered with potted geraniums to a side door.

Alsatian chef Michel Keller and his Culinary Institute-trained American wife Cynthia run their top-rated establishment very personally. A third-generation pastry chef, Michel spends his time in the kitchen and bakes the breads and desserts. Cynthia does the soups and some of the fish dishes, but is in the front of the house to welcome guests in the evening.

Through the small bar-lounge, decorated with plump piggies (the logo of the restaurant) with a few tables for overflow, you reach the small dining room. Along one wall, two sets of french doors open onto the brick walk for welcome breezes on warm nights. A sideboard between the doors contains the night's desserts and a large floral arrangement. A few lighted oil paintings adorn the stucco-type walls. A high shelf over the front windows displays antique plates.

The air of elegant simplicity is enhanced at the thirteen tables by white cloths and napkins, carafes of flowers, votive candles, open salt and pepper dishes, and blue sprigged service plates.

What may be the best French bread you will taste in this country is brought to the table with generous cocktails. Crunchy and chewy, made of Hecker's unbleached flour that gives it a darker color, the baguette is cut into thick chunks. Each diner is served an individual crock of sweet butter. If you get near the last piece of bread – and most do – the basket is whisked away and refilled, which could be detrimental to one's dietary health. On one of our visits it came back three times.

Of the six appetizers, standouts are the cassoulet, a small copper casserole filled with sautéed shrimp in a light curry sauce; the house-smoked trout with walnut bread and horseradish sauce, and the escargots with wild mushrooms in puff pastry. We also like the baked French goat cheese on herbed salad greens with garlic croutons. The soup changes daily, but often is a pureé of vegetables or, on one summer night we dined, a cold cucumber and dill.

The ten or so entrées might include steamed fillet of salmon wrapped in a leaf of savoy cabbage with salmon mousse, Rhode Island striped bass in parchment, rabbit flamande (a specialty of Belgium), pan-seared veal cutlet with a flan of wild mushrooms obtained by a local purveyor from nearby woods, leg of herb-marinated lamb with flageolets and rosemary jus, and Cynthia's specialty, a stew of veal, lamb and pork with leeks and potatoes. These are accompanied by treats like dauphinoise potatoes with melted gruyère, and yellow squash and zucchini with a sherry vinegar-shallot flavoring. The salad of exotic greens is tossed with a creamy mustard dressing that packs a wallop.

The well-chosen, mostly French wine list features vintages from Alsace.

Desserts change daily and are notable, too. At a recent visit, Michel was preparing an open fruit tart with blueberries and peaches in almond cream, a gratin of passion fruit, and paris-brest, in addition to his usual napoleons and soufflés glacé.

(860) 526-5301. Entrées, $24 to $27. Dinner, Tuesday-Saturday 5:30 to 9, Sunday 5 to 9. Closed Tuesday in winter.

Steve's Centerbrook Cafe, 78 Main St., Centerbrook.

What a difference a change in concept can make. Master chef Steve Wilkinson decided it was time to lighten up the interior of Fine Bouche, his small French restaurant and patisserie that had been a culinary beacon in the area since 1979. Next we knew, Fine Bouche was out and Steve's Centerbrook Cafe was in. A big change? Yes, and no. As the owner put it, "we didn't want to throw out the baby with the bath water."

The interior, even lightened up, still resembles the old Fine Bouche. The menu, although more varied and appearing more affordable, retains some traditional specialties. And, a welcome touch, fifteen quality wines are available for $15, although the full, 250-selection cellar especially strong in French Bordeaux retains the Wine Spectator award of excellence.

Steve's is possibly the highest-style cafe around. Cheery with cream-colored or sunlight yellow walls and accents of light pastels, it seats 45 at well-spaced tables in three small rooms and an enclosed, lattice-trimmed wraparound porch. Works of local artists provide colorful decoration. The white cloths are covered with butcher paper, a stash of bread sticks and a container of olive oil. Fiestaware is interspersed with the traditional Villeroy & Boch place settings.

Steve, who trained in London and San Francisco, offers a with-it menu that spans the globe. Pastas come in two sizes, the better for teaming with an appetizer or salad to make a lighter meal. Consider a roasted beet and goat cheese timbale salad, paired with a pasta of lobster and ricotta wonton or garlic roasted chicken cannelloni. Or graze through starters like a velvety lobster bisque laced with cognac, an Asian duck and shiitake mushroom spring roll, or fried green tomatoes with shrimp rémoulade.

Main courses – incredible values considering their ingredients and execution – range from sautéed crab and salmon cakes to rack of lamb with artichokes and polenta. We go for treats like Steve's fabulous Bombay shrimp curry with jasmine rice, grilled salmon fillet with corn pudding and mango salsa, tuna rossini topped with seared Hudson Valley foie gras, and duck, crayfish and sausage étouffée with green rice.

Desserts are superlative, particularly the almond-hazelnut dacquoise, a light but intense chocolate cake with chocolate chantilly, and the marjolaine, a heavenly combination of almond praline, hazelnut meringue, crème fraîche and bittersweet Belgian chocolate. To the roster of old favorites (crème brûlée and sacher torte) have been added "a chocolate home run (a fanciful diamond of delicacies) and occasionally Julia Child's classic strawberry tart, described on the menu as "the one from her first book thirty-something years ago."

That's Steve, mixing the trendy with the tried and true, keeping his superb restaurant up with the times. We only wish Sweet Sarah's, his great patisserie and takeout shop in back, hadn't succumbed along the way.

(860) 767-1277. Entrées, $14.95 to $19.50. Dinner, Tuesday-Sunday 5:30 to 9, Sunday 4:30 to 8.

Café Routier, 1080 Boston Post Road, Old Saybrook.

The subtitle for this French bistro is "The Truck Stop Café," because it used to be a breakfast diner. Owners Robert Rabine and chef Jeffrey Renkl had fun with the concept. The unimposing roadhouse façade opens into a pristine interior of white-clothed tables set with fresh flowers and votive candles, café curtains on the windows and a gleaming copper wine bar. "People were shocked," claims Jeffrey. Ever since its opening, the phone has been ringing off the hook as those in the know try to make dinner reservations.

The first-rate fare is Yankee bistro with a pronounced French accent, although no one involved is French. Jeffrey attributes it to his training at the Culinary Institute of America, followed by stints at Max on Main in his native Hartford and at Auriele, Union Square Café and Les Halles in New York.

Here he mixes starters like a classic mussels marnière, homemade pommes frites with dipping sauce and frisée aux lardons with a trendy potato and goat cheese gratinée, fried oysters with chipotle rémoulade and lamb sausage with an apple-onion-rosemary compote. He might even stray into the Middle East with baba ghanoush, an eggplant spread with pita crisps.

Main courses, served with a house salad, tend to be more mainstream French. You might find "camp-style" grilled trout with mustard sauce and lyonnaise potatoes, herbed chicken provençal with garlic smashed potatoes and steak frites, and grilled New York strip steak topped with whole-grain mustard butter. How about grilled calves liver with polenta and arugula salad? Or grilled lamb paillard with sautéed spinach and seasoned white beans?

Desserts could be crème brûlée flavored with fresh lavender picked outside the door, napoleons, or homemade ice creams and sorbets – ginger and lemon-crème fraîche at our visit.

The wine list is amusingly categorized by white and red "plonk" and is far better than what most would consider plonk. About half are French favorites priced in the teens and twenties. Many are available by the glass.

(860) 388-6270. Entrées, $15.50 to $20. Dinner nightly except Monday, from 5.

Timothy's, 181 Bank St., New London.

Chef-owner Timothy Grills quickly found a niche in New London for his nifty restaurant transformed from the space that formerly housed a drug store and later James' Gourmet Deli. He started offering three meals a day, but quickly had to abandon breakfast service because more than 1,000 people were coming through for lunch and dinner each week.

Timothy, a Johnson & Wales culinary graduate, trained in the Hartford area at Carbone's, Cavey's and the Simsbury 1820 House before venturing out on his own. Portrayed in 1999 by Connecticut magazine as one of Connecticut's four outstanding chefs, he describes his fare as continental and American. Others call it simply contemporary. A favorite starter from the get-go has been the lobster and mushroom crêpe with a madeira-chive cream sauce. Other dinner appetizers are cilantro-flavored salmon cakes topped with a sherried roasted pepper coulis and grilled szechuan tuna served over field greens with a sesame-ginger glaze and wasabi sauce.

Typical main courses are Atlantic salmon medallions stuffed with roasted leeks over a bed of swiss chard and red onion with horseradish cream sauce, sautéed pistachio-crusted pork loin with a mango-sage demi-glace and grilled leg of lamb with port wine-glazed apples. White chocolate-raspberry ganache tart, berry trifles, and apple napoleon with maple gelato are favorite desserts.

For lunch ($4.50 to $10.95), Timothy touts the shrimp and scallops over tomato basil pasta, the chicken and duck confit with fettuccine and the "focaccia vegwich."

The kitchen is partially on view at the far end of the urbane, high-ceilinged dining room, handsome in mauve and gray-green. Tall glass-enclosed shelves along the sides display antiques and vases, with bins of wine stored on top. Black cushioned chairs flank well-spaced tables dressed in white linens.

The extensive wine list is priced mainly in the twenties and thirties.

(860) 437-0526. Entrées, $16.95 to $24.95. Lunch, Monday-Saturday 11:30 to 2:30. Dinner, Monday-Saturday 5:30 to 9 or 10.

Water Street Cafe, 142 Water St., Stonington.

The dining fortunes in the tony borough of Stonington have been elevated by Walter Houlihan, former chef at the UN Plaza Hotel in New York. He and his wife Stephanie, who oversees the front of the house, first upscaled the small storefront space previously occupied by Kitchen Little to considerable acclaim. Then they acquired the Water Street Market across the street and followed with an ice cream store down the street in 1999.

The base of the intimate operation is the cafe's pint-size kitchen, where Walter fulfills a with-it, contemporary, all-day menu, supplemented by specials that change nightly. They're served in an arty and funky, bright red and blue dining area with a curving solid Honduras mahogany bar almost as big as the restaurant. White linens have been replaced by hand-painted tables left bare. The 35 seats are so close together that if you don't know your neighbor, you soon will.

Dig into starters like tuna tartare, escargot pot pie, a wild mushroom tartlet or a warm duck salad with asparagus and sesame-orange dressing. A grilled petit New York steak with pomme frites and grilled lamb loin paillard with watercress, fried capers and creamy mint vinaigrette are the priciest items ($10.95) on the all-day menu. Added at night are up to a dozen specials, perhaps pepper-seared halibut with roast corn-shiitake salsa, herb-crusted salmon with fennel-beet risotto, duck and scallops with oyster mushrooms, and pan-roasted veal porterhouse with littleneck clams and arrabiata sauce.

Desserts vary from pear-mango bread pudding and coconut-walnut-chocolate cake to crème caramel and poached pears with ginger ice cream.

Walter's fans can get some of his prepared foods, cheeses, breads and salads to take home from **Walter's Market & Deli** across the street. The blackboard lists wonderful sandwiches, and we found a loaf of his boule (peasant bread) to be exceptional. People also enjoy his intense, European-style ice creams and gelatos as well as chocolates at the new **Walter's Chocolates & Gelato** at 125 Water St.

(860) 535-2122. Entrées. $10.95 to $18.95. Lunch, Thursday-Monday from 11:30. Dinner nightly, 5 to 10 or 11. Sunday brunch, 10 to 2:30.

A Midsummer Night's Dream

The Golden Lamb Buttery, Hillandale Farm, Bush Hill Road (off Route 169), Brooklyn.

We fell in love with this rural restaurant more than twenty years ago and every time we go back we are smitten again. It's a Constable landscape, a working farm, a hayride, folk music and much more.

It's also the home of Bob and Jimmie (for Virginia) Booth, who set the stage for the most magical evening imaginable. Bob is the genial host who makes wonderful drinks (the manhattan is garnished with a fresh cherry because the Booths don't like to use preservatives) and oversees the dining rooms. Jimmie does most of the cooking with originality, energy and love.

The evening begins around 7 with cocktails in summer on a deck off the barn overlooking a farm pond or on a wagon drawn by a tractor over fields while you sit – with drink in hand – on bales of hay, listening to the fresh voice of Susan Smith Lamb, who accompanies herself on the guitar. Before you set off on this adventure, your gingham-clad (and sometimes pigtailed) waitress takes your order from the four or five entrées written on the blackboard.

Dinner ($65, complete) starts with a choice of about four hot or cold soups. We have never tasted one that wasn't wonderful. Using herbs and vegetables from the farm's gardens, Jimmie makes soups like cold lovage bisque, a green vegetable one using "every green vegetable you can name," raspberry pureé, scotch barley, cold cucumber and an unusually good cabbage soup made with duck stock.

Almost always on the menu are duck (a crispy half, done with many different sauces), châteaubriand for one, grilled lamb and fish (perhaps salmon or swordfish), cooked over applewood on the farm's smoker. Lately, Jimmie has added the occasional pasta entrée. Salt is not used, but many herbs, and essences of lemons and limes, are. Crisp and thinly sliced onion bagels are the only starch.

What we always remember best are the vegetables – six to eight an evening brought around in large crocks and wooden bowls and served family style (yes, you can have seconds). They could be almost anything, but always there are marinated mushrooms and nearly always cold minted peas. Tomatoes with basil, braised celery and fennel, carrots with orange rind and raisins, a casserole of zucchini and summer squash with mornay sauce – they depend on the garden and the season.

Desserts like coffee mousse, raspberry cream sherbet, heavy butter cake with fresh berries, pies (made by neighborhood women) and a chocolate roll using Belgian chocolate, topped with chocolate sauce and fruit, are fitting endings.

Owners Jimmie and Bob Booth relax at entrance to Golden Lamb Buttery.

During all this, you are seated in a dining room in the barn or in the attached building with a loft that once was a studio used by writers. The old wood of the walls and raftered ceilings glows with the patina of age, as do the bare dark wood tables in the flickering candlelight. The singer strolls from table to table taking song requests.

It's all so subtly theatrical, yet with a feeling of honest simplicity, that you feel part of a midsummer night's dream.

Lunch, with entrées in the $13 to $18 range, might be oyster stew, salmon quiche, seafood crêpes or the delicious Hillandale hash. It may not be as romantic as dinner, but you get to see the surroundings better.

Folks reserve a year in advance for the December madrigal dinners, when a group of renaissance singers wanders the dining rooms singing carols, and pork tenderloin is the main course.

Although we have had more interesting entrées on our wanderings, we never have had such a satisfying total dining experience. It's not inexpensive, but what price can you put on pure enchantment?

(860) 774-4423. Prix-fixe, $65. Lunch, Tuesday-Saturday noon to 2:30. Dinner, Friday and Saturday, one seating from 7. Dinner reservations required far in advance. Closed January-May. No credit cards.

More Dining Choices

J.P. Daniels, Route 184, Old Mystic.

Off the beaten path – as are many of the Mystic area's treasures – is this high-ceilinged old dairy barn, handsomely restored, elegantly appointed and operating since 1981 at a generally high level, although some report it has slipped a bit of late. Tables on two floors are set with linens and fresh flowers. The subdued lighting

Farm wagon greets diners outside J.P. Daniels restaurant in restored dairy barn.

is by oil lamps and lanterns on the rustic barnwood walls. The welcome by owners Larry St. Clair and Brian Henry is friendly, a pianist or harpist entertains some evenings, and the atmosphere is quite enchanting.

The menu, formerly continental, has been broadened to include regional American and ethnic influences. Most dishes come in full and lighter portions, priced accordingly.

Appetizers run the gamut from shrimp cocktail supreme to lobster pasta fritters with ricotta cheese. Three "pastabilities" are available in two sizes. Entrées include seafood crêpes, chicken Vermont topped with Canadian bacon and cheddar cheese, and twin filet mignons paired with bordelaise and béarnaise sauces. A tempting recent concoction is called mirlton porro, a pear-shaped Southwestern vegetable with a squash-like flavor, filled with jumbo shrimp, lobster, scallops and andouille sausage in cajun spices and topped with béarnaise sauce. A specialty from the beginning is boneless duck stuffed with seasonal fruits and finished with apricot brandy.

Almost everyone orders a side of Nicholas potatoes, a specialty of diced potatoes sauced with sour cream, bacon, scallions and a hint of brown sugar.

Desserts include rum crisp, chocolate mousse and chocolate-raspberry torte. The wine list contains a description of all the selections.

(860) 572-9564. Entrées, $11.95 to $19.95. Dinner nightly, 5 to 9 or 9:30. Sunday brunch buffet, 11 to 2.

Restaurant Bravo Bravo, 20 East Main St., Mystic.
Well-known area chefs Robert Sader and Carol Kanabis produce contemporary Italian fare at this 50-seat restaurant, which includes a large and popular sidewalk cafe off to the side.

The extensive menu rarely changes but offers plenty of excitement, especially among the specials. For dinner, sirloin carpaccio, grilled shrimp wrapped in prosciutto with skewered artichokes, seafood sausage stuffed with lobster and scallops, and grilled mozzarella skewered between croutons topped with a savory garlic sauce make good starters.

Creative pastas include lobster ravioli with a lobster chive sauce and black pepper fettuccine with grilled scallops, roasted tart apples and a gorgonzola cream sauce.

Typical entrées are Maryland crab cakes topped with lobster-chive sauce, a saffron-seasoned seafood stew, and braised lamb shanks. Grilled local ostrich with a watermelon barbecue and sweet corn sauce was an appealing special at our latest visit.

The lengthy dessert roster includes the obligatory tiramisu as well as tartuffo, fresh fruit napoleon with mascarpone cheese, ricotta cheesecake with grand marnier sauce and chocolate truffle torte with raspberry sauce.

The mainly Italian wine list is one of the area's more affordable.

The down sides are the service, sometimes aloof and rushed, and the atmosphere. Dining is in a spare, noisy and rather cheerless room at tables quite close together. Much more appealing is the canopy-covered terrace with white molded furniture. The outdoor **Cafe Bravo** menu features grilled pizzas (we're partial to the one with pesto, sundried tomatoes and goat cheese), pastas and entrées from $10.95 to $14.95.

(860) 536-3228. Entrées, $14.95 to $25.95. Dinner, Tuesday-Sunday 5 to 9:30. Also lunch, 11:30 to 2:30, October-May. Cafe, May-October 11:30 to 9.

Noah's, 113 Water St., Stonington.

Owners Dorothy and John Papp have a winning formula: good food, informal atmosphere and affordable prices. Their two storefront dining rooms, colorfully decorated with pastel tablecloths and fresh flowers beneath a pressed-tin ceiling, are usually packed with loyal regulars.

Everything is made on the premises, including the breads displayed in the window – an assortment of which begins every meal.

Regional and ethnic specialties are posted nightly to complement traditional dinners on the order of broiled flounder, cod Portuguese, pasta, and grilled breast of chicken, with everything priced under $12.25 except for filet mignon – and that only $12.95. The night's numerous specials have been upscaled lately and are pricier, as you'd expect for dishes like spice-rubbed grilled bluefish with mango-lime relish, grilled rare salmon with wasabi and pickled ginger, and lobster and monkfish sauté.

The fare is mighty interesting, from the house chicken liver pâté with sherry and pistachios to the Greek country or farmer's chop suey salads at lunch. A bowl of clam chowder with half a BLT and a bacon-gouda quiche with side salad made a fine lunch for two for about $10.

Save room for the scrumptious homemade desserts, perhaps chocolate-yogurt cake, bourbon bread pudding, or what one local gentleman volunteered was the best dessert he'd ever had: fresh strawberries with Italian cream made from cream cheese, eggs and kirsch.

Noah's is fully licensed, offering many wines in the teens.

(860) 535-3925. Entrées, $7.75 to $19.95. Breakfast, 7 to 11, Sunday to noon. Lunch, 11:15 to 2:30. Dinner, 6 to 9 or 9:30. Closed Monday.

The Real Thing

Abbott's Lobster in the Rough, 117 Pearl St., Noank.

Gourmet it's not, but it's the closest thing to a Down East lobster pound this side of Maine, and goes through 80 tons of lobster a summer. We've been Abbott's fans for years, drawn by the rocky setting where the Mystic River opens into Fishers Island Sound, thus providing a parade of interesting craft to watch. And when our sons were little, they could keep occupied finding briny treasures on the rocks. Now grown and far away, they return whenever in town for a lobster fix, as do we with out-of-state visitors in tow.

You can eat inside at Abbott's, but it's much more fun outdoors at the brightly painted picnic tables set on mashed-up clam shells beside the water. The menu is fairly limited and the wait for a lobster can be long – we bring along a cooler with wine or beer and snacks for sustenance.

A 1¼-pound lobster (about $14.95) comes with coleslaw and a bag of potato chips, while a New England feast goes for $21.95. Ram Island oysters are served on the half shell. Clam chowder or steamed clams, shrimp in the rough, lobster or crab rolls, steamed mussels and clams are other offerings. The only non-seafood items are barbecued chicken and hot dogs. Desserts include apple crisp, New York cheesecake and strawberry shortcake.

Beside the restaurant operation are the large lobster tanks that youngsters like to look at, and a retail store. Here you may purchase a couple of lobsters or cans of Abbott's clam chowder to take home.

In 1996, Abbott's opened **Costello's Clam Co.** just beyond in the Noank Shipyard, an open-air place beneath a blue and white canopy right over the water. It's smaller, less crowded and less known. Although you can get a lobster dinner here, it's best for its fried clams and fried scallops. The aroma of fried seafood is pervasive. The water on three sides compensates.

(860) 536-7719. Open daily, noon to 9, May through Labor Day; Abbott's also open weekends through Columbus Day. Both BYOB.

Breakfast Gourmet

Kitchen Little, 135 Greenmanville Ave. (Route 27), Mystic.

People line up for breakfast on hottest summer and coldest winter days at this little gem beside the Mystic River. We waited our turn in the January chill for a dynamite breakfast of scrambled eggs with crabmeat and cream cheese, served with raisin toast, and a spicy scrambled-egg dish with jalapeño cheese on grilled corned-beef hash, accompanied by toasted dill-rye bread.

The coffee flows endlessly into red mugs, the folks occupying the nine tables and seats at the counter are convivial, and you can eat outside at picnic tables beside the water in season. Florence Klewin's open kitchen certainly is little (she says the entire establishment measures nineteen feet square). But it doesn't prevent her from putting out some remarkable omelets and other breakfasts "like Momma didn't used to make" with a creativity and prices that put bigger restaurants to shame.

She also serves more ordinary lunches on weekdays, but it's breakfast where Kitchen Little shines.

(860) 536-2122. Entrées, $3.25 to $7.95. Breakfast and lunch, Monday-Friday 6:30 to 2. Weekends 6:30 to 1, breakfast only.

Dining and Lodging

Bee and Thistle Inn, 100 Lyme St., Old Lyme 06371.

When Bob and Penny Nelson decided to leave corporate life in northern New Jersey and buy a New England inn, little did they think of southern Connecticut or the Bee and Thistle. But on their rounds they took one look at this tranquil yellow house with its center entrance hall and graceful staircase, parlors on either side and three dining rooms, and said, "this is it."

That was in 1982. The Nelsons since have refurbished the inn's eleven guest rooms and public rooms, added a riverside cottage and elevated the dining situation to approach perfection. They won ten awards, more than any other restaurant, in Connecticut magazine's annual readers' choice poll two years in a row. "Romantic dining" and "best desserts" are their hallmarks.

Executive chef Francis Brooke-Smith, who trained at the Ritz-Carlton in London, delights in innovative touches and presentations, including garnishes of edible flowers and fresh herbs grown hydroponically year-round. His sous chef is the Nelsons' son Jeffrey, a CIA grad who trained at the 21 Club in New York and the Ritz in Boston.

Cocktails may be taken club-style in the comfortable front living room, where the seamless service begins and continues through after-dinner coffee. Dinner is served on intimate side sun porches or in a rear dining room. We like to start with one of the exotic appetizers, most lately ??? a cured rabbit spring roll served on a green olive and pickled ginger relish and a goat cheese torte layered with basil and sundried tomato pestos and served with grilled french bread. Cold charred spiced beef served rare with haricots verts and crispy potato salad is a perennial favorite.

Main courses range from fillet of sole Breton style and lobster pot pie to peppered pork medallions sauced with Jack Daniels and grilled veal chop with a sweet corn and basil broth. The thin-sliced breast of duck is served rare, one time with a roesti potato and orange-tarragon-jicama-pecan salad and another time served on a passion-fruit purée with a spiced pear beggar's purse. For a celebratory birthday dinner, one of us indulged in a perfectly seared roasted filet mignon sauced with a tomato-oregano vinaigrette, served with a gorgonzola-onion-potato flat bread and garnished with a roasted yellow and red pepper black olive salad. The other enjoyed the dijon-crusted rack of lamb with house-made tomato-mint chutney and mashed potatoes.

Apricot bread pudding with brandied caramel sauce, banana flan over mango purée, white chocolate mousse with black currant and cassis sauce, and fresh fruit sorbets are among the luscious desserts.

Bob Nelson, who studied wines at the Cornell University Hotel School, put together the wine list with an eye to price "so people can afford a good bottle."

A harpist plays on Saturday and a guitar-playing duo sings love songs on Friday in this "inn designed for people to get away from their stresses and to relate to each other," in the words of Penny Nelson.

Lunch overlooking the lawns on the cheery sun porches – one with loads of plants hanging from the ceiling and the other full of Penny's collection of baskets – also is a delight. Choices are of the brunch and dinner variety: smoked salmon-stuffed blini, shrimp and mozzarella tart, sautéed crab cakes with a mango-apple chutney and twin lamb chops with a tomato-mint chutney. The only salad might be grilled Thai chicken, the only sandwich, homemade sausage with swiss cheese and roasted red peppers on French bread.

A fairly extensive breakfast at modest extra cost may be enjoyed by guests in their rooms or on the sun porches or in one of the parlors beside a fire. The Bee and Thistle popover filled with scrambled eggs, bacon and cheese and the beef and bacon hash with eggs draw the public as well as overnighters. So do the finger sandwiches and scones served with preserves and whipped cream at English tea ($12.95) in the parlor from 3:30 to 5 on Monday, Wednesday and Thursday from November to April.

Sunday brunch ($12.95 to $16.95) features sticky buns and the chef's potatoes with such entrées as scallops in brioche, stuffed french toast, grilled smoked pork loin and a variety of omelets.

Games and books are on the two stairway landings leading to guest rooms on the second and third floors. Rooms vary from large with queensize canopy beds and a loveseat to small with double or two twin beds. All come with antique, country-style furnishings. The cottage beside the Lieutenant River offers a waterside deck off the bedroom wrapping around to the reading room with fireplace, a TV room and a kitchen. Its rate includes continental breakfast.

(860) 434-1667 or (800) 622-4946. Fax (860) 434-3402. Eleven rooms and one cottage with private baths. Doubles, $79 to $159, EP. Cottage, $210.

Entrées, $22.95 to $29.95. Lunch, daily except Tuesday 11:30 to 2. Dinner, nightly except Tuesday from 6. Sunday brunch, 11 to 2. Jackets required on Saturday.

Old Lyme Inn, 85 Lyme St., Old Lyme 06371.

In contrast to the antique charm of the Bee and Thistle across the street, the Old Lyme Inn is pristine and chic, quietly sedate in royal blue and white. Inside a beautifully restored 1850s mansion is a formal restaurant with inventive French cuisine and seating for more than 200, as well as thirteen guest rooms upstairs and in a newer wing.

The setting in the main dining room is elegant if a bit austere – very tall and formally draped windows, walls papered in a gold pattern and chairs upholstered in royal blue velvet at tables angled in perfect formation. A single rose in a crystal vase is on each large, white-linened table, and tapestries and oil paintings (appropriately, some by the famed Lyme Impressionists) in elaborate frames adorn the walls. Beyond are two more dining rooms, one with an intimate windowed alcove embracing a table for four.

Under the aegis of owner Diana Atwood-Johnson, the inn's restaurant has been awarded top ratings three times by the New York Times and its desserts were featured in successive issues of Bon Appétit magazine. Her chefs implement ambitious dinner menus. Among main courses might be planked swordfish roasted with a lemongrass-basil butter, sesame tuna steak on a bed of seaweed salad garnished with a trio of caviars and wasabi sauce, tandoori turkey medallions, and grilled filet mignon aged in rare bourbon and spices.

Irish smoked salmon with brown bead, capers and onions is a signature appetizer. Others might be tuna tartare, rock shrimp martini and escargots bourguignonne. The soup might be artichoke and hazelnut; the salad, Asian greens with Florida shrimp and fried wonton shreds.

For dessert, try the award-winning chocolate truffle tart, pumpkin cheesecake with cranberries, or layered gingerbread with butter cream, peaches and

Mirror reflects tables in perfect formation in Old Lyme Inn dining room.

raspberries. Homemade ice creams include caramel and eggnog. We can vouch for a chocolate truffle cake with mandarin-flavored pastry cream topped with a layer of sponge cake soaked in cointreau. Cafe Diana with chambord and chocolate liqueurs is a fitting finale.

The indexed wine list, honored by Wine Spectator, is unusual in range and scope. It's particularly strong on Californias.

A light supper menu is available in the stylish Grill Room bar-lounge, where a fire crackles in cool weather and a pianist or a jazz guitarist entertains on weekends.

Luncheon brings some of the dinner appetizers, plus salads like tandoori chicken and shrimp Louis, a grilled portobello and goat cheese rollup. Entrées ($8.95 to $12.95) could be chicken and asparagus shepherd's pie, grilled pizza, sweetbreads and "wild American meatloaf," a blend of wild boar and buffalo, served with mushroom gravy. The Sunday brunch menu ($10.95 to $16.95) might include house-made corned beef hash and poached eggs, zucchini pancakes with smoked ham, pecan belgian waffles, and smoked salmon with eggs and onions.

Eight guest rooms in the north wing are decorated in plush Empire or Victorian style. Marblehead mints are perched atop the oversize pillows on the canopy and four-poster beds, comfortable sofas or chairs are grouped around marble-top tables, and gleaming white bathrooms are outfitted with herbal shampoos and Dickenson's Witch Hazel made in nearby Essex. The five smaller rooms in the older part of the inn are not as elegant. All rooms have televisions and telephones.

Homemade croissants and granola are served for continental breakfast in the Rose Room.

(860) 434-2600 or (800) 434-5352. Fax (860) 434-5352. www.oldlymeinn.com. Thirteen rooms with private baths. Weekends: doubles, $130 to $160 May-December, $120 to $150 rest of year. Midweek: doubles, $99 to $130.

Entrées, $21.95 to $32. Lunch, Monday-Saturday noon to 2. Dinner, Monday-Saturday 6 to 9. Sunday, brunch 11 to 3, dinner 4 to 9.

Copper Beech Inn, 46 Main Street, Ivoryton 06442.

This imposing mansion, shaded by the oldest copper beech tree in Connecticut, is back on top as one of Connecticut's premier dining spots. Owners Eldon and Sally Senner, he formerly with the World Bank in Washington and she an interior designer, have upgraded the accommodations as well.

The Senners offer four period guest rooms upstairs, as well as nine deluxe guest rooms in an old carriage house behind the inn. Each of the latter has a whirlpool tub and french doors onto an outdoor deck or balcony overlooking the gardens. Second-floor rooms have cathedral ceilings. Mahogany queensize beds, TVs and telephones are the rule. The Senners have added their own antiques and 19th-century art to the inn, and show fine oriental porcelain for sale in a small second-floor gallery, open by appointment.

They also have added an elegant, plant-filled Victorian solarium in the front of the inn, replacing a rear greenhouse that was accessible only in summer. Guests find it a pleasant and quiet retreat in which to relax.

A continental breakfast buffet of fresh fruit, cereals, breads and two kinds of French pastries is set out in the clubby blue Cooper Beech Room, where tables are spaced well apart and the windows afford views of the majestic tree outside.

Dining of distinction is offered in four elegant rooms, including the chandeliered main Ivoryton Room with a floral Victorian motif, where twisted napkins stand tall in the water glasses, looking from afar like candles. The paneled Comstock Room with a beamed ceiling retains the look of the billiards parlor that it once was. Between the two is a pretty garden porch with intricate wicker chairs at four romantic tables for two set amidst the plants. Windows in the clubby blue Copper Beech Room afford views of the great tree outside. Tables in each dining room are centered by a perfect red rose.

This is a place to be pampered. Expect dinner to take up to two and one-half hours, and pick out a choice selection from the Wine Spectator award-winning cellar that gets better all the time.

The Senners credit the rise in the inn's dining fortunes to executive chef Robert Celentano, a Culinary Institute of America grad who also trained at LaVarenne Culinary School in Paris. Together, their success prompted the AAA to upgrade its dining rating to four diamonds.

The fare is country French, light but highly sophisticated. The menu is printed in French with English translations. The ten hors d'oeuvre start with pâté of pheasant and truffles and top off with ossetra caviar with blinis. The chilled lobster salad with mango vinaigrette, the mussels steamed with white wine in a lavender-scented butter sauce and the phyllo-wrapped artichokes, spinach and goat cheese are among recent favorites.

Typical of the dozen or so entrées are poached salmon stuffed with arugula and shiitake mushrooms, sweetbreads with a shiitake and sundried tomato sauce, and roasted pheasant filled with a mousseline of pheasant and morel mushrooms and served with a madeira wine and black truffle glaze. Recent autumn choices were fillet of salmon pan roasted with a light coating of honey and crushed black pepper, served on a bed of lightly sautéed greens, and medallions of venison loin with a pear-flavored venison glaze and a warm pear and sundried cranberry galette.

Desserts might be a white chocolate and cherry terrine with brandied cherry compote, a chocolate banana cake and dark chocolate praline mousse in a delicate pastry floret with caramel sauce, and blackberry sorbet with a coulis of red berries and a vanilla shortbread. Finish with one of the fancy liqueured coffees, dessert wines or fine brandies for an occasion to remember.

(860) 767-0330 or (888) 809-2056. www.copperbeechinn.com. Thirteen rooms with private baths. Doubles, $105 to $175. Two-night minimum weekends. Entrées, $23.75 to $28.75. Dinner, Tuesday-Saturday 5:30 to 8:30 or 9, Sunday 1 to 8. Closed Tuesday in winter.

Stonecroft, 515 Pumpkin Hill Road, Ledyard 06339.

His international travels with Chase Manhattan Bank heightened their interest in running an inn, and his love of sailing led them to the Mystic area. Her interest in psychosynthesis as a way of life seemed attuned for innkeeping. Add their youngest son's service as a chef.

The result is this soothing ten-room country inn, which began as four-room B&B in the main house and, with the 1999 renovation of a three-story hay barn, added luxury lodging and a distinguished restaurant.

Lynn and Joan Egy started in phases, first renovating the handsome yellow 1807 Georgian Colonial that had stood empty for five years. The four downstairs common rooms are beauties, from the Snuggery library that once was a borning room to a luxurious rear great room with nine-foot-wide fireplace. The country French furnishings throughout lend an elegant and comfortable, uncluttered look. To the rear of the great room is the Buttery, smallest of the guest rooms with a beamed ceiling, queen bed, full bath and its own terrace. The lumber here dates to the 1700s.

A young artist-friend of the Egys painted the mural of a hot-air balloon scene along the front staircase to be "cheerful and uplifting, as in the inngoing experience," said Joan. The stairway leads to two front corner bedrooms, both with queen beds. All are equipped with top-of-the-line mattresses and bath amenities that include inflatable tub pillows and aromatherapy bath salts for relaxation. Up a steep rear stairway reached through an unusual cut-out door is the prized Stonecroft Room with kingsize four-poster bed, loveseat and 22-inch-wide chestnut floorboards. The walls above the wainscoting bear the young artist's wraparound mural depicting a day in the life of Stonecroft about 1820. Look for the faces of the Beatles in the string quartet entertaining beside a stone wall and for the house ghost in the covered bridge.

New accommodations in the renovated Grange hay barn are more upscale. Each has a sitting area, a gas fireplace with a built-in TV overhead, original fir or new lodge pole pine floors, and a large bath with double whirlpool tub and separate shower. They're elegantly furnished in country French or English styles, plus one in Colonial décor for Yankee purists.

The enormous bathrooms in the two top-floor suites are awesome. One part is commode and bidet, with towel warmers and his and her vanities opposite each other. The other half is a huge walk-in shower, alongside the oversize jacuzzi. Shutters open above it for a view of the fireplace in the bedroom. One suite has a kingsize bed; the rest of the beds are queensize. All rooms open to private or shared wraparound balconies.

Fluffy comforters, terrycloth robes, bath sheets rather than towels, Crabtree & Evelyn toiletries and soft music throughout the common areas help Joan provide a serene, therapeutic stay. Guests respond with their thoughts in words and sketches in the room diaries. The six-acre rural property, surrounded by 300 acres of

Granite-walled Grange restaurant is furnished like a country manor.

Conservancy woodlands and stone walls, add to the tranquillity. Guests report deer and coyote sightings and lots of birds, Lynn says.

Breakfast is an event, served in the dining room, the new restaurant or on the tiered flagstone terrace beneath a venerable maple tree. Juice and Lynn's baked bananas, pineapples and mangos in a lemon-rum sauce might precede buttermilk waffles with strawberries and whipped cream, herbed scrambled eggs with turkey bacon or a cloud omelet (so-called because it's four inches high) layered with smoked salmon or cheese. The ginger scones and cheese-almond danish are addictive.

The Grange at Stonecroft Inn is the inn's crowning glory. Opened in 1999, it earned stellar reviews (including best new restaurant statewide in the annual Connecticut magazine readers' poll). The expansive, granite-walled dining room seats 60. It is furnished like an English country manor, with a lounge area of high-back couches facing a fireplace and well-spaced tables set with cream-colored linens and Villeroy & Boch china. Floor-to-ceiling, multi-paned windows yield a glorious view of a landscaped stone terrace for outdoor dining, a grapevine-covered pergola and a water garden.

It is a pastoral, thoroughly delightful setting for sensational fare prepared in a custom-designed kitchen by European-trained chef de cuisine Drew Egy and his pastry chef, Felicia Mahoney.

Dinner begins with an amuse-bouche, usually morsels – perhaps a spring roll with apricot-fennel filling, a shumai dumpling and a mushroom tart – that hint of the heavenly tastes to come. Herbed focaccia spread with caramelized onion butter accompanies.

Typical starters are lobster cappuccino served tarragon froth and all in an Irish coffee mug, Thai shrimp satay with sesame noodles and a spicy peanut dipping sauce, chile and garlic-grilled squid on arugula drizzled with lemon-tahini sauce, and grilled corn and roasted pepper quesadilla teamed with a cumin-accented guacamole, a zesty cilantro salsa and red onion-flecked sour cream. The smoked salmon plate is elevated by crisp fried capers and a little salad of avocado and basil.

Asian grilled tuna is a signature main course, sliced and fanned on the plate around a dollop of pungent wasabi, sliced maki rolls, sticky rice and julienned vegetables. Another signature is peppercorn-roasted rack of Australian lamb with rosemary and garlic jus. The choices range from garlic-grilled salmon on a French bean and arugula salad to sage-grilled pork tenderloin in a lingonberry and xeres sauce.

Desserts are knockouts. The house specialty is the night's chocolate trio, at our visit a little pot of intense chocolate mousse, three homemade truffles and a chocolate fudge brownie, plus a bonus, chocolate ice cream with a stick of white chocolate.

Those with lesser appetites might settle for coconut crème brûlée topped with bananas and served with mango sorbet.

If it's offered, try Felicia's remarkable "Blue Lagoon," an architectural marvel inspired by her daughter's sand castle at the beach – a tasty and photogenic combination of white chocolate sea shells, blue curaçao and more. It epitomizes the artistry that goes into the food and presentation here.

(860) 572-0771 or (800) 772-0774. Fax (860) 572-9161. www.stonecroft.com. Eight rooms and two suites with private baths. Weekends: doubles $130 to $195, suites $250. Midweek: doubles, $110 to $155, suites $200.

Entrées, $16 to $25. Dinner by reservation, nightly except Tuesday 5 to 9.

The Inn at Mystic, Route 1, Mystic 06355.

This is the crown jewel of the Mystic Motor Inn, the area's nicest motel and inn complex situated beside Pequotsepos Cove. Above the motor inn (which also boasts deluxe inn-style rooms in its East Wing) is an eight-acre hilltop estate with a white-pillared Colonial revival mansion and gatehouse offering sumptuous bedrooms – spacious, full of antiques, and with whirlpool-soaking tubs and spas in the bathrooms. It's said that Lauren Bacall and Humphrey Bogart spent their honeymoon here.

As a guest in one of the five rooms in the mansion, you may feel like a country squire soaking in your private spa, relaxing on a chintz-covered sofa by the fire in the drawing room with its 17th-century pin pine paneling, or rocking on the wicker-filled veranda overlooking manicured gardens, with Long Island Sound in the distance.

Behind the inn, the four guest rooms with fireplaces and jacuzzi tubs in the secluded Gatehouse, redone with Ralph Lauren sheets and coverlets, could have come straight out of England.

Sisters Jody Dyer and Nancy Gray, whose father started this as Mystic's first motor inn of size in 1963, revamped the twelve rooms in the motor inn's East Wing, all with Federal-style furniture, queensize canopy beds, wing chairs and fireplaces, plus balconies or patios with views of the water. Six rooms here have huge jacuzzis in the bathrooms with mirrors all around.

The 38 rooms in the original two-story motor inn are handsomely furnished as well.

Although breakfast is no longer included in the rates, complimentary tea and pastries are served from 4 to 5 at the **Flood Tide,** the inn's glamorous restaurant, which serves some of the area's fanciest meals.

The spacious two-level dining room in elegant Colonial decor has large windows onto Pequotsepos Cove. Tables are appointed with white linens, etched-glass lamps, hammered silverware and small vases holding a single rose each.

Executive chef Robert Tripp is known for his wine list and a popular Sunday brunch ($17.95). We certainly liked the $13.95 luncheon buffet, which contained everything from seviche, caviar and seafood salad through eggs benedict, beef stroganoff, seafood crêpes and fettuccine with lobster alfredo, to kiwi tarts and bread pudding. You also can order dishes like curried chicken salad and baked fillet of sole with lobster and béarnaise sauce, à la carte.

At night, start with the chef's special baked escargots with portobello mushrooms and garlic in puff pastry, duck strudel, or a crêpe filled with lobster madeira. A creamy herbed mushroom soup is a house specialty. Entrées range from salmon scaloppine with pernod beurre blanc, fillet of sole française and shrimp niçoise to baked chicken in banana leaves, and grilled medallions of ostrich. Rack of lamb, beef wellington and châteaubriand are carved tableside for two.

Bananas foster, strawberries romanoff, raspberry-kiwi parfait and chocolate fondue are among the renowned desserts.

A smaller menu, featuring some of the house specialties as well as lighter fare, is offered in the **Crystal Swan Lounge** with its plush leather chairs, piano and a wine bar. An outdoor deck is popular in summer.

(860) 536-9604 or (800) 237-2415. Fax (860) 572-1635. Sixty-seven rooms with private baths. Mid-June to late October: Inn, Gatehouse and East Wing: $250 to $275 weekends, $170 to $215 midweek. Motor inn: doubles, $165 to $240 weekends, $115 to $160 midweek. Rest of year: Inn, Gatehouse and East Wing: doubles, $225 to $275 weekends, $125 to $235 midweek. Motor inn: doubles, $95 to $240 weekends, $75 to $145 midweek.

Entrées, $18.95 to $29.95. Lunch, Monday-Saturday 11:30 to 2. Dinner, 5:30 to 9 or 10. Sunday brunch, 11 to 2.

Gelston House, 8 Main St., East Haddam.

No major restaurant along the Connecticut River has experienced more ups and downs than the Gelston House, a landmark white confection alongside the famed Goodspeed Opera House. Over the years, owners and chefs have come and gone seemingly with the theater seasons. Despite a sensational riverfront location, a captive audience and the best of intentions, none seemed truly to satisfy and survive.

The Carbone family of Hartford restaurant fame took over in 1999. They scaled back the menu and simplified the décor of the vast main dining room, a summery sea of white-clothed tables and upholstered chairs with big windows on three sides onto the river. They renamed it the **River Grill.** Early reviews were mixed, but hopeful.

The cuisine is in the contemporary American idiom. Dinner might start with a smoked salmon spring roll with goat cheese and dill crème fraîche, sautéed Maine crab cake with lemon wasabi aioli, or a portobello and shrimp salad on baby spinach with parmesan.

Main dishes at our visit included almond-crusted salmon with saffron aioli, lobster-stuffed lemon sole with sherried lobster crème, caramelized duck breast with white port wine glaze and grilled strip steak with roast garlic and charred

Chef cooks hearthside dinner at Randall's Ordinary.

tomato aioli. Seasonal desserts could be pumpkin cheesecake with cinnamon crème anglaise, pecan tart with bourbon-spiked whipped cream and chocolate truffle cake with raspberry sauce.

The restored Victorian bar, lit by a stunning chandelier, offers a tavern menu and weekend entertainment. The side **Terrace Café,** formerly known as the Beer Garden, offers a casual al fresco menu in season.

Upstairs on the second and third floors are six prim guest rooms and suites furnished in Victoriana. All have queensize beds and TVs. Three suites afford great views onto the river. A complimentary continental breakfast basket is offered in the morning.

(860) 873-1411. Fax (860) 873-9300. Three rooms and three suites with private baths. Doubles, $100 to $125. Suites, $225.

Entrées, $18.25 to 25.95. Lunch, Wednesday-Sunday 11:30 to 2:30. Dinner, 5 or 5:30 to 9 or 10, Sunday 4 to 8.

Gourmet from Days Past

Randall's Ordinary, Route 2, Box 243, North Stonington 06359.

Here's a unique Colonial inn and restaurant, where you can hearken back to pre-Revolutionary War times, enjoying hearthside dinners and historic accommodations in a rural farmhouse dating to 1685, sequestered in the midst of 27 acres at the end of a dirt road. Or you can partake of the more modern amenities of newer guest rooms in a restored 1819 barn dismantled and moved to the property from Richmondville, N.Y.

Using antique iron pots and utensils and cooking in reflector ovens and an immense open hearth, the staff serves food from the Colonial era to patrons in a thoroughly authentic 18th-century setting. Diners gather in a small taproom, where they pick up a drink along with hearth-roasted popcorn, crackers and cheese. Then they watch cooks in Colonial costumes preparing their meals on the open hearth.

Seating is in three beamed dining rooms at long old tables with hand-loomed placemats, Bennington black and white pottery, flatware with pistol-grip knives and three-tined forks, and such unusual accessories as a pewter salt plate and a sugar scoop. Some of the chairs are so low that we had to switch to reach the table comfortably.

The $39 prix-fixe dinner offers a choice among four or five entrées – Nantucket scallops, sage roasted capon, roast leg of lamb and roast goose with wild rice stuffing when we were last there. The meal includes soup (butternut squash or Shaker herb, perhaps), whole-wheat walnut bread or spider cornbread, vegetables like cauliflower duBarry and corn pudding, and a dessert of bread pudding, apple-rhubarb crisp or Vermont ginger bread. Choose a house Napa Ridge chardonnay or côtes du rhône from the small wine list to complement your meal.

Lunch is à la carte and the menu much more extensive. Start perhaps with parsnip and apple soup with spider cornbread. Consider New England cod cakes, Yankee pot roast, a hearth-roasted turkey sandwich with cranberry relish or venison sausage skewered with peppers, onions and mushrooms for $7.95 to $10.95. We tried the succulent Nantucket scallops with scallions and butter – "the best you'll ever eat," advised innkeeper Gary Baker. He was right. They're lightly breaded and cooked with herbs and paprika in a wok-like skillet. Accompanying were sides of zucchini and broccoli as well as sweet-potato purée.

The restaurant also offers breakfast to the public, perhaps maple toast with fried apples and Shaker apple salad, griddle cakes and breakfast pie. All are in the $5 range, except for the "Ordinary breakfast" bringing the works for $9.75.

The restaurant sells its homemade sausages, brick-oven baked breads and packaged cornmeal. A cookbook of its Colonial recipes was in the works.

Three guest rooms in the main house have ornamental fireplaces and queensize four-poster beds with hand-loomed coverlets, as well as modern baths with whirlpool jets in the tubs. Twelve rooms and suites are located to the rear in the old-style English barn with open bays, to which a milking shed and a silo have been attached. The framing was left exposed, random pine floors are covered with area rugs, and rooms are furnished to the period. With mostly queensize beds, modern baths, built-in sofas, phones and TVs, they are quite contemporary. Four have loft bedrooms with skylights and spiral staircases from the sitting rooms. The circular, three-story Silo Suite with a huge jacuzzi tub on the top floor is enormous. Formerly rather spartan, the rooms were refurbished in 1999 with art works and new period furniture for a warmer ambiance. "We are what we are, rustic but with modern amenities," says innkeeper Baker, who manages the place for the new ownership, the Mashantucket Pequots. "Our niche is unique."

The tribe, owners of the nearby Foxwoods Casino, maintained the Randall's tradition. It also was upgrading its other nearby properties, the Mystic Hilton and the Norwich Inn & Spa.

(860) 599-4540. Fax (860) 599-3308. Ten rooms and five suites with private baths. Weekends: doubles, $140; suites $175 and $300. Midweek: doubles; $125; suites, $150 and $250.

Prix-fixe, $39. Breakfast daily, 7 to 11. Lunch, noon to 2 (to 3 on weekends). Dinner, 5:30 to 9.

Lodging

Riverwind, 209 Main St., Deep River 06417.

Her contractor didn't blanch when Barbara Barlow said in 1987 that she wanted to build an addition 100 years older than her existing 1850 inn. The result is a skillful blend of old and new, embracing eight guest rooms with private baths and an equal number of common rooms that afford space for mingling or privacy. An unexpected but happy side result: the innkeeper married the contractor, and Barbara and Bob Bucknall are both now Riverwind's innkeepers.

Antiques from Barbara's former shop, wooden and stuffed animals in all guises (especially pigs), folk art, hand-stenciling, and tasteful knickknacks and memorabilia are all around. Each bedroom has thick robes in colorful patterns, some matching the decor. Poland Spring water and candies are put out in each.

The Hearts and Flowers Room has flowers on the bedroom wallpaper, hearts on the bathroom wallpaper and a specially made, heart-filled, stained-glass window. Every room is charming, but the ultimate is the Champagne and Roses Room with a private balcony, a wonderfully decadent (according to Barbara) bathroom with a shower and a Japanese steeping tub, a bottle of champagne cooling on a table between two wing chairs, and a fishnet canopy bed too lacy and frilly for words.

Barbara grew up in Smithfield, Va., where her father was a hog farmer. Naturally, she serves slices of red, salty Smithfield ham for breakfast every morning at a table for twelve in the new dining room and at a smaller table in the adjacent room. She may offer coffee cake, Southern biscuits, fresh fruit in summer and hot curried fruit in winter, as well as homemade jams and preserves. Lately she has added more breakfast casseroles to her repertoire. One that particularly appeals is like a quiche and incorporates swiss cheese, eggs, asparagus, mushrooms, cream sauce and french-fried onion rings.

Besides a delightful living room with fireplace, a library and a trophy room for games, guests enjoy a keeping room with a huge fireplace in which Barbara was cooking stews, chili and soups at one of our winter visits. Guests also make quite a to-do over the life-size mounted moose, a century-old antique sited smack dab in the center of the living room – staring head-on at the decanter of sherry, which is always at the ready in this hospitable B&B.

(860) 526-2014. Fax (860) 526-0875. www.information.com/ct/riverwind. Doubles, $95 to $165.

Steamboat Inn, 73 Steamboat Wharf, Mystic 06355.

This inn, transformed from a vacant restaurant along the Mystic River, offers ten luxurious guest rooms right beside the water in the heart of downtown Mystic.

Named after ships built in Mystic, all have whirlpool baths (five of them double size), telephones and televisions hidden in cupboards or armoires and six have fireplaced sitting areas facing the river. A local decorator outfitted them in lavish style: mounds of pillows and designer sheets on the queensize canopy or twin beds; loveseats or sofas with a plush armchair in front of the fireplaces. Mantels and cabinetwork make these rooms look right at home.

Our favorites are the second-floor rooms at either end, brighter and more airy with bigger windows onto the water, a couple with half-cathedral ceilings. Rooms in the middle are darker in both decor and daylight. Four rooms on the ground floor are suite-size in proportion and come with double whirlpool tubs and wet bars with microwaves, but are on view to the constant stream of passersby on the wharf. Each room is distinctively different and has its own merits. "One couple stayed here four times in the first month and worked their way around the inn, staying in different rooms," reported co-owner John McGee.

There's a common room with all the right magazines and glass tables for continental breakfast. Innkeeper Diane Stadtmiller puts out fruit compote, homemade muffins, cereal and granola each morning.

(860) 536-8300 or (800) 364-6100. Fax (860) 572-1250. www.visitmystic.com/ steamboat. Ten rooms with private baths. Doubles, $210 to $275 summer and fall weekends, $185 to $250 summer midweek, $165 to $210 fall midweek. Rest of year: $160 to $235 weekends, $110 to $175 midweek.

House of 1833, 72 North Stonington Road, Mystic 06355.

Built by banker Elias Brown in 1833, this pillared, Greek Revival mansion on three hillside acres must have been the most imposing house in Old Mystic. Or so it's depicted by an artist in a stunning mural that wraps around its curving staircase and shows the way the hamlet looked at the time.

Californians Carol and Matt Nolan spent two years touring 36 states to find the perfect place to run an inn. They purchased this substantial residence and undertook renovations to create a luxurious B&B. They gutted the bathrooms, which had been modernized, and say they redid them to the period, although which period might be debatable. They installed a Har-Tru tennis court next to the pool and produced an assistant innkeeper, bright-eyed son Alexander, a year after opening.

This is one gorgeous house, from the formal dining room that dwarfs a long breakfast table set for ten, to the five large guest bedrooms, all with queen beds and wood-burning fireplaces, some of them quite spacious and unusual. The double parlor is a knockout: the front portion, outfitted in Greek Revival, opens into a Victorian section notable for a crystal chandelier, a grand piano and an antique pump organ. A heavy door opens off the front parlor into the Peach Room, the former library. Here's a guest room with a mahogany canopy bed draped in peach fabric, a plush settee with matching chair on an oriental rug, a private wicker porch facing the pool, and a bathroom with a walk-in shower through which one passes to get to the double whirlpool tub.

Upstairs are three more guest rooms with thick carpeting and fine fabrics. Although Carol oversaw most of the decorating, each picked one room to do themselves. Hers was the rear Verandah Room in cream and celadon green with a light pine queen bed enclosed in wispy sheer curtains and a ladyslipper clawfoot tub. Matt's was the third-floor Cupola Room in plum and gold with a four-poster bed draped from the ceiling, a potbelly stove, a double whirlpool tub in the bathroom in one corner and a separate stall shower off by itself under the stairs. The stairs rise to a cupola, holding two seats from which to observe the sunset.

Chocolate-chip cookies and tea or lemonade greet guests upon arrival. At 9 the next morning, breakfast begins with Matt's decorative fresh fruit plates ("he gets very creative," says Carol). His artistry continues as he plays light contemporary music on the baby grand during the main course, which might be baked custard french toast, eggs florentine in puff pastry with honey-mustard sauce or a specialty quiche with eggs, cottage cheese and corn chips.

(860) 536-6325 or (800) 367-1833. Five rooms with private baths. Memorial Day to mid-November: doubles, $155 to $225 weekends, $115 to $165 midweek. Rest of year: $115 to $165 weekends, $95 to $135 midweek. Two-night minimum on weekends.

Table is set for elegant breakfast by candlelight at Antiques & Accommodations.

Antiques & Accommodations, 32 Main St., North Stonington 06359.
Ann and Thomas Gray, who are really into cooking, nearly enrolled in the Johnson
& Wales culinary program but decided instead to open a B&B. Their 1861 yellow
house with the gingerbread trim of its era became the focal point for a complex
that includes five guest rooms, a garden cottage suite, an antiques shop in the barn
and extensive gardens.

Tom puts his cooking skills to the test with an outstanding English breakfast,
served by candlelight at 8:30 or 9:30 in the formal dining room, on the flower-
bedecked front porch or the stone patio in the garden. It always includes fresh
fruit in an antique crystal bowl, perhaps melon with a yogurt, honey and mint
sauce or cantaloupe-melon soup with viola garnish. Main courses could be eggs
benedict, crab soufflé, a stilton and aquavit omelet with dill sauce, an apple-rum
puff garnished with strawberries and a signature sweet bread pudding laced with
dried apricots and cream sherry. "Breakfast goes on for hours," says Ann, who
was still serving at 11 the December weekday we first called in. These hospitable
hosts also have been known to dispense wine late into the evening on the patio.

Memories of traveling in England inspired the Grays to furnish their home in
the Georgian manner with formal antique furniture and accessories. Six rooms
come with private baths, and all have canopied beds, fresh flowers and decanters
of sherry. Besides a parlor with TV, the main house offers a recently redecorated,
elegant downstairs bedroom with yellow painted walls glazed with gold, a queen
poster bed and a working fireplace. Upstairs are two bedrooms, one a bridal room
filled with photographs of honeymooners who have stayed there.

Families and couples traveling together tend to book the suites in the 1820
Garden Cottage, a two-story affair beside landscaped gardens in back. Each floor
contains a sitting room and a kitchen. The lower-floor suite called Kerri's Cottage

offers three queensize bedrooms and a bath. The second floor has two bedrooms (each with Eldred Wheeler lace canopy queen beds, gas fireplace and private bath), and a fireplace and wet bar in the common room. Rooms here contain some remarkable stenciling, sponge-painted furniture, marbleized dressers and floral curtains, along with the antiques that characterize the rest of the establishment, although here most of them are early American and country. One bedroom is furnished by Whitmore of Middletown, and the contents are for sale. "You can sleep in the canopy bed and take it home," advises Ann. "We keep replenishing the stock with new discoveries, which keeps the house interesting." At our latest visit she had just sold $1,600 worth of flatware off the dining-room table to a guest who took a liking to that aspect of their growing silver collection.

Another draw here, besides the antiques and breakfasts, are the exotic gardens. They provide plenty of herbs and edible flowers with which to garnish the breakfasts, as well as hours of enjoyment for guests.

(860) 535-1736 or (800) 554-7829. Fax (860) 535-2613.www.visitmystic/com/antiques. Five rooms and one three-bedroom suite with private baths. Doubles, $169 to $199; suite $229. December-April midweek, doubles $99 to $149, suite $169.

Gourmet Treats

Wheatmarket at 4 Water St., Chester, is a well-stocked specialty-foods store where you can order a prepared picnic (the Lovers' includes orange-passion fruit sodas, bliss potato salad and chocolate kisses) or eat at one of the small tables in the front. Nineteen sandwiches include country pâté with sweet and rough mustard, turkey breast with cranberry conserve and cheddar, and roast beef with garlic and herb cheese. Also on the docket are salads, soups, stews, a handful of hot entrées (all under $5) and deep-dish pizzas (the chicken with artichoke and the eggplant with sundried tomatoes are especially popular). Owner Dennis Welch also does low-calorie dishes. A specialty is custard-filled cornbread (obviously not low-calorie). Browse among the racks for Belgian butter-almond cookies, Coryell's Crossing jams, Guiltless Gourmet dips, beluga caviar, saffron and such.

Pasta Unlimited at 159 Main St., Deep River, is where to get the freshest pasta imaginable. Michelle St. Marie's pasta machine is in the window, and nothing gets cut until a customer orders it. Available types include spinach, pumpkin, tomato, lemon-dill and a dynamite black-peppercorn pasta that we tried with Michelle's good clam sauce. At another visit, we took home pumpkin pasta and topped it with the raphael sauce (artichoke hearts, plum tomatoes and romano cheese) – oh, so good. A recent addition is scallop and lobster raviolis. The little shop also has a new coffee bar, as well as cookware and gourmet items. Sandwiches ($3.50 to $4.50) include one with roast beef, Vermont cheddar, red onions and beer mustard. Soups, salads and desserts like key lime zest or black and white espresso cake are on display. The fantasy rice salad includes snow peas, scallions, radishes, water chestnuts, almonds, sesame seeds and more.

Fromage at 1400 Boston Post Road, Old Saybrook, is an upscale shop where Christine Chesanek purveys wonderful cheeses, fine foods and coffees. She stocks ten kinds of olives, like french black olives in sunflower-seed oil and roasted garlic. Aged chèvre, her own cheese spreads, Harney & Sons teas, pâtés, pastas and more are on the shelves. Christine also has an Italian machine that makes a good cup of latte for $2.30.

Ex-restaurant chef Lissa Loucks, a Culinary Institute of America grad, heads up **Vanderbrooke Bakers and Caterers,** 65 Main St., Old Saybrook. She produces dynamite breads, pastries, salads, sandwiches and hot entrées, available at the retail shop or from the deli to eat in or take out. The bread repertoire includes country french, flanders (a Belgian white with oats), squaw, mustard-tarragon, sourdough, and gorgonzola and roasted red pepper, about eight changing varieties each day. The pastry case is full of delights. The deli also impresses with sandwiches, salads (Moroccan chicken, minty barley, ginger coleslaw), soups like shrimp and corn chowder and the day's entrées.

The original clam hash draws food lovers to **Pat's Kountry Kitchen** at 70 Mill Rock Road (Route 154 at the junction of Route 1), Old Saybrook. It's an utterly delicious blend of clams, onions and potatoes, topped with a fried egg and sensational for breakfast or lunch with coleslaw. The hash, for which Pat Brink closely guards the recipe, resulted from an accident (her kids threw out the broth distilled from two bushels of quahogs destined for the day's chowder, and she improvised to use up the dried clams). Pat's serves good, old-fashioned country meals daily, from 7 a.m. to 9 p.m.

For pizzas with a difference, head to the new **Pizza Grille,** Route 27, Mystic, just north of I-95 and the Mystic Carousel & Fun Center. Timothy Doyle from Providence, who says he's the only Irishman offering pizzas in that city's Little Italy called Federal Hill, offers wood-fired grilled pizzas here. This is no ordinary pizza parlor. It's paneled in pine, upholstered in burgundy leather and has a bar. The thin-sliced pizzas come from a wood grill and thicker, traditional pizzas from a traditional oven. The wild mushroom pizza (portobello, crimini and shiitake, with diced tomatoes and grilled onions, $11.95) teamed with a mesclun salad makes a good meal. Open daily, 11 to 10 or 11.

We've seldom seen so many unusual flavors as at **Mystic Drawbridge Ice Cream Shoppe,** 2 West Main St., Mystic. Rod Desmarais and his wife Cheryl, a pastry chef, say they get their ideas from their travels. Among the 25 changing choices, you might find macadamia nut, kahlua-mocha fudge, praline-pecan, spiked apple pie (with a touch of rum), ginger-chocolate chunk, pumpkin pie ("sorry, no crust") and the perennial favorite, Mystic mud – chocolate ice cream combined with anything else at hand. With less air overrun than usual, Mystic ice creams are creamier and richer than most. Shakes, sundaes, gourmet coffees and pastries are also served. Check out the mural on the wall: it's an endearing picture of Mystic, to which staff and customers keep adding local folks and landmarks. The ice creams are made daily at the couple's new shop in the Mystic Carousel & Fun Center.

The area's best gourmet shop and deli is **Culinary Capers,** 63 Williams Ave. (Route 1), on the eastern outskirts of Mystic. Here you'll find sleek kitchen shelves full of specialty foods as well as a coffee bar and deli and pastry cases laden with treats. Sample a few salads (saffron-marinated cauliflower, horseradish coleslaw, kamut and currant waldorf) or a sandwich (Connecticut smoked turkey and swiss cheese on a baguette). Save room for one of the delectable desserts – perhaps fruit tart, peach cobbler or lemon bar – beckoning from the counter top. The rear kitchen is on view through windows from the counter area. Tables beside the big front windows look out onto the passing scene along Route 1. Open daily, 7 to 7.

Watermark at 2 Wyassup Road, North Stonington, is an aromatic segue into the rural past. Area women formerly associated with the famed Caprilands Herb Farm in Coventry opened this 200-year-old structure overlooking the Shunock

River in the ever-so-quaint crossroads of North Stonington to showcase their herbs, teas, specialty foods, candles and garden books. A gallery in one room offers changing exhibitions, and floral and food demonstrations are among activities on tap. At the rear is a small, funky café where the blackboard menu might offer Greek salad, a hummus club or a turkey roll-up. Desert could be a slice of oreo cookie pie. Comments written in the guest book range from "earthy, soothing" to "full of treasures." Open Tuesday-Saturday 9 to 5, also some Sundays and evenings.

French Gourmet

Quimper Faience, 141 Water St., Stonington.

Who would guess that the world headquarters of the famed hand-painted French dinnerware and decorative pottery is located along the main street of downtown Stonington? It seems that Paul and Sarah Janssens, Stonington residents who had imported and distributed the ware through their Quimper retail store here since 1979, helped save the 300-year-old Quimper factory from bankruptcy in 1984. They and several investors purchased the faiencerie (the second oldest company in France), continued its operations and turned their storefront and an upstairs apartment here into the retail and mail-order headquarters. This is the flagship store, and Quimper/Stonington now has four company stores (one in Paris) and wholesales to others. Quimperware, best known for its colorful Breton peasant motifs and always hand-painted and signed by the artist, is still produced at the factory in Brittany. Fifty-eight artists paint the patterns on the pieces, no two of which are the same.

(860) 535-1712. Open Monday-Saturday 10 to 5.

A Choice Winery

Chamard Vineyards, 115 Cow Hill Road, Clinton.

The owner of this money-is-no-object winery is William R. Chaney, chairman and CEO of Tiffany & Co., so you know things are done with class. And classy all the way is Chamard, reached via an unremarkable residential street off Exit 63 of I-95, not far from the Clinton Crossing factory outlet stores. Overlooking a farm pond, one of the Northeast's best wineries occupies a gray shingled house built in 1988 as "a New England château" near the front entrance to a 40-acre property that is half planted with vines. Wines are tasted with crackers and cheese in a richly furnished living room with vaulted ceiling, a fieldstone fireplace and the air of a deluxe hunting lodge. Larry McCulloch has been the active winemaker since Chamard began in 1985, but Bill and Carolyn Chaney remain involved on weekends, from planting and picking to leading tours and pouring wines. Eighty per cent of the 7,000-case annual output is white wines, primarily a premium chardonnay that sells here for $10. About 150 cases of cabernet and 75 of pinot noir sell out as quickly as they are released. Bill Chaney acknowledges that his connections helped place Chamard's chardonnay in some of New York's finest restaurants, but merit keeps them there. Chamard's emerging chardonnay style is more European than Californian, and wine writers have ranked it among the best wines produced in this country.

(860) 664-0299 or (800) 371-1609. Tours and tastings, Wednesday-Sunday 11 to 4.

Commodore's Room at the Black Pearl restaurant looks onto the Newport waterfront.

Newport, R.I.
In Pursuit of Pleasures

Few cities its size can match in quality or quantity the astonishing variety of restaurants of Newport.

Little wonder. Newport has been a symbol of high living since the Victorian era when America's affluent built summer "cottages" that now form the nation's most imposing collection of mansions in one place. Visitors from around the world come to view the mansions as well as the restorations of some of America's oldest buildings. Sailing and tennis have given modern Newport a sporty face, too.

With all the attractions come the trappings. Restaurants, inns, B&Bs and shops are part of a tourist/building boom that has transformed Rhode Island's most visited city in recent years.

It was not until the early 1970s that Newport's restaurants became known for much more than fresh seafood, served to the masses on venerable waterfront wharves. An immensely popular establishment called The Black Pearl changed that. The first of the town's innovative restaurants, it blended elegant cuisine with more casual fare in a mix that triggered a trend.

Now Newport is home to notable small French restaurants, the nation's oldest continuously operating tavern, small eateries with pace-setting chefs, contemporary seafood houses, assorted ethnic spots and sidewalk cafes. everywhere in a growing smorgasbord of fine and fast food. "The best of the lot here match the best restaurants in Boston," said the mâitre-d' at the Clarke Cooke House, whose owner also owns Locke-Ober in Boston.

Summers and weekends in Newport are pricey and crowded; dinner reservations a week in advance are the alternative to two-hour waits. It's best to visit mid-week or in the off-season.

The myriad pleasures of this small historic city will surprise you. So will the numbers of people pursuing them. On a sunny day, it may seem as if the whole world has come to Newport and its restaurants.

Dining

The Best of the Best

The Place, 28 Washington Square, Newport.

This wine bar and grill keeps Newport abuzz with its exciting cuisine. An adjunct to Yesterday's Ale House, a pubby downtown institution, it was opened by owners Maria and Richard Korn as a showcase for their longtime chef, Alex Daglis. Alex moved to a separate kitchen, hired a staff and devised a contemporary American menu with a European flair that, Richard says, "expands and challenges your tastes."

Everyone raves about the entrées, which range from fennel-crusted tuna finished with a mandarin-ginger vinaigrette and served on stir-fried vegetables and a julienne of crunchy wontons to grilled tournedos with ancho chile sauce and wild mushrooms. Pan-seared red snapper served on lobster and guava sauces with black and white angel-hair pasta, roasted leg and grilled breast of duck with a sweet and spicy chipotle-cherry sauce, and pecan-crusted lamb loin with balsamic vinegar sauce also entice.

But we never got beyond the appetizers, which were so tantalizing that we shared and made a meal of five. The Asian lobster and shrimp pot stickers, terrific scallops with cranberries and ginger, the gratin of wild mushrooms, and the crab raviolis with goat cheese and ginger were warm-ups for a salad of smoked pheasant with poached pears and hazelnuts that was out of this world. Each was gorgeously presented on black octagonal plates. Strawberry margarita sorbet with fresh fruit and a warm apple crêpe with apple fries and apple sorbet were worthy endings.

All this is stylishly served at white-clothed tables on two levels of a long, narrow dining room with brass rails, oil lamps and sconces. A vaudeville curtain from a New Bedford theater, framed and back lit on one wall, dominates the decor.

To accompany, 33 wines are offered by the glass and 150 by the bottle. "Flights" offer a tasting of four wines for $13.50.

From the adjacent Ale House come not flights but "schooners" featuring 36 microbrews. Four seven-ounce pilsener glasses for $6 arrive in an elaborate homemade wooden schooner. A recent lunch here produced a stellar cheddar and bacon soup, mussels dijonnaise and a pasta special blending a portobello mushroom with olives and asparagus. There were interesting sandwiches and salads but, alas, no appetizers at all, let alone any with the appeal of those available at dinner next door. Yesterday's is deservedly popular, but we'll stick with The Place.

(401) 847-0116. Entrées, $17.95 to $25.95. Dinner nightly, 5:30 to 10 or 11. Closed Monday and Tuesday, December-March.

The Black Pearl, Bannister's Wharf.

Since this rambling establishment opened in 1972 as the first of Newport's innovative restaurants, it's been one of our favorites, serving a staggering 1,500

Framed vaudeville curtain is dominant decorative piece along wall at The Place.

meals a day in summer from what owner Tom Cullen calls "the world's smallest kitchen."

Outside under the Cinzano umbrellas, you can sit and watch the world go by as you enjoy what we think is Newport's best clam chowder – creamy, chock full of clams and laced with dill, served piping hot with a huge soda cracker ($4.75 a bowl, and seemingly better every time we order it). You also can get a Pearlburger with mint salad served in pita bread for $6.25, and a variety of sandwiches or stew of the day.

Inside, the tavern is informal, hectic, noisy and fun, offering much the same fare as the outdoor cafe plus heartier offerings (baked cod with pepper jack cheese, "21 Club" chicken hash and grilled calves liver, $9.75 to $22) that can serve as lunch or dinner. In fact, after a bowl of chowder, the crab benedict with french fries was almost too much to finish. You also can get several desserts – we remember a delectable brandy-cream cake – and espresso as strong as it should be, plus cappuccino Black Pearl, enhanced with courvoisier and kahlua.

The pride of the Pearl is the **Commodore Room,** pristinely pretty with white linens, dark walls, low ceiling, ladderback chairs and a view of the harbor through small-paned windows.

Chef Daniel Knerr's dinner appetizers range from fried brie and pâté de maison to Scottish smoked salmon. Start, perhaps, with a shrimp, crab and lobster cocktail with three sauces, "black and blue" tuna with roasted pepper sauce or a salad of exotic lettuces with goat cheese and sundried tomatoes. Typical entrées are salmon fillet with mustard-dill hollandaise, gray sole meunière, medallions of veal with morels and champagne sauce, breast of pheasant with perigueux sauce and special, dry-aged sirloin steaks obtained from a New York butcher.

It's an ambitious menu, the more so considering the size of the kitchen. But the Black Pearl can expand or contract its service with the season and the crowds. While others have come and gone, it remains a pearl on the Newport scene.

(401) 846-5264. Entrées, $17.50 to $28.50. Tavern and outdoor cafe open daily from 11. Dinner in Commodore Room, 6 to 11, jackets required. Closed six weeks in winter.

Restaurant Bouchard, 505 Thames St.

After training in France and sixteen years as executive chef at the famed Le Château in New York's Westchester County, Albert J. Bouchard III decided in 1995 it was time to be on his own. He, his wife Sarah and their three youngsters moved to Newport because of its water and yachting (they live on their yacht in the summer). They sought a small establishment where he could exercise "total artistic control," which turned out to be the former tea room at the Hammett House Inn.

The two-section, 43-seat dining room is a beauty in celadon and cream. Assorted chairs with upholstered celadon or mauve seats are at well-spaced tables dressed in cream-colored, floor-length cloths and topped with Wedgwood china, expensive stemware and tall oil lamps bearing small shades. Four shelves of demitasse cups and saucers, part of his father's collection, separate the front section from the back, and a small bar in the front room looks to be straight out of Provence.

The food is classic French with contemporary nuances in the style of Albert's former domain. It has received rave reviews and, combined with the elegant sense of comfort and flawless service, contributes to a memorable dining experience.

Entrées at our latest autumn visit ranged from roasted cod with creamy mustard sauce to lobster cardinal, stuffed with scallops, gruyère and cognac-truffle lobster sauce. Dover sole with sorrel sauce, Atlantic salmon with sautéed foie gras and port wine sauce, sweetbreads in citron sauce, and sautéed duck breast with ginger-honey demi-glace testify to the small kitchen's scope.

Typical starters are lobster vol-au-vent, escargots in sourdough with mushrooms and garlic, and roquefort and eggplant cheesecake with tomato butter sauce. Warm pear salad with walnuts, blue cheese and greens was a mid-winter refresher.

Albert, with two talented assistants in the kitchen, prepares the crusty sourdough rolls as well as the desserts, which range from a mocha phyllo napoleon to chocolate crêpes and grand marnier soufflés. Some of the wines, which date back to the 1960s, come from his personal cellar.

The Bouchards landscaped a rear brick patio for drinks and hors d'oeuvres in summer, and had an option to buy the five-room B&B operation upstairs.

(401) 846-0123. Entrées, $18.75 to $26. Dinner nightly except Tuesday, 6 to 9:30 or 10. Sunday brunch, 11 to 2.

Asterix & Obelix, 599 Lower Thames St.

With worldly talents, youthful bravado and Danish good looks, John Bach-Sorenson alighted at age 33 in Newport – "it reminded me of home" – and looked for a restaurant site. The scion of a family of Copenhagen restaurateurs found it in a working auto-repair garage. Three whirlwind months of sweat equity later, he had transformed it into an airy, high-ceilinged and colorful space with a partly open rear kitchen, a remarkable hand-crafted bar along one side, and black chairs at white-linened tables topped with circular white butcher paper, votive candles and vases of alstroemeria. In summer, the two front garage doors open to the street for a European sidewalk cafe atmosphere.

John, his partner-become-wife Tracy Tarigo and an artist friend are responsible for the splashy effects and artworks. The artistry continues in the kitchen, where this 1986 World Culinary Olympics winner holds forth seven nights a week after arising at 5 a.m. to start baking in his new **Boulangerie Obelix** at 382 Spring St. Asked how he could maintain the pace, he enthused: "This is my hobby, my life."

Albert and Sarah Bouchard in front of display of demitasse cups at Restaurant Bouchard.

He calls his fare Mediterranean-Asian. Ever-changing main courses range widely, from a classic sole meunière to steak au poivre with spinach anglaise and french fries. You might find Thai-style grilled prawns with green curry and coconut milk, crispy salmon with mushroom-asparagus-orzo risotto, and crispy duck with honey and ginger. The filet mignon might be à la milanaise (a mouthful of a menu description: tomato espagnole sauce, shredded ham, mushrooms and white truffle oil with roasted pasta).

Among appetizers at our latest visit were escargots bourguignonne, crab cakes rémoulade, tempura tuna roll, carpaccio of black angus beef with arugula, and a salad of bibb lettuce and radicchio with grapes and aged cheddar. Raspberry torte, key lime pie and chocolate mousse are favorite desserts.

A rack of newspapers for reading and an energetic young staff contribute to a laid-back, brasserie atmosphere. The place is named for John's two favorite French comic-strip characters, known for fighting the bureaucracy, which John was doing in pursuing a liquor license. He finally received a beer and wine license.

(401) 841-8833. Entrées, $19 to $24. Dinner nightly, from 5.

The West Deck, 1 Waite's Wharf.

Modern bistro cuisine and a cozy grill room with a waterside deck are the hallmarks of this local haunt off the tourist path. Chef-owner James Mitchell, whose cooking we first encountered when he was at the Inn at Castle Hill, took over a century-old structure that once served as a garage for an oil company.

Here, in a small, rather garage-like space that's one-third cooking area, he seats 30 diners at tables dressed in pink and white and ten more at an L-shaped eating bar facing the open kitchen. A potbelly stove warms an enclosed sun porch for dining on a chilly day. In summer the seating of choice is on the outside deck, where there's a wood grill.

The dinner menu, printed nightly, is surprisingly extensive. It offers some of Newport's best seafood as well as adventurous modern variations of the classic French dishes that are the chef's forte. At a recent December visit, the fifteen entrées ran the gamut from potato-crusted salmon with mushroom duxelle and pinot noir sauce to a mixed grill of filet, lamb chop, game hen and spicy andouille sausage. Jim might enhance sesame-crusted mahi-mahi with coconut and lemongrass and offer grilled shrimp lo mein, over oriental noodles and vegetables. Braised beef shortribs, sliced duck breast and confit with raspberry sauce, and venison Baden-Baden with chestnuts and mushrooms indicate the range.

Fourteen appetizers included sole mousseline with dill and steamed mussels in lobster jus, escargots on a portobello mushroom with garlic-red wine sauce, and goat cheese salad with a parmesan crisp and roasted beets. The night's terrine of duck, rabbit, quail and foie gras with hazelnuts and port wine glaze sounded fabulous. Among the rich desserts were a peach bread pudding with whiskey-caramel sauce, chocolate fondant, and cappuccino-praline mousse with espresso sauce. Most of the well-chosen wines, refreshingly priced in the twenties and thirties, are available by the glass. A captain's select list adds more expensive choices.

In season on the waterfront deck, the outdoor grill furnishes the bulk of the dishes on a simpler, all-day menu that ranges from a fish sandwich to teriyaki steak.

(401) 847-3610. Entrées, $16 to $25. Lunch in summer, noon to 4. Dinner nightly in summer, 6 to 10, Wednesday-Sunday in off-season. Sunday brunch in winter, noon to 3.

The White Horse Tavern, corner of Marlborough and Farewell Streets.

Claiming to be the oldest operating tavern in the United States, established in 1673, the tavern was restored by the Newport Preservation Society and opened as a restaurant in 1957. It's also known for some of the best – albeit expensive – food in town.

The White Horse is a deep red Colonial building that imparts an unmistakable feeling of history. We find it most appealing for cozy, cold-weather dining, with its dark interior, wide-plank floors, beamed ceilings, huge fireplace and classical music. The dark rose and white draperies complement the handsome burgundy and off-white china and the winter arrangements of silk flowers and dried berries. Brass candlesticks with Colonial candles inside large clear hurricane chimneys are on each table.

Service by a tuxedo-clad staff is formal and even at lunch, prices start at $9 (for a grilled chicken or turkey club sandwich) and top off at $17 for bouillabaisse or sautéed veal pommery.

On a spring afternoon, we tried the day's soup, an interesting chilled mixture of yogurt, cucumber, dill and walnuts. Baked marinated montrachet with garlic purée and herbed croutons was a delicious appetizer. The fish of the day, halibut in a sauce with grapefruit pieces and a hint of brandy, was excellent. The chicken salad resting in a half avocado was decidedly bland.

Decor is elegant Colonial at historic White Horse Tavern.

Wines are, as you would imagine, expensive, but many are available by the glass. The old bar room in one corner of the building is atmospheric as can be.

The classic continental fare takes on decidedly trendy twists at night. Expect appetizers like Atlantic salmon tartare with wasabi crème fraîche and salmon roe, peeky toe crab napoleon with house-made tuiles garnished with flying fish roe, a lobster and shrimp "tower" stacked with crispy wontons and roasted corn salsa, and a watercress and beef tenderloin salad tossed with a spicy lime dressing and roasted peanuts.

Seafood entrées can be complex, as in seared yellowfin tuna with Hudson Valley foie gras in a red wine and wild mushroom sauce, Pacific halibut over a roasted red pepper and scallion risotto cake with sautéed bok choy, and pan-seared mahi-mahi with lobster and roasted corn hash topped with swirls of crispy onions in a citrus-ginger jus. More traditional are such menu staples as grilled duck breast, individual beef wellington and châteaubriand for two.

You might like to finish with a triple silk torte on a bed of raspberry-melba sauce. It's not exactly Colonial fare or prices, but well-heeled folks who like good food and formal ambiance keep the White Horse busy most of the time.

(401) 849-3600. Entrées, $28 to $36. Lunch, daily except Tuesday noon to 3. Dinner nightly, 6 to 10, jackets required. Sunday champagne brunch, noon to 3.

La Petite Auberge, 19 Charles St.

Dining on classic French cuisine in the historic Stephen Decatur House has been a fairly serious matter since chef-owner Roger Putier opened his small and charming restaurant in 1975. He has lightened up with a new courtyard/bistro menu, although traditionalists still like the rich French sauces and the air of romance.

The dark green house, warmed by roses climbing fence posts and trellises, is typical of many in old Newport, smack up against the sidewalk.

In two main-floor dining rooms, each with a handful of tables, the atmosphere is convivial and intimate – not for naught is this called petite. To the side and rear are a cozy bar with a sofa in front of a fireplace and a courtyard with five tables for outdoor dining. Up steep stairs are three more small dining rooms. Elegant lace tablecloths are layered over blue or gold linens, and the large menu is in French with English translations. The printed menu rarely changes, but is supplemented by many nightly specials.

The only description for the sauces is heavenly – from the escargots with cèpes, a house specialty (the heavily garlicked sauce fairly cries out to be sopped up with the crusty French bread) to our entrées of veal with morels and cream sauce and two tender pink lamb chops, also with cèpes and a rich brown sauce.

Appetizers and soups are predictable, from smoked salmon to lobster bisque. They include a fish soup Marseilles style, mussels in a light cream sauce, and duck and goose liver pâtés.

Entrées, including vegetables (crisp green beans and creamy sliced potatoes topped with cheese at our visit), run from frog's legs provençal to beef wellington with truffle sauce. Other choices are salmon in cream sauce with pink peppercorns, trout with hazelnuts, and four presentations of beef.

Service by black-suited women is efficient. Most dishes are finished at tableside, even the tossed salad with choice of dressings.

We ended with strawberries romanoff, one of the old favorites. The desserts are mostly classics like crêpes suzette, pear hélène and cherries jubilee. The excellent wine list is mainly French and reasonably priced.

The bistro menu, served on the trellised courtyard or in the charming rear bar, is short and to the point. Start perhaps with fish soup, crab cakes or a charcuterie assortment of pâtés and dry-cured sausage. Move on to swordfish with citrus-chile butter, sirloin strip steak, grilled quail or grilled lobster with fresh herbs ($12.95 to $17.95). Finish with chambord cheesecake or amaretto tartuffo.

(401) 849-6669. Entrées, $21 to $33. Dinner, Monday-Saturday 6 to 10 (courtyard to 11), Sunday 5 to 9.

The Clarke Cooke House, Bannister's Wharf.

Dining is on several levels and a breezy yet formal upper deck in this 1790-vintage Colonial house, another venerable Newport establishment. Two kitchens, offering different renditions of contemporary European fare, are under the aegis of executive chef Ted Gidley, who returned to the Cooke House in 1994 after several years at Pronto.

The most casual venue is the ground-level Candy Store cafe and espresso bar. Up a level on the other side is the Grille, a middle-of-the-road bistro offering lunch and dinner. Proceed up past the Midway Bar on the stairway landing to the winter Gilbert Stuart dining room, the semi-private Skybar and the glamorous summer Porch with a panoramic harbor view.

Casual fare is served at down-to-earth prices in the Candy Store. We can vouch for a lunch dish of eggs benedict, salad vinaigrette and great french fries, and a thick and creamy cup of clam chowder – one of the best we've had lately – with a juicy hamburger on an onion roll, again with those addictive french fries. The dinner menu is priced from $15.95 for sesame-grilled rare tuna fanned on mesclun salad to $22.95 for Mediterranean fish stew.

The food gets considerably more expensive, the service more polished and the atmosphere more haute in the Porch and Skybar. The dining area is formal in green and white, with high beamed ceiling, green high-back chairs and green banquettes awash with pillows. Hurricane chimneys enclose silver candlesticks,

Waterfront is on view from glamorous upper Porch at The Clarke Cooke House.

and fresh flowers and ornate silver top the white-linened tables. The doors open onto a canopied deck called the Porch, overlooking the harbor scene.

The upstairs menu has gone through contemporary French and northern Italian phases lately before settling into what the chef calls modern European, incorporating elements of both. Among recent appetizers were carpaccio of yellowfin tuna, ravioli of lobster and wild mushrooms, and pan-seared duck foie gras with a croquette of English peas in a pistachio crust, caramelized raisin-black peppercorn sauce and roasted garlic jus. A signature salad of lobster, mango and avocado is dressed with a citrus-ginger vinaigrette.

Entrées run from sautéed fillet of sole lyonnaise and native George's Bank cod with a smoked codfish brandade and a bouillabaisse coulis to wood-grilled veal rib chop with turnip-infused veal jus, a ravioli of celery root and foie gras, shallot confit and English peas. Others include peppered tuna steak, pan-seared magret duck and rack of lamb persillade.

Among desserts are chocolate mascarpone terrine, a signature "snowball in hell" teaming chocolate roulade and vanilla ice cream, and Indian pudding à la mode – the last a fixture at Locke-Ober, the Boston institution also owned by proprietor David Ray.

The wine list ranks as the city's priciest, with many in the triple digits.

(401) 849-2900. Entrées, $22.50 to $31. Dinner nightly in season, 6 to 10 or 10:30, weekends in off-season. Candy Store and Grill, lunch daily, 11:30 to 5, weekends in winter; dinner nightly from 5, Wednesday-Sunday in winter.

Pronto, 464 Thames St.

Some of the most innovative cooking in the city emanates from the partially open kitchen of this dark and cozy cocoon of Victorian romance. Owner Janne Osean's vintage decor is a melange of gilt mirrors, heavy dark draperies, potted palms, crystal chandeliers (a different one over almost every table), pressed-tin walls and ceiling, and oriental rugs on the floors. One innkeeper calls it the most romantic dining spot in the city, but we find the tables too close for comfort, let alone romance. A new upstairs room doubles the seating capacity with tables spaced a bit farther apart.

Soft jazz played as we lunched, fortunately for us nearly alone, here one winter weekday. The vegetable soup was hearty and the wild mushroom crostini quite tasty. Truly terrific was a special of chicken breast encrusted in pistachios and walnuts, served on a bed of many greens with red and yellow pepper vinaigrette, the plate colorfully decorated with flecks of parsley and squiggles of vinaigrette. It was so good we asked the chef afterward how he prepared it. We also could understand how Newporters felt a favorite haunt, once perceived as quite reasonable, had become more expensive. Bread was extra (50 cents for half a loaf). A masterful apple tart with praline ice cream (razor-thin apple slices flecked with cinnamon and fanned around the perimeter of a dinner-size plate) turned out to be $6 on the bill. Add a couple of glasses of the house Sicilian wine and our luncheon tab escalated to more than $50 for two.

Yet we'd gladly go back (on an uncrowded night) for a dinner repertoire that yields nightly specials as well as some wonderful (and quite reasonable, $11 to $14) pastas. Consider the signature farfalle with shiitake mushrooms, kalamata olives, spinach, roasted red peppers, pinenuts and chèvre – all the currently "in" ingredients in one dish. The specials here are indeed special, perhaps calamari and shrimp scampi, pan-seared red snapper with a ginger-jasmine sauce, grilled ahi tuna with orzo pilaf and mango chutney, and spicy duck breast and smoked mozzarella quesadilla. Start with Thai shrimp nachos, grilled lobster and sea scallops with a wilted spinach and endive salad, or beef carpaccio with arugula, shaved reggiano and white truffle oil. Finish with key lime pie or white and dark chocolate mousse. Be enticed by the specials, and happy to pay the piper.

(401) 847-5251. Entrées, $16 to $24. Breakfast daily in summer, 9 to 3; lunch rest of year, 11:30 to 4; dinner nightly, 5 to 10 or 11.

More Dining Choices

Scales and Shells, 527 Thames St.

This local favorite perhaps epitomizes the Newport restaurant phenomenon. It was standing-room-only in its first week without so much as a word of advertising. Later, it expanded with a second-floor addition called **Upscales,** a smaller and quieter room open from May-September with a rather more sophisticated menu ($16.25 to $22.25, for the likes of grilled marinated toro tuna with haricots verts and baby bliss mashed potatoes).

On the main floor, plain and exotic seafood – simply prepared and presented in stylishly simple surroundings – is offered by retired sea captain Andy Ackerman. He and his staff cook up a storm in an open kitchen near the door, as fast as the seafood can be unloaded from the docks out back.

The delicious aromas almost overpowered as we read the blackboard menu with an immense range but nary a non-fish item in sight. Start with deep-fried calamari, grilled white clam pizza, Sicilian mussels or mesquite-grilled shrimp from the list of appetizers. From this you could make a meal and, Andy says, many people do, ordering Chinese style. Monkfish, scallops, shrimp, swordfish, snapper, scrod – you name it, it comes in many variations as a main dish, wood-grilled, broiled or tossed with pasta. Shrimp or clams fra diavolo are served right in their own steaming-hot pans.

Tabasco, red pepper and parmesan cheese are on the tables, which are covered with black and white checked cloths. The floors are bare, and the decor is pretty much nil except for models of fish on the walls. You can pick and choose from the raw bar near the front entrance.

Italian gelatos (apricot and hazelnut are a couple) and tarts comprise the dessert selection. The short list of Italian and California wines is affordably priced.

(401) 846-3474. Entrées, $10.95 to $19.95. Dinner, Monday-Saturday 5 to 9 or 10, Sunday 4 to 9. No credit cards.

Cheeky Monkey Cafe, 14 Perry Mill Wharf.

The owners of Providence's acclaimed Gatehouse Restaurant branched out to mixed reviews with this small, two-level dining room, bar and an upstairs cigar lounge with a great view of the harbor.

The name refers to the British expression of endearment for a fun-loving, devilish person. Owner Henry Kates chose it to reflect a cheeky point of view on foods and spirits, and provided a dark and vaguely jungle-look decor of black wood tables and faux-leopard skins on the benches and wainscoting. Dining is on two levels, facing an open kitchen.

The chef works with executive chef Steven Marsella, who moved on to open the latest Cheeky Monkeys in Miami's South Beach, to deliver contemporary cuisine with Southern and Asian accents. The short dinner menu might harbor such eclectic starters as a gumbo ya-ya of chicken, greens and andouille sausage, New Orleans-style barbecued shrimp with green onion popcorn rice, and tuna nori rolls with a tamari dipping sauce,

Main courses range from sesame-seared tuna with wasabi jasmine rice to grilled ribeye steak glazed with worcestershire sauce. Typical are lobster paella, grilled Atlantic salmon with tamarind glaze, skillet-seared chicken breast with creole tomato salsa, and grilled pork tenderloin with banana plantain chutney, smothered collard greens and blackeyed peas.

Dessert could be bananas foster, raspberry tart with vanilla ice cream or chocolate suicide torte with peanut butter whipped cream.

Start with a drink in a separate bar across the hallway. Finish with an after-dinner cordial the upstairs cigar lounge, with a parlor-like ambiance of sofas, overstuffed chairs, floor lamps and – what every parlor needs – a humidor cabinet.

(401) 845-9494. Entrées, $19.95 to $24.95. Dinner, Wednesday-Sunday 6 to 9 or 10.

Café Zelda, 528 Lower Thames St.

This deco-style bar and bistro has been around for some time, but its food has been elevated lately by chef Marjorie Knerr, formerly of the Commodore Room at the Black Pearl. In our opinion, Zelda had suffered from terminal funkiness (when we popped in a few years ago we could hardly see through the smoke and beat a hasty retreat). Now with its act together, the food is affordably priced and gets high ratings.

The international dinner menu entices with starters like a chunky lobster bisque, roasted garlic bruschetta with warm gorgonzola, pan-seared tuna with peanut satay on a twist of soba noodles, and Zelda's steamed or fried dumplings with wasabi soy sauce. Typical main courses are New England fisherman's stew, seafood nantua in puff pastry, pan-seared duck breast with maple-apple glaze, osso buco, and rack of lamb with rosemary-mustard sauce. There are a few sandwiches for those who prefer. Chef Midge's desserts are renowned.

Dining is in a long, narrow two-level room with glass-shaded oil lamps on tables topped with white paper over white cloths. There's a cozy, century-old bar at the main entry.

(401) 849-4002. Entrées, $14.25 to $24. Lunch daily in season, from 11:30. Dinner nightly, from 5. Sunday brunch, from 11:30.

Tucker's Bistro, 150 Broadway.
For romance, there's no more idyllic place in Newport than this new French bistro in the heart of the out-of-the-way restaurant row beloved by locals along Broadway. Co-owners Tucker Harris and Ellen Coleman have fashioned a 1920s deco bistro in a double storefront, The bar is in a small room with a library look. Most of the dining takes place in a larger room with a dozen tables amidst red lacquered walls and a ceiling draped in vine branches, rhinestone strands and tiny white lights.

The fare is primarily Mediterranean. The partners tweak the regular printed menu with a trio of daily specials, including soft-shell crab tempura and baked striped bass fillet with gorgonzola sauce at our visit. Otherwise, expect about a dozen entrées, from seafood creole and grilled sea scallops with a lobster-mango cream sauce to beef wellington and rack of lamb with raspberry-rosemary sauce. The duck breast is stuffed with spinach and pistachio nuts and served à l'orange, and the roasted chicken breast rubbed with Moroccan spices and served over couscous.

Appetizers go international, as in crab cakes rémoulade, fried calamari topped with a banana pepper and butter sauce, garlicky escargots sautéed in a sundried tomato pesto beurre blanc, and coconut shrimp with a horseradish-orange marmalade. Desserts are Tucker's forte. His specialty is a signature banana pudding, but he may offer a pecan bread pudding with white chocolate and dried cranberries as well.

(401) 846-3449. Entrées, $12.95 to $20.95. Dinner nightly, 6 to 10.

Dining and Lodging

Castle Hill Inn & Resort, Ocean Drive, Newport 02840.
Originally called "a country inn by the sea," the old Inn at Castle Hill has a new name and a new vitality. The main-floor restaurant has been refurbished, the food service enhanced and the accommodations vastly upgraded.

The locally owned Newport Harbor Corp. reassumed control of the oceanside Victorian mansion in 1995. The father-and-son ownership team of Tim and Paul O'Reilly first renewed the richly paneled lobby, the inner Castle Hill dining room, our favorite Sunset Room with expansive windows jutting out toward the water, and the smaller Agassiz and Newport dining rooms. Only the elegant, romantic bar – long a favorite hangout of the in crowd – remained untouched.

The opulent setting became known for fabulous, contemporary-to-the-max food for several years under executive chef Wayne Gibson, who departed in November 1999. Paul O'Reilly, the on-site general manager, was interviewing chefs from around the country in hopes of maintaining a similar level of Northeastern regional cuisine.

There's no more refined place for an oceanside lunch in Newport than the oval Sunset Room, redecorated with a billowing pale yellow canopy on the ceiling. This is also the place for Castle Hill's long-popular Sunday brunch.

While elevating the food, the O'Reillys also upgraded the accommodations to some of the best along the New England coast. Six outlying Harbor House units were winterized and given kingsize beds, single whirlpool baths, televisions, fireplaces and french doors onto semi-private decks overlooking Narragansett Bay. Also refurbished were nine Victorian guest rooms and a suite upstairs in the main inn, most with king or queen beds, double whirlpool marble baths, fireplaces and original antiques. The side Swiss-style Chalet, former laboratory of original owner Alexander Agassiz, the Harvard marine biologist, also was renovated. Kingsize canopy beds, double whirlpool baths and fireplaces were provided for its upstairs bedroom and a bridal suite.

Latest to bear the O'Reilly touch are eight of the eighteen beachfront efficiency cottages, which formerly were spartan at best and rented only in the summer. The first eight were refurbished and enlarged in 1999. Now elegant with vaulted ceilings, beadboard paneling and beachy décor, Paul ranks them with the best in New England. Each has a granite-counter galley kitchen, kingsize bed, TV and distressed leather couch that converts into a queen bed in the sitting area, fireplace, double whirlpool tub and separate shower and an outdoor deck facing the ocean. From the whirlpool tub in several, you can look out onto the beach – and be out there in no time. The remaining ten beachfront cottages were to be renovated in 2000 and 2001.

A complimentary breakfast with a choice of juices, fruits and entrées is served to overnight guests in the Sunset Room. The fare includes lobster omelets, eggs benedict, French toast made with raisin challah and smoked salmon with breakfast garnishes.

(401) 849-3800 or (888) 466-1355. Fax (401) 849-3838. Twenty-three rooms and cottages and two suites with private baths. Early May to mid-November: doubles, $325 to $495 weekends, $225 to $450 midweek; suites, $450 to $495 weekends, $350 to $450 midweek. Rest of year: doubles, $255 to $375 weekends, $145 to $225 midweek; suites, $375 weekends, $225 midweek. Two-night minimum weekends. Closed in January.

Entrées, $22 to $36. Lunch, Monday-Saturday noon to 3. Dinner nightly, 6 to 9, to 10 in summer; jackets requested. Sunday brunch, 11:30 to 3. Off-season: lunch/brunch on weekends and dinner Wednesday-Saturday 6 to 9.

Vanderbilt Hall, 41 Mary St., Box 840, Newport 02840.

This deluxe "mansion house hotel" was created in 1997 from a former YMCA building in the heart of Newport's Historic Hill district. Partners in the $10 million venture were a management team that opened the opulent Inn at Perry Cabin in Maryland and Keswick Hall in Virginia and Providence investor Arnold Chace, who was familiar with the property. Built in 1909 by Alfred Vanderbilt to be granted to the town for a YMCA in memory of his father, Cornelius, it had been unoccupied for twenty years.

The red-brick hotel's 52 guest accommodations, including 28 on the second and third floors of the restored hall and the rest in a new wing, are divided into five categories, from four "cozy house rooms" to a couple of 700-square-foot suites.

Twenty-eight are "state rooms" that turned out not as large as you might expect. Ten of the more unusual on the third floor are classified as "executive studies," with spiral staircases leading to skylit lofts with office equipment. All are appointed with period furnishings and rich wallpapers, fabrics and linens in the style of Perry Cabin and Keswick. The king and queen bed canopies and treatments are distinctive here; a couple of rooms have kingsize beds in the center draped in fabric. Towel warmers and makeup mirrors are among the amenities.

The main floor is a ramble of elegant rooms with fireplaces, polished hardwood floors and showy furniture. Tea and cookies are offered (by reservation for the public, $9.50 per person) in the main lobby, where a young pianist played (somewhat errantly, we must say – or was she simply practicing?) – the Friday afternoon we were there. The stately living room has countless overstuffed chairs and a rolling cart laden with fine brandies. A game room and a cheery reading room go off the living room at the far end.

Downstairs are a clubby billiards room, a spa and fitness center and the Y's restored, marble-decked indoor pool with a mural of a clipper ship at one end. Indeed, art seems to be a major theme, from the realistic trompe-l'oeil painting on a doorway to murals in the elevator to fine art hung on the corridor walls.

Graceful arches off the lobby lead to a bright and airy garden conservatory full of wicker and tropical plants and an outdoor courtyard with terrace and herb garden. Its menu offers a handful of treats priced from $6.50 for clam chowder and half a club sandwich to $15.50 for New York strip sirloin. The paneled, richly appointed main dining room is named **The Alva** (for a Vanderbilt boat). It is handsome in rich paneling, yellow walls, a coffered ceiling and the finest table appointments (the white napkins are rolled to stand upright). The Alva is flanked by three smaller private rooms: a wine-tasting room with bottles in racks along the walls, a cigar room with humidors and a club-like "en famille" room for single diners to join a common table.

Executive chef Alan Maw from England offers an upscale menu of traditional and modern cuisine. Dinner is available à la carte or prix-fixe, $55 for a five-course tasting menu. Roast halibut, lobster thermidor, chicken en croûte, Mediterranean pork and châteaubriand were choices at a recent visit. The breakfast menu carries prices that might make a Vanderbilt blanch.

In keeping with the "grand house" experience, Vanderbilt Hall operates on a no-tipping policy. Instead, a "discretionary service charge" is added to the bill.

401) 846-6200 or (888) 826-4255. Fax (401) 846-0701. Forty-five rooms and seven suites with private baths. Rates EP. Memorial Day to Columbus Day: doubles, $195 to $430; studios and suites, $495 to $795. Early spring and late fall: doubles $155 to $340; studios and suites, $395 to $615. January-March: doubles $95 to $225; studios and suites, $345 to $495. Two-night minimum peak weekends.

Entrées, $19.50 to $29. Conservatory/terrace, daily 11 to 11. Dinner nightly in Alva, 6 to 10.

Lodging

Rooms in Newport are a glut on the market or scarce to come by, depending on the day and season. A deluxe room that goes for $300 a night on a summer weekend may be available for $100 or so on a winter weekday. Some of the largest and most advertised "inns" tend to be time-sharing condos on the water; a couple of innkeepers own several B&Bs. Breakfasts are usually continental and, in general, the owners are seldom to be seen. We focus here on some of the exceptions.

Cliffside Inn, 2 Seaview Ave., Newport 02840.

Big bucks and great taste have been rendered unto this sumptuous Victorian charmer – the ultimate gourmet getaway. In a textbook example of how to transform a small and quirky place, former broadcast executive Winthrop Baker of Connecticut has created one of the most elegant and comfortable B&Bs in the land. For those who crave the latest in creature comforts, innkeeper Stephan Nicolas and chef Mark Spring have turned it into an epicurean indulgence.

Breakfast table at Cliffside Inn.

The summer villa, a short block from the ocean, was built in 1880 by a governor of Maryland. It later was owned by Newport artist Beatrice Turner, a fact that prompted its current owner to gather many of her paintings from hither and yon and mount a fascinating retrospective exhibit that commanded wide attention for the inn. The Cliffside now offers sixteen air-conditioned bedrooms and suites, the largest of which Win Baker considers the most upscale in Newport with their jacuzzi baths, fireplaces and sitting areas with TVs. Even the smallest of rooms now have been ingeniously expanded to include jacuzzi tubs and sitting areas facing TVs hidden behind mirrors above their new corner fireplaces.

No room in the house has escaped his touch, be it the sumptuous Governor's Suite with its working fireplace visible from both the bedroom and the jacuzzi in the bathroom or the newly enlarged Garden Suite, a great summer space with a bay window off the front porch and a 28-foot-long "habitat bathroom" beneath, so-called "because you can live in it," what with a Victorian book nook at one end and french doors at the other opening onto a private courtyard. The inn's many floor-to-ceiling and bay windows bathe the rooms with light, blending rich Victoriana with an airy Laura Ashley freshness.

The newest accommodations are in the Cliffside Cottage, a onetime ranch house at the foot of the property. It's been transformed into three suites, each with three fireplaces and sound-system bathrooms. The new Seaview on the lower floor is a stone-walled hideaway with a wood-burning fireplace and a kingsize bed dressed in florals as well as a plush sitting room with a see-through gas fireplace shared with the marble bathroom. Here you'll find the first Allure tub sold by Jacuzzi. It's quite a sight, with whirlpool tub, hand-held shower, steam bath, TV, CD player and operating gadgets all integrated into one glass enclosure that looks as if it belongs in a hospital – the intrepid might hesitate to even step inside, but innkeeper Stephan assures that "all the guests love it." Upstairs are two equally majestic suites, both newly configured as the Cliffside repositions to stay in the vanguard. The Atlantic enjoys an ocean view as well as a new sitting room. The Cliff with a kingsize bedroom has two sitting rooms, having taken over what had been a joint common room. Who needs two living rooms? "People can spread out," responds Stephan, acknowledging one of our favorite themes, carried here to the extreme. "Maybe we'll turn the second one into a second bathroom – his and hers."

Every guest room has not only a fireplace (some have two or three) but a whirlpool tub except for one that has a steam bath and separate shower. All also have extra amenities, from robes and mineral water to morning coffee service with a choice from thirteen newspapers. Every room also holds at least one of the fascinating Beatrice Turner portraits, among more than 140 restored by the Cliffside and on display everywhere, but particularly in the main hallways and staircases.

Although the guest quarters are so self-sufficient one feels no need to leave, the Cliffside is a convivial place, thanks to a young and personable staff, a large and welcoming veranda, and an expansive parlor, cheerfully decorated in shades of orange-coral and moss green with handsome faille draperies. Classical music or opera plays in the background as Victorian tea is presented . with an impressive array of finger sandwiches and sweets in the afternoon. Guests choose from a remarkable collection of one-of-a-kind heirloom, antique and specialty cups. Crab-stuffed mushrooms, spinach and portobello puff pastry squares, cucumber pinwheel sandwiches, meringues, baklava, shortbread, maraschino tea cake, lemon bars – they're offered here, and detailed by popular demand in the new *Cliffside Inn Tea and Breakfast Cookbook.*

The food dimension is overseen by innkeeper Stephan, a Johnson & Wales University hospitality graduate whose experienced demeanor belies his youth. The 28-year-old son of a French chef and cookbook author, he's a font of culinary knowledge and puts together a handsome album of local restaurant menus photocopied and scaled to size on cream-colored stock. "We think it's the best menu book in America," says Stephan, who borrowed the idea from a California B&B and – as with everything else about the Cliffside – took it a step beyond.

The chef works full-time to prepare the tea treats as well as nightly turndown sweets and a lavish breakfast in the morning. Ours began with fresh orange juice, two kinds of muffins and a remarkable (for winter) array of raspberries, blackberries and strawberries to lather upon homemade granola and yogurt. The main event was eggs benedict with a subtle hollandaise sauce. The calories were worked off with a jaunt along the oceanside Cliff Walk nearby.

(401) 847-1811 or (800) 845-1811. Fax (401) 848-5850. www.cliffsideinn.com. Eight rooms and eight suites with private baths. Doubles, $205 to $325; suites, $295 to $425. Add $30 weekends, May-October.

Elm Tree Cottage, 336 Gibbs Ave., Newport 02840.

Here is one beautiful "cottage," situated in a quiet neighborhood a block from the sea. Large and comfortable rooms appointed in elegant country style and artist-innkeepers with outgoing personalities help make the place special. Priscilla and Tom Malone and their three young daughters acquired the mansion, built in 1882 and later owned by Mrs. Crawford Hill, the Pennsylvania Railroad heiress and member of Newport's 400. "Our entire house fit into this living room," Priscilla said, recalling their move from Long Island and how they furnished the huge home "from auctions and estate sales."

Furnish it they did, quite grandly yet unpretentiously. There's an 87-foot sweep from dining room to parlor, which ends at expansive windows overlooking Easton's Pond and First Beach. Chintz sofas and a grand piano welcome guests to a living room that could be pictured in a design magazine. To the side are a morning garden room great for lounging and a bar room furnished in wicker. Here the Malones put out munchies for guests to BYOB and sit at the great old bar with 1921 silver dollars embedded in its top and pictures of the former owner's Pekinese dogs reverse-painted on the mirror behind.

Expansive living room is furnished with comfort in mind at Elm Tree Cottage.

At three tables in the fireplaced dining room, the Malones serve extravagant breakfasts by candlelight: perhaps heart-shaped waffles, Portuguese sweet bread french toast or apple crêpes in the shape of calla lilies. "No bacon and eggs here," says Priscilla. "I try to treat guests the way I want to be pampered when I'm away from home." Our autumn breakfast started with juice and homemade oatmeal (the dish arrived on a saucer delightfully decorated with five varieties of dried leaves) and culminated in delicious pumpkin waffles. The day's menu, beautifully calligraphed by Priscilla, went home as a souvenir.

On the second floor are four large bedrooms and a master suite; all with private baths and four with fireplaces. The suite, all 23 by 37 feet of it, is pretty in salmon and seafoam green. It has a Louis XV kingsize bed with a crown canopy, two sitting areas (one in front of the fireplace) and a huge bath with a dressing table and Austrian crystal legs on the washstand. Its newest addition is a two-person whirlpool tub. Country French and English linens and antiques dress this and the other four rooms, which pale only modestly in comparison. The newest room is the main-floor corner library-bedroom, lovely in wine and teal colors and outfitted in an equestrian theme with a TV.

After more than a year of renovations and flat-out work in getting the place furnished, Priscilla has fulfilled her desire to "fluff up the rooms" with such touches as dried flowers, mounds of pillows, racks with old hats and individual stained-glass pieces reflecting the couple's artistry. At one visit, her eye for fluff produced a goat cart in the foyer, brought in for fall to showcase the harvest.

Priscilla's background in fine arts and woodworking and Tom's in interior design have stood them in good stead for the inn's refurbishing as well as for their thriving stained-glass business. Lately, she resumed her painting in the American Impressionist style and has become "our artist-in-residence," in Tom's words. A portfolio of her work is on display at the inn.

(401) 849-1610 or (888) 356-8733. www.elmtreebnb.com. Six rooms with private baths. July-October: doubles, $195 to $425. November-April: $155 to $325. Three-night minimum weekends, July-October and holidays; two-night minimum other weekends. Closed Christmas to Valentine's Day.

The Francis Malbone House, 392 Thames St., Newport 02840.

This imposing residence, built in 1760 for a shipping merchant and later occupied by a physician, has been converted into one of Newport's more inviting inns. The five partners recently added a handsome rear wing around a rear courtyard, doubling its size and doing so with such exquisite taste and attention to detail that the first-time visitor would think it had been part of the B&B all along.

They started in the original residence with eight attractive bedrooms and a suite, all with private baths and six with fireplaces. For space and privacy, we've always liked the sunken Counting House suite (formerly the physician's office) with its private entry, a queensize four-poster bed facing the TV, a sitting area with a sofabed and two chairs, and a two-part bathroom with shower and dressing room-vanity.

Although still the premium accommodation, the suite has competition from the nine new courtyard rooms in the rear, all with kingsize poster beds and jacuzzi tubs, writing desks, fireplaces and TVs hidden in recessed bookshelves. Bigger, more private and quiet because they're away from the street traffic, they encompass all the nuances that "we couldn't have in the original house and wanted here," in the words of innkeeper Will Dewey. A couple open onto private courtyards with wrought-iron furniture; the courtyard suite adds a wet bar and a sitting area. Oriental rugs, rich appointments, down comforters and duvet covers monogrammed in white are the rule.

Guests enjoy a couple of lovely, high-ceilinged front parlors, a library with TV and a small dining room that served as the kitchen when the house was built in 1760 for a shipping merchant. Check out the hidden servants' stairway leading to the attic beside the tiled fireplace and the old bread oven in the hearth.

A spectacular new dining room goes off a corridor walled with glass and Portuguese tiles leading to the courtyard wing. It's a beauty in pale yellow and gray with a domed ceiling, four round tables and two tall shelves displaying Will's collection of blue and white English china.

Will, a culinary graduate of Johnson & Wales University in Providence, and his staff prepare a full breakfast. The fare includes fruits, breads, perhaps raspberry croissants or cinnamon-raisin strudels, and a main course ranging from eggs benedict to belgian waffles. Homemade cookies and beverages are offered in the afternoon.

(401) 846-0392 or (800) 846-0392. Fax (401) 848-5956. Sixteen rooms and two suites with private baths. April-October: doubles, $205 to $295; suites, $345 and $395. Rest of year: doubles, $135 to $225; suites, $255 and $295.

The Old Beach Inn, 19 Old Beach Road, Newport 02840.

Look beyond the ornate Victorian facade, colorful in grayish beige, yellow and green, and you might see an old anchor embedded in the third-story turret of the home built as the Anchorage in 1879. It's one of the surprises that abound in this stellar B&B run very personally by Luke and Cyndi Murray.

They offer seven guest rooms with private baths. Cyndi says she likes "a lot of different styles." They are reflected in the English country decor in the rooms, named after flowers or plants and full of whimsical touches. In the Rose Room, a white iron canopy bed angles from the corner beneath a black bamboo-beamed ceiling. Done up in black and pink, it has a fireplace and a hand-painted dresser with hand-carved rose drawer pulls, and even the white toilet seat cover is sculpted like a rose. Hand-painted Victorian cottage furniture, a faux bookcase along one wall and an antique wood-burning fireplace grace the Ivy Room. Check out the bishop-sleeve draperies with valances and the fireplace in the first-floor Wisteria Room, and the wicker loveseat and chair in the Forget-Me-Not Room.

The newest rooms are two with separate entrances in a rear carriage house, part of which the Murrays converted into meeting space for small groups. These have TVs and a more contemporary air. The Sunflower, lovely in pale yellow and burgundy, contains a wicker queensize sleigh bed, a wicker loveseat and two chairs, and a sunflower motif, from the lamps on the nightstands to a hand-painted shelf. Cyndi decorates for the season, but the front hall's original stained-glass window representing the four seasons shines at all times.

Guests gather in a small front parlor or in a new and larger Victorian living room where two plush chairs and a couch face a glass cocktail table resting on four bunnies. Here are a pretty tiled fireplace, a rabbit fashioned from moss and a copper bar in the corner. Outside are a back porch and a brick patio overlooking a pleasant back yard with a gazebo and a fish pond. The Murrays serve continental breakfast at four tables in the dining room or outside on the porch patio. It usually involves juice, fruit, homemade granola and pastries like muffins, croissants and coffeecake. They add a main dish such as egg casserole, quiche or blueberry stuffed french toast on Sundays.

The Murrays also have put together a categorized collection of restaurant menus, drawing on Luke's experience as a restaurant consultant and beverage manager for the Black Pearl.

(401) 849-3479 or (888) 303-5033. Fax (401) 847-1236. www.oldbeachinn.com. Seven rooms with private baths. May-October: doubles, $135 to $250. Rest of year: $85 to $175. Three-night minimum weekends in season.

Rhode Island House, 77 Rhode Island Ave., Newport 02840.

Cooking instructor Michael Dupré makes this elegant B&B special for those with an interest in matters culinary.

Trained at La Varenne in Paris, the former private chef for Mrs. Hugh D. Auchincloss at Hammersmith Farm now offers culinary weekends in winter and serves breakfasts to remember in a dining room with Chinese Chippendale chairs at tables for four. The meal starts with a buffet on the sideboard: bowls of fresh fruit, whole-grain cereals, scones, pumpkin or lemon-poppyseed breads, and a "dessert" like banana-rum bread pudding or peach-cranberry crisp. These are preliminaries to the main event, perhaps eggs benedict with asparagus and tomato or popovers with basil-scrambled eggs, grilled tomato, asparagus and sausage. These treats originate in a great professional kitchen, where Michael caters and gives cooking lessons, including wintertime classes in which everyone participates and then sits down to eat. "I used to peek in the windows and say 'I want that kitchen,'" Michael said as he told how he acquired the property in 1993. The kitchen came with an 1882 Victorian estate that a previous owner had turned into a low-profile B&B.

As most of the restoration work had been done. Michael, an avid collector, had only to furnish the house. This he has done with taste and flair, in both common rooms and bedrooms. The great hall/foyer is remarkable for yellow faux-marble walls. Off one side is an airy sunroom. In front is a cozy library and on the other side is an inviting living room with a remarkable set of elaborate arched windows.

Upstairs are five guest rooms with private baths and queensize beds, each with its own distinction. The bath in the small Mary Kay Room, for instance, occupies a sun porch and retains the original pink and gray fixtures. The antique headboard on the bed matches the chest of drawers in the creamy white and floral green front Garden Room. The Auchincloss Room is "dainty, lovely and nice – just like her," says Michael of Mrs. Auchincloss, who was his favorite grande dame. It has a fireplace and a full bath with an enormous jacuzzi, as does the rear Hunter Room, masculine in hunter green and complete with a private balcony overlooking the back yard. All the rooms have large windows and are bright and airy, unusual for Victorian houses of the period.

(401) 848-7787. Fax (401) 849-3104. Five rooms with private baths. Doubles, $165 to $250, May-October. Rest of year: $145 to $195.

Savanas' Inn, 41 Pelham St., Newport 02840.

Her experience as comptroller for her family's construction business paid off when Andrea Savana and her husband Phil decided to retire and move from Long Island to their favorite vacation spot. She had picked up interior design talents along the way, and their new 1865 Second Empire residence in the Historic Hill district gave her plenty of chance to play. They commuted weekends for nearly three years of restoration, doing most of the work themselves, prior to opening their dreamed-of B&B in 1998.

Andrea's designer instincts are everywhere evident, from the intricate fabric bed canopies to the fifteen kinds of wallpaper whose patterns she hand-cut and installed on walls and ceiling of the Louis XV Suite. Indeed, showy wallpapers are a Savana trademark. So are the frogs that are the inn's logo and now turn up in various guises all over the house. Not that you'd necessarily notice, since the stunning haute Victorian décor is what catches the eye.

The Savanas live on the third floor, but give up the first two floors to guests. Four second-floor bedrooms are equipped with TVs and telephones as well as chandeliers. They vary from the rear Casino Room, masculine in tartan red and green with a brass double bed and a distant view of the harbor, to the lush English Cottage Room with a queensize iron bed and dainty canopy. The front Blue Room is, well, blue and also white in many patterns and comes with a tiled fireplace. Andrea calls the Louis XV "my gaudy room" because of the gilt. But gaudy? Hardly. The bay-windowed sitting room holds two Victorian arm chairs and the bedroom, with a queensize sleigh bed in another bay window, is done up in those fifteen wallpaper patterns.

The main parlor is pristine without wallpaper in the English country style. It opens into a rich library with wallpapered walls and ceilings. Evening cordials are offered here. The chandeliered dining room is given over to a Chippendale table with chairs for ten. Here, Andrea cooks and Philip serves a full breakfast. Following juice and a fruit plate, the main event might be a frittata or puff pancakes with fruit.

Outside are a front veranda and a rear hot tub overlooking a small English garden, with fountains, statuary, benches and pathways of the intricate detail you'd expect from the interior of the house.

(401) 847-3801 or (888) 880-3764. Three rooms and one suite with private baths. May-October: weekends, doubles $185 to $235, suite $275; midweek, doubles $150 to $200, suite $235. Rest of year: weekends, doubles $135 to $165, suite $195; midweek, doubles $100 to $130, suite $150.

Gourmet Treats

With everything from delis to food boutiques, the Newport area is a paradise for the palate of the wandering gourmet. Among the possibilities:

Newport Mansions. On most visitors' must-see lists, several of Newport's principal tourist attractions also hold special culinary appeal. The dining rooms in all are on display, and at the Marble House is a gold ballroom in which the owner once gave a ten-course dinner for 100 dogs in full party dress. At the fabulous Breakers, you get to see a number of kitchens and butler's pantries, an area larger than most houses. The dining room at Kingscote, an oft-overlooked Greek Revival cottage, is one of the nicest rooms in all the mansions – decorated with Tiffany glass tiles and stained-glass panels of dahlias.

The Market on the Boulevard, 43 Memorial Blvd., is a large, upscale grocery store with a market cafe and espresso bar, a bakery, deli and "gourmet to go." And what wonderful things do go – in our case, a dish of oriental beef with a vegetable medley for supper at home, plus a ginger-pear tart and lemon-raspberry roulade for dessert. There are wonderful breads, choice meats, exotic produce, select condiments, fresh pastas – you name it, Newport's beautiful (and ordinary) people come here to buy it. From salads to pastries to sandwiches (the last delightfully named for behind-the-scenes workers at the mansions), all the makings for a gourmet picnic, lunch or dinner are here.

Boulangerie Obelix, 382 Spring St., is the place where restaurateur John Sorenson and crew bake and sell their marvelous breads and pastries. Besides an ample supply to go, there are novel sandwiches to try here. One mouthful – in more ways than one – is composed of roasted eggplant, zucchini, peppers, green onions, spinach, tomatoes, Vermont goat cheese, extra-virgin olive oil and balsamic vinegar. Another combines prosciutto and asiago, with arugula and artichoke tapenade. You can order soups, a ham and swiss quiche, scones or a peach tart.

For casual dining, **Cappuccino's** at 92 William St. is a pleasant breakfast and lunch cafe in the uptown Bellevue Avenue area. The salads are great, the chicken-onion-bacon quiche was hearty and we drooled over the white-chocolate and strawberry bars. **Ocean Breeze Cafe** at 580 Thames St. stocks gourmet coffees and teas, baked goods and an array of sandwiches and salads.

Coffee and espresso are the rage in this seaport town, as elsewhere. A new **Starbucks** occupies a prime corner at Thames & Church, beside the Trinity Church green. Across the way where Thames and America's Cup meet is **Espresso Your Self Café,** also good for sandwiches and salads. Farther along Lower Thames are the excellent **Steaming Bean Espresso Cafe,** where old magazines displayed in the windows draw browsers inside for pastries, sandwiches and desserts; and **Espressibles of Newport,** which advertises collectibles, gifts and antiques but seems to be mainly coffee.

Fragrant dried flowers hang from the ceiling and jars of loose teas, herbs and teapots line the shelves at **Tea & Herb Essence,** 476 Thames St. Proprietor Laureen Grenus offers everything from passionfruit to hibiscus heaven teas to herbal remedies and health-care products, handmade soaps, gifts and more. Some of the herbs and flowers come from her gardens out front. Lower Thames harbors not one but two gourmet pet stores, **Salty Paws** ("gifts for cats and dogs and the people who love them") and **The Gourmet Dog,** with a fire hydrant at the entrance and a "dog bakery" dispensing all-natural premium dog biscuits.

A most colorful kitchen shop is **Runcible Spoon** (the title taken from "The Owl and the Pussycat") at 180 Bellevue Ave. Amid the garlic salsa and the lobster platters, we were taken with a line of Portuguese pottery with tiny vegetables like radishes and scallions depicted thereon.

Another good shop is **Kitchen Pot Pourri** at 42 West Main Road, Middletown, a house full of kitchen gadgets and accessories, baking items, pots and pans, placemats, cookbooks and the like. Nearby, the fledgling **Newport Vineyards & Winery** at 909 East Main Road (Route 138) harvested its first grapes in 1996 under the ownership of John Nunes. Its new port wine is one of the few ports released along the East Coast. The winery is open for tours and tastings daily, 10 to 5, Sunday noon to 5. Also of interest in Middletown is **Coddington Brewing Co.,** Newport County's first brew pub and restaurant, open daily from 11:30 at 210 Coddington Hwy.

Gourmet Side Trips

Take a side trip down Route 77 along the picturesque East Bay. In Tiverton, stop at **Past and Presence** at 2753 Main Road, where Judy Galway stocks tea sets, linens and "Angel Duds" made from old chenille bedspreads in her gift shop. Adjacent is her **Here & Now Tea Room** with a wall-size mural of an English garden, a water view and a deck for lunch or English cream tea (by reservation at 4). In the quaint hamlet of Tiverton Four Corners is **Provender,** a specialty-foods store and upscale sandwich shop, where you can obtain lunch to eat in or take out. Farther along are **Walker's Farm Stand,** where the folks from suave Little Compton shop for produce and preserves, and **Olga's Cup & Saucer,** a small place next door, where you can stop for coffee, biscotti or pizzas.

Sakonnet Vineyards, the largest and oldest continuously producing winery in New England, is nearby at 162 West Main Road in Little Compton. Owners Earl and Susan Samson are known for some of the East's better wines. Among their annual output of 50,000 cases are a distinguished estate chardonnay and a pinot noir, both retailing in the $16.95 range. In 1999 Sakonnet produced its first sparkling wine, a samson brut made in the traditional methode champenoise. You can sample the offerings in a large tasting room with oriental rugs on the floors, daily 10 to 6. The winery hosts numerous special events of culinary interest, including a Master Chef Series. The Roost, the original farmhouse on the property, offers three bedrooms with private baths and breakfast for overnight guests (doubles, $85 to $95).

To the northwest of Newport is the historic, bayside village of Wickford, one of New England's most picturesque. For gourmands, the highlight among many fine shops and historic structures is **Wickford Gourmet Foods** at 21 West Main St., (800) 286-8190. Here, Joe and Donna Dube offer two floors chock full of great specialty foods, condiments, cookbooks, a coffee bar, Rhode Island's largest selection of cheeses and pâtés, chocolates and superior takeout foods to go. Or you can choose from **The Café at Wickford Gourmet** menu of soups, salads, panini and entrées in the $4 to $6.95 range and eat upstairs. In an historic barn behind is **Wickford Gourmet's Kitchen & Table.** This expanding enterprise with a mail-order catalog even has a new factory outlet in North Kingston. Little wonder Gourmet Retailer magazine ranks it one of the top twelve retailers in the country.

Crowds enjoy festivities in new Waterplace Park in downtown Providence.

Providence, R.I.

Cinderella of Cuisine

Not all that long ago, Rhode Island's capital city was known for its colleges, its historic architecture and its earthy Little Italy. If you had to find a place to eat here, your choices were pretty well limited to the downtown MacDonald's and the dated, gaudy shrines to spaghetti along Federal Hill.

In terms of culinary excitement, however, Providence has gone from rags to riches. This Cinderella of cuisine has vaulted into the national food limelight and become a destination for food lovers. Thousands of restaurant seats have been added in a city whose population has remained roughly static at 160,000. More than one-third of the city's 565 restaurants opened in four years between 1996 and 1999. A Providence entry was ranked among the year's best new restaurants nationally by Esquire magazine every year but one since 1994. Budding chefs and restaurateurs have been drawn to Providence. And successful Providence restaurateurs have branched out – in Boston, Miami and Los Angeles.

In the spring of 2000, food experts from across the world set their sights on Providence. It was the first "second-tier city" to host the International Association of Culinary Professionals conference, according to host city chairman Bob Burke, owner of one of the oldest of the city's good restaurants.

Some credit longtime mayor Vincent A. (Buddy) Cianci Jr. for the city's heightened culinary awareness. A food lover as well as civic booster, he initiated a revolving loan fund for new restaurant start-ups and helped cut through the red tape for liquor licenses. He also marketed his own brand of marinara sauce and followed with the Mayor's Own Coffee and lately the Mayor's Own Olive Oil.

Others credit the expansion of Johnson & Wales University, whose College of Culinary Arts students and graduates provide a steady stream of well-trained kitchen, dining room and management staff.

Still others credit George Germon and Johanne Killeen, who opened Al Forno in 1980 and turned it into one of the best-known restaurants in the country. Not only have they trained many a leading chef (a dozen played starring roles in a 1999 alumni dinner they hosted in Boston). They also have helped several open their first restaurants.

Providence's culinary revival has gone hand in hand with the city's restored downtown riverfront, which is undergoing a $1.5 billion facelift as part of the most ambitious renewal project in America. The Providence River, for years obscured by the world's widest bridge, has been uncovered and flows like a canal beneath graceful new Venetian-style spans connecting downtown with College Hill and the historic East Side. Cobblestone riverwalks, an amphitheater and food vendors enhance Waterplace Park with its celebrated WaterFire "singing bonfires" blazing in the middle of the river on summer nights. The huge new Providence Place shopping mall is drawing people downtown day and night.

Providence offers countless riches for the gourmand. They go beyond the indigenous jonnycakes and quahogs to the home-grown Italian markets of Federal Hill and the fresh seafood from the Rhode Island shore. Nowhere are the riches more evident than in its restaurants. They helped spark this Cinderella city's rejuvenation, and now share in its success.

Dining

The Best of the Best

Al Forno, 577 South Main St.

Food at its gutsiest is served at this widely honored restaurant, a bustling yet comfortable establishment that generates national publicity and turnaway crowds.

Rhode Island School of Design graduates Johanne Killeen and George Germain applied their artistic talents to northern Italian cooking and developed a cult following for Al Forno, which literally means "from the oven."

Their followers love the grilled pizzas done over the open fire with ever-changing toppings, they love the salads dressed with extra-virgin olive oil and balsamic vinegar, they love the oven-baked pastas bearing such goodies as grilled squid and spicy peppers, they love the grilled items done on the wood grill using fruitwoods and even grapevines from nearby Sakonnet Vineyards, and they love the fabulous desserts cooked to order. They also don't seem to mind long waits for a table.

The husband-and-wife team, then in their twenties, started modestly enough in 1980 in pintsize quarters on Steeple Street at the foot of College Hill after working in Italy. They had no room for a wood-fired pizza oven so cooked thin pizza dough over a wood grill. Their grilled pizzas caught on, and the couple expanded beyond northern and southern Italian confines to offer cuisines from other regions of Italy and its Mediterranean neighbors.

Even with a relocation in 1990 to a much larger, 19th-century brick building near the waterfront, there still are usually lines at the door when the restaurant opens for dinner, since the demand exceeds the supply and no reservations are taken.

Al Forno occupies two floors of a building that once served as the municipal stables for Providence. Dining is at close-together tables seating a total of 140, casual downstairs and a bit more formal upstairs. The rest of the space seems to be half kitchen, one for each floor with ten cooks in each. The fare is deceptively simple. Al Forno's magic is in transforming the simplest, most seasonal

ingredients into something intensely flavorful.

On the clamorous, two-level main floor, we enjoyed one of our more memorable meals in a long time. Grilled pizza has always been Al Forno's signature dish. With a crackly thin crust and different toppings every day (ours had onion, gorgonzola, chicken, tarragon and tomato coulis), it is sensational. We also loved a starter of cool vermicelli with five little salads (cucumber, jicama, carrot, red pepper and Egyptian beans).

The menu changes daily, but you might find a clam roast with hot spicy sausage and endive in a tomato broth, pepper-grilled chicken with arugula and parmigiano, and grilled veal tenderloin with roasted crimini and portobello mushrooms on

Johanne Killeen and George Germain at Al Forno.

grilled polenta. Lasagna, made with light sheets of pasta folded over freestyle, might contain sliced grilled chicken breast with fresh tomato salad or turkey, béchamel sauce and diced vegetables. Our choucroute garni included three of the fattest sausages we ever saw topping mild sauerkraut, accompanied by wide noodles sparked with fresh coriander. The skirt steak, seared right on the coals, came with wilted watercress and a green chile sauce. Portions are huge and we saw many others leave, as we did, with doggy bags.

The wine list, featuring many Italian vintages, starts reasonably and goes sky high.

Dessert, which must be ordered with the main course, is the icing on the cake. We'd try any of Johanne's special tarts; the lemon soufflé version is ethereal. Another masterpiece is a sourdough waffle with caramel-walnut ice cream and chocolate. The "grand cookie finale" has been widely imitated. Here a large tray on a pedestal holds two kinds of chocolate cookies, ricotta fritters, pinwheels, ginger molasses cookies and chocolate truffles – a mix and match play on textures and flavors that's heaven for cookie lovers.

The decor is secondary to the food. Short lace curtains hang from the high beams, tables are covered with sheets of paper, the wine is poured into stemless glasses like those used for vin ordinaire in France, and the atmosphere is jolly and just right. George designed the upstairs room in a classic and sophisticated European style, using lots of dark slate and bluestone marble. The couple turned to Italy for many of their accessories, including cutlery from Florence in the trattoria style, with long-tined pasta forks and pasta spoons. They are artists and restaurant designers as well as highly inventive cooks who wrote the cookbook, *Cucina Simpatica.*

In 1998, after helping inspire many another restaurant locally, Al Forno's principals moved into the Boston market. They took over the fashionable Café Louis and installed a young friend, David Reynoso, as chef de cuisine.

The accolades continue to flow freely to the unassuming, down-to-earth couple, who travel widely to teach cooking and share their secrets. The James Beard Foundation has named them the best chefs in the Northeast and cited them in 1999 for having the best restaurant.

(401) 273-9760. Entrées, $18.95 to $27.95. Dinner, Tuesday-Friday 5 to 10, Saturday 4 to 10.

New Rivers, 7 Steeple St.

The intimate space where Al Forno got its start is now the setting for nationally honored chefs Bruce and Patricia Tillinghast, he in the kitchen and she generally out front. After training with Madeleine Kamman, both Tillinghasts had been chefs in executive dining rooms in Boston, before they returned to his hometown to open their own operation, happily unpretentious and lacking in attitude. Nice things happen to nice people, and it wasn't long before they were finalists for the annual James Beard Award, "Best Chefs of the Northeast."

New Rivers tucks tables for 40 and a small bar into a pair of rooms in an 1870 building at the base of College Hill, near the confluence of the two recently uncovered rivers for which the restaurant is named. A striking picture of six red pears glistening against a dark green wall sets the theme in the main dining room, where white butcher paper covers pale yellow tablecloths beneath a rust-colored ceiling. The smaller side dining room has more pale yellow, from cloths to walls, and a yellow-tiled bar at which some folks perch and eat. The only downsides are that tables are uncomfortably close together and reservations may be hard to come by.

The Tillinghasts make a point of supporting sustainable agriculture and favor organic products. They change their creative, contemporary fare frequently, borrowing from Tuscan, Thai, Portuguese, Middle Eastern and Caribbean cuisines. The menu is nicely categorized by nibbles, starters and salads, small meals and pasta, and main dishes from the grill and oven. Three-course bistro meals for $18, available Tuesday-Thursday, are the best deals in town.

Nime chow spring rolls combining lobster meat, julienned vegetables, sprouts and pungent basil rolled in cool Thai rice wrappers, served with a gingery dipping sauce, are the specialty appetizer. You could also start with grilled figs with prosciutto and shaved reggiano parmigiano, or grilled shrimp on sugarcane skewers with spicy pineapple salsa and crispy cassava. Move on to one of the small meals or pastas, as basic as a half-pound burger on a Portuguese sweet roll or as exotic as sundried tomato and artichoke tortellini with Tuscan sausage, roasted fennel, olives and mint. The polenta with wild mushrooms is like eating a cloud. These plus a dessert of fresh fruit and cookies will satisfy most diners.

Heartier appetites are well served by items from the grill and oven: perhaps baked sand dab with crab and corn stuffing, grilled Atlantic halibut on Thai purple rice, and bulgogi (Korean beef with spicy pickle and shiitake mushrooms over rice and soy sprouts).

Diners enjoy riverfront tables outside Cafe Nuovo at sunset.

A made-to-order lemon tartlet, garnished with blueberries or other seasonal fruit, is the specialty dessert. Other standouts are homemade ice creams like huckleberry or a rum-spiked praline and a cookie plate bearing eight New Rivers favorites.

The extensive, affordably priced wine list has been honored by Wine Spectator. *(401) 751-0350. Entrées, $15 to $21. Dinner, Tuesday-Saturday 5:30 to 10.*

Cafe Nuovo, One Citizens Plaza.

The owners of Capriccio, a glamorous Italian restaurant of the old school in the city's financial district, branched out with this dramatic newcomer along the revived downtown riverfront. The views of water and skyline are sensational from the soaring windows that make up one side of the angular dining room off the lobby rotunda of the Citizens Bank tower. The best riverfront tables in town are those for 60 diners on the outdoor terrace beside the Providence River.

The large and airy interior seating 120 is spectacular in gray, white and red. Sleek red lacquered chairs and banquettes flank well-spaced tables set with white cloths, votive candles, fresh flowers and clear-glass salt and pepper shakers. A partly open kitchen plays a starring role at one end. The sedate bar area wraps around the curve of the rotunda near the other end. Abstract artworks provide color.

The setting matches the trendy food that's architectural as well as unusual. Chef Timothy Kelly, formerly in Manhattan, has been with owner Dimitri Kriticos since Café Nuovo opened in 1994. He calls the cuisine fusion, although his classic French training is evident in his terrific sauces.

His wide repertoire certainly is appealing. As we dipped excellent rustic breads into a saucer of olive oil garnished with roasted red peppers, one of us said she could happily eat everything on the menu, which is seldom the case. She settled for a couple of stellar appetizers, the nime chow shrimp rolls with cellophane noodles, tiny vegetables and a lemongrass dipping sauce, and a chopped salad of cucumbers, tomatoes, asparagus, snap peas and more, standing tall in a radicchio cup. Both were as exciting to taste as to look at. Against these high-rise theatrics the low-rise smoked salmon club sandwich with side potato and tossed salads looked somewhat mundane, though it proved to be good and filling.

Pastry chef Emily Pascal's desserts are the talk of the town. San Francisco-trained, she is partial to her crêpes, touting one with grand marnier and sweet cream cheese. Her "citrus circus" is a tantalizing combination of a petite lemon cake with lemon ice cream, orange parfait and a zesty lime mousse. The "bonanza" of banana pastry crème with a white chocolate macadamia cookie, spiced rum caramel and coconut froth is another knockout. We enjoyed a crystal bowl filled with a selection of fruit sorbets and ice creams, studded with a candy stick.

For dinner appetizers, the chef traverses the world for the likes of a towering portobello napoleon, Aegean salad, escargots with a baguette and a wedge of brie, and sesame-crusted ahi tuna with lemon-tamari dipping sauce. The arugula salad with warm pecan-coated Vermont goat cheese, baby pear tomatoes and lemon-thyme triangular tuiles is a work of art.

Nuovo's innovative pasta and risotto dishes give new meaning to the genre: perhaps a summer vegetable risotto with pan-seared Maine sea scallops, penne tossed with tomatoes and basil and topped with grilled veal tenderloin, and lobster-stuffed raviolis with half a lobster tail over wilted spinach in a grappa-tomato cream sauce. One of the main courses could be rainbow trout wrapped in crisp potato strands, stuffed with mustard greens and portobello mushrooms and served around an arugula salad with raspberries and frizzled leeks. Another could be marinated Hudson Valley duck breast fanned around sweet potato falafel, crisp plantains and pepper-studded pineapple jam.

The wine list covers a wide range from $21 to $225. Waiters take orders without notes and seem to get everything right.

(401) 421-2525. Entrées, $18.50 to $27.95. Lunch, Monday-Friday 11:30 to 3. Dinner, Monday-Saturday, 5 to 10:30 or 11.

Neath's, 262 South Water St.

West meets East in Cambodian chef-owner Neath Pal's stylish New American bistro. Neath (pronounced Nee-it) immigrated to Providence with his family in 1975 and worked summers in Newport restaurants before going off to study at LaVarenne in Paris. He returned for a job at Al Forno, "the best restaurant in my home city." In the kitchen there he met his Irish-Italian wife Beth Toolan, now a physician. He moved on to help start L'Epicureo and Grappa before opening his own place in 1998 in the former Grill 262, a short-lived, industrial-look restaurant in a restored warehouse along the river.

He kept the angular main-floor bar but warmed and softened the upstairs space with bold yellow and red walls beneath a high wood ceiling. White cloths, votive candles and small vases with fresh flowers top the widely spaced tables seating 75, some next to big windows overlooking the developing parkland along the river. The whole family pitched in, from his sister, a restaurant designer in California, to his mother-in-law, who made aprons for the waitstaff. Neath paused to reflect beside a montage of photos of family and staff along the stairway that tells the story.

Although he table-hops nightly and his wife hostesses weekends, there's nothing he'd rather do than "be back behind the line cooking." His is the vision that fuses

Chef-owner Neath Pal in dining room at Neath's bistro.

New England ingredients with French and Asian preparations for a highly personalized cooking style. It showed up in an appetizer of shrimp and shiitake-mushroom dumplings, steamed and then grilled and served with a shoyu dipping sauce, wood-grilled baguette slices lathered with a coconut and scallion sauce and a bowl of extra dipping sauce for good measure. The star of the evening was a special salad of chilled Maine crab with diced cucumbers and tomatoes and delicate potato gaufrettes, the crabmeat stunningly pure and the wafers so thin and intricately latticed as not to be believed.

Signature main dishes are lobster with snow peas and shiitake mushrooms, simmered in coconut milk with red curry and served over chow foon noodles; grilled pork loin chop with stir-fried Asian broccoli and sweet-potato gratin, and pan-roasted Hudson Valley duck breast and confit with a subtle ginger glaze over sweet-potato gratin and wilted spinach. We were pleased with the oven-roasted Chilean sea bass, succulent and of the melt-in-the-mouth variety, teamed with a cool cucumber salad. The chicken breast rubbed with lemongrass was wood-grilled and served with a Thai basil salad, but we couldn't find the green papaya that the menu promised. The lapse was redeemed by extra ginger ice cream on the signature dessert of crunchy fried wontons filled with molten chocolate, which everyone raves about but must be an acquired taste. Passion-fruit crème brulée served in an almond lace cookie is another house favorite.

Pleasantly priced, the primarily American wine list included a Bonny Doon Pacific Rim riesling that was quite appropriate for the fare. Flawless service was provided by a waitress who not only recited the complicated specials but also took the orders without notes. As darkness fell, the interior walls glowed and the lights of the city gleamed across the river shimmering outside the window – a fitting backdrop for some interesting food.

(401 751-3700. Entrées, $17 to $25. Dinner, Tuesday-Sunday 5:30 to 10 or 10:30.

XO Café, 125 North Main St.

"Life is uncertain, order dessert first," begins the menu at this unconventional restaurant. It then proceeds to list the sweets, prior to the "egg-free caesar" salad and the seared coriander tuna appetizer. John Elkhay, executive chef and co-owner, wants you to save room for the grand finale.

Peripatetic John, whom we first met many years ago at the late great Café in the Barn in nearby Seekonk, Mass., has always been in the vanguard – at In-Prov, Angels, Atomic Grill and now here, in the space once occupied by Angels and a succession of short-lived restaurants. He and co-owners Rick and Cheryl Bready doubled the size, expanding into an adjacent storefront to produce an open wood-oven kitchen and the most offbeat, eclectic decor in town. It's an avant-garde fantasy in ivory, gold and black, augmented by pop art and mirrors. A banquette along one wall serves close-together tables topped with black lamps trimmed in gold roping. The opposite wall is home to two sensuous black-mesh nude sculptures and four art panels endearingly if mysteriously labeled Picasso-Pepin, Warhol-Bocuse, Manet-Elkhay and Schnabel-Child. The convivial, cigar-friendly bar in the original dining room has engraved inscriptions identifying seats of regulars. Exotic martinis are served in what the barmaid calls the city's fanciest stemware.

Ultimately, all the whimsy and hype play second fiddle to the food, which measures up in the Elkhay tradition of on-the-edge style, innovation and presentation. It's contemporary, regional and Asian – fusion to the max. The best starter is the bento box sampler, if only because the shiny black Japanese box yields four of the best: crunchy, rice-flour-battered calamari rings with smoked jalapeño mayonnaise and chopped hot peppers, lobster wonton ravioli with Thai mango dipping sauce, light tempura-battered portobello mushroom fries with star anise dipping sauce and chicken satay with coconut-lime dipping sauce. Those seeking less incendiary tastes might opt for the lobster and corn chowder "cappuccino," the wild mushroom and goat cheese tamale or the chinois chicken salad inspired by Wolfgang Puck. But, as you can tell, everything here comes with a bite.

For main dishes, consider a pizza of lobster with white truffle oil and yukon gold potato gratin or angelhair pasta with ancho chile-crusted diver scallops, corn and cilantro. Typical of the other choices are cornmeal-crusted trout with tomatillo mojo and finnan haddie brandade cake, and wood-oven roasted chicken breast cooked under a brick with garlic, lemon and rosemary.

The crème brûlée tray is a selection of three tiny pots of caramelized custards whose flavors could be banana, ginger, mango, coconut, maple, clove or rosewater. The white chocolate cheesecake is swathed in a brittle sheath of dark chocolate and flavored by a blood orange coulis. The warm mango-rhubarb crisp with guava ice cream was a hit at our autumn visit.

The café is named for a zesty Asian sauce, but also plays on the word extraordinary. Exactly how Elkhay fans describe it.

(401) 273-9090. Entrées, $18 to $24. Dinner nightly, 5 to 10 or 11.

The Gatehouse, 4 Richmond Square.

A chef's table for ten takes center stage at this chic restaurant on the banks of the Seekonk River. This kind of table, usually placed in the kitchens in other restaurants, is one where patrons eat what special treats the chef puts before them. Here, the kitchen is too small for a table, so the biggest table in the house is ready for takers (about $50 per person, depending on the meal) close to the kitchen in the main interior dining room. We couldn't help but notice it as we passed through on our way to lunch on the enclosed porch that seems to float right over the river.

Founding executive chef Steven Marsella, a Providence native who cooked in New Orleans, entertained his mentor, Emeril Lagasse, as well as Julia Child at the chef's table. He has since moved on to open owner Henry Kates's latest culinary outpost, a Cheeky Monkey in Miami's South Beach. He was succeeded by Jim Maxwell, who moved from the Quilted Giraffe in New York to become executive chef for the Gatehouse's Rhode Island operations. They include this restaurant, the first Cheeky Monkey in Newport and two catering companies, one of which had just catered the gala Nordstrom opening soiree prior to our latest visit.

The contemporary menu combines the tastes of the Mediterranean with those of New Orleans and New England for a distinctive flavor of its own.

Seated at a window table beside the water, we felt as if we were on a cruise ship as the waves rippled by. One of us ordered the lobster club sandwich ($12.95), a good but unexceptional version enhanced with avocado. The other enjoyed a grilled chicken sandwich with creole salsa on a homemade bulkie roll ($7.95), a hefty, knife-and-fork affair. All sandwiches come with an unusual sweet-potato salad, a house signature that turned out to be surprisingly tasty and not at all sweet. Dessert choices include chocolate-hazelnut velvet cake, banana-caramel crème brûlée, and refreshng berries and melon served over lemon-lime granita in a martini glass.

At night, the darkened interior of one of southern New England's prettiest restaurants shimmers with the moon reflecting off the river and the glow of rich wood and brick walls, candlelight and charming paintings of old Providence scenes all around. Appetizers could be an award-winning Rhode Island lobster jonnycake with sherry lobster cream, New Orleans barbecued shrimp served with a golden roasted garlic cloud, and baked mission figs stuffed with stilton cheese, wrapped in prosciutto and phyllo pastry.

Main courses run from lavender-scented chicken breast to a signature filet of beef paired with tender lobster in a flavorful bordelaise sauce and truffled mashed potatoes. Almond-encrusted tilapia with meunière sauce, and wood-grilled pork porterhouse with smoked apple demi-glace are among the changing possibilities.

The restored gatehouse, appearing small from the outside, expands into stylish dining areas on two levels. Beneath the more formal upper level is an inviting Victorian-style lounge. Here, an enclosed wraparound porch holds the tables of choice. For those who wish to imbibe and partake of a small but appealing lounge menu, bar stools and a counter are up against floor-to-ceiling windows for a boat's-eye view of the river. The extensive wine list is quite moderately priced.

The place delights with a sense of humor. A life-like, bespectacled codger named Willy appears to be snoozing on a bench in the vestibule outside the men's room, which is artistically enhanced by trompe-l'oeil shelves of books. His counterpart, Agnes, slouches in a more prominent position in the dining room, where she can keep an eye on some serious culinary goings-on.

(401) 521-9229. Entrées, $19.95 to $28.95. Lunch, Wednesday-Friday noon to 2. Dinner nightly, 5:30 to 10. Sunday brunch, 11 to 2.

Walter's La Locanda del Coccia, 265 Atwells Ave.

Clay-pot cookery and Italian-Jewish cuisine are two hallmarks of Walter Potenza's charming restaurant, which represents a homecoming in Federal Hill, the shrine to Italian cuisine. The peripatetic native of Abruzzo was the first chef at the Blue Grotto down the street before moving on to suburban East Greenwich and Cranston to establish his own considerable imprint. Now he's back in the

Dinner is served on DiPasquale Square courtyard in front of Walter's La Locanda del Coccia.

thick of things, with an inviting two-story restaurant facing DiPasquale Square, plus a sleek new European tapas bar and restaurant across the street.

Loosely translated as "the inn of the clay pot," the establishment lives up to its name. Quilts and tapestries on Mediterranean-colored walls create a warm and convivial gathering spot for fat-free food prepared in terra cotta pots in the ancient Etruscan manner. Walter showed us his stash of clay dishes that are soaked in water and then filled with food and placed on a stone floor inside his oven. The clay acts like a sponge and, when heated, releases moisture that self-bastes the food without the use of oil or butter. He cooks pastas, chicken, seafood and rice in the shallow pots about ten inches across, then serves pot and all atop oversize pewter service plates delivered to the table.

The technique imparts earthy flavors to several concoctions detailed on the menu, among them chunks of fresh snapper baked with potatoes and kale, farfalle with sliced chicken and prosciutto, and rigatoni with veal ragu topped with pecorino-crusted bread. More traditional dishes range from a sauté of shrimp and shiitake mushrooms to tender veal medallions with roasted peppers and artichokes.

Walter puts out a lavish spread of antipasti on a table near the entry, which almost everyone orders to start. Homemade desserts include cranberry-pecan tart, a chocolate timbale and a sponge cake with flambéed strawberries.

A food historian as well as a chef, this former soccer pro (in Italy) also prepares five appetizers reflecting his Italian-Jewish heritage – a prix-fixe sampler (non-kosher regulated) of seven courses may be reserved in advance for $35. This facet earned him an invitation to prepare an Italian Passover dinner – the first of two appearances at the James Beard Foundation in New York.

Always on the go with new ideas and cooking classes, Walter opened in 1999 the sleek **AquaViva Eurobistro** at 286 Atwells Ave., a large tapas restaurant and bar featuring small dishes from sixteen European countries. The place looks like a sea of chrome as you enter and everything is in cool tones of gray, blue and aqua. The curving tiled bar seats fifteen for quite a selection of martinis, wines, beers and cognacs. We had our choice of a multitude of round tables for four for a late lunch of tapas from the all-day menu: chilled roasted peppers stuffed with gorgonzola and prosciutto, Swedish chicken livers in tomatoes and cream, and – the stars of the show – Portuguese clams with chorizo and New Zealand mussels sauced with pernod and cream. They made for an expensive lunch, but would have been an inexpensive dinner. "We're introducing the tapas culture and had to make the portions bigger for Rhode Island appetites," explained Walter's wife Carmela, who was holding the fort while he was teaching a culinary course in Minnesota. "It's tough being in the vanguard." But that's where Walter wants to be.

The second floor of the new restaurant – transformed at great expense from an abandoned warehouse, the first macaroni plant in New England – also is home to the Providence branch of his Etruria International Cooking School in Umbria. He was instrumental in founding the first Chefs Association of Rhode Island to showcase local culinary expertise. He hosts "Flavors & Knowledge," an ABC television cooking series that won an Emmy Award in 1999. His latest venture was opening the first cooking school for children in New England.

Walters: (401) 273-2652. Entrées, $14 to $24. Dinner, Monday-Saturday 5 to 10.
AquaViva Eurobistro: (401) 273-8664. Tapas, $5 to $10. Open Tuesday-Saturday noon to 10 or 11, Sunday 4 to 10.

Agora, One West Exchange Street.
A centerpiece of the new Westin Hotel, this culinary star basks in the limelight of the national food media, the style of a magnificent setting and a drop-dead view of the new Waterplace Park with the domed state capitol in the background.

Greek for "gathering place," Agora rests comfortably on the second floor at the head of a long escalator from the hotel's lobby rotunda. The 75-seat dining room has the look and intimacy of the living room of an East Side mansion, what with four couch-like settees with side-by-side seats at tables for two facing the view. Beyond is an array of formally clad tables flanked by Chippendale-style mohair-covered armchairs amid deep reddish amber wood paneling, dark brocade walls hung with fine oils, a barrel-vaulted gold arched ceiling and floor lamps all around. But for the glassed-in cases displaying the restaurant's cigar and wine offerings and the discreet marble-topped bar where a pianist plays and sings, this could be some very rich person's home.

The Westin's consulting chef, Frank McClelland of the top-ranked L'Espalier in Boston, dispatched his sous-chef of six years, Casey Riley, to be Agora's executive chef. Together they put L'Espalier's imprimatur on the food and service, winning accolades from Esquire magazine in 1995 as one of America's best new restaurants. Barely 28 at the time, New Mexico-born Casey still imparts a youthful playfulness and derring-do to his food that excites seasoned diners.

Part of it comes from the unusual wood-fired rotisserie custom-made for the kitchen. It might yield four spicy grilled shrimp with chipotle-cilantro glaze and lime cream for an appetizer or a main dish of juniper-rubbed venison with sundried tomato-vermouth sauce. The choices on the menu may be relatively straightforward and unadorned, as in a section labeled "simply styled entrées" (any seafood selection, grilled over natural wood or steamed, or grilled chicken or beef).

Ironically these choices are placed beside a section of side dishes called "extra pleasures and other desires" (among them, truffled mashed potato, and white bean and tarragon cassoulet). The rest of the menu is rather more complex ("prepared with our own unique exuberance and style.") That might translate to a fricassee of monkfish and vegetables with clams, sherry and sweet pepper cream or seared guava-glazed yellowfin tuna with Costa Rican chile relish

The best deal may be the four-course tasting menu ($48). At our visit it opened with two appetizers from the regular menu, the aforementioned grilled shrimp, and fall-spiced ravioli filled with sweet potato, cheddar and bacon on sautéed broccoli rabe and forest mushrooms. The main dish was a wood-grilled beef tenderloin with porcini-gorgonzola crust and green onion duchess potatoes. Dessert was a sampler of the night's offerings, among them Belgian chocolate fudge terrine with Tahitian vanilla ice cream and a napoleon of baked apples, caramel mousse and pecan florentines.

The wide-ranging wine list is distinguished as much by its inflated prices (only a few local offerings in the twenties) as by its flowery headers ("berries and earth," "bold and beautiful.")

(401) 598-8011. Entrées, $24 to $32. Dinner, Monday-Saturday 5:30 to 9:30 or 10.

L'Epicureo, 238 Atwells Ave.

From a funky deli and lunch adjunct to Joe's Quality Meat Market, this evolved into one stylish, beautiful restaurant dispensing some of the best food in town. Such a class act is not what you'd expect to find in Providence's Federal Hill section, long a tight little enclave of ethnic eateries, most of them southern Italian.

Here is a romantic European bistro with New York flair, in the words of chef Tom Buckner, co-owner with his wife Rozann. The unusual walls convey a mahogany leather look created by a local artist, the wood paneling is mahogany and ash, and Italian marble and granite dress the service counter in front of the partially open kitchen. White-linened tables topped with shaded oil lamps seat 50 in tasteful elegance. A recent rear addition with a fireplace seats 50 more for functions and overflow.

The food is up to the surroundings, thanks to Tom's twenty-year association in the meat market with his late father-in-law, Joseph DiGiglio. "He was known for the best meat market in the country," says Tom. "And we're trying to be the best restaurant." Tom ages the restaurant's beef for six weeks as his mentor taught him, smokes his own salmon on the restaurant's state-of-the-art wood grill, cuts his own halibut, stuffs his calamari ("nobody does that any more"), bakes all the rosemary-perfumed focaccia and makes his own ice creams. When his wife utters the usual buzzwords that "everything is made from scratch," you know that's the case here.

We would gladly try every single item on the menu. Expect such starters as straciatella (the classic Roman egg soup), white bean and tomato polenta with grilled veal sausage, a warm goat cheese crostini with pan-seared tomatoes on field greens, and an Italian crêpe filled with shrimp and braised spinach in a gorgonzola cream sauce. The signature pasta dish is clams in white wine sauce and diced tomatoes over angelhair pasta. Other main courses include handmade lobster raviolis with grilled sea scallops in a cognac-shallot cream sauce, pan-seared pork loin with a merlot sauce over wilted spinach and a terrific wood-grilled veal tenderloin served with spinach and cheese raviolis.

Baking is Tom's forte, so desserts are exemplary. Among them are his special tiramisu over espresso crème anglaise, and a warm apple tart with honey ice cream studded with pinenuts, served with caramel sauce. The all-Italian wine list is nicely priced in the high teens and twenties.

This engaging establishment's attention to detail extends to the napkins folded like birds of paradise or imperial fans – "we let the staff have fun and see what they can create each week," says Tom. There's even a brandy snifter filled with roses in the ladies' room.

(401) 454-8430. Entrées, $16.95 to $27.95. Dinner, Tuesday-Saturday 5 to 9 or 10.

Other Top Choices

Pot au Feu, 44 Custom House St.

The first of Providence's fine downtown restaurants, this split-level establishment (a charming bistro in the basement; a glamorous French salon upstairs) has long been one of our favorites. Lovingly tended by Bob and Ann Burke, it helped inspire the city's initial culinary renaissance, but like many old-timers clings to a comforting niche.

No less an authority than Julia Child is partial to its food, which received the first five-star rating granted by Rhode Island Monthly magazine reviewers on the occasion of its twentieth anniversary in 1992. Wine Spectator honors its wine list, and Bob Burke was one of the first in New England to be inducted into Moet's Club des Sabreurs for those who pop champagne corks with sabers. The Burkes branched out in 1996 with an opulent restaurant in a former bank rechristened Federal Reserve, but quickly gave that over to private functions, including a series of festival dinners that Providence hosted in 1999 for its sister city of Florence, featuring fifteen visiting Italian chefs.

In the Bistro, with its zinc bar, ancient stone and brick walls, and tiny lights illuminating a brick shelf lined with empty wine bottles, you may order typical bistro food – omelets, onion soup, pâtés (one of duck foie gras), salmon gravlax, quiche and salade au chèvre, all at reasonable prices. The vanilla mousse with praline sauce is not to be missed. The twenty or so dinner entrées might include shrimp provençal, broiled salmon with a citrus-ginger butter, roasted chicken with a pecan and maple syrup glaze, and the namesake pot au feu, the traditional French "pot on fire" of braised meats and vegetables.

Upstairs, amid crisp white linens, lacquered black chairs and wall panels painted black with gold, you may order the same bistro items for lunch or choose again from daily specials. We'd rather save up for dinner here; it's a special-occasion place with perfect lighting, service and classical music. The haute menu is traditional, except perhaps for a recent offering of grilled medallions of ostrich with a caramelized onion and madeira sauce. You can order à la carte, but we prefer the three-course table d'hôte dinners, good value for an extra $10.

On the night we dined we were celebrating a double birthday. Fond memories of escargots bourguignonne and clams épinard dance in our heads, as do thoughts of the mushroom soup, the salad with fresh mushrooms and cherry tomatoes, the French bread served from a huge basket with sweet butter, the pink roast lamb, the tournedos with blue cheese, the crisp vegetables, the crème brûlée, the mousse au citron, the espresso. Memories are a bit blurred by a couple of the best martinis

Refurbished dining room at Chez Pascal is setting for country French bistro fare.

we've had and a bottle of La Cour Pavillon Medoc – well, it was a birthday! We can't wait to go back before too many more roll around.

(401) 273-8953. Salon: Entrées, $19.50 to $29. Lunch, Monday-Friday noon to 1:30. Dinner, Thursday-Saturday 6 to 9 or 9:30.

Bistro: Entrées, $13.95 to $20.95. Lunch, Monday-Friday 11:30 to 2. Dinner, Monday-Saturday 5 to 9 or 11, Sunday 4 to 9.

Chez Pascal, 960 Hope St.

Providence is the new restaurant home of Pascal and Lynn Leffray, he a French-born chef from Chartres and she a native Rhode Islander who "dragged him home with me from New York" in 1993 to launch their own place in a former diner in downstate Narragansett. There, the food received instant "outstanding" status from a Rhode Island Monthly reviewer. She wrote that it was "as close to a five-star restaurant as Rhode Island has to offer," were it not missing "a few of the essentials of a fine dining experience (a liquor license and a lush interior, for instance")."

When their lease ran out, the Leffrays moved to Providence to quarters once occupied by La France restaurant. They refurbished the dining room in pale yellow and hung framed French culinary posters on the walls above rich wood wainscoting. They relocated the bar to the front end of the dining room, facing the écru lace café curtain that Lynn sewed to screen part of the picture window onto the street. They hand-painted the tiles of the patterned tin ceiling in shades of green. They set the tables with white cloths, oil lamps and fresh flowers. Cabaret songs in the Edith Piaf tradition play in the background.

With the "essentials of a fine dining experience" now provided, the food expectations were readily met. "Everything is superb," raved the Providence

Journal reviewer. Pascal's is country French bistro cooking at its best – "nothing trendy," he says. "The flavors on the plate are what matters."

They're at their most redolent in such starters as Mediterranean fish broth with saffron and rouille, port-sauced sweetbreads in brioche, and baked oysters gratinée with a champagne and basil mousseline. More good flavors are evident in a salad of scallops and shrimp provençal or Pascal's favorite: mixed greens with gruyère, walnuts, olives, tomatoes, shallots and julienned garlic sausage.

The treats continue with the main courses, perhaps skate fish grenobloise, roasted chicken with truffles and port wine sauce, hanger steak with shallot sauce and french fries, and New Zealand rack of lamb garnished with goat cheese, spinach, potatoes, onions and fennel.

Dessert is no letdown, not with Pascal's French almond pear tarte (Gourmet magazine requested the recipe), his profiteroles au chocolat or his chocolate fondant spilling molten decadence from its center.

Shortly after opening, Chez Pascal undertook an expansion into an adjacent building to double its dining capacity to 100. With his long-awaited liquor license, he also was offering Tuesday night tastings pairing flights of wines with appropriate foods. His French and American wine list is notable for its proportion of bistro offerings at modest prices.

(401) 782-6020. Entrées, $15.50 to $23. Lunch, Tuesday-Saturday 11:30 to 2:30. Dinner, Tuesday-Saturday from 5:30. Sunday, brunch 11 to 2, dinner from 5.

Empire, 123 Empire St.

It's named for the downtown street. Its space, fashioned from a former Packard automobile showroom, is stark. Its food began as Tuscan but added some old-fashioned Americana. And Empire has more than the usual ties to Al Forno.

Chef-owners Eric Moshier and his wife, Loren Falsone, trained at Al Forno for seven years following graduation from Johnson & Wales University. In 1999, they were persuaded by mentors George Germon and Johanne Killeen to open their own restaurant in a condemned building that had been an X-rated bookstore, lately purchased by developer Arnold Chace Jr. across from the Trinity Repertory Theater. George, who taught architecture at Rhode Island School of Design before opening Al Forno, designed a monochromatic, L-shaped space with floor-to-ceiling windows onto the streets. The windows facing Washington Street yield a view of the showy theater, while those on the Empire Street side swing open, extending the dining room to sidewalk tables in summer. The restaurant's atmosphere has been described as gothic/art deco, although Eric was as nonplused as we were in trying to categorize it. He said that George calls it modern European, with a touch of Greco-Roman and Provence. Others find its grays, olive greens and unusually subdued paint colors rather, well, monochromatic. Faux-marble tables, a granite bar and carved ceiling moldings are notable attributes.

The extensive menu is tweaked daily and bears many an imprint from Al Forno, especially the desserts (to be ordered at meal's start), and the pizzas (although here they are baked Neapolitan style rather than grilled).

"We cook the way we like to eat," says Eric, who demurs to Loren in culinary matters, He puts his pastry training to good use on some of the desserts and oversees the business end of the venture. The warm apple butter served with seared foie gras on homemade Empire toast reflects his upbringing in Lancaster, heart of Pennsylvania Dutch country. The roasted julienne of summer squash and zucchini atop portobello, chanterelle and lobster mushrooms reflects the vegetarian bent of Loren, a Long Islander. Her potato and cabbage soup, accented with zucchini croutons, proves that vegetables can fill one as satisfyingly as meat. But she's also partial to Nana's meatball soup, a treat borrowed from her grandmother. Other standout starters are prosciutto and black mission figs with parmigiano and aged balsamic, and griddled shrimp with shaved fennel salad. The signature pizza is the margarita with mozzarella and basil; the pasta, crespelle layered in an earthenware dish with wild mushrooms, two cheeses, pumpkin and tomato.

Chicken is a staple on the menu, showing up four times among ten entrée choices the night we were there. The double marinated half chicken with tartly sweet preserved lemons, herbs, crispy potato torta and roasted red onions is a masterpiece. So is the fried chicken impanato, soaked overnight in buttermilk and then dredged in seasoned flour to be crisp outside, tender and juicy inside. It's accompanied by house-made slaw, a tangle of mixed greens, and french fries so good that they often show up alone as an appetizer, offered with lemony mayonnaise. Other favorites include fresh hake and mixed vegetables en papillote, roasted veal chop with fried sweetbread giblets, and flank steak braciole stuffed with polenta, mozzarella and prosciutto. The veal chop and the delmonico steak are apt to be "griddled" – cooked quickly on a very hot flat-top griddle to seal in the juices.

You may wonder whether you can handle the dessert you had to order at meal's start. Be assured it will be worth it. Eric's feathery lavender panna cotta with caramelized apples shimmers on a thin pistachio crust. The roasted grape tart is teamed with bitter chocolate sauce, and the dense Gothic chocolate cake floats on a cloud of meringue. You may find lemon meringue crêpes with roasted plums, crème caramel with fig jam and sour cream, or poached cranberry bread pudding with caramel crust. No ice creams or sorbets here. The proof is in the puddings, pastries and whipped creams.

The dessert list offers a few coffees, but most of the space is devoted to teas by the pot – more than two dozen options at our visit.

(401) 621-7911. Entrées, $18 to $26. Dinner, Monday-Saturday 5 to 11 or midnight, Sunday 4 to 9.

Adesso, 161 Cushing St.
By far the best and most enduring of the ever-changing eateries on College Hill is this chic California cafe in a converted garage. Celebrated for its flashy "Cal/Ital" cuisine, it was founded by the owner of the old Anthony's restaurant downtown, opened by a pizza chef from Spago in Los Angeles and lovingly tended since by David Drake.

Adesso means "now" in Italian, and this is a now place. Casual and noisy, it's done up crisply in grays and mauve, with heavy European cutlery rolled up inside gray napkins atop charcoal gray oilcloths, neon signs on the walls and changing pots of flowering plants on the tables year-round. Pots of daffodils brightened a shelf on a rainy April day at one visit. Skylights and huge windows make the rear room an oversize greenhouse, while the dark interior dining room yields a view of the open mesquite grill.

From the wood oven come interesting pizzas like barbecued chicken with smoked gouda, mozzarella, red onion and cilantro. We lunched on a good pizza with lamb sausage, roasted red and yellow peppers, and wild mushrooms. Also delicious was grilled squid with a salsa of red peppers, onions and black olives, accompanied by excellent zucchini, potatoes and snap peas. Desserts were pear bread pudding with bourbon sauce and a warm walnut tart with crème chantilly.

At a subsequent dinner for three, the mesquite grill yielded swordfish with a relish of cucumber, red apple and onion; yellowfin tuna with crushed black pepper and a warmed artichoke, thyme, tomato and enoki mushroom concasse, and Canadian pheasant served on wild rice with a madeira and black truffle sauce. The substantial entrée salads and exotic pastas also enticed. Worthy endings were warm chocolate-bourbon truffle cake with french vanilla ice cream and a chocolate terrine capped with white chocolate ganache and served with raspberry sauce.

Strong coffee is served in stainless-steel cups. The sleek chrome and glass salt and pepper grinders are so handsome that we bought a pair to take home.

(401) 521-0770. Entrées, $15.95 to $23.95. Lunch, Monday-Saturday 11:30 to 2:30. Dinner nightly, 5 to 10:30, weekends to 11:30, Sunday from 4:30.

Rue de L'Espoir, 99 Hope St.

Once consciously French, this old favorite of the academic crowd is now consciously international – and may have lost something in the transition. When it opened more than two decades ago, the Left Bank-style bistro was perhaps the city's most exciting eatery. With the proliferation of restaurants of late, it has lost that distinction, but remains an authentic cafe that could have been lifted from the streets of Paris.

The unusual tables are made of quarry tile, copper pans and plants hang from the pressed-tin ceiling, and decorative panels and woodwork are sponged in cranberry and peach colors around an interior dining room on several levels. In changing to an international menu, owner Deb Norman still offers a classic onion soup gratinée and a salade niçoise – but no more of the wonderful pâtés we enjoyed in the past. You're more likely to find starters like Thai crab cakes, grilled chiles rellenos stuffed with sweet potato mash, spinach and mushroom raviolis with smoked gouda and ricotta cheese, and stuffed brie della robia with sautéed spinach, sundried tomatoes, black olives and garlic pesto. Main courses include crispy-skin salmon with avocado vinaigrette, a duet of duck breast and sea scallops with two sauces, and "leaning tower of portobello," a grilled mushroom atop a layered stack of wilted greens, risotto cake, roasted red peppers and ricotta cheese.

From the dessert tray we recall a memorable charlotte malakoff (lady fingers, whipped cream, nuts, kirsch and strawberry preserves). A large selection of beers is available, as are interesting and reasonable wines.

This remains a good place for breakfast. Although famous for its honey oatbread french toast with yogurt and fruit, we could only manage the $3.95 special: two eggs, coffee, corn muffin and crispy home fries. The fries were so addictive that most were stolen by the person who only came in for orange juice and caffe au lait.

(401) 751-8890. Entrées, $16.95 to $21.95. Breakfast, Tuesday-Friday 7:30 to 11, weekends 8:30 to 2:30. Lunch, Tuesday-Sunday 11:30 to 2:30. Dinner nightly, 5 to 9 or 10:30.

Pizzico, 762 Hope St.

Here is one of the more engaging Italian trattorias we've seen: two side-by-side dining rooms – one done up in Mediterranean peach and yellow painted walls and the other in white brick walls – both nicely offset against the dark ceilings. Generally well-spaced tables sport white butcher paper over white cloths and bottles of mineral water.

Folks rave about the food, orchestrated by chef-owner Fabrizio Iannucci, who sold his celebrated little Il Piccolo in suburban Johnston in 1997. He and his wife Alison from England kept this when they moved to southern California, where they opened a similar restaurant with a shared menu in Brentwood., Cal. The food here is said to have suffered a bit in their absence, "but their hearts are still here," according to their local manager-sommelier.

The rather lengthy menu opens with "center of the table" plates to be shared, among them crostini with assorted toppings, a thin-crust chestnut pizza with roasted asparagus and mozzarella, and an "assortimento" platter of prosciutto, mozzarella, fried olives, artichokes, cannellini beans and what have you. Smaller starters could be roasted portobello mushrooms over prosciutto, Roman-style bruschetta and gnocchi genovesi as well as soups and salads (some of the last are available as entrées).

The dozen pastas might include barilla in a spicy tomato and goat cheese sauce or black-ink ravioli stuffed with lobster and ricotta, served in a creamy cognac-basil and lobster sauce.

Main dishes range from pan-roasted rainbow trout with a garlicky wine sauce and herb-crusted Norwegian salmon served over sautéed mixed greens to grilled turkey breast accented with black olives and artichokes and grilled lamb chops with rosemary and balsamic vinegar. Both of the latter are served with "bubble and squeak" potatoes.

The 1,000-bottle, Wine Spectator award-winning wine list might be supplemented by a blackboard listing "special chiantis and super Tuscans."

(401) 421-4114. Entrées, $13.95 to $21.75. Lunch, Monday-Friday and weekend brunch, 11:30 to 2:30. Dinner nightly from 5.

How Cav?

CAV, 14 Imperial Place.

What to make of a place whose name is an acronym for Coffee, Antiques and Victuals, and also alludes to a French wine cellar (cave, pronounced *cahv*)? Gourmet, you ask? Very much so, avows owner Sylvia Moubayed from Alexandria, Egypt, citing endorsements by Bon Appetit magazine and the New York Times. The former executive director of the Providence Atheneum library opened this coffeehouse cum restaurant cum antiques shop in 1989. "My taste for decor was more expensive than my pocketbook," she said, so selling the decor pays the bills.

The former factory space with fourteen-foot-high ceiling is rather dizzying and overwhelming, what with chairs and rugs hanging from the rafters, dining tables tucked between glass cases of art objects and displays of Asian bronzes and carved wooden masks, a staff of young women in black, and people emerging here, there and everywhere. The tables are set with kilim rugs, a couple of booths are topped with hoods and the enormous menu comes in an album. It runs to at least eight typewritten pages, not counting specials of the day and night.

This is much more than an ambient pause for coffee or tea and pastries. It's a lunch stop for ladies who shop, a celebratory venue for a special-occasion dinner,

Kilim rugs cover tables and wooden sleigh hangs from ceiling in dining room at CAV.

and a jazz club with live music on weekends. The eclectic, international menu covers all the bases and all price ranges. Sit back, watch the scene and enjoy.

(401) 751-9164. Entrées, $13.50 to $20.95. Lunch and dinner daily. Open weekdays from 9, weekends from noon.

Coffee and Breads, Country Style

Olga's Cup and Saucer, 103 Point St.

Coffee with the best artisan breads and pastries in town is the claim to fame of this small café with a bakery of great note. It's the offspring of the much-loved Olga's Cup and Saucer in Little Compton, which baker Olga Bravo opened in 1988 next to our favorite Walker's Farm Stand. She was joined two years later by Rebecca Wagner, an Al Forno alumnus who's known for her soups.

They added a year-round bakery in a charming English-style cottage in the Point section in the Jewelry District just south of downtown Providence in 1997. Their summer following expected lunches as well as breads, so the partners obliged. The thin-crust corn and tomato pizzas, sandwiches, pastas, tempting entrées and yummy desserts pack in the noonday crowds. Morning coffee, enormous muffins, scones and breads for toasting proved so popular that we could barely get in the door.

There's a handful of tiled tables made by the owners, who also are artists. Most choice are those outside beneath apricot trees beside a showplace little English garden, full of raised and potted beds bursting with flowers, vines and herbs. It's a touch of country in the midst of the city.

(401) 831-6666. Entrées, $6 to $9. Open Monday-Friday, 7 to 6, Saturday 8 to 5. Lunch, 11 to 3.

Hope on Hope

Trent, 748 Hope St.

The small sign out front says "Bistro/Kafe/Pastries." Trent Ferrara offers these and more at this combination gourmet eat-in, takeout establishment. It had to be a combination, at least to start. Small and stylish, the small storefront holds only eight glass-topped tables in a modern gray and white setting, with a glass deli case at the back. Here you find the day's offerings, an appetizing and changing array of pastries, salads, pastas, risottos and entrées. There's no menu – "I just keep cooking and bringing things out all day," says Trent. We admired a tomato stuffed with salmon salad for lunch, pan-seared scallops and roasted leg of lamb for dinner. Everything is à la carte, so order, say, poached salmon for $8, add rice and a vegetable and the tab might total $15. Trent does everything himself, even waiting on tables when his waitress didn't show up the day we were there. He'd been open only a short time, but already was being recommended by foodies in the know. The place was full for lunch, but we hoped to return – if only to take out. You just knew it had to be good.

(401) 861-5363. Entrées, $8 to $15. Lunch and dinner, Tuesday-Saturday 11:30 to 9. BYOB.

Lodging

The Westin Providence, 1 West Exchange Street, Providence 02903.

Built and owned by the state as part of the new Rhode Island Convention Center complex, this is New England's fanciest hotel outside Boston. From the striking, 25-story-high gabled roof that denotes its Neoclassic presence on the Providence skyline to the majestic four-story lobby rotunda with its marble floor and columns, the Westin exudes class.

Each of the 364 handsomely appointed rooms and suites comes with kingsize or two double beds, at least one easy chair with ottoman, a spacious writing desk, a TV hidden in an armoire, two telephones, a mini-bar and a coffee-maker stocked with Starbucks coffee.

Our quiet cocoon of a room came with a triple-sheeted kingsize bed topped with six big pillows, two upholstered chairs and large windows that opened. A deluxe corner room on the nineteenth floor, it was bright and cheery by day and yielded a knockout view of the city lights at night. The contemporary European décor in champagne tones supposedly reflected the interior of a Newport mansion. The more memorable Newport touch was the immense bathroom, where for some strange reason the rack with hand towels was clear across the room from the washstand. Chocolates and a weather forecast arrived at nightly turndown, and the day's newspaper was at the door in the morning.

Guests enjoy the hotel's fitness center with indoor pool beneath the dome atop the rotunda building. The Library Bar & Lounge off the lobby rotunda is the ultimate in plush surroundings and a refuge for creative appetizers, single-malt scotches and cigars. Take the long escalator up to the second-floor lounges, which include a sports bar serving light lunch and dinner fare. Besides the elegant **Agora** restaurant, **The Café** offers less lofty fare for breakfast and lunch.

(401) 598-8000. Fax (401) 598-8200. Three hundred sixty rooms and four suites. Doubles, $149 to $265.

Westin Hotel offers elegant dining in sumptuous Agora restaurant.

The Providence Biltmore, Kennedy Plaza, Providence 02903.

An early feather in Providence's cap, this restored downtown hotel appears just slightly dowdy in comparison with its new neighbor across Kennedy Plaza. The imposing brick edifice opened in 1922 to a special trainload from New York, a 50-piece band and a sea of roses, but fell on hard times and closed in 1973. It reopened with great fanfare in 1979 after local business interests renovated it for $15 million. All was ultra-new and deluxe when we stayed here shortly thereafter.

At the top of the three-story lobby you can see the wonderfully ornate, original gilt ceiling, and the crystal chandelier and palm trees remind one of the Plaza in New York. **Davio's,** a member of the small Italian restaurant chain out of Boston, offers a quiet, arched dining room with a semi-open kitchen on the main floor.

The original 500 bedrooms have been converted into 224 comfortable, large and deluxe rooms, done in soft and soothing colors. Many are called junior suites with kingsize or two queen beds, plus armchairs and sofabeds in elegant sitting areas, and TVs hidden in armoires. We liked the huge closets and the bathrooms with separate dressing areas and vanities. Two presidential suites on the fifteenth floor are some of the largest we've seen – each impeccably outfitted with antiques, two bathrooms, dining room, living room and kitchenette. (The price? If you have to ask, you won't be staying).

(401) 421-0700 or (800) 294-7709. Fax (401) 455-3050. Two hundred twenty-four rooms and suites. Doubles, $100 to $150.

The Old Court, 144 Benefit St., Providence 02903.

You can stay on historic Benefit Street and relive the Providence of yesteryear, thanks to the conversion of an 1863 Episcopal church rectory into a fine B&B. Owners Jon and Carol Rosenblatt, who also own a series of small East Side restaurants, spared no expense in the restoration. Italianate in design, the Old Court has ornate mantelpieces, plaster moldings and twelve-foot-high ceilings.

Each of the ten guest rooms is decorated differently, if rather sparely. Some have brass beds, some four-poster, and most have exotic wallpapers. All beds are queen or kingsize except for one with two doubles and another with twins. The large Eastlake Room is done with Eastlake furniture and offers a sofa and wet bar. Lace curtains and old clocks convey a feeling of the past. Air-conditioning, telephones and televisions are concessions to the present.

Because there is no common room, the Old Court seems like a small hotel. A full breakfast is served in a pink breakfast room, graced with an oriental rug and fresh flowers. The specialty is crêpes, but the day's menu might dictate eggs, pancakes or french toast.

(401) 751-2002. Fax (401) 282-4830. Ten rooms with private baths. March-November: doubles, $155 weekends, $135 midweek. Rest of year: $135 weekends, $115 midweek.

The Cady House. 127 Power St., Providence 02906.

The owner's eclectic collections of folk art are everywhere evident in this imposing 1839 residence with pillared entrance on College Hill.

Their offspring gone, Anna Colaiace and her husband Bill, a radiologist, offer three much-decorated Victorian guest quarters with queen beds and private baths. A side suite contains a daybed with trundle bed in the living room and a sturdy armoire and dresser in the bedroom. A rear bedroom has a luxurious settee in a windowed alcove and a giant bathroom with clawfoot tub, separate shower and a circular stand holding a multitude of plants. Guests enter a front bedroom through the bathroom to find a spacious room with sofa and tiled fireplace. The wild wallpapers throughout "are my interpretation of Victorian," says Anna, who did the decorating herself.

A former caterer who used to make desserts for CAV, she serves an ample breakfast of eggs, frittata or french toast on the weekends (continental during the week) in a formal dining room opening onto a delightful screened porch. The porch overlooks a curved terrace and showy gardens on a triple lot. Folk art and sculptures continue in the lower garden.

"We just got a little crazier," Anna said at our latest visit, noting her husband's display of African masks all over the living room. "He went crazy on E-Bay for two months after a trip." Along with their growing collections, the couple's two dogs are much in evidence.

(401) 273-5398. Two rooms and one suite with private baths. Doubles, $90 to $95.

Annie Brownell House, 400 Angell St., Providence 02906.

Choices are a feature of this new B&B in an 1899 Colonial Revival on the historic East Side. You get a choice of rooms, since it has three bedrooms but zoning allows use of only two. And you get a choice of breakfast fare served in your choice of dining rooms.

Annie Tunderman, the owner-innkeeper from England, and her husband Steve bought the house when he accepted a job with a computer software company around the corner. She had warmed to the challenge as a manager for a quasi-B&B in West Concord, Mass.

The Tundermans offer a choice of three rooms in the three-story house crowned by a widow's walk. Most in demand is the main-floor rear Magnolia Room, so named for the bedding on the queensize four-poster. It offers a dressing room/closet and a large bathroom with a shower. Upstairs are a small side queen bedroom, this with a private hall bath, and a rear room with two twin beds and "an en-suite bath – is that what you call it?" Annie asks. She was toying with changing their quarters in front into a guest suite because of its fireplaced den.

The main floor harbors a pleasant parlor and two rooms furnished with dining tables on either side of the hallway (Annie prefers the more casual breakfast room that's sunnier in the morning). She offers a full breakfast starting with juice, fresh fruit and hot or cold cereals. The main dish could be frittata, a Spanish omelet, french toast or pancakes with a cranberry-orange compote. You decide.

(401) 454-2934. Two rooms with private baths. Doubles, $80 to $115.

Gourmet Treats

Providence Place, a huge and appealing downtown mall, bills itself as New England's premier shopping and dining destination. For shopping, you have not only Filene's, Lord & Taylor and Nordstrom but **Crate & Barrel,** the **Pottery Barn, Williams-Sonoma, Lindt Chocolates** and **Godiva Chocolatier.** There's a food court as well as free-standing restaurants like **Fire & Ice, The Cheesecake Factory** and the **Napa Valley Grille.** Our favorite here is **Café Nordstrom,** a dark and elegant corner space hidden away on the third floor of the Seattle-based Nordstrom. The cafeteria-style food offerings are far more innovative than the norm – and rationally priced.

The **Union Station Brewery,** 36 Exchange Ter., produces specialty ales, lagers and stout in a section of the old Union Station, along with some snacks and light fare to go with. More award-winners emanate from **Trinity Brewhouse,** across from the Providence Civic Center at 186 Fountain St.

L'Elizabeth, 285 South Main St., is a romantic spot for a tête-à-tête coffee or drink. It has a true European feeling, with the look of a salon where there are different groupings of sofas and chairs, and is very dimly lit at night. No meals are served, but L'Elizabeth's torte cake with raspberry, apricot and chocolate, and perhaps chocolate mousse pie are offered with tea or coffee. Espresso, cappuccino, international coffees, hot toddies and a large selection of single-malt scotches and liqueurs are available.

Wickenden Street, just southeast of downtown, offers a panoply of food: Café Zog (coffee, sandwiches and juices), the Coffee Exchange, I-Scream, O-Cha Thai cuisine and sushi bar, Sweet Street Café and Taste of India. It's a funky street that USA Today dubbed bohemian in a 1999 feature highlighting how a wave of movies and the hit TV show have helped turned Providence into a getaway destination for the young and hip.

Culinary Treasures

Culinary Archives & Museum, 315 Harborside Blvd.

The 1989 gifts of Chef Louis Szathmary of Chicago's famed Bakery restaurant launched this little-known museum in a vast, unlikely-looking warehouse on an outlying campus of Johnson & Wales University. They were the nucleus of holdings that have quickly yet quietly grown into the largest archive of cookbooks and food-related objects in the world. Students lead hour-long tours that show a portion of the more than 500,000 items billed as "the Smithsonian of the food service industry." There's so much stuff and so little budget that relatively little is marked, so the effect is quite endearing if primitive. On a whirlwind tour, director Barbara Kuck pointed out highlights: a special exhibit of stoves and another tracing the history of cooking schools back to the 15th Century, an early Michelin guide, a history of chef's uniforms, publisher Earle MacAusland's collection of Gourmet magazines, a letter from Escoffier planning a dinner for Gilbert and Sullivan, a menu signed by California chefs who cooked an 80th birthday dinner for Julia Child. You might see a circular sofa from Boston's Copley Plaza Hotel and a 5,000-year-old flint kitchen knife from Egypt. A presidential collection traces "The History of the First Stomach." All these artifacts will get their just due with a planned move in 2003 into the old Gladding's department store downtown.

(401) 598-2805. Guided tours, Tuesday-Saturday 10 to 5. Adults, $5.

A Touch of Italy, Plus

An entire book could be written on Federal Hill, Providence's enclave of ethnic eateries, bakeries, markets and pasta stores. Lately, its stress on heavy Neapolitan cuisine has been broadened with the likes of **L'Epicureo** and **Mediterraneo.** Not to mention the sleek **Eclectic Grille, Gracie's Bar & Grille, AquaViva Eurobistro,** the New American bistro **Lucy's,** the Japanese outpost **Fuji,** the Caribbean **Montego Bay on the Hill,** the **Bombay Club** and the authentic, inexpensive **Mexico.** Traditionalists still dote on the **Blue Grotto** and **Camille's Roman Garden.** Visitors mix with regulars at old kitchen tables in **Angelo's Civita Farnese,** an unlikely-looking spot where you roll up your sleeves for family-style food like Mama really did make.

The heart of the area is DePasquale Square, a charming cobblestone plaza with a fountain, pots of flowers, tiny white lights in the trees, and outdoor tables and benches. Here you can lunch on an Italian tuna sandwich or one of prosciutto, fresh mozzarella and tomatoes followed by an imported dessert at **Caffe Dolce Vita.** You can sup on a "legendary grilled pizza" from **Bob & Timmy's,** or have a festive dinner at **Walter's La Locanda del Coccio.** You can also "see your chicken alive," according to the sign in the window of **Antonelli's Poultry.**

Newly relocated and vastly expanded across the plaza from its original space is **Venda Ravioli,** which sells handmade pastas and sauces (the cheese ravioli with wild mushroom sauce is heavenly). Owner Alan Costantino now stocks many exclusive imported items and offers a cappuccino bar, gelatos and sit-down lunches.

Around the corner at 92 Spruce St. is **Pastiche,** a bakery and gourmet dessertery par excellence. Partake of an exotic homemade dessert (perhaps toffee-walnut torte or a fabulous looking fruit tart ($5 a slice) with cappuccino or café au lait in stylish digs beside the fireplace.

Pick out panini sandwiches or dinner to go from a remarkable selection at **Tony's Colonial Food Store** at 311 Atwells Ave. Anthonio DiCicco bought an original Greek grocery and kept the Colonial name. He cut back on groceries in favor of gourmet items, mostly Italian, but still has a grand assortment of cheeses and deli meats. There's an amazing selection of olive oils, vinegars and pastas, plus colorful ceramic pasta dishes and spoon rests at the entry. We enjoyed Tony's chicken cutlets, broccoli rabe and garlic breadsticks at home after a long day in Providence. The newer **Roma Gourmet** across the street is equally fun to browse in. It has a butcher and a small cafe and bakery at the side. **Scialo Brothers Bakery** at 257 Atwells, a fixture since 1916, offers terrific muffins, breads and pastries.

Water scene is on view from corner table for two at The Regatta restaurant in Falmouth.

Cape Cod

New Capers on the Old Cape

The time was not all that long ago when dining on Cape Cod meant, for many, the three C's: Chillingsworth, the Christopher Ryder House and clam shacks.

When you thought of places to stay, you hoped to luck into a friend's summer house or you rented a cottage, preferably somewhere near the water. The few inns tended to be large and posh and were far outnumbered by all those funny-looking motels with glassed-in swimming pools near Hyannis.

Well, Chillingsworth is still there, better than ever. The Christopher Ryder House has been converted into condominiums, and the clam shacks are overshadowed by a burst of serious restaurants.

There are more summer houses, cottages, deluxe inns and funny-looking motels than ever, of course. But there's also a new breed of country inns – not full-service like their predecessors, but more than bed-and-breakfast houses.

In spring, the season starts gearing up, yet crowds and prices are less than at summer's height. Then comes the July and August crush, and the high season ends abruptly after Labor Day.

Knowledgeable visitors have long preferred the Cape in the off-season. They avoid the tourist trappings of busy Hyannis and Provincetown, whose restaurants this chapter purposely omits. For the Cape is a place for escape, for relative solitude, for respite in a sandy, seaside setting unsurpassed in New England.

Note: Although the Cape's season is lengthening every year and more places remain open year-round, the owners' plans may change. Restaurant hours vary widely. Reservations are required in advance for peak periods. Minimum stays for lodging are not unusual. Planning, flexibility and/or luck overcome such caveats.

People who haven't been to the Cape lately – or who haven't ventured far from the beach if they have – might be surprised by the "new" Cape that co-exists with the old.

Dining

The Best of the Best

Chillingsworth, Route 6A, Brewster.
The revitalized dowager of Cape Cod restaurants offers what some reviewers call the best serious resort-area dining in New England. For two years in a row it outranked all 500 Boston restaurants in the Zagat survey. In 1999, chef-owner Robert (Nitzi) Rabin won Gourmet magazine's Great American Chef award. In an era of shortcuts and cost-shaving, he is one of the last of a breed maintaining a tradition of fine dining.

For most, this is a special destination – so special, in fact, that we stopped by to reserve a table six weeks in advance for a mid-October Saturday. As it turned out, we didn't get the specific time or the table we had picked out, but that was our only complaint from a memorable dinner that lasted past midnight.

The restored 1689 house is named for Chillingsworth Foster, son of its builder. Its quaint and unassuming Cape Cod exterior gives little clue to the treasures inside – room after room full of priceless furnishings, antiques and museum pieces. The large Terrace Room in which we ended up dining is not, to our mind, as special as one of the smaller rooms like the Empire, where we had booked, or the table for four in an alcove off the living room, which one innkeeper of our acquaintance thinks is the most exquisite around.

A hurricane oil lamp, Limoges china and a vase of flowers graced our heavily linened table. A harpist was playing in the background as the waiter asked if we had questions about the menu, which is typewritten daily. The meal consists of seven courses at a fixed price of $49.50 to $64, depending upon choice of entrée. Although locally considered pricey, Chillingsworth offers better value than do its peers elsewhere – far better in that you get seven exotic courses. And the bistro menu is a relative steal.

We chose a French vouvray to accompany our appetizers, grilled duck and pepper quesadilla with coriander and tomatillo salsa and a feuilleté of oysters with spinach and lemon-butter sauce with roe. A dozen appetizers are offered, from crab cakes with cucumber julienne and golden caviar to carpaccio of veal tenderloin with truffle oil, baby greens and grilled olive bread.

The cream of mussel soup that followed was superb, as was the consommé of mushrooms. A second helping of the night's squash bread – after all, we weren't seated until 9:30 – was followed by a salad of four baby leaf lettuces, arugula, radicchio and sorrel, enriched with a crouton of warm chèvre and dressed with a zesty vinaigrette. A grapefruit sorbet with a sprig of mint, served in a crystal sherry glass, cleared the palate.

All that was literally prelude to the main event – stunning entrées, beautifully presented. The breast of duck was garnished with citrus rind and fanned in slices around the plate, interspersed with kiwi and papaya slices. A side plate contained julienned carrots and a spinach soufflé with nutmeg and wild rice. Our other entrée was an equally imaginative treatment of lamb with veal kidneys, grilled with herbs

Chef-owner Robert (Nitzi) Rabin outside Chillingsworth.

from Chillingsworth's garden. With these we had a 1982 Rodney Strong cabernet, among the least expensive California vintages on a choice wine list priced well into the hundreds.

Chillingsworth teamed grilled rare tuna loin with wasabi butter sauce long before it became the rage. Now it offers rare seared tuna tournedos with foie gras and loin of lamb with rosemary-wine sauce and a fig and chèvre tart. The loin of elk comes with a fig and sundried cranberry sauce.

Desserts here are anything but an anti-climax. One of us chose a raspberry tulipe, an intriguing presentation atop a speckled-striped pattern of napoleon. The other enjoyed a hazelnut dacquoise with coffee butter cream. Before these came the "amusements" – a plate of gingerbread men, rolled cookies around citrus and macaroons. The finale was a serving of chocolate truffles, intense to the ultimate.

Nitzi Rabin made the rounds of diners as they lingered over coffee. He and wife Pat, whose youthful appearances belie their forty-something years, work fourteen-hour days overseeing the expanding operation they purchased in 1975. Both had worked summers at Chillingsworth, he advancing from busboy to captain to manager and managing to pick up an MBA at the Tuck School at Dartmouth. The Rabins winter in Colorado ski country and travel to France or California to continue to enhance their highly creative American version of new French cuisine.

Lunch and dinner are available in a contemporary bistro and greenhouse lounge area with skylights, walls of glass and plants. The lunch menu embraces some of the dinner items as well as other creative fare at more down-to-earth prices (entrées, $9.75 to $13.50). A broader bistro menu at night offers exotic appetizers in the $7 to $8 range and main courses from $12.50 for grilled chicken with spicy field salad and warm mushroom vinaigrette to $23.50 for grilled veal chop with garlic-mashed potatoes and red onion marmalade. This is the place for those who want to sense the Chillingsworth flair but feel that the main dining room serves more than they can eat, or who don't like precise seatings at perhaps awkward hours.

Off the lounge, **Le Bistrôt** gift shop offers many Chillingsworth specialties for sale. Nitzi calls it "a nice catering business without the delivery problems." The shop was crowded on a summer Sunday with tourists seeking to get a taste of Chillingsworth without paying full price. Frankly, we'd go all-out and splurge – the experience is worth the tab.

Upstairs, the Rabins offer three elegant guest rooms and suites for overnight stays. Rates are $95 to $135, B&B.

(508) 896-3640 or (800) 430-3640. Prix-fixe, $49.50 to $64. Lunch in summer, Tuesday-Sunday 11:30 to 2:30. Dinner by reservation, Tuesday-Sunday, seatings at 6 and 9; weekends only in spring and fall. Closed after Thanksgiving to mid-May.

The Regatta of Falmouth By-the-Sea, 217 Clinton Avenue, Falmouth.

One of the Cape's best waterfront locations, a jaunty pink and white decor, inventive food and a smashing wine list – it's little wonder that Upper Cape folks rate this long-established restaurant right up there with Chillingsworth and keep it consistently crowded and lively. And to offer New England specialties in an historic setting, owners Wendy and Brantz Bryan took on a year-round venture, the Regatta at Cotuit (see below), which some now consider the best restaurant on Cape Cod.

The original Regatta takes its name, no doubt, from its location in a gray- shingled building with black and white awnings and a profusion of pink geraniums and purple impatiens beside Falmouth's inner harbor. The structure was totally rebuilt in 1992 after suffering severe damage during Hurricane Bob. Most of the 100 seats in the main dining room take advantage of the view.

The walls are mirrored and masses of fresh flowers are all around. Pink cloths, dusky rose napkins fanned in the water glasses, pink bows on the pillars and pink banquettes around the perimeter set the color scheme. Chairs and plates are white. As the hurricane lamps are lit before dusk, the setting is colorful and romantic, to say the least.

Wendy Bryan is in charge of the wine list, which has many available by the glass since no liquor is served. The unusual selection, mainly French with a nod to California, is priced from the high teens to $250.

Appetizers are oriented toward the sea: caramelized Martha's Vineyard bay scallops paired with a phyllo napoleon filled with grilled red peppers, summer vegetables and roasted fennel coulis; seared soft-shell crab with smoked bacon vinaigrette, arugula and crispy onions, and tuna tartare with bok choy, wakame seaweed salad and crisp wontons. We gobbled up a rich chilled lobster and sole terrine, served with a saffron sauce garnished with truffles, and loved the broiled Wellfleet oysters with black American caviar.

A complimentary sorbet follows the appetizer course. Our dinner could have ended happily there, but on came the entrées. The seafood fettuccine contained more shrimp, scallops, lobster and artichoke hearts than it did spinach pasta, and the seared Norwegian salmon came with oysters and a leek and chardonnay sauce. Vegetables, served on clear glass side plates, were two kinds of squash, piquant red cabbage and new potatoes.

At our latest visit we sampled a palette of two fish, each with its own sauce (yellowfin tuna with pinot noir sauce and roasted shallots, and swordfish with caramelized-lemon and white-butter sauce), and the grilled breast of pheasant. Although seafood is the specialty, the veal sirloin, filet mignon and seared lamb loin offered in varying presentations measure up as well.

Desserts are inventive: among them, a towering striped almond cake filled with chocolate hazelnut mousse and crowned with chantilly and praline, and the Regatta's "soup des fruits" with house-made sorbets and fresh fruit garnishes. Best bet is a tasting trilogy of three favorites ($13.50 for two). Ours brought a chocolate truffle cake, almond torte with framboise sauce and hand-dipped chocolate strawberries. With dessert comes coffee in delicate cups.

The nautical flags fluttering outside in the breeze are a wonderful sight, matched by the colorful trousers of Brantz Bryan, who explains that he wears them "to make people laugh and feel at ease." He and Wendy were the first high-end restaurateurs on our travels to anticipate the change in eating habits and offer alternatives. Since rebuilding following the hurricane, they have added three-course early dinners, as well as a lighter menu with entrées priced from $12.50 to $18.50. Perhaps such flexibility is why the Bryans have been so successful at the Regatta for more than 30 years.

(508) 548-5400. Entrées, $25.50 to $29. Dinner nightly, 4:30 to 10, mid-May to mid-September.

The Red Pheasant Inn, 905 Main St. (Route 6A), Dennis.

The exterior is strictly old New England – a rambling, red, 200-year-old saltbox house and barn. Inside is a reception area-living room (used for wine tastings), a couple of dining rooms and an enclosed porch, a mix of upholstered chairs and white linens, barnwood and walls with painted flowers, hanging plants and flickering oil lamps. It's a very comfortable place. Tables are well spaced, background music is at the right level, and the service is deft and unobtrusive.

The food is on the cutting edge, with inspired touches of regional New England cuisine with fusion accents. The creative hand in the kitchen belongs to chef Bill Atwood Jr., son of the founder. Bill's wife Denise oversees the front of the house and is responsible for the beautiful side gardens around a castle sculpture in the center.

Bill, elected to the Master Chefs of America, says his efforts have evolved over the years into a Cape Cod cuisine with "a truly local flavor." He smokes his own bluefish, cod cakes and venison sausage, mixes local cod and calamari in new presentations, and stuffs quails with duck sausage. He also experiments with Asian and Mediterranean fare, "which keeps me fresh."

For starters, we were impressed with a caesar salad as good as we can make at home and the fried goat-cheese raviolis on a lovely tomato coulis, with asparagus spears and frizzles of leek radiating out. Current choices include a trio of house-cured seafood (monkfish pâté, salmon gravlax and scallop seviche), lobster and pistachio dumplings with a Japanese salsa, braised escargots in a crêpe bearing greens scented with white truffle oil, and seaweed and squid salad – a chiffonade of mixed greens with salmon cracklings, homemade ponzu and sesame vinaigrette.

Among main courses you might find cedar-planked salmon with a cumin-curry-tomato coulis, and pan-roasted halibut with a broth of saffron and ginger. Asian-style barbecued chicken comes with kim chee salsa, and grilled ostrich with tapioca flan. The native bouillabaisse, in a tomato-saffron broth, is served in custom-designed bowls from the nearby Scargo Pottery. Our choices could not have been better: roast boneless Long Island duckling served with a rhubarb, dried cherry and caramelized-ginger sauce, and grilled pavé of beef with fried oysters, wrapped in leeks with bordelaise sauce. Side plates carried different assortments of grilled and roasted vegetables, including sliced potatoes, zucchini, yellow squash and green tomatoes, as well as some barely cooked green beans. We were too full to sample the desserts, which for a warm summer night seemed rather heavy. Recent choices were crème brûlée, strawberry charlotte, profiteroles, strawberry-rhubarb tart on lemon curd and chocolate flourless cake with crème anglaise.

The distinguished wine list, priced starting in the high teens, has been cited by Wine Spectator.

(508) 385-2133 or (800) 480-2133. Entrées, $16 to $26. Dinner nightly, 5 to 8:30 or 9. Reduced schedule in January.

Abbicci, 43 Main St. (Route 6A), Yarmouth Port.

Veteran Cape restaurateur Marietta Hickey returned to the town where she had founded La Cipollina down the street. She took over the beloved Cranberry Moose and soon closed it for redecoration and a reconfiguration of the kitchen. The restaurant reopened with a new name, a new look and a new menu.

"Business is up big-time," says Marietta, "even though the average check has dropped." No longer merely a special-occasion place, Abbicci offers a variety of dining options in a Cape-style house painted butterscotch yellow with the date 1755 engraved on the chimney. Locals crowd into the 75 seats in four dining areas and a reception area with mod bar seats and tables against the windows for food that ranks among the Cape's best.

The kitchen executes an ambitious menu created by Marietta, who oversees the front of the house. A dozen entrées range from calves liver veneziana to grilled veal chop with wild mushrooms and truffled madeira demi-glace. Options include roasted fillet of salmon with a chervil-scented tangerine sauce, free-range chicken breast with Moroccan spices, veal saltimbocca and pistachio-crusted rack of lamb. Asparagus, haricots verts or sautéed spinach come with.

The antipasti and pastas are first-rate, among them the carpaccio, the fried calamari and the tagliatelle with lobster in a saffron-infused lobster cream sauce. Desserts are to die for, especially the warm peach tartlet with vanilla ice cream and raspberry sauce, the banana fritters with vanilla ice cream and rum-caramel sauce, and the frozen lemon soufflé with raspberries and pistachio. Finish with the seductive Abbicci cappuccino, a heavily liqueured concoction that might just finish you off. The extensive wine list is mostly Italian, well chosen in a broad price range.

We returned lately for a lunch that got off to a shaky start with too-loud jazz playing in the background and niggardly glasses of white wine. Things improved with crumbly, piping-hot rolls and our main choices: a kicky steak sandwich with arugula and gorgonzola, served on grilled country bread, and an assertive linguini and shellfish, with all kinds of vegetables from squash and peppers to tomatoes and asparagus. Warm raisin gingerbread with lemon mousse and applejack brandy sauce was a memorable dessert.

The decor is spare, with rooms painted different colors, white tablecloths and an array of cactus plants and artifacts. The subdued maps of ancient Italy on the walls were hand-drawn by Marietta's son, a San Francisco architect who oversaw Abbicci's redesign.

(508) 362-3501. Entrées, $19.50 to $28.50. Lunch daily, 11:30 to 2:30. Dinner nightly, from 5. Sunday brunch, 11:30 to 2:30.

Academy Ocean Grille, 2 Academy Place (Route 28), Orleans.

The hottest restaurant on the Lower Cape emerged in 1999 under the aegis of two former moteliers-turned-innkeepers. Robert Messina and Joseph Zelich sold their stylish Brewster Farmhouse Inn unexpectedly in 1996 when they received a purchase offer they could not refuse. They resurfaced at Bob & Joe's Sesuit Café at the end of Sesuit Harbor Road in the North Side Marina, turning – in Bob's words – "a dump into a gold mine," serving 500 breakfasts and lunches a day. The café is still going strong, but the partners devote full attention to this contemporary-style grill fashioned from the old Wheel House, a German restaurant. They renovated the dining room and lightened it up in white and blue, with nautical accents. The 65-seat space, casual by day, is dressed up by white tablecloths and candlelight at night. A verdant terrace adds outdoor dining in season.

Bob Messina designed the menu, but fine-tuned it with chef Brian Jenkins, who joined him after fifteen years as executive chef at the innovative Impudent Oyster in Chatham, and Christian Schulz, formerly of Christian's in Chatham. Quickly becoming signature dishes were bouillabaisse laden with at least seven kinds of seafood and garnished with lobster, pan-fried sole Mediterranean with olives and roasted tomatoes, and cod Messina, "a dish I dreamed up – kind of like oysters Rockefeller but with a piece of cod" and a pernod-accented velouté. All the fish is obtained from day boats, so it's super-fresh. Several pasta dishes, grilled Tuscan chicken, filet mignon and rack of veal are available for those who prefer.

Starters include a creamy and briny quahog chowder, Mediterranean salad, crab cakes with mango-chipotle ketchup, and avocado tostada with lime crème fraîche. A pastry chef from our favorite Fancy's Farm Market prepares sensational desserts like raspberry-almond torte, chocolate cream cheese layer cake and chocolate-pistachio layer cake.

You can sample many of the house specialties at lunch, as we did. The bouillabaisse is a sure winner, as is the lobster focaccia, which turned out to be lobster salad and avocado served with herbed focaccia and thick house fries on the side. A plate of the day's ginger-lemon and campari-grapefruit sorbets, decorated with various and colorful kinds of coulis, was a refreshing finale.

The partners also offer four pleasant guest rooms upstairs. Small but nicely furnished, they have private baths, queensize beds and TV. Continental breakfast is included in the rates.

(508) 240-1585. Entrées, $15.95 to $24.95. Lunch daily, 11:30 to 2:30. Dinner, 5:30 to 9:30. Closed Monday in off-season and November-April. Doubles, $85 in summer, $65 in off-season.

The Cape Sea Grille, 31 Sea St., Harwich Port.

A few tables on the sun porch in this former sea captain's house offer a view of the ocean down the street. The scene inside the pale yellow and green main dining room is handsome as well with white linens and Lalique-style lamps atop nicely spaced tables. It's a serene setting for some highly regarded food offered by chef-owner Jim Poitras and his wife, Beth.

Both working in the kitchen (they met while cooking in Miami), the couple have changed the emphasis from country French to new American since they took over the old Cafe Elizabeth. They offer a short, straightforward menu that changes only modestly. The food is first-rate, and the primarily local clientele considers it good value.

The emphasis is on seafood: crispy sole piccata with lemon and tomatoes, seafood paella over toasted pasta, seared rare tuna and crunchy tempura shrimp with vegetable stir-fry, and a mixed grill of roasted lobster, bacon-wrapped swordfish, salmon with herb butter and barbecued shrimp. The only other options on a recent menu were Mediterranean-style chicken stuffed with sundried tomatoes and goat cheese, and grilled tenderloin with roquefort butter and spicy pecans.

The chefs get more adventurous with starters: perhaps smoked garlic soup with charred lobster, salmon carpaccio with grilled exotic mushrooms, and crab cakes with herbed rémoulade, salsa and pepper slaw. Desserts include twin brûlées (one vanilla, one espresso), lime pie with banana whipped cream, and warm apple tart with cinnamon sauce and vanilla bean ice cream.

On busy nights, the rear garden room that used to be a country lounge is opened for overflow. It's a delightful space with a remarkable, full-length mural of a Cape Cod scene on the far wall.

(508) 432-4745. Entrées, $14.95 to $24.50. Dinner nightly, 5 to 9 or 10. Closed Tuesday in spring and fall. Closed November-March.

The Regatta of Cotuit, 4631 Falmouth Road (Route 28), Cotuit.

This elegant restaurant in a handsome 1790 Federal-style house has been lovingly run since 1987 by Wendy and Brantz Bryan of the Regatta in Falmouth. "You couldn't have two more extremes," admitted Wendy. While the Falmouth restaurant features seafood and is summery, New Yorkish and on the waterfront, the Cotuit venture serves up regional dishes and Americana on a year-round basis. It has a full bar and a broad tavern menu.

Eight dining rooms, one with only two tables, are beautifully appointed in shades of pink and green, with authentic print wallpapers, needlepoint rugs and furnishings of the period. Tables are set with pink and white Limoges china, crystal glassware and fine silver.

Executive chef Heather Allen has helped the Regatta earn a reputation for fine dining every bit as stellar as that of Chillingsworth, which is more widely known.

Entrées range from sautéed fillet of halibut with key lime beurre blanc to seared filet mignon with cabernet sauce. Among the possibilities are sautéed arctic char, seared rare sesame-encrusted tuna sashimi with ginger-wasabi vinaigrette, and roasted rack of lamb with balsamic-port wine sauce. The trilogy of seafood, each with its own sauce, is a house specialty. Brantz claims his restaurant sells more tenderloin of buffalo and elk than any restaurant on the East Coast.

Typical starters are a crabmeat and mango salad on toasted brioche, grilled half lobster Thai style, and bay scallops and sautéed foie gras with citrus vinaigrette and mango chutney. The brandied lobster bisque with a confetti of lobster and fresh chervil also merits attention. Desserts are similar to those of the Regatta at Falmouth, including house-made ice creams and sorbets and a trilogy of three favorites. The chocolate seduction on a lovely patterned raspberry sauce and the crème brûlée garnished with red and gold raspberries and blackberries are among the best we've tasted.

Wendy and Brantz Bryan outside Regatta at Cotuit.

The Regatta's lighter fare menu is perfect for grazing. It modifies some of the regular appetizers, salads and entrées, at prices from $8.50 to $19.95.

The wine list, which emphasizes good reds, is priced from the high teens.

(508) 428-5715. Entrées, $24 to $28. Dinner nightly, 5 to 10, from 4:30 in winter.

More Good Dining

Inaho Japanese Restaurant, 157 Route 6A, Yarmouth Port.

The little white house that long harbored La Cipollina restaurant is the home of a Japanese restaurant that relocated from Hyannis. Ugi Wantanabe, who had worked as a sushi chef in New York and Newport, and his Portuguese-American wife Alda live upstairs, in the European fashion, and travel every other day to Boston for fresh fish and provisions.

A long sushi bar where singles can be comfortable faces one wall of the rear dining room; three Japanese-looking booths flank the other. The far end is all windows gazing onto a courtyard garden, where spotlights focus on a few Japanese plantings (the Japanese garden in front seemed to be thriving better at our visit). There are two front dining rooms as well. The bare wood tables topped only with chopsticks and napkins hint that here you'll find the real thing.

An order of gyoza dumplings staved off hunger as we nursed a bottle of Chalk Hill sauvignon blanc from a small but well-chosen wine list. One of us sampled the nine-piece sushi plate for $15; the sushi was fresh and delicious. The other was pleased with the bento box ($16) yielding salad, a skewer of chicken teriyaki, tempura and a California roll. Sashimi, teriyaki, tempura and katsu items completed the menu, although specials such as grilled tuna steak were offered at our latest visit. Also available are shabu shabu and sushi special dinners, $42 for two.

Among desserts are bananas tempura, a poached pear on ice cream with ginger sauce and a frozen chocolate cake as thick as fudge, served with vanilla ice cream.

But we could not be dissuaded from our favorite ginger ice cream, rendered here to perfection.

(508) 362-5522. Entrées, $14.50 to $23. Dinner nightly, from 5.

Aardvark, 134 Route 6A, Yarmouth Port.
Upon its opening, this homey little restaurant in a gingerbread-trimmed house became so popular that a policeman had to direct traffic in and out of the parking lot. Co-owners Peter Watson and chef Missy Minor started it as a coffee shop but soon evolved into cooking what Peter called "North American cuisine with ethnic influences." The food, which now upstages the coffees and teas and full bar, is taken in four small dining rooms and a porch, plus three outdoor tables on the front lawn. Cotton bandannas depicting perhaps elephants or zucchini are under the glass-topped tables. The walls are a veritable art gallery.

At lunch, look for sandwiches like the piggly wiggly (black forest ham, pineapple, avocado and honey-mustard, topped with melted swiss cheese) and roast turkey with sliced cucumber, onions, yogurt, dill spread and mixed greens. The long list of specials might include a terrific grilled chicken caesar roll-up or a lemon-pepper penne tossed with mushrooms, sundried tomatoes, pinenuts and basil. We thought the gazpacho and the grilled chicken-bulgur salad, brimming with tomatoes, olives, goat cheese and green beans, were sensational. And when a sort of cobbler/pie of strawberries, rhubarb and apples appeared on the countertop fresh from the oven, one of us couldn't resist a wedge.

Chef Missy has added Vietnamese accents to the fusion dinner menu that changes weekly. We'd gladly have made an entire dinner of her appetizers: Vietnamese shrimp salad rolls, chicken satays with a spicy peanut dipping sauce, and the night's special of shrimp cortez coated in a Brazilian spice rub and served with pineapple. But then we'd have missed such entrées as grilled Atlantic salmon marinated in miso and served with stir-fried rice noodles, and grilled Vietnamese pork tenderloin marinated in lemongrass and soy. At our latest visit you could also make a meal of pho, the tasty Vietnamese dinner soup featuring thin-sliced prime sirloin in a spicy broth.

(508) 362-9866. Entrées, $13.95 to $18.95. Breakfast, Monday-Saturday 7:30 to 10:30, Sunday 9 to 3 Lunch, Tuesday-Sunday 11:30 to 3, Dinner, Wednesday-Saturday 5 to 9.

Contrast Bistro & Espresso Bar, 605 Route 6A, Dennis.
Picture walls of bright yellow and red, beneath a blue ceiling. Well-worn oriental rugs on old wood floors. Rustic hand-painted tables. A counter at the espresso bar.

You've got plenty of contrasts, which the hostess said accounts for the name of this funky venture that draws a young crowd. The concept proved so popular that partners Christian Soderstrom, who does some of the cooking, and David Burbank opened a second Contrast in 1999 in Mashpee Commons.

The extensive menu, quite similar day and night, stresses contrasts in flavors. It features unusual salads, grilled lavasch pizzas, hot and cold sandwiches served with mixed greens and such bistro fare as cod cakes with citrus rémoulade, wild mushroom and chèvre crêpes, noodle cakes with curried chicken, moussaka, meatloaf and chicken pot pie. At lunch, add specials like portobello sandwich on a toasted focaccia roll, franks with three-bean casserole and ancho cornbread, a brisket sandwich with lime coleslaw and grilled Thai chicken sausages.

The dinner menu sparkles with such entrées as tuna steak served on sautéed Asian greens, striped bass with roasted garlic over rainbow chard, grilled free-range duck breast with green olive sauce, and grilled tenderloin of beef with stilton and sundried pesto. Even the burger is a cut above: a "lamburger" filled with chèvre, wrapped in bacon and served with Scottish mint jam.

The pastry case is laden with luscious looking berry tarts and chocolate cakes. There's a short, well-chosen list of wine, beers and cordials.

(508) 385-9100. Entrées, $15 to $19. Open daily, 11 to 9 or 10, later in summer.

The Brewster Fish House Restaurant, 2208 Route 6A, Brewster.

David and Vernon Smith took over what had been a fish market and converted it into one of the Cape's best seafood restaurants. For years it was so low-key that, despite countless trips through the area, we were unaware of its existence until a knowing innkeeper tipped us off. Good thing, for we found a simple but stylish little cafe where the brothers, both self-taught chefs, man the kitchen and produce a satisfying array of treats incorporating the freshest fish available. And now, for some it's their favorite restaurant along the length of Route 6A.

Small and personal, this is a pure place – nothing like the take-a-number-and-hope-for-the-best of the ubiquitous fried-fish ilk. There's no meat on the printed menu, although one of the three nightly specials involves a beef, lamb or poultry dish. Otherwise it's all seafood, from fish and chips to lobster pan-seared in chipotle butter and served on fried leeks. In between are treats like grilled Atlantic salmon with spinach and prosciutto, grilled swordfish on a Tuscan roasted red pepper sauce, baked pollock under a horseradish crust with a grilled corn and red-onion salad, and walnut-crusted catfish sautéed with marsala wine. The mixed grill combines swordfish, shrimp, scallops and andouille sausage with a creole dipping sauce. Specials at a recent visit were poached salmon with raspberry sauce and poached leeks, and grilled tuna over bok choy with sesame-soy sauce. Three pastas can be ordered as appetizers or main courses.

All the appetizers save one – fried artichoke hearts with a Thai roasted pepper sauce – involve seafood. Deep-fried oysters on wilted spinach with a rouille, crab cake with a mixed fruit and bell-pepper marmalade, and fried calamari with a tomato and red-pepper aioli are favorites. Or you can start with fish chowder, lobster bisque or billi-bi.

The day's three desserts could be crème brûlée, flourless chocolate torte with raspberry sauce and roasted hazelnut cheesecake. The wine list is as well chosen as the rest of the menu. Many wines are available by the glass.

Dining is at white-clothed tables topped with glass, candles and fresh flowers.

(508) 896-7867. Entrées, $13 to $24. Lunch daily, 11:30 to 3. Dinner, 5 to 9:30 or 10. Closed Monday in off-season. Closed December-March.

The Impudent Oyster, 115 Chatham Bars Ave., Chatham.

With a name like the Impudent Oyster, how could this restaurant miss? An avid local following jams together at small, glass-covered tables beneath a skylit cathedral ceiling, with plants in straw baskets balancing overhead on the beams.

The changing menu, based on local seafood, roams the globe to blend regional, French, Mexican, Chinese and Italian cuisines, among others.

We couldn't resist starting with the drunken mussels, shelled and served in an intense marinade of tamari, fresh ginger, szechuan peppercorns and sake. The

Mexican chicken, chile and lime soup, spicy and full of interesting flavors, was one of the best we've tasted. Other starters could be Basque shrimp simmered in garlic with red chiles, Portuguese mussels steamed with chorizo sausage in a spicy diablo sauce, and "devils on horseback" (Cape sea scallops wrapped in bacon and served on toast points).

Entrées vary from scrod amandine to bouillabaisse, a house specialty. Another specialty is grilled yellowfin tuna in soy sauce and cumin. Sole and crab piccata, celestial oysters poached in champagne and mixed seafood fra diavolo over fettuccine are some of chef-owner Peter Barnard's changing offerings. You might find sautéed tenderloin tips with a sweet and spicy oriental sauce, steak au poivre and even a mesclun salad garnished with grilled shrimp, tuna and chicken. At one visit we liked the feta and fennel scrod (a Greek dish touched with ouzo) and the swordfish broiled with orange and pepper butter. A plate of several ice creams made with fresh fruits was a cooling dessert.

Creativity extends to the wine list – which, like the food, is reasonably priced – and to the lunch menu with a changing array of salads, sandwiches and entrées. Some of this is the exciting kind of food of which we never tire, although we'd like to have it in more tranquil and less crowded surroundings.

(508) 945-3545. Entrées, $17.95 to $23.95. Lunch daily, 11:30 to 3, Sunday noon to 3. Tavern menu, 3 to 5. Dinner nightly from 5.

L'Alouette, 787 Main St. (Route 28), Harwich Port.

Chef Jean-Louis Bastres, who converses with his kitchen staff in the French of his native Pyrenées, and his wife Danielle run this charmer of a restaurant in a shingled Cape Cod house with blue-gray shutters and awnings and dormer windows upstairs. A series of three low-ceilinged dining rooms, open one to the next, hold large and well-spaced tables. As oil lamps flicker at night, the look is ever-so-old-school European.

The menu is classic French with a contemporary accent. Expect such main dishes as sesame-crusted scrod served over spinach with a ginger beurre blanc, peppered fillet of salmon sautéed with a roasted shallot vinaigrette, grilled swordfish with a roasted red pepper coulis, bouillabaisse, beef tenderloin au poivre, and rack of lamb encrusted with mustard and garlic.

Among appetizers are smoked trout with radicchio, pink grapefruit and walnuts; grilled shrimp and scallop sausage with caramelized leek vinaigrette, and country-style duck liver pâté with pink peppercorns and pistachios, Onion soup gratinée and lobster bisque are other starters. Macadamia nougatine cream genoise with belgian chocolate sauce, assorted berries romanoff and chocolate truffle cake with raspberry coulis are some of the good desserts.

(508) 430-0405. Entrées, $16.95 to $28.50. Dinner nightly except Monday, 5 to 9 or 10.

Chapaquoit Grill, 410 West Falmouth Hwy. (Route 28A), West Falmouth.

People wait up to two hours on busy nights for one of the 95 seats in this trendy but affordable grill. The throngs don't seem to mind, although local gourmands say they would prefer less of a wait and less of a rush once they're seated.

But the owners of the Chappy, as it's called, are on to something hot. They offer wood-fired pizzas from a huge brick oven that occupies an open room off the entry, "big-flavored" appetizers and entrées, specials that are truly special and a wine list with many choices priced under $20.

Unassuming on the outside, the place is much bigger than it looks (and encompasses a basic cafe alongside for daytime coffee, pastries, sandwiches and pizzas). The main building has a bar and waiting area and a large rear dining room with a vaguely tropical theme: splashy patterned cloths on the widely spaced tables, colorful sea prints on the salmon-colored walls and the odd fish silhouette hanging from a trellis screening the two-story-high ceiling.

The printed menu offers appetizers like littleneck clams steamed Portuguese style, deep-fried calamari, and the chef's antipasti. Entrées range from linguini marinara to shrimp creole. Specialty pizzas are available in small and large sizes. They include margarita, shrimp diavolo, southwestern and the chef's favorite – grilled chicken with broccoli, mushrooms and provolone.

The specials board generates the most excitement. Consider a sampling of one night's selections: snapper marinated in tequila and ginger and served with coconut-mango relish, cumin-rubbed swordfish with roasted jalapeño butter, roasted coffee-encrusted pork tenderloin with raspberry and hoisin sauce, and grilled sirloin marinated in tequila and cilantro with a chipotle demi-glace.

Desserts follow suit: mango cheesecake with macadamia-nut crust, a classic tiramisu, exotic gelatos and sorbets made by a neighbor down the road.

"We keep things changing so people will come back," says the chef. People certainly do.

(508) 540-7794. Entrées, $10.95 to $17.95. Dinner nightly, 5 to 10, pizzas weekends until 11. Cafe, Monday-Saturday 8 to 5.

Dining and Lodging

The Bramble Inn & Restaurant, 2019 Main St. (Route 6A), Brewster 01631. White linens, pretty floral china in the Victoria pattern from Czechoslovakia,

candles in hurricane lamps and assorted flowers in vases grace the five small dining rooms seating a total of 60 at this inn renowned for its restaurant. Ruth and Cliff Manchester, who got their start at his parents' Old Manse Inn nearby, have continued the tradition here.

Ruth is an inventive cook, whose four-course, prix-fixe dinners ($42 to $55, depending on choice of entrée) draw rave press reviews and a devoted following. Her soups are triumphs: perhaps chilled cherry with port and crème fraîche, four-onion soup with brie croutons or a lettuce and scallion bisque. Other starters might be smoked salmon and scallop seviche, a tuna chile quesadilla with roasted corn and sweet red pepper salsa, an artistic smoked

Front dining room at Bramble Inn.

seafood palette "with painter's spatter sauce," and quail with a chilled lentil and feta salad. We were impressed with the New England seafood chili: cod, clams and tuna in a spicy tomato sauce with black beans, jack cheese and sour cream.

The eight main-course choices could include salmon crêpes with cod and smoked salmon mousse, grilled lobster with Ethiopian spice butter and exotic fruit chutney, veal tenderloin with shiitake mushroom and whole-grain mustard sauce, and – a novel twist on surf and turf – parchment-roasted chicken breast with a grilled chicken lobster, served with lobster-champagne sauce. A signature dish – assorted seafood curry – combines lobster, cod, scallops and shrimp in a light curry sauce with banana, coconut, almonds and chutney.

Desserts are inventive: white-chocolate coeur à la crème (a recipe requested by Bon Appétit magazine), a strawberry mousse and angel cake tower layered with vanilla crème fraîche, and a treat called lemon jewel tarte, a toasted pistachio butter pastry lined with blueberries and topped with a baked lemon filling, brandied whipped cream and blueberry-maple nectar.

The small, paneled Hunt Room houses a service bar. The limited but serviceable wine list offers good values.

Upstairs in the main 1861 house are three guest rooms with sloping floors, furnished in a comfortable country style. Five more rooms are in the 1849 House, a Greek Revival structure two doors away. Guests enjoy a full breakfast on the cheery dining porch of the main inn.

Lately, Ruth's daughter, Suzanne Plum, who had worked with her mother for two years in the kitchen at the Bramble Inn, returned to the family's early beginnings. She and her husband David purchased the nine-room Old Manse Inn and restaurant from her grandparents.

(508) 896-7644. Eight rooms with private baths. Doubles, $95 to $125.

Prix-fixe, $42 to $55. Dinner by reservation, nightly except Monday in summer, 6 to 9; Thursday-Sunday in spring and fall. Closed November to early to May.

High Brewster, 964 Satucket Road, Brewster 01631.

Only a discreet sign in front of the large brown Colonial house on a hill with beautifully landscaped grounds gives a clue that this is more than someone's private home. And for 25 years, it was indeed the home of two gentlemen in the old-fashioned sense of the word, who – with little fanfare, no advertising and much acclaim from those in the know – welcomed guests to their home for dinner four nights a week.

It has changed hands several times since they sold it in 1987, and old-timers lament that it's not the same. But veteran Cape Cod chef Robert Hickey now oversees the kitchen. At least for the first-time visitor, the atmospheric dining experience in the shingled house overlooking Lower Mill Pond remains the essence of Cape Cod, much as it was when we first ate here with the original owners.

Dinner is available prix-fixe in four courses, the price varying according to entrée, or à la carte. Basically the same choices are available on each menu. The fare straddles both contemporary and classic American/French lines, as in appetizers of crab cakes with red pepper aioli, grilled quail with lemon-sage butter on wilted swiss chard, and a pâté of brandied chicken livers served with the traditional cornichons, red onions and capers. If you go the prix-fixe route, a salad of mesclun greens dressed with a citrus vinaigrette is served between appetizer and main course. The choices could be oven-roasted salmon with kalamata-caper-roasted pepper sauce, pan-seared duck breast with raspberry and cranberry demi-glace, and rack of lamb with mustard and tarragon demi-glace. Dessert could be lemon roulade, strawberry-rhubarb crisp or chocolate mousse cake.

Traditionally, High Brewster lacked a liquor license but allowed patrons to bring

Outdoor terrace at High Brewster looks toward Lower Mill Pond.

their own. Now it serves beer and wine, inside in the cozy lounge or outside in summer on a terrace overlooking the scenic pond.

The 18th-century Cape Cod house, its age wearing well, contains three cozy, low-ceilinged dining rooms seating a total of 75. Tables are of deeply polished dark wood, and those in the keeping room are set with crisp off-white linens and Blue Willow tableware. Dark beams, wide paneling and barn boards are displayed to advantage by candlelight and track lights, as are the oil paintings and antiques all around.

Owners Timothy and Catherine Mundy offer two upstairs guest rooms with private baths, sloping ceilings and a lived-in, historic feel. Outside are an efficiency cottage for two as well as two fireplaced houses sleeping up to four adults, rented by the night or week. A substantial continental breakfast is included in the rates.

(508) 896-3636 or (800) 203-2634. Fax (508) 896-3734. Two rooms, one cottage and two houses with private baths. Doubles, $95 and $115. Cottage and houses, $165 to $220.

Prix-fixe, $34 to $58. À la carte entrées, $18 to $36. Dinner nightly by reservation in summer, 5:30 to 9, Wednesday-Sunday in off-season. Closed Thanksgiving to Easter.

Wequassett Inn, Pleasant Bay, Chatham 02633.

Cape Cod has perhaps no more majestic water view amid more elegant surroundings than from the restored, 18th-century "square top" sea captain's mansion that houses this venerable inn's dining room.

Floor-to-ceiling windows on three sides is all the decor necessary in the expansive main dining room that looks quite summery with rose-cushioned chairs, linens from France and oil lamps. A two-tiered garden deck off the lounge is a treat for lunch or cocktails overlooking Pleasant Bay.

Fresh seafood and continental cuisine are the themes of longtime chef Frank McMullen, a Culinary Institute of America graduate who came here from Pier 66 in Fort Lauderdale. Our dinner began with a special terrine, one part scallop and the other part salmon, garnished with grapefruit and a tangy sauce, and escargots with pinenuts in puff pastry.

Among entrées, we liked the grilled lamb loin marinated in garlic-rosemary mustard and the twin beef tenderloins with smoked cheddar sauce, both accessorized with crisp snow peas, carrots, cauliflower and roast potatoes. Recent options were pan-seared swordfish finished in a ginger-lobster broth, seared Atlantic salmon glazed with truffle honey and sautéed veal loin layered with lobster claws and fresh mozzarella.

Desserts included cranberry mousse in an almond tuile with a red and white sauce underneath looking as lacy as a doily, and a frozen chambord mousse in a parfait glass. With all the candles lit and reflecting in the windows, it was a romantic atmosphere in which to linger over cappuccino and cordials.

We had only to amble off to our room, one of several in duplex cottages right by the bay, with a deck almost over the water. The 104 handsomely furnished rooms with all the amenities are in eighteen Cape-style cottages, motel buildings and condo-type facilities. They range from water-view suites to tennis villas with cathedral ceilings and private balconies overlooking the woods and courts.

(508) 432-5400 or (800) 225-7125. Fax (508) 432-1915. Ninety-three rooms and eleven suites with private baths. Rates EP. Late June to Labor Day: doubles $255 to $490, suites $510. Late spring and early fall: doubles $175 to $295, suites $375 to $400. April and November: doubles $100 to $200, suites $225. Closed December-March. Entrées, $23 to $34. Lunch daily, 11:30 to 2. Dinner, 6 to 10.

Lodging

Cobb's Cove, Powder Hill Road, Barnstable Village 02630.

Down a country lane off Route 6A, this house was built to look old in 1974 by engineer Henry Chester, whose wife Evelyn is innkeeper.

You can tell they have a sense of humor when you see the Scargo Pottery bird feeder in the back garden. It's a replica of St. Basil's in the Kremlin and the birds (including "Cardinal Richelieu") really flock to it.

In the dining room/library is a piano surrounded by a fascinating collection of books of all kinds, many of the coffee-table variety. Behind it is the Keeping Room with its Count Rumford fireplace, unusually shallow and designed to send out much heat, and beyond that is the sunny terrace where guests keep an eye on the many feathered visitors.

Six unusually large guest quarters are on two floors. The honeymoon suites on the third floor afford spectacular views of Barnstable Harbor and Cape Cod Bay, each with two chairs in front of a huge window from which to enjoy. Windows dip to the floors in all the rooms. Most walls are of barnsiding for a pleasantly rustic look, the floors are tiled and the closets huge. King or queensize beds, loveseats or wing chairs, antiques, pottery, vases of pampas grass, baskets of pine cones, terrycloth robes, magazines and bowls of nuts make each room special, since "we're trying to make this a secluded getaway for couples," says Evelyn. Each tub has a whirlpool, and Pears soap and bath oil are provided.

Guests are served wine in the afternoon and a full breakfast, sometimes peach crêpes with mint, fish cakes with scrambled eggs or french toast made with raisin-nut bread. Outspoken Henry, in his other guise as Henri-Jean, serves dinners by request to groups of six to eight or more. The gala five-course meal with wine ($50 a head) could include Portuguese soup, asparagus vinaigrette, a whole bass garnished with herbs from the garden, salad and a fruit tart or crème caramel with espresso or sambuca-laced coffee.

"We try to get a full table," says Evelyn. "The fun is having our guests sitting down together." Knowing the Chesters, it would be a lively dinner party indeed.

(508) 362-9356. Six rooms with private baths. Doubles, $149 to $189.

Wedgewood Inn at Yarmouth Port occupies restored 1812 house.

Wedgewood Inn, 83 Main St. (Route 6A), Yarmouth Port 02675.

Built in 1812, this distinguished white house with black shutters was restored from top to bottom in 1983. The result was one of the first in the new breed of Cape Cod B&Bs offering superior lodging, and this keeps getting better and better.

All nine air-conditioned guest quarters are spacious with private baths and sitting areas. A third-floor room affords a view of Cape Cod Bay. The two main-floor rooms have screened porches and one has a separate sitting room. Four rooms hold working fireplaces and pencil-post beds. All are comfortably and artfully furnished with quilts, wing chairs, oriental rugs on wide-board floors and spiffy period wallpapers, mostly in shades of Wedgwood blue, pink and white. Fresh flowers and fruit are in each room, and a tea tray with munchies is offered about 4 p.m.

The most coveted accommodations are those in the recently renovated carriage barn. Off a soaring center entry hall are three spacious suites with kingsize poster beds, fireplaces, soaking tubs, private phones and handsome sitting areas. TVs are ensconced in entertainment-center cabinets beautifully hand-painted by Gerrie. The two suites facing away from the road offer private decks.

Back in the main inn, the cream-colored dining room is unusually attractive. Windsor chairs flank tables for two set with china patterned with swallows (from the Country Diary of an Edwardian Lady) and sunlight streams through a plant-filled bow window. Four kinds of pastries, cold cereals, fresh fruit and yogurt are set out on the sideboard for breakfast. Guests have a choice of scrambled eggs, french toast or belgian waffles.

Innkeepers Gerrie and Milton Graham (she a former teacher and he a retired FBI agent who played pro football with the Ottawa Rough Riders and the old Boston Patriots) continue to make improvements. They have added Williamsburg gardens and a walk leading to a new entry and common room with oriental rugs, a small TV and a Colonial air. Lately, they built a gazebo in the perennial gardens.

(508) 362-5157. Fax (508) 362-5851. www.wedgewood-inn.com Three rooms and six suites with private baths. June-October: doubles, $135 to $165; suites, $185 and $195. November-May: doubles, $105 to $125; suites, $145.

Ashley Manor, 3660 Olde Kings Highway, Box 856, Barnstable 02630.

One of the more gracious houses on the north shore is a serene and elegant B&B hidden behind huge privet hedges. Notable breakfasts are prepared by innkeeper Don Bain, a dropout from the New York corporate scene.

In summer, the morning extravaganza is served on a delightful brick terrace in back of the house, with a fountain garden, a tennis court and spacious lawns beyond. In other seasons, guests breakfast by the fire on Chippendale chairs in the dining room, the original 1699 part of the house, with candles lit in crystal candelabra. It's a fairly elaborate affair – "almost like an early brunch," says Don – accompanied by the house coffee with "our own spices." We enjoyed watching the birds flit in and out of a remarkable Scargo cathedral birdhouse as we feasted on fresh orange juice, a stuffed baked apple, the best raspberry muffins we've ever tasted (Don even packed a couple to go), his delicious and not too sweet homemade granola and, the crowning touch, stuffed crêpes with farmer's cheese, strawberry sauce and sour cream. Other main courses include omelets that guests

Outdoor breakfast table at Ashley Manor.

say are the world's best (light and fluffy, with changing fillings), quiche and a french-toast sandwich with cream cheese, nuts and currants.

Both a keeping room and a well-furnished living room with a grand piano and three navy blue sofas contain fireplaces; the massive one in the living room has a beehive oven. Decanters of wine, sherry and port are set out for guests. The master bedroom suite in which we stayed on the main floor has a floor that is painted, stained and turpentined, giving it an elegant sheen; the same treatment is in the living room as well. By the fireplace in the bedroom is a secret stairway to the second-floor suite above. The bathroom contains a large double whirlpool tub.

Upstairs are two rooms and two suites, all but one with fireplaces. Each is welcoming, but we especially like the end suite with a kingsize canopy bed, a double jacuzzi in an old closet, a beautiful breakfront, two pumpkin-colored velvet wing chairs beside the fireplace, and deep blue wallpaper and bedspread. The other suite has a queen bed, sitting room with a fireplace and a corner jacuzzi. Interestingly furnished in antiques, all rooms have flowers, magazines, bedside candies, coffee and tea service, and wine glasses tied with white ribbons. Some rooms sport colorful Nantucket spackled floors.

The newest accommodation is the Hideaway Suite, formerly the innkeeper's quarters with private entrance and patio out back. Here Don opened up two rooms to create a sitting area with two wing chairs in front of the fireplace, TV and mini-refrigerator. The bedroom has a queen lace canopy bed. The bath has a double jacuzzi and separate shower.

(508) 362-8044 or (888) 535-2246. Fax (508) 362-9927. www.capecod.net/ashleymn. Two rooms and four suites with private baths. Doubles, $135 to $145. Suites, $185 to $195. Deduct 20 percent November-April.

The Candleberry Inn, 1882 Main St., Brewster 02631.
White with black shutters, this handsome 250-year-old Georgian residence has been taking in guests under various names since 1945. Gini and David Donnelly acquired it in 1996 and have been upgrading ever since.
The main house is distinguished by wide pine floors, oriental rugs, wainscoting and original windows with bubbled and wavy glass. There's a pump organ in the parlor. A couple of bedrooms are in front on the main floor, one with twin carved pineapple beds and a gas fireplace and the other with a queensize canopy bed. Upstairs are four more guest quarters, two in front with queen poster beds and gas fireplaces and a third a cozy room with a double bed. A new rear suite has a sitting room opening through french doors into a room with a queensize bed. They're furnished eclectically in Colonial style with antiques and family heirlooms. The walls of several are hung with the enlarged framed photographs by Gini, a photographer of note.
The Donnellys recently gutted the rear carriage house to create three new guest accommodations. The ground floor is a suite with a kingsize pine sleigh bed, plush sofa and a summer country look in blue and yellow. Its enormous bath harbors an unusually deep, double whirlpool tub from which the less agile might never get out, as well as a separate shower. A private entrance opens off a terrace. Upstairs are two loft rooms, one with queen bed and another with two doubles, sharing a large balcony.
A substantial breakfast is served at three tables in the formal dining room, the oldest section of the house, or on a pretty covered brick terrace furnished in wicker and overlooking the spacious side lawn of the two-acre property. The fare when we were there was fresh fruit, cinnamon-rhubarb muffins and poppyseed pancakes with homemade hard cider syrup. Other mornings bring orange spiced french toast or a scramble with feta cheese, sundried tomatoes and spinach. Complimentary sherry and soft drinks are available later in the day.

(508) 896-3300 or (800) 573-4769. Fax (508) 896-4016. Seven rooms and two suites with private baths. July and August: doubles $95 to $135, suites $155 and $195. Spring and fall, doubles $90 to $135, suites $140 and $165. November-April, doubles $80 to $120, suites, $135 and $145. Two-night minimum in summer and most weekends.

The Captain Freeman Inn, 15 Breakwater Road, Brewster 02631.
The innkeeper teaches cooking classes at this twelve-room inn in an 1860s sea captain's home. Carol and Tom Edmonson, both formerly in computer marketing, reopened the inn following a total renovation in 1992. Trained by her grandmother, a professional chef, Carol conducts cooking schools on winter and early spring weekends in the inn's spacious, updated kitchen. Participants take part in a hands-on Saturday afternoon class in which they prepare a four-course dinner to be served that evening. Her 1999-2000 series featured the cuisines of Italy and Provence. Some of the recipes are detailed in *The Captain Freeman Inn Cookbook.*
Guests share the bounty of her expertise at breakfast, the menu for which is placed in the rooms each day. At our visit it started with a variety of juices, ginger-poached pears and scrumptious blueberry muffins served with strawberry and orange/grand-marnier butters. Homemade oatmeal and cranberry granola accompanied. The main event was a prosciutto and cheddar quiche. Other days might see eggs Brewster with a cranberry compote, prosciutto and tabasco-

hollandaise sauce; cinnamon french toast with homemade blueberry-rum syrup, or homemade granola pancakes with dried cranberries and currants. Tom furnishes the herbs, wild berries and fruits from his gardens and trees on the two-acre property.

Guest rooms come in three configurations. The Orleans, with shiny, patterned inlaid parquet floors and a high, hand-carved ceiling medallion from Italy, is typical of the six traditional rooms with private baths. It has a lace-canopy queensize bed, a reading area with a loveseat and a wing chair, and five tiny straw hats on the wall of the bathroom. Three rooms on the third floor were converted in 2000 into two luxury rooms with fireplaces, large baths and whirlpool tubs, and what Carol called "great tree-top views over Brewster." Most deluxe are three air-conditioned suites at the rear, each with its own whirlpool spa on an enclosed balcony, a sitting area with fireplace, reading lamps with three-way bulbs, cable TV/VCR, telephone, mini-refrigerator, queensize canopy bed and full bath. Carol, who did the decorating, is partial to floral patterns, roman shades on the windows, lace swag curtains and straw hats.

The common areas are comfortable as well, from the Victorian parlor to the fireplaced dining room to the wraparound veranda outfitted in wicker and wrought iron. An inviting screened porch overlooks the large pool area. Guests enjoy woodland trails and a Victorian specimen garden along a hillside in back. They report the results of their dining ventures in a guest diary beside a basket full of menus. Afternoon refreshments might be iced tea or hot mulled cider with almond biscotti and a basket of fruit.

(508) 896-7481 or (800) 843-4664. Fax (508) 896-5618. Eleven rooms with private baths. Doubles, $125 to $250, June-October; $110 to $220 rest of year. Two-night minimum stay in season.

The Whalewalk Inn, 220 Bridge Road, Eastham 02642.

It's easy for a New England inn to get indigenous food for the evening meal, says innkeeper/cook Richard Smith, but breakfast is another matter. That's why he occasionally incorporates seafood into the morning feast, as in a dynamite crustless crab quiche. And why he adds cranberries to the Cape Cod pancakes. And bakes pumpkin and squash breads. And serves strawberry shortcake or apple crêpes à la mode as "a dessert surprise" to start his guests' day.

The culinary treats continue with hot mulled cider or tea and cookies at mid-afternoon and with assorted hors d'oeuvres during the BYOB cocktail hour that Dick and wife Carolyn host nightly.

The food at this suave, welcoming refuge in a quiet residential area is Dick's bailiwick. The decor is his wife's. She has outfitted their sixteen guest quarters with English country antiques and family heirlooms. "Sophisticated country charm" was her goal. She achieved it with a light and airy style that's more often associated with California than New England. There are no bed canopies or knickknack clutter. Expect plump chairs and down comforters, interesting art, fresh flowers, dhurrie rugs and whimsical accents – a floral wallpaper border in place of a chair rail here, a lush potted geranium in a bathroom window there. Suites include kitchen facilities, from tiny to full. Eleven rooms in five buildings come with fireplaces and six with private balconies or patios.

Most in demand are a deluxe room with kingsize four-poster off the patio, the studio suite in the secluded Salt Box cottage, and four suites with living/dining

Breakfast treats include "dessert surprise" at The Whalewalk Inn in Eastham.

rooms and wet bars in the attached barn or the outlying Guest House. In Carolyn's favorite Ivy Room you can "lie in bed and feel you're in the treetops," thanks to a lineup of windows onto the greenery. Her decorative scheme here incorporates ivy, from bed linens to the Kleenex box in the skylit bathroom.

A new Carriage House addition off the Guest House offers luxury guest rooms on the first floor and two larger accommodations with sitting areas upstairs. Each has a gas fireplace and a private patio or balcony overlooking a wildflower meadow. Three have whirlpool tubs. The upstairs rooms add king beds, phones, TV/VCRs in cabinets, and extra-large bathrooms containing wet bars and small refrigerators.

Accommodations vary in size, but guests have plenty of space to spread out. The main inn harbors a handsome living room, a cozy den with windows onto a large and colorful courtyard terrace (a festive setting for breakfast in summer), a sun porch where breakfast is served at a long antique table for ten in the off-season and a butler's pantry with a guest bar. The three-and-one-half-acre property is laced with gardens and pleasant outdoor sitting areas.

The place emits a palpable air of warmth, comfort and verve. So you are not surprised to learn that both Smiths had successful advertising careers in New York and Boston before taking over an 1830 homestead-turned-inn in 1990 and elevating it into one of Cape Cod's finest.

(508) 255-0617. Fax (508) 240-0017. www.whalewalkinn.com. Eleven rooms and five suites with private baths. Memorial Day to Columbus Day: doubles, $160 to $275; suites, $235. Rest of year: doubles, $135 to $225; suites, $185. Closed mid-December to mid-February except holiday weekends.

The Nauset House Inn, 143 Beach Road, Box 774, East Orleans 02643.

Here's a B&B with exceptional personality and character, reflecting the tastes and energies of its owners, Diane and Al Johnson, now joined by their daughter

Lush plants surround sitting area in inviting conservatory at The Nauset House Inn.

and son-in-law, Cindy and John Vessella. It's also a B&B of great value, given all the food, comfort and charm.

Well-known for her stained-glass objects, artistic Diane has refurbished the inn with many of her works, and has painted artistic touches here and there. She and Cindy stenciled most of the sweet bedrooms where quilts, crewel work and afghans abound. Named for native wildflowers, eight of the fourteen rooms in the main inn and a couple of outlying buildings have private bathrooms with showers. Diane painted a trompe-l'oeil cabinet on the wall of the Sea Oats Room to make it appear bigger. She painted a curtain for the bathroom window of the pale yellow Rosebud, which comes with a queen bed, rattan loveseat and two chairs plus a rear balcony enhanced by flowers in window boxes. We were happily ensconced in the Beach Plum, largest of four rooms in the Carriage House, where a wall of windows stretches toward the top of the cathedral ceiling. It has a kingsize bed and a sitting area with couch and side chairs around a coffee table. The most coveted accommodation may be the Outermost Cottage, where the bed is situated beneath a stained-glass window and a sunken bathroom awaits beneath a faux painted sky.

Breakfast is served in the beamed, brick-floored dining room with its huge open hearth, looking for all the world like a British pub. Guests have so enjoyed Diane's treats (homemade granola, strawberry frosty, ginger pancakes and Southern-style french toast) that she has published the recipes in a small cookbook. We can attest to her veggie frittatas and raspberry pancakes.

The dining room separates the plush and comfortable living room, where guests congregate around the fire and play board games, from the fabulous Victorian glass conservatory, filled with wicker furniture and plants centered by a weeping cherry tree. The rhododendron and clematis were in bloom at one visit; at another, grapes from the vines garnished the breakfast plates. Folks hang out in the spacious conservatory in the off-season and feel is if they've been transported to a tropical island.

Every afternoon around 5:30, Diane sets out hors d'oeuvres like guacamole, an olive-nut spread, or a cream-cheese and chutney spread with crackers to accompany complimentary wine and cranberry juice. Guests debate the spirited reviews of their predecessors in a guest book called "Where Did You Eat and How Did You Like It?"

The inn is so comfy and the grounds so pretty that you might not want to leave, but Nauset Beach is nearby. Don't miss the shop out back where Diane sells her stained glass, painted furniture, picture frames, little boxes and other handicrafts.

(508) 255-2195. Fourteen rooms, eight with private baths. Doubles, $75 to $135. Closed November-March. Two-night minimum weekends.

The Captain's House Inn of Chatham, 371 Old Harbor Road, Chatham 02633.

There's more than a touch of Britain amid all the Americana of this supremely elegant inn that originated in Captain Hiram Harding's restored 1839 home, set on shaded lawns screened by high hedges in a sedate residential section north of the village.

Their predecessors built this into one of the first small AAA four-diamond inns in New England. Through attention to detail and a knack for knowing what the luxury market wants, Jan and David McMaster have taken it to a higher level. They expanded and beautified the dining porch, added a few whirlpool tubs and built four deluxe rooms with fireplaces. They also developed new English perennial gardens with a three-tiered fountain pond in a rear corner of the two-acre property. "That manicured lawn was made for croquet," said Dave, a former California computer company CEO.

And proper British accents are heard often as the McMasters continue the tradition of staffing their inn with English students from the University of Bournemouth, which happens to be Jan's hometown.

The heart of the main house is the dining porch, a beauty in white and dusky rose. An addition projects eight feet out into the gardens with floor-to-ceiling windows. The floor is tiled and trailing wisteria is stenciled on the walls. Two fancy serving areas along the sides simplify breakfast service at individual linen-covered tables set with sterling silver and fine china.

Here is where Jan McMaster serves a true English tea in the afternoon. She also has enlarged the breakfast offerings to include smoked salmon corncakes with broiled tomatoes and cheese, waffles with strawberries or blueberries, quiches and apple crêpes to supplement the traditional fresh fruit, breads and muffins.

Poland Spring water is in each guest room. Turndown service is available, and guests find an evening snack.

Thirteen of the nineteen guest accommodations now have fireplaces and five have TV/VCR combinations, refrigerators and coffee makers. All are furnished with antiques, comfortable chairs for reading, pretty sheets, thick towels and French toiletries.

A couple of rooms with beamed and peaked ceilings are among the more deluxe in a rear carriage house. Also coveted is the Captain's Cottage, where the sumptuous Captain Hiram Harding suite looks like a library with dark walnut paneling and beamed ceiling, fine oriental rugs on the wide-plank floor, large fireplace, plush sofa and side chairs, and lace-canopied kingsize four-poster bed. A jacuzzi tub has been added here, as well as in the newly enlarged Lady Mariah Room adjacent. In the latter, an old kitchen was converted into what Jan calls a "fantasy bathroom," a smashing space with a double whirlpool flanked by four pillars and two wicker chairs facing a corner fireplace. The fireplace is also on view from the extra-high, step-up kingsize bed.

Top of the line are three jacuzzi accommodations in the Stables, a new building behind the cottage. The upstairs suite has fireplaces in both living room and bedroom, a kingsize bed and french doors leading to a full-length balcony. Each of the two downstairs rooms has a queen canopy bed, fireplace and a private deck, and a TV/VCR is hidden in an 1875 chest or the armoire.

(508) 945-0127 or (800) 315-0728. Fax (508) 315-0728. Eighteen rooms and one suite with private baths. Memorial Day through October: doubles, $125 to $275, suite $350. Rest of year: doubles, $105 to $215, suite $275. Three-night minimum July-September; two-night minimum other peak periods.

The Simmons Homestead Inn, 288 Scudder Ave., Hyannis Port 02647.

"I can't abide empty spaces," says Bill Putman, who has filled every available space, and then some, at this winner of a B&B. Built by a sea captain, the restored country estate was acquired in 1988 by Bill, then recently widowed, and turned into a B&B of great personality.

Part of the personality comes from Bill, an outgoing, marketing type who proudly displays his varied collections throughout the house. But most comes from the inn and its furnishings. Start with the 32-foot-long living room, comfortable as can be and now a jungle of hanging plants as "the only empty spaces left are on the ceiling." The room is notable for all the brass birds on the mantel and inanimate wildlife everywhere, a remarkable tapestry of animals done by his late wife, and large parrots from Pavo Real. Parrots are a theme repeated in many rooms. For instance, they are on the chandeliers in the 20-by-40-foot dining room, which has a fantastic collection of mugs depicting different fruits to coordinate with the fruit du jour china. Here guests gather at two tables for a full breakfast with perhaps cheese omelets or blueberry pancakes. Bill does the cooking – "I learned quickly," says he, although he did defer once to a skeptical guest, Dinah Shore. He serves complimentary wine on the breezy porches in summer beside a new outdoor hot tub and in front of the roaring fireplace in winter. The wine hour is "from 5:30 to 7:30 or whenever – that's p.m., but we are flexible," he stresses.

Along with a lively house-party atmosphere ("the place is simply fun," Bill says in a letter to prospective guests), it is the accommodations and all the accouterments that are most unusual.

Room 3 has a working fireplace and a queensize four-poster with a fishnet canopy. Its theme is elephants, and they are everywhere – inside the shutters, on the windows, on the mantel. Room 6 is the rabbit room, with a kingsize bed and bunnies all around. Room 7, Bill's concession to country decor, has a cherry four-poster bed and a country goose theme. It also serves as a transition to Room 8, which is simply wild: beneath the cathedral ceiling is a loft that's a jungle of plants and animals, including a purple rhinoceros. Animals are appliquéd all over the walls, the queensize bed is purple and the floor is painted green, and somehow it all works. Traditionalists might prefer the newer rooms in the old servants' quarters. Room 10, the largest and brightest, has its own little patio bedecked with spirea. The Bird Room, it's outfitted in white wicker with a kingsize bed and blue summery prints, and birds and butterflies hang from the vaulted ceiling.

The latest accommodations are in the old Barn Annex, which Bill rebuilt as his house but now shares with guests. Upstairs are the skylit Captain's Quarters (the largest room with queen canopy bed and an understated theme of Cape critters), and a two-room family suite embracing the twin-bedded Little Critter Room and the hunt-themed Horse & Hound Room with a queen bed. The open main floor holds a guest living room with the inn's only TV, the innkeeper's bedroom that's home for four cats he calls "the children" (except when he vacates it for guests), and his office named Hyannis Port. The open kitchen is stocked with 230 different single-malt Scotches – more than we've seen in any one place in Scotland, and he professes never to have even been to Scotland. Winter weeknight guests are invited to sample a few.

Back in the main house, Bill, a former race-car driver, displays the hoods of his race car and Paul Newman's on the upstairs landing and racing photos in a long upstairs hallway. That's mere prelude to the ten bright red racecars parked in the garage area, including a newly restored 1967 right-hand drive Bentley that he commandeers to shuttle guests. There's also a bulletin board with letters from guests, sheets of personalized ideas and directions for what to do around the Cape, and a map with pins showing where guests have come from. Not to mention several plants adorned with tiny white lights. Or the sixteen ten-speed bikes he loans out to guests. Or a billiards room with a stocked refrigerator and wine and wall space giving more room for his signs and plaques downstairs in the barn annex.

"I wanted to create a place where you feel at home," Bill says. Although it's not like any home we know, we'd be quite at home as guests.

(508) 778-4999 or (800) 637-1649. Fax (508) 790-1342. www.capecod.com/ simmonsinn. Eleven rooms and one two-bedroom suite with private baths. Doubles, $150 to $200, family suite $300. Off-season: doubles, $120 to $160; suite, $200.

La Maison Cappellari at Mostly Hall, 27 Main St., Falmouth 02540.

In the heart of Falmouth's historic district, this 1849 house with the wrap-around veranda looks as if it came right out of New Orleans. As a matter of fact, it was built by a sea captain as a wedding present for his bride from New Orleans, and is named for its extra-large hall. The former innkeepers said it got its name from a young child who entered the home and blurted, "Why, Mama, it's mostly hall!"

Actually, new owners Christina and Bogdan Simcic, Romanians who grew up in Italy and Austria, say it was built as an Italian mansion with Greek Revival elements, so their goal was to "bring that look and feeling back." Formerly interior designers in New York, the Simcics took over in early 2000 and renamed it for one of his ancestors. They closed to refurbish three prime bedrooms facing the rear courtyard. They also added tapestries, statues and "the European feeling that the house is asking for," according to Christina.

Off the main hall with a thirteen-foot-high ceiling are two guest rooms and a long living room with oriental rugs, European furnishings and a dining table at one end. Four more guest rooms go off the second-floor hall. Christina, an artist, was painting murals on the room walls, in the public areas and on the wraparound porch ("I'd been painting everyone else's walls and figured it was time to do my own"). For the future, they planned to add a small studio, exercise room and sauna to the rear garage.

An enclosed widow's walk with a TV/VCR is a great retreat, from which you can see the garden gazebo out back. Adirondack chairs are scattered around the deep back yard, a secluded and quiet refuge seemingly far from the heart of town.

The Simcics serve afternoon lemonade or coffee and pastries in the living room or on the veranda, which are also the sites for a European-style breakfast in the morning. Christina said it would start with "a variety of things to pick from – pastries, cold cuts, caviar, tapenades, octopus salad, French and Italian cheeses. We'll do some things like eggs, but not things you do at home."

(508) 548-3786 or (800) 682-0565. www.mostlyhall.com. Six rooms with private baths. Doubles, $185 to $225. Two-night minimum in season, on weekends and holidays.

Gourmet Treats

The Cape is full of kitchen and specialty-food shops, along with every other type of shop imaginable. Among our favorites:

Green Briar Jam Kitchen, 6 Discovery Road, East Sandwich. The first stop on the Cape might be this charmingly low-key place, where four paid cooks and many volunteers employ turn-of-the-century methods to produce jams, continuing a tradition begun in 1903. You get to see the old wood stove that founder Ida Putnam started with, as well as probably the oldest solar-cooking operation in the country – the hot-house windows in which ingenious racks slide in and out to make the prized sun-cooked strawberries with vodka, as well as blueberries with kirsch. Of course, you get to watch – and smell – some of the 20,000 bottles of jams, chutneys and relishes as they are lovingly prepared for sale in the gift shop. You also see Thornton Burgess's framed, handwritten description of the Jam Kitchen in 1939: "It is a wonderful thing to sweeten the world which is in a jam and needs preserving." Adjacent to the kitchen is the Green Briar Nature Center, including the Old Briar Patch conservation area, home of Brer Rabbit and his animal friends. Kitchen open Monday-Saturday 10 to 4, Sunday 1 to 4; winter hours vary. Shop open Monday-Friday 9 to 4, year-round.

Madden & Co., at 16 Jarves St. in the center of historic Sandwich, purveys unexpected gourmet treats among its antiques and "gatherings for the country home." Owner Parke Madden offers choice specialty foods and cookbooks, including those by his niece, Sarah Leah Chase of Nantucket.

Oven-ready prepared foods are the forte of **Mill Way Fish & Lobster Market** at 275 Mill Way beside Barnstable Harbor. Chef Ralph Binder, a Culinary Institute of America grad who worked at Chillingsworth, makes everything himself, according to season. "People are looking for prepared foods, even fish," says Ralph. He obliges with takeout treats like seafood sausage (composed of crawfish, shrimp and scallops), salmon manicotti, lobster pie, bouillabaisse and finnan haddie. A meal in itself is the seafood Tuscan bread, which he likens to a deep-pan pizza with shrimp, pesto, spinach, sundried tomatoes and parmesan cheese. You can get anything from a clam roll to a calamari salad to an oyster platter, to eat outside at picnic tables or to go.

The **Lemon Tree Village** complex along Route 6A in Brewster is worth a visit. The **Lemon Tree Pottery** is full of interesting pottery and other crafts. **The Cook Shop** offers specialty foods and kitchen essentials while its large new offshoot across the way, **The Tabletop Shop,** is a terrific, two-story kaleidoscope of hard-to-find fine china, flatware, glassware, table linens and cookbooks to please the most discriminating of hostesses. **Brewster Sweets** offers fine chocolates and confections. **Cafe Alfresco,** with tables inside and out, is a great place for an interesting meal or to get something to take out. Marcia Clark and her son, Dale, who used to own the Tower House Restaurant in Brewster, offer excellent food at refreshing prices. We enjoyed a smoked salmon sandwich with avocado and sprouts and a lobster club with pancetta and the works. A raspberry square made for a tasty dessert. Pick up a homemade pastry from the deli case, or order a dinner special from the blackboard. Open daily, 9 to 8:30 in summer, shorter hours in winter.

The open-air showroom of **Scargo Stoneware Pottery** is quite a sight off Dr. Lord's Road South in Dennis. Harry Holl and his family have been producing the stunning stoneware for decorative and kitchen purposes since 1952. Harry, whose majestic bird feeders grace the back yards of some of our favorite B&Bs in the area, turned to painting lately. His daughters and a son-in-law continue at the potter's kiln.

The Chocolate Sparrow at the Seatoller Shops in North Eastham is where dietitian Marjorie Sparrow produces her luscious chocolates, chocolate-covered cranberry cordials, English toffee crunch, assorted nut barks and more. Its offshoot is **Hot Chocolate Sparrow,** the quintessential coffee and dessert bar along Route 6A at Lowell Square, Orleans. We stopped at the espresso bar here for fat-free cranberry muffins and a latte and watched touring families devouring the candies and terrific ice-cream concoctions, among them a raspberry-sorbet lime rickey and a frozen espresso shake. More exotic coffees and ice creams are served up across the street at **Emack & Bolio's,** a branch of a Boston outfit.

Fancy's Farm Stand, 199 Main St., East Orleans, is the Cape's ultimate produce stand. It also purveys potpourris and wreaths (we coveted a huge one with all kinds of geese for $100), fancy cheeses and local jellies, baked goods and soups. You can make up a meal to go with, perhaps, kale and corn chowder, the offerings from an extensive salad bar, a deli, prepared foods from turkey pie to chicken noodle casserole, roll-ups, a pastry or a piece of pie.

A favorite stop almost across the street in East Orleans is the **Sundae School Ice Cream Parlor,** which dispenses ice creams and frozen yogurts in flavors from crème de menthe to kahlua chip. We thought a small cone of ginger ice cream tasted like ginger ale, only to be told no one had ever said that before. Those with heartier appetites can splurge for a hot fudge sundae or a giant banana split.

Chatham Cookware, 524 Main St., Chatham, offers all kinds of kitchen items and colorful pottery as well as fine foods to eat in or to go. Proprietor Vera Lynne Champlin no longer gives cooking demonstrations in her open kitchen based on the one at La Varenne, but she and her staff certainly put out some delectable sandwiches, soups, salads, quiches and desserts. There are a few tables in a little yellow room at the rear and on a side courtyard.

Founded by Art and Meredith Fancy of Fancy's Farm Stand, the **Cornfield Market** complex at 1297 Main St. in West Chatham is a gourmet haven. The **Fancy's Farm of Chatham** market is now run by Norm and Linda Weiner and her sister, Debra Scotch. Besides a bakery, meats, vegetables and such, you will find prepared dinners ranging from pinenut-stuffed chicken breast to beef wellington, priced at our visit for $5.95. The Weiners stage cooking demonstrations Thursdays at 3, and have a new wine section where tastings are scheduled summer Saturdays from 2 to 5. **The Pampered Palate** is an excellent deli and gourmet foods shop. Pick up a lobster salad sandwich on a croissant or a smoked salmon sandwich on a french roll with cucumber and wasabi mayo for a super picnic. It offers all kinds of salads, prepared foods and desserts to go. Supplement this with Fancy's produce or the extensive selection at **Chatham Fish and Lobster** next door and you have the makings for a great party. Of note across the street is the **Chatham Herbary.**

If you're looking for exotic French breads like those served in some of the Cape's best restaurants, head for **Pain D'Avignon** in a business park at 192 Airport Road in Hyannis. It's primarily a wholesaler, even designing a French onion roll especially for the Academy Ocean Grille in Orleans. The retail shop sells some of the treats.

The Casual Gourmet, a catering service in the Bell Tower Mall at 1600 Falmouth Road, Centerville, has a large deli section dispensing salads, sandwiches, baked goods and prepared foods. Try the egg, bacon and cheddar calzone for breakfast or a hefty tarragon chicken salad sandwich for lunch.

Mashpee Commons, an expanding new-town shopping marketplace, offers a number of places of interest to foodies. Besides restaurants like Contrast, Gone Tomatoes and Zuni, look for Fountain of Juice, an all-natural juice bar, and The Tea Shoppe.

In Falmouth, the understated **Bean & Cod** at 95 Palmer Ave. is a paradise of specialty foods and gourmet items, from cookbooks to napkins to dishes. The selection of crackers, cheeses, vinegars, pâtés, preserves and candies is exceptional, and surprises unfold on shelf after shelf. The blackboard might list prepared foods and breads, from crab cakes and lobster ravioli to dessert squares.

Gourmet Chips

Do you think, as we do, that Cape Cod potato chips are absolutely the best? Then stop in Hyannis at their place of origin, **The Cape Cod Potato Chip Co.,** 100 Breed's Hill Road, in an industrial park area off Route 132. There's an informative, self-guided tour of the plant, which evolved from Steve and Lynn Bernard's storefront kitchen that started in 1980 producing 200 bags of Cape Cod Potato Chips a day. Still hand-cooking their chips in kettles one batch at a time, they produce 200,000 bags a day and go through more than 50 million pounds of potatoes a year. This is big business, and we were surprised by the number of people touring on a summer weekday. You can pick up samples as well as buy more in the gift shop at tour's end. Tours, Monday-Friday 9 to 5.

Arty Place

One of our favorite shops for browsing at the Cape is **Tree's Place,** Route 6A at 28, Orleans. An art gallery, a tilery (the largest selection of designer tiles in the country, they say) and a gift shop occupy several rooms filled with such diverse items as Russian lacquer boxes, jewelry, Swiss musical paper weights, Hadley stoneware, Salt Marsh Pottery, carved birds – even tartan ties. We love the biscuit baskets of glazed stoneware made by Eucalyptus Pottery in California. You can choose any of the tiles to be framed for use as a trivet. One of us could spend hours mooching around here, but the other always says that it's time to be moving on.

Table at Straight Wharf Restaurant overlooks Nantucket harbor.

Nantucket
The Ultimate Indulgence for Gourmets

For an offshore island with a year-round population of 6,000 (augmented by up to 40,000 high-livers and free-spenders in the summer), Nantucket has an uncommon concentration of good restaurants.

Ever since French chef Jean-Charles Beret took over the rose-covered Chanticleer Inn in the hamlet of Siasconset in 1969, knowledgeable diners have been flocking to Nantucket in droves. Other restaurateurs and culinary businesses have followed.

"I don't know of another resort area that can beat Nantucket for good restaurants per square mile," says Neal Grennan, chef-owner of Le Languedoc.

Given its small size and island remoteness, "it's amazing," adds Chick Walsh, owner of the highly acclaimed 21 Federal, who started as maître-d' at the old Opera House restaurant in 1970 when it was about the only game in town. "When I arrived here, we couldn't have had a restaurant like this. We used to have difficulty flying in Haagen-Dazs ice cream. Now, fancy food products are at our doorstep, and we make ice cream ourselves. Thirty years ago, the local population wouldn't have supported this restaurant, and now they do. The whole food awareness has changed."

Indeed it has. The island now has a dozen superior restaurants, another dozen good ones, and countless more of the ordinary variety. At one of our visits, two cookbooks by Nantucket chefs had just been published and another was in the works. The 21 Federal restaurant opened a "branch" in Washington, D.C., and local chef Peter Wallace opened a second restaurant in New York's Tribeca section.

What other seaside resort dines so fashionably late? Many restaurants don't open for dinner until 6:30 or 7 – the 4:30 early-bird specials of Cape Cod don't play here. Dining is an event and a pricey one, given local chefs' preoccupation with fresh and exotic ingredients, their island location and a captive, affluent audience.

Lately, prices have raised a few eyebrows. That you might expect when menus list baked codfish at $24 for lunch at Brant Point Grill, a plate of sorbets for dessert costs $25 at the Chanticleer and some restaurants specify hefty per-person food minimums. Such prices are "insulting," according to local chefs like Michael Geller. The explanation is not the island's remoteness, adds innkeeper Bob Taylor, a former restaurateur. Rather it's a perception that "if you don't charge enough, you're no good. So people charge what the traffic will bear."

We know people who vacation at Nantucket for a month every summer, eating out almost every night, and relishing every minute as the ultimate gustatory experience. Book a room, reserve the ferry or an airplane seat, bring your wallet and indulge in the gourmet splendors of Nantucket yourself.

Dining

The Best of the Best

The Chanticleer Inn, 40 New St., Siasconset.

Lunch in the rose garden is a tradition, as is an after-dinner drink in the old Chantey Bar, now called the Grille Room. But the four-course dinners and the extraordinary wine cellar are what draw the knowing from hither and yon to the world-class restaurant built by Jean-Charles Berruet since he took over in 1969.

Prix-fixe dinners are $70 "and worth every penny," all kinds of fans had told us. The setting, the service and the food are nearly perfect, which is exactly the way Jean-Charles wants it.

You are greeted at the door and directed to your table. It could be in the sought-after, formal main-floor dining room with a fireplace at the end and a greenhouse on one side (rather brightly illuminated, we thought – the better to see and be seen, perhaps?) Or in the convivial, informal grill (a bit too bistro-ish, we felt, considering the tab). Or in the upstairs dining room to which we were assigned, serene in gray and white and dim enough to be just right.

The complex French menu and the endless wine list are so staggering that both first-timers and knowing regulars put themselves in the hands of a solicitous, knowledgeable staff to help with their selections. Also available is an à la carte menu, equally complex and astonishingly pricey (appetizers $20 to $28, desserts $19 to $25).

We, like most, chose the prix-fixe route. A tiny cheese gougère was served with drinks, "compliments of the chef." For starters, one of us had Nantucket oysters served in a warm mussel broth topped with American sturgeon caviar (a small portion, but ever so delicious). The other had lobster and sole sausage poached with a purée of sweet red peppers (ever so presented, but super).

From a choice of six entrées (all of which we gladly would have tried), we decided on the Nantucket-raised pheasant, stuffed with mushrooms, herbs and ricotta, and the roasted tenderloin of lamb served with a venison sauce. A triangle of potato pancake, spinach and ratatouille niçoise accompanied. A salad of greens with two kinds of cheeses was unwieldy to eat because the leaves were too large.

Chef Jean-Charles Berruet takes break outside The Chantecleer Inn.

For dessert, the assortment of sorbets was a pretty plate of small scoops interspersed with fresh fruit on a raspberry sauce. Creole-style lime meringue pie was an ethereal second choice. Over demitasses of decaf and espresso, we savored an experience that ranks with the ultimate in fine dining.

Not that it's for everyone. Without background music, the atmosphere is hushed until the room fills up. The tastes are complex and the portions small. Riffling through the more than 1,200 selections on the wine list – winner since 1987 of Wine Spectator's Grand Award as one of the world's best – is so mind-boggling that you're apt to ask the waiter to make the choice, and ours chose on the high side.

And yet, young and old alike go back time after time, such is the spell of the Chanticleer and the output of the energetic owner and his kitchen staff of eleven. Jean-Charles proudly showed us his expansive facility, including a big walk-in cooler in back. "You can tell how good a kitchen is by the condition of its cooler," said he. His was organized and spotless.

If you can't get in for dinner (tables are booked far in advance), splurge for lunch in the garden, beneath trellised canopies of roses and surrounded by impeccably manicured hedges. Expect entrées ($25 to $28) like lobster en croûte with arborio risotto, a mousse of eel and salmon rolled in a crêpe, or scrambled eggs put back in the shell and topped with sevruga caviar, garnished with a purée of potatoes with olive oil. Start with the signature lobster bisque and finish with the French cheese tray or the vanilla crème brûlée.

If you can't get here for a meal, look through Jean-Charles's beautiful cookbook, *Here's to Nantucket: Recipes for the Good Life and Great Food.* This could be the slogan for all Nantucket. And Jean-Charles certainly knows the recipes.

(508) 257-6231. Prix-fixe, $70. À la carte, entrées, $35 to $45. Lunch in summer, noon to 2. Dinner, 6:30 to 9:30. Closed Monday. Open May to mid-October. Reservations and jackets required except in grill.

21 Federal, 21 Federal St., Nantucket.

If Chanticleer is the venerable old-timer, everyone else is a "newcomer," among them 21 Federal. It did so well that only two years after opening in 1985 it added a second establishment in Washington, D.C. Executive chef Bob Kinkead was dispatched to the D.C. operation, called 21 Federal as well. It consistently won high ratings until it closed in 1993 and reopened to rave reviews as Kinkead's in a new Foggy Bottom location.

Owner-manager Chick Walsh runs a tight ship here on the island. Known for its new American grill cuisine, 21 Federal presents a limited menu, but one that's compelling and not in the vanguard of Nantucket's highest prices. The 1847 Greek Revival structure offers six intimate dining rooms – some with their white-linened tables rather close together – on two floors of museum-quality, Federal period decor. In summer, lunch is served on a nifty outdoor courtyard ringed with impatiens, where the whine linens on the tables are topped by herbs in clay pots and classical music wafts across the scene.

Our courtyard lunch arrived on large wicker trays. The pheasant and wild rice soup of the day was sublime, as was the linguini salad with shrimp and pinenuts. The five-salad sampler was less interesting, the chicken with green salsa and oriental noodles outshining the ratatouille and the eggplant, which were too much of the same thing. Calvados ice cream and an intense pineapple-mint sorbet served with wonderful small coconut or lemon squares topped off a flavorful meal.

Chef Russell Jaehnig changes the short dinner menu weekly. You might start with asparagus soup with fiddlehead ferns and crème fraîche, tuna tartare with Asian salad and fried wontons, or lobster and warm spinach salad with chardonnay hollandaise.

Entrées could be sautéed halibut with foie gras butter and chive risotto cakes, seared yellowfin tuna with littleneck clams and lemongrass broth, braised lamb with tuscan white bean ragoût and, from the grill, aged sirloin steak or veal loin chop with potato-leek gratin. Dessert might be a chocolate-mocha roulade with raspberry sauce, blueberry/montrachet tart with whipped cream or homemade sorbet with fresh berries. The fare changes with the seasons, but always appeals and asserts.

(508) 228-2121. Entrées, $23 to $33. Lunch daily in summer, 11:30 to 2:30. Dinner, 6 to 9:30 or 10. Closed Sunday. Open April-December.

Le Languedoc, 24 Broad St., Nantucket.

After a brief stint with a hired chef, longtime chef-owner Neil Grennan is back in the kitchen, where he can keep better rein on what he admits are Nantucket's steep prices and where he produced one of our best meals in Nantucket a few years back. A local institution of 25 years, Le Languedoc continues to please an expanding clientele.

Our autumn dinner began with an appetizer of smoked Nantucket pheasant with cranberry relish, very good and very colorful with red cabbage and slices of apples and oranges on a bed of lettuce. For the main course, one of us tried the noisettes of lamb with artichokes in a rosemary sauce and the other enjoyed sautéed sweetbreads and lobster in puff pastry. Nicely presented on piping-hot white oval plates, they were accompanied by snow peas, broccoli, puréed turnips, yellow peppers, sweet potatoes and peach slices. We ended with a dense chocolate-hazelnut torte spiked with grand marnier.

Settings are elegant in dining rooms at 21 Federal.

Recently, we liked the sound of cream of crab soup, lobster and St. André ravioli and a "short stack" of foie gras, potato brioche and duck rillette, followed by cedar-planked salmon with lobster mashed potatoes, grilled rare tuna with seaweed salad, and porcini-dusted loin of lamb with wilted red chard..

The dessert list included banana-butterscotch meringue tart with caramel drizzle, vanilla crème brûlée and three-chocolate terrine with praline chantilly.

These treats are served in four small upstairs dining rooms amid peach walls and white trim, windows covered with peach draperies and valances, and changing art from a local gallery. Windsor chairs are at well-spaced tables topped by candles in hurricane lamps and vases, each containing a salmon-hued rose.

The downstairs has a small pub-like dining room with checkered cloths. Off the side entrance is a canopied terrace for summer lunches. Everyone loves the cafe menu, from which you can dine very well in the $10 to $20 range for things like a napoleon of grilled tuna or a grilled open-faced lobster reuben with frizzled leeks. The warm duck hash with poached egg, asparagus and gaufrette potatoes makes a super lunch.

(508) 228-2552. Entrées, $21.75 to $37. Lunch in summer, Tuesday-Saturday noon to 2; dinner nightly, 6 to 9:30. Open mid-April through December.

Oran Mor, 1 South Beach St., Nantucket.

Our old favorite Second Story restaurant had slipped and finally gave way in 1997 to this highly rated successor. Peter Wallace, whose food we had enjoyed at the Wauwinet where he was executive chef for six years, and his wife Kathleen renamed the place for a Gaelic phrase meaning "Great Song." She's Irish and he's of Scottish descent and they "thought it sounded nice," he said.

They took over a summery, second-story space with windows toward the harbor and did a major rehab and reconfiguration. A copper and wood staircase rises to a reception podium in the front room. There you find a couple of booths and a neat small, semi-circular bar fashioned from the portico of the local electric company, which they rescued on its way to the dump. Three small, off-white dining rooms with seafoam green trim are dressed with paintings by local artists.

Peter considers it a soothing backdrop for international cuisine that is at the cutting edge. "I'm taking a few more risks," he said, than a hotel dining room would allow. For starters, we were mighty impressed with Peter's champagne risotto with sweetbreads and wild mushrooms, and his Asian fried quail with sticky rice. Expect other choices like tuna tartare with essence of celery and ossetra, a seafood bourride with aioli and a salad of soft-shell crab over field greens. Main courses vary from grilled halibut with chorizo and mahogany clam sauce to roast rack and grilled leg of lamb with mashed fava bean bruschetta. We liked the seared tuna with shallot jus and fresh spinach, and grilled swordfish with orange and black sesame seed butter.

Kathleen's desserts include fresh fruit croustade in a tulipe, quenelles of chocolate mousse topped with pralines, and molten chocolate cake with a trio of ice creams.

In the fall of 1999, Peter opened a new restaurant called Laight Street in New York's trendy Tribeca section. He said his sous chef of ten years would man the Nantucket restaurant in the off-season and "nobody would know I was gone." With his children in school on Nantucket, "I'll be doing a lot of flying back and forth."

(508) 228-8655. Entrées, $25 to $32. Dinner nightly in season, 6 to 10. Closed Sunday-Wednesday in winter.

The Boarding House and The Pearl, 12 Federal St., Nantucket.

When it opened in 1973, the Boarding House was the summer's success story and provided our first great meal on Nantucket. It since has moved around the corner to considerably larger quarters, and several owners (and chefs) have come and gone. It's better than ever lately, having been taken over by Seth and Angela Raynor, he a former sous chef at 21 Federal and both having worked at the Chanticleer. In 1999, they expanded upstairs with their crowning fillip, a showy, aquatic-look, designer restaurant called **The Pearl,** specializing in high-style coastal cuisine. Billed as a separate restaurant for more leisurely dining, "it's like two siblings in a family," said Angela.

The original Boarding House is a beauty, its cathedral-ceilinged Victorian lounge with small faux-marble tables on a flagstone floor opening into a sunken dining room. The latter room is striking in rich cream and pink, with a curved banquette at the far end in front of a mural of Vernazzia, a culinary destination featured in Gourmet magazine the month after the mural went up. The Raynors own the originals but sell lithographs of the exclusive Nantucket series "Streets of Paris," which hang on the walls. Villeroy & Boch china of the Florida pattern graces the nicely spaced tables, which allow for one of Nantucket's more pleasant dining situations.

Upstairs, Pearl is serene in white and blue, with an aquarium at the entrance and a scrim curtain giving the illusion of floating at sea. Indeed, facing the leather-like banquette against the fish tank, you might feel as if you're diving beneath the sea. An onyx bar lit from beneath contributes to a surreal look that catches the eye of restaurant design magazine editors. Off a large new custom-designed kitchen is a chef's table for eight on an outside deck overlooking fountains and gardens. Here is where Seth offers special meals at $150 a head.

Equal to the dramatic settings is the cooking of Seth, who was one of 30 chefs chosen to appear on the "Great Chefs of the East" public television series only

Archways and mural evoke Mediterranean feeling at The Boarding House.

nine months after taking over the Boarding House. We certainly liked our latest dinner here. Starters were mellow sautéed crab cakes with scallion crème fraîche, and grilled quail with crisp fried onion rings and baby mixed greens. Main dishes were pan-roasted salmon with Thai curried cream and crispy rice noodles, and a spicy Asian seafood stew with lobster, shrimp and scallops. Accompanying was a powerful Caymus sauvignon blanc from a well-chosen wine selection with less than the normal Nantucket price markup. Coffee ice cream with chocolate sauce and a dense chocolate-kahlua terrine were worthy endings.

With the opening of The Pearl, the Boarding House is billed more as a year-round bistro with a cocktail bar and an outdoor terrace, appealing for a bistro lunch and drinks. We've also found it a felicitous setting for an after-dinner liqueur while watching the late-night parade pass by.

Chef de cuisine David Buchman oversees the Boarding House, while Seth directs the larger Pearl, a spectacular showcase for leisurely, seafood-oriented dinners. Typical starters here are an island-style seafood platter featuring Nantucket oysters, sashimi of striped bass, a martini of yellowfin tuna and steamed ginger shrimp dumplings. Main courses might marry miso-marinated local codfish with Asian greens and jasmine rice or dish up wok-seared lobster with Thai curry, coconuts and cilantro. The grilled angus tenderloin comes with seared foie gras and caramelized cippolini onions.

(508) 228-9622. Boarding House, entrées $24 to $30. Lunch daily in summer, noon to 2; dinner nightly, 6 to 10, fewer nights in winter.

The Pearl, entrées, $26 to $40. Dinner nightly, 6 to 10:30. Closed January-March.

Straight Wharf Restaurant, Straight Wharf, Nantucket.

Chef Marian Morash of television and cookbook fame put this summery restaurant on the culinary map. She left in 1987 to finish a seafood cookbook, but the menu style and the spiffy decor remained the same. The level of food has been raised lately by partner Steve Cavagnaro, chef-owner of the much-acclaimed Cavey's restaurant in Manchester, Conn., who cooks here summer evenings. His wife Kate, who runs the front of the house, has warmed the welcome as well. They spend the season in Nantucket, but return to Connecticut the rest of the year.

The interior is a pristine palette of shiny floors and soaring, shingled walls topped by billowing banners and hung with striking paintings by an island artist. There's also a bar at the side, noisy and usually with crowds spilling outside onto a terrace in front. The dining and bar areas are well separated, so one does not interfere with the other. The same kitchen serves both, with a sophisticated seafood menu in the dining room and a more rustic, casual grill menu that locals consider among the town's most appealing in the bar.

We wish that the June night we first dined here had been warm enough to eat outside on the canopied, rib-lit deck beside the water, and that the then-acclaimed vegetables had been more exciting than plainly cooked broccoli and carrots. But the complimentary smoked bluefish pâté with drinks, the grilled salmon with tarragon-mustard sauce and the lobster crêpes were first-rate, the peach bavarian laden with raspberry sauce was outstanding and, a nice touch, the elaborately written bill came with two chocolate shells.

A recent September evening was warm enough to relax on the deck as we waited for the 7:10 ferry back to the mainland. We expected only to stave off hunger, but ultimately made a meal of the smoked bluefish pâté with focaccia melba toasts, the basket of breads to dip into a pool of olive oil made tart by the addition of raspberry vinegar, a rich lobster bisque heavily laced with sherry, and an appetizer of seared beef carpaccio with shards of parmigiano-reggiano, white truffle oil and mesclun. The new Hy-Line catamaran arrived so quickly we had to forego the dessert trio of sorbets and rush off to catch the ferry with only the cookies that came with. It was enough that we couldn't even think of a snack back in Hyannis.

Most recently we ate in the wildly popular bar/grill, which is Nantucket's nightly gathering spot for the under 40 crowd, all of whom seem to know each other. Here we enjoyed a sensational appetizer of local black bass with a vegetable mignonette, quite delicate like a seviche, and a main course of grilled rare tuna with white beans, escarole and roasted garlic. Dessert was the previously missed trio of plum-banana, lemon-thyme and mango-pineapple sorbets.

Other favorites among appetizers are Nantucket sea scallops and crisp potato with seared foie gras, and peeky toe crab ravioli with morels and nettle broth. Main dishes range from pan-roasted local cod with clams and smoked sausage to rosemary-grilled rack of lamb with eggplant and lamb cassoulet. The dessert specialty is warm Valrhona chocolate tart with orange cardamom gelato.

(508) 228-4499. Entrées, $29 to $36. Dinner by reservation, nightly except Monday 6 to 10. Open Memorial Day to late September. Grill, $15 to $22, no reservations.

American Seasons, 80 Centre St., Nantucket.

This innovative, off-the-beaten-path establishment is a find for those who want distinguished, ever-changing regional cuisine at reasonable prices. Chef-owner Michael Getter, formerly of 21 Federal, retained the concept and decor launched by his predecessor.

The 50-seat dining room is notable for high-backed banquettes serving as room dividers and polyurethaned tables whose tops are game boards. A local artist painted the tabletops as well as a stunning wall mural of a vine-covered Willamette Valley hillside in Oregon. A couple of dim wall sconces and candlelight provide illumination. Outside is a pleasant patio for dinner in summer.

Local artist painted colorful mural and tabletops at American Seasons.

Michael says he "cranked up the menu a notch" in terms of sophistication, He changes it monthly to highlight regional and seasonal ingredients.

As our meal unfolded, we discovered why people had said that the presentations were so striking and that every plate was different. It turned out it wasn't the plates (most are white) but the decorative garnishes on the rims that made them look different.

Interestingly, the menu is categorized by four regions – Pacific Coast, Wild West, New England and Down South – each with two or three appetizers and entrées. You're supposed to mix and match, pairing, say, Florida rock shrimp gumbo with andouille sausage, okra and biscuits with a lobster and corn enchilada in a blue cornmeal crêpe. Those and a lentil salad with goat cheese, frisée and grilled leeks made a memorable meal. Or you could start with a Pacific tart of roasted rabbit and morels, and enjoy a main dish of crispy salmon with Turkish figs. Louisiana frog's legs and crispy grits with a Western tenderloin of veal with niçoise olive hash is another interesting pairing.

We shared a dessert of raspberry-mango shortcake with raspberry coulis, presented artistically with fresh fruit on a square plate decorated with squiggles of chocolate and crème anglaise. Other choices might be chocolate lava boule with french vanilla bean ice cream and crystalized blackberries, and peanut-butter brittle tart with bourbon chocolate sauce.

The all-American wine list has been honored by Wine Spectator.

(508) 228-7111. Entrées, $23 to $29. Dinner nightly, 6 to 10, April to mid-December.

The Club Car, 1 Main St., Nantucket.

Chef-owner Michael Shannon is a local institution, as is his sumptuous establishment. You enter through a red train car used as a lounge (open from 11 o'clock and lately the scene of chowder and sandwich lunches in season) and a lively piano bar. The lounge represents a bit of history: it is the last remaining club car from the old Nantucket Railroad Co., which operated from here out to 'Sconset. Beyond the lounge is an expansive dining room of white-over-red-linened tables topped by enormous wine globes, upholstered cane-back chairs, an array of large artworks and a colorful shelf of copper pans.

The continental menu, which varies only modestly from year to year, has traditionally ranked as the town's priciest. There's a minimum charge of $26 per person, and a separate plate charge of $15. Appetizers start at $11 for broiled sesame eel and go to $28 for seared New York State duck foie gras ($75 for beluga caviar and vodka). Roasted quail with truffle polenta, cold Nantucket lobster with citrus and avocado and "squid in the style of Bangkok" are among the possibilities.

Typical entrées are shrimp scampi dijonnaise, Norwegian salmon with roasted red pepper coulis, veal sweetbreads grenobloise, roasted poussin stuffed with goose liver pâté and roast rack of lamb glazed with honey mustard and served with minted madeira sauce.

Finish with one of a dozen desserts, perhaps fresh berries with devonshire cream or chocolate-mousse cake with crème anglaise.

(508) 228-1101. Entrées, $30 to $45. Lunch daily in summer, 11 to 3. Dinner nightly, 6 to 10. Closed Monday-Wednesday in off-season and Christmas Stroll to Memorial Day.

Moona, 122 Pleasant St., Nantucket.

Just the ticket to contrast with Nantucket's surfeit of pricey restaurants is this casual grill. The food sparkles and the prices make you think the island might have a middle class, after all. Located on the outskirts of town and upstaging many in-town restaurants, it's run by chef Everett Reid, who founded American Seasons with his brother in 1988. Everett and his wife Linda decided in 1995 it was time to move on.

Here, in what was described as a former roadhouse, a designer covered the walls with black burlap, shellacked the windows and added copper-topped tables for the look of an 18th-century home. They called it Moona for its location: a tract of land designated on old Nantucket maps as part of South Pasture. With candles lit and light jazz playing, it's a dark and casual spot for an innovative dinner. And, unusual for Nantucket, most of the menu is available for takeout – a boon for those who want an interesting picnic supper for the beach.

A Culinary Institute of America graduate who had worked in Boston, New York and at the Summer House in Siasconset, Everett was featured on the PBS series "Great Chefs of the East" and has been invited three times to prepare James Beard Foundation dinners in New York. His is gutsy cooking, without nouvelle conceits. The short menu ranges widely, from an appetizer of crispy fried Portuguese sardines with parmesan toast and a lobster caper mayonnaise to a main-course omelet of Italian spring truffles with a salad of morels and frisée. The seared breast of muscovy duck might be sauced with blackberries and rhubarb and the grilled whole sea bass teamed with a chowder of whelks, slab bacon and fingerling potatoes.

One of us happily made a dinner of three first courses: a bowl of smooth, chilled tomato and leek soup with herb brioche croutons and goat cheese, with sprinkles of parsley on the accompanying plate. This was followed by lamb and goat cheese "poverty" hash with a poached egg and spicy ketchup, the plate decorated with stripes of red pepper purée interspersed with specks of green herbs. Then came an interesting warm "James Beard" lobster salad with asparagus and beet orange dressing. The other diner enjoyed wild-mushroom and tomato pasta with garlic, olive oil and clams, which entered the annals as one of the most powerful-tasting ever. A side dish of crisp carrots, zucchini, beets, summer squash, turnips and a section of corn on the cob accompanied.

Desserts ranged from a sweet potato pancake with candied pecans and butterscotch ice cream to a banana split with coconut ice cream, roasted macadamia nuts and rum-chocolate sauce.

Beers from microbreweries are featured. The dessert menu lists American dessert wines, single-malt scotches and single-barrel bourbons.

(508) 325-4301. Entrées, $17.50 to $26. Dinner nightly, 5:30 to 10. Closed January-March.

Company of the Cauldron, 7 India St., Nantucket.

Originally the home of the Boarding House restaurant, this brick-red Colonial building with ivy-covered windows has been home to this intimate little restaurant since 1977. Lately it was purchased by Allen Kovalencik, a Hungarian from New Jersey who had been its chef since 1987, and his wife Andrea. They liken the experience to dining in a private home with your own personal chef. The prix-fixe, no-choice menu changes nightly, although it's available for viewing a week in advance. Patrons make reservations for the night's seatings and take what's served, which is reputed to be excellent.

Behind an antique wrought-iron baker's rack laden with flowers at the entry are a number of small tables rather close together, colorful with a mix of orange and purple floral cloths on old wood tables. A small service bar at the rear is open to the kitchen. Copper pots, cauldrons and ship's models hang from the stucco walls. Classical harp music often plays and it's all very close, dark and romantic.

A typical dinner brings a wild mushroom and brie soup, tossed Nantucket greens with fiddlehead ferns and lemon-basil vinaigrette, individual beef wellington with port wine sauce, roasted potatoes and green bean bundles, and a mocha-coffee tart. Another could be white gazpacho with lobster meat, field greens and pecan-breaded oysters with a honey-shallot vinaigrette, baked Atlantic sole in parchment with julienne leeks and champagne, and chocolate soufflé cake with raspberries. The vinewood-roasted Atlantic salmon in puff pastry is a house favorite. The small but select wine list is rationally priced.

(508) 228-4016. Prix-fixe, $48 to $50. Dinner nightly, seatings at 7 (also at 9 on busy nights). Open Memorial Day to Columbus Day.

Cioppino's, 20 Broad St., Nantucket.

This old house in the heart of the town's restaurant district has been home to many an eatery. Its latest incarnation by Tracy and Susan Root (he the former mâitre-d' at Chanticleer and she a bartender at the Summer House) has endured, the Roots proving to be hands-on restaurateurs in a town where that's not always the case. "We're working this ourselves, staying open year-round, and it's paying off," said Tracy.

Dining is in a couple of small rooms on the main floor, pretty in white, black and mauve. Upstairs are larger rooms, one with a skylit peaked ceiling and a stunning mural of what looks to be Monet's Garden by a Nantucket artist. In season you can dine at umbrellaed tables on the side and rear patio, a charming setting that draws the locals.

At a September lunch, the special fried oysters with béarnaise sauce was a nouvelle presentation with rice, broccoli, strained zucchini and swirled yellow squash. Also excellent was the caribbean shrimp and asparagus salad. Good sourdough rolls came first; a mellow key lime pie was the finale. The folks at the next table were exclaiming over the soup and half a sandwich ($8.75 for conch chowder and roast beef with boursin) and the shrimp, tomato and mozzarella pizzetta. On our way out, we paused to look at the wine labels inlaid in the bar, representing a few of the owner's collection of 12,000 labels.

The dinner menu is short but sweet. You might start with beef carpaccio or a chilled lobster and asparagus salad. Main courses range from Italian herb-crusted sea bass and grilled fillet of salmon with a tomato-basil vinaigrette to scaloppini of pork piccata and twin tournedos of beef with lobster and hollandaise. The namesake San Francisco cioppino is served over linguini.

Finish with key lime pie, peach and blueberry cobbler with vanilla bean ice cream or the chocolate-kahlua fantasy cake.

Tracy has developed the wine cellar to the point where it earns the Wine Spectator award of excellence. He also has started bottling a couple of special sauces for sale. One enlivens the house drink, the "bloody cioppino," a bloody mary made with clamato juice.

(508) 228-4622. Entrées, $19.75 to $31. Lunch daily, 11:30 to 2:30. Dinner nightly from 5:30.

Christian's, 17 Old South Road, Nantucket.

A shingled Cape Cod-style house on the outskirts of town holds a simple but elegant new restaurant in which chef-owner Christian Dennae is a one-man dynamo. Formerly strictly a caterer, he now features "eclectic coast-to-coast cuisine" and live jazz on weekends in a summery gray and white dining room with white tablecloths, potted palms and artworks for accents.

Classically trained at L'Ecole du Lausanne in Switzerland, Christian offers an inspired menu. Consider appetizers like lobster crab cakes with hot red pineapple and kiwi salsa, Sonoma foie gras with sweet corn salsa, tempura coconut tiger prawns glazed with Thai mustard or "crustaceans in concert:" roasted prawns, lobster and scallops wrapped in phyllo with a champagne beurre blanc.

Main courses range widely from fiery lobster and shrimp savannah to peppercorn-crusted medallions of elk with a roasted red pepper coulis. Among the choices: applewood-grilled Atlantic salmon with pomegranate butter, smoked shrimp and wild morels with a white truffle risotto, and wood-grilled muscovy hen breast with garlic-sesame aioli.

Typical desserts are kona chocolate torte with sweet coconut cream, kahlua poached pears and praline soufflé with white chocolate custard sauce.

The choice American wine list, selected by Christian and wife Rhonda, has been honored by Wine Spectator.

(508) 228-5818. Entrées, $28 to $38. Dinner nightly in summer, 6 to 10; rest of year, Wednesday-Sunday from 6.

West Creek Cafe, 11 West Creek Road, Nantucket.

Our favorite little Beach Plum Cafe gave way to this creative establishment owned by Patricia Tyler, whom we first knew at the Second Story. Taking over from chef Jean Dion, who moved around the corner to Moona and then on to Fahey & Fromagerie, she reconfigured the layout and eliminated the former bakery. Now there are three small rooms, each sponge painted in shades of yellow, burnt orange or gray, with the tablecloths in each room color-coordinated with the walls and a mix of sprightly pillowed banquettes and old-fashioned cane chairs.

The menu is brief and innovative in the New American style. Typical entrées are pan-fried catfish with tomato beurre blanc, Maine diver scallops with a citrus vinaigrette, chile-rubbed ribeye steak with bourbon butter, and grilled lamb tenderloin with sweet garlic demi-glace. Accompaniments vary from scallion and jack cheese grits to chive lyonnaise potatoes to creamy collards and jalapeño corn cakes.

For starters, how about local oysters on the half shell with champagne mignonette, cumin-glazed shrimp over roast corn risotto or crisp duck confit with grilled pears, arugula and onion jam? Desserts are the owner's prerogative. She might make rum torte, a pecan tart or profiteroles.

A couple of Nantucket Vineyard wines are available on the well-chosen list.

(508) 228-4943. Entrées, $21 to $26. Dinner nightly except Tuesday, 6 to 9.

Casual Dining Choices

Even the most determined Nantucket gourmand may tire of fancy, high-priced meals. Luckily, the island has other possibilities, among them:

Black-Eyed Susan's, 10 India St., Nantucket.

This quirky place where you may sit on a picnic bench in a back alley while awaiting a table is a local favorite. It's a small storefront run by partners Susan Handy and chef Jeff Worster, both with long backgrounds in local restaurants, the most recent being the Summer House. The space was formerly a breakfast bar, said Susan, and "all we had to do was clean it up." They still serve breakfast, probably a bit more fancy than before, with the likes of sourdough french toast with orange Jack Daniels butter and pecans and a spicy Thai curry scramble with broccoli and new potatoes. Most dishes come with a choice of hash browns or black-eyed peas, and you can add garlic, cilantro and/or salsa to your omelet for 25 cents each.

From his open kitchen behind the counter, Jeff, a chef-taught chef with experience in Los Angeles, where he got many of his creative ideas, offers eclectic dinner fare – a mix of salads, pastas and seafood and chicken items, with nary a beef dish in sight. One spring night's menu yielded things like Tunisian chickpea soup, Brazilian hearts of palm salad, lime-marinated red snapper, a ragoût of penne with New Zealand lamb and crimini mushrooms, and barbecued pork with szechuan pineapple fried rice and rapini. Venetian whitefish and parmesan polenta with eggplant and onion compote, and Moroccan lamb stew on minted couscous were a couple of the intriguing dishes on a fall dinner menu. We liked the sound of lemon-parsnip soup with peppered grilled tomato. Lighter eaters could order a hearts of romaine salad with caesar dressing (a whole head of romaine, says Susan) for $8. The one dessert a night might be a cobbler or bread pudding.

There's a social, European cafe atmosphere, and singles love to eat at the long bar. The owners only recently got a telephone, to take reservations for the 6 p.m.

seating. Otherwise, summer diners face waits of more than an hour. Says Susan: "you put your name in and then go off and have a cocktail somewhere." She added that the idea was to be here for the local population more than for the tourists, but the word got out.

In 1996, the partners opened a casual restaurant called **Patio J,** behind the mini-golf course out near the airport at 12 Nobadeer Farm Road. Most of the fare is Mexican and Latin-American, and it's available for takeout.

(508) 325-0308. Entrées, $13 to $26. Breakfast daily, 7 to 1. Dinner, Tuesday-Saturday 6 to 9. BYOB. No credit cards. Closed six weeks in winter.

Nantucket Tapas, 15 South Beach St., Nantucket.

Tapas from around the world are the hallmark of this restaurant opened in a former gourmet food store and deli. It's run by Terry Noyes, formerly of the White Elephant, in partnership with Yoshi Mabuchi, who staffs Sushi by Yoshi (see below). "We saw a need for tapas on the island – not just from Spain but the kind a Nantucket sailor would have found all over the world," Terry advised.

You can make quite an exotic meal of some of the 40-odd offerings, many with an Asian accent. The menu is all over the lot, in no particular order. Consider cold smoked scallops with arugula salad and roasted peppers, seared tuna carpaccio with greens and crème fraîche, lobster ravioli, tomato-basil bruschetta, Maine crab cakes, tempura fried calamari, oriental-style boneless ribs with white rice, grilled lamb chop with potato lasagna, and grilled Szechwan filet with steamed white rice. Can't decide? Try the dim-sum sampling of tapas for $13.40.

All is available to eat here or to go. Here is one part reasonably fancy with tablecloths, the other a family-style picnic area with designer boards perched on barrels. Bright and unusual by day, it's dark and appealing at night.

(508) 228-2033. Tapas, $5 to $10.60. Lunch daily, 11:30 to 2:30. Dinner, 5 to 9 or 10.

'Sconset Cafe, Post Office Square, Siasconset.

The founder of the famed Morning Glory Cafe, Pam McKinstry, moved on to the 'Sconset Cafe before giving it up to lead treks to Africa. Now it's run by Rolf and Sue Nelson, who continue to pack in habitués at eight tables for three meals a day amid a casual green and white decor, track lighting and arty accents. We enjoyed a delicious lunch of croque monsieur and boboli, a pizza-like creation with pesto and artichoke hearts. Finishing touches were homemade rum-walnut ice cream with chocolate sauce and a slice of frozen key lime pie, both heavenly.

Dinner dishes could be Thai seafood pasta, grouper rubbed with Indian spices, bouillabaisse provençal, or lamb dijon. Start with filetto carpaccio, pot stickers or the cafe ravioli with artichokes and cheese. Save room for desserts like fresh peach pie, bête noir and bread pudding flavored with grand marnier. Some of the recipes are detailed in the cafe's three cookbooks.

(508) 257-4008. Entrées, $19 to $26. Lunch daily, 11:30 to 2:30; dinner, 6 to 9:30. Open mid-May to early October. BYOB. No credit cards.

Centre Street Bistro, 29 Centre St., Nantucket.

Another of Nantucket's ubiquitous cafes, this small place is on the upswing under chef-owners Ruth and Tim Pitts, whom we last knew at the Summer House in 'Sconset and before that at DeMarco.

They offer creative breakfasts in the $6 to $8 range – perhaps scrambled eggs with sliced tomato and herbed goat cheese toast, a breakfast burrito with black beans and salsa or a potato pancake with smoked salmon and sour cream. The kitchen and the counter are bigger than the six-table bistro, which is augmented by a sidewalk cafe in the summer.

The bistro branches out at night with elegant dinners of what Ruth calls "Nantucket comfort cuisine." You might start with a warm goat cheese tart or a layered version of the morning's potato pancake with smoked salmon. Typical among the half-dozen entrées are sautéed shrimp with red curry and coconut rice noodles and tenderloin of beef with wild mushrooms and goat cheese. One innkeeper reported that two of her guests ate there several times and pronounced it better than anything in New York.

(508) 228-8470. Entrées, $18 to $23. Breakfast daily, 8 to 11. Lunch, 11 to 2, Dinner, 6 to 9. No credit cards.

Sushi by Yoshi, 2 East Chestnut St., Nantucket.

This is the latest takeout endeavor associated with the folks at 21 Federal. Actually, they lease the space to Tokyo-born Yoshi Mabuchi, whom we remember from his partnership with Donald Noyes in the halcyon days of Hatsune in New Haven. Here he seats up to eighteen people at three tables and a small sushi bar, and offers his sensational sushi to go.

Besides more kinds of sushi than you probably thought existed in so small a place, Yoshi offers other Japanese appetizers and entrées at moderate prices, here or to take out. By reservation, he's been known to offer a seven-course Japanese dinner some nights at 9 o'clock. Lately, he has expanded his horizons, opening a second location in Hyannis and adding an oriental flair as a partner with the Noyes family in Nantucket Tapas (see above).

(508) 228-1801. Entrées. $8.60 to $13.35. Open daily, 11:30 to 2:30 and 4:30 to 9, weekends 11:30 to 9:30. Closed Tuesday and Wednesday in off-season and mid-December to April.

Espresso Cafe, 40 Main St., Nantucket.

The foods of a local caterer moved into this snazzy location with an interior in black and white and an appealing, two-level rear garden patio that's an oasis away from the hustle and bustle, with ivy twining all over the stucco walls. We know people who go here just for the desserts, perhaps lemon-almond pound cake or one of the gigantic cookies with cappuccino or the best cup of coffee in town. Scones, bagels and Mexican eggs are among the breakfast items. At lunch, we were impressed by a garden burger with Mexican sage cheese and salsa and a grilled spinach and mozzarella sandwich with garlic and roasted red peppers, both served with zesty cafe potatoes. Another time, a big chocolate-chip cookie and a mocha cappuccino made a nice mid-afternoon break. Light entrées supplement the lunch items in the evening.

(508) 228-6930. Entrées, $5 to $9. Open daily in summer, 7:30 a.m. to 10 or 11 p.m. Off-season, 7:30 to 4:30.

Natural Gourmet

Something Natural, 50 Cliff Road, Nantucket.

Gourmet magazine requested the recipes for the carrot cake and the herb bread made at this rustic cottage at the edge of town. There are old school desks on the deck and picnic tables on the grounds for enjoying one of the nineteen sandwiches available on the wonderful whole wheat, oatmeal, rye, pumpernickel, herb, six-grain and Portuguese breads baked here and served at many a restaurant in town. We found half a sandwich of smoked turkey with tomato and swiss cheese plenty for a late lunch. You also can get salads, Nantucket Nectars and, for breakfast, muffins and raisin rolls. Owner Matt Fee branched out with the **Nantucket Bagel Company**, across town at 5 West Creek Road, and the downtown **Nantucket Bagel Company/Yogurt Plus** for bagels, sandwiches, yogurt and more at 6 Oak St. *(508) 228-0504. Open daily 8 to 6 in summer, shorter hours in off-season. Closed November-April.*

Dining and Lodging

The Wauwinet, Box 2580, Wauwinet Road, Nantucket 02554.

Gloriously situated on a strip of land between Nantucket Bay and the Atlantic, the Wauwinet House had seen better days before it was acquired by Stephen and Jill Karp of Weston, Mass., island vacationers who restored the place to the tune of many millions of dollars for a grand reopening in 1988.

The original building in a rural section of parkland was gutted to make a dining room with french doors and windows taking advantage of the view, a common sitting room with a fireplace, and 25 air-conditioned rooms with private baths, antique pine armoires, and iron or wicker headboards. Across the road in five courtyard cottages are seven more rooms and two suites.

Our bayview bedroom – as opposed to deluxe or suite – was not large but was nicely located on a third-floor corner facing the harbor so that we were able to watch spectacular sunsets at night. Fresh and pretty, it had a queensize bed, upholstered armchairs and a painted armoire topped with a wooden swan and two hat boxes (one of the inn's decorating signatures). The modern bathroom contained a multitude of thick white towels and a basket of Crabtree & Evelyn amenities. During turndown, the towels were replenished and mints placed by the bed.

All the rooms we saw had different, striking stenciled borders (some turning up in the most ingenious places), interesting artworks and sculptures, ceiling fans, and such fillips as clouds painted on the ceiling. TVs and VCRs are hidden in armoires and trunks. A wide selection of videotapes is available – they're delivered to the room with complimentary popcorn.

Outside are chairs lined up strategically on the back lawn and a beachside platform where guests may play "beach chess" with lifesize pieces. You can swim from a dock in the bay, or walk through the dunes in front of the hotel to the most gorgeous, endless and unoccupied strand we've seen along the Atlantic coast. A 21-foot runabout will transport guests to town or to a remote beach for the day.

A full breakfast is included in the room rate. Guests order from a menu spanning a spectrum from strawberry and rhubarb pancakes to egg-white omelets with spa cheese and fresh vegetables.

General manager Russell Cleveland (earlier of Williamsburg Inn and Salishan Lodge renown) ensures that everything is first-rate as far as lodging goes, even as he oversees the owners' new in-town properties including the Harbor House, the White Elephant and the Breakers. The restaurant and wine cellar are overseen by his wife Debbie, food and beverage manager as well as co-innkeeper.

Topper's, named for the owners' dog, is a refined summery setting for some of

Topper's is luxurious dining room at the Wauwinet.

the island's best food. Two elegant, side-by-side rooms harbor masses of flowers and well-spaced tables with upholstered chairs in blue and white. The outdoor terrace overlooking lawn and bay is favored for lunch and drinks.

Executive chef Christopher Freeman is known for refined regional cuisine. Among appetizers, we were impressed with the signature lobster crab cakes with smoked corn, jalapeño olives and a divine mustard sauce, and the coriander-seared yellowfin tuna sashimi with soba noodles and pickled vegetables, served on hand-made sushi boards of purple heart wood.

Every main course we've had here has been superior. Included were roast rack of lamb with potato-fennel brandade and grilled veal chop with wild grape compote, both accompanied by baby vegetables (tiny pattypan squash and carrots about a big as a fingernail) and a wedge of potatoes. The hearty Nantucket lobster stew – incorporating abundant lobster, salsify, leeks, island tomatoes and tomalley croutons – is the latest hit. The caramelized sea scallops with french green lentils and seared foie gras vinaigrette is a close second.

Desserts include a signature chocolate marquise with raspberries and grand marnier and a n "ABC tart" comprised of almonds, rum-soaked bananas and chocolate that's to die for.

The sparkling Wauwinet Water pours freely from antique cobalt blue bottles, the breadsticks and baguettes are crusty, salt and pepper are served only on request, and all courses are delivered on sterling silver pendulum plate carriers. Martinis and manhattans are served by the pitcher, and brandy arrives in innovative footless glasses. The Wine Spectator grand award wine list is strong in American and French vintages from a selection of more than 800.

(508) 228-8768 or (800) 426-8718. Fax (508) 228-7135. Thirty-two rooms and two cottage suites with private baths. Mid-June to mid-September: doubles, $540 to $870; suites, $850 to $1,010. Rest of year: doubles $230 to $750, suites $550 to $900. Four-night minimum in summer. Closed November to early May.

Entrées, $32 to $42. Lunch, Monday-Saturday noon to 2. Dinner nightly, 6 to 9:30, jackets requested. Sunday brunch, 10:30 to 2. Closed November to early May.

The Summer House, 17 Ocean Ave., Box 880, Siasconset 02564.

A more romantic setting for dining could scarcely be imagined than the front veranda of this low-slung, Southern-style house or its summery interior dining room. It's a mix of white chairs (many with billowing blue-cushioned backs) and painted floors, good 'Sconset oils and watercolors on the whitewashed walls, and fresh flowers and plants everywhere.

We chose one of the handful of tables on the veranda yielding a view of the moon rising over the ocean that we could hear lapping at the foot of the bluff across the road. The setting remained etched in our memory longer than our dinner, which was more ordinary than the tab would have suggested. The leased restaurant operation is said to have improved lately under chef Carl Keller, whose fare we sampled when he was at 21 Federal and the old Morning Glory Cafe.

You're paying for the setting as well as the food, of course. Appetizers might be a smoked salmon, lobster and scallop sausage with black caviar, Jamaican grilled shrimp and artichokes with beet juice and mango salsa, and a spring roll of goat cheese, citrus, mint and snap peas with fennel and watercress. Assertive, complex flavors continue with such entrées as tuna nori and Szechuan seared tuna with tempura lobster tail and grapefruit-braised greens, amandine roast trout and littlenecks with asparagus and truffle risotto, and grilled beef tenderloin with a jonah crab cake, marrow-crusted potato roesti and elephant garlic crème fraîche.

A brandy tart with dollops of whipped cream, blueberries and slices of kiwi proved a memorable choice from a dessert selection that included frozen key lime mousse with raspberries, Mexican chocolate cake on a pool of cinnamon crème anglaise and rum-spiked white chocolate coconut cake with lemongrass syrup. The extensive wine list concludes with a page of cigars.

Our meal was enlivened by piano music that makes you want to linger over one of the island's largest selections of single malts, cognacs and ports. We were content to toddle off to our room in one of eight Bermuda-like cottages strung in a horseshoe pattern around a garden between restaurant and sea.

Beneath a canopy of trees and ivy with bridal veil spilling over the roofs, the charming, rose-covered cottages have been redecorated with antiques, eyelet-embroidered pillows and lace-edged duvets on the beds, lace curtains, and painted floors and chests. A New York artist hand-painted floral borders along the tops of the walls for the finishing touch. Interesting roof lines, stained glass, leaded windows, and little nooks and crannies contribute to the charm. Modern amenities include telephones and renovated marble bathrooms, each with a jacuzzi.

Jimmy Cagney cherished the privacy of the cottage-suite named in his honor. Although each has its own or a shared small terrace, we felt on display reading on ours as arriving diners passed at cocktail hour. There are no real sitting areas, public or private, inside the cottages or main building.

An elaborate continental breakfast buffet – juices, fresh fruit, granola, bran cereal and baked goods – is offered in the morning on the sun-drenched veranda, where you can savor the sun rising over the open expanse of azure-blue ocean. It's a magical setting, like none other we know of on the East Coast.

Lunch is available on a landscaped bluestone terrace beside the pool, sequestered halfway down the bluff in the dunes, a long stone's throw from the beach. Everything's pricey ($8 to $18), but there's a good selection and the eight-ounce burger is advertised as the best on the island. Look at it this way: lunch patrons get to use the pool (others are charged $15), and the view is free.

Summery dining room at The Summer House in Siasconset.

In 1999, Summer House owner Peter Karlson and his wife, Danielle DeBenedictis, acquired two in-town B&Bs to add 23 more rooms, extend the season and become more of a full-service hotel. A jitney shuttled guests back and forth between town and beach.

First to open was the house at 27 Fair St., formerly an inn known as Fair Gardens and once owned by noted hand-hooked rug designer Claire Murray. Here guests stay in twelve rooms and suites decorated in pastels with roses and garlands hand-painted by the same artist whose work enhances the Summer House cottages. Four rooms in the main house and three in the rear guest house were to get jacuzzi baths. Peter showed a garden area where he planned to install a terraced lap pool.

He also led a tour as construction proceeded at the house at 31 India St., formerly the Great Harbor Inn. Here guests find a common room with fireplace, eleven guest rooms (seven with jacuzzis), whimsical artistry and a lighter, more open feeling than at the others. There's a hot tub in the garden out back. Both houses were to be painted white with green shutters for a common identity.

Inn: (508) 257-4577. Fax (508) 257-4590. Nine cottage rooms with private baths at Siasconset and 23 B&B rooms and suites in town. Mid-June to Labor Day, cottages, $450 to $525; rooms and suites, $200 to $425. Late spring and early fall: cottages, $275 to $375; rooms and suites, $125 to $300. Rest of year: cottages, $175 to $250; rooms and suites, $100 to $225. Closed January-March.

Restaurant: (508) 257-9976. Entrées, $34 to $41. Lunch at poolside, daily 11 to 3. Dinner, 6 to 10. Closed mid-October to May.

Cliffside Beach Club, Jefferson Avenue, Box 449, Nantucket 02554.

The Cliffside Beach Club, situated for more than 70 years on the marvelous open beach on the north shore, has been owned since 1954 by the Currie family, whose offspring now run a deluxe small inn/hotel and an oceanfront restaurant.

Club members coveted the same umbrella and assortment of chairs and used to wait years to reserve one of the more prestigious spots on the west beach,

Canopied outdoor deck offers seaside dining at The Galley on Cliffside Beach.

according to general manager Robert F. Currie. Now guests don't have to wait – they simply walk out of their rooms onto the beach. Some of the old bathhouses have been converted into fourteen contemporary bedrooms with cathedral ceilings and modern baths. All the beds, doors, tables, vanities and even the pegs for the beach towels were fashioned by Nantucket craftsmen. Angled wainscoting serves as the headboards for the built-in queensize beds. Prints by local artists and oriental rugs on the dark green carpets set off the old wood walls. Wicker furniture, antique wooden toys and black leather couches are among the appointments.

Nine air-conditioned beachfront studio apartments, each with a private deck and the phones and TVs characteristic of all the rooms, and several suites are of newer vintage. A new health club is said to be one of the busiest spots in town.

A continental breakfast is served in the club's spectacular high-ceilinged lobby that Monique Currie decorated in South of France style. It has quilts on the ceiling and is full of smart wicker furniture and potted flowers, so prolific and splashy that tending them has "become my full-time job," says Monique.

Lunch and dinner are available to guests and the public at **The Galley at Cliffside Beach,** situated between the club and the studio apartments, with an L-shaped, canopied deck facing the ocean. Here you sit on blue wicker chairs at tables with floral cloths, backing up to planters filled with petunias and geraniums with hanging pink paper globes overhead. It's enchanting by day or night.

We thoroughly enjoyed a couple of the best bloody marys ever before a lunch of salade niçoise and chicken salad Hawaiian. Service is by waiters who spend their winters working at a club in Palm Beach, which helps explain the level of professionalism here.

A jazz pianist plays at night, when the place conveys a clubby air. The seafood-oriented dinner menu ranges from seared yellowfin tuna with sticky rice stacks and a kumquat sambal to roasted lobster and local shellfish with riesling-braised leeks, fire-roasted baby corn and "young" potatoes. The only meat options on a recent menu were filet mignon with a portobello roasted shallot compote and maytag blue cheese whipped potatoes, and horseradish-crusted rack of lamb in a tomato-rosemary jus. Start with a lobster spring roll, cornmeal-crusted calamari, or a goat cheese-stuffed squash blossom on grilled focaccia. Finish with homemade cognac ice cream, blueberry-peach pie or chocolate-soufflé cake.

Retired owner Jane Currie Silva's sons David, who used to be sous chef, and Geoffrey, the mâitre-d, oversee the front of the house. Many of the Galley's paintings and the menu cover are by Belgian artist Lucien van Vyve, the first chef at the old Opera House here, whom Jane considered her mentor.

(508) 228-0618. Thirty-one rooms and suites with private baths. Mid-June to Labor Day: doubles, $335 to $535, suites, $655 to $1,310; off-season: doubles $275 to $395; suites, $495 to $990. Lodging open Memorial Day to Columbus Day.

Entrées, $30 to $40. Lunch daily in summer, 11:30 to 2:30. Dinner nightly, 6 to 10, mid-June to mid-September; Thursday-Monday until Columbus Day.

Ships Inn, 13 Fair St., Nantucket 02554.

Built in 1831 by whaling captain Obed Starbuck, this has been restored by chef-owner Mark Gottwald and his wife Ellie. It now claims some of Nantucket's most comfortable accommodations as well as a highly regarded restaurant.

The ten guest rooms, named after ships that Starbuck commanded, contain many of original furnishings and retain the look of the period. They have been refurbished with new wallpapers and tiled baths and come with interesting window treatments, down comforters, Neutrogena toiletries and mini-refrigerators in cabinets beneath the TV sets. Most have reading chairs and half have desks. All but two tiny single rooms are more spacious than most bedrooms in Nantucket inns.

Guests enjoy afternoon tea with coffeecake and cookies. Innkeeper Meghan Moore sets out a continental-plus breakfast of fruit, cereal, scones and muffins.

Dinners here have received considerable notice since the Gottwalds took over. Chef Mark, who trained at Le Cirque in New York and at Spago in Los Angeles, oversees the cooking duties with a sizable kitchen staff. He calls the style California-French. Among entrées, you might find crispy salmon with cabernet sauce and niçoise vegetables, grilled halibut with braised leeks in a sweet carrot and ginger coulis, and roast muscovy duck breast with wild mushroom ragoût and plum wine duck jus, Or consider a pasta, perhaps rigatoni with duck confit, tomato and port demi-glace or lobster with gnocchi, shiitake mushrooms, artichokes, leeks and sauternes.

Start with chilled cucumber-watercress soup with lobster garnish, smoked trout salad with horseradish vinaigrette on Smithfield ham, or a roquefort and walnut terrine with Asian pear. Finish with chocolate voodoo cake or passion-fruit crème brûlée studded with fresh cherries. A well-chosen wine list starts in the twenties.

The dining room is attractive with apricot walls over white wainscoting, exposed beams, a white fireplace in the center of the room, candles in the many-paned windows, and white-linened tables dressed with candles and fresh flowers. There also are tables for eating in the adjacent Dory Bar.

The Gottwalds winter with their young children in Vero Beach, Fla., where they opened Ellie's, a new American restaurant on the waterfront. They and their staff go back and forth between the two establishments.

(508) 228-0040. Ten rooms with private baths. Doubles, $195 to $210. Closed November-March.

Entrées, $18 to $32. Dinner, Thursday-Monday 5:30 to 9.

Breakfast is a highlight for guests at The Pineapple Inn.

Lodging

The Pineapple Inn, 10 Hussey St., Nantucket 02554.

Breakfast is a high point of a stay at this deluxe new B&B. That's no surprise to anyone familiar with the innkeepers, Caroline and Bob Taylor. They were known for their breakfasts during the fifteen years they owned and operated the Quaker House Inn and Restaurant here before they turned their attention to the Pineapple.

More than half the comments in the inn's guest book relate to the food. "We like different things," says Bob, who rises early every day to bake the pastries and prepare the entrée. "You won't get muffins here." What you will get, perhaps, are scones with flavored creams or blueberry-coffee crumb cake. Or clafouti, the recipe for which appeared in Gourmet magazine. Or, in our case, a savory tart of spinach, cheese, basil and sundried tomatoes, teamed with a slice of the day's nectarine and blueberry tart, a delicious and custardy affair. These followed a choice of cereals: berndt muesli or dry mix with granola. Fresh orange juice, a fruit cocktail and an endless reservoir of café latte came with. "The only holdovers here from our restaurant are the espresso and juicing machines," Bob advised. He puts both to good use.

The leisurely repast takes place between 8 and 10 at a table for ten in an elegant, chandeliered dining area on the inn's lower level. In good weather, it's served outside at umbrella-covered tables beside a fountain on a large, plant-bedecked rear terrace. Roses were bursting into bloom there at our June visit.

The Taylors are among the few Nantucket innkeepers who live on the premises and attend to their guests personally. They spent nearly $1 million in 1997 to transform an 1838 Greek Revival ship captain's house into one of the town's more comfortable B&Bs. "We wanted to bring our accommodations to the highest standard possible on the island," says Bob.

The house is conveniently situated along a quiet, one-way residential street at the edge of downtown. The building had to be gutted to install private baths, all finished in white marble. The twelve air-conditioned guest quarters, named for whaling ship captains whose biographies are in the appropriate room's welcome book, are spread over four floors. Each features a handmade Eldred Wheeler four-poster canopy bed of tiger maple, king or queen size, covered by a Ralph Lauren duvet in a Williamsburg pattern. Sitting areas have wing chairs or small sofas. Amenities include TVs hidden in highboys, telephones, handmade oriental carpets, and 19th-century antiques and artworks. Three rooms have ornamental fireplaces. The Captain Pollard on the lower level adds a private patio.

In cool weather, guests gather on tapestry sofas in front of the fireplace in the side parlor in this B&B that lives up to its name, the Colonial symbol for hospitality. The Taylors do it up right.

(508) 228-9992. Fax (508) 325-6051. www.pineappleinn.com. Twelve rooms with private baths. Mid-June to late September and special events and weekends: doubles $175 to $295. Off-season, $110 to $225. Closed Christmas Stroll to Daffodil Weekend.

Centerboard Guest House, 8 Chester St., Nantucket 02554.

A Victorian guest house of quiet country elegance is how its brochure describes it. That doesn't entirely do justice to this appealing B&B, which is a cut above most of the rest in town. Each of the seven air-conditioned guest quarters has a plush feather mattress, color TV, phone, mini-refrigerator and air-conditioning. They were furnished with panache by longtime owner Marcia Wasserman, a Long Island artist and interior designer who now runs the burgeoning local food operation known as Peter Piper Market (see Gourmet Treats). New owner Debbie Wasil also bought the Martin House next door in 1998. She took over turnkey operations and kept the properties separate and distinct.

We lucked into the main-floor suite, with a library-style living room in dark woods and hunter green, a bedroom with a queensize canopy feather bed, and a glamorous bathroom in deep green marble, with a jacuzzi in one section, a large marble-tiled shower in another, and the sink and toilet in still another. The suite had two TVs, plush masculine furnishings, and no fewer than six bouquets of fresh and dried flowers scattered here and there.

The upstairs rooms are romantic, if not quite so glamorous. All with queens or two double beds, they show decorative flair, with lacy pillows, flouncy comforters and the odd mural on the wall. Terrycloth robes, baskets of Caswell-Massey toiletries, a bowl of toffee and a welcoming basket of apples and cheeses are in the rooms. A pine-paneled studio apartment in the basement has built-in double beds and a small kitchen.

A resident innkeeper puts out a bountiful continental breakfast buffet: bowls of fresh fruit, cereals, granola, and a wide variety of muffins and breads for toasting. This can be taken in the dining room, on the front porch or at the window seat in the living room.

(508) 228-9696. Six rooms and one suite with private baths. Mid-June to mid-October: doubles, $185; suite, $325. Rest of year: doubles, $110 to $155; suite, $185 to $225.

Cliff Lodge, 9 Cliff Road, Nantucket 02554.

Twelve guest rooms, designed for comfort and decorated with flair, are offered at this 1771 sea captain's house in a residential neighborhood overlooking town and harbor. Owners John and Debby Bennett have imparted a summery, beach look inside and enhanced the gardens, a talent he learned from his father, a professional landscaper. A Nantucket native, he met his wife-to-be at the local hospital, where both were employed.

Bedrooms here are notable for spatter-painted floors, Laura Ashley wallpapers, frilly bedding, fresh flowers and antiques. Many boast kingsize beds and fireplaces, and all have telephones and TVs nicely built into the walls or concealed in armoires.

Few B&Bs have so many neat places to sit and relax, inside or out. There are five sitting rooms on three floors, a rooftop deck with a view of the harbor, reading porches and a couple of brick patios beside the lovely gardens.

Debby serves a buffet breakfast in one of the sitting rooms, or guests can adjourn to the said patio, where she matches the tablecloths with the flowers that are in bloom. Fresh fruit, cereal, muffins and Portuguese toasting bread are typical fare. Apple-cranberry crisp is her specialty. She offers hot or iced tea and snacks like cucumber sandwiches or homemade cookies in the afternoon.

(508) 228-9480. Twelve rooms with private baths. Doubles, $140 to $180, mid-June to late September; $75 to $140, rest of year.

Union Street Inn, 7 Union St., Nantucket 02554.

A hotel manager from Connecticut and his wife, Ken and Deborah Withrow, took over this newish inn and gave it the professional, in-residence care it needed. The restored 1770 house, converted from a guest house into a luxury B&B by previous owners, offers twelve spacious accommodations with air conditioning, antique furnishings and cable TV. Scatter rugs dot the original wide-plank pine floors. Six rooms have working fireplaces, including a suite with queen canopy bed, mini-fridge and sitting room with VCR and telephone. Another premier room has a king poster bed and fireplace. Others have queensize or two twin beds, except for one with a double bed.

Because of its location (and zoning), the Union Street can offer more than Nantucket's highly regulated continental breakfasts. The Withrows serve things like scrambled eggs and bacon, blueberry pancakes, french toast and, every fourth day, eggs benedict. These are in addition to a cold buffet that includes a fresh fruit platter, cereals and muffins. The repast is taken in a large dining room or at three handsome garden tables on the side patio beneath an ivy-covered hillside.

"Debbie cooks and I'm the bus boy," quips Ken, who had been manager of the Hyatt UN Plaza Hotel in New York and the Ambassador East Hotel in Chicago. They wanted their own business and a family life for their young son, and found both here.

(508) 228-9222 or (800) 225-5116. Fax (508) 325-0848. Twelve rooms with private baths. Mid-June to mid-September: doubles, $140 to $210; suite, $245. Rest of year: doubles, $80 to $195; suite, $215.

Anchor Inn, 66 Centre St., Box 387, Nantucket 02554.

Charles and Ann Balas, who used to own the Nantucket Fine Chocolates store, are the hands-on innkeepers at this venerable B&B. They feel their in-residence position helps set the Anchor apart. Built by a whaling ship captain, this was the home in the 1950s of the Gilbreths of "Cheaper by the Dozen" fame, who wrote of their experience in the book *Innside Nantucket.*

Ten guest rooms, named after whaling ships, have queen beds and period furnishings amid the original random-width floorboards and antique paneling. An eleventh room on the third floor has twin beds. Most bathrooms have showers only, but are equipped with hair dryers. Guests help themselves to continental breakfast on an enclosed wraparound side/rear porch with individual tables and cafe curtains. Charles's homemade muffins are served to the accompaniment of classical music.

The Balases, who by nature and avocation know all the food goings-on around the island, share their insights with guests in the front parlor, where the fireplace is lit in cool weather.

(508) 228-0072. Eleven rooms with private baths. Doubles, $130 to $185, June to mid-September and most weekends; rest of year, $65 to $135.

Gourmet Treats

Rarely have we encountered a small area so chock full of gourmet shops, specialty-food takeouts, caterers and other services pertaining to matters culinary.

Many cheeses, gazpacho, Thai noodle and curried couscous salads, muffulettas, apple-peach muffins and sandwiches in the $6 to $7 range are available from **Provisions** at 3 Harbor Square, behind the bandstand on Straight Wharf. Also part of the food complex here are **Stars,** a seasonal ice cream and frozen yogurt shop with a porch where you can sit right by the water, and the **Straight Wharf Fish Store,** where soft-shell crab and swordfish steak sandwiches were going for $8.95 last we knew. The store carries some specialty foods along with fresh fish.

Satisfy your sweet tooth at **Sweet Inspirations** at 26 Centre St. You can indulge in handmade chocolates, pecan and caramel tuckernucks, award-winning cranberry truffles, chocolate-almond buttercrunch, and an exclusive line of Nantucket fruit preserves and chutneys. A recent favorite is cranberry bark, available in dark, milk or white chocolate, each studded with bright red dried cranberries. The confections are made here daily the old-fashioned way, smoothed and cut by hand.

The Complete Kitchen at 25 Centre St. offers Nantucket jams, jellies and ketchup made just for the store, caviars, crème fraîche and California tortas with basil, garlic and pinenuts or smoked salmon, mustard and dill. All those items the beautiful people need for their cocktail parties are here, as are a good selection of cookbooks and cookware. Around the corner is the **Nantucket Gourmet,** with more specialty foods, a deli case for salads and sandwiches, and a lot of high-tech kettles, toasters and such, as well as a practical oyster opener for $13.95.

If you're interested in pepper grinders, check out the Peppergun, invented and made on the island. Ads headlining it as "Nantucket Native" tout the fast-grinding one-hander as the world's most efficient peppermill. It's on sale at local stores.

The Lion's Paw at the foot of Main Street carries wonderful hand-painted pottery, including great fish plates. We think it's the nicest of several gift shops of interest to gourmets.

Majolica at 1 Old North Wharf specializes in hand-painted, one-of-a-kind pieces of the imported Italian pottery and ceramics. The colorful store displays teapots, trays, vases, salad bowls, demitasse cups and the trademark rooster pitchers in several sizes. You can even buy a set of hand-painted animal plates from Tuscany.

Only in Nantucket would you not be surprised to come across **Cold Noses,** a small gourmet shop for cats and dogs near Straight Wharf. As well as gourmet natural dog cookies, you'll find "doggie duds," cat beds, pearls pour le pouch and perfect purrls for cats, and even cologne from Paris for Fluffy or Spot.

Gourmet Destinations

Fahey & Fromagerie, 49A Pleasant St., Nantucket.

The choicest prepared foods, cheeses and wines in town come from this intimate new establishment. Michael Fahey gave a sample of brin d'amour from Corsica to go with a taste of a fine bordeaux while French chef Jean Dion worked with a baker and a Thai chef in the kitchen. Their specialty is fine foods to go, as in a deli case brimming with the likes of salmon mousse, spinach and roquefort pâté, salads, stuffed zucchini boats, roasted free-range chicken, and sliced beef tenderloin. Buddy Dion, who was featured on the PBS series "Great Chefs of the East" after opening the island's old Beach Plum Cafe, now is involved in this venture's catering, cooking demonstrations and wine tours to France.

(508) 325-5644. Open Monday-Thursday 10:30 to 6:30, Friday and Saturday 9 to 7:30.

Peter Piper Market, 19 Boynton Lane, Nantucket.

This versatile new establishment off Surfside Road south of town is the result of a vision hatched by a former Long Island interior designer-turned-innkeeper. Marcia Wasserman, who started the stylish Centerboard Guest House here, sold it in 1997 to fulfill her dream of "a virtual food factory" combining the attributes of California wine-country markets and the specialty food stores in New York. She started with take-out meat loaf at the Centerboard for nourishing winter dinners. The idea evolved into a custom-designed building with a large deli, salad bar, soup and brew bar, wine store, meats and seafood, cheeses, essential and specialty groceries, plants, a bakery and more – what Boston magazine called "Nantucket's answer to Dean & DeLuca." All the food is prepared from scratch in the basement "factory" kitchens and is available for takeout. Although it is geared for Nantucketers too busy to cook, transients find it a great place for a reasonable lunch or picnic. We enjoyed a trio of interesting salads at a table on the side porch.

(508) 228-9842. Open daily 7 to 7 in summer; 7 to 7 weekdays and 8 to 4 weekends rest of year.

They're Juice Guys

Nantucket Nectars, juices that seem to be turning up everywhere, got their start in Nantucket. Tom First and Tom Scott, fresh out of Brown University in 1988, started Allserve, a floating convenience store, to serve boats in Nantucket Harbor. During the off-season, they repeated for island friends the taste of a peach nectar that Tom First had enjoyed in Spain. They began making it in blenders and selling it in cups off the stern of the Allserve boat in 1990. Starting with three flavors, the pair known as "Tom and Tom – we're juice guys" expanded to the point where they were the fastest-growing New Age beverage company in the country. These beverages that some locals contend are a bigger and better phenomenon than Snaffle and Celestial Seasonings are now headquartered in Boston and produced in five plants around the country. They come with distinctive purple caps and colorful labels that depict fond memories of days spent in the Allserve General Store behind the Hy-Line terminal at 44 Straight Wharf. Most varieties cost $1.25 a bottle there, more around town and on the mainland. The bottle caps contain nuggets of Nantucket lore, and it's the in thing locally to rate mention on a cap.

Boston skyline as viewed from the Rotunda at Boston Harbor Hotel.

Boston, Mass.

Baked Beans to New Cuisine

If California is America's last culinary frontier, as one food magazine has suggested, Boston is our first. This city situated not far from where the Pilgrims landed has had more than 350 years to refine and redefine itself, to become civilized in cuisine as well as in culture.

No American city has given its name to, nor been associated with, more indigenous foods. Boston baked beans, Boston scrod, Boston lettuce, Indian pudding, Boston brown bread and Parker House rolls got their start here. The nation's first French restaurant dates back to 1793 in Boston. The Parker House opthe staples remain, but the new regional cuisine is everywhere – reigning a tad preciously in some of the East's great restaurants (most of them creations of the 1980s and '90s), simply evolving or being accommodated in more traditional places. Boston was among the first to take to bistro cooking, as the economy softened in the early 1990s. And Boston restaurants were among the first to upscale again as the recession eased.

Boston is at the heart of an emerging New England cuisine, with chefs developing original recipes employing regional ingredients and. Several have been ranked by national magazines among the country's best. Lydia Shire, who led the revolution in Boston food circles while at the acclaimed Seasons, returned to Boston to open her own restaurant after a brief stint in southern California, where she said she could not find as good local provisioners. Todd English has vaulted onto the national stage, opening more restaurants across the nation than, say, Mark Miller or Wolfgang Puck Several of the city's hotels are in the forefront of the city's growing culinary reputation, and the chefs they import tend to stay to open their own restaurants.

The leading chefs in America's largest small town consider themselves a family, it seems. They've reached the big time here, and have little inclination to move on. All of which makes Boston an exciting destination for those seeking adventure in food and wine.

Dining

More than ever, Boston offers a roster of "hot," high-profile restaurants, whose members come and go. While they receive a lot of the media buzz, others of earlier consequence continue to appeal.

The Best of the Best

L'Espalier, 30 Gloucester St.,

The first – and, most agree, still the best – of Boston's great restaurants, L'Espalier offers cuisine, setting and style for a special occasion. It makes such demands upon your palate that we cannot imagine dining here every week, as habitués are known to do. Nor could we often sample the chef's tasting menu, so extravagant that even those of us who were taught to eat every last morsel simply couldn't. It was too much of a great thing.

L'Espalier opened in 1978 under the auspices of Tunisian-born French chef Moncef Meddeb, who sold it a decade later to his sous chef, Frank McClelland. Frank and his wife Catherine, who until recently lived upstairs with their children, devote full-time-plus to the effort. "We're putting lots of energy into upgrading every aspect of the cuisine, service and decor so that we have something very special here," says Frank. Their energy and expertise pay off as L'Espalier keeps raising the bar for perfection, lately surpassing Aujourd'hui at the Four Seasons as Boston's best in Gourmet magazine's ranking of top tables. Frank's evolving new French-American cuisine keeps getting better and better.

L'Espalier has a totally prix-fixe menu, charging $65 for three courses of multiple choices. There are three seven-course tasting menus: $72 for the vegetarian, $82 for the James Beard Ultimate Dinner, $125 for the chef's dégustation of caviar. The last two basically offer smaller portions with extra courses of the regular menu plus add-ons. Since we wanted to taste as much as possible, our party of four put ourselves in the chef's hands – which is a princely way to go. About half the 120 diners here each night do likewise.

An amuse-bouche of a fall vegetable tart with smoked pork on toasted brioche and a sampling of five exotic breads got the meal off to a tasty start. First courses included warm Wellfleet oysters in a champagne, leek and pumpkin nage with blinis, herb salad and caviar; a terrine of smoked salmon with leeks, watercress and potato and, for good measure, an incredible dish of roasted foie gras with a savory prune, dried cherry and oatmeal crisp. We'll never forget the cappuccino of chanterelles and white truffles, a vegetarian broth with a foamy topping of essence of mushrooms and truffles steamed in the manner of cappuccino, enhanced with oysters baked with cider and cracked white-pepper glaze.

Main courses were melt-in-the-mouth poached halibut with black truffles and crabmeat gratin; roasted apple-smoked chicken in a mille-feuille of sweet potato, apple and turnip; braised stuffed Vermont veal shoulder, served under a dome, and roasted Vermont pheasant with foie gras croutons and côtes du rhône plum sauce.

Chef-owner Frank McClelland in elegant dining room at L'Espalier.

Honestly, it was the exotic accompaniments – doled out family style for sampling on plate after plate – that finished us off. Not to mention the grand assortment of cheeses, a tray of eleven of the best from Massachusetts to Tuscany. We picked out three and the waiter returned with five each.

Desserts, to which we could no longer do justice, were a roasted banana soufflé with toasted coconut crème anglaise, a molten-centered chocolate fondant cake with grand marnier sabayon, a refreshing passion-fruit sorbet and raspberry frozen yogurt with a meringue swirl and – the ultimate – "L'Espalier's study of pears." The last was an artistic rendering of a pear stuffed with ice cream, a grilled pear and a puff-pastry tart called pithiviers. The work was colorfully outlined with chocolate, raspberry and kiwi sauces around the edge of the plate.

More than most, the straightforward menu descriptions belie the complexity of flavors and tastes. Frank cooks in an intellectual style, working daily in a test kitchen on taste and composition so that the diner senses the essence of the food. Perfection is his goal (he received the current Boston Globe food critic's first four-star rating and, in 2000, a five-diamond rating from AAA). He also has a passion for vegetables. His was the first mainstream restaurant we encountered to offer a dégustation vegetarian menu.

The venison, lamb, rabbit, produce – most grown organically – come from L'Espalier's own purveyors. Frank personally buys the selections for the thirteen-page wine list, which is especially strong on Bordeaux and wines from Alsace and Rhône, well aged in three cellars. Although he has twelve professional cooks in the kitchen, he works a station and personally oversees every dish that goes out. You also can be assured that he's on the scene – when he goes to France for his annual busman's holiday to study with three-star chefs, he closes the restaurant.

His renovated Back Bay Victorian townhouse is a supremely elegant atmosphere in which to dine. After buzzing a doorbell to gain entry, diners proceed to the second floor, which has two high-ceilinged dining rooms in shades of taupe and cream, or to the third floor, where the dining-room walls are a warm lacquered and stenciled terra cotta and the kitchen is next door. There are marble fireplaces, carved moldings, flower arrangements in niches, pin spotlights on well-spaced tables set with damask linens and fresh flowers, and luxurious yet comfortable lacquered chairs with curved arms.

Frank, besides keeping on top of everything in the kitchen, pops out to greet customers in his dining rooms as well. L'Espalier was not only full of what he termed "discerning diners" but was catering to two private functions that night. It turned out the obviously discerning party of ten at the corner table by the window across the way from ours was hosted by the Baroness Nadine Rothschild, in town to promote her Lafite and Mouton wines. The sommelier treated us to a rather nice taste of one of their leftovers.

For 2000, Frank was preparing to open **Sel de la Terre,** a 150-seat Provence-style restaurant at 255 State Street, in partnership with his sous chef, Geoff Gardner. He designed it to be a more accessible establishment with café, bar, retail bakery and takeout, located in the busy downtown area between Faneuil Hall and the waterfront. "Simple, gutsy" food at moderate prices was the goal. Frank said he was looking forward to being involved in the "new focal point of the city," where more people could get a taste of the best of Boston.

(617) 262-3023. Prix-fixe, $65. Dinner by reservation, Monday-Saturday 6 to 10.

Radius, 8 High St.

Boston's culinary sensation du moment – at least until the next superstar comes along – is this chic restaurant destined for greatness. Ex-New York chef Michael Schlow left the tiny Café Louis in a fashionable Back Bay clothing store for a big ticket at the edge of the Financial District.

Radius takes its straightforward geometric name from a large, circular dining room that once housed a bank. This is one restaurant that's designed rather than decorated. "We tried to create Boston's first fully conceptualized modern restaurant," said co-owner/manager Christopher Myers. That translates, apparently, to a lack of signage on the exterior and a stark, minimalist interior of curves within curves in shades of charcoal gray and poppy red. Precise rectangular cuts of dentil molding ornament the lofty white ceiling. Comfortable upholstered chairs and banquettes seat 90 at nicely spaced tables dressed with double sets of thick white linens and topped at our autumn visit with bud vases holding rare Chinese orchids. Eighteen solo diners can join a raised communal table for an overview.

Expert service is provided by an army of staff in loose-fitting gray designer suits with white T-shirts that look like something your mod kids might wear.

The much-honored chef is known for seasonally driven menus that substitute reductions, juices, oils and emulsions for the butters and creams of classic French fare. Good, crusty rolls were doled out one at a time during a leisurely meal that proved this to be a midday destination rather than a mere lunch break. (How could it be otherwise when the tab for two soared to $74 before tax, tip and parking?)

True, we splurged on the most expensive of appetizers: halibut tartare and fingerling potato tart with ossetra caviar and "three-minute egg sauce." Very unusual, it was an exquisite blend of tastes and textures for a cool $16. Main courses, priced at similar levels, were a superior spice-crusted tender duck confit with tarbias bean cassoulet, carrots and red wine sauce, and a great-sounding Australian farm-raised loin of lamb salad with mesclun, goat cheese and baby beets. The sliced lamb was perfect, though not as abundant as the mesclun. We filled up on rolls and a shared dessert of lemon chamomile cake, served with blueberries, crème fraîche ice cream and honey-thyme syrup.

Designer-modern dining room is feature of Radius.

At night, the noise level rises with the prices. Serious diners join the beautiful people in partaking of an extravagant repertoire on the cusp of pretense. The appetizer terminology gives a hint: a French butter pear and Pierre Robert terrine with lacquered quail, walnut dust and port syrup; and tender escargot, prosciutto and swiss chard tortellini with late summer vegetables, garlic crème and parsley sauce. Main courses sound simpler but turn out sublime: roasted black grouper with manilla clams and saffron sauce, crispy lemon chicken with black olives and roasted peppers, and Vermont pheasant suffused with foie gras.

Boston's best pastry chef, Paul Connors, has collaborated with Michael since their New York days. Here his signature Tahitian vanilla crème brûlée might be upstaged by his "black and tan" – bittersweet chocolate with caramel mousse, cappuccino ice cream and glazed bananas.

Radius also offers a six-course tasting menu for $85 and a nine-course "grande luxe" tasting menu for $125. Wine tastings, matched with each course, add $40 and $75 respectively. The prices of the 200-plus wines, incidentally, are tilted toward those who are inclined to spend more for beverage than food.

(617) 426-1234. Entrées, $23 to $42. Lunch, Monday-Friday 11:30 to 2:30. Dinner, Monday-Saturday 5:30 to 10 or 11.

Mistral, 223 Columbus Ave.

The other brightly shining star in Boston's current culinary constellation is the new venture of chef Jamie Mammano, who elevated Aujourd'hui at the Four Seasons Hotel to five-diamond status. Here he's backed by nightclub impresario Seth Greenberg and developer Paul Roiff, who spared no expense in providing cutting-edge cachet.

The facade of the restored black building looming above the Massachusetts Turnpike is unobtrusive, marked only by its name spelled out in wrought-iron in the window above the door. Inside is a drop-dead beautiful, tasteful space sectioned

Chef Jamie Mammano relaxes in dining room at Mistral.

into lounge, bar, bistro and dining area seating 200. Twelve-foot-high arched windows on three sides shed light on sandstone walls and slate floors. Shaded curling wrought-iron chandeliers are suspended from the sixteen-foot-high ceilings. Green rattan chairs are at angled tables in the front section of the room accented with pillars and plants. Yellow-print fabric banquettes flank the perimeter. Named for the winds that sweep through the South of France, the décor is Beaux Arts elegant rather than Provençal cute. Intriguing details everywhere catch the eye, not the last of which is a broad lineup of sawed-off branches inexplicably standing upright above the stone-topped bar.

While his partners provided wall-to-wall buzz, chef Jamie simplified and made accessible his French-Mediterranean fare that commanded top dollar at Aujourd'hui. It's a shrewd move, one applauded by the more sanguine of his peers and guaranteed to keep the place packed well into the new millennium. The menu is short and spans a broad price range.

Two signature starters at either end of the spectrum illustrate. The "cheapie" is the portobello mushroom "carpaccio." Roasted red peppers, baby arugula and marinated raisins frame thin slices of grilled portobello drizzled with balsamic vinaigrette, a counterpoint of tastes from tart to sour to sweet. The splurge is for foie gras, a substantial slice of goose liver served atop a hollowed-out brioche filled with warm confit of duck, complimented by a tart sauce of dried cherries. Other recommended starters are tuna tartare with crispy wontons and ginger, Dungeness crab ravioli and any of the grilled thin-crust pizzas. (With a side salad, these can make a satisfying meal for the price-conscious.)

Main courses range from grilled salmon with rosemary-cider crème fraîche to rack of lamb presented as a small sculpture, four ample chops soaring skyward beside a gratin of celery root and a side of pepper caramel squash. Portions are substantial and the accompaniments enticing. Straightforward braised beef shortribs might come with roasted garlic mash and sweet vidalia crisps, and a skillet-roasted veal chop with gorgonzola polenta and fried green tomatoes. The primarily French and American wine offerings are as extensive as they are expensive. The reserve wine list raises the bar from the high double digits well into three and four figures.

Desserts present a difficult choice, from a warm chocolate torte with vanilla sauce to a caramelized pear upside-down cake with candied ginger ice cream. The "mini dessert assiette" for two simplifies the problem. It yields a themed sampling of the night's offerings in small clay pots perfect for passing.

(617) 867-9300. Entrées, $18 to $40. Dinner nightly, 5:30 to 11, later in bistro.

Hamersley's Bistro, 553 Tremont St.
Anticipating the trend to downscaled food and prices, this bistro was an instant hit when it opened in 1987 in the South End. Then it relocated to larger quarters nearby, upscaling the food and prices along the way. It remains a big player on the Boston scene, without so much as a press agent or a media kit. Instead, it offers a welcoming and chatty web site appealing directly to the customer.

That's to be expected from this amiable, with-it, 120-seat place. It's run very personally by two redheads, Gordon Hamersley, once apprentice to Wolfgang Puck at Ma Maison in Los Angeles and then executive sous chef to Lydia Shire at Seasons, and his English-born wife Fiona, former New England director of the American Institute of Wine and Food. Gordon and his assistants wear red baseball caps in the open kitchen along the side of the long, buttercup yellow dining room (the ceiling at his former place was too low for a white toque, he explained). The bobbing baseball caps came to symbolize a refreshing lack of pretense that pays dividends in durability.

The Hamersleys envision theirs as an elegant Boston translation of the homey, family-run country bistros of France. Rough wooden ceiling beams salvaged from a Connecticut barn are counterpoints to French floral tapestries. In typical bistro style, large squares of white paper are clipped over the tablecloths, the silverware is rolled inside white napkins, bottles of S. Pellegrino water serve as centerpieces, track lights provide illumination and the noise level is high enough that you can't really overhear the couple at the next table. Fiona presides at the bar, which is part of a cafe that offers both a bistro and the full menu. Outdoor dining is available on a section of the brick patio beside the Boston Center for the Arts.

"We serve high-quality food stripped down to the basics," Gordon says. "Rustic, peasant food" is what he calls it. We call it gutsy.

Our dinner began memorably with the signature grilled mushroom and garlic "sandwich" on country bread, not really a sandwich but two toasted bread slices flanking an abundance of mushrooms and watercress, and a tasty but messy whole braised artichoke stuffed with olives and mint.

Among main courses, we loved the duckling with turnips, endive and apple slices – an enormous portion, including an entire leg and crisp slices of breast grilled and blackened at the edges like a good sirloin steak – and a Moroccan lamb stew with couscous and harissa that everybody raves about. The basic roast chicken with garlic, lemon and parsley is a standout. But that's for the timid. More exciting are the haddock wrapped in crisp potato leaves with a stew of mussels, garlic and watercress; the pan-roasted lobster with pears, ginger and

Asian greens, the slow-roasted and grilled organic Vermont pig with onions, apples, red cabbage and calvados; the fall gamebird mixed grill of quail, grouse and duck with a crêpe filled with wild rice, walnuts and quince. Those aren't concoctions you readily prepare at home.

Ever experimenting at the edge, Gordon offered a three-course autumn mushroom tasting menu ($49) at our latest visit. An appetizer of braised wild mushrooms with polenta and asiago cheese was followed by a cream of black trumpet soup with white truffle oil. The main dish was a complex salmi of guinea hen with golden chanterelles and foie gras sauce.

The wine list, like the menu, changes with the seasons. Fiona seeks out the unique among wines from around the world and there was scarcely a vintner we recognized. Symbols distinguished the type of grape for the uninitiated.

Desserts have been elevated lately. Typical are a sticky date and toffee cake with toasted pecans and caramel, a warm brioche with blue cheese, grilled figs and port sabayon, and souffléd lemon custard, a menu fixture. Gordon is partial to the apple tarte tatin with thyme-infused buttermilk ice cream. We still remember the trilogy of sorbets – brandied pear, green melon and concord grape – served with biscotti, a refreshing end to a memorable meal.

(617) 423-2700. Entrées, $23 to $38. Dinner, Monday-Friday 6 to 10, Saturday 5:30 to 10:30, Sunday 5:30 to 9:30.

No. 9 Park, 9 Park St.

A distinguished looking gentleman was polishing the silver door pull shaped in the form of a nine at the front entry as we arrived for lunch. He turned out to be the husband of the chef, Barbara Lynch. Although he has his own business, he shows up at mealtime to keep things polished in one of Boston's most au courant restaurants.

His wife, who grew up in South Boston, is happiest in the kitchen, which is out of sight in an era when others are open to the dining arena. Cooking her way through the top restaurants in Boston and Cambridge, she emerged as one of Food & Wine magazine's top new chefs while executive chef at Galleria Italiana. In 1998, she moved a few blocks up Tremont Street to a Beacon Hill brownstone, facing the Boston Common across from the State House. She named it for its address.

A quick winner of Best of Boston honors, this was designed to evoke a European bistro atmosphere. It's unexpectedly small, with a 30-seat café around the bar and two intimate dining rooms seating a total of 65. The main room in the rear, an austere affair with mahogany wainscoting and a montage of black and white photos of the Boston Common, is notable for its lack of windows – in contrast to the side dining room in front with big wraparound windows onto the Common. Actually, you don't notice the muted decor. It blends into the background as the food moves into the foreground.

Barbara is known for robust yet refined country European fare. She delivered it at our autumn lunch, which began with an amusé, a demitasse cup of the day's chestnut bisque – delicate, studded with wild mushrooms and surprisingly good. One of us ordered the three-course, prix-fixe meal for $24. It yielded a perfect bibb salad, a plate of lamb ravioli with an ethereal white bean ragoût (these earthy beans never before received such refined treatment) and a rich chocolate-hazelnut terrine with espresso anglaise. The other ordered the chilled lobster salad, which arrived squashed in a cylinder shape in the center of a large plate. What appeared to be red caviar atop layers of lobster, mache, watercress and golden potato brunoise turned out to be the tiniest bits of red tomato. The layered effect was deceptive, the salad proving to be far larger than it looked. After espresso, the bill

came with a china box holding macaroons.

The lunch menu lacked the chef's signature dishes, which are offered for dinner. Don't miss her crispy duck, served any number of ways but at our visit with a cider reduction, alsatian cabbage and a quince confit. Otherwise go for the grilled arctic char with chanterelles and citrus beurre blanc or the ballotine of pheasant with chestnut cream, We've heard raves for the rabbit three ways – seared loin, baked rack and braised leg, each with its own accompaniment of parsnip-potato purée, porcini flan and lentils.

Chef-owner Barbara Lynch in dining room at No. 9 Park.

The pasta sampler is a favorite starter for two to six. But then you'd miss the belon oysters au gratin with ossetra caviar, the foie gras roulade on brioche toast and the parmigiano-reggiano soufflé.

The pastry chef is known for her bread pudding served with brandied figs and caramel sauce. Black mission figs five ways yields stewed and roasted figs, fig tart, sorbet and strudel. Or you might try the lemon vacherin, the hazelnut bombe, the trio of glacés or the selection of artisan cheeses.

The wine list here is extraordinary, which is predictable given its creation by wine expert Cat Silirie, a friend who was rated Boston's top sommelier in a male-dominated profession. She and Barbara collaborated with a Santa Barbara County winery to create their own house wines labeled No. 9.

The café menu, served in the convivial bar area, offers bistro fare at its best.

(617) 742-9991. Entrées, $28 to $35; café, $11 to $19. Lunch, Monday-Friday 11:30 to 2:30. Dinner, Monday-Saturday 5:30 to 10.

Olives, 10 City Square, Charlestown.

Celebrated chef Todd English and his staff build three wood fires a day in the open kitchen of his much-loved restaurant at the foot of America's oldest main street, just across the Charles River from Boston. One fire is in the brick oven, a second is in the grill he designed himself and the third is for a rotisserie – all the better for his roasts and grills fired by such New England hardwoods as apple, oak and ash. And all the better for his stand-in-line clientele who appreciate robust cooking and spirited surroundings.

Olives has come a long way since it opened in 1989 in small quarters up the street. Todd and wife Olivia, both Culinary Institute of America grads, kept the original space and rechristened it **Figs,** a cafe/pizzeria, now with offshoots in Beacon Hill (42 Charles St.), Wellesley and Chestnut Hill. Though the family lives in Brookline, Todd has become a national player. His culinary stage now includes restaurants in Westport, Conn., Washington, D.C., Las Vegas (two) and even Israel. He's written two cookbooks and launched his own frozen line of "Todd's Real Pasta."

Back home, the new Olives is upscale in price and setting, and takes no reservations. Lines start forming at 4:30 and the 110 seats are filled most nights before 6.

Once inside the noisy, high-ceilinged space with walls of brick and tall windows on two sides, you'll find a mix of plush and rustic. Upholstered banquettes and booths are situated side-by-side with bentwood chairs at bare wood tables. Lights in the form of stars hang over the bar, which is separated from the dining room by a divider with arched windows. Most of the color comes from the crowd and the activity in the huge open kitchen at the rear.

Diners munch on marinated olives and crusty focaccia as they watch Todd's crew whip up starters like big-eye tuna tartare served over a spun asparagus salad with crispy oysters and whipped hummus, a wood-oven fired porcini tart with seared foie gras and toasted fennel cream, and a spring artichoke waffle with crispy artichoke ragoût, whipped goat cheese and shaved black truffles. Pastas come in three sizes and in such unusual combinations as shrimp agnolotti on a roasted asparagus hash and bucatini with sea urchins and lobster tossed with hot cherry peppers.

The chef, known for the robust flavors of Italy where he did most of his training, has mellowed a bit from the time when he said "I couldn't see myself doing all that nouvelle, prissy stuff. It just wasn't lusty and full-bodied enough."

Now many of his entrées, still hearty and abundant in portion, have been prissied up. Irish salmon fillet is oven-steamed with wild mushrooms, truffle essence and stewed fiddlehead ferns. Golden trout is layered with prosciutto and sage on charred asparagus and fingerling potatoes and called trout saltimbocca. The spit-roasted ribeye of pork rests on a "pot roast" of black beans with chorizo, creamy honeyed semolina polenta and mustard-almond romesco. The veal steak is braised in morel cream and served over a "moppin' cake" stuffed with peas, fava beans and pea tendrils.

Desserts are a high point: perhaps pumpkin-brioche pudding with pumpkin anglaise and poached cranberries, tiramisu crêpe soufflé with rum-raisin sauce and espresso glaze, or fried banana ravioli with banana flan gâteau.

This is not leisurely or intimate dining (the lights are bright and the music loud to discourage lingering). But there's no denying the food, which is the rage in Boston.

(617) 242-1999. Entrées, $19 to $29. Dinner, Monday-Friday 5:30 to 10:30, Saturday 5 to 10:30.

Biba, 272 Boylston St.
Lydia Shire, who established Seasons at the Bostonian Hotel as an early culinary landmark before launching the Four Seasons Hotel in Beverly Hills, returned in 1989 to open a restaurant of her own. It's one like no other, which is not surprising to those who know Lydia.

The two-story emporium in the tony Heritage on the Garden shopping/residential complex seats 50 in a main-floor bar serving tapas and such, and 150 in a colorful dining room up a curving staircase. The bar features a Winston Churchill-style

Chef-owner Lydia Shire at Biba.   Chef-owner Todd English at Olives.

smoking couch, a mural of chubby, well-fed people, a lineup of photos taken by Lydia on her various travels, and framed shopping bags from the late Biba, her favorite London store.

The Biba Food Hall upstairs is notable for a glassed-in wine cellar along the staircase, an open space with a tandoori oven, pale yellow walls, ceilings with patterns taken from Albanian carpets, warm woods and white-clothed tables covered with butcher paper and placed rather close together.

Lydia refutes those who classify her decor as Southwest. "If anything, it's Mediterranean in feeling," she counters. Her menu defies classification as well. It's categorized according to fish, meat, starch, legumina, offal and sweets, lately clarified with labels for "apps" and "mains." Full of surprises, it's hard to follow (and figure) but delightfully quirky, as in – we quote – an unusual yellow beet napoleon of lobster knuckles and crisped cod cheeks, and a salad of red chicory, roasted rare pigeon, ripe peach and black pepper. Or netted whitebait and bay scallops, crisp fried with vinegared cider aioli; venison steak charcoaled with spiced concord grape butter, and unusual salad of chestnut whipped potato in crisp potato shell, dark garden greens and grilled bacon...with or without. Without what, you might wonder. But you get the idea. Or do you? Executive chef Susan Regis, Lydia's longtime sidekick who now plays a more prominent role, seems to have toned down some of the menu rhetoric lately.

At a springtime lunch, we devoured the yummy onion, tandoori and French breads that preceded our entrées: chickpea and potato rolled in thin pasta with Moroccan tenderloin of lamb ($15) and citrus salmon with crackling skin and parsley cakes ($17). Artfully presented on rectangular white plates, each was an explosion of tastes. A bottle of Hogue fumé blanc from the Yakima Valley accompanied from an unusual, fairly priced wine list starting at $18 for a Canadian vidal. We finished a memorable meal with a terrific warm tarte tatin with cinnamon ice cream and a cassis and champagne sorbet with linzer cookies.

Dinnertime brings the ultimate grazing menu, as Biba ignores the rules regarding appetizers, entrées and such. Under fish, you might order a white pumpkin and oyster stew or wood-roasted lobster spiked with single-barrel bourbon and a spoon of speckled heart grits. Ditto for meat: horseradish gnocchi with oxtail ragoût or chestnut-crumbed lamb chop with sherry-braised shank and chestnut-floured crespelle of sheep's milk ricotta. Legumina items vary from a panna cotta with crisped kale leaves and chanterelles in a bowl of butternut squash soup flamed with grappa to a "simple salad of leaf greens, $10."

While food reviewers swoon and restaurateurs of our acquaintance think this is the most exciting eating in New England, mere mortals are not universally charmed. Some think it's awful for a restaurant to present a menu with three items listed as "offal." Others complain of a high decibel level and slow service. Although the early hype has long since passed, we found that the dining experience fully measures up to its billing. Biba's success spawned another Shire venture, **Pignoli,** an upscale Italian restaurant around the corner at 79 Park Plaza – same restaurant designer, same Lydia theme, with sidewalk seating in summer and a bakery for Biba breads, delectable desserts and takeout lunch. The lunch and dinner menus bear Lydia's touch, but the execution is left to chef Daniele Baliani, whose Italian-French background comes through strong and clear.

(617) 426-7878. Entrées, $27 to $45. Lunch, Monday-Friday 11:30 to 2:30, Sunday 11:30 to 3. Dinner nightly, 5:30 to 10 or 11; Sunday brunch, 11:30 to 3. Desserts and bar menu, nightly 5:30 to midnight.

Maison Robert, 45 School St.

As pace-setting as the pioneer of one of the first restaurant web sites and as traditional as its dover sole meunière, this bastion of French cuisine celebrated its 25th anniversary with a new chef and something of a new look. Jacky Robert, who helped his uncle open Boston's then most glamorous restaurant in 1971, returned after twenty years in San Francisco, where he was chef at Ernie's before opening the four-star Amelio's. Meanwhile, chef-proprietor Lucien Robert from Normandy and his wife Ann, the hostess of Norwegian descent, had evolved their restaurant with the times, particularly since daughter Andrée joined the operation in the early 1990s. "We've hung around long enough that French is back," noted Andrée. Her kitchen weathered the era when Italian cuisine dominated and now, with Jacky at the helm, is in the vanguard of French restaurants in the Northeast.

Always formal and to some a tad forbidding, this sizable operation on two floors of Boston's old City Hall has been lightened up in decor and cuisine lately.

The Empire-style Bonhomme Richard dining room with its lofty molded ceiling, three majestic crystal chandeliers, twenty-foot-long velvet draperies and warm peach-colored walls with rich butternut paneling is elegant and expensive. Ben's Cafe downstairs is less so. New silverware and Villeroy & Boch china dress its tables, the walls are hung with a revolving art show and the curtains have been removed to open the window wells to art of another sort: stunning displays of tulips in spring, geraniums and herbs in summer, mums and pumpkins in the fall, and evergreens in the winter.

The menus in both venues reflect the culinary flair and Asian accents of Jacky, whose wife is of Korean background. He oversees both kitchens, with help from Andrée downstairs. The upstairs dinner menu, still printed in French but with oversize English translations, bears little resemblance to the haute cuisine with classic sauces that prevailed when one of us dined regally here some 25 years ago as the guest of an entertaining businessman. Fans consider the hot-smoked (yes)

Jackie and Andrée Robert toast the future at Maison Robert.

Maine lobster the best in Boston. It turns up in a smoked lobster cream soup with a "salmon floating island" and in a signature entrée, cooked over applewood with corn and braised lettuce. Other appetizers include a crab cake with a core of cayenne-mango atop a caesar salad, parmesan soufflé in a pumpkin with a crab and sea urchin sauce, and clams and Virginia ham "baked in a large bone." Entrées could be salmon baked in parchment paper soaring like a sail above the plate and bearing pears and mango-walnut dressing, sautéed fillet of manta ray with cabbage confit and black rice, and ostrich marinated in pomegranate juice and roasted with a potato basket. Desserts run from traditional soufflés and flambéed crêpes to upside-down apple tart with cinnamon sabayon, and homemade sorbets in a giant cookie shell.

The fare is more earthy and bistro-like in **Ben's Cafe.** Dinner entrées range from calves liver with bacon and onions to grilled filet mignon with béarnaise sauce. Many of the nighttime items are available on an expanded lunch menu.

The 10,000-bottle wine cellar, strong on older vintages of Bordeaux back to 1959, holds some terrific values. The elegant bar does not have a television set because, the Roberts advise, "we believe in human contact – it's the place to go if you want to carry on a conversation."

Lately, Maison Robert has been offering monthly Scandinavian dinners, wife Ann's counterpart to Lucien's traditional monthly French table, which draws up to 75 people to speak French and enjoy a thoroughly French meal. Ever evolving and not afraid to change with the times, theirs is a restaurant with tradition and soul.

(617) 227-3370. Entrées, $23 to $32; Bens, $12 to $28. Lunch, Monday-Friday 11:30 to 2:30. Dinner, Monday-Saturday 5:30 to 10 or 10:30.

Café Louis, 234 Berkeley St.

For Bostonians whose favorite restaurant was Al Forno in Providence, this is a dream come true.

Johanne Killeen and George Germon took over the intimate café in the rear of the ultra-suave men's clothing store called Louis in 1998. They installed in the kitchen chef David Reynoso, a native of Mexico whom they had kept their eyes on since they had met while he was cooking in Chicago. He was restless at age 27 after opening a Disney restaurant in Florida and ready for their challenge. They collaborated on the menu – "it's half ours, half his," says Johanne, though the format and the section of Al Forno classics might testify otherwise. And the owners commute from Providence to keep an eye on things. They were hosting a wine-tasting at our visit, and George was staying on over the weekend to paint and redecorate to reopen with "an all-new look" on Monday.

The TLC lavished by the owners pays off in crowds who squeeze into the 48-seat café and a small bar. They cherish the signature grilled pizzas, the baked pastas, the roasted vegetables and the "grills and roasts," among them roasted monkfish with wild New England mushrooms, baby chicken roasted under a brick, and grilled brine-cured pork tenderloin with stewed legumes. Start with a crunchy fennel and radish salad with shaved parmigiano. Finish with the made-to-order desserts, perhaps one of the distinctive fruit tarts for two (the plum and anise beckoned at our fall visit), a coconut ice cream sandwich or the grand cookie finale.

Much the same fare is available at lunch, when shoppers take a break for the grilled pizza margarita, an apple and arugula salad or an open-faced egg salad and cured salmon sandwich with fennel. The innovative choices range from ten-vegetable stew with yellow pea purée to grilled salmon with eggplant caviar and "one thousand year old balsamic vinegar."

Here, unlike Al Forno, you can make reservations for dinner. And, big bonus, the store's parking lot is free, if you can find a spot.

(617) 266-4680. Entrées, $23 to $34. Lunch, Monday-Saturday 11:30 to 3. Dinner, Monday-Saturday 5:30 to 10.

Hotel Dining

More than in most cities, some of Boston's best eating takes place in its hotels. And many a local chef has launched or fine-tuned a career there before striking out on his or her own.

Aujourd'hui, Four Seasons Hotel, 200 Boylston St.
A window table at Aujourd'hui is a prospect on the finer things in Boston life, among them a view of the swan boats plying the pond of the Public Garden, and the cooking of world-class chefs.

The second-floor restaurant's setting is serene: floral-fabric banquettes, rich oak paneling, antique Royal Doulton china atop white damask cloths and floor-length skirts, nicely spaced tables, and a solicitous staff in subdued outfits that match the colors of the spacious, 124-seat room. A series of meals here attests to its status as the first five-diamond rated restaurant in New England.

At lunch when celebrated chef Jamie Mammano was at the helm, we loved the subtle tomato and fennel soup with toasted focaccia and the smoked duck pieces encased in tiny herbed rice pancakes with a sesame-flavored dipping sauce. Entrées were a tasty grilled pork tenderloin with plum-pepper marmalade and potato pancakes and a special of medallions of wild boar with pearl onions and madeira. The fruit tart that we'd admired in the enticing pastry display near the entry was perfection, filled with oversize blackberries, blueberries and strawberries in a pastry

Wiudow tables at Aujourd'hui overlook Boston Public Garden.

cream with a shortbread-like crust. The sorbet lover among us blissed out on the day's trio – pear, mixed berry and mango.

A recent dinner under executive chef Edward Gannon's tutelage was even more memorable (and showed Aujourd'hui hadn't missed a beat since Jamie Mammano left to open Mistral). A couple of tasting menus (the chef's six courses for $98, the four-course fall tasting for $76) gave the opportunity to sample the range of exceptional fare. Dinner begins, compliments of the chef, with an amusé like salmon mousse with black-pepper vodka and crème fraîche, and a bowl of six exotic breads (the most distinctive a profiterole filled with cheese). Appetizers were a parade of caramelized diver scallops with calypso bean lobster ragoût, hamachi with spicy tuna tartare and oven-roasted beets, and an unforgettable, thick slice of seared foie gras with a duck confit spring roll and sour cherry compote. Fish courses were succulent baked arctic char with vegetable relish and seared ahi tuna with pickled eggplant, their multiple accompaniments creating bursts of flavors. One main dish was perfectly roasted aged beef sirloin with peppercorn sauce, ragoût of chanterelles, a potato nest, leeks and pearl onions. The other was tender lamb noisettes with black olives, preserved lemon and Moroccan spices, haricots verts and baby garbanzo beans. A trio of cheeses paved the way for dessert. One was crème brûlée, fancifully decorated with spun sugar. The other was a platter of tea-scented panna cotta, lemon tart and warm chocolate cake with liquid milk chocolate truffle. A tray of "les mignardises" ended a truly superb meal.

The regular menu is enticing (how about roasted Maine lobster with crabmeat wontons, pineapple compote and fenugreek broth)? A number of selections designate reduced levels of calories, cholesterol, sodium and fat. A four-course vegetarian dinner is available for $52.

The wine list, one of Boston's best, includes a full page of wines by the glass and two pages of domestic chardonnays. We've found a couple of good, better than usual low-end sauvignon blancs, a merlot and a pinot noir in the $40 range. *(617) 338-4400. Entrées, $33 to $45. Lunch, Monday-Friday 11:30 to 2:30. Dinner nightly, 5:30 to 10:30. Sunday brunch, 10 to 2.*

Rowes Wharf Restaurant, Boston Harbor Hotel, 70 Rowes Wharf.

Since 1990, the Boston Harbor Hotel has garnered national attention for its annual Boston Wine Festival, fifteen weeks of wine tastings, dinners, seminars and other events involving many of the world's leading winemakers. A principal reason is the distinguished food offered by executive chef Daniel Bruce in the hotel's harborfront dining room.

Boston's longest-lasting celebrity hotel chef, Dan is an innovator in New England cuisine and a promoter of healthier dining (he spearheaded the first "Food and Wine for Life" conference at the hotel in 1996). His menus change daily, although red flannel hash (a Boston mainstay of beef, beets and potatoes) is offered for breakfast year-round.

He forages for the fungi that turn up in a signature appetizer of wild mushrooms over stone-ground cornmeal polenta. Other starters at dinner could be maple-smoked salmon with potato cake and caviar, Maine lobster sausage over lemon pasta, and pepper-crusted Long Island duck breast with mushroom risotto and sautéed spinach. Typical entrées are pan-seared striped black bass with New Zealand cockle clams, fricassee of lobster and chorizo, and cabernet-marinated venison loin with dried cranberries.

A five-course wine-pairing menu showcases the best of the evening as offered during the Boston Wine Festival. For $75, you get five glasses of appropriate wines to go with the likes of sea scallops in a coconut-ginger nage, sautéed sea bream with macomber turnips and black trumpet mushrooms, slow-roasted moulard duck with foie gras, a compote of cheeses and baby dandelion greens, and a warm vanilla almond cake with honey kumquat sauce and cinnamon ice cream.

For a winter lunch, we began with the caramelized sweet onion soup with New Hampshire cheese croustade and the crab, salmon and cod cakes with celery root rémoulade. A salad of grilled sea scallops over baby spinach, red onions and hickory-smoked bacon and the grilled duck breast with braised red cabbage and currants made fine main dishes. A chocolate-chestnut dacquoise and the trilogy of raspberry, mango and blackberry sorbets were grand endings.

The setting is masculine and clubby with dark mahogany walls, recessed lighting in the ceiling, and a deep blue decor from chairs to vases to carpeting. About 250 people can be seated in a variety of rooms, all with at least a glimpse of the water. A seasonal outdoor cafe serves lunch and dinner overlooking the harbor. The Sunday brunch is considered one of the city's best.

(617) 439-3995. Entrées, $28 to $38. Lunch, Monday-Saturday 11:30 to 2:30. Dinner, 5:30 to 10 or 11. Sunday, brunch 10:30 to 2, dinner 5 to 9.

Julien, Hotel Meridien, 250 Franklin St.

The setting is historic: the former Members Court of the stately Federal Reserve Building built in 1922, across from the site of Boston's first French restaurant, opened in 1793 by French-émigré Jean-Baptiste Julien. But its spirit is ephemeral – sometimes classic, sometimes contemporary, depending on the succession of chefs who seem to come and go with increasing frequency. Julian was in the midst of a soar in 1999 under Alain Rayé, who had left Michelin-starred restaurants in Paris to move to Boston and was gone within the year. Executive chef at our subsequent visit was Mark Sapienza, the first non-French chef in memory at a classic that begs for ineffably French cuisine in the Meridien tradition.

Some of Boston's most distinguished food is served in this palatial room with towering gilded ceiling, five crystal chandeliers and lattice work on the walls with lights behind. Mushroom velour banquettes or Queen Anne wing chairs flank tables set with heavy silverware, monogrammed china, tiny shaded brass lamps and Peruvian lilies.

Dinner begins with a complimentary hors d'oeuvre – a small vegetable quiche at our visit. If you're not up to an appetizer like juniper-rubbed venison carpaccio or pan-seared foie gras with szechuan peppercorns, splurge on one of the masterful soups, perhaps jonah crab with green onion beignets.

A recent menu was downscaled from the dazzling heights of those we sampled over the years, adding Italian components like wild mushroom and swiss chard cannelloni with parma ham and porcini foam. The five-spice roast magret of duck with steamed dumplings and bok choy bespoke of Asia. Roast monkfish in crepinette with braised cabbage and french green lentils and braised veal persillade with petit white beans and tomato and green olive cassoulet upheld the French tradition. We'll never forget our earlier lobster ravioli, the lobster reconstructed from its head and tail, the body made from ravioli filled with lobster mousse, the legs and feelers represented by green beans and asparagus or snow peas, and the whole topped with tomatoes and truffles – presentation personified.

Among pastry chef Christophe Feyt's desserts are caramelized cinnamon apple tower with caramel ice cream, banana crème brûlée flambéed with rum, and a chocolate trilogy of white chocolate ice cream, milk chocolate mousse and dark chocolate cherry cake. The bill is sweetened with a plate of homemade candies and cookies.

Although offering an impressive variety of French wines that helped win Wine Spectator's Best of Award of Excellence, the sommelier also recommends a number of Californias.

The formal atmosphere and service are lightened by piano music in the adjacent Julien bar, the bank's former counting room, where two original N.C. Wyeth murals embellish the paneled walls.

(617) 451-1900. Entrées, $26 to $36. Lunch, Monday-Friday noon to 2. Dinner nightly, 6 to 10:30 or 11.

Clío, 370A Commonwealth Ave.

This is the dining room for the upscaled Eliot Suite Hotel, which is why it serves breakfast in such stylish surroundings. At night, it turns into what chef-owner Kenneth Oringer likens to a Parisian supper club, which offers some of the best food in town. Serene in white and taupe, it seats 60 at curved and square banquettes or on chairs topped with patterned fabric backs in the hotel style. Floor lamps convey the look of a living room salon, quite in contrast to the sunken lounge on the other side of the bar at the entry.

It's a comfortable setting for serious eating in the contemporary French-American idiom. The chef started cooking for his family in Paramus, N.J., making stocks and sauces from scratch at age 10. Voted most likely to succeed in his class at the Culinary Institute of America, he worked first at Brooklyn's River Café and then at Al Forno in Providence, where he became known for his pastries. Culinary stints in Connecticut, San Francisco and the Boston suburb of Hingham prepared him for his own venture, which opened in 1997 to national as well as local acclaim.

He's known for exotic starters, perhaps Jerusalem artichoke soup with pork and russet apples, a seviche of abalone, bay scallops and lobster with grapefruit and mint, or hamachi tartare with beets, caviar and baby leeks. His foie gras steak is roasted to a melt-in-the-mouth tenderness, its sweet and sour glazed richness at once soothed with spiced apple and heightened with szechuan pepper.

Main courses vary from crisped skate with beurre noisette and caramelized swordfish au poivre to roasted organic rack of pork with sage and juniper, and roasted wild Scottish venison with forest mushrooms. The Maine lobster is basted in sweet butter and served partially out of its shell with carrot-clove emulsion, lemon balm and sweet-pea purée.

Desserts are generally light and refreshing: frozen lemon verbena soufflé with hot chocolate mousse, chilled concord grape soup with vanilla bean ice cream and ginger lace tuile, a vanilla bean panna cotta with sassafras sorbet and root-beer float. A must-try is the "flight" of ice creams and sorbets, showcasing six distinctive tastes.

Everything is rather pricey, including the French-American wine list. It starts at $35 for a muscadet and goes to $200.

(617) 536-7200. Entrées, $24 to $36. Dinner nightly, 5:30 to 10.

Anago, 65 Exeter St.

From a small but precocious start in an industrial building in Cambridge, the former Anago Bistro has gone big-time. Not that it didn't have the credentials. Owner Bob Calderone cooked for Bruce Frankel for nine years at the restaurant we loved as Panache. When Bruce "retired" (way too early) in 1992, his chef took over, gave it the name of an Italian aunt whose cooking secrets inspired him, and won a ranking by Bon Appétit magazine as one of the nation's top new restaurants, an honor earlier accorded Panache. In 1997, Anago dropped the bistro from its name and tripled its size with a move into Boston's renovated Lenox Hotel. Here it became one of Esquire magazine's best new restaurants of 1998. Not bad for a young man who started flipping burgers at McDonalds. As they say, you've got to keep moving to stay in the forefront.

With his wife Susan Finegold as hostess, the new Anago is a pleasant, elegant space in the Beaux Arts style. Subdued lighting from sconces and chandeliers illuminate tall arched windows, mauve walls, mauve banquettes and dark blue chairs beneath a vaulted fifteen-foot ceiling. At the far end is a partially open kitchen with a custom-built wood-burning oven, wood grill and rotisserie.

Tables are nicely spaced for enjoyment of the straightforward, Mediterranean-inspired dishes for which Anago is known. Boston's ubiquitous autumn foie gras is served in the form of a terrine, with dried cherries, apple, toasted pecans and brioche. Other starters are tuna tartare with wasabi aioli and tobiko, grilled Vermont quail with sausage polenta, huckleberry syrup and mache, and an antipasto platter of roasted pear, prosciutto, olives, roasted red peppers and buffalo mozzarella.

Anago's main dishes are comforting and pleasantly priced. Typical are grilled halibut steak with saffron aioli, grilled beef sirloin with red wine sauce and lamb loin with red pepper-dijon mustard sauce. In these days of fancy terminology, the duck entrée on the menu here is described as "roast Long Island duck, mixed grain pilaf, fruit chutney, orange sauce, nuts." As one reviewer noted, "good grub, prepared with gusto, sets Anago apart."

Pastry chef Lee Napoli's dessert menu turns exotic. The choices might be a trio of soufflés, warm chocolate poblano tarts with chocolate pots du crème and honey vanilla ice cream, a roasted fig gratin with crispy goat cheese and port sorbet, and a bento box of fruit, cookies and chocolates for two.

(617) 266-6222. Entrées, $18 to $35. Dinner, Monday-Saturday 5:30 to 10 or 10:30. Sunday, jazz brunch, 11 to 2, dinner 5 to 9.

Seasons, The Bostonian Hotel, 4 Faneuil Hall Marketplace.

This is the culinary heart of the Bostonian Hotel, its curved, windowed dining room on the fourth floor looking out over Quincy Market. Part of the ceiling is stainless steel and part glass, and a billowing fabric canopy affair moves back and forth electrically, depending on sunshine and temperatures.

Generally well-spaced tables seat 125 on several tiers to take full advantage of the view. Gold-rimmed service plates, heavy cutlery and a pristine freesia in a bud vase on each table add to the feeling of warm, contemporary elegance. Service is by an army of fresh-faced, tuxedoed waiters.

The food has been ranked among Boston's best since noted chef Jasper White helped open Seasons in the mid-1980s. Locally high-profile successors including Lydia Shire, Gordon Hamersley, Jody Adams, Tony Ambrose and Bill Poirier maintained the concept and a menu that changes with the seasons.

At our stay, an appetizer of smoked fish – red sturgeon with scallops and salmon in a horseradish-champagne vinaigrette, with a side presentation of cucumbers, watercress and capers – was superb, as was the smooth lobster and sweet-corn chowder. Current chef Brian Houlihan added starters like pan-seared Maine crab cakes with a roasted pepper tartare, shiitake-stuffed Vermont quail with truffled greens and duck confit salad with soy-dressed Asian vegetables and greens.

Main courses include seared Atlantic salmon atop a shellfish risotto and lobster nage, pancetta-wrapped veal tenderloin with a white bean and artichoke ragoût and pumpkin-seed-crusted rack of lamb with rosemary and sweet-potato purée. We liked the signature roast duckling with ginger and scallions, surrounded by Chinese vegetables, and grilled red snapper with thin jonnycakes and mustard greens.

An array of sorbets – papaya, pear, apple and raspberry – was most refreshing. The sweet potato cheesecake and sekel pear and camembert tart also tempted. Cappuccino and decaf coffee were served in silver pots. The not unreasonable bill arrived with chocolate truffles and a macadamia-nut pastry on a doily.

The choice all-American wine list is enormous, with no fewer than 58 California cabernet sauvignons priced from $23 to $205.

(617) 523-4119. Entrées, $31 to $42. Lunch, Monday-Friday 11:30 to 2. Dinner nightly, 6 to 10 or 11.

More Dining Choices

Icarus, 3 Appleton St.

A statue of the mythological Icarus, poised for flight, looms above tree branches lit with tiny white lights high on the rear wall of this comforting restaurant. It oversees a sunken, split-level room full of rich dark wood and a mix of booths and round mission oak tables. The tables are left bare except for dusky pink napkins folded sideways between fluted silverware. Recessed aqua lighting outlines the perimeter of the ceiling.

It's an altogether pleasant, clubby backdrop for the fare of longtime chef Chris Douglass, whose low public profile masks his standing as one of the best in town. His menu, brief and thankfully unpretentious, is the equal of any in the city. It also has held the line on the price inflation that has afflicted many of its peers.

Seasonal New England ingredients take precedence in such autumn entrées as pan-roasted lobster with pumpkin, chestnuts and bourbon, and monkfish bourride, a Mediterranean fish soup bearing leeks, beans, Wellfleet littleneck clams and saffron aioli. Other choices could be brook trout topped with crab and chanterelle-herb sauce, paella with saffron and handmade chorizo, seared duck breast and confit with quince preserves, and farm-raised veal chop with black trumpet mushrooms and celery root. .

Appetizers span the globe: grilled shrimp with mango and jalapeño sorbet, pizzetta with duck confit, roasted pear and gorgonzola, and dark and spicy turkey mole over a chile tortilla quesadilla. The soup could be pumpkin, fontina and truffle, and the salad goat cheese with beets, arugula and grilled flatbread.

Save room for dessert, perhaps profiteroles filled with chocolate ice cream drizzled with caramel sauce or warm apple tart with dried apricots, toasted pinenuts and vanilla bean ice cream. The ginger ice cream sandwich with a whole roasted peach and blackberry-ginger sauce is to die for.

(617) 426-1790. Entrées, $21 to $32. Dinner, Monday-Friday 6 to 10, Saturday 5:30 to 10:30, Sunday 5:30 to 9:30.

Lala Rokh, 97 Mt. Vernon St.

Home-style Persian cuisine is offered up by Azita Bina-Seibel and her brother Babak Bina at the only eastern Mediterranean restaurant of its kind in New England. The pair also ran Azita, a Tuscan charmer at 560 Tremont St. in the South End, where we had a memorable lunch a few years back. They sold that space because Azita feels more at home with the food of her native Azerbaijan, which she considers every bit as sophisticated as that of Tuscany.

Ensconced in the former quarters of our late favorite Another Season, the two cozy dining rooms in a Beacon Hill townhouse have been redone country style in mustard yellow and burgundy. The family's notable collection of early Persian memorabilia – framed photographs, antique maps and calligraphy dating to the ninth century – adorn the walls. Classical Persian music plays in the background.

It's a subdued setting for food that is anything but subdued. Although unfamiliar in terminology and combinations of ingredients, it's aromatic, heavily spiced and ever so good. The waitstaff can steer you to a succession of mix-and-match appetizers, entrées and side dishes that make for novel taste sensations. The breadth of the offerings defies description. Eggplant, a staple of the cuisine, appears in several appetizers, one of the best being kashk-e-bademjan, a warm dip of roasted eggplant, caramelized onions and goat's milk yogurt, to stand alone or be spread on the complimentary sesame-topped bread.

Main courses are categorized by cooking style and yield flavorful combinations mainly of chicken, beef, lamb and veal with basmati rice. Diners are encouraged to complement them with mazze (side dishes) and torshi (pickled chutneys and relishes). Particularly tempting are abgusht (lamb shank in spiced broth with string beans, chickpeas, okra and eggplant) and joojeh (a kabob of grilled chicken breast marinated in saffron, lemon and onions and served with saffron-perfumed basmati rice). A short, wide-ranging wine list is modestly priced.

Desserts are as exotic as the rest of the fare. You might try ranghinak, squares of layered dates stuffed with walnuts and dusted with pistachio, or Persian ice cream scented with saffron and rose water and studded with chunks of frozen cream.

Lala Rokh (pronounced la-la-roke) is the name of a fictional Persian princess seduced by a storytelling suitor in the epic poem of the same name by 19th-century Irish poet Thomas Moore (a slightly faded copy of the work is displayed near the entrance). The spell of the food and the ambiance here will likely seduce you, too.

(617) 720-5511. Entrées, $13 to $17. Dinner nightly, 5:30 to 10.

The Cafe Budapest, 90 Exeter St.

The late Edith Ban, a Hungarian who came to Boston after the 1956 uprising and who was the grande dame of Boston restaurateurs, had a reputation for imperiousness, one no doubt enhanced by her commanding presence always garbed completely in white. So we were stunned after staggering through a January blizzard back in the '70s for a 1 p.m. lunch reservation to learn that Mrs. Ban had decreed that the first patrons of the day were to be her guests, and that we were they.

Many are the times since that we and friends have dined in regal splendor in our favorite oak-paneled dining room, all red and white with old Hungarian flasks, walking sticks, wine jugs and decorative plates on the walls. The tradition has been maintained by Mrs. Ban's sister, Dr. Hedda Rev-Kury, who practices medicine by day and restaurateuring at night.

Our first memorable lunch began with a hearty peasant soup topped with fried noodles and exquisite chicken paprikas crêpes. It continued with gypsy baron rice pilaf and the authentic beef goulash that an Austrian friend who manages a fine hotel thinks is the best anywhere. The finale was a sensational Hungarian strudel, accompanied by fragrant Viennese coffee, made from beans ground fresh hourly and served in glass cups.

Meals here are fit for royalty, and the setting is so old-world romantic that you'd almost expect to see Zsa Zsa Gabor dallying with an admirer in one of the intimate alcoves off the lounge (actually, she has dined here, on chicken paprika, we're told). At night, when things get busy and up to 500 meals may be served, the Hungarian menu carries French accents. For appetizers, you can get the great chicken paprikas crêpe, or you can try Hungarian goose liver with truffles or caviar à la russe.

Most of the 26 entrées are Middle European and seldom change, for the clock here has stopped in, say, the Europe of the fifties. Sweetbreads à la hongroise under glass, veal gulyas and wiener schnitzel vie for attention with broiled lemon sole and châteaubriand with mimosa salad. Each comes with different vegetables and salads. One night, three in our party declared spectacular the veal served with rice, string beans and carrots tied in a bundle, and a special salad of grapes and endive arranged like a star. Desserts like a champagne torte, apple strudel and crêpes suzette bring back the old days.

If you're of a certain age and have any romance in your soul, you'll love Cafe

Budapest – particularly the small pink dining room with pink chairs off the lounge, almost too pretty for words, and the Empire-style lounge where, ensconced in gilt and brocade chairs, you can have dessert crêpes flambéed tableside while a pianist and a violinist entertain nearby.

(617) 734-3388. Entrées, $19.50 to $33. Lunch, Monday-Saturday noon to 3. Dinner, 5 to 10:30 or 11:30, Sunday 1 to 10:30.

South End Values

Not every good eating spot in Boston caters to high rollers and beautiful people, who often seem to be one and the same. Hamersley's Bistro blazed the trail into Boston's close-in South End, ever since the foodies' hot spot. Others have followed. Three outstanding newcomers offer good vibes and quality food that won't set you back a day's pay or two. Indeed, these are where hip young Bostonians like to eat – and do, regularly.

Aquitaine, 569 Tremont St.

Across trendy Tremont Street from each other are two wildly popular restaurants owned by a husband and wife cooking team who have been likened to George Germon and Johanne Killeen, the owners of Providence's Al Forno. They share a passion for French and Italian food and decadent desserts, delivered in lively rooms packed with happy diners.

After launching **Metropolis Café** in a former ice-cream parlor next to the first home of Hamersley's, Seth and Shari Woods went big-time in 1998, following Gordon and Fiona Hamersley across the street. They took over the old Botolph's on Tremont restaurant and created a true Parisian bistro. Tall plate-glass windows, cast-iron columns and exposed ducts beneath a gray, twenty-foot-high ceiling create a European industrial look, softened by chocolate brown cushioned booths and leather-look banquettes facing tables and beige walls with linear mirrors at eye level. Wine bottles climb to the ceiling above the zinc-lined bar at the entrance.

The blackboard menu, as orchestrated by Seth and executed by chef de cuisine Michele Malley, transports the visitor to France. The plat du jour changes daily (a Toulousian cassoulet on Tuesday, an Alsatian choucroute on Thursday, a slow-roasted confit of lamb with flageolets and truffled radish salad for Sunday supper). Look for entrées like pan-based monkfish with mahogany clams and provençal vegetables, venison au poivre with garlicky gratin potatoes, and steak and frites with perigord black truffle vinaigrette. Even the least expensive dish is full of extravagant ingredients. It's duck ravioli with caramelized oyster mushrooms, truffle oil and foie gras sauce.

Foie gras also turns up in a terrine with traditional accompaniments as an appetizer. Or you could start with crisp sweetbreads with caramelized quince, escargots with celery root purée and crispy parsnips or steak tartare with cornichons and shallots. A selection of three artisan cheeses is offered with fruit and country bread to start or to finish.

Desserts are extravagant and priced accordingly. Consider Vahlrona chocolate bread pudding with caramelized cardamom bananas, a pear and fig chousson (puff pastry stuffed with port-glazed figs, pears, blackberries and honey chèvre cream) and maple-toasted pumpkin soufflé with lavender crème anglaise.

This being a wine bar, many are available by the glass. The markup on wines is

High-ceilinged dining area at Aquitaine conveys Parisian bistro look.

one of the lowest in Boston, with plenty of good choices in the mid-twenties to mid-thirties.

With the wholeheartedly French thrust at Aquitaine, the 35-seat Metropolis took on more of an Italian accent for dinner in the tiny, buttercup yellow space where the Woodses got their start.

(617) 424-8577. Entrées, $17 to $24. Dinner nightly, 5:30 to 11 or midnight.

Truc, 560 Tremont St.

Occupying the lower-level space vacated when Azita's owners decided to concentrate on their Persian winner Lala Rokh (see above), this is a favorite of the young, professional city-dwellers who are fueling much of Boston's current restaurant boom. Co-owners Amanda Lydon, who formerly cooked at Radius, and manager Karen Densmore named it for the French colloquialism for "that little thing." Truc indeed is little, a long, narrow room with a gray banquette facing tables squeezed together in a lineup against a bright yellow-green wall whose exact shade defies description. The "decor" is stark, a backdrop for the food rather than a statement itself. A more cheery solarium at the rear contains a handful of tables overlooking a garden.

Amanda cooks in a narrow, semi-open kitchen behind a front display counter. Her menu is necessarily short (a choice of five appetizers and five entrées). But the pleasing, stylish yet unfussy French country fare warms Gallic innards.

For starters, garlic is employed freely in the creamy fish soup laden with crispy squid and in the frogs' legs with green lentils and bacon. The French sausage boudin blanc is served over a grilled onion salad with violet mustard. The duck foie gras is seared for a crisp exterior, contrasted against a fluff of mashed potatoes and flavored with a pomegranate vinaigrette.

Typical main courses are sea scallops over a purée of cauliflower with saffron, toasted pinenuts and oranges, tender veal over chive spaetzle, and grilled leg of lamb with spicy chickpea fries, quince chutney and braised greens.

The assorted cheese plate takes equal billing with the desserts. Indulge in tarte tatin with thyme ice cream, espresso pots de crème with sable cookies or warm chocolate gâteau with crème fraîche.

This "little thing" is a true place, too.

(617) 388-8070. Entrées, $21 to $24. Dinner, Tuesday-Saturday 6 to 10, Sunday 6 to 9.

Tremont 647, 647 Tremont St.

The "thrill of the grill" now tantalizes the South End. Chef-owner Andy Husbands opened here at age 27 after serving as executive chef with famed Chris Schlesinger at the East Coast Grill in Cambridge. He quit the grill briefly to motorcycle around the West Coast, working on an organic farm in New Mexico and cooking at restaurants in California.

That may account for the daredevil element in his "adventurous American cuisine." It explains the lack of pretense in his rustic, rough-edged restaurant a long block beyond Tremont Street's restaurant row. Beside and beyond a bar at the front, simple pine tables are set with utensils rolled-up in napkins. There supposedly are seats for 70, but is that for two sittings? The most open of open kitchens is as big as the dining area. Here, you not only see and hear but smell the grill as the cooks do their thing. The owner, who dyed his hair purple in the eighth grade, is the one with the pierced tongue and many tattoos.

Andy, who had the smarts to name his restaurant so people could find it, is known for bold flavors that straddle the globe. Consider his "Five-Course Rave" dinner that opens with house-made breads and crackers with a plate of "too stinky cheeses." Next is his favorite Tibetan momos of fiery pork and gingery vegetables with a soy-sake dipping sauce, followed by a Southeast Asian consommé with grilled shrimp, mango brunoise, galanga and lemongrass. The main course could be northern Italian braised lamb shank, accompanied by fried capers, pickled red onions and portobello-ricotta raviolis. A salad of arugula and roasted pears precedes dessert – chocolate espresso cups filled with vanilla bean ice cream. Each course is matched with wines from Oregon's Willamette Valley.

Other signature creations are hoisin-glazed squid with "lots of fire power," Chilean sea bass steamed and wrapped in a banana leaf, prosciutto-crusted monkfish with lemon zest aioli, duck confit served on a duck breast quesadilla and grilled ribeye steak with a grilled shrimp herb butter and "truffle-scented, fontina-stuffed 'tater tots." Banana cream pie with a slab of pecan brittle and caramel sauce is the staple dessert.

Andy, who co-chairs Taste of the Nation for hunger relief, is at the cutting edge. His menu proclaims, "ask about our chef's table." And "join us on Sundays for pajama brunch." Now *that* would be fun to see.

(617) 266-4600. Entrées, $16.50 to $20. Dinner, Tuesday-Sunday 5:30 to 10 or 10:30. Sunday brunch 10:30 to 3.

Offbeat Gourmet

Sonsie, 327 Newbury St.

What's this? A "kitchen/bar/bakery" on Newbury Street? Opened by Boston's leading nightclub entrepreneur? Overseen by one of the city's top chefs? With healthful foods?

The name provides a clue – a Celtic word for relaxed and comfortable. A front wall of french doors opens onto Newbury Street. An air-curtain allows patrons to sip cappuccino at little marble tables just inside as they "watch the world go by right out front, even in the dead of winter," in the words of co-owner Patrick Lyons, the local night club czar. Inside is a corner salon harboring a clutch of antique stuffed leather club chairs for lounging. A multi-colored curtain parts to yield a vista of bar and dining room beneath a high pressed-tin ceiling. The vision is one of close-together tables, terra-cotta colors, wainscoted walls, red swagged draperies and Moroccan hand-blown glass chandeliers.

This is like nothing Boston had seen before, and its consistently hot scene has helped it survive. Chef-partner Bill Poirier, whom we first met at Seasons at the Bostonian Hotel, directs a cast of dozens – big enough to staff an entire hotel without the rooms, says Lyons, who obviously put his money where his mouth is. Poirier's wide-ranging international menu covers all the bases, from spiced onion and ale soup with homemade pretzels and inside-out tuna sashimi rolls with ocean salad through assertive pastas, brick-oven pizzas and main dishes to decadent desserts. A note on the menu says the dishes are designed to keep fat and cholesterol levels low; "we use little or no dairy products and lean meats whenever possible." About the only beef word on the menu turns up in an appetizer of steamed Korean beef dumplings with house-made kim chi and a main course of grilled sirloin steak, straight or au poivre. The trendoids who populate the place appreciate entrées like monkfish "osso buco" with roasted fennel, katsu tuna steak with crispy shrimp and wasabi mayo and charcoal grilled duck breast and roasted leg with cranberry-apple butter. Those into starches can order the five-potato sampler; one each of five offered as sides.

Indulge in dessert, perhaps espresso pizzelle with caramelized bananas and mocha ice cream or Sonsie's award-winning chocolate bread pudding with chocolate drizzle.

There's lot to look at: a cache of newspapers from across the world, a 1902 hand-carved oak mantel behind the bar from a Commonwealth Avenue mansion, a waterfall of colored droplets on the way to the downstairs bakery, a ladies' room papered with racy tabloid covers and polyurethaned toilet seats embedded with coins or, ouch, barbed wire. "We wanted to inject a little theater," deadpans Patrick.

(617) 351-2500. Entrées, $18 to $29.50. Breakfast, lunch and dinner daily, 7 a.m. to 1 a.m.

Gourmet's Digest

Parish Cafe, 361 Boylston St.

Sandwiches created by some of the area's best-known chefs – many of them mentioned in this chapter – are featured at this funky establishment.

The nearly two dozen choices are priced up to $14 (for the Lydia – lobster salad with lemon, parsley, celery leaves and balsamic mayo on Lydia Shire's peppercorn brioche). The Schlesinger is warmed banana bread topped with melted monterey jack, smokehouse ham and mango chutney. The Ambrosian spreads chilled leg of lamb with Asian mayo on Tuscan bread. Parish's own chefs have added appetizers, salads and entrées like fishcakes, BLT pasta and grilled duck.

Superior desserts are served in plush, colorful setting at Finale.

There's an impressive list of wines and ales to go with. The prominent bar plays a major role, and a rear mural portraying laid-back diners on an outdoor patio sets the theme. Given their pedigrees, most of the sandwiches are first-rate. And the large terrace on the broad Boylston Street sidewalk is pleasant on a nice day.

(617) 247-4777. Entrées, $9 to $15. Open daily, 11:30 to 1 a.m., Sunday from noon.

Grand Finale

Finale, 1 Columbus Ave.

In a variation on the eat-dessert-first credo, this large new desserterie/bistro/bakery/bar in a prime corner of the Statler Building inspires you to eat nothing but. Just one sample of pastry chef Nicole Coady's creations will indicate why.

You can get sandwiches and appetizers, but they're mere "preludes" to the sweet priorities: perhaps a light and creamy cheesecake with sautéed peaches and blueberries, plum isle (rum butter cake on poached plums), a large bowl of perfect crème brûlée topped with chopped fresh fruit, a succulent berry tart or pear-chestnut crisp with cinnamon ice cream.

Chocaholics find euphoria in the chocolate plate for two ($25). Its focal point is a tower of chocolate embossed with the Finale logo and filled with a creamy orange-chocolate mousse. Among the plate's panoply of treats are a wedge of bittersweet chocolate cake beside chocolate-hazelnut bavarian pyramids, a baked-to-order molten chocolate gâteau, and an orb of white chocolate gelato topped with crunchy milk-chocolate almonds, finished with raspberry sauce.

Each of the dozen or so dessert choices is accompanied by a wine recommendation. Cordials, teas, espresso and international coffees also are available.

Red velvet and chocolate brown banquettes and booths, yellow walls and plate-glass windows onto the street convey an urbane bistro look to match the fare.

Overhead mirrors above the dessert station let you watch the treats being assembled in this, the first establishment of its kind in the country. It's the brainchild of Kim Moore and Paul Conforti, who designed it as a prototype for a Harvard Business School project. They found a sweet niche.

(617) 423-3184. Desserts, $7.95 to $13.95. Lunch, Monday-Friday 11:30 to 3. Open Monday-Friday, 11:30 to midnight, Monday to 10; Saturday, 6 to midnight; Sunday, 4 to 11.

Lodging

Four Seasons Hotel, 200 Boylston St., Boston 02116.

From the hotel's eighth-floor health spa that has Caribbean-style patio furniture around a swimming pool and whirlpool, you can look out over the Boston Public Garden and, at night, the lights of Boston. "Very romantic while relaxing in the jacuzzi," our guide advised.

It's also very serene and comfortable, this grand luxury hotel with 288 guest rooms and suites reflecting the understated style of a traditional Beacon Hill home. All rooms were refurbished for the new millennium. They have Henredon cherry furniture, plush fabrics, writing tables, TV in an armoire, a minibar, two or three telephones, hair dryers, terrycloth robes and such, plus bay windows that open – a rare blessing for those who cherish fresh air. The 64 mini-suites add alcove seating areas. Executive suites with a living room contain two TVs and stereos with CD players. The over-all guest experience reflects the hotel's five-diamond rating.

Complimentary town car service to downtown locations is a bonus, one that's useful if you're headed out to dinner or to a business engagement.

The luxurious health spa offers massage therapy, treadmills with TVs and VCRs, and spin-dry machines for wet swimsuits. Continental breakfast and the hotel's healthful alternative cuisine may be ordered for service beside the pool.

Public rooms are quietly decorated with antiques and fine art. A five-foot crystal chandelier lights the grand stairway to the elegant, second-floor Aujourd'hui restaurant. The airy, main-floor **Bristol Lounge** serves three meals a day. It also offers Viennese dessert buffets (a dozen fabulous concoctions, $16) on weekends from 9 to midnight. Afternoon tea is served by the fireplace here daily from 3 to 4:30. An elegant Sunday breakfast buffet for $32 is considered one of the best in the city. Speaking of breakfast, among the room-service options is a Japanese breakfast, from grilled salmon and nori to miso soup, for $18.50.

(617) 338-4400 or (800) 332-3442. Fax (617) 351-2051. Two hundred eleven rooms and 77 suites. Doubles, $465 to $595. Suites, $655 to $3,950.

Hotel Le Meridien, 250 Franklin St., Boston 02110.

Known for its gastronomic flair (its chefs offer periodic cooking classes for guests) as well as its trademark red awnings, Le Meridien is run in European splendor by Air France. It occupies the 1922 Federal Reserve Bank building, a National Historic Landmark, reincarnated 60 years and $40 million later into an elegant hotel.

Facing Post Office Square but rather hard to find in the maze of the Financial District, it has 326 recently renovated guest rooms on nine floors. There are more than 150 variations, from two-story loft suites to rooms on the three top floors with sloping windows and mansard roofs. Contemporary sofas, artworks (striking caricatures by local artist Ken Maryanski), live plants and minibars are in each room. Beds are made up in the French style (an extra sheet on top of the blanket), and maids provide turndown service at night with mints and a written weather forecast. A French news sheet is distributed to the rooms, and French cable television is available in the evening. The large bathrooms contain scales, telephones and baskets of assorted amenities. The third-floor health club has a glassed-in pool with skylights.

The Meridien offers a chocolate lover's weekend package from September through May. It features the ultimate chocolate bar, an all-you-can-eat buffet of light and dark chocolate desserts, served Saturdays from 1 to 3 for $16.50 in the **Cafe Fleuri,** the hotel's airy Mediterranean brasserie. Chocolate raspberry mousse cake, chocolate croissant pudding and orange chocolate tart, each identified by a handwritten label, are among the 25 creations. On a typical afternoon, pastry chef Christophe Feyt goes through more than 40 pounds of chocolate, much of which is flown in from France. A nine-station Sunday brunch ($38), voted Boston's best, is served in the cafe's interior courtyard-atrium soaring six stories high.

(617) 451-1900 or (800) 543-4300. Fax (617) 423-2844. Three hundred nine rooms and seventeen suites. Doubles, $355 to $695. Suites, $635 to $1,400.

Boston Harbor Hotel, 70 Rowes Wharf, Boston 02110.
A more sumptuous hotel could scarcely be imagined. The floors are marble, the sides of the elevators are brocade, and the walls of the public spaces are hung with fine art and antique nautical prints. Redwood furniture surrounds the 60-foot lap pool. A large lounge at the rear of the main floor has huge sofas in plums, golds and teals for relaxing as you enjoy live piano music and absorb the view of boats and airplanes around the harbor.

Luxury and care extend to the 230 rooms and suites on Floors 8 through 16 (the lower floors are offices). Our oversize room had a kingsize bed, a sofa and an upholstered chair with good reading lamps in a sitting area, lovely reproduction antiques, and an enormous bathroom full of amenities from fine soaps to terrycloth robes and a hair dryer. Breakfronts concealed the TV and a minibar, atop which were three kinds of glasses – highball, lowball and wine. Luggage racks, removable hangers, soundproof windows that open and enormous towels are other assets. Doorways are recessed well back from the corridor.

Afternoon tea and drinks are offered in a handsome Harborview Lounge on the main floor, and private parties and special events take place in the two-story Rotunda, a copper-domed observatory with views of harbor and city. Guests enjoy the health club and spa, which besides a lap pool has steam rooms and saunas, a hydrotherapy tub and an exercise room.

The hotel is "elaborate, dramatic, even operatic," gushed the Boston Globe's architectural critic shortly after its 1987 opening. It is "an expression of the new wealth of Boston." Stay here, indulge, and you'll surely feel part of it.

(617) 439-7000 or (800) 752-7077. Fax (617) 330-9450. Doubles, $235 to $510. Suites, $350 to $1,600.

The Ritz-Carlton, 15 Arlington St., Boston 02117.
The original Ritz in Boston is not just a hotel. It's an institution – *the* place where proper Bostonians put up visitors or go themselves for lunch in the cafe, tea in the lounge, or drinks and dinner in the Ritz Bar and the Dining Room. Even with all the new hotel competition in which the Ritz risked becoming passé, it remains Boston's bastion of Brahmin elegance.

The elevator operators wear white gloves – yes, there still are elevator operators, to say nothing of white gloves – as they take guests up to the 275 rooms, perhaps one of the 42 wood-burning fireplaced suites billed for romance. Could romance be why the Ritz perpetuates its tradition of nightly big-band dancing on The Roof and weekly Thursday tea dances in the French and Adam Room? And why the Ritz presents "a day of social savvy" for budding socialites aged 8 to 12?

Yes, romance and the Ritz are legendary: Rodgers and Hammerstein wrote many of their musical favorites here, and in the 1930s and '40s, more romantic Broadway musicals were worked on at the Ritz than at any other location in the country.

The martinis in the Ritz Bar are legendary, as is English tea while a harpist plays in the Victorian parlor-salon (full tea, $22; light tea, $18; tea royale with a glass of Mumm's, $27). New is the "Caviar Indulgence," offered nightly in the lounge from 6 to midnight.

The Dining Room fare has been contemporized lately under chef Mark Allen, who had his own restaurant in California's Napa Valley and quietly took this to the cutting edge. He's the youngest and only American chef to take over the Escoffier-inspired Dining Room. Gone are the classics like dover sole meunière. In their place are such novelties (for the Ritz habitué) as potato-wrapped turbot with braised artichokes and beans and lobster jus. The dinner menu at our visit had become all prix-fixe: $61 for three courses, $69 for four, $75 for five. The host called it the best deal in town since it did not specify which courses – you could order four main dishes, as if anyone would.

French provincial furnishings, imported fabrics, distinctive artworks, windows that open onto a view of the Public Garden and all the amenities of a four-diamond hotel are here, even if some think they've seen better days.

The "some" include the Millennium Partners of New York, who bought the Ritz in late 1999 and undertook major renovations. They also started construction of another 155-room Ritz to open in 2001 across the Boston Common as part of the $500 million Millennium Place development along Tremont Street.

And then there will be two Ritzes. Cesar Ritz would be proud.

(617) 536-5700 or (800) 241-3333. Fax (617) 536-1335. Two hundred thirty-one rooms and 44 suites. Doubles, $295 to $495. Suites, $395 to $695.

The Bostonian Hotel, 4 Faneuil Hall Marketplace, Boston 02109.

Its location next to Quincy Market might lead you to think this is good for families, but the Bostonian is quiet, deluxe and, above all, grown-up. Although the original 163 rooms on three floors are rather small, they are beautifully decorated and equipped, and the bathrooms with deep tiled tubs, French soaps and huge towels are a delight. In most rooms, french doors open onto tiny balconies with wrought-iron railings and planters filled with flowers. The television set is tucked discreetly into the armoire. There are two telephones (one in the bathroom), and two AM/FM radios (one in the bathroom). You get the picture.

Since its 1982 opening, the Bostonian has been acclaimed for its European style, its small residential lobby with a corner fireplace, its spacious Atrium Lounge where you can sink into upholstered chairs and sofas to order a fine wine by the glass, espresso or a light lunch, and for Seasons, its rooftop restaurant.

Eleven suites come with fireplaces and some have oval tubs and jacuzzis. The hotel started basically in two wings – one called the contemporary, especially attractive to business travelers, and one in the 19th-century Harkness wing.

Thirty-eight new rooms were added in 1999 in an adjacent eight-story building. Top-of-the-line are five new penthouse-level rooms and suites, each with floor-to-ceiling windows onto the Boston skyline. The addition includes a fitness suite and space for a planned ground-floor restaurant.

(617) 523-3600 or (800) 343-0922. Fax (617) 523-2454. One hundred eighty-nine rooms and twelve suites. Doubles, $225 to $375. Suites, $450 to $775.

Fifteen Beacon, 15 Beacon St., Boston 02108.

This 61-room luxury boutique hotel was billed as the city's finest as it was being readied for a late 1999 opening. Built on the site of a 1722 mansion, it was transformed from a ten-story Beaux Arts office building occupied by the Boston School Committee for most of its 100 years.

Owner Paul Roiff, a local real estate developer with an abiding interest in food and wine, went for the ultimate. His designer was Celeste Cooper, who previously designed Mistral, the restaurant of which he is part-owner, as well as L'Espalier. Here she decorated in elegant modernist style, combining up-to-date conveniences with the intimate touches of a private residence. Each of the upper nine floors has seven rooms and suites, no two of which are alike. The only common elements are the queensize beds (some of them canopied), dressed in Italian 300-thread-count linens, plus working gas fireplaces and windows that open. State-of-the-art technology is concealed within muted Old World decor in shades of taupe, cream and espresso. Each room has a business center with three phones (one cordless), a combination fax and color printer, and direct Internet access. A bedside keypad operates the gas fireplace and activates digital satellite music from a surround-sound stereo system. Among amenities are TVs and heated towel racks in the bathrooms, imported Italian fabric robes, and in-room bars stocked with the finest liquors and half bottles of Chateau Lafite Rothschild, Opus One and Krug champagne.

The main-floor corner restaurant, **The Federalist,** was far from finished at our visit a month after its scheduled opening. About all we could detect was that it would be clubby in gray and black and have pillars as focal points. The menu was not available, but Robert Fathman, previously at Boston's Grill 23 & Bar, was on board as executive chef. He was working on in-kitchen fish tanks and a rooftop herb garden. Owner Roiff had already collected some of world's finest wines for a cellar he said would be unsurpassed in Boston.

(617) 670-1500 or (877) 982-3226. Fax (617) 670-2525. Sixty-one rooms and suites. Doubles, from $395. Suites, $475 to $1,200. Lunch daily, 11:30 to 2:30. Dinner, 5:30 to 10:30.

Gourmet Treats

Faneuil Hall Marketplace, the East's busiest tourist destination after Disney World, is a festival arena for foodies, from the great **Crate & Barrel** store to the approximately twenty restaurants and thirty snackeries, salad bars and food stalls in Quincy Market. It wasn't always thus, but now, wouldn't you know, **Starbucks** is first as you enter from the west. As you stroll through, pick up a wild berry bagel from **Finagle a Bagel,** a non-alcoholic banana daiquiri from the **Monkey Bar,** a spanakopita from **Mykonos Fair,** sweet and sour chicken from **Ming Tree,** a swordfish kabob from **Boston & Maine Fish Co.,** a fajita salad at **El Paso**

Enchiladas or a Philly cheesesteak sandwich at **Philadelphia Steak & Hoagie.** Finish with a cookie from **Boston Chipyard.** There aren't many foods you can think of that you can't find here, and prices are gentle. **Boston Cooks** purveys a selection of cookbooks and cooking accessories. The larger restaurants, though frequented by tourists, are nothing to write home about, with the possible exceptions of historic **Durgin-Park,** the trendy Tex-Mex **Zuma** and the new **Plaza III Kansas City Steakhouse.**

Under the market's north canopy is **Le Saucier,** where Lisa Lamme stocks, at latest count, more than 700 sauces from 37 countries. There are many items to taste; we tried a potent potion called Mad Dog Inferno made in Boston, and eyed a couple more called Dare Double Dare Sauce and Mike's Kissed by Fire salsa. The first hot sauce store in the country ("we started a trend," Lisa says), the place also offers mustards, oils and vinegars, condiments, hot lollipops, New England products and gift baskets.

One of the better places in the waterfront area to pick up lunch or a snack is **Rudi's Cafe Bistro** at 30 Rowes Wharf, near the Boston Harbor Hotel. Billed as a boulangerie, pâtisserie and croissanterie, the upscale spot offers delectable salads, prepared foods and colorful pastries in a curved display case, along with gourmet foods and books. You can eat in a pleasant dining area at the side or take out to the waterfront.

Across town are the tony stores at **Copley Plaza** and the mixed bag that make up the renovated **Shops at Prudential Center.**

The 100 block of increasingly fashionable Newbury Street holds special interest for food lovers. An artist from MacKenzie-Childs Ltd. in New York's Finger Lakes region was painting a table in the front window during a special exhibition when we visited **LaRuche** at 168 Newbury, notable for unique place settings and decorative accessories. **Kitchen Arts** at 161 is chock-full of neat gadgets, including a good little hand-held knife sharpener ($8.95) that went home in our shopping bag. Vermont's **Simon Pearce** glass has a branch at 115 Newbury, next door to **Pierre Deux.** Next to the Armani designer store at 214 Newbury St., the showy **Emporio Armani Express** offers designer Italian fare for lunch and dinner. **Teuscher** at 230 Newbury airlifts its chocolates weekly from Zurich.

The old Coffee Connection (at 165 Newbury St. and countless other locations around town) has been absorbed by **Starbucks,** which helps account for the latter's omnipresence across Boston. More coffee is available, along with tea, chocolates and Italian sodas, on a little sunken patio in front of **Espresso Royale Caffe,** 286 Newbury. Adjacent is **Emack & Bolio's,** one of a small local chain offering ice cream, yogurt and a juice bar offering "Boston's best smoothie;" the day's special at our visit was a "thick as a brick oreo frappe."

The finest in pots and pans, plus some cookbooks, are featured at **Seasonings,** a good cookware and accessory store at 65 Beacon St., near Charles Street.

Savenor's at 160 Charles St. is considered Boston's best gourmet market. It made its name as a butcher (everything from farm-raised lamb to lion meat). Choosy cooks head here for choice groceries, specialty foods, sauces, oils and breads, including imports from Poilane, the legendary all-organic baker in Paris.

Nearly every top restaurant in Boston offers a special course of artisan cheeses. Most get them from **Formaggio Kitchen** at 244 Huron Ave. in Cambridge. Food & Wine magazine ranked it one of the five best cheese shops in the nation.

Monadnock Region

A Step Back in Time

"The Quiet Corner," the Monadnock area is called. Also "the Currier and Ives Section." Both with good reason.

Many of the trappings of contemporary civilization have passed this region by. So have many tourists. The restaurant scene here seems to be in a continual state of flux, and we've had to stretch the region's borders a bit to find enough good places to eat. But exciting things have been happening lately in terms of food, particularly in Peterborough, the region's biggest community (population 5,000).

Otherwise, during our explorations through the heart of the region, we noticed only two motels worthy of the name, nary a fast-food outlet and only a single shopping plaza, that on the outskirts of Peterborough.

Instead there are picture-book villages with Colonial houses, churches and perhaps a general store, antiques shops but rarely a boutique or gift shop, the occasional inn or restaurant, countless streams, lakes and hills, and Mount Monadnock, the ubiquitous, 3,165-foot mountain that is supposedly the world's most climbed. It seems fitting that the area's most popular tourist attraction is the Cathedral of the Pines, an outdoor shrine on a garden-bedecked knoll of pines east of Rindge; the sounds of the carillon are soothing and the view of Grand Monadnock inspiring. Even there, in the 1850s Cathedral House on the grounds, is one of the area's growing number of B&Bs.

It's a distinct pleasure to stray off the beaten path to encounter a place like the old mill town of Harrisville, which is striking for its red brick structures surrounding a duck pond. They stand quite in contrast to the white frame buildings elsewhere in the region and perhaps epitomized in nearby Dublin, New England's highest village and home of Yankee magazine.

The Quiet Corner is ripe for such rural discoveries. You can find tranquil, postcard New England settings around almost every turn. And like the rest of Monadnock, many of the restaurants and inns are rustic and low-key, capitalizing on the fact they have changed little over the years. Nor have their prices.

They invite you to relive the old days.

Dining

Acqua Bistro, 9 School St., Peterborough.

Boston restaurant consultant David Chicane decided he'd helped open enough restaurants for others and it was time to open his own. Peterborough and the Monadnock Region are the beneficiary of his change of heart, not to mention his cooking skills.

He took over a vacant restaurant space in the town's bustling downtown retail and arts area in 1999. After a total rehab and installation of a bar and a modern kitchen, he opened a stylish dining room on the upper level and a wine and jazz bar on the lower level. Rear windows look onto the Nubanusit River, which is spotlit at night. Old benches from a Dartmouth College auditorium provide banquette seating. A substantial, gold-gilded wine rack fills one wall. Framed French posters and colorful fig-green walls up, burgundy walls down, impart a cheery bistro air. The brown butcher paper atop white linen cloths signifies a casual yet elegant theme.

Chef-owner David Chicane in wine bar at Acqua Bistro.

The theme is reflected in the cuisine, which is modern city bistro at affordable prices. The name is Italian for water – "one of the basics of life," David says, "and we're right on the water." He highlights the simple flavors of basic foods and elevates them to a higher level. "Comfort food taken to the nth degree," he calls it.

"I'm basically doing what they're doing in Boston for $38 a plate, only here it's $12 to $15," says David, whose fifteen-year career included a cooking stint at Upstairs at the Pudding in Cambridge before he decided to help open restaurants.

The Mediterranean menu changes almost daily as Acqua attempts to draw repeat business regularly. It's also the kind to appeal to theater-goers before and after the show.

Soups and salads star on the starter list: perhaps a chilled spring pea soup with crème fraîche and mint, or a salad of bitter greens, spiced walnuts, blue cheese and mission figs. Stuffed banana peppers, a cheese plate with Spanish manchego and crostini, or a beef carpaccio with a ricotta salata appease hungrier palates.

Creative pizzas share top billing with bistro plates for the main course. Consider a pizza of four cheeses, one of lamb sausage or another of spicy shrimp. Typical "plates" are cavatelli with braised artichokes and arugula, seared scallops with tomato-saffron risotto and wilted spinach, hand-rolled saffron pappardelle with lobster bolognese and veal meatloaf with wild mushroom pan sauce.

Desserts are standouts. Early favorites were individual warm chocolate cake with a Belgian chocolate truffle center, lavender pot de crème and fallen strawberry cake with macadamia nut shortbread. Cappuccino is the beverage of choice to go with.

Twenty wines are offered by the glass from a good wine cellar.

(603) 924-9905. Entrées, $10.95 to $16.95. Dinner, Tuesday-Sunday 4 to 11.

Nicola's Trattoria, 39 Central Square, Keene.

Nicola Bencivenga was studying law in Rome when he met Cheryl Frez while she was on an art history tour with Keene State College. They were married two years later and settled in Keene, where a lawyer from Italy could not find work. Instead, he taught Italian language classes and took up cooking for area hospitals

Cheryl and Nicola Bencivenga in dining room of Nicola's Trattoria.

and restaurants. In 1997, the space occupied by the late Mangos and Manners restaurant became available and, as Cheryl tells it, "we decided to go for it."

They redecorated the former storefront in warm earth tones that make people "feel like they're in a home in Italy." A revolving art show enhances the walls. Nicola works from a wide-open kitchen at the rear of the dining room.

Sourdough Italian bread and a container of olive oil are on a butcher block on each table. A complimentary sauté of broccoli rabe, chick peas and garlic is served each diner.

The fare is classic Italian and highly regarded. Veal and chicken are served with fettuccine alfredo or ziti, or with marsala, milanese or piccata sauces. Saltimbocca is a standard, and osso buco is offered on weekends. Cioppino, risotto milanese, and pasta with shellfish are among the offerings.

Appetizers include bruschetta, fresh mozzarella, crostini with prosciutto and provolone, baked shrimp and fried calamari. Desserts vary, but some folks will order nothing but Nicola's signature tiramisu.

(603) 355-5242. Entrées, $10.95 to $18.95. Lunch, Tuesday-Friday 11:30 to 2. Dinner, Tuesday-Saturday 5 to 9 or 10.

Red Maples Restaurant, 12 Maple St., Bennington.

After a break as a restaurant consultant in Boston, chef Jerry Willis returned home to reopen a restaurant of his own. Jerry, who had garnered quite a following at his old Powder Mill Pond Restaurant nearby, turned up in 1998 in the quarters long occupied by the old Petite Maison, a French restaurant.

One of Bennington's oldest Cape Cod houses, the structure had been abandoned by a previous owner. Jerry freshened up the two intimate dining rooms and hung on the walls the paintings of his parents, Barbara and Sidney Willis, artists who show in Massachusetts galleries and work out of their home – the site of their son's former restaurant. While the Powder Mill quarters were summery and colorful, the new location is country-charming, with a decidedly Colonial look and homey feeling. The raftered, wainscoted rooms are decked out with white cloths and cut-glass oil lamps on the tables and lace curtains over the windows. Chef Willis trained at the Culinary Institute of America and in San Francisco, where he acquired an oriental flair. It still shows up in appetizers like Thai clams and spring roll dumplings, but he maintains that the rest of the fare is more upscale than before. Options are constantly changing. Pan-seared haddock, filet mignon with rich mushroom sauce and pot roast were favorites on a recent menu that ranged from grilled salmon with herbed butter to lamb chops dijonnaise.

Desserts include such popular Willis standbys as lemon mousse with raspberry sauce, bread pudding royale, chocolate truffle cake and ice cream puff with chocolate or amaretto sauce.

A consultant put together the short but wide-ranging wine list priced mostly in the $20s.

In the winter, Jerry closes Red Maples to continue his work for a Boston restaurant group.

(603) 588-3588. Entrées, $14.25 to $19.50. Dinner, Tuesday-Sunday 5:30 to 9. Closed January-April.

Del Rossi's Trattoria, Route 137 at Route 101, Dublin.

The aroma of garlic wafts through this pretty Colonial house – the setting for some fine Italian fare, cooked up by chef David Del Rossi, co-owner with his wife Elaina. The two Jaffrey natives also run a music store, which accounts for the fact they feature live music (mostly bluegrass and folk with name entertainers) on Saturday nights on a stage in a corner of the main dining room.

With its wide-plank floors and post and beam construction, the dining room is plain and comfortable with sturdy captain's chairs at the tables, some left bare and some with beige linens and burgundy napkins. There are a couple of smaller rooms (away from the entertainment) plus a sun porch with a stained-glass window, where we enjoyed lunch.

For dinner, you might begin with crostini with calamari or polenta topped with a tomato and basil (from the chef's garden) sauce and melted gorgonzola, and go on to a pasta – all made in house by this talented chef who recreates dishes he tasted as a child with his grandparents from Abruzzi. Among the favorites are gnocchi bolognese, four-cheese ravioli, and fettuccine with shiitake mushrooms.

Entrées include seafood fra diavolo, shrimp scampi, scallops broiled in a wine sauce topped with bread crumbs and grated romano, pork scaloppine with prosciutto and cheese, and steak cacciatore. Loaves of homemade Italian bread, vegetable of the day and a side of pasta accompany. The lengthy wine list is well chosen and reasonably priced, and beers are a bargain.

"Once you try my Sicilian cake, you want it again and again," says David. The homemade pound cake has ricotta cheese and chocolate filling between its layers and couldn't be more lush. Another favorite is Roman cheese pie, an old recipe featuring ricotta with a marsala wine crust on a bed of honey with grapes.

The menu for lunch, recently served seasonally on a somewhat iffy basis, changes every day. Our quiche of smoked oysters and cheese with a generous salad and a PLT version of a BLT (prosciutto, lettuce, and tomato on grilled garlic bread) were super.

(603) 563-7195. Entrées, $10.95 to $16.95. Dinner, Tuesday-Saturday 5 to 9, Sunday 4 to 8.

Lilly's On the Pond, Route 202, Rindge.
The core of "the Old Forge," the last remaining of seven mills in Rindge, dates back to 1790 when it was a sawmill. It's been given new life by two women who had managed area restaurants, Suanne Yglesias and Helen Kendall. They and their husbands painted the interior white with dark trim for a Tudor tavern look, hung quilts on the walls, scattered oriental rugs on the floors, enclosed a porch overlooking the mill pond and installed a wood stove on the site of the original forge in the pub. The large main dining room is properly historic looking with captain's chairs at bare wood tables, wagon-wheel chandeliers overhead and wide-plank floors beneath. The porch offers the best view of the water wheel and ducks on the mill pond.

The owners keep their large place busy with an extensive menu that encourages grazing as well as full-course meals. The chef is known for pork spare ribs with a spicy Jamaican jerk sauce that comes in three degrees of heat: "wimpy, hot or industrial." Those with less incendiary tastes can opt for grilled salmon fillet with artichokes and béarnaise sauce, tequila-lime or kiwi-apple chutney chicken, pork tenderloin in a creamy dijon sauce, wiener schnitzel or blackened sirloin.

The all-day menu also offers eight kinds of burgers, snacky appetizers like nachos and potato layers ("better than skins," according to the menu) and countless sandwiches, from philly cheese steak and reubens to veggie stir-fry pitas. There's also a full page of specials for lunch and dinner. No one goes hungry here, nor will the bill break the bank.

Lilly's chocolate-topped peanut-butter cheesecake won first prize in a chocolate contest. The raspberry pie and grand-marnier chocolate mousse also are highly rated.

(603) 899-3322. Entrées, $9.95 to $15.95. Lunch, Tuesday-Saturday 11:30 to 5. Dinner, 5 to 9. Sunday, brunch 10 to 3, dinner noon to 8. Closed Monday.

Martinos, 276 West St., Keene.
"Rome all you like without leaving Keene," says the business card of this wildly popular restaurant that started as Martinos Spaghetti House.

Chef-owner Donna Sears, following some of her grandmother's recipes, cooks creatively with a penchant for garlic and oregano. The short menu is posted on a couple of hard-to-read blackboards on either side of the small, jam-packed and dimly lit dining room. You'd best determine your choices from the blackboard posted in the rear waiting area downstairs, where an assortment of magazines and complimentary hot spiced cider and pretzels keep would-be diners contented. Fortunately, reservations are advised (and honored), but walk-ins may slip into an open slot. "There's one table available for 45 minutes," the hostess advised the Friday night we stopped by to find the place otherwise filled at 5:45.

Spaghetti is featured, but here you can order it with sausage, fresh vegetables or rosemary chicken. The specials change daily. One night's offerings were typical: starters of creamy lobster bisque and baked stuffed focaccia; the "spaghetti and..." section, and up to five other main dishes, perhaps sautéed salmon in mushroom caper glaze, a suave scallops and saffron risotto, and chicken, shrimp, sausage and artichoke hearts in tomato-pesto cream sauce. Portions are huge, and nearly everyone leaves with a foil-wrapped doggie bag shaped like a swan.

Italian bread and garlic-oregano butter are served as you are seated. Main dishes come with an interesting mixed salad, dressed in creamy gorgonzola. Dessert could be German chocolate cake, cappuccino silk pie, or spumoni.

Old farm cart displays season's bounty at Twelve Pine market and cafe.

The place is dark and intimate and nicely outfitted in a simple country look (note the changing displays of healthful foods on the glass shelves in the front window). It's convivial and welcoming, and much admired for good food at bargain prices.

(603) 357-0859. Entrées, $12.95 to $15.95. Lunch, Tuesday-Friday 11:30 to 1:30; dinner Tuesday-Saturday 5 to 9, Sunday to 8. Closed Sunday in summer.

Twelve Pine, 11 School St., Peterborough.

Although not a restaurant as such, this gourmet takeout spot is the "in" place for area food-lovers. Daniel Thibeault, who worked his way through art school in Boston in the employ of hotel restaurants, and his wife Joan started a catering business at their home (from whose address was derived the name). Success prompted a small downtown takeout operation, which moved in 1996 into an old grain warehouse at Depot Square.

Large and stylish, the barn of a place is a perfect showcase for the specialty foods, bakery, produce, cafe and deli items offered by the couple. This destination for gourmands – obviously a gathering spot in town – has a juice and espresso bar.

Old farm carts and wagons display the season's bounty in a fresh and airy, market-type setting with beamed ceiling, shiny floors and mustard yellow walls. There's cafe seating at tables inside or outside on the side train platform. About half the space is given over to cafeteria-style counters and display cases full of delectable-looking treats. White chocolate mousse cakes, raspberry-strawberry shortcakes and hazelnut-cappuccino cheesecakes might be lined up in one case next to another full of salads, phyllo rolls, polenta triangles and pesto ovals.

You can pick up the makings for lunch or a picnic or get an entrée for dinner, to eat here or to go (there's no table service or liquor). The changing blackboard and deli choices are legion. How about one of the soups (perhaps Russian peasant, gazpacho or tomato and cheddar), with a ham and potato tart or a crabmeat quiche? Or one of about a dozen enticing salads? We made a picnic of three – an assertive grilled chicken with peppers and corn and chipotle dressing, Vietnamese pork with green beans and cilantro dressing, and red cabbage slaw with capers and almonds – plus a couple of peanut-butter chocolate-chip cookies, and trundled off to partake on the side porch. Moussaka, chicken rosemary, and stuffed cornish game hens are some of the heartier entrées. Burritos and gourmet pizzas also are offered.

(603) 924-6140. Entrées, $4 to $8. Open Monday-Friday 8 to 7, Saturday and Sunday 9 to 4.

Monadnock School for Natural Cooking and Philosophy, 77 Route 137, Peterborough.

Here, for those who missed it, is the successor to the late **Latacarta,** a restaurant with a host of followers and a reputation far beyond the region.

Japanese master chef Hiroshi Hayashi's all-natural restaurant opened in 1990 in the old Gem Theater on School Street in the center of Peterborough. It moved a couple miles south in 1997 into bigger, splashier quarters formerly occupied by the Boilerhouse at Noone Falls. Latacarta closed in 1999, and consolidated operations as a non-profit corporation affiliated with New Hampshire College.

The scaled-down restaurant is now based in the home of its owner. He had moved to Peterborough from Newbury Street in Boston where, he says, "I never had to serve meat, but I do here." He is a student of cosmic philosophy (explained on the back of the menu) and gave seminars in natural-foods cooking at his home before launching the cooking school fulltime.

Although the school's new 24-seat restaurant was unfinished at our 1999 visit, Barbara Sustik, manager and dining instructor who has been with him for 25 years, said it would be up and running by spring 2000 after a year of catering private functions. She pledged that the inspired cooking and New Age feeling for which Latacarta was known would continue. "If anything," she said, "the food is better" because much of it is grown on the 100-acre property, the rest is ordered daily and it's prepared for smaller numbers with more attention to detail.

Dinner is offered prix-fixe, $37 for appetizer, breads, salad, entrée, side dishes and dessert. The main course involves a choice of vegetarian, fish, chicken or beef. You'll likely find things like stuffed sole or poached salmon with dill sauce, ginger or tarragon chicken, and beef wellington or tenderloin with red wine sauce. The vegetarian entrée might be a zucchini boat filled with mushrooms, tomatoes, eggplant and cheddar cheese, vegetables in phyllo, green beans and roasted almonds with olive oil. Appetizers vary from gyoza dumplings to hummus served with pita bread. Sushi, spring rolls, smoked seafood and shrimp tempura with sweet potato and carrot fritters are typical offerings. A large salad is topped with tofu, which the chef calls "sage's protein." Using little salt and sugar, he and his staff turn out desserts like mocha custard, apple pandowdy, banana supreme, strawberry mousse and lemon meringue pie.

At the original Latacarta, a lunchtime taste of the two soups of the day, cream of butternut squash and a chunky fish chowder, convinced us to return. A subsequent meal produced black bean soup, the Latacarta grilled tofu sandwich served on sourdough bread with fried potatoes, and a special of linguini with vegetables provençal, served with a salad – all in more than generous portions. The delicious and piping-hot pear crunch with ice cream was enough for two to share. The new dining room is simple but stylish and oriental in feeling. A gorgeous kimono made by Hayashi's wife is spotlit in a place of prominence, as it always has been.

(603) 924-6878. Prix-fixe, $37. Lunch, Monday-Saturday noon to 2. Dinner by reservation, Monday-Saturday 5:30 to 9:30. BYOB.

Dining and Lodging

Chesterfield Inn, Route 9, West Chesterfield 03466.

Young corporate dropouts Phil and Judy Hueber from Connecticut stayed in 80-odd country inns before deciding to purchase the two-year-old Chesterfield Inn in 1987, proclaiming the guest rooms here "the finest we'd seen." That, it turns out, was just the beginning. They added six more luxury rooms, a beautiful new dining room and plush common areas to create what they call "a luxurious country hotel" that justifies an AAA four-diamond rating.

The spacious guest rooms are striking with cathedral ceilings, exposed beams and barn boards. Each has a comfortable sitting area, three-way reading lamps, a full bath beyond a separate dressing area, period antiques and quilts. All have kingsize or two double beds.

The Huebers have stocked mini-refrigerators in the rooms with a variety of beverages and have outfitted the bathrooms with Gilchrist & Soames toiletries. All rooms have televisions and telephones, all different and some cleverly tucked away in boxes. "These are really elegant and beautiful rooms," says Judy, "but we want them to be comfortable and livable."

The latter was a prime consideration when the Heubers added a new structure to the side with four spacious bedrooms in the same style. These come with corner fireplaces and private brick patios overlooking the gardens – "great places

Elegant porch dining at Chesterfield Inn.

to sit and watch the sunset," says Judy. The latest addition holds two more deluxe rooms with kingsize beds, double jacuzzis, gas fireplaces and private balconies.

Another addition, to the rear off the entry lobby, produced a stylish living room, a commercial kitchen and a dining room with windows on three sides and french doors onto a patio. Now 50 people can dine by candlelight at tables set with white over pink linens, Dudson floral china, big wine globes and crystal water glasses.

Chef Carl Warner, who has been with the Huebers from the beginning, changes the short dinner menu seasonally. A complimentary starter like smoked salmon pâté is on the table as guests are seated. Appetizers might be lobster and corn chowder, crab cakes with rémoulade sauce, lobster ravioli with tarragon butter sauce or lamb sausage with goat cheese. Main courses could be scallops with citrus-ginger vinaigrette, hoisin-glazed duck breast and leg with nectarine salsa, and beef tenderloin with wild mushroom and cabernet sauce.

For dessert, try Carl's fresh berry trifle, flourless chocolate cake with custard sauce, pumpkin cheesecake or walnut pie. The wine list is a well-chosen mix of American and French, with some not-often-seen Californias.

Judy Hueber or their chef cooks a hearty breakfast for overnight guests. The choices might include blueberry pancakes, cinnamon maple french toast, eggs any style or omelet of the day. Corn fritters, potato pancakes, hash browns, and homemade muffins and scones accompany.

(603) 256-3211 or (800) 365-5515. Fax (603) 256-6131. Thirteen rooms and two suites with private baths. Doubles, $125 to $200. Suites, $175. Add $25 for foliage and one-night Saturday stays.

Entrées. $17 to $24. Dinner Monday-Saturday (also Sunday in foliage), 5:30 to 9.

The Hancock Inn, 33 Main St., Hancock 03449.

New Hampshire's oldest operating inn (1789) doesn't look that old because of the later addition of a mansard roof. Its elegant, pillared facade enhances the main street of the picturesque hamlet of Hancock. It also doesn't feel that old, thanks to the redecorating and upgrading done by owners Linda and Joe Johnston, formerly of the New England Inn at Intervale, N.H. They have lavished much time and money in redoing the inn, from top to bottom, to create in Linda's words, "a genuine inn experience for our guests."

They started with the tavern, "because we strongly believe that an inn should be an inn – with a common room." Here is a welcoming place where folks gather not only to imbibe but to play checkers and other board games or to simply read in the corner. Remarkable Linda painted a Rufus Porter-style mural around the walls of the tavern. It bears an uncanny resemblance to the artist's trademark murals that adorn the upstairs Rufus Porter bedroom.

The Johnstons also put new emphasis on the inn's dining. They have gussied up all three dining areas, sponging the walls of the main room a Colonial red color, nicely trimmed in grayish-blue, which with a blazing hearth is a favorite in winter. The tables are elegantly set with cream-colored linens, modern glass oil lamps, oversize pewter cutlery and napkins stashed in wine glasses. In summer, we prefer the more casual, beamed dining room in the rear, with barnwoods walls and windows onto the lawns. Here is where house guests also enjoy a breakfast buffet of homemade granola, scones, juices, fruits and a cooked-to-order dish, perhaps banana-pecan pancakes with sausage or a sausage and egg casserole.

The dinner fare has been upgraded as well since we supped here a few years back. Instead of vegetable juice, cellophane-wrapped crackers with crocks of Wispride and tossed salads of iceberg lettuce, chef Michael Mack offers starters like a ragout of lobster and artichoke hearts, Maine crab cakes with a plum tomato and scallion concasse, or a salad of field greens with endive and a blueberry-pistachio vinaigrette. The eight entrées range from pan-seared salmon fillet and shellfish cioppino over tomato fettuccine to slow-roasted half duckling with dried cherry sauce and grilled beef tenderloin with roasted shallot bordelaise sauce. Although the fare has contemporary overtones, the house specialty (brought here from the New England Inn) remains Shaker cranberry pot roast – "which outsells anything else on the menu, two to one," says Linda.

Desserts also mix the traditional with the trendy. Indian pudding à la mode and bread pudding with caramel sauce vie for attention with chocolate-chestnut tart, three-chocolate terrine and a crème brûlée napoleon with hazelnuts.

Pillars dignify facade of The Hancock Inn, New Hampshire's oldest but nicely upgraded.

Most of the inn's fifteen guest rooms are done in handsome period furniture. The Johnstons have added telephones, air-conditioning, queensize and king or twin beds, bath toiletries and cassettes with tapes for music. Four new deluxe rooms fashioned from a former ballroom wing come with gas fireplaces and whirlpool or soaking tubs. One retains its domed ballroom ceiling, and another bears wall murals painted by Linda. The new downstairs Drovers Room adds a private patio and a realistic looking faux-fieldstone fireplace.

(603) 525-3318 or (800) 525-1789. Fax (603) 525-9301. www.hancockinn.com. Fifteen rooms with private baths. Doubles, $126 to $210 weekends, $106 to $192 midweek. Entrées, $16 to $22.50. Dinner nightly, 6 to 9, Sunday 5 to 8.

The Inn at Crotched Mountain, 534 Mountain Road, off Route 47, Francestown 03043.

This rambling red brick inn, with a renovated red and white barn attached, is at the 1,300-foot level with the former Crotched Mountain ski area almost at the front door, so the air is sparkling and the view, 40 miles across the Piscataquog Valley, is grand.

Owners Rose and John Perry have operated the inn since 1973. Both are schooled in the restaurant business and their dining room is highly regarded in the area. Lately they have curtailed its operations to weekends only, leaving house guests somewhat high and dry – and hungry – at other times, now that several nearby restaurants have closed.

The aromas emanating from the kitchen indicate a culinary master at work. Chef Rose, a native of Singapore, offers nightly specials that strike us as more interesting than the regular menu. Treats like lobster strudel, grilled tuna with cucumber dressing, babi ritja (an Indonesian dish with pork and ginger), roast pork with seasonal fruit sauce and potstickers supplement the regular entrées of shrimp scampi, cranberry pot roast, calves liver with onion and bacon, and filet mignon béarnaise. Entrée prices include cellophane-noodle or apple-curry soup, salad with one of the inn's homemade dressings, homemade breads and vegetables grown on the premises. A surcharge brings appetizers like herring in wine, shrimp cocktail or smoked mussels. Desserts specialties are a dense dark chocolate mousse and raspberry sherbet.

After dinner, guests often congregate in the library/tavern for a nightcap by the fireplace.

Guests eat in two dining rooms or at a couple of tables set up in the huge living room, which has lovely oriental rugs and a fireplace at either end. A display case shows off jars of the Perrys' homemade goodies, including jams, tarragon vinegar and celery seed dressing, which are for sale. The inn has eight other working fireplaces, three of them in guest rooms. All told, the inn has thirteen rooms (eight with private baths). They are furnished with antiques befitting, in John's words, a country estate. Breakfast is included in the rates.

Two clay tennis courts and a large swimming pool taking full advantage of the view give guests a choice of activities. This is a place where you can really feel secluded and almost on top of the world.

(603) 588-6840. Fax (603) 588-6840. Eight rooms with private baths and five rooms with shared baths. Doubles, $70 to $90; add $20 for holiday weekends and foliage. Closed April and November. Two-night minimum weekends.
Entrées, $14.95 to $19.95. Dinner, Friday-Saturday 6 to 8:30.

Colby Hill Inn, The Oaks, Box 779, Henniker 03242.
Vastly upgraded lately in terms of food, hospitality and decor, this sixteen-room inn with a good dining room was a working farm until 1959 and the old barn is still attached to the inn. You go through it to get to the secluded swimming pool, with views of hills and meadows and a pond that is used for ice-skating.

Built about 1800, this is a cheery, cozy and delightfully unpretentious inn with two sitting rooms, one with a flickering fireplace and the other with games, television and rear windows looking onto gardens and a new gazebo. Business transplants from Maryland, Ellie and John Day and their daughter Laurel, took over the inn in 1990 and have infused it with enthusiasm and good taste. They redecorated six rooms in the rear carriage house and ten rooms in the main inn with antiques. All have private baths, telephones and air-conditioning, and four of the most prized in the main house have working fireplaces. One with an ornate brass kingsize bed is especially appealing in blue and white Waverly fabrics.

Pots of coffee and tea and a cookie jar full of the best crunchy oatmeal-raisin cookies are at the ready for guests in the entry to the dining room. A full country breakfast is served in the morning. A couple of large, friendly dogs are much in evidence in the common rooms.

The dining room has become increasingly known for good food under the aegis of CIA-trained chef Michael Mack, who was with the Days since they took over and officially became part of the family when he and Laurel were married. Sous chef Dana Hansen took over the kitchen when Michael left in 1999 to become chef at the nearby Hancock Inn.

The dozen or so dinner entrées include a signature breast of chicken stuffed

Twining grapevines are strung with tiny white lights in Colby Hill Inn dining room.

with lobster, leeks and boursin cheese; horseradish-crusted haddock with mustard-dill cream sauce, and rack of American lamb rubbed with pommery mustard and herbs and finished with minted red wine demi-glace.

The starters are no less enticing, among them roasted garlic soup or lobster bisque, jonah crab cakes with whole-grain mustard sauce, lobster spring roll with curried aioli, and mushrooms stuffed with smoked bacon, tomatoes, spinach and cream cheese. Ellie Day prepares the scrumptious desserts, always a cheesecake (pecan-pumpkin-praline at an autumn visit) and a napoleon and perhaps amaretto crème caramel, blueberry-cream pie and cream puff swans with raspberry purée. The short but good wine list is priced in the twenties and thirties.

All this is served in a couple of serene dining rooms. One is a wainscoted tavern room and the other a stenciled room with big windows onto the back gardens. Twining grapevines above the windows are strung with tiny white lights all year. Upholstered chairs, cream-colored linens, pink napkins, candles in hurricane chimneys and oriental rugs contribute to the country elegance.

The inn now sponsors a series of five wine-tasting dinners that are sold out each year. Five courses are offered for $85, all-inclusive.

(603) 428-3281 or (800) 531-0330. Fax (603) 428-9218. www.colbyhillinn.com. Sixteen rooms with private baths. Doubles, $95 to $185.

Entrees, $18 to $31. Dinner nightly, 5:30 to 8:30, Sunday 4:30 to 7:30.

The Birchwood Inn, Route 45, Temple 03084.

Judy and Bill Wolfe, originally from New Jersey, have been operating this red brick inn, built around 1800 and now listed on the National Register, since 1980. They have earned wide acclaim for their bargain-priced dinners, served to the public as well as inn guests, and one area booster thinks they serve the best meals in the region.

The small dining room, its walls covered by Rufus Porter murals, is candlelit. The blackboard menu usually lists three entrées that could be seafood chautauqua (a medley of shrimp, scallops and lobster in herbed butter sauce over rice), roast duckling with grand marnier sauce, and tournedos of beef béarnaise. Meals start with relishes like cottage cheese with horseradish and curried kidney beans and a choice of two homemade breads from Judy's repertoire of 100. Then comes juice or soup, among them minestrone, French onion, she-crab and lobster bisque. Dessert could be an apple-raspberry cobbler, tortes, cream cheese-pecan pie and ice cream with a homemade sauce, perhaps rum-maple.

The four-course meal varies from $17.95 to $23.95, depending on choice of entrée. "We do everything ourselves – that's how we can keep these prices," Bill explained.

Upstairs are six small guest rooms with private baths. Each is charmingly decorated around family collection themes: a seashore room, music room, editorial office (with an ancient typewriter and wallpaper of front pages) and the like. A newer bedroom on the ground floor, where a large shop used to be, has TV, private bath and a brightly-colored quilt, with old produce signs on the walls. Room rates include a full country breakfast, which also draws the locals (as you might expect, considering its $4.95 price).

Guests gather in the country parlor, and in front is a small shop and a game room.

(603) 878-3285. Fax: (603) 878-2159. Five rooms with private baths and two with shared baths. Doubles, $69 to $79; foliage, $89.

Breakfast, Tuesday-Sunday, 7:30 to 9:30, weekends only in winter. Dinner, table d'hôte, $17.95 to $23.95. Tuesday-Saturday 5 to 8:30. BYOB. No credit cards.

Lodging

Amos A. Parker House, 146 New Hampshire Route West, Fitzwilliam 03447.

A travel agent in Chicago, Freda Houpt had been nearly everywhere in the world except India and New England when she first visited her son in Boston. After that visit, she went home, sold her house the next day and wound up in Fitzwilliam, where she runs one of the region's most appealing B&Bs.

A Renaissance woman if ever there was one, energetic Freda does everything at the four-room B&B herself. She still finds time to develop and tend the incredible gardens with more than 1,500 perennials in back, dabble in sculpture and host workshops on drying flowers. And, on a rare busman's holiday, she traveled around Russia staying at B&Bs.

Her spacious 1780 house, backing up to fields and forests at the western edge of town, is a beauty. The main floor harbors a cozy "great room" (her words) with newly sanded pine floors ("which never had been sanded before"), comfortable furniture, wood stove, barnwood walls, shelves of books and old crockery, dried flowers hanging from the beams and one of the six fireplaces that warm the house. There also are a charming fireplaced dining room painted in cream and striking burnt orange, a kitchen in which guests tend to congregate, and a TV room with sliding doors to a rear deck overlooking the gardens and a pond "with 250 frogs," Freda specifies.

The main floor also contains a suite with a private entrance. It has a large bedroom with queensize bed, a sitting area with a sofabed and a fireplace, a small kitchen and stenciling all around. Upstairs are two front guest rooms with fireplaces and private baths (one a two-room affair with a w.c. and sink in one and the smallest shower ever in the other). Two back rooms form a suite with sitting room and a full bath with a bidet. Two area women were responsible for a couple of stunning trompe-l'oeil wall murals: a floral trellis behind the bed in the suite, and a vase of flowers over the fireplace mantel in a front room. Oriental rugs warm the wide-plank floors and lace-edged pillows and comforters cover the beds. Fresh flowers, colorful towels and terrycloth robes in every room are among caring touches. As guests arrive, a silver tray on the dining-room table awaits with hot or cold drinks, fruit, cheese, crackers and cookies.

Breakfast is quite a feast, starting with cold fruit under a glass dome garnished with flowers in the summer and hot fruit like apricot and blueberry compote in long-stemmed Waterford glasses in the fall. The main course might be a "pullapart," a huge puffy pancake done in an iron skillet and sprinkled with lemon and powdered sugar, or an apple soufflé pancake with sour cream. Spinach soufflé crêpes with mushroom sauce are garnished with vegetables like snow peas or squash with walnuts and cranberries. Another favorite is a dish of rice and dried fruits topped with maple syrup, accompanied by a medley of breakfast meats. Freda loves to experiment, so who knows what yummy dishes you will find at the breakfast table.

She had planned to open a perennial garden nursery behind her home, but was too busy expanding her gardens – a showplace of bloom from spring through fall. It is the equal of any perennial garden we've seen, the more remarkable in that she does virtually all of it herself. Pathways wind past colorful lupine, "show-stopper" allium, a Japanese fern bed, a frog pond and a new wet shade garden for which she was seeking out skunk cabbage at our visit. They culminate in an idyllic, circular brick terrace beside a rose and dahlia garden overlooking a bog.

(603) 585-6540. Two rooms and two suites with private baths. Doubles, $85. Suites, $95.

Hannah Davis House, 106 New Hampshire Route 119 West, Fitzwilliam 03447.

Innkeepers Kaye and Mike Terpstra "always traveled on our stomachs" and expect their guests to do the same. So extravagant breakfasts and afternoon refreshments are a priority in their elegant, 1820 Federal house.

The heart of the operation is an enormous, open country kitchen made cozy by prolific plants (including one hanging from a butcher scale). Guests breakfast here at a large table beside the fireplace. Afternoon treats, from popcorn to chocolate-chip cookies, are served in a common room or on the rear deck overlooking colorful gardens and a pond occupied by a resident beaver. Another common room holds a piano and stereo system.

Upstairs are three guest rooms with private baths. All the beds are angled into the corners and the large bathrooms have clawfoot tubs and pedestal sinks. Kaye's collection of quilts, teddy bears and an old nightdress and cap decorate the rooms. A high chair in the hall contains the necessities a guest might forget, including a hair dryer, a steam iron and a wine pull.

Two large and airy guest suites out over the garage and carriage barn have private entrances. One is called Popovers because its deck and elevated walkway to the breakfast area "pops over" the back yard and bog. A spacious affair where room divisions occur with oak furniture rather than walls, it has an angled antique cannonball queen bed, a sofa and another bed tucked into a corner. The fireplace may be enjoyed from both bedroom and sitting room. Mount Monadnock is on view from the window of the bathroom, which, Kaye quips, has the best seat in the house. The lofty bedroom in the Loft Suite opens onto a sitting room below with a queensize sofabed, corner fireplace, walk-in closet and a bathroom with clawfoot tub and separate, glass-enclosed shower. A new main-floor suite has two fireplaces, a kingsize bed, a sofabed in the sitting room and a private porch.

The hearty breakfast one day we visited included juice, homemade granola and applesauce, cinnamon-raisin bread and banana bread with fresh ginger, pears poached in syrup and ginger, and french toast stuffed with ham and cheese topped with a dijon sauce. Nasturtiums and snow peas garnish the main courses, which could be scrambled eggs with green beans, ratatouille-stuffed crêpes or a sandwich of stuffed french toast with peaches and cream cheese. Occasionally Kaye stuffs the french toast with seafood and cream cheese.

(603) 585-3344. Three rooms and three suites with private baths. Doubles, $60 to $85. Suites, $105 to $115.

The Benjamin Prescott Inn, Route 124 East, Jaffrey 03452.

This handsome pale yellow 1820s Greek Revival house in a rural setting east of town was the first of Monadnock's upscale B&Bs. Since 1988 it's been run by Barry and Janice Miller, he with 26 years in the hotel business – half of them at Henry Ford's Dearborn Inn in Michigan.

The Snyders have added their own hallmarks and upgraded the nine guest rooms, all with private baths and ranging from standard size to a suite that can sleep eight. Rooms are stenciled and furnished with antiques, handsome quilts, items from the owners' seemingly myriad collections and interesting touches like handpainted antique irons used as door stops. The John Adams Attic Suite on the third floor is a delight with a living room/wet bar and a balcony overlooking the rural back yard, plus another room with a kingsize bed. Both rooms have unusual sleeping alcoves that Barry calls "closet beds" – a Scottish practice using the eaves to cram in extra sleeping space.

A full country breakfast is served at a large table in the dining room or at smaller tables in the common sitting room with a fireplace and TV. Juices and three of Janice's fruit breads precede the main course, perhaps scotch eggs, eggs benedict or Prescott rarebit, or a bread dish like cinnamon-sourdough french toast shaped in a fan of maple leaves, multi-grain waffles with raspberry butter, or dutch apple pancakes made with granny smith apples. Check out Barry's collection of sands from across the world, stocked in test tubes and displayed on three shelves in the common room. And don't miss the inn's mailbox across the street, an intricate replica of the house itself.

(603) 532-6637. Nine rooms and one suite with private baths. Doubles, $75. Suite $140.

Apple Gate Bed & Breakfast, 199 Upland Farm Road (Route 123), Peterborough 03458.

Tiny electric candles glow year-round in the windows of this handsome 1832 Colonial surrounded by prolific gardens, trees and apple orchards. The wraparound veranda with its dark green Adirondack chairs is a perfect spot for taking in the rural surroundings.

Apples are the theme inside, done in exquisite taste by Dianne and Ken

Legenhausen, formerly of Long Island, where she was a music teacher and he a police officer. Colorful stenciling leads guests up the front staircase to three of the four fresh-looking guest rooms, all with private baths. We like best the buttery yellow Cortland corner room with a queensize bed, hooked rugs on the wide pine floors and basket of Woods of Windsor amenities in the bathroom. The small McIntosh room with a clawfoot tub in the bath is barely big enough for a three-quarter bed.

Particularly attractive are the main-floor common rooms, including a fireplaced parlor opening into a library, where a stuffed bear is perched on the bench at the piano. A full breakfast is served by candlelight at a table set for six or eight beside the fireplace in the beamed dining room. Specialties are oven-baked apple pancakes and various kinds of omelets.

(603) 924-6543. Fax (603) 924-1633. Four rooms with private baths. Doubles, $65 to $80. Two night minimum weekends in summer and fall.

Gourmet Treats

Peterborough is the center of the area's culinary, cultural and shopping attractions, and art galleries are especially drawn to the area around Depot Square.

The **Sharon Arts Center** at 457 Route 123 south of town has a super shop with items from the League of New Hampshire Craftsmen and exhibits in the Killian and Young Galleries. A good sampling is on display in the center's large new fine art and crafts shop in Depot Square.

The North Gallery at Tewksbury's, Route 123, is a favorite shop of many, representing more than 500 American craftsmen and carrying everything from cards to toys to paintings to collectibles and a small section of specialty foods and jams, not to mention all the crafts, on three floors of a newly reconstructed, post and beam barn. Other good gift shops with specialty foods and dishware as sidelines include **At Wit's End, The Winged Pig** and **The Field Mouse. Wild World** at Depot Square specializes in New England farmstead cheeses, pastas, chocolates and epicurean treats. **Maggie's Farm Natural Foods** at 14 Main St. is a large and good natural-foods store with healthful cookbooks, vinegars, sundried tomatoes, salsas and such, plus organic produce, wines and coffee. It opens into **Cook's Complements,** a nice kitchen shop next door, which stocks all the proper equipment from gadgets to coffee makers to pretty placemats.

Aesop's Tables at 12 Depot Square is a coffee bar and tea room with a difference. For one thing, it's in a corner of the Toad-Stool Bookstore, and is a comfy refuge of mismatched tables and chairs. For another, it dispenses pastries, sandwiches and desserts to go with. Owner Janice Hurley offers soups and sandwiches in the $4 range (cajun meatloaf and chicken burrito, at our recent visit) along with pastries and sweets.

Two other eateries have their devotees. **Nonie's Restaurant & Bakery,** 28 Grove St., serves breakfast all day and is known for hearty homemade soups and an extensive menu, all available for takeout. The **Café at Noone Falls,** south of town at 50 Jaffrey Road, is a cafeteria-style eatery offering informal breakfast, lunch and dinner, to eat at little tables or to go. The rough-edged, glassed-in dining area looks out toward Noone Falls. The tables are dressed with cloths at night.

For a taste of rural New England, **Parker's Maple Barn,** Brookline Road, Mason, is a favorite stop of many for breakfast – for pancakes, of course – and breakfast is served all day, until dinner service starts at 4:30. Besides old-fashioned home cooking in a 19th-century barn, there's a country store with gifts and maple items produced on site. Open daily from 7 or 8 a.m., March-December.

If your taste runs to Thai, head for **Thai Garden**, 118 Main St., Keene. Local innkeepers and chefs tout it as an exceptional, urban-quality ethnic restaurant that's a surprise given the prevailing marketplace.

Garden Gourmet

Rosaly's Farm Stand, Route 123, Peterborough.

Some of the salads at local restaurants bear the name Rosaly, as in "Rosaly's Garden" at the former Latacarta. They contain fresh organic baby greens, tomatoes, cucumbers and whatever and come from the certified organic gardens of Rosaly S. Bass just southeast of Peterborough. The farm stand, the retail adjunct to the 26-year-old Rosaly's Garden enterprise, is a fascinating stop for people interested in exotic produce and flowers. It also offers cookies, scones and the odd prepared foods and vinegars, among them hot pepper. We bought some yukon gold potatoes, lavender peppers and pattypan squash and admired the pick-your-own flower and herb gardens, a well-marked showplace of prolific blooms and color.

(603) 924-7774. Open daily in season, 10 to 6.

Herbal Gourmet

Pickity Place, Nutting Hill Road, Mason.

Usually it's "over the river and through the woods" to Grandmother's house, but in this case it's up, up, and up a mountain on some bumpy dirt roads and, if you didn't see the odd small sign tacked to a tree, you would swear you were on a wild goose chase.

It's worth the jolts, for eventually you come to a 1786 house and barn embracing a restaurant, herb shop, museum, garden shop, greenhouse and, in the Little Red Riding Hood Room (because Elizabeth O. Jones used the house to illustrate her version of the book), you guessed it, a big bad wolf in a nightcap, lying in grandmother's canopied bed.

The shop smells marvelous, with its wares of herbal teas, potpourris, pomanders, soaps, dried apple wreaths and even a dill pillow (which apparently will help soothe a baby to sleep). We picked up a tea drinker's gift box ($12.95 – four teas, bamboo strainer, honey and honey dipper) for a tea-loving grandpa.

Pickity Place also offers herbal luncheons, five courses for $13.95. You're encouraged to bring your own wine (not too much, or you'll never negotiate down the mountain). In a room where bunches of herbs hang on the walls and a huge swag of bay leaves is over the mantel, you will be served foods appropriate to the season (and often in honor of the ancient farming festivals of Europe). The October menu, for instance, might have creamy spinach dip, tomato-barley soup, eight-grain bread, herbed pasta salad, a choice of beef crêpes with horseradish sauce or vegetable stroganoff, spinach mornay and pumpkin squares.

(603) 878-1151. Lunch, $13.95. Seatings at 11:30, 12:45 or 2, daily except major holidays. Reservations required.

Summer Suite at Inn at Harbor Head yields view toward ocean from Cape Porpoise.

Southern Maine

Sophistication by the Sea

It wasn't so long ago that proper Bostonians thought fine dining ended at Portsmouth and the New Hampshire-Maine state line.

The Southern Maine coast was known for lobster shacks and seafood roadhouses, and about the only restaurant of note was the Whistling Oyster in Ogunquit.

How times have changed. Such popularity and sophisticated summer resort areas as York Harbor, Ogunquit and Kennebunkport have spawned countless new restaurants and inns. Most of the better establishments today did not even exist twenty years ago. A restaurant supplier said that in one boom year in the late 1980s, twelve major restaurants had popped up along the Maine coast since the previous summer. The boom continues, with more opening in the late 90s, when other locales barely held to the status quo.

The region's focus of culinary interest is Portland (see next chapter), which offers more quality and variety in dining and food attractions than cities many times its size.

But the treats begin almost at the Maine border, where the new headquarters and company store of the rapidly expanding Stonewall Kitchen specialty foods business greets visitors at a prime location next to the large new York visitor center.

The other centers of culinary interest are in Ogunquit and Kennebunkport, two of the more luxurious summer colonies along the coast south of Portland. Ogunquit's famed Whistling Oyster closed, but worthy successors remain. And George Bush and his summer neighbors in Kennebunkport no longer have to go to Ogunquit for a fine meal – they have plenty of good restaurants of their own.

Dining

The Best of the Best

Arrows, Berwick Road, Ogunquit.

Two chefs who apprenticed with Jeremiah Tower at Stars in San Francisco came east in 1988 to take over this off-again, on-again restaurant that had great potential. Clark Frasier and Mark Gaier quickly fulfilled that potential and more. With great attention to detail, they have painstakingly crafted a chic and uniquely personal destination restaurant that offers some of the most exciting – and probably the most expensive – food in Maine.

Their setting is hard to beat: a 1765 Colonial farmhouse that imparts a vision of pastoral paradise just west of the Maine Turnpike. Through leaded panes reminiscent of the Mission style, patrons in the spacious rear dining room look out onto fabulous gardens. On the entry table, flowers and branches of berries rise to the ceiling from a bowl flanked by produce spilling out of baskets. The dark wood ceiling, wide-plank floors, handsome service plates, crisp white linens, fresh flowers, and new cherry and walnut chairs with upholstered seats are as pretty as a picture.

The affable owners' insistence on purity and perfection goes to extremes. Their full-time staff of 35 includes two gardeners on the property. One, Marcia MacDonald, tends a showplace acre of vegetables and herbs, presenting a detailed list of what exotica is available each day to the chef. Raised beds and cold-frame covers allow her to produce lettuces for salads from April to early December, and their garden-to-table freshness is manifest in every delicious bite. The owners recently replaced every piece of glassware with fine crystal, the better for connoisseurs to enjoy the most extensive wine cellar in Maine, which includes twenty by the glass, many by the half bottle and an impressive selection of rare Bordeaux from the 1960s.

Surrounded by fields and flowers (spotlit from above and below) as well as trees and bushes bedecked in lights, up to 70 diners feast on the view of jaunty black-eyed susans and a sea of zinnias as well as some of Maine's most sophisticated fare. Formally clad waiters in black and white take orders without making notes, quite a feat since the contemporary American menu with Pacific Rim overtones changes nightly.

For starters, how about the nightly Arrows bento box, a tiered, wooden Asian lunch box filled one night with a crispy crab pillow, shiitake mushroom salad and a spicy beef brochette, and the next night with paper-wrapped chicken, crispy catfish with carrot and papaya salad and a vegetable spring roll? A roulade of foie gras might be teamed with poached pears and a vidalia onion confit. We liked the tea-smoked quail with a garlic-ginger vinaigrette and red-chile mayonnaise (the description cannot do justice to its complexity) and one of the evening's three salads, a trio of Japanese delicacies: zucchini with soy, carrot with sweet peanut dressing and mushroom with green onion. Each was a visual as well as a gustatory work of art, as was each dish to come.

Among the six entrée choices, you might find grilled yellowfin tuna with fried green tomatoes and cornmeal spoonbread or plank-roasted Atlantic salmon with haricots verts and a creamy corn purée. The tea-smoked duck breast and ginger

Chef-owners Clark Frasier and Mark Gaier and staff raise perfect produce for meals at Arrows.

confit duck leg with garlic greens, jasmine rice and a scallion and Chinese black bean sauce was a masterpiece. The only dish we weren't wild about was the grilled tenderloin of beef, which we thought had too intense a smoky taste. The accompaniment of fire-roasted red onion, grilled radicchio, green and yellow beans, tarragon mayonnaise and the best thread-thin crispy french fries ever more than compensated.

A dessert of pineapple, peach-plum and mango sorbets, each atop a meringue and each with its own distinctive sauce, was a triumph. But we'd return anytime for any of pastry chef Lucia Velasco Evans's offerings, say the apple and pear croustade with pecan frangipane, double chocolate ice cream and vanilla crème anglaise or the lemon tart with pistachio cookie crust, blueberry sorbet, raspberry coulis and crème chantilly.

At meal's end, chef-owners Clark and Mark table-hop and chat about food with their customers.

Clark, who studied cooking in China, hails from California. Mark trained with Madeleine Kamman and was executive chef at the late Whistling Oyster in Perkins Cove. Mark is usually in the kitchen and Clark out front, although they sometimes trade places so each can keep tabs on what's going on. And they take advantage of their winter break to travel, research food ideas and rejuvenate. "Instead of burning ourselves out," says Clark, "we come back re-energized and ready to go again. After a dozen years, we're still excited." So are their fans.

(207) 361-1100. Entrées, $36.95 to $39.95. Dinner nightly except Monday, 6 to 10, Thursday-Sunday in off-season. Open mid-April to mid-December.

Cape Neddick Inn, 1233 U.S. Route 1 at Route 1A, Cape Neddick.

Combine an artistic setting and an innovative menu and you have one of the more interesting restaurants in southern Maine. Michele Duval, the founding chef in 1979 at what was then known as the Cape Neddick Inn and Gallery, returned in

1997 to rejoin maitre-d' Glenn Gobeille. They bought out his partners and spiffed up the image, downplaying the gallery theme and upgrading the restaurant. The attractive, low-slung building with porte-cochere in front retains something of a gallery feeling. Artworks are displayed to great advantage in the entry foyer and on the walls of the main dining room and the bar/lounge. Equally a focus now are the custom-made wine racks along one side of the dining room, holding a selection that earned the Wine Spectator award. Michele enhanced the windows with sheer "Matisse-look curtains" from France and upgraded the place settings. The monogrammed CNI white china is rimmed in sage green, matching the color of the walls in the two-level dining room. "It looks more like a restaurant now," she declares.

Sophistication extends to the contemporary American fare executed by Michele, who wears proudly her title as chef of the year, as determined by the area chapter of the American Culinary Federation. Appetizers range widely from New England fish chowder to a salad called "tip of the iceberg," a wedge of lettuce topped with maytag blue cheese dressing, cob-smoked bacon and chopped tomato. Among the favorites: a cognac-laced pâté of chicken liver and Italian sausage, a citrus-marinated angus steak taco with manchego cheese and roasted grape salsa, and applewood-smoked seafood stacked with Rhode Island jonnycakes.

For main courses, expect novel takes on basic New England fare. The pan-roasted haddock might be paired with Maine crabmeat and potato hash and an herbed velouté sauce. A timbale of Maine scallops and baby spinach is served with lobster raviolis and garnished with ossetra caviar. The duck breast comes with Chinese oyster-ginger sauce atop lo mein noodles. A truffled bread and butter pudding accompanies the chargrilled club steak with four-peppercorn sauce.

At our visit, a macadamia-lobster tart served on mushroom duxelles was an extraordinary appetizer. We passed up one of the night's specials of swordfish grilled with ginger and gin for a fantastic fettuccine with lobster, shrimp, scallops and artichokes, and a Korean-style lamb kabob with sesame sauce and a spicy vegetable relish.

Desserts have always been a Cape Neddick Inn strong point. Recent winners were floating islands filled with coffee-cognac mousse, ginger cake with molten chocolate center and ginger crème anglaise, and a Mexican parfait of chocolate-tequila and cinnamon ice creams with butterscotch sauce and tortilla strips.

The bar offerings include a rare brandy poured from an oak cask. Periodic dinners in Cape Neddick's Marriage of Food and Wine series are highly regarded.

(207) 363-2899. Entrées, $16 to $25. Dinner nightly, from 5:30.

Hurricane, Oarweed Lane, Perkins Cove, Ogunquit.

This trendy establishment has been upgraded by Brooks and Luanne MacDonald, he the working chef who has elevated its already high reputation. "Our view will blow you away – our menu will bring you back" is its slogan, a realistic claim based on our meals there and the crowds waiting to be seated for lunch at 2 o'clock on a September weekday.

The decor is nil, since floor-to-ceiling windows in two small summery rooms look out onto the ocean. Every table has a view. The all-day menu is categorized by soups and salads and small plates that change seasonally, and lunch and dinner entrées posted daily. Among the former, you could make a good meal of lobster gazpacho ("so hot it's cool") or lobster chowder (the house specialty) with the

Wine, bread and pottery displays are backdrop for dining at Cape Neddick Inn.

house salad of cracked-peppercorn-dressed field greens with roasted shallots and pistachios. Also consider deviled lobster cakes with teardrop tomato and avocado salsa or a shrimp spring roll with a mandarin orange and wasabi dipping sauce. Or how about Royal Caspian ossetra caviar for a cool $50? With the meal comes a loaf of rustic hearth-baked sourdough bread, served in an unusual cylindrical stainless steel container with a bottle of extra-virgin olive oil.

The lunch entrées from a lengthy and interesting repertoire range from pan-seared yellowfin tuna served over a sweet corn coulis and truffled mashed potatoes to an open-faced swordfish sandwich and caesar salad with shrimp, chicken or lobster. We liked the gloppy five-onion soup crusted with gruyère cheese and the Thai beef salad with greens, soba noodles and a peanut sauce so spicy it brought tears to the eyes. At the other end of the taste spectrum was a soothing sandwich of delicate grilled crabmeat and havarti cheese on butter-grilled sourdough bread. Big eaters at the next table praised desserts of apple-walnut-cinnamon bread pudding and lemon blackberry purse with ginger anglaise.

Dinner dishes include baked lobster and haddock baklava with brie, lobster cioppino, fire-roasted black grouper with a spicy wakame and lobster salad, and grilled veal chop with a pistachio crust and vegetable "linguini." Unusual items on a recent menu were seared Hawaiian opah with coconut cream sauce on a sautéed mango, and an herb-encrusted venison tower with shaved garlic sauce and roasted vegetables.

Like the menu, the choice wine list encourages experimentation. Its introduction suggests pairing pinot noir with salmon or a big cabernet with chocolate decadence for dessert – "what a great match!" Fifty wines are available by the glass and five by the half-bottle.

Beside the restaurant is **Hurricane Provisions,** an offshoot stocking some of the products used at Hurricane as well as a good selection of wines.

(207) 646-6348. Entrées, $16 to $35. Lunch daily, 11:30 to 3:30. Dinner, 5:30 to 9:30 or 10:30.

98 Provence, 104 Shore Road, Ogunquit.

Team a local restaurateur and his French-Canadian wife with her talented brother as chef. The result is this winner, a true place seemingly transplanted from the countryside of France to the hubbub of Ogunquit. Johanna Gignach had run a small French restaurant in Old Montreal during the Olympics before being wooed to Ogunquit to marry Paul Haseltine, known to everyone at Barnacle Billy's Etc. restaurant as "Hez." It seems her brother, Pierre Gignach, was too young then to be a chef, but after training at Chez la Mère Michel, one of our favorite Montreal restaurants, and working in Winnipeg, he was ready. The Haseltines fashioned a country-pretty dining room and living room/lounge from the old 98 Shore Road breakfast eatery, added a new kitchen and bar, and awaited the arrival of Pierre with his visa.

Chef and visa arrived in the nick of time for the 1996 summer season. They started serving breakfast, "which was the best advertising for us," said Johanna, and soon opened for dinner. Breakfast has fallen by the wayside, since it was dinner for which Pierre had prepared.

He excels with the classic dishes of Provence, perhaps roasted black sea bass with potato and fennel gratin or pan-seared St. Peter fish with a pistachio-butter sauce. He might serve a lamb shank confit on stewed green lentils, produce a traditional venison stew with porcini, mirepoix and red wine, and top a provimi veal tenderloin with a wild mushroom cream sauce. Where else could you find an entrée of langoustines paired with goat cheese ravioli gratin?

Francophiles are in heaven with the starters, perhaps duck foie gras poached in a traditional pot-au-feu, a terrine of roquefort and armagnac goat cheese or Normandy sardine fritters with a niçoise-style mayonnaise. Desserts are prepared in the French style. Savor fondat au chocolat, profiteroles, strawberry bavarois or poached pear with homemade sorbet.

The dining room with its cafe curtains, barnwood walls decked out with plates, and its colorful floral tablecloths and service plates will charm you into thinking you're in the South of France. The food will convince you.

(207) 646-9898. Entrées, $18.95 to $25.95. Dinner nightly except Tuesday, 5:30 to 9. Closed Wednesday in off-season and December-March.

Seascapes, On the Pier, Cape Porpoise, Kennebunkport.

The smashing table settings at this elegant seaside restaurant won a national tabletop competition sponsored by Restaurant Hospitality magazine as "the prettiest tables in America." No wonder. The plates and candle holders are of hand-painted Italian pottery in heavenly colors, the napkins are ringed with fishes, and the unusual wineglasses are fluted. Angela and Arthur LeBlanc, then owners of the Kennebunk Inn, found them on their travels and knew they were perfect for their restaurant, with its sea of windows onto the waterscape. The colorful table – pictured on the cover of our book, *The Restaurants of New England* – is the match for the view of boats in quaint Cape Porpoise Harbor.

Chef Martin Carlton from California enjoys a reputation for pan-Asian and Mediterranean fare that gets better and better. Excellent dark wheat rolls get dinner here off to a good start. For appetizers, we've relished a stellar seafood and corn chowder, the marinated portobello napoleon with roasted peppers, zucchini, smoked mozzarella and shaved peppered fennel, and the fabulous lobster and crab egg roll with a lively mango coulis and Asian slaw, almost a meal in itself. Also

Country French dining room at 98 Provence.   Prize-winning table setting at Seascapes.

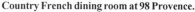

almost a meal is the novel Seascapes caesar salad like none we've seen – chiffoned lettuce wrapped in a grilled flour tortilla and served sliced with prosciutto, parmigiano-reggiano and chives.

A sorbet precedes the entrées. At one dinner they were a classic Mediterranean bouillabaisse with rouille and a breast of chicken coated with pistachio nuts and stuffed with scallops; at another, a rich lobster tequila over linguini, a garlicky shrimp Christina with feta, kalamata olives and plum tomatoes, and grilled salmon with a sesame-soy-sherry marinade and a trio of julienned vegetables. Lately, as chef Martin toyed with the vertical style, the rack of lamb arrived looking like flying buttresses. He paired lobster with pheasant, an unusual combination of delicacies, served with a mushroom-corn salad and wild rice-ginger pancake.

We're usually too full after the main courses to order dessert, but you might succumb to a creamy blueberry cheesecake with vanilla bean ice cream and a chocolate-chip cookie, almond puff pastry with raspberries in a port wine sauce or tiramisu with coffee bean brittle, caramel and ginger meringue sauce.

The select, primarily California wine list is reasonably priced and merits annual Wine Spectator awards. The "Silver Collection" offers a selection for $25.

Ever-improving, the LeBlancs have added a fireplace to the dining room and a pianist for the piano bar in the reception area. In the walkout basement beneath Seascapes, they also run the casual **Porpoise Pub,** serving a light menu in summer from noon to sunset.

(207) 967-8500. Entrées, $19.50 to $29. Dinner nightly, from 5. Wednesday-Sunday in off-season. Closed December to mid-April.

Salt Marsh Tavern, 46 Western Ave. (Route 9), Lower Village, Kennebunkport.

If the makeover of the old Hennessy's restaurant reminds people of the old White Barn, that's the way its new owner planned it. Artist Jack Nahil recreated the White Barn restaurant he used to own after a brief hiatus in Florida. "There's a lot of déjà-vu here," he acknowledged. "Barns speak to me, I guess."

This barn speaks with a piano bar in the center beneath a soaring ceiling, oriental scatter rugs on the wide plank floors, the owner's oil paintings on the barnwood walls, farm implements and wood carvings on the lofts, and large rear windows onto gardens and a salt marsh stretching toward Kennebunk Beach. Tables dressed with white over forest green cloths and brass candlesticks are spaced throughout the open main floor and the upstairs loft.

The exterior speaks with a showy array of exotic gardens, lovingly tended by Jack and a gardener as "art – an extension of my painting." Diners find the beauty "an extension of the dining experience," Jack says.

The food blends the classic and the creative with equal flair. Among main courses, the grilled salmon fillet might be served with pommery mustard, crème fraîche and a chiffonade of spinach and radicchio; the pan-seared halibut finished with a champagne and saffron beurre blanc, raspberries and fried leeks. The free-range chicken could be served with blueberry-pear chutney and grilled corn on the cob and the black angus sirloin strip steak napped with bourbon-garlic butter and accompanied by onion marmalade and chive-mashed potatoes.

Among starters, roasted chicken and green-chile soup with cilantro cream is a counterpoint to the traditional lobster bisque. Baked oysters come with leeks, pancetta and romano cheese, and sweetbreads with asparagus and capers. Dessert could be profiteroles, bittersweet chocolate torte or fruit tartlets.

A pianist entertains nightly.

(207) 967-4500. Entrées, $21.95 to $25.95. Dinner, Tuesday-Sunday 6 to 9 or 10. Closed in March.

Grissini Trattoria & Panificio, 27 Western Ave., Kennebunkport.

If you think the folks at the White Barn Inn know how to do things right, wait until you see their casual but elegant Italian bistro. Owner Laurie Bongiorno bought the old Cafe Topher and undertook a big-bucks renovation right down to the studs. The result is a perfectly stunning space, with vaulted beamed ceilings three stories high and a tall fieldstone fireplace – looking straight out of the Adirondacks – that fits right in. Sponged pale yellow walls, large tables for four spaced well apart, comfortable lacquered wicker armchairs, white tablecloths covered with paper, rather bright pinpoint lighting, and fancy bottles and sculptures backlit in the windows add up to a thoroughly sophisticated feeling, not exactly what one expects in a small seaside town. The talented chef, Sebastian Pfeiffer, happens to be French, but much of the kitchen staff is direct from Italy. The waiters are young, handsome, Italian and ever-so-discreetly flirtatious. And what charming accents!

Opera was playing in the background as a plate of tasty little crostini, some with pesto and black olives and some with gorgonzola cheese and tomato, arrived to start our dinner. We liked the bread, prepared in the in-house bakery and served in slabs unexpectedly plunked – in most un-White Barn-like fashion – smack onto the table, with the server pouring an exorbitant amount of olive oil into a bowl for dipping. Everything else came on enormous white plates, except for the wine (in beautiful stemmed glasses) and the ice water (in pilsener glasses).

The exciting, oversize menu changes weekly and is made for grazing. Among antipasti, we loved the wood-grilled local venison sausage on a caramelized onion salad and the house-cured Maine salmon carpaccio accompanied by pasta salad. Pizzas come in small and large sizes. We were tempted by the "porto livorno" with scallops, mussels, calamari, tomato and mozzarella, but finally chose the barbarucci with duck sausage, goat cheese and pesto.

Fieldstone fireplace and beamed ceiling contribute to Adirondack lodge look at Grissini.

Pastas are creative and a meal in themselves. Equally good values are the secondi, dishes like osso buco, wood-grilled tuna with olive mashed potatoes, warm spinach and sundried tomato salad, and – you know there has to be a lobster dish here somewhere – pan-seared lobster tail with extra-virgin olive oil, herbs and smashed potatoes (it's the only item priced over $20). We split the wood-grilled leg of lamb steak with Tuscan white beans, pancetta, garlic and rosemary. The steak was a bit tough but had great flavor. The "insalata mista" was a nice mixture of field greens, kalamata olives, tomato, gorgonzola and pinenuts. Accompanying the meal was a fine reserve chianti for $18 from an affordable, mostly Italian wine list.

A sampler plate of tiramisu, a chocolate delicacy and strawberries in balsamic vinegar with mascarpone cheese ended a memorable dinner.

The turnaway crowds spill on warm nights onto a tiered outdoor courtyard that looks rather like a grotto. It was easy to understand why one local innkeeper who knows her food had dined at Grissini eleven times the first two months it was open, and another at our latest visit called it the best value in town. Eating well here could easily become a habit.

(207) 967-2211. Entrées, $14.95 to $19.95. Dinner nightly, 5:30 to 9 or 9:30.

Windows on the Water, 12 Chase Hill Road, Kennebunkport.

The windows are architecturally interesting at this expansive restaurant on a hilltop above the Kennebunk River, although their views have been obstructed by the Federal Jack's Restaurant & Brew Pub complex below. Chef-owner John Hughes, inducted into the Master Chefs Institute of America, has earned quite a collection of awards. One is for his lobster-stuffed baked potato, teamed with scallions, jarlsburg cheese and sweet cream and available for $10.95 as a dinner appetizer or as a lunch entrée (we found the latter more appropriate). Other Maine Culinary Festival gold-medal winners are lobster ravioli, lobster bisque, free-range chicken tortellini alfredo and prosciutto-wrapped grilled shrimp on a bed of mango and pineapple salsa.

The dinner menu is laced with novel twists as well as award-winning standbys. For starters, how about lobster potstickers, "Texas-style mallard fingers" (otherwise known as duck tenders with grilled corn and cactus salsa), cajun smoked beef carpaccio with sweet molasses oil and chipotle aioli, or a salad of house-smoked salmon, wilted spinach and wild mushrooms? Tempting main courses include miso-marinated halibut fillet with szechuan-spiced vegetables and wasabi whipped potatoes, and pinenut-encrusted rack of lamb with a vidalia onion vinaigrette and mint essence.

Dessert could be lemon cheesecake, chocolate oblivion torte and charlotte au chocolat. The wine selection has been expanded lately, with more than 80 available by the glass.

The setting is quite elegant, given the restaurant's billing as "casual gourmet." The main dining room is handsome with high ceiling, track lighting, well-spaced tables dressed in linens and a peach color scheme accented by vases of fresh flowers. An even nicer small room beyond has a bowed front window. There's a two-level Garden Room at the side, half enclosed and half screened. Upstairs is a lounge with a cathedral ceiling and a Palladian window overlooking the river.

(207) 967-3313. Entrées, $19.95 to $36.95. Lunch daily, 11:45 to 2:30. Dinner, 5:30 to 9:30 or 10:30. Closed Monday in winter.

Healthful Gourmet

Frankie & Johnny's, 1594 Route 1 North, Cape Neddick.

It isn't much to look at, this gourmet natural-foods restaurant originating in a manufactured home beside the highway, painted with colorful triangles and sporting a Haagen-Dazs sign in front. But stop, venture in and have a healthful meal, either inside in a whimsical dining room, outside at a couple of picnic tables or to go.

Amiable Frank Rostad handles the front of the house while partner John Shaw, formerly with the late Laura Tanner House restaurant in Ogunquit, cooks in a state-of-the-art kitchen. Everything is made from scratch and almost all of it on site, say these purists (it took them fourteen months to find an all-natural cone to serve with their Haagen-Dazs ice cream). They even squeeze juices at their juice bar.

John produces "gourmet food that's good for you." The soups could be vegetarian or vegan (dairy-free). Six remarkable "entrée salads" are served on dinner plates. They're based on mixed greens and classic caesar with additions of grilled veggies, blackened chicken and cheeses, blackened salmon and shrimp, and more. Under pastas and spaetzles you might find tofu and rice noodles, chicken, Sicilian shrimp, vegetable harvest and, at one visit, broccoli alfredo ("there is a little Italian in all of us," the menu noted). Favorites among entrées are grilled or blackened Atlantic salmon, served on a giant potato pancake with wilted spinach in a nutmeg sherry cream sauce, topped with crème fraîche and caviar, and a timely newcomer, roasted tenderloin of ostrich with a red wine and portobello mushroom sauce.

The pair are best known for their trademarked crustolis ($10.75 or $13.75), ten-inch or fourteen-inch round French bread crusts made from unbleached flour and not unlike pizzas. For dinner, we ordered one with shrimp, pesto and goat cheese and another with capers, olives, red onions and feta cheese, split a house 'salad and had more than enough left over for lunch the next day.

Dinner is by candlelight and the food is serious, but it's dispensed in a relaxed and playful environment. Decor in the recently expanded dining room is nil except for a few abstract oils by Frank's sister and a handful of rocks and perhaps a miniature dinosaur on each table. "It's hard to take yourself seriously with rocks and a little dinosaur in front of you," says Frank, whose aim is for customers to have a good time. It's also hard to imagine that reservations are advised, but this place is very popular. So popular that they've discontinued lunch to concentrate on dinner. How many other natural-foods restaurants can say the same?

(207) 363-1909. Entrées, $14.75 to $20.75. Dinner from 5, nightly except Tuesday in summer, Thursday-Sunday in spring and fall. Closed late December through March. BYOB. No credit cards.

Dining and Lodging

White Barn Inn, Beach Street, Box 560C, Kennebunkport 04046.

Long known for its restaurant, the White Barn has been vastly upgraded in terms of accommodations as well.

Such has been the infusion of money and T.L.C. by the hands-on Australian owner, personable Laurie Bongiorno, that the inn was only the second in New England to be accepted into the prestigious Relais & Châteaux, the world-wide association of deluxe owner-operated hotels. Its restaurant was the first to be accorded five stars for all three categories of food, service and atmosphere by the Maine Sunday Telegram. In 1993, the restaurant became the AAA's first five-diamond dining in New England outside Boston. In 1999, the restaurant won the highest ranking of any resort restaurant worldwide in the annual Condé Nast Traveler Best of the Best awards.

And yes, it's really that good.

Dinner is served in a three-story barn attached to the inn, where you can look out through soaring plate-glass windows onto an incredible backdrop that changes with the seasons – lush impatiens in summer, assorted mums in fall, and spruce trees dressed with velvet bows and tiny white lights for Christmas. Up to 120 diners can be seated at tables spaced blessedly well apart in the main barn and in an adjoining barn. They're filled with understated antiques and oil paintings dating to the 18th century, and the loft holds quite a collection of wildlife wood carvings. The tables are set with silver, Schottsweizel crystal and Villeroy & Boch china, white linens and white tapers in crystal candlesticks. At one of our visits, a Russian pianist, here on a scholarship, played seemingly by ear in the entry near the gleaming copper-topped bar. A table of imported Indian granite centers seats fourteen in a new private dining room called the Wine Room, part of the expanded, 7,000-bottle wine cellar.

The food is in the vanguard of contemporary New England cuisine with a European flair. Dinner is prix-fixe ($67 in four courses), with at least half a dozen choices for most courses. The complex menu changes weekly. It's executed by a kitchen staff of sixteen and served with precision by a young waitstaff who meet with chef Jonathan Cartwright beforehand for 45 minutes each night. Guests at each table are served simultaneously, one waiter per plate.

Our latest dinner began with a glass of Perrier-Jouët extra brut (complimentary for house guests) and the chef's "welcome amenity," an herbed goat-cheese rosette, an onion tart and a tapenade of eggplant and kalamata olives. Interesting olive bread and plain white and poppyseed rolls followed. We'd gladly have tried any of the appetizers, but settled on a lobster spring roll with daikon radish, savoy cabbage and hot and sweet glaze, and the seared Hudson Valley foie gras on an apple and celeriac tart with a calvados sauce. Both were sensational.

Champagne sorbet in a pool of Piper Heidsieck extra-dry cleared the palate with a flourish for the main courses, of which a recent entry – "grilled cutlet of lamb and medallion of farm-raised veal filet on oregano-scented garden tomatoes with a parcel of forest mushroom risotto and chardonnay jus" – might be considered typical. One of us settled for a duo of Maine rabbit, a grilled loin with roasted rosemary and pommery mustard and a braised leg in cabernet sauvignon, accompanied by wild mushrooms and pesto-accented risotto. The other chose pan-seared tenderloin of beef topped with a horseradish gratin and port-glazed shallots on a pool of potato and Vermont cheddar cheese, with a side of asparagus. A bottle of Firestone cabernet accompanied from an excellent wine list especially strong on American chardonnays and cabernets.

Dessert was anything but anti-climactic: a classic coeur à la crème with tropical fruits and sugared shortbread and a trio of pear, raspberry and mango sorbets, served artistically on a black plate with colored swirls matching the sorbets. A tray of petits fours came with the bill. After an after-dinner brandy in the inn's living room, the little raisin cookies we found on the bed back in our room were somewhat superfluous.

The 25 guest accommodations in the main inn and outbuildings vary considerably, as their range in prices indicates. A renovated cottage beside the elegant pool area is the ultimate in plush privacy with a living room, porch, kingsize bedroom, double-sided fireplace and double jacuzzi. Almost its equal is the new loft suite, adjacent to the main inn with king bed, fireplace and oversize marble bath with whirlpool and separate steam shower. A private deck overlooks the inn's grounds.

The six fireplaced suites in the refurbished May's Annex also are the height of luxury. Each has a library-style sitting area with chintz-covered furniture, wood-burning fireplace, dressing room, spacious bathroom with a marble jacuzzi and separate shower, Queen Anne kingsize four-poster bed, secretary desk and a TV/VCR hidden in the armoire.

We felt quite pampered in the Green Room here, thanks to a personal note of welcome from the innkeeper, fresh fruit, Poland Spring water, terry robes and Gilchrist & Soames toiletries.

Four large renovated rooms in the Garden House also claim fireplaces and jacuzzis, as well as cathedral ceilings, queensize sleigh beds and sitting areas with wing chairs. Rooms upstairs in the inn, although nicely furnished and cheerfully decorated with whimsical hand-painted furniture and trompe-l'oeil accents, could not possibly be as spacious or sumptuous. Except, that is, for the new junior suite, which incorporated two older rooms. It's appointed in rich damask fabrics and boasts a sumptuous marble bath with whirlpool, separate steam shower and matching Victorian-style porcelain sinks with hand-painted cabinets.

Floral backdop outside window changes seasonally in glamorous dining room at White Barn Inn.

A lavish continental breakfast is served in the elegant Colonial dining room. Fresh orange juice and slices of cut-up fruits are brought to your table by a tuxedoed waiter. You help yourself to assorted cereals, yogurts and an array of muffins and pastries the likes of which we've seldom seen before – including a sensational strawberry-bran muffin with a top the size of a grapefruit and a cool crème d'amandes with a sliced peach inside. Entrées are available for a surcharge.

In 1999, owner Bongiorno acquired two nearby waterfront properties, the Yachtsman Lodge and the Sundial Inn. The 30-unit lodge was renovated and quickly won a four-diamond rating. The 34-room Sundial was renamed the Beachhouse and was undergoing renovation in two phases during 2000 and 2001. Although both were being upgraded, Laurie stressed they are "positioned quite differently" from each other and the White Barn.

(207) 967-2321. Fax (207) 967-1100. Sixteen rooms and nine suites with private baths. May-December: doubles, $230 to $365; suites and cottage, $395 to $495. January-April: doubles, $190 to $325; suites, $365 to $425. Two-night minimum weekends; three-nights holiday weekends.

Prix-fixe, $67. Dinner nightly by reservation, 6 to 9:30, Saturday from 5:30. Closed first two weeks of January. Jackets requested.

Cape Arundel Inn, Ocean Avenue, Kennebunkport 04046.

A choice location facing the open ocean and an excellent dining room commend this Shingle-style inn that reflects the essence of Maine.

Veteran restaurateur Jack Nahil of the Salt Marsh Tavern, who formerly owned the White Barn Inn, acquired the Cape Arundel in 1997 and started upgrading. He added larger beds and in-room telephones in the seven upstairs rooms, created more windows for what he rightly bills as "bold ocean views" and completely refurnished the 1950s motel units to convey a country inn motif. He also refurbished the inn's living room, through which diners pass to get to the restaurant. An artist and avid gardener, he has maintained the appropriately simple grandeur without adding the glitz so common today.

Dinner here is better than ever, thanks to the assured Nahil touch. Executive chef, Rich Lemoine, who has been with him since White Barn days, presents exotic contemporary fare. It enhances the romance of dining at a window table, watching wispy clouds turn to mauve and violet as the sun sets, followed by a full golden moon rising over the darkened ocean. For gourmands who like their food with a view, it's a dream come true.

The 60-seat, two-level dining room itself is a study in white and cobalt blue. An arty display of cobalt glass is on a shelf above a painting of cobalt glass.

Our latest dinner began with remarkably good crusty basil-parmesan-rosemary bread. Appetizers were a composed spinach salad with prosciutto and oyster mushrooms and an exemplary chilled sampler of ginger poached shrimp, a Maine crab-filled spring roll and tea-smoked sirloin with wasabi citrus rémoulade, each artfully presented and interspersed with colorful slaw.

Oversize dinner plates speckled with herbs yielded a superior sliced leg of lamb teamed with cavatelli pasta and wilted arugula, and a mixed grill of duck sausage, veal london broil and lamb loin chop. Other choices ranged from broiled halibut with a macadamia crust to grilled duck breast marinated in plum wine with confit dumplings, green tea rice and sesame honey demi-glace.

The dessert of cinnamon ice cream with strawberries over lady fingers was enough for two to share. A $23 Blackstone merlot from California accompanied from a small but unusually interesting wine list.

Happily, we had only to adjourn to our room in Rockbound, the former motel section. Each room here has a full bath and TV, and a small balcony with a front-on view of the ocean beyond the wild roses. Our end room was spiffily furnished in florals and reproduction furniture. A queen bed with a sturdy white wood headboard was angled from the corner. At an earlier visit, we enjoyed Room 4 on the far-front corner of the main inn, where white organdy curtains fluttered in the breeze. From two chairs in the corner we could take in the bird's-eye panorama of the ocean and the George Bush family compound at Walker Point.

The inn's spacious front porch is a super place to curl up with a good book or the morning newspaper before breakfast. Breakfast is a hearty continental buffet. Ours began with fresh orange juice, cereal, muesli, fruit and yogurt, and superior scones and croissants. The highlight was the day's extra: toasted basil-parmesan bread and a small spanakopita, "presented" in the dinner style on an oversize plate.

(207) 967-2125. Fax (207) 967-1199. Thirteen rooms and one suite with private baths. Doubles, $150 to $205, mid-June to mid-October; $85 to $180, rest of year. Two-night minimum weekends, three nights on holidays. Closed late December to early April. Entrées, $21 to $25.95. Dinner, Monday-Saturday 5:30 to 8:30 or 9.

Lodging

Hartwell House, 118 Shore Road, Box 393, Ogunquit 03907.

The British flag flies alongside the American in front of this sophisticated B&B on the main road between the center of Ogunquit and Perkins Cove. Owners Jim and Tricia Hartwell have an English background, which explains their extensive use of English antiques in the thirteen guest rooms and three suites, all with modern baths, and the lush lawns and sculpted gardens out back, which provide the profusion of flowers inside.

The enclosed front porch is a lovely space with arched windows, colorful French chintz on the loungers and wicker chairs, and an array of plants and flowers. Here is where guests gather for an afternoon pick-me-up of iced tea, poured from a glass pitcher topped with strawberries and orange slices on a silver tray. Everything except the wood floor in the stunning living room is white. The formal dining room has one long table, willowware china and a silver service on the sideboard. Hooked rugs dot the wide-board floors. A full breakfast of fresh fruit and a hot dish, perhaps stuffed crêpes, frittatas, baked chicken in puff pastry or belgian waffles, is served here or on the enclosed porch. Chef-innkeepers Christopher and Tracey Anderson also serve intimate, seven-course dinners for eight on Saturday nights in the off-season as part of a weekend package.

Most of the nine rooms in the main house have french doors onto terraces or private balconies looking over the rear yard. Across the street in an addition to the house where the innkeepers reside are seven more luxurious rooms and suites. The latter includesliving room, dining area, kitchen with refrigerator and wet bar and a balcony or terrace. Trisha's favorite is the James Monroe Suite, a two-level affair all in white.

(207) 646-7210 or (800) 235-8883. Fax (207) 646-6032. Eleven rooms, three suites and two studio apartments with private baths. July to mid-September: doubles, $125 to $150; suites, $170 to $190. Late spring and early fall: doubles, $100 to $130; suites, $150 to $170. November–April: doubles, $90 to $100; suites, $140.

The Inn at Harbor Head, 41 Pier Road, R.R.2, Box 1180, Kennebunkport 04046.

The location of this rambling shingled home on a rocky knoll right above the picturesque Cape Porpoise harbor is one of the attractions at this small B&B. Out front are gorgeous gardens with a sundial. A rear terrace and lawns lead down to the shore for swimming from the dock or just relaxing in one of the oversize rope hammocks, watching the lobster boats go by.

Breakfast is another attraction. From the country kitchen of innkeepers Eve and Dick Roesler come such dishes as bananas foster, poached pears with custard sauce and raspberries, or broiled grapefruit with kirsch and brown sugar. The "Maine" course could be marinated artichoke and broccoli frittata, honey-pecan french toast, crabmeat and bacon quiche, or wild Maine blueberry pancakes with warm maple syrup. Homemade lemon-poppyseed or cranberry muffins might accompany this feast. The meal is served at 9 a.m. in the dining room at a long table where there is much camaraderie. Coffee for early risers is put out at 8 in the kitchen.

The five guest quarters, three up and two down, have king or queensize canopy beds. They are decorated to the nth degree with exquisite hand-painted murals.

The newly expanded Harbor Suite's murals are of Cape Porpoise on the walls, with clouds and sky on the ceiling, mirroring the view from the window. Its sitting room boasts a gas fireplace, tiled with ivy and birds crafted by local artist Lou Lipkin of Goose Rocks Pottery. A kingsize pewter canopy bed is positioned in front of the window of the bedroom. A bath area with a clawfoot soaking tub and a chaise lounge opens through french doors onto a balcony overlooking the harbor and the gardens.

The entrance to the Garden Room is paved with stones and a little fountain, and original drawings of peach and plum blossoms float on the wall. French doors open onto a private, trellised deck overlooking the harbor. The downstairs Greenery, where we stayed, has a mural of fir trees by the shore, a bathroom with hand-painted tile and jacuzzi tub, and a view of the front gardens. Next time we'd opt for the upstairs Summer Suite, with the best view of the harbor from its balcony. It's painted with clouds drifting across the ceiling and comes with a kingsize wicker bed, gas fireplace and a cathedral-ceilinged bathroom with skylight, bidet and jacuzzi tub.

The Ocean Room is different from the rest – bold and masculine with a library of books about sailing, the sea and shipwrecks, plus a trompe-l'oeil window scene painted in its skylit bathroom to simulate a window.

Rooms are outfitted with thick towels, terrycloth robes, hair dryers, irons and boards, books and magazines, good reading lights, CD players, clock radios, a decanter of port and fresh flowers from the backyard cutting garden.

Eve serves afternoon tea with home-baked desserts in the living room from February to May and, in warm weather, offers afternoon wine and cheese on the back deck overlooking the harbor. After guests leave for dinner, the Roeslers turn down their beds, light soft lights and leave seashell dishes of chocolates on the pillows. It's little wonder that some guests stay for a week or more, and that many are honeymooners.

(207) 967-5564. Fax (207) 967-1294. www.harborhead.com. Three rooms and two suites with private baths. Doubles, $190 to $265; off-season, $130 to $205. Suites, $305 to $330; off-season, $205 to $260. Two-night minimum weekends. Closed Dec. 15 through January.

Bufflehead Cove Inn, Gornitz Lane, Box 499, Kennebunkport 04046.

Past a lily pond at the end of a long dirt road is this hidden treasure: a gray shingled, Dutch Colonial manse right beside a scenic bend of the Kennebunk River. Owners Harriet and Jim Gott have turned their family home since 1973 into a stunning B&B – the kind of waterfront home we've always dreamed of.

The public rooms, the setting and the warmth of the welcome are special here. A wide porch faces the tidal river and downtown Kennbunkport in the distance; there are porches along the side and a huge wraparound deck in back. A large and comfy living room contains window seats with views of the water. The dining room, which is shaped like the back of a ship, has a dark beamed ceiling, paneling, stenciling and a carpet painted on the floor. There are a dock with boats and five acres of tranquility with which to surround oneself.

All bedrooms are bright and cheerful. The spacious Balcony Room is perhaps the most appealing of those in the main house. It offers a wicker-filled screened balcony overlooking the river, a kingsize bed dressed with a plump floral comforter, a fireplace, a window seat and a chaise lounge. Its large bathroom has a shower.

refrigerator/wet bar and, most spectacular, a corner jacuzzi for two, positioned dramatically beneath hand-painted pots of apple blossoms stretching overhead.

Reflections of sun on the river shimmer on the ceiling of the River Room, which has a queen bed and a balcony. The walls and ceilings are hand-painted with vines in the Cove Suite, two rooms with lots of wicker, a gas fireplace and a private bath. Although it lacks a river view, the Garden Studio in back is ever-so-engaging with its own entrance and patio, a wicker sitting area, gas fireplace, a handcrafted queensize bed and grapevine stenciling that echoes the real vines outside the entry.

The crowning glory is the secluded Hideaway, fashioned from the Gotts' former quarters in the adjacent cottage. Mostly windows, it holds a kingsize bed, a tiled fireplace open to both the bedroom and the living room, rattan chairs, and an enormous bathroom with a double jacuzzi surrounded by a tiled border of fish. Pears seem to be a decorative theme, showing up on the fireplace tiles and at the base of a huge twig wreath over the mantel. Outside is a private deck where early-morning coffee was provided and we would gladly have spent the day, had we not been working.

Breakfast at 8:30 on the inn's front porch brought fresh orange juice and an elaborate dish of melon bearing mixed fruit and homemade pineapple sorbet. The main event was a delicious zucchini crescent pie, teamed with an English muffin topped with cheddar, tomato and bacon, and roasted potatoes with onions and salsa. Lobster quiche, soufflés, asparagus strata, green-apple stuffed french toast, waffles and popovers are other specialties. Jim often cooks breakfast when he's not out on his rounds as a lobster fisherman.

Wine and cheese are served in the early evening. Decanters of sherry and bottles of sparkling water are in each room.

(207) 967-3879. www.buffleheadcove.com Three rooms and two suites with private baths. June-October: doubles $145 to $275, suites $165 to $295. Rest of year: doubles $115 to $210, suites $140 to $210. Two-night minimum weekends.

The Captain Lord Mansion, Pleasant Street, Box 800, Kennebunkport 04046.

Rick Litchfield and his wife Bev Davis bought this structure, which they consider "probably the finest example of Federal architecture on the coast of Maine, if not the country," in 1978 when it was a home for elderly women. The couple totally restored the place, putting in private baths for each of the sixteen bedrooms on three floors, and creating an inn of such historic interest that public tours are given in summer.

Two chocolates are placed every evening in the bedrooms, which are elegantly furnished in antiques, most with four-poster or canopied beds. All but the smallest room have gas fireplaces, much in demand in autumn and winter. Five have new whirlpool tubs, and two more have deep clawfoot soaking tubs. A number have minibars.

The prime quarters seem to change with every upgrade, of which these peerless innkeepers never seem to tire. They first opened an annex called Phoebe's Fantasy with four more guest rooms, all with king or queen beds and fireplaces. Guests here take breakfast at a seven-foot harvest table in a gathering room with a chintz sofa, fireplace and television.

Lately they have made remarkable enhancements in the main building, particularly in terms of bath facilities. The first-floor Merchant Room was expanded into a deluxe suite with king canopy bed, two fireplaces, and a bathroom with heated marble floor, a ten-jet hydro-massage waterfall shower, double jacuzzi, bidet and three vanities. The Mary Lord and Excelsior rooms on the second floor gained renovated baths with heated Italian tiled floors and double whirlpool tubs. Now expanded as two-room suites are the Champion, which has a clawfoot soaking tub, the Mousam, whose new bath comes with a heated black granite floor and double-headed shower for two.

The corner rooms in this square, cupola-topped yellow mansion are especially spacious and airy. All rooms have period reproduction wallpaper and nice touches like sewing kits, Poland Spring water, and a tray with wine glasses and a corkscrew.

Guests gather beneath crystal chandeliers in the richly furnished parlor for herbal tea or Swedish glögg, or beside the fire in the Gathering Room. Downstairs in what was once the summer kitchen is another common room with a fireplace.

A three-course breakfast for guests in the main inn is served family-style at large tables in the big, cheery kitchen. The meal begins with fresh fruit, French-vanilla yogurt and whole-grain muesli cereal. Next come a variety of homemade muffins. The main course could be baked egg casserole, vegetable quiche, cheese strata, cinnamon french toast or belgian waffles. Bev's zucchini bread is renowned, as are some of the hors d'oeuvres she prepares for wine gatherings for guests at Halloween and New Year's.

(207) 967-3141 or (800) 522-3141. Fax (207) 967-3172. www.captainlord.com. Seventeen rooms and three suites with private baths. June-October and weekends through December: doubles, $179 to $325, suites, $225 to $399. Rest of year: weekends, doubles $125 to $249, suites $189 to $349; midweek, doubles $99 to $249, suites $129 to $299.

Old Fort Inn, Old Fort Avenue, Box M, Kennebunkport 04046

Away from the hubbub of town and out near the ocean in a secluded, landscaped setting with a large pool and tennis court, this is the kind of place that appeals to Californians, to say nothing of Connecticut friends who return year after year.

David and Sheila Aldrich, transplanted Californians, offer fourteen large luxurious guest rooms in a stone and brick carriage house, plus two suites upstairs in the main lodge. They are furnished with style and such nice touches as velvet wing chairs, stenciling on the walls and handmade wreaths over the beds. "My wife agonizes over every intricate detail," says David. "I call her Ms. Mix and Match." Her decorating flair shows; even the towels are color-coordinated. In the hall, her framed shadow boxes containing Victorian outfits are conversation pieces.

Each air-conditioned room has a phone, TV and deluxe wet bar with microwave, since this is a place where people tend to stay for some time. In the most deluxe rooms, of which there seem to be more at every visit, the TV may be hidden in a handsome chest of drawers, the kingsize four-poster beds are topped with fishnet canopies, and the baths are outfitted with jacuzzis, Neutrogena amenities and heated tile floors.

Besides the pool, the gathering spot of choice is the main lodge in a converted barn. At the entry is the reception area and Sheila's antiques shop. Beyond is a large rustic room with enormous beams, weathered pine walls and a massive brick fireplace, the perfect setting for some of her antiques.

It's also where the Aldriches set out their breakfast buffet. Guests pick up wicker trays with calico linings, help themselves to bowls of gorgeous fresh fruits and platters of pastries, and sit around the lodge or outside on the sun-dappled deck beside the pool. Sheila bakes the sweet breads (blueberry, zucchini, banana, oatmeal and pumpkin are some). The croissants are David's forte and there are sticky buns on Sundays. They added granola and yogurt to the spread, and quickly found they were going through twenty pounds of granola a week. Quiche or waffles are the latest additions to the daily fare.

A plate of chocolate-chip cookies greets guests at check-in. Chocolates are at bedside at night.

(207) 967-5353. Fax (207) 967-4547. www.oldfortinn.com. Fourteen rooms and two suites with private baths. Doubles, $150 to $310, mid-June to late October; $110 to $285 rest of year. Two-night minimum stay in summer and all weekends; three nights on holiday weekends. Closed mid-December to mid-April. No smoking.

Crosstrees, 6 South St., Box 1333, Kennebunkport 04046.

Artistry and cooking are the hallmarks at this new B&B, handsomely transformed from the old Kylemere guest house by a pair of Kansans. Lawyer Keith Henley and artist Dennis Rafferty wanted to run a B&B and found Kennebunkport a more compelling market than Topeka. They moved from a 6,000-square-foot house there to this unassuming but deep 1818 Federal house on a residential street, where they set undertook a total renovation. They restored its original name, given by Maine artist/architect Abbott Graves, for the two maples that once crossed in the front yard.

The late artist's studio in the attached rear barn is now the prime accommodation. It's hung with oils and watercolors by Dennis, a present-day painter whom we caught up with here in his other role as chambermaid. His meticulous cleanup as well as his artworks enhanced what is now a suite with a kingsize sleigh bed and a gas fireplace beneath the beams and skylights in the former studio, a bath with double whirlpool and separate shower, and a sitting room with a sofabed.

Other guest quarters are in the front of the house and are quite spacious, given their antiquity. Upstairs, the formal Victorian with a king bed and gas fireplace is furnished according to its name. Across the hall is the Abbott Graves, a master bedroom with queensize poster bed and a sofabed. On the main floor is the corner Library, with a queen poster bed, wood-burning fireplace, Waverly floral wallpaper and windows screened by Indian shutters.

Guests gather in a front parlor, furnished to the Federal period. Breakfast is served amidst much sterling, crystal and china in the formal dining room. Here is where another kind of artistry is evident – that of the culinary variety. Keith is the breakfast cook of distinction. The day of our visit, he prepared a three-course feast of mixed melon with honey-glazed sauce, herb-baked eggs with sautéed portobellos and a broiled tomato topped with olive oil and parmesan. "Dessert" was an individual blueberry-peach cobbler. Other favorites are crab quiche, artichoke-broccoli frittata and pecan french toast hailed by guests as out of this world.

(207) 967-2780 or (800) 564-1527. Fax (207) 967-2619. Three rooms and one suite with private baths. July-October, doubles, $160 to $175; suite, $225. Rest of year: weekends: doubles, $130 to $145, suite, $185; midweek: doubles, $100 to $115, suite, $155.

Gourmet Treats

Their Wooden Goose Inn was one of the fanciest, most gourmet-oriented B&Bs ever. In 1999, owners Tony Sienicki and Jerry Rippetoe traded innkeeping life for retail, opening **TJ's at the Sign of the Goose**, Route 1, Cape Neddick. Former guests will immediately detect their sense of style in furnishings and accessories for home and garden. Like their inn, it's the kind of stuff of which design-magazine editors' dreams are made; not the least of which are the magnificent crystal candelabra collected over the years by Jerry and the incredible decorative bird-houses (some more like high-rise hotels) made by Tony and scattered about the gardens. Open daily, 10 to 6.

In Ogunquit, several places of culinary interest distract passersby from the traffic travails at the horrendous main intersection in the center of town. No doubt contributing to the pedestrian traffic, at any rate, are the side-by-side **Latest Scoop** for ice cream, **Native Grounds** for coffee, **Fancy That** for baked goods and sandwiches, and the **Village Market.** Out near the entrance to Perkins Cove, **Cafe Amoré** is just the ticket for those into exotic coffees and food more creative (and healthful) than fried clams. Go for the blackboard specials: omelets and lobster benedict, interesting salads and sandwiches (the "crabster roll" is the specialty for $9.50), good bagels and desserts like peach pie. For provisions, head for **Perkins & Perkins,** purveyors of fine foods, wines and gifts along Route 1 north.

A must stop for baked goods is **Borealis Breads,** supplier to many a restaurant and with retail outlets along Route 1 in Ogunquit and Wells. More than twenty varieties of crusty, moist and tangy artisan loaves are baked daily, including French peasant, orange-date (which makes fabulous french toast) and savory herb. Scones and sandwiches also are available.

In Kennebunkport, **Keys to the Kitchen** out Port Road (Route 35) in the Lower Village is well worth a visit. Owner Dodie Phillips has an unusual flair for displays. The cookbook area is distinctive, and upstairs around an open atrium we found some pretty and summery placemats that now grace our patio table at home. Out back under separate ownership is **Stonehouse Port & Cheese,** where Shawn O'Neil stocks wines, cheeses, pâtés and hard-to-find sauces and condiments.

Incredibly gourmet is the new **Market Day,** just beyond on Route 35. Racks of olive oils, specialty foods, cookbooks, wines, cheeses and fresh produce vie for attention. Among the takeout food offerings are sandwiches in the $5.95 range.

Out of town in Cape Porpoise, the market of choice is **Bradbury Brothers,** with the usual, plus essentials for summer residents like bread from When Pigs Fly in York, Greek olive pesto, Rose's lime juice and local jams.

The high-end, dark beers are particularly good, we're told, at the **Kennebunkport Brewing Co.** at the Shipyard Shops, 8 Western Ave., facing the river in the Lower Village. You can tour the main-floor brewery and sample the beers upstairs at its **Federal Jack's Brew Pub,** where lunch and dinner are available daily at sturdy wood communal tables in a big room beside the water. On the ground floor is **KBC Coffee and Dry Goods,** billed as a European-style coffee shop with a section selling gourmet foods.

Cherie's Sweet Treats & Other Eats at 7 High St., Kennebunk, was jammed at our noontime visit with folks picking up moderately priced lunches. Most took out, as we did, but there are a few stools at a counter for those who wish. "That Sandwich" is a perennial favorite: the mixture of artichoke hearts, red pepper, red onion, pesto and olives was delicious. But we also could have gone for the seafood quiche, the peanut-ginger or lentil-mint salads, the jambalaya or one of the six soups of the day. And we wouldn't have minded at all having a slice of fresh strawberry pie.

A huge grapevine moose was at the entrance to **Marlows,** 39 Main St., Kennebunk, a gift shop stocked with "swell stuff and terrific things," itemized literally from A to Z. There's a section for specialty foods, local mustards and jams, as well as cookbooks.

Gourmet Success

Stonewall Kitchen Company Store, Stonewall Lane, York.

The jams and condiments turning up in specialty-food stores across the nation are sold here in a small, upscale retail setting in the front of its production facility, which was fashioned from an old grocery store in York Corners. Jonathan King and Jim Stott, who met as waiters in leading restaurants in Portsmouth, N.H., started selling homemade jams and vinegars at the Portsmouth farmers' market in 1991 for extra spending money. One customer bought out their entire inventory for her store, and therein began a phenomenon that quickly projected them into Dean & DeLuca, Williams-Sonoma and 6,000 stores nationwide. Now with 130 products and as many employees, they are the talk of the gourmet food industry. In 1996, they became the first company to win the Outstanding Product Line award at the International Fancy Food and Confection Show in Philadelphia two years in a row – a feat that neither they nor anyone else has matched. Their ginger-peach tea jam was named the outstanding new product of the year, followed a year later by a maple-chipotle grill sauce. "We love to create new products," says Jonathan, who loves to cook and first gave his jams to his family as Christmas presents. "Some people think in words or in pictures, but I think in terms of tastes." Those tastes have led to all kinds of jams (how about lemon-pear marmalade or one with roasted garlic and onion?), oils, vinegars, mustards, coffees, crackers, dessert toppings, relishes, salsas and more. They sell here for $3 to $20 and appeal to the high-end market. A new line, inspired by their children, is called "Kids Like Good Food, Too." Stonewall Kitchen has since opened company stores in Portsmouth, Portland and Camden. In 2000, it relocated up Route 1 to a new headquarters building housing a large production facility and a much-expanded retail store. Future plans for the property include a restaurant showcasing its products.

(207) 351-2712 or (800) 207-5267. Open daily, 10 to 5 or 6.

Lobster With a View

Cape Pier Chowder House, Pier Road, Cape Porpoise.

If you like your lobster in an informal outdoor setting, head right to the pier at Cape Porpoise. This is the successor to the Lively Lobster run for several years by the adjacent Seascapes restaurant. The nearby Cape Porpoise Lobster Co., which does a land-office wholesale and mail-order business, took over in 1997. It offers the usual lobster-pound seafood items, from chowders and fish sandwiches to fried haddock and lobster dinners. They're served inside or out on a spacious deck with a gull's-eye view of the harbor.

(207) 967-0123 or (800) 967-4268. Open daily for lunch and dinner, 10:30 to 9 or 10 in summer, to dusk in off-season. Closed December-March. BYOB.

Diners enjoy lofty seating while customers shop for Maine foods in Portland Public Market.

Portland, Me.

Bounty by the Bay

Perhaps no other Northeastern state has such close associations with indigenous foods as Maine. Think Maine lobsters. Think Maine crabs. Think Maine blueberries. Think fiddlehead ferns. Think smoked mussels and salmon.

As a coastal area where such bounty is found in abundance, it's no surprise that Maine inspired good restaurants earlier and in greater numbers than other northern New England states. And, when some found they couldn't survive year-round in the seasonal tourist areas, they converged on Portland, the state's largest and most sophisticated city and a seaport facing Casco Bay.

"There's no other place in Maine with a year-round food audience," says top chef Sam Hayward, who opened one of Maine's first great restaurants in Brunswick in 1981. It lasted ten years, as did David Grant's pioneering Aubergine, Maine's first nouvelle cuisine restaurant launched in Camden in 1979. But after a decade, both knew they had to move to Portland for economic reasons. "This is where the customers are," Grant said after relocating Aubergine.

Other top chefs gravitated from outlying areas to the city. As a result, Portland claims the nation's densest concentration of restaurants per capita after San Francisco. It ranks third in per-capita restaurant spending after New York and San Francisco. Its food scene has garnered national attention lately in the New York Times, Bon Appétit and Travel & Leisure.

Although Commercial and Congress streets boast more enduring restaurants (Boone's dates to 1898 and The Roma Café to 1924), the heart of the food area is the restored Old Port area between downtown and the waterfront. A single block of quaint Wharf Street harbors eight restaurants (with more on the way). A restaurant row has blossomed along outer Middle Street.

Not only does Portland have more good and more varied restaurants than cities several times its size (population, 65,000), it also has "fierce regionalists" as proclaimed by Aubergine's Grant. He eschews the ubiquitous Chilean sea bass, for instance, in favor of fresh fish from a local purveyor. Most other chefs do likewise, helping support what may be the largest and most varied food producing industry in New England.

Nowhere is the import of food in Portland more evident than in the new, privately funded Portland Public Market, a model of its genre. Two dozen purveyors of Maine-raised meats and produce as well as regional fishmongers and bakers find a receptive clientele in the block-long downtown food hall.

Portland also is home to specialty food stores, kitchen shops and wine stores that rank with the best anywhere.

The culinary treats are affordable, approachable and seemingly endless here.

Dining

The Best of the Best

Fore Street, 288 Fore St., Portland.

Two of Maine's best-known restaurateurs, Sam Hayward and Dana Street, joined to open this hot-ticket establishment in 1996. The menu is as understated as the name, but rest assured, there's more here than meets the eye.

Start with the exterior, a garage-like brick low-rise at the edge of the historic Old Port area. It still looks like the tank-storage warehouse it was built as during World War II. Inside is a soaring space with brick walls, tall windows, and assorted booths and tables on two levels, all overlooking a large and busy open kitchen. Indeed, this kitchen is so open that it forms a large portion of the restaurant. With tables set around the perimeter, the dozen cooks manning the applewood-fired grill, rotisserie and oven are actors nightly for dinner theater-in-the-round. There's a small, intimate cocktail lounge with a waiting area in front.

"Refined peasant food" is how Sam, the operative chef, describes the fare. We first sampled his product at the late 22 Lincoln, his early Brunswick restaurant, which was ahead of the times. He then took a prime post as executive chef at the Harraseeket Inn in Freeport. He moved here for a simpler operation, one that he could call partly his own. The emphasis, as at his former venues, is on Maine ingredients and produce. The exotica and complexities of his past performances are understated here, as they always have been at his partner's Street and Co. seafood restaurant in the Old Port (see below).

The menu, printed nightly, offers about a dozen main courses. They're categorized as roasted (turnspit-roasted pork loin, wood-oven roasted Maine lobster, farm-raised loup de mer, Gulf of Maine hake fillet). Or grilled (Pacific opah and dorado fillets, Atlantic yellowfin tuna loin, New England farm venison chop, hanger steak). That's it – no highfalutin language, just a few surprises like an autumn mixed grill of lamb sirloin, game sausage, duck confit and farm-raised elk liver, teamed with a chestnut garlic mash and wild Maine chanterelles.

We could make a meal of appetizers: a platter of seasonal salads that resembles an antipasto plate, roasted jumbo oyster mushrooms, wood-oven baked goat cheese on chanterelle toasts, seared rabbit livers with shiitakes. Plus perhaps a pizzetta of tomatoes, mushrooms and spinach, or Fore Street's ultimate "BLT" layering lobster, apple-smoked bacon, bibb lettuce and basil mayonnaise on toasted country bread.

No wonder the place is so popular that we couldn't get a reservation on a Thursday night. Fellow inn guests who did snag a table, both high-living Californians, were mighty impressed with the food and style. So are innkeeper friends who trek often from Connecticut to Portland, mainly to eat at Fore Street.

We'll try again, if only for the desserts, no fewer than fourteen to-die-for choices like pear pain perdu, white chocolate espresso napoleon, wild huckleberry tart, and a trio of passion-fruit, blackberry and peach sorbets. How about a selection of cheeses? Or perhaps an assortment of handmade chocolates for two?

The wine list is short but select, and reflects Sam's award-winning expertise.

Although some find Fore Street rushed and noisy, no one doubts the success of its kitchen theatrics. Simple is best, they say. Reserve a ringside seat and enjoy the show.

(207) 775-2717. Entrées, $13.95 to $21.95. Dinner nightly, from 5:30.

Aubergine, 555 Congress St., Portland.

Maine celebrity chef David Grant had long been looking toward "the city," as he called Portland. A Philadelphia native who trained at the Restaurant School there and in France, he became chef in 1977 at America's first nouvelle cuisine restaurant, the Red Balloon in Philadelphia. Two years later he launched the nouvelle movement in Maine with the charming Aubergine inn and restaurant in Camden. He eventually sold Aubergine but retained rights to the name as he bided time for a site to open up in Portland.

That opportunity occurred in 1996, when he took over a former firehouse-turned-bookstore café and opened his dreamed-of city bistro and wine bar. The wine bar and dining area is augmented by loft seating on a wraparound mezzanine. Decor is understated in black and white. The tables of maple were made in Maine and retained from David's interim restaurant, the Reunion Bar & Grill in Camden. Color emanates from a large mural of the Andalusian seacoast and a huge still life painting of an aubergine in Paris, with the Eiffel Tower as the backdrop. It's the landmark work of Ted A. Dyer, a nationally known graphic illustrator in Philadelphia, who got his start washing dishes as a teen-ager at Aubergine,

The cuisine is modern French bistro with a Gascon accent. That means an emphasis on duck, drawing from David's training in Gascony with Jean-Louis Palladin. At our visit, it showed up in an appetizer of duck liver pâté with a brioche and blueberry chutney and in a main course of spiced duck breasts with green peppercorns (the short menu changes daily). It also means an emphasis on North Atlantic seafood, as in main dishes of brioche pan-fried oysters with garlic and basil rouille and seared Georges Bank scallops with mussels and herbs. "I'm a fierce regionalist," says David, who relies on local purveyors for seasonal products.

The menu typically opens with such starters as creamy onion soup laced with tarragon and white wine, a gratin of snails and a jumbo scallop with fennel and garlic, and a warm mango and duck crackling salad with ginger and soy. Among main courses, look for sweetbreads with locally foraged wild mushrooms, thyme-grilled lamb brochettes, and the signature grilled rump steak with red leek béarnaise. The menu descriptions are straightforward; the results are complex.

The three dozen wines on the predominantly French wine list are priced from $24 to $48. All are offered by the glass, and a couple by the carafe.

Pioneering regional chef David Grant mans stove at Aubergine.

Aubergine's food, service and atmosphere merited perfect five-star ratings in each category as reviewed in the Maine Sunday Telegram.

(207) 874-0680. Entrées, $17 to $22. Dinner, Tuesday-Saturday 5:30 to 10.

Street and Co., 33 Wharf St., Portland.

Pure, pure, pure is the feeling of the small, Mediterranean-style "eating establishment" run by Dana Street in the heart of the Old Port. You enter past an open grill/kitchen and face a blackboard menu, both good indicators. Ahead is a small room with bare pegged floors and 40 seats, where strands of herbs and garlic hang on a brick wall. Dana acquired an adjacent space that gave him twenty more seats as well as a wine bar that doubles as a waiting area. Outside are about two dozen more seats along Wharf Street for summer dining. The tables might turn four times on a busy night, which seems to be the norm.

The freshest of seafood and a purist philosophy draw a steady clientele. Self-taught chef Abbie Harman, who apprenticed under Dana, offers six varieties of fish that could be grilled, blackened or broiled. Mussels marinara, clams, shrimp and garlic are available over linguini. Other possibilities are scallops in pernod and cream, sole française, grilled lobster with butter and garlic over linguini and lobster fra diavolo ($34.95 for two). That was it – at our first visit, and at every subsequent visit. Nothing outré or adjectival here. There may be a "whole fish" offering, and a pasta alfredo and primavera. Nary a meat item or even free-range chicken is in sight. Meals come with French bread and fresh vegetables (asparagus, zucchini and red bell peppers at one visit) sautéed in butter and white wine.

Equally straightforward are the appetizers: mussels provençal, steamers, calamari and seasonal salad. The formula works, so why change?

Most of the wines are priced in the twenties.

(207) 775-0887. Entrées, $15.95 to $19.95. Dinner nightly, 5:30 to 9:30 or 10.

Gabriel's, 47 Middle St., Portland.

Pair a 22-year-old percussionist turned hotshot cook with a frustrated restaurant manager/sommelier. The result is Gabriel's, Portland's newest marquee dining emporium.

Gabriel Bremer spent fourteen years studying classical percussion and ran a short-lived coffeehouse in the Old Port before becoming part of Sam Hayward's opening crew at Fore Street. He turned down a full scholarship to Chicago's American Conservatory of Music and moved to Seascapes in Kennebunkport, where manager Michael O'Neill quickly noticed "all these amazing specials coming out of the kitchen." He and Gabriel decided to open their own place in Portland to give their creativity free rein.

Their launching pad was the space formerly occupied by Café Always, which provided some of our best meals in Portland during its heyday. The partners gutted the place to reconfigure the entry, open up the kitchen, and add a bar and overflow dining tables upstairs. The star of the decor is the remarkable wall landscape mural painted during a vacation in Ireland by Michael's wife Piper, an artist. About the only Café Always holdovers are the black strings used to tie the yellow napkins at each place setting.

Gabriel calls his cuisine "seasonal fresh American, with French and Japanese accents." It adds innovative twists to the discipline of integrity and simplicity he learned at Fore Street. Everything on the short seasonal menu entices.

Consider the halibut en papillote with aromatic herbs and vegetables – a heady melange of aromas when released by the diner from the parchment paper in which they were steamed. The whole French turbot is roasted with vegetables and sea salt. The John Dory fillet comes with seared foie gras and a salad of fennel, celery root and pomegranate. The chef works wonders with slow-roasted Long Island duck, crusted with preserved lemon and flavored with Asian spices. The tamarind-glazed pheasant with its stewed shiitakes and baby vegetables en papillote explodes with flavor. Vegetarians find nirvana in an Asian-style beggar's purse of squash, baby leeks, exotic mushrooms and pumpkin seed oil, or a roasted "bear's head mushroom" with sweet-potato/malanga gnocchi and baby spinach.

The pear and mache salad with hazelnut vinaigrette and chèvre and the artisan cheese plate with fruit and nuts quickly became signature starters, half of which are salads. Other tempting options at our autumn visit were heirloom squash soup with ginger confit, and a blue cheese tart with caramelized walnuts and onion confit.

The treats continue with desserts, perhaps an Asian pear and star anise crème brûlée with crispy pear chip, caramel apple upside-down cake with green apple sorbet or seckel pear butter cake with silken praline sauce. Or refresh the palate with a seasonal fruit ice "martini" laden with fresh fruit.

Fancy hand-blown stemware is used for the wines, a superb compendium of choices priced from the low twenties to $225.

(207) 775-1510. Entrées, $20 to $25. Dinner, Tuesday-Saturday 5:30 to 10, Sunday to 9.

Back Bay Grill, 65 Portland St., Portland.

A twenty-foot-long mural along one wall attests that this grill isn't in Back Bay Boston. Done by local artist Ed Manning Jr., it is a fanciful rendering of restaurant scenes and characters that are very much the Back Bay Grill. It's also so life-like

Artist's mural of local scenes enlivens dining room at Back Bay Bistro.

that it makes the intimate room seem bigger, according to personable owner Joel Freund.

The mural is a focal point of his highly regarded and urbane establishment, "dean" of Portland's gourmet restaurants at the ripe young age of ten or so. The chic interior has high ceilings, track lighting, antique mirrors, modern upholstered chairs (obtained from an office furniture company) and mahogany tables rather close together. Roses and candles are atop the tables.

The chefs change the handsome menus seasonally. Entrées might be Maine lobster with garlic chives and black truffle-cognac sauce, horseradish-crusted Atlantic salmon in puff pastry with a roasted beet and sorrel salad over whole-grain mustard spaetzle, filet mignon with braised garlic sauce and stilton, and rosemary-crusted rack of lamb with figs and chanterelles. These could be accompanied by haricots verts, spring asparagus, corn with sugar snap peas and fingerling or olive-oil smashed potatoes.

Start perhaps with chilled cantaloupe soup in summer; black bean and pancetta soup in winter. Appetizers might be peeky-toe crab cakes with an Indian curry vinaigrette, sautéed foie gras and a chanterelle ravioli in a sauternes butter sauce, and carpaccio of tuna with an avocado-sesame salad. Typical desserts are an acclaimed crème brûlée, chocolate banana mousse, and pecan bourbon tart with caramel ice cream.

The 100-bottle wine list, which changes every week or two, is fairly priced. Many wines are available by the glass. Also available are $12 samplers giving a choice of three from the list of single-malt scotches and small-batch bourbons.

(207) 772-8833. Entrées, $18 to $27. Dinner, Monday-Saturday 5:30 to 9:30 or 10, also Sunday 5 to 9 in July and August.

Bibo's Madd Apple Cafe, 23 Forest Ave., Portland.

Some of the best cooking and best values among serious restaurants in town are found at this old favorite, nicely reborn in 1999. Bill Boutwell, a talented chef whom we first knew at Seascapes in Kennebunkport, later put Cafe

Stroudwater at Embassy Suites on Portland's culinary map. From that unlikely location he ventured out on his own with partner Andrea Raymond, turning up at the Madd Apple, where we'd enjoyed many a delectable treat under previous owners.

Here he quickly stamped his imprint on an intimate cafe that we always felt was under-rated. He added a quirky appellation derived from the opening letters of his first and last names and tweaked the curtain and floral treatments in the prominent front windows, but otherwise kept the colorful, arty surroundings the same. He embellished the menu with the latest accents.

Well situated next to the Portland Performing Arts Center, the cafe finds its business driven by the theater, which may explain why we were the only customers for a late lunch one September weekday. It won't be our last, however, given the caliber of the food and the reasonable prices. A shrimp and avocado sandwich on toasted rye bread and a juicy lamb burger arrived on oversize plates. Both knife-and-fork affairs, they were flanked by abundant mesclun salad, roasted potatoes and garnishes of what the menu calls garlic-marinated cucumbers and we call pickles. A trio of the day's sorbets – raspberry, apple and orange-cranberry – was served atop squiggles of matching coulis. With tax and tip, the tab came to less than $20.

Although the focus is on straightforward salads and sandwiches at midday, the menu becomes much more complex at night. Expect entrées like seared rare tuna loin wrapped in leeks and prosciutto, Asian-style pork loin rubbed in five spices and sauced with ginger and soy, braised leg of rabbit with a juniper-infused red wine reduction, and roasted loin of lamb dusted with cornmeal spices and served with a sweet corn broth. The accompaniments, each different, are novel as well.

Starters could be a chunky gazpacho topped by a crab-cheddar cheese quenelle, shrimp and vegetable maki rolls with a spicy peanut sauce or a rose of smoked salmon stuffed with goat cheese and drizzled with a raspberry-horseradish crème fraîche. Desserts follow suit, among them chocolate-macadamia stout pâté ("also known as fudge with an attitude") and chocolate-banana-coconut dumplings with coconut and chocolate sauces. One delight is called "Bibo's crackerjacks" – peanut-butter mousse atop a bed of old-fashioned caramel corn garnished with bittersweet chocolate sauce.

Amidst all the fun and culinary sizzle is a choice wine list, almost every bottle pleasantly priced in the teens and twenties.

(207) 774-9698. Entrées, $15.95 to $19.95. Lunch, Wednesday-Friday 11:30 to 2. Dinner, Wednesday-Saturday from 5:30. Sunday, brunch 11 to 3, "supper" from 4.

Ribollita, 41 Middle St., Portland.

Still another chef drawn to the city from the hinterlands, so to speak, Ron Boogaard opened this intimate Tuscan-style place after ten years at the Cape Arundel Inn in Kennebunkport. Here he was joined by Kevin Quiet. Both are equally at home in the kitchen.

Occupying the space of a former Mediterranean restaurant called Luna D'Oro, Ribollita is convivial, warm and intimate. It seats a mere 35 people inside and a few more outside in season. The owners make their own pastas for such treats as roast squash and Tuscan sheep's cheese ravioli with sage butter, mushroom and pesto lasagna, pan-seared gnocchi with prosciutto and peas, and roast chicken putanesca with pappardelle.

Those are meals in themselves, especially when preceded by the hearty Tuscan vegetable and bread soup from which the restaurant takes its name. Or perhaps a caramelized onion tart with black olives and goat cheese, or polenta-crusted calamari with roasted peppers. Secondi await those who prefer. Consider radicchio-wrapped salmon with pesto and roasted pepper sauce, chicken breast saltimbocca, and osso buco with creamy polenta. A specialty is farmer's market risotto, changing nightly depending on what's available at the market – mussels, saffron and spinach, when we were there.

Dessert could be vanilla bean flan, apple croustade with cinnamon ice cream, and chocolate torte. The wine list is all-Italian.

(207) 774-2972. Entrées, $12.25 to $16.50. Dinner, Monday-Saturday from 5.

Rachel's Wood Grill, 90 Exchange St., Portland.

Little known and never advertised, this storefront sleeper is run very personally by Laura and Bob Butler. They share the cooking duties in a tiny kitchen, as well as the buying of some extraordinary wines. "We do it all ourselves," says Laura.

The couple moved in 1996 from Rhode Island, where they also had a restaurant called Rachel's (named for his grandmother) and Laura had worked at the famed Al Forno, whose influence is felt here. They chose to open in Portland because "it was up and coming," while the Providence restaurant scene "was too busy."

The Butlers devote much time and thought to their establishment, which we first met when it was Afghan Restaurant. Laura painted the walls above the charcoal gray wainscoting a cheerful ragged red-orange. Bob built the bar. They cover the white-clothed tables with white butcher paper, place a few plants here and there, and dim the lighting for romance.

As you arrive for dinner and dunk dense Tuscan bread into the olive oil poured at every table, cast your eyes over a long and select wine list. Many are from favorite wineries the owners have visited in California and Italy. The waitstaff has a handle on their attributes, but you're free to visit the kitchen to ask the Butlers for a special recommendation. Then prepare for a leisurely, two-hour meal.

The couple's offerings are categorized under salads and small plates as well as large plates, and portions are substantial. The day's specials hint of the couple's scope: grilled pompano with island spices, grilled escolar with basil and sundried tomato pesto over saffron risotto, and grilled yuan-glazed hamachi over Japanese-style soba noodles and spinach stew. The printed menu offers meats like grilled pork chop and fixins' paired with grilled chicken and apple sausage, ribeye steak with red pepper butter and parmesan, and rack of lamb glazed with cabernet. The couple are known for interesting greens and vegetables, many of them grilled.

Start with Brazilian seafood chowder, grilled garlic shrimp over homemade flatbread, a grilled pear and endive salad with stilton cheese and caramelized pecans, or a traditional caesar salad. Finish with a chocolate soufflé cake, white and dark chocolate crème brûlée or bread pudding with bourbon glaze. You'll know why the regulars keep coming back.

(207) 774-1192. Entrées, $15 to $23. Dinner, Tuesday-Saturday 5 to 10.

Joe's Boathouse, 1 Spring Point Drive, South Portland.

This is one of those rarities where the food is equal to the view. The view is of boats bobbing in the marina where Portland Harbor opens into Casco Bay and, beyond, the enchanting islands out in the bay itself. The food is sophisticated and first-rate.

Brothers Joe and Mark Loring opened the sleekly nautical establishment surrounded by decks in 1997 and immediately drew city-slickers as well as the yachting set. They come as much for the fare as the watery ambiance. There's an eat-at bar popular with single diners just inside the main entrance. Beyond are a couple of simple, low-slung dining rooms, the main one with a fireplace and large windows. The tables of choice in summer are outside by the harbor, where torches are lit at night.

Lunch was a festive treat as 1950s music played in the background. Word of the portobello and asiago club sandwich preceded our arrival. It turned out to be a knife-and-fork whopper, paired with homemade chips and served on the restaurant's colorful Fiestaware. Another treat was the orange-ginger crispy salmon salad – a plateful of greens, rice noodles, bamboo shoots, red peppers and scallions, with a spicy-sauced salmon fillet on top and many contrasting tastes in competition with each other. It took desserts of chocolate-kahlua mousse and homemade sorbets to clear the palate.

Aforementioned spicy orange-ginger sauce shows up for dinner on stir-fried sea scallops with vegetables, pineapple and cashews over Asian rice noodles, topped with crispy wontons. The evening salmon is Southwest-style, grilled with toasted almonds and basil pesto. Other possibilities are lobster fettuccine, mango chicken, and hickory-smoked pork ribs with a blueberry barbecue sauce. Best of the starters are cajun chicken and corn egg rolls with a honey-mustard dipping sauce, and crab cakes drizzled with rémoulade over fried potatoes and greens.

Folks from the Casco Bay islands like to sail over here for Sunday brunch.

(207) 741-2780. Entrées, $12.95 to $19.95. Lunch, Monday-Saturday 11 to 3. Dinner nightly, 5 to 9:30. Sunday brunch, 9 to 3.

Other Dining Choices

Walter's Cafe, 15 Exchange St., Portland.

Noisy and intimate, this "now" kind of place has been packed to the rafters since it was opened by Walter Loeman and Mark Loring. The two have since parted, Mark holding onto this and Walter opening Perfetto across the street. The emphasis on spirited food at pleasant prices continues here.

We faced a twenty-minute wait for a weekday lunch in July, but were glad we stayed. A BOLT – bacon, lettuce, tomato and red onion sandwich with sweet cajun mayonnaise – arrived in a pita, served with a pickle and "gnarly" fries. The "chilling pasta salad" yielded a zesty plateful tossed with chicken, avocado and red peppers.

From our table alongside a brick wall in the long and narrow, high-ceilinged room we could see the cooks splashing liberal amounts of wine into the dishes they were preparing in the open kitchen. Green plants backlit on a shelf above the kitchen area provided accents amid the prevailing brick. Glass covered the black vinyl tablecloths.

Dinner entrées have been known to be categorized by "flippin' pans" and "thrill of the grill." One signature dish is "crazy chicken" with prosciutto, peas and scallions in a red wine and cream sauce over cappellini. Other possibilities range from a gingered stir-fry of Shanghai scallops over jasmine rice to filet mignon with red pepper and bourbon pan gravy. Start with cod and corn cakes, asiago cannelloni or a concoction called "non-traditional greens," which are rolled in lavasch bread and spread with goat cheese dressed with "Loring's own" vinaigrette.

Irish cream cheesecake, orange mousse with wild blueberries, and varied chocolate creations typify the dessert list. Lots of good wines are priced in the teens and twenties.

(207) 871-9258. Entrées, $14.95 to $18.95. Lunch, Monday-Saturday 11 to 3. Dinner nightly, 5 to 10.

Cafe at Wharf Street, 38 Wharf St., Portland.

Former Minneapolis caterer Steve Massing and partner Janet Berry are back with a new name at their former Wharf Street Cafe. Although Janet started the cafe as a sandwich shop across the street, in their latest incarnation they have abandoned lunch service in favor of a contemporary American bistro menu for dinner.

Upstairs in what once was a banana storage room for a produce company is a funky wine and espresso bar, full of couches and stuffed chairs and a piano, where you can get appetizers, desserts and wines by the glass. The candlelight setting is dark and romantic.

The main floor is funky but chic, what with purple walls beneath a charcoal-gray ceiling. A copy of Food Arts magazine was on each table at one visit. The ceiling is low and the room dark, a perfect setting for the eclectic fare that Steve serves up. His short menu offers preliminaries like crabmeat and asparagus quesadilla, caesar salad with grilled shrimp, and a changing succession of pizzettes: perhaps with sundried tomato pesto, feta and greek olives or another with grilled pear, gorgonzola and candied walnuts. The signature lobster and brie ravioli with roasted grapes in a caramelized onion sauce is so popular it's available as both appetizer and entrée.

Other main courses could be pistachio-crusted salmon fillet with Japanese soba noodles and sweet chile mirin, grilled halibut with roasted corn and red pepper coulis, and grilled filet mignon with mushroom-cabernet sauce.

For dessert, consider key lime cheesecake, blueberry crumb tart or warm chocolate truffle torte with raspberry coulis. Adjourn to the upstairs wine bar for an after-dinner espresso.

(207) 773-6667. Entrées, $14 to $21. Dinner nightly in summer, 5:30 to 9:30 or 10; Tuesday-Saturday, rest of year.

Perfetto, 28 Exchange St., Portland.

Inspired by the success of Walter's Cafe, co-owner Walter Loeman opened this engaging northern Italian eatery across the street. Two side-by-side storefronts contain a bar/lounge on side and a dining room in the other, with an open kitchen at the rear. High-back cane chairs are at butcher-block tables amidst a backdrop of brick and green walls, exposed piping, lava lamps and colorful artworks.

The fare speaks with an Italian accent. For dinner expect appetizers like the day's bruschetta, a roasted red pepper caesar salad with chèvre, fried calamari with lime-basil aioli and baked brie and sweet potato torte. Shrimp or chicken may be added to vegetarian pastas like milan linguini, cappellini parma and tuscan rigatoni. Main dishes range from roasted haddock with caramelized grapefruit and hazelnuts over a vegetable ragu to pan-seared paillard of salmon over wild mushrooms and sticky rice, finished with a sweet Italian parsley sauce. Pomegranate-glazed chicken and veal tenderloin with a blueberry-port wine sauce are other possibilities.

Typical desserts are chocolate raspberry-torte, gingered apple strudel and lemon almond cheesecake.

The Perfetto group has grown to include **Cotton Street,** a tropical grill and bar at 10 Cotton St., and **Mazza,** a wine and spirits bar offering tempting "small plates" at 30 Market St.

(207) 828-0001. Entrees, $15.50 to $18.50. Lunch, Monday-Friday 11:30 to 3. Dinner nightly, from 5. Sunday brunch, 10 to 3.

Worldly and Vegetarian

Pepperclub, 78 Middle St., Portland.

"World cuisine" is the theme of this hip organic-vegetarian-seafood establishment, part of the Middle Street "Restaurant Row." It's the creation of Jaap Helder, a Danish-born chef-artist who owned the late, great Vinyard restaurant (Portland's earliest gourmet restaurant) nearby. He re-emerged here with his paintings and a partner, former art editor Eddie Fitzpatrick, to produce something of a showplace of quirky culinary design. A crazy paint job with many colors on the walls, fresh flowers on the tables and a bar made of old Jamaican steel drums, painted and cut in half, create a vivid setting.

The food is colorful as well. The blackboard menu might list such soups as sweet potato-cauliflower, swiss chard and red bliss potatoes, and curried corn chowder. Otherwise, consider starters of baked brie with apricot preserves and almonds, Caribbean shrimp cakes, and vegetarian samosas with beet chutney.

Main dishes range from an organic pepper burger to ginger-lime chicken with mango salsa and Moroccan lamb with zatat bread and couscous. Most of the offerings are seafood: Atlantic scallops with Vietnamese coconut curry sauce over jasmine rice, fillet of salmon with roasted red pepper and basil sauce, a quesadilla of Maine crabmeat, roasted corn and asparagus. Or vegetarian: Indonesian vegetables gado-gado with marinated tempeh, Indian curries with dahl and chutney, and roasted red pepper and basil béchamel lasagna. Salads and molasses-oatmeal bread come with.

Among desserts are a chocolate soufflé roll, orange chiffon cake, and mocha-hazelnut dacquoise. Organic wines and coffees are featured.

(207) 772-0531. Entrées, $10.95 to $13.95. Dinner nightly, 5 to 9 or 10.

Extra Value

Cafe Uffa! 190 State St., Portland.

This storefront eatery facing Longfellow Square is known for creative, healthful fare and good value. It gained inordinate fame when featured in Bon Appétit magazine's 1999 spread on Portland. The Louisiana writer – taken, no doubt, by its rustic wood tables, bare wood floor, funky art and high ceiling – likened it to being transported to New York's East Village.

It was portrayed as primarily vegetarian, although in the year's interim between the time of research and publication the restaurant had changed hands. New owners Russ and Jackie Pierce from California distanced themselves from the vegetarian image.

The fare prepared by Jackie, the chef, reflects her California Culinary Academy training. Her short menu changes weekly. At our autumn visit it offered spicy

Everyone likes to eat lobster beside the ocean, as here at Two Lights in Cape Elizabeth.

seafood sausage with garlic tomato sauce on linguini with an asiago and basil chiffonade, grilled Atlantic farm-raised salmon with lemon thyme butter on mashed potatoes, pan-seared halibut with sauce romesco on a corn risotto cake with asparagus, and grilled marinated ribeye steak with gruyère scalloped potatoes. A couple of polenta and pasta dishes appeased vegetarians.

Starters were french onion soup, three salads and veggie dumplings with hoisin dipping sauce, grilled shrimp with curried coconut-peanut sauce, and smoked trout on a corn-leek pancake with horseradish crème fraîche and salmon roe.

The mainly California wine list is pleasantly priced in the teens and twenties.

The breakfast menu ($3.50 to $6.25) turns up treats like huevos rancheros and omelets of smoked salmon and dill or spinach, feta and cheese.

(207) 775-3380. Entrées, $9 to $16. Breakfast, Wednesday-Saturday 7 to 11. Dinner, Wednesday-Saturday 5:30 to 10. Sunday brunch, 9 to 2.

Lobster by the Ocean

Two Lights Lobster Shack, 225 Two Lights Road, Cape Elizabeth.

Near Two Lights State Park and almost in the shadow of the two lighthouses south of Portland, this is located on a bluff overlooking nothing but rocks and open ocean. You can eat inside, but we prefer to sip a drink outside at a picnic table (BYOB) as we await our order. This is a great place to bring youngsters because they can clamber around on the rocks while waiting for dinner and because the Lobster Shack offers hot dogs, hamburgers, fried chicken and clam cakes as well as boiled lobsters, fried seafood, chowder and steamers. A lobster dinner went for $11.95 at a recent visit.

(207) 799-1677. Open daily from 11 to 8, April to mid-October, to 8:30 in July and August.

Dining and Lodging

The Inn by the Sea, 40 Bowery Beach Road (off Route 77), Cape Elizabeth 04107.

Nearly $7 million went into this luxury resort launched in 1987 on the site of the former Crescent Beach Inn in the Portland suburb of Cape Elizabeth. And it looks it, from the marble-tiled lobby and the twelve Audubon hand-colored engravings gracing the inn's walls to the luxury suites with two TVs (the one in the sitting room hidden in the armoire) and no fewer than three telephones. There's an ocean view from every room's patio or balcony.

Handsomely done in Maine shingle style, the angled complex consists of 25 one-bedroom suites in the main building and eighteen condo-style one- or two-bedroom suites in four attached cottages. The loft suites on the second floor are most in demand, each with a kitchenette, a large living room opening onto a private balcony, and a loft bedroom and an enormous bathroom/dressing area upstairs. We liked our first stay in a garden suite facing the lawn and ocean on the first floor, its living room – with reproduction Chippendale furnishings and a blue chintz sofa – opening through sliding doors onto an outside patio. Its small bedroom with a four-poster queen bed was quite adequate, even though the windows opened onto the parking lot. Next time we reveled in the extra space of a loft suite, which offered a better water view from its balcony and a three-section bathroom bigger than the kingsize loft bedroom. Furnishings are most comfortable and the decor understated in a Maine woods theme.

Owner Maureen McQuade, a Maine native who had managed large properties, lucked into buying this inn in foreclosure in 1993. A hands-on innkeeper, she's very much at home here and her enthusiasm shows. The friendly young staff is dressed in khakis and bids everyone "a nice Maine day." Families are in evidence, at least in summer. So are pets. The four-diamond, four-star inn not only accepts but encourages travelers' pets, pampering them almost as much as guests of the human persuasion. (The "gourmet pet menu" offers not only doggie tapas but chargrilled New York sirloin strip steak with pan-fried potato and summer vegetables and a dessert of French vanilla ice cream with crumbled granola and whipped cream.)

Pets or no, you can swim in a pleasant pool or saunter down a boardwalk to a private entrance to the beach at Crescent Beach State Park. The tea garden with rose bushes and fish in a fountain pool is a quiet retreat.

Breakfast and dinner are served in the Audubon Room, a harmonious space striking in white, with comfortable chairs and an enclosed porch around two sides. Tables are topped with white linens, English bone china and fresh flowers. The dinner fare has been elevated as well as condensed in recent years. We hear the rack of lamb is to die for, but were quite content at one visit with a couple of salads (spinach with grilled portobello mushrooms and caramelized walnuts, and fanned breast of duck on baby spinach and arugula) and main dishes of grilled medallions of jerk-spiced pork on a papaya and sundried-cherry relish, and shrimp szechuan, tossed with broccoli rabe, snow peas and a zesty orange-ginger sauce on cellophane noodles.

Another occasion produced a fabulous seafood fettuccine, loaded with lobster, diver scallops and tiger shrimp in an ethereal seaweed and saffron cream sauce, and a rich seafood strudel. The latter was accompanied by asparagus, pattypan squash, carrots and red peppers. Though there were no chilled desserts on the menu, the kitchen managed to turn up a dish of chocolate ice cream garnished with blueberries.

Breakfast (not included) is a feast as well. You can order a lobster and cheese omelet, amaretto or grand-marnier french toast, or eggs benedict with lobster. Portions are abundant, and the lady at the next table exclaimed that her pancakes and blueberries were the biggest she ever saw.

They do things up big here. Even the bill comes on an oversize computer printout.

(207) 799-3134 or (800) 888-4287. Fax (207) 799-4779. www.innbythesea.com. Forty-three one and two-bedroom suites with private baths. Summer: Doubles, $269 to $319; cottage suites, $359 to $549. Late spring and early fall: doubles, $179 to $239; cottages, $239 to $399. November-April: doubles, $139 to $179; cottages, $169 to $279.

Restaurant: (207) 767-0888. Entrées, $18.95 to $27.95. Lunch, daily 11 to 1. Dinner nightly, 5:30 to 9.

Black Point Inn Resort, 510 Black Point Road, Prouts Neck 04074.

But for the elegant antique car parked out front, this gray shingled inn built in 1925 is not all that imposing – although very attractive and impeccably kept up. Inside all is rustic and refined in an old Maine way. The location not far south of Portland on Prouts Neck is smashing, with Sand Dollar Beach on one side and Scarborough Beach on the other.

The delightful public rooms range from old-fashioned lobby to porches to library to a salon with grand piano. They're notable for overstuffed chairs, fireplaces, game tables and books to read, and many are the guests who seem to hang out there from morning to evening. The ambiance is low-key social, and jackets are required in all public areas after 7, as they always have been.

Breakfast and dinner are served in a big, dark and old pine-paneled dining room. Only the window tables get much of a view, but they do catch a glimpse of the open ocean. On good days a buffet lunch is set out outside beside the large heated saltwater pool overlooking the ocean (there's also an indoor freshwater pool). Five-course dinners with several choices for each course are offered by reservation. Maine seafood fettuccine, roasted chicken with sauce piquant and roast tenderloin of beef with merlot sauce were options at our visit. The fare is continental with a New England accent. Chef Bruce Orr employs herbs from the inn's garden for some of his delicate sauces.

Staying in one of the 80 inn rooms or cottages is also one way to get to see the exclusive summer community of Prouts Neck. The famous Cliff Walk passes Winslow Homer's studio, and the pine woods between inn and ocean are a national bird sanctuary. Guests enjoy an adjacent eighteen-hole golf course and fourteen tennis courts hidden away in the woods.

Although the resort had been seasonal, the experience was in such demand that Black Point stayed open year-round starting in 1999-2000.

(207) 883-4126 or (800) 258-0003. Fax (207) 883-9976. Eighty rooms and cottages with private baths. Rates, MAP: doubles, $355 to $580 in summer, $280 to $90 in spring and fall, $255 to $430 in winter. Three-night minimum stay in summer.

Prix-fixe, $40. Dinner by reservation, nightly 6:30 to 9. Jackets required.

Portland Regency Hotel, 20 Milk St., Portland 04101.

This downtown hotel is superbly located in the heart of the Old Port, which might justify the extra charge for valet parking. The fact that it's in the restored

1895 armory, providing some unusual architectural treatments, is a bonus. It wears its designation as a member of the Historic Hotels of America proudly. Most of the 95 guest and suites go off a three-story atrium above the dining room. Rooms are plush, many with kingsize four-poster beds and minibars. There's nightly turn-down service. Complimentary coffee and newspapers are placed at the door in the morning.

The health club is up-to-date, and the Armory Lounge offers complimentary hors d'oeuvres with cocktails and nightly entertainment in a warren of downstairs rooms.

The **Armory Restaurant** has a traditional menu for breakfast, lunch and dinner. Dinner entrées range from haddock fillets sautéed with Maine shrimp and cheese to roast rack of lamb with a red-wine demi-glace. Baked stuffed lobster, veal marsala and steak diane are among the possibilities.

(207) 774-4200 or (800) 727-3436. Fax (207) 775-2150. Ninety-five rooms and suites with private baths. Doubles, $199 to $249, July-October; $149 to $219, rest of year. Entrées, $15.95 to $27.95. Lunch daily, 11:30 to 2. Dinner, 5:30 to 9:30.

Lodging

Pomegranate Inn, 49 Neal St., Portland 04102.

Isabel Smiles and her late husband Alan picked Portland as the small city in which to launch a B&B when they decided to move from Connecticut. They "turned the conventional idea of a bed and breakfast on its side and created a funky, relaxed and stylish inner-city space," in the words of the Portland Press-Telegram. They also made heads turn in local art circles, not to mention those of their B&B colleagues.

Called the "queen of the B&Bs" by no less than the New York Times, the Pomegranate is an art lover's paradise – part museum, part gallery, part antiques collection and part inn. The last attribute gives the unlikely-looking, 1884 Italianate Victorian with Colonial Revival facade in Portland's residential West End its raison d'être. It's filled with antiques (Isabel was in the decorating and antiques business in Greenwich) and contemporary art.

The seven bedrooms on the second and third floors, all with modern tiled baths, televisions and telephones, are a kaleidoscope of design. Each is unique, blending antique rugs, colorful fabrics, antique and contemporary furnishings, charming eccentricities and prized artworks. Even the bed configuration is mixed: five rooms come with queensize beds, another with kingsize and one has twins. Four have gas fireplaces.

A deluxe, two-room suite has been added upstairs in the renovated carriage house across a terrace beside the main inn. We happily splurged for the downstairs garden room in the carriage house. It had two plush chairs and a puffy duvet on the bed, a marble bathroom and walls painted with riotous flowers. It opened onto a secret courtyard, so quiet and secluded it was hard to imagine we were in the midst of a city.

Walls in guest rooms, hand-painted by Portland artist Heidi Gerquest Harbert, are themselves works of art. Most striking is one on a robin's-egg-blue wall with a swirl design taken from a pattern on a Japanese kimono. Paisley, birds and flowers are painted in other rooms, and the hallways are sponged a golden color. Isabel's daughter, Amy Russack, painted faux finishes on moldings, fireplace mantels and columns. The downstairs parlors are almost a gallery of marble columns, Greek statuary, contemporary artworks and, near the long hand-painted Italianate dining

Stylish bedrooms at Pomegranate Inn are a kaleidoscope of design.

table, three huge papier-maché vegetables, each perched atop a small clay pot on a shelf in the front window.

Breakfast is served between 8 and 9:30 at the aforementioned communal table, or at a couple of small tables for those who prefer. Poached eggs with capers, creamy quiches and pancakes with sautéed pears turn the meal into another show of artistry. Our tasty waffles with bananas and raspberries were preceded by a dish of dainty nectarines with tiny blueberries and vanilla yogurt and a glass of mystery juice, whose contents no one at the table could fathom. "Just orange and cranberry," Isabel said breezily. "I should tell everybody it's pomegranate juice."

(207) 772-1006 or (800) 356-0408. Fax (207) 773-4426. Eight rooms and one suite with private baths. Doubles, $135 to $175, mid-May through October; $95 to $135, rest of year. Two-night minimum weekends.

The Danforth, 163 Danforth St., Portland 04102.

Energetic owner Barbara Hathaway from Connecticut never dreamed she'd be running an inn, let alone a landmark 1821 brick Georgian mansion that used to be the rectory for the Archdiocese of Portland. She opened in 1994 with two rooms, finished the ninth and last guest room a year later, and added an efficiency apartment in an annex down the street in 1997. She caters private functions and offers more common rooms and areas than most inns twice the size.

The nine accommodations (one a two-bedroom suite) on the second and third floors are spacious, light and airy with tall windows and thick off-white carpeting. They're outfitted with updated baths, queensize beds bearing pillow-top mattresses, remote-control television, telephones, loveseats or wing chairs, antique armoires, writing desks with data-port terminals and all the accouterments of the good B&B life. Indian shutters cover the windows and Baccarat crystal knobs open the doors. All the tiled fireplaces are working and wood-burning. The only shortcoming in some is the lack of good lights where one might like to read.

Restored 1821 Georgian mansion now offers elegant accommodations as The Danforth.

On one side of the main floor is a double parlor. The front portion is a plush living room and the rear portion has been restored as a dining room, with a sun porch alongside. On the other side of the wide entry hall are a function room and a garden solarium that serves as the reception area. To the rear is a cozy library with a wet bar in an old vault and one of the mansion's thirteen fireplaces. The day's newspapers are set out here with morning coffee. Late afternoon brings cookies and lemonade or tea and, in cool weather, hot soups with rustic breads. Decanters of port, brandy and sherry await in the evening.

Downstairs is the original billiards room, paneled and looking much as it did a century ago. Way upstairs on the rooftop is the enclosed widow's walk, occasionally used for sunrise breakfasts. With moon and stars painted on the ceiling, it offers wraparound views of downtown Portland and the waterfront, plus a quite unexpected vista to the west of countless brick chimneys – a remarkable scene "straight out of England," says Barbara.

There's more. A vacant third-floor room was converted into a garden "conservatory" because the owner believes guests on every floor should enjoy a common area. Occupants of the six second-floor rooms have a parlor opening onto a deck overlooking the colorful side garden.

The day's breakfast fare – usually a savory and a sweet – is posted on a menu at the reception desk. At our latest visit, the choice involved artichoke-mushroom crustless quiche or raisin bread pudding with bourbon sauce. Another day might pair scrambled eggs in puff pastry with french toast. "I love to cook," says Barbara. She hoped to publish her recipes in a cookbook to be called *Maine Mornings.*

As we paused to take everything in atop the widow's walk, Barbara acknowledged she "saw the building, fell in love with it and turning it into an inn was the only way for me to have it." Her guests are lucky to share it.

(207) 879-8755 or (800) 991-6557. Fax (207) 879-8754. Eight rooms and one two-bedroom suite with private baths. Doubles, $135 to $285, Memorial Day through October; $115 to $225, rest of year.

The Percy Inn, 15 Pine St., Box 8187, Portland 04104.

Travel writer Dale Northrup, peripatetic and unencumbered, transformed a vacant 1830 Federal-style brick townhouse in his hometown into the kind of B&B he finds travelers want. "After 24,000 hotel reviews in nineteen years," he said, "it was the only way I saw to get back here and spend some time at home."

Eighteen months of renovations produced four upstairs guest rooms, a main-floor living room with fireplace and library, and a second-story breakfast room and wet bar, which remains open 24 hours for snacks and board games. The same schedule prevails for a top-floor pantry called the Poet's Corner and containing a coffee and tea station. Beyond, a new rooftop deck yields a view of Portland roofs and, in the distance, Mount Washington and the Presidential Range.

Air-conditioned bedrooms on the second and third floors come with queen beds, cedar closets and marble or stone bathrooms. The largest room is the second-floor front Longfellow Suite with an ornamental fireplace, pumpkin pine floor, and an adjoining study. Of similar size overhead is the Dorothy Parker Suite, where a dressing room separates the bedroom from the bathroom with double shower. Period décor and designer fabrics vary, but common amenities include wet bars, stocked refrigerators, TVs, CD players, weather radios and candles. "I paid attention to what I'd miss if I stayed here," says Dale. He occupies a rear main-floor bedroom when he's not traveling across the world to evaluate hotels for the Star Search guides for travel agents or scouting out places for Fodor's and Frommer travel guides. "Bathroom and kitchen facilities are important."

Poetry is the theme, though not exactly of the kind you might expect. Given Henry Wadsworth Longfellow's ties to Portland and the inn's location in the city's arts district, Dale named the rooms for poets, including Percy Bysshe Shelley. That accounts for the inn's name? Not exactly. The innkeeper's father did most of the renovations and his name is Percy. So it was a good fit.

(207) 871-7638 or (888) 417-3729. Fax (207) 775-2599. Four rooms with private baths. Doubles, $129 to $179, Memorial Day through October; $89 to $159, rest of year.

Gourmet Treats

The new Portland Public Market and the burgeoning Theater Arts District have shifted some of the visitor focus away from the Old Port area to another part of downtown. Otherwise, along with its restaurants, the restored Old Port area remains the center of shops appealing to those interested in food.

Portland Public Market, Preble Street and Cumberland Avenue, Portland.

New England's biggest farm market gives new dimension to the term, at least regionally. Maine philanthropist Elizabeth Noyce, ex-wife of the co-founder of the microchip and Intel Corp., was on a personal campaign to revitalize downtown Portland when her advisor happened across Seattle's famed Pike Place Market. That inspired her privately funded, $9 million beauty of timbered beams, walls of windows and soaring ceilings, built on land that had been awaiting a higher use than a parking lot. The 37,000-square-foot structure, a block long and half as wide, is just off busy Congress Street and linked by a skybridge to a 650-car parking garage with free validated parking. Inside, more than two dozen carefully selected Maine food growers and vendors purvey everything from elk to eels.

Opened in 1998, the market looks new and a bit antiseptic, at least in comparison with older models. But that is not to negate in any way its riches, or its bevy of national awards for architecture, economic development and urban revitalization. The state's famed Borealis Breads bakes many of its treats on site daily. Bayley Hill Butcher Shoppe and Wolfe's Neck Farm sell exotic meats raised on their farms. One of the principals in the large Hanson Brothers Seafood operation is Walter Compare, who left his job at Pike Place to replicate his seafood market – minus the fish-throwing camaraderie – in his wife's home state.

Besides all the market stalls, there's a state-of-the-art demonstration kitchen where food and wine classes are conducted several times weekly. Not to mention the granite central fireplace flanked by stone benches, or an informative newsletter that noted in a recent issue that Barbara Bush, Julia Child and Harrison Ford had been spotted shopping there. Eventually, a large restaurant called The Market on Elm is to open at one end of the market. Meanwhile, Hanson Brothers offers a good seafood cafe and there are plenty of takeout opportunities and tables on the mezzanine upon which to eat.

On the mezzanine stands a private tribute to Mrs. Noyce, who died shortly before her dream was realized. It's a small sculpture of a woman pushing a cart laden with vegetables and feeding corn to a crow. Originally titled "Henry and the Heckler" by its Colorado artist, her lawyer aptly renamed it "Betty Sharing the Bounty." *(207) 228-2000. Open Monday-Saturday 9 to 7, Sunday 10 to 5.*

Portland's century-old outdoor farmers' market, featuring local food purveyors of more modest means, was continuing on Wednesdays at Monument Square in the heart of downtown and Saturdays at Deering Oaks Park.

The owners of **The Whip and Spoon,** a fascinating store for serious cooks at 161 Commercial St., say "if it's worth using in the kitchen, we have it." From lobster picks to expensive food processors, you can find everything including magazines for cooks, a great collection of cookbooks and local products like herbs and spices from Ram Island Farm in Cape Elizabeth. All kinds of supplies are available for wine and beer makers, too. You could spend hours here, browsing and buying.

Modeled after a European coffee bar, the **Portland Coffee Roasting Co.** at 111 Commercial St. draws folks for a coffee fix or the "eggspresso" breakfast (scrambled eggs, bagel and coffee, $3.25). Small sandwiches, pastries like sticky buns and almond crescents and delicious Samantha juices (made in nearby Scarborough – we loved the strawberry-orange) are also on the board. Tall windows reveal the passing scene as you sip cappuccino or cafe au lait at modern little tables beneath a high pressed-tin ceiling. Owner Gerrie Brooke offers a traditional cream tea, with scones and double devon cream. As we nursed a latte and caffe mocha outdoors on a ledge with a view of the waterfront and the sounds of the seagulls, we could picture ourselves in Seattle, the latte capital of the world.

For interesting pottery and dishware, check out **Maxwell's Pottery** at 384 Fore St. (we liked the blue and white pottery bearing sailing ships) and, across the street, **Maine Potters,** a co-op, where we admired dishes for dips depicting different shellfish.

With plump red radishes on its sign, **The Portland Greengrocer** on Commercial Street is the place to pick up breads like peach focaccia from Black Crow Bakery in Litchfield, imported beers, wines, oils and vinegars. The deli looks fantastic and the produce section pristine, with such fancy items as imported Italian onions.

Della's Catessen, located in the thick of things at 92 Exchange St., is a fun place where Della Parker, who once was a sous chef at Cafe Always, sells soups like carrot-ginger, haddock chowder and gazpacho, bacon corn muffins, chicken pot pie, Peruvian pâté, salads and quiches. Sandwiches are in the $3 to $5 range. Top off your lunch with a chocolate fudge grand slam brownie. Beers and wines, herbs, oils, gift baskets and exotic jars of pickled fiddleheads, cajun ketchup and rhubarb chutney are displayed around the cheery yellow and red room, with several tables and framed old Life covers on the walls.

Restaurateurs and locals in the know get their breads and pastries from the **Standard Baking Co.,** located at 75 Commercial St., behind and beneath the Fore Street Restaurant. Country boules, baguettes, rosemary focaccia, black olive rolls, morning buns, cranberry-walnut scones, fruit tarts, almond biscotti – you name it and this sparkling place probably has it.

Tastes of Tuscany

The Clown, 143 Middle St.

This stylish newcomer to the Old Port area is an antiques, arts and wine shop par excellence. Taking over the old Carbur's restaurant property, Kyle A. Wolfe and Martin Kolk opened in 1999 a year-round and considerably larger offshoot of their seasonal shop they'd run for three years in rural Stonington. Here they stock the main floor with European antiques and accessories, among them stunning ceramics, plus paintings and sculpture by contemporary artists, most with a European focus. The downstairs seemingly was made for Maine's largest wine cellar. Among the more than 1,100 labels are two excellent chiantis – one a reserve classico and one a table wine – from the 350 cases produced annually at the couple's vineyard in Tuscany. The owners were planning to double the size of their Tuscan farm to add more grapes as well as olive trees, the fruits of which turn up in some mighty fine olive oils for sale. Wine tastings are scheduled here monthly as part of what the couple call "the art of considered living."

(207) 756-7390. Open daily, 10 to 5 or 7, Sunday noon to 5.

Ultimate Gourmet

Aurora Provisions, 64 Pine St., Portland.

"The selections are choice" is the apt credo for this upscale market and cafe in Portland's West End. Chef Cheryl Lewis and partner Norine Kotts resurfaced here with a popular and very visible adjunct to their catering business after selling Cafe Always, for ten years our favorite Portland restaurant. The shelves are stocked with the finest specialty foods, but the focus of the establishment are the espresso bar and the central deli and pastry cases, dispensing more – and more innovative – treats than you might think existed. Stop here for a morning "ginger rabbit" fruit smoothie, a cranberry scone or a cafe au lait. Lunchtime brings sensational soups, salads and sandwiches in the $5 to $6 range. Later in the day, the possibilities for takeout dinners are endless. There are tables inside and out upon which to partake. We seldom can pass Portland by without indulging in something extravagant from Aurora.

(207) 871-9060. Open Monday-Saturday 7:30 to 7.

Mid-Coast Maine

Where the Real Maine Starts

The sandy beaches of Southern Maine yield to Maine's more typical rockbound coast north of Portland. There are those who say that this is where the real Maine starts.

The coastline becomes more jagged, its fingers protruding like tentacles toward the sea between inlets, rivers and bays. Poke down remote byways to Bailey Island, Popham Beach, Westport, Christmas Cove and Pemaquid Point. You'll find life quieter here and the distances between points long and roundabout. One look at the map as you eye the shore across the inlet and you'll understand why the natives say "you can't get theah from heah" – except by boat.

Here also are two of Maine's leading tourist destinations – crowded Boothbay Harbor, a commercial fishing village surrounded by a choice and remote shoreline beyond and on either side, and upscale Camden, where the mountains meet the sea and the windjammer fleet sets sail from the colorful harbor.

These two resort areas have long been favored by visitors, whose arrival has produced the inevitable influx of souvenir shops and golden arches nearby. But the Mid-coast's increasing gentrification also has attracted new and better restaurants, inns and B&Bs, and – a surprise at a recent visit – a little landmark called Lighthouse Espresso, "serving Downeast coffee," a beacon on Route 1 above Rockland.

Side by side with touristy Boothbay and Camden are postcard fishing hamlets like Ocean Point and Port Clyde. The busy towns of Brunswick, Bath and Rockland co-exist with salt-washed villages like Rockport and South Harpswell.

Before you head Down East, tarry along the mid-coast. Here, as elsewhere in Maine, entries are generally presented geographically, from southwest to northeast.

Dining

The Best of the Best

The Robinhood Free Meetinghouse, Robinhood Road, off Route 127, Georgetown.

Yes, this place with the odd name really was a church until 1989. In 1996, it was transformed into a restaurant-cum-gallery by chef-owner Michael Gagné, who moved up the road after putting the Osprey restaurant at Robinhood Marine Center on the culinary map.

Well known in the area for his catering and cooking classes, he oversees an ambitious, contemporary fusion menu that has gone beyond its original New American base to embrace continental and oriental cuisines (some dishes are marked "very peppery" and "spicy hot"). He and his staff make their own breads, pastas, sausages and ice creams. From their dream of a kitchen, they turn out up to three dozen entrées a night, not to mention three soups, six salads, twelve appetizers, four pastas and a staggering fourteen desserts. Skeptics call it overkill, but they recognize Michael as one of Maine's best chefs.

In leaving the Osprey, Michael gave up a waterfront location for a better arena in which to show his stuff. The lower floor of the meeting house bears a clean

Chef-owner Michael Gagné in dining room of The Robinhood Free Meetinghouse.

stark New England look. It's pristine in white and cream, with oriental runners on the wide-board floors and Shaker-style chairs at tables clad in white. Arty sculptures dress a window ledge, and the upstairs meeting house has been turned into a gallery.

Michael invites customers to "mix and match appetizers, pastas and salads to make up a meal that fits your appetite." The smoked seafood sampler served with a baguette and horseradish-mustard mousseline is sensational, as are the corn-fried oysters with fresh salsa and chipotle cream. The grilled sausage sampler is a meal in itself, with two six-inch sausages (one garlic, one chicken) and a sliced baguette. A tart cherry-lemon sorbet cleared the palate for our entrées. We found the gutsy scallops niçoise in puff pastry with saffron rice and the grilled chicken with sundried tomatoes over fettuccine both so ample as to require doggy bags, since we wanted to save room for the trio of ice creams – ginger, raspberry swirl and childhood orange. The signature "obsession in three chocolates" – white, dark and milk, all flavored with different liqueurs – is as good as it gets. No wonder the Maine Sunday Telegram reviewer awarded the ultimate five stars in his latest review.

Quite a selection of wines is available by the glass. The wine list is priced mostly in the teens and twenties, with less than the usual markup. The dessert list has been known to offer a flight of six ports, as if anyone could manage.

(207) 371-2188. Entrées, $19 to $23. Dinner nightly, 5:30 to 9, fewer nights in off-season.

Star Fish Grill, 100 Pleasant St., Brunswick.

A former New York attorney and a free-standing storefront location overshadowed by a video store are an unusual combination for a hot new seafood restaurant. Alyson Cummings moved to Portland, where she practiced law by day and apprenticed nights in the kitchen at the acclaimed Street & Company seafood restaurant. In 1998, she and a friend, Tom Cary, took over a former pizza establishment and opened the Star Fish to four-star reviews and a lengthy feature by Down East magazine in 1999 about "what might be Maine's best new restaurant." The name originated in a brainstorming session among friends, Alyson recounts. They settled on starfish, "because they're mollusk eaters, like our customers. They love feeding on them." They decorated the place in "peaceful blues" – navy on the ceiling, aqua on the walls and vividly bright on the tiled floor – with hundreds of tiny starfish stenciled on the front windows. It gives some diners the illusion of being underwater, a feeling enhanced by pinpoint "star lights" on the ceiling and wavy illumination from scallop-shaped sconces on the walls. The butcher-block tables are dressed with fresh flowers and votive candles, but no tablecloths. "We wanted this to be accessible for the locals, who might otherwise think it was too fancy and just for visitors," Alyson advised.

Given her legal training, everything was carefully calculated, from the straight-ahead presentation of the freshest of fish to the credo that here was a place to have fun (she was singing and joking with staff in the prep kitchen, her hands covered with pastry dough, when we stopped by one mid-afternoon). She even was thinking about somehow reconfiguring the restaurant to take advantage of the rushing Androscoggin River in back rather than busy Route 1 out front.

Meanwhile, from the open kitchen in the center of the establishment comes an assortment of grilled fish and seafood, each basted with the house citrus oil – a blend of extra-virgin olive oil and lemon and lime juices. Also available are more complex choices: shrimp sautéed with crunchy jícama over pasta in a subtle champagne-lobster beurre blanc, spicy mussels and calamari in a Thai-style green curry sauce over rice, and pan-seared sea scallops in brandy cream. The only non-seafood items are pasta primavera and grilled organic Maine sirloin steak with a side of horseradish cream sauce. But almost everyone here, at one time or another, orders the signature lobster paella for two ($34.95), an extravagant takeoff on the Spanish classic. It features a sizable split lobster, loads of mussels, calamari, chorizo, chicken morsels and Mediterranean vegetables served in the traditional pan, redolent of sea flavors and so ample that some of it usually goes home for another meal.

Those who go for the lobster paella are advised to skip the appetizers, which are presented as a "tasting menu" for sharing or to make a lighter meal. Among the options are escabeche of barely sautéed sea scallops served cool over mesclun greens, mussels steamed in wine, garlic and fennel, and sautéed calamari accented with lemon and garlic. Caesar salad may be paired with shrimp, scallops, calamari, salmon or tuna.

Desserts could be the chocolate of the evening, orange pound cake latticed and pooled with chocolate sauce, or a tangy pink grapefruit sorbet spiked with campari. Wines, many available by the glass, are priced from $17 to $50.

(207) 725-7828. Entrées, $13.95 to $17.95. Dinner, Tuesday-Sunday 5 to 9:30. Sunday brunch in winter, 9 to 2.

Christopher's Boathouse, 25 Union St., Boothbay Harbor.

New world cuisine prepared over a wood-fired grill is featured at this with-it new restaurant and wine and cheese emporium. That the waterfront location at the head of the harbor is so picturesque is a bonus.

Floor-to-ceiling windows bring the outdoors inside the candlelit interior with pine walls, white-clothed tables and a few plants for accents. The low ceilings reflect its boathouse past, and a deck is used on warm nights. A recent adjunct called the **Winecellar** purveys not only wines but cheeses, breads, picnic makings and prepared entrées to go.

"Never trust a skinny chef," proclaims the business card of chef-owner Christopher Russell. Instead, put yourself in his hands for creative fare that makes dinner an event. You might start with his award-winning lobster and mango bisque with hot and spicy lobster wontons, pan-seared peeky-toe crab cakes with black bean sauce and scallion cream, or a napoleon of crispy potatoes and wild mushrooms with herb cream sauce. Or how about the chef's "new world caesar" salad with charred tomatoes, grilled scallops, caperberries, white anchovies and maytag cheddar?

Typical main courses range from local pistachio-battered haddock, deep fried and served with homemade tartar sauce, to pan-seared medallions of milk-fed veal flamed with brandy and finished with black truffle oil. From the wood grill come such treats as lobster with roasted red pepper-tarragon butter, spice-painted salmon with pickled onion sauce, and tamarind-glazed pork chop with chipotle and pecan demi-glace.

Dessert could be black-bottom chocolate-hazelnut mousse cake, raspberry-almond flan, or a lemon cream torte.

(207) 633-6565. Entrées, $16.75 to $21.95. Dinner, Tuesday-Sunday 5:30 to 9 or 9:30.

Amalfi, 421 Main St., Rockland.

When a Maine coast restaurant is launched in the dead of winter and acquires a wide reputation before summer arrives, you know it's worth seeking out. That was the happy circumstance in 1999 for this intimate Mediterranean eatery near the famed Farnsworth Museum in Rockland. Chip Ewing, who grew up in his family's Whitehall Inn in Camden, converted a downtown storefront into a colorful space with purple runners and pink napkins on the tables and a mural of a Tuscan vineyard painted on the wall by a friend from Kennebunkport.

Why Mediterranean in Maine? "I've traveled there many times and the food appeals to a wide range of people," answers Chip. "It's healthy and light, and it's a broad region that lends itself to a lot of creativity."

Chef David Cooke turns out dinner dishes like Spanish paella, grilled chicken over roasted vegetable risotto, beef bracole in tomato sauce and Moroccan lamb kabob. Tempting starters are butternut squash ravioli with gorgonzola cream, warm goat cheese with mixed greens, and local shrimp scampi. Dessert could be a signature chocolate soup with berries, lemon tart, or homemade ice cream or sorbet.

The interesting lunch menu offers a Greek gyro, toasted brie on a baguette, a pesto chicken focaccia sandwich, Tuscan cannellini bean soup and salade niçoise. The Mediterranean-inspired wine list is priced in the teens and twenties.

With tasty food at modest prices, it's little wonder that Amalfi's 35 seats fill quickly – often, Chip says, two or three times a night.

(207) 596-0012. Entrées, $11.50 to $15.50. Lunch, Monday-Friday 11 to 2:30. Dinner, Monday-Saturday 5:30 to 9 or 9:30.

Primo, 2 South Main St. (Route 73), Rockland.

Melissa Kelly, cited by the James Beard Foundation as the best chef in the Northeast in 1999, teamed up with Price Kushner, her fiancé and a baker and

Top chef Melissa Kelly and baker Price Kushner cater event as owners of Primo.

pastry chef of note, to open their own restaurant in spring 2000. Primo, named for her Italian grandfather, Primo Magnani, occupies the Victorian house that formerly housed Jessica's restaurant just south of town.

The pair were doing major renovations and planting vegetables and herb gardens on the four-acre property for what promised to be a sparkling, creative restaurant. The fare reflects the award-winning cuisine and baked goods for which they were known at the famed Old Chatham Sheepherding Company Inn in Old Chatham, N.Y., which closed suddenly in mid-1999 following the departure of Melissa, its founding chef.

"This is the fifth restaurant I've opened but the first for myself," she said. "We're here for the long-term." Both were looking for a place to settle down and chose the Maine coast for its access to "great fish and farms." Her family from Long Island used to have a home in Maine. Price went to summer camp there and his family just built a summer house there.

The partners renovated the existing kitchen to serve their purposes and installed a wood-fired brick oven. They imparted a cozy, country elegant look to three small, white-tablecloth dining rooms on the main floor. Three rooms upstairs were opened up into one large space featuring a bar and "a more funky dining area where you might come by yourself after a movie," in Melissa's words. A bar menu, pizzas, paninis and "fun finger-type foods" were planned here.

Price employs the brick oven to bake his memorable breads and desserts. Melissa considers the oven less a focal point than a reflection of Primo's food style, "rustic and seasonal," drawing its roots from the Mediterranean and its ingredients from Maine.

Sample menu items were starters of orange-dusted Maine sea scallops with a beet and blood orange salad, an arugula and prosciutto pizza from the wood oven, and hand-rolled ravioli filled with Maine lobster in a celeriac sauce. Melissa anticipated main courses like seared Maine salmon with sorrel mashed potatoes and garden vegetables, and Kelmscott Farm lamb Moroccan style with couscous and harissa. For dessert, Price was planning apple crostata with rum-raisin ice cream, wood-oven roasted nectarines with sabayon, zinfandel poached pears with vanilla bean ice cream, and a vanilla and chocolate gelato sundae with espresso and cinnamon beignets.

A moderately priced wine list was in the works.

Melissa, who trained with celebrity chefs Larry Forgione and Alice Waters after graduating first in her class from the Culinary Institute of America, has her own cult following. So does self-taught baker Price, whose hearth-baked breads had early morning buyers lining up outside the inn's bakery in Old Chatham. Accompanying them to Primo from Old Chatham were Melissa's sous chef, three cooks and several people to run the gardens.

Look for much the same spirit and style that we and food lovers from across the world came to enjoy at Old Chatham. We can't wait for a primo meal at Primo.

(207) 596-0770. Entrées, $10 to $25. Dinner nightly in summer, from 5:30. Closed Tuesday and possibly Wednesday in off-season, also January to mid-February.

Cafe Miranda, 15 Oak St., Rockland.

The beige and green colors of the exterior are repeated inside this trendy cafe at the edge of downtown Rockland. Run by chef Kerry Altiero and his wife, Evelyn Donnelly, a craftswoman by day, the cafe draws throngs from throughout the meat-and-haddock Rockland area for its laid-back atmosphere and the gutsy cooking emanating from the wood-fired brick oven in the open kitchen.

At our first visit, patrons were extolling the carrot-ginger soup served with herbed flatbread, the bruschetta with grilled chicken, artichoke spread and greens, and the mushroom pizza with three cheeses and red onions. The ambitious menu denotes small plates and "big, bigger, biggest" plates, ranging from appetizers for one to dinner for one or appetizers for two. Kerry cooks almost everything in the brick oven, even the fish of the day, going through a cord of wood a month.

His offerings range widely, from pasta with sundried tomatoes, ricotta and artichoke hearts to ziti bolognaise with pork, veal and wine cream sauce. Lest Cafe Miranda be categorized as Italian, Kerry injects Thai and North African influences, as in a pork dish with gorgonzola, polenta and three chiles with avocado salsa or grilled salmon with mandarin oranges, cilantro and roasted peppers and served with couscous. Expect innovations like chargrilled pork and shrimp cakes with peanuts and stir-fried veggies in a coconut-peanut sauce, and stir-fried salmon strips tossed with Thai chiles, lime, mint and greens. Consider the Thai curry shrimp, grilled chicken with roasted peppers and basil on saffron risotto, the lamb korma, or the sliced duck breast with ginger-plum sauce. There are a number of vegetarian items, too.

We would gladly make a meal of small plates like roasted salmon cakes, shrimp tossed with avocado-corn salsa on roasted romano grits, or mussels steamed in saffron cream.

Evelyn's talents are evident in the desserts, perhaps zabaglione with fresh fruit, trifle with chocolate sauce and blackberries, or frozen lemon mousse pie.

Rainbow-colored cloth napkins and candles grace the blond wood tables. Single diners enjoy gathering at one of the three counters – two smack in the middle of the room and one facing Kerry in the kitchen. There's a select and varied, reasonably priced wine list.

(207) 594-2034. Entrées, $11 to $17. Dinner, Tuesday-Saturday from 5:30.

Atlantica, One Bayview Landing, Camden.
Local art is served up alongside Atlantic cuisine at this self-styled "Gallery & Grille" on the Camden waterfront. Opened in 1996, the place is both highly rated and wildly popular, so much so that the first time we tried to eat here we couldn't endure the lengthy wait for a table. When we tried to case out the art, so many people were milling about that we could barely get the picture.

We did get the picture at a subsequent visit in the off-season, when we managed to get a table on the second floor near a window, although the night was so foggy we were unable to see much of anything. The picture doesn't really matter here. The food is assertive, the surroundings convivial and the contemporary nautical ambiance pleasing.

Dining is on two floors, including a much-coveted upstairs turret with a single table for five, as well as outdoors on a covered terrace and an upper deck.

Chef-owner Kristine Kane, a Lincolnville native who cooked in Hawaii, is in the kitchen with co-owner James Tafoya, the sous chef. They mix Pacific accents into Atlantic fare. Consider Kristine's "unusual crab cakes" blended with rice noodles, green onions, corn and Japanese spices and served with lemongrass-coconut sauce and wasabi vinaigrette. Or her red curry scallops with vegetables, ginger, lemongrass and cilantro. The lone beef item on the menu, an angus tenderloin, is pan-seared and served with a roasted garlic-cabernet sauce.

One of us made a satisfying dinner of two appetizers: spicy Maine mahogany clams steamed with oriental black beans and cilantro, and crispy spring rolls filled with Maine shrimp and served with a zippy sweet Thai chili dipping sauce. The other enjoyed the caesar salad that came with the seafood pasta entrée. One of the best we've had, it was brimming with lobster, scallops, whitefish and shrimp in a pineapple-ginger sauce with basil and roasted macadamia nuts. Unusually good hot rolls and a Gieson sauvignon blanc from New Zealand accompanied.

Typical desserts are orange creme brûlée, decadent chocolate cake filled with ganache and, our choices, ginger ice cream and red raspberry sorbet.

(207) 236-6011. Entrées, $14.95 to $18.95. Lunch, Monday-Saturday 11:30 to 2:30. Dinner, from 5:30. Closed Monday in off-season and month of April.

More Dining Choices

Kristina's, 160 Centre St., Bath.
From a tiny bakery with a few tables and a display case full of sticky buns, Kristina's has evolved into a full-service restaurant and lounge. You can still get sticky buns and other good things to take out from the display cases at the entrance, but now there are two dining rooms, a front dining deck with a tree growing through it and, upstairs, **Harry's Bar,** an attractive room that is all blond wood and deck chairs, with windows onto the outdoors. Jazz groups play here at night.

For breakfast we like to feast on such treats as a Mexican omelet, belgian waffles or a seafood quiche. Soups, quiches, salads (shrimp and peanut noodle or crabmeat in avocado), sandwiches, burgers and entrées like Santa Fe chicken make up the lunch menu.

At dinner start with one of the changing seafood bisques, a rich lobster stew spiked with Spanish sherry and topped with nutty cornbread croutons, cornmeal and basil crêpes with ratatouille and chèvre, a trio of crostini or spicy Jamaican half moons (jerked chicken folded in a cream cheese pastry drizzled with a honey-ginger glaze). Typical entrées are shrimp marsala with pinenuts and currants atop grilled parmesan polenta triangles, pepper-roasted salmon fillet with quinoa primavera and vidalia onion beurre blanc, and grilled sirloin steak in a Nicaraguan citrus marinade, sliced and served over rice and beans. You know you're in creative culinary hands when Kristina's stuffs that Maine staple, haddock, with crabmeat and serves it in a brandied mushroom cream sauce. You really know when you try the Caribbean pepper pot (seafood in coconut milk and scotch bonnet pepper broth with sweet potatoes and coconut jonnycakes). Desserts from the bakery case, perhaps strawberry mousse torte or blueberry cream cake, taste as wonderful as they look.

For weekend brunch, try the Swiss panfkuchen (a pancake topped with berries), Kristina's french toast made with cinnamon swirl bread, smoked salmon quesadilla, a breakfast sandwich or one of the five kinds of benedicts.

(207) 442-8577. Entrées, $14.95 to $17.95. Breakfast, 8 to 11; lunch, 11:30 to 2:30; dinner, 5 to 9. Sunday brunch, 9 to 2. Closed Sunday night and Monday.

Ristorante Black Orchid, 5 By-Way, Boothbay Harbor.

Rather New Yorkish in a seaside kind of way is this intimate Italian trattoria run by chef-owner Steven DiCicco, a Culinary Institute of America grad. The unpretentious interior is done up in black and white, with pink stenciling on the walls, beams strewn with odd-looking grapevines and baskets of hanging fuschias. The upstairs cafe and raw bar overlook the downtown harbor scene.

The highly rated food includes fourteen pasta dishes with salad, from $10 for linguini with meatballs to $18 for the signature fettuccine alfredo with lobster and mushrooms. Lobster also appears alla diavolo and teamed with sundried tomatoes over linguini. Poultry and veal dishes head the list of entrées. Look for things like chicken stuffed with ricotta and crab, veal saltimbocca, salmon with mushrooms and cream, pork tenderloin with raisins and pinenuts and petite filets diavolo.

Desserts include amaretto bread pudding and chocolate-chambord torte.

(207) 633-6650. Entrées, $12 to $18. Dinner nightly in summer, 5:30 to 10, fewer nights in off-season. Raw bar from 5. Closed mid-October to mid-May.

Harbor View Tavern, 1 Water St., Thomaston.

Want good food with a water view? Try this hard-to-find, funky eatery with a darkened dining room/tavern that's too atmospheric for words and, beyond, an enclosed porch and a new deck overlooking the Thomaston harbor. It's a favorite with locals, and probably only locals could find it down an unmarked roadway near the town landing.

Would-be diners line up outside at peak periods. Inside the entry, an upside-down perambulator is on the ceiling. Ahead, every conceivable inch of wall space is covered with old license plates, photos, books, signs, masks and such, and musical instruments hang from the ceiling. But there's much up-to-date in this old boat-building facility, from the day's USA Today sports page posted in the men's room to the artful presentations of the lunches we were served. The chicken and basil pasta salad was garnished with sliced strawberries, oranges and watermelon. Ditto for crab cristo that came with french fries and coleslaw. Two candies arrived with the bill.

Votive candles in little pewter dishes flicker on the tables set with mismatched cloths and colorful napkins at night. The varied menu stays the same, with prices inserted by hand. It lists appetizers, light fare and entrées like baked stuffed haddock, scallops au gratin, chicken imperial and sirloin steak St. Jacques, smothered with scallops and mushroom-cream sauce. Owner Bernard Davodet says the place is famous for its brownie à la mode, grapenut parfait, "strawberry fields forever" cake and apple crisp.

(207) 354-8173. Entrées, $14.95 to $16.95. Lunch daily, 11:30 to 4; dinner, 5 to 10. Shorter hours in winter.

Cork, 51 Bayview St., Camden.

This colorful establishment is an outgrowth of a sixteen-seat wine bar upstairs over a gourmet food and wine store known as Lily, Lupine & Fern.. "Nobody knew we were there," said Aimee Ricca. They do now. Aimee, her parents Gary and Bunni Anderson, and her partner, Brian Krebs, restored a 200-year-old house into a soaring interior space painted purple and focusing on a central staircase. Besides a wine bar where more than 100 wines are available by the bottle, taste or glass, a full menu is served at tables covered with floral cloths and flanked by upholstered chairs.

Self-taught Aimee says she moved into the kitchen by default. "At the original wine bar, everyone wanted more food, so that's how I started cooking." Her food is available à la carte, table d'hôte or by menu dégustation, the latter two involving variations of the former. The menu is a mix of contemporary and continental, accented with occasional French terminology, as in châteaubriand avec shallot-lemon butter, soupe à l'onion and salade de césar.

Dinner might start with warm Saint André cheese served over toasted bread and baby greens, tiger shrimp with guacamole, or crab cakes with caper sauce. Entrées, served with a house salad, range from grilled mako shark with citrus sauce and lime-ginger pork chop to lamb chops with Irish onion sauce and aforementioned châteaubriand. Desserts include the chef's "own authentic" cannoli, hazelnut-praline mousse cake and blueberry cobbler.

Most choices are duplicated on a four-course table d'hôte menu ($33 to $41, depending on choice of entrée) and on the six-course dégustation menu ($54).

(207) 230-0533. Entrées, $17 to $25. Dinner, Tuesday-Saturday 5:30 to 9 or 9:30, fewer days in off-season.

The Waterfront Restaurant, Harborside Square off Bayview Street, Camden.

Rebuilt following a damaging 1995 fire, this popular restaurant is notable for its large outdoor deck partly shaded by a striking white canopy resembling a boat's sails, right beside the windjammers on picturesque Camden Harbor, and for its affordable, international menu. Purists say the location surpasses the food, though we've been satisfied each time we've eaten here.

At lunch, the most costly entrées are crab cakes and sautéed lobster (both in the $14.95 range, including salad or gazpacho and french fries). Eight delectable salads in glass bowls are dressed with outstanding dressings, among them sweet-and-sour bacon, lemon-parmesan, dijon vinaigrette and blue cheese.

Billowing canopy shades dining deck at Waterfront Restaurant in Camden.

At night, when the luncheon salads are still available, the menu turns more eclectic. Among appetizers are calamari and shrimp, baked brie and soups, perhaps chilled raspberry accented with grand marnier. The superlative smoked seafood sampler has been our choice for sharing.

Among main dishes, we've enjoyed the Maine crab cakes with creamy mustard sauce, an assertive linguini with salmon and sundried tomatoes, shrimp with oriental black beans over angel-hair pasta and a special of swordfish grilled over applewood with rosemary, which was juicy and succulent. Lemon and chive glazed chicken, grilled sirloin steak and prosciutto-wrapped rack of lamb are the only meat offerings. Mint chocolate chip pie with hot fudge sauce and whipped cream proved to be the ultimate dessert at one visit. The next time we passed on the heavy offerings and walked up the street to Camden Cone for some raspberry frozen yogurt.

All sorts of shellfish and light fare from hamburgers to lobster rolls are available at the raw bar and outdoor grill.

The Waterfront is understandably a busy, convivial spot on a sunny summer day. Its owners run an offshoot, The Cannery, at Lower Falls Landing in Yarmouth.

(207) 236-3747. Entrées, $14.95 to $22.95. Lunch daily, 11:30 to 2:30. Dinner, 5 to 10. Raw Bar, 2 to 11.

Frogwater Cafe, 31 Elm St., Camden.

Healthful and innovative fare at kindly prices is offered by Erin and Joseph Zdanowicz, young New England Culinary Institute graduates who moved across the country from Tacoma, Wash., to open this homey little storefront cafe in 1995. The name was inspired by a favorite lane on Bainbridge Island in Puget Sound, and some of the primarily domestic wines (most priced in the teens) come from Washington and Oregon.

Food with a flair is featured in simple surroundings. Joseph's menu ranges widely, from garlic ziti and homemade vegetable ravioli to seafood stew and chicken stuffed with crabmeat. Among the choices are grilled Atlantic salmon served over homemade sundried tomato gnocchi in a pesto broth, braised game hen with green olive polenta, and grilled portobello mushroom topped with sautéed veggies and brie and served over couscous and wilted spinach. The only red-meat item on a summer menu was the signature Frogwater burger, topped with blue cheese and bacon on homemade bread served with potato wedges

The appetizers are some of the most interesting in town. Start with an order of the luscious jumbo Spanish onion rings, steamed mussels in a curry-ginger broth, sweet potato cakes topped with lobster, or "shrimp in a skirt," stuffed with boursin cheese fried in a wonton served with a sesame seaweed salad

Finish with Erin's peach bread pudding with butterscotch sauce, chocolate-hazelnut layer cake or berry crisp with vanilla ice cream. Her pastries were in such demand that she was opening **Erin's Maine Street Bakery** in downtown Rockland at our latest visit.

Some of the fare sounds simple, but takes on complex tastes, as we found at lunch (since discontinued, when the couple decided after two years to concentrate on dinner). We enjoyed a hearty bacon-leek-potato soup, an open-faced grilled baguette with feta cheese, tomato, cucumber, black olives and sundried tomato pesto, and a "BLT and Then Some Club" sandwich adding onions, cucumber and cheddar cheese on Texas toast. Sides of nippy macaroni and vegetable salads came with each, and the meal indicated the style that this couple added to the Camden dining scene. The locals return the favor by packing the place at night.

There's a belted galloway cow at the door (this used to be Galloway's, a family restaurant), and the walls bear hand-painted windows for art.

(207) 236-8998. Entrées, $14 to $19. Dinner nightly, from 5.

Dos Amigos, 144 Bayside Road, Northport.

Pink stucco with aqua trim, the exterior of this unlikely-looking Mexican cantina alongside Route 1 deceives. It appears small, but inside is a colorful space with quite a collection of sombreros on the walls and seating for 125. The food is authentic and packs a wallop as well.

Chips and excellent salsa laced with cilantro get meals off to a good start, along with, perhaps, a zinger of a "cadillac" margarita incorporating cointreau and grand marnier. For a summer lunch, the chorizo and corn chowder was excellent, and the fire-roasted chicken fajita salad assertive. So was the open-faced steak fajita sandwich, accompanied by spicy island fries. Our mouths were left tingling, even after sharing the margarita cheesecake for dessert.

The interesting menu covers all the usual bases and then some: scallops acapulco, spicy crab cakes with smoky chipotle cream sauce, cancun soft lobster tacos, lobster and brie chile rellenos, blue crab enchiladas, and roasted red chile pork over rice., All dishes are considered mild to mildly spicy, but can be made hotter and spicier on request. Ask for the red-hot firecracker salsa if you like really hot. The jalapeño corn fritters, the crab empanadas, and the smoked duck and jalapeño jack flautas are recommended starters. The kahlua mousse and chambord torte are refreshing endings.

Don and Tarijita Warner have themselves a winner of a place.

(207) 338-5775. Entrées, $8.95 to $13.95. Lunch daily, 11 to 3. Dinner to 9. Closed January and February.

Extravagant buffet is set out for lunch and brunch at Harraseeket Inn.

Dining and Lodging

Harraseeket Inn, 162 Main St., Freeport 04032.

In Freeport, where the supply of rooms can hardly keep up with the onslaught of shoppers, sisters Nancy Gray and Jody Dyer of Connecticut's Inn at Mystic got their foot in the door in 1984 with an elegant, five-room B&B in an 1850 Greek Revival farmhouse. A few years and many millions of dollars later, a handsome, three-story white building connecting smaller existing structures houses a fine 85-seat restaurant, a large and informal tavern and 84 posh guest rooms and suites. Nine townhouse units of two and three bedrooms each were added in 1999 for longer-term stays.

Standard rooms contain two double beds or one queensize with blue and white fabric half-canopies, a single wing chair, and baskets of Lord & Mayfair amenities on the pedestal sinks in the bathrooms. Our large third-floor room offered a kingsize bed with a partial-canopy headboard and botanical prints, a sofa and wing chair beneath a paladin window, a working fireplace, a wet bar and a small refrigerator, TV hidden in an armoire, and an enormous bath with a jacuzzi. Turndown service produced chocolates at night.

The newest wing holds 30 more rooms, a mix of luxury units with fireplaces and jacuzzis and others with two double beds for traveling families. All told, the inn offers 41 accommodations with whirlpool tubs, 23 of those with fireplaces.

Also in the new wing are a function facility accommodating up to 400, a 45-foot-long indoor lap pool in a garden solarium and a relocated tavern, enlarged to handle increased numbers of casual diners who had been turned away in the old quarters. You'd never guess this was the site of the original B&B a few years earlier.

Fine artworks, fresh flowers and many of Nancy Gray's personal antiques are evident throughout. Afternoon tea with quite a spread of pastries and sandwiches is served in a large and sumptuous drawing room notable for mahogany paneling.

The relocated Broad Arrow Tavern now fronting on Main Street is a beauty in hunter green, with seating for 100 – nearly triple the size of the basement original – plus a pleasant outdoor patio that draws in the passersby. The tavern is outfitted with old snowshoes, paddles, fly rods and a moosehead. "It's my life in review," says Nancy, recalling her upbringing in a Maine sporting camp. The extensive tavern menu features hot-rock cooking, as well as grills from a wood-fired oven and grill in an open kitchen.

The stylish Maine Dining Room, divided into three sections, is pretty as a picture. Substantial black windsor chairs and a few banquettes flank tables set formally with white linens, heavy silver, silver service plates and pink stemware.

From a custom-designed, state-of-the-art kitchen, executive chef Chris Moran oversees some highly rated new American and updated continental fare. The stress is on products from area farmers and growers, all of whom are nicely credited on a page at the back of the menu. Main courses range from free-range chicken stuffed with mushrooms and spinach to three "tableside classics" for two – Maine lobster and shellfish, rack of lamb and châteaubriand. Recent choices included pan-seared halibut with littleneck clams in pesto broth, pan-seared salmon with cucumber broth and shiitake couscous, and grilled duck breast with blackberry barbecue sauce and foie gras. Interesting accompaniments support the main events: among them, gingered baby vegetables, cornmeal chive cake, stewed mustard greens, red onion confit and yellow pepper risotto.

Lobster turns up in such starters as sherried lobster stew, lobster risotto and lobster bruschetta. Other possibilities are swiss chard ravioli, beef carpaccio and caesar salad prepared tableside for two or more. Finish with a flourish: rum-flamed Jamaican bananas, chocolate overdose flamed with grand marnier, a choice of crêpes, the evening's soufflé or one of the exotic homemade ice creams and sorbets. The wine list has been honored by Wine Spectator.

A full breakfast buffet, from fresh fruit and biscuits to scrambled eggs and french toast, is included for overnight guests. The buffet lunch at $10.95 is exceeded in bounty only by the Sunday brunch ($15.95, with music by a classical guitarist).

(207) 865-9377 or (800) 342-6423. Fax (207) 865-1684. Eighty-two rooms and two suites with private baths. Mid-May-October: doubles, $165 to $245; suites, $265. Rest of year: doubles, $100 to $230; suites, $235 to $250.

Entrées, $19 to $30. Lunch, daily 11:30 to 2:30. Dinner, 6 to 9 or 9:30. Tavern, daily from 11:30.

The Squire Tarbox Inn, Route 144, Westport Island (Box 1181, Wiscasset 04878).

Here is a wonderful anomaly: a "sensitive" yet thrivingly successful inn and restaurant of the old school, but with an appealing twist. It's the real Maine – the way inns used to be, before they decided to offer cable TV/VCRs and two-person jacuzzis and dining rooms full of nouvelle conceits.

Owners Karen and Bill Mitman are part of a vanishing breed. Like others, they tired of urban corporate life and acquired a 1763 farmhouse-turned-inn on twelve acres on remote Westport Island, eight miles and light years distant from the mainstream of coastal Route 1. "We added baths and goats and cheese," recalled Bill, who had been marketing director for Boston's Copley Plaza Hotel.

Originally novices in country living, they have raised it to an art form.

Bill and Karen Mitman tend nubian goats on grounds of The Squire Tarbox Inn.

The attractive beige farmhouse with green trim occupies twelve acres sloping to a cove. The "squire's" main house retains its original floors, beams, moldings and fireplaces, as well as four spacious bedrooms upstairs and down. The dining room and three common parlors open to the rear in a carriage barn that connects to the stables, which have been converted into seven more rustic bedrooms. The goats that are the heart of the operation are stabled in a nearby hay barn. Their bounty is pasteurized and fermented in two small, sparkling white cheese-making rooms in the basement beneath the kitchen.

Guest accommodations in the main house are Colonial in style, with hooked rugs, quilts on the walls, unpretentious objects picked up at yard sales over the years and not a TV, telephone or jacuzzi in sight. A couple do have kingsize beds. The side stables contain seven more rooms with queensize (save for one double) beds, all odd shapes and full of beams. "Some guests prefer these as more in keeping with the old farmhouse style," says Bill. "The main house is more like what they have at home."

Common spaces abound. First comes a parlor notable for its cookie jar and old music box amid comfy farmhouse furnishings. There's what Bill calls the world's smallest bar, fully stocked and with a small but select wine list. A buffet breakfast is put out in the squire's breakfast room, an adjunct to the beamed and paneled dining room. Beyond is a large screened and canopied deck, overlooking grounds abloom with wildflowers and birds pecking at feeders. (A path leads to the cove where guests enjoy a rowboat and a screened shed.) Occupying prime space in the soaring carriage barn is the "adult playroom," where jigsaw puzzles, board games and a player piano beckon.

Dinner is the epitome of the Squire experience. Overnight guests and knowing diners from afar gather in the parlor at 6 for a cocktail hour starring some of the three house-made goat cheeses: the pungent, creamy, spreadable Farmstead chèvre flecked with garlic and chives or jalapeño peppers; the aged, waxed hard cheese

Caerphilly for slicing, and the aged Crottin, eaten plain or rolled in cracked sweet tellicherry pepper. Squire Tarbox makes cheese twice a week and produces 1,500 pounds a year. It sells most to guests – in a package with a trademark goat bell – and to nearby restaurateur Michael Gagne, who considers it world-class.

Tables in the 26-seat dining room are set simply with pink tablecloths, wild-flowers and a card denoting the four-course meal to come. Soothing live harp music accompanies what Karen calls "healthful, good-quality country food." The first course is generally a chèvre strudel incorporating asparagus and smoked ham. Next comes a changing salad, perhaps marinated tomato with basil and feta or caesar with the Squire's own dressing, and the inn's signature warm buns, made sweeter and softer with whey. There is usually a choice of main course – at our spring visit, crab lasagna with goat cheese and beef tenderloin with raisin-basil butter, teamed with snow peas, harvard beets and wild rice. Dessert was the specialty sin pie with chocolate sauce. Others might be chocolate brownie torte with goat cheese or a velvety chèvre pound cake with blueberry sauce. "We try not to over-cheese them," Bill says of his guests, "but that's part of what they come here for."

As the meal winds down, guests are invited to adjourn to the hay barn to watch as Karen, the chief goat honcho, milks her six nubian goats at 9. The after-dinner finale is country theater at its best.

There's a repeat performance the next morning. It follows a buffet breakfast of assorted fruit, hot cereal or cold granola with goat's milk, a selection of five breads and a panoply of quiche, pancakes and bacon. The spread "grows every year," says Bill, as the Mitmans share a serene, pastoral, adult-oriented farm experience with like-minded guests. Or, as the latter-day marketer in Bill calls it, "a restful journey into simplicity."

(207) 882-7693. Fax (207) 882-7107. Eleven rooms with private baths. MAP, doubles, $174 to $241, mid-July through October, $152 to $214, early May through mid-July. B&B, doubles, $90 to $179. Closed November to Mother's Day.
Prix-fixe, $34. Dinner nightly except Tuesday at 7.

Lawnmeer Inn and Restaurant, Route 27, Box 505, West Boothbay Harbor 04575.

Virtually every table has a water view in the long, pine-paneled dining room of this Southport Island restaurant. Redone in burgundy and white with green napkins that match the carpet, it's dramatic by day and romantic by candlelight at night.

Chef Bill Edgerton supplements the regular menu with a page of daily specials – things like garlicky linguini tossed with smoked salmon and peas alfredo as an appetizer and a trio of fish (swordfish with pesto, tuna with soy and garlic, and sole with crabmeat and tomato) as an entrée, both of which proved exceptional. When one of us chose the fish trio over the lobster Johnny Walker but wanted to sample the sauce, the chef obliged with a taste on the side.

We also can vouch for the shrimp in parchment with julienned vegetables, new potatoes and crisp yellow squash and zucchini, and the poached salmon with dill-hollandaise sauce. Other main dishes could be Maine lobster risotto, herb-crusted filet mignon with green peppercorn butter and grilled london broil of venison with oyster mushrooms and bordelaise sauce.

Vermont maple crème brûlée, blueberry bread pudding with crème anglaise, grand marnier mousse and key lime pie are among the delightful desserts.

Owners Lee and Jim Metzger have renovated thirteen inn rooms and suites, all with private baths and TV. Twenty more modern rooms, some with king beds or queen four-posters, are in two motel buildings on either side of the inn. There's a charming cottage for two with a queen poster bed and a sun deck at the water's edge. Lee, who is constantly upgrading, has recovered the beds in the motel buildings in lovely fabrics. She did the stunning, free-flowing stenciling that graces many of the rooms and bathrooms as well as the diverse wreaths in each room. Breakfast is extra, but the roast-beef hash topped with two poached eggs and the tomato and herb omelet with whole-wheat toast are worth the tab.

(207) 633-2544 or (800) 633-7645. www.lawnmeerinn.com. Thirty-two rooms and suites with private baths. EP: Doubles, $90 to $145 in summer and weekends in fall; $68 to $130 in spring and midweek in fall. Open mid-May to mid-October.

Entrées, $15.95 to $22.95. Dinner nightly, 6 to 9, mid-June to Labor Day (Thursday-Sunday until mid-June; Tuesday-Sunday after Labor Day). Sunday brunch, 8 to 11.

The Newcastle Inn, River Road, Newcastle 04553.

Rebecca and Howard Levitan arrived from Boston in 1995 to maintain this inn's dining tradition of fine dining. They have enhanced some of the accommodations, common areas and grounds at the fifteen-room inn and restaurant beside the Damariscotta River as well.

The Levitans opened the rear dining room onto a deck overlooking the broad lawns and lupine gardens sloping toward river's edge. Breakfast and cocktails may be served out here. They installed a small pub area with bright red walls and green chair rail off the rear parlor, redid the front living room with a more traditional look and hung a picture of lupines ("our logo") over the sofa, and outfitted a cheery side sun porch with wicker furniture and a wood stove.

More improvements were made to the guest lodgings upstairs and in the Carriage House. Two small rear bedrooms with a bath in between became the inn's premier accommodation. It has a kingsize bed, corner fireplace, sitting area and a jacuzzi for two. A room in which we once stayed became a second suite with sitting area, fireplace and jacuzzi. A fireplace, king bed and double jacuzzi were added to a third room and more changes were in the works. "We have lots of ideas," Rebecca advised. All rooms in the Federal-style Colonial house and annex have private baths and are furnished with a mix of antiques and New England crafts. Canopy beds, hand stenciling, floral wallpapers and wreaths on the doors are among their attributes.

The newest room, called the Cottage, is across from the Carriage House. It's a split-level space with a sitting room with TV on one level and a queen sleigh bed and bath above. Rebecca decorated it like a Maine cottage with Waverly fabrics.

The inn's talented chef is Terry Foster, who trained at the Culinary Institute of America. He moved here in 1999 for year-round stability after nine summers of cooking at the Pilgrim's Inn in Deer Isle.

Dinner seatings are staggered throughout the evening in two country-charming dining rooms. Candlelit tables are covered with quilt-look squares over white cloths. Complimentary hors d'oeuvres are offered at 5:30 in the full-service pub.

Available to the public as well as house guests, the meal is prix-fixe for four courses. One summer menu started with a choice of shrimp and tomato bisque or sautéed Maine crab cake with rémoulade sauce and arugula. A mesclun salad accented with snow peas and pinenuts and dressed with a citrus-basil vinaigrette came next. Main courses were pan-seared haddock fillet with a lime-caper vinaigrette, mixed grill of Gulf shrimp and pheasant breast with cherry peach glaze, and loin of lamb with a rosemary-dijon crust and wild mushroom burgundy sauce. Desserts are a high point: a choice of frozen raspberry soufflé with raspberry coulis, lemon tart with blueberries or baked alaska with crème anglaise. Overnight guests enjoy a full breakfast of juice, fruit, pastry and a hot entrée. The last might be eggs benedict, cheese and vegetable strata or an acclaimed Santa Fe french toast made with crushed corn flakes. The fruit course becomes extra hearty in winter: perhaps hot baked bananas (like bananas foster), poached pear or apple-cranberry crisp.

The Newcastle Inn is a stylish but relaxed place where guests like to read and contemplate the river from hammocks or Adirondack chairs on the lawn, watch the many birds in the feeder off the deck and enjoy the gardens that change with the seasons. The Levitans were adding more gardens and beautifying the adjacent property that had been a town fire pond.

(207) 563-5685 or (800) 832-8669. Fax (207) 563-6877. www.newcastleinn.com.
Twelve rooms and three suites with private baths. Doubles, $110 to $210, June-October;
$90 to $175, November-May.

Prix-fixe, $39.50. Dinner by reservation, Tuesday-Sunday 6 to 7:30; Thursday-Sunday
in winter.

The Belmont, 6 Belmont Ave., Camden 04843.

An 1886 Victorian house on a residential side street, Camden's oldest inn has been charmingly restored into a small and intimate, year-round village inn with six guest rooms and a distinguished dining room. It took on new life and a new look in late 1999 under owners Dan and Liz White from Florida in partnership with innkeepers Joshua and Ruth Perry from Camden. Their predecessors had tired of the pace and closed the dining room unexpectedly in the summer of 1999, just after having earned a coveted four-diamond AAA rating for the restaurant. They had a ten-year run as the Belmont following in the footsteps of David Grant, who gave it earlier fame as Aubergine, Maine's first new American restaurant.

The new partners were redecorating and refurnishing both common areas and guest rooms. Three bedrooms gained gas fireplaces, and all have new TVs and CD players. Two suites offer separate sitting rooms. The two third-floor rooms we once occupied with our sons have been converted into one extra-large deluxe room called the Hideway, with a queen bed, gas stove, window seat and a clawfoot tub/shower.

Wicker rockers on the side porch invite dalliance with a cocktail from the small bar off the comfortable parlor. With a nifty window seat and small built-in benches beside the fireplace, it leads into the main dining room, now known as **Marquis at The Belmont** and leased to chef-caterer Scott Marquis, whose previous restaurants were in Bangor and Brunswick. It's serene and lovely with well-spaced tables dressed in white linens and floral china. The adjacent sun porch that we like best contains a handful of pristine white tables and chairs.

Scott, who smokes his own seafood and game, executes a changing menu of innovative American cuisine. His opening repertoire tempted with such entrées as haddock in phyllo with watercress, roasted peppers and passion-fruit cream, and roast rack of lamb with berry and thyme vinaigrette. His chicken breast took the form of a roulade with apricot-pecan-caramelized onion stuffing and sage beurre blanc. He gave an Asian twist to his mixed seafood grill: sesame-crusted yellowfin tuna with wasabi aioli, diver scallops with orange-cashew pesto, and jumbo shrimp with tomato-soy relish and lemongrass.

Early starters included Maine crab cakes encrusted with peccorino-romano and sauced with mango coulis and chipotle-scallion mayonnaise, baked brie with figs in puff pastry, and local quail with French & Brawn homemade sausage, onion jam and roasted pumpkin coulis.

Scott's fiancée, Rebecca Brown, manages the dining room and makes the breads and desserts. Among her offerings were white chocolate bread pudding with peaches, mascarpone mousse with puff pastry stars and strawberry-kiwi coulis, and a trio of raspberry, passion-fruit and key lime sorbets.

The opening wine list was exceptionally priced, mainly in the teens and twenties.

The Perrys offer a full country breakfast in the dining room or sun porch. The day's entrée might be potato quiche rancheros or peaches and cream french toast.

(207) 236-8053 or (800) 238-8053. Four rooms and two suites with private baths. Doubles, $115 to $175; suites, $155 to $175. Off-season: doubles $95 to $115, suites $110 to $125.

Restaurant: (207) 230-1226. Entrées, $15.50 to $23. Dinner nightly except Sunday, 5:30 to 9; fewer days in off-season, Thursday-Saturday in winter.

The Youngtown Inn & Restaurant, Route 52 and Youngtown Road, Lincolnville 04849.

The restaurant in this restored 1810 Federal-style farmhouse, which we enjoyed so much when it opened in the mid-1980s, reopened after being abandoned for five years. The dining rooms are exceptionally pretty, the setting is rural and the food is French-inspired and getting better all the time, according to local consensus. It's run by Manuel Mercier, a chef who trained in Cannes, and his wife Mary Ann, a former Wall Street bond trader whom he met on a cruise ship. They live on the premises in the French style with their young family.

The two pristine dining rooms and a sun porch seat 60 at well-spaced tables covered with white linens, oil lamps and fresh flowers. Floral stenciling and oriental rugs add color.

Manuel describes his cooking as "strictly traditional French, using American products." The short menu lists perhaps nine entrées, of which the baked grouper provençal, the grilled duck with red currants and port, and the rack of lamb with thyme are house favorites. The diver scallops might be grilled with a tomato-basil sauce and the filet mignon served with foie gras pâté and cabernet sauce. Starters include a stellar lobster ravioli with saffron sauce, provençal fish soup, and pork and duck foie gras mousse. Dessert brings a crème brûlée that one reviewer said was the best he ever tasted, classic soufflés, cappuccino mousse cake and homemade sorbets in a meringue shell.

Upstairs are six guest rooms, four with access to balconies. Two on the second floor offer gas fireplaces. Among them are a family suite with a queensize iron bed in the bedroom and a sitting room with a sofabed and TV/VCR. Newer are two rooms nestled under the eaves with beamed cathedral ceilings on the third floor. One has a painted sleigh bed and a sitting area with a sofabed, the other a wicker iron bed and a twin bed. Both have TV/VCRs. Each room is decorated simply but attractively in country French style with colorful comforters and hand stenciling. A small second-floor common room with TV opens onto a deck with four umbrella-covered tables above the front porte cochere.

A full breakfast, from homemade croissants to omelets or french toast stuffed with apples and walnuts, is served to overnight guests.

(207) 763-4290 or (800) 291-8438. Five rooms and one suite with private baths. Doubles, $99 to $140, Memorial Day to Columbus Day; $89 to $120, rest of year. Entrées, $18 to $25. Dinner nightly, 5:30 to 9; closed Monday in off-season.

A Regal Experience

Norumbega, 61 High St., Camden 04843.

Ensconced in one of the finest "castles" along the Maine coast is this elegant B&B with great style and a combination lock on the front door to deter curious passersby.

The cobblestone and slate-roofed mansion, built in 1886 for the inventor of the duplex system of telegraphy, was for a few years the summer home of journalist Hodding Carter. The hillside property was acquired in 1987 by the Keatinge family, Californians who summered in Camden. Longtime innkeeper Murray Keatinge "retired" lately and son Kent of Boston assumed control. News accounts of family litigation seemed at our 1999 visit to have had little effect on the guest experience as directed by general manager JoAnne Reuillard. Indeed, Norumbega had just become a full-service inn, offering dinner to house guests in a salon-style setting and fulfilling a longtime Keatinge goal.

The exterior is said to be Maine's most photographed piece of real estate. Inside are endlessly fascinating public rooms (the woodwork alone is priceless), eleven bedrooms and two suites, all with private baths, sitting areas and telephones and some with TVs. The ones in back have breathtaking views of Penobscot Bay. Most have fireplaces and canopy beds, all kingsize except for a queen in the smallest garden-level room. The ultimate is the penthouse suite, a bit of a climb up a spiral staircase from the third floor. It offers a kingsize bed, a regal bath with pillows around a circular ebony tub big enough for two, a wet bar, a sitting room in pink and green, and a see-through, three-sided fireplace, plus a little porch with two deck chairs and a fabulous water view.

Guests have the run of the common areas and a small library, an intimate retreat for two beside a fireplace on the landing of the ornate staircase, as well as flower-laden rear porches and balconies on all three floors overlooking expansive lawns and the bay.

Until dinner service started, breakfast was the day's highlight. Served at a long table in the formal dining room or at a round glass table beside the telescope in the conservatory, it is a feast of juices and fruits, all kinds of breads and muffins, and, when we stayed, the best french toast ever, topped with a dollop of sherbet and sliced oranges. Eggs florentine or benedict, vegetable omelets, crêpes with an almond filling and peach topping, and ginger-apple pancakes are other favorites.

At night, the front parlor and deck become dining areas. Following a cocktail hour with complimentary hors d'oeuvres, guests have the option of dining regally from a small menu offering four or five choices per course. Young chef Wayne Cousins from Belfast comes from a family of chefs. His initial menu listed, for starters, a soup du jour, a "signature" salad dressed with blueberry-balsamic vinaigrette, a marinated shrimp sampler and artichoke hearts stuffed with crabmeat and caviar. Main courses included seafood pasta, free-range chicken in a red currant sauce with golden raisins, and hazelnut-glazed sirloin. Desserts were a cold rhubarb

Breakfast is served in formal dining room at Norumbega.

soufflé, frozen raspberry meringue in a lace cookie cup and rum-soaked chocolate cake. There's a full-service bar and a short but select wine list.

(207) 236-4646. Fax (207) 236-0824. Entrées, $19 to $26. Optional dinner for house guests, nightly 6:30 to 10.

Eleven rooms and two suites with private baths. Doubles, $160 to $340; suites, $365 to $475. Off-season, doubles $95 to $225; suites, $250 to $295. Children over 7.

Lodging

181 Main Street Bed & Breakfast, 181 Main St., Freeport 04032.

One of the more engaging and enduring B&Bs popping up around busy Freeport is this 1840 Greek Revival cape, run with TLC since 1986 by Ed Hasset and David Cates in a residential area of substantial homes, many of which are being converted to guest houses. They offer seven upstairs guest rooms with private baths and queensize beds, nicely furnished but rather small, as rooms in some historic homes are apt to be. They compensate with extra common space – twin front parlors, one like a library with TV and the other containing quite a collection of ceramic animals in a sideboard and a long coffee table made of glass atop an old ship's rope bed.

Two dining rooms dressed with calico tablecloths and Hitchcock chairs are the settings for breakfasts to remember. When we were there, the feast began with a choice of juices and zucchini muffins. A fruit platter bearing slices of three kinds of melon, kiwi, pineapple, strawberries and cherries followed the main dish, cheese strata with English muffins and bacon. The day before produced apple-walnut coffeecake and belgian waffles with baked apple and sausage.

A bonus here is a secluded rear swimming pool, surrounded by flowers, blessedly removed from the hubbub of the Freeport shops a couple of blocks away.

(207) 865-1226 or (800) 235-9750. Seven rooms with private baths. Doubles, $110, June-October; $95, rest of year.

Log Cabin, Box 41, Bailey Island 04003.
This started as a restaurant in a log cabin, but you'd never know it following its 1996 upgrade. Downsizing and ultimately closing (to the public) their popular restaurant to add lodging, Sue and Neal Favreau offer eight comfortable accommodations, each with its own deck upon which to savor the water views.
We liked the looks of the bright and airy second-floor York Room with queen bed, TV and telephone, kitchenette, jacuzzi tub and separate shower. The Mount Washington suite atop a former garage comes with a full kitchen, separate kingsize bedroom, two TVs, stereo and a deck with a private hot tub, from which you can see New England's tallest peak 90 miles away on a clear day. Along with the TV/VCR standard in all rooms, the new Sunset and Westview rooms offer gas fireplaces as well as jacuzzi tubs and queensize beds. All the summery lounge chairs on the decks and in the rooms are display models for the line Sue carries in her gift shop.
In preparation for closing the restaurant to the public in 2000 and concentrating on lodging and meals for house guests, the Log Cabin added a great swimming pool.
Dinner is available for inn guests in a cozy, lodge-like room with a moosehead above the fireplace, in an intimate front bar and on enclosed porches with water views. Sue, who has been in the restaurant business since she was 13 and originally ran the late Rock Ovens nearby, oversees the kitchen. A typical menu includes lobster, filet mignon, a chicken dish and two or three special appetizers, entrées and desserts.
Guests enjoy a complimentary breakfast of eggs or french toast with meats and home fries.
(207) 833-5546. Fax (207) 833-7858. www.logcabin-maine.com. Seven rooms and one suite with private baths. Summer: Doubles, $109 to $165, suite $199. Off-season: doubles, $98 to $148; suite, $169. Closed mid-October to April.

Five Gables Inn, Murray Hill Road, Box 335, East Boothbay 04544.
Perched on a hillside overlooking Linekin Bay, this five-gabled establishment dates back more than 110 years and was the last remaining summer hotel in the area. It was love at first sight for Mike and De Kennedy, who had just concluded a "mid-life break" in which they crewed on a yacht in French Polynesia and backpacked for six months from Bali to Nepal.
Previous owners had renovated the old Forest House into their dream B&B by the water. The Kennedys had only to add their personal touches and experiences, which they have in abundance. Mike, a graduate of the Culinary Institute of America when it was in New Haven, has worked his way around much of the world. He and De moved to Maine from Atlanta, where he renovated old homes, performed in TV commercials and gave historic tours. De, an artist, comes from an old Southern family and prepped for innkeeping by organizing house parties at her family's ante-bellum retreat in the Georgia hills.
Here they entertain guests in sixteen rooms on three floors, all with a water view. All have modern baths and queensize beds (one kingsize), and five have working fireplaces. Lace curtains and quilts color-coordinated to De's artistic accents and the pictures on the walls enhance the decor, all of which is light, airy and new. De hand-crocheted the afghans that grace many of the rooms.
Mike puts his cooking background to the test at multi-course breakfasts, served in a spacious common room appointed with wing chairs and bouquets of fresh

Windward House is decked out in Christmas finery.

flowers. His repertoire lasts for two weeks, a daily procession of, say, zucchini-walnut pancakes, quiche lorraine, blueberry french toast or basil-tomato frittata. Potatoes anna, fried tomatoes, blueberry crisp and pear in puff pastry might accompany, along with fresh-ground Columbian coffee.

De offers afternoon tea in the English manner, served with chocolate-chip cookies and poppyseed or banana bread and taken in the airy living room or on the wraparound veranda, where a hammock and abundant sitting areas take in the view of the bay. Port, sherry and madeira are put out on the sideboard in the evening.

(207) 633-4551 or (800) 451-5048. Sixteen rooms with private baths. Doubles, $100 to $175. Open mid-May through October.

The Camden Windward House, 6 High St., Camden 04843.

Warm hospitality and bountiful breakfasts await guests at this cool blue 1854 Greek Revival, a stylish B&B being upgraded by new owners Charlotte and Del Lawrence. Longtime owners of the Nutmeg Inn in Wilmington, Vt., they sold it and retired to Florida, only to find they missed New England and innkeeping. An extensive search for a small B&B ended in Camden, where they'd never been, and this handsome property.

The Lawrences immediately set to work on improvements, based on what they had found inn guests wanted in Vermont. They installed air conditioning, feather beds, TVs and telephones in all eight guest quarters, and added extra insulation and new double windows around the front and side of the house to reduce road noise. They renovated the kitchen and altered the set breakfast format, offering a choice of items and of times at which to partake.

That breakfast remains a highlight. Served by candlelight at individual tables in the dining room, it might begin, as ours did, with a compote of roasted peaches and plums with vanilla yogurt or escalloped baked apples with mixed fruit. The day's main courses were blueberry pancakes, peaches and cream french toast and creamy egg casserole with white sauce and a baked tomato, offered with sausage or bacon and multi-grain toast.

The treats continue in the afternoon, when the Lawrences offer tea and cookies in the library, where they also added a guest refrigerator and wet bar. Decanters of sherry and port are here in the evening, and chocolates await at bedside.

The common rooms in this rambling structure also include a comfortable living room where the unusual soapstone fireplace seems to be ablaze morning and night and a smaller parlor stocked with puzzles and board games. The rear deck looks onto a long back yard, where the Lawrences were busy restoring the gardens.

Upstairs are five guest rooms, each with queensize bed and private bath, and a suite with sitting room and a clawfoot tub in the large bathroom. In the rear Garden Room, a favorite of honeymooners, light pours through a skylit cathedral ceiling to reveal walls papered in a Laura Ashley floral pattern, a treasured brass bed of roses, a Vermont Castings stove and a TV/VCR. We were happily ensconced in the new Carriage Room: an elegant, blue and white space in the front carriage section of a restored barn. A crocheted canopy bed, two wing chairs in front of the gas stove, a radio with compact disc player, a TV/VCR and a collection of blue jars were in the room. The oversize bathroom added a clawfoot soaking tub and a corner shower. Caring touches came in extras like a small sewing dish, a hair dryer and three-way reading lamps.

(207) 236-9656. Fax (207) 230-0433. www.windwardhouse.com. Doubles, $110 to $195, mid-May through December; $90 to $120, rest of year.

A Little Dream, 66 High St., Camden 04843.

Piles of thank-you notes on the table at the entry, books of love letters and poems, an abundance of lace and a welcoming lemonade, served in a tall glass with a sprig of mint plus blueberries and strawberries, signify that this charming place is special. It's a little dream for Joanne Fontana and her husband, Billy, a sculptor and handyman-remodeler. From the looks of all the dolls and teddybears, the Fontanas must have brought their entire inventory with them when they sold their toy stores in New York City and Boston. Joanne has decorated and accessorized their turreted Victorian house with great flair.

She pampers guests in a parlor furnished in wicker and chintz, an elaborate dining room beside a conservatory and a wraparound porch, the side portion of which has lately been enclosed in glass for year-round use. Three spacious bedrooms in the house are decorated to the hilt with Victorian clothing, lace, ribbons and at least eight pillows on each bed. All have private baths, as do three more in a rear carriage house with wet bars and small refrigerators. Always perfecting, the Fontanas transformed its middle floor into a huge room with kingsize iron canopy bed, a chintz sofa and wing chair, and a window seat looking onto a glorious private porch. The porch, furnished with wicker rockers and a hanging glider/swing, yields a great view of Penobscot Bay, Curtis Island and the lights of passing boats at night. The bath contains a double soaking tub and separate shower. There's also a hidden TV, its whereabouts a pleasant surprise – one of several "surprises" with which Joanne entices her guests.

Breakfasts, served on lace-clothed tables topped with floral mats and heavy silver in the dining room or on the side porch, are gala here. Guests choose from a fancy menu placed in their rooms the night before The choice might involve lemon-ricotta soufflé pancakes with fresh raspberry sauce, banana-pecan waffles with maple country sausage, or three kinds of omelets: smoked salmon, apple-cheddar and ham-swiss. The coffee is breakfast blend or chocolate-raspberry or hazelnut. Orange or cranberry juice, fresh fruit and muffin of the day come with.

(207) 236-8742. www.camdeninns.com. Six rooms with private baths. Doubles, $129 to $225, mid-May through October; $95 to $185, rest of year. Closed in March.

The Inn at Sunrise Point, Box 1344, Camden 04843.

This is the inn of former inn reviewer Jerry Levitin's dreams. The California travel writer, who took over Norman Simpson's *Country Inns & Back Roads* guidebooks and ruffled the feathers of a few longtime innkeepers along the way, opened his own secluded B&B in 1992 on four forested acres at the foot of a dirt road leading from Route 1 to Penobscot Bay in Lincolnville.

"I built what I'd like to stay at," says Jerry with characteristic candor. The result is mixed –contemporary and Californian in style, but small and pricey for some Yankee tastes. Jerry offers three rooms in the main house plus four cottages. The Winslow Homer Cottage that we occupied right beside the water featured a kingsize bed, a fireplace and an enormous bathroom with a jacuzzi for two and a separate shower. It was luxurious indeed, but there was nowhere to stash luggage other than in the bathroom, and the waterfront deck was so narrow as to be useless (the front porch of the main house compensated). Though small, the three upstairs rooms have fireplaces and music systems, queensize beds, swivel upholstered or wicker chairs in front of the window, built-in desks and armoires holding TVs and VCRs. The two newest cottages possess queensize beds and the other inn amenities, and one has a kitchenette. All have been upgraded with paintings, deck chairs and accessories to "make the rooms more warm and homey," in the words of a resident innkeeper.

Arriving guests are welcomed in the main inn with tea, coffee, wine and hot and cold appetizers, which are substantial enough that some forego dinner. The main floor offers a wonderful living/dining room that's mostly windows onto Penobscot Bay, an English hunting-style library with a fireplace and a small conservatory for tête-à-tête breakfasts. We feasted here on fruit, pecan coffeecake, a terrific frittata with basil, bay shrimp and jack cheese, potatoes dusted with cayenne, crisp bacon and hazelnut coffee.

Upon departure, we found a card under our windshield: "Our porter has cleaned your windscreen to allow you to get a clear picture of our Penobscot Bay."

(207) 236-7716 or (800) 435-6278. Fax (207) 236-0820. Three rooms and four cottages with private baths. Summer: doubles, $175 to $225; cottages, $275 to $350. Off-season: doubles, $150 to $190, cottages, $195 to $295. Closed November-April.

Gourmet Treats

The treats in this area begin at **Clayton's,** 106 Main St., Yarmouth, a must stop right off Route 1. Starting as a gourmet market affiliated with Treats in Wiscasset (see below), Martha and David Clayton made good use of their space in the old Masonic Hall, adding a coffee bar in the center and a cafe for lunch on the stage. The latter serves good sandwiches, salads and vegetarian items in the $5 range. We also like Clayton's for all its copper pots, cheeses, specialty foods, baked goods and even a canoe stocked with bargain wines.

In Freeport, home of outlets to serve almost every interest, a large **Ben & Jerry's Ice Cream** stand is set up right beside L.L. Bean. All the flavors of one of Vermont's best-known exporters are available, but not exactly at outlet prices. And you thought **L.L. Bean Co.** was just for great sportswear and equipment. This ever-changing and expanding emporium has a gourmet food shop with Maine-made and New England mail-order products, including its own line of raspberry jams, bittersweet fudge sauce, maple syrup and the like. From saltwater taffy and dandelion greens to Bean's-blend coffee beans, this place has it – or will soon.

If you tire of the Freeport outlet scene, head for South Freeport Harbor wharf and the **Harraseeket Lunch & Lobster Co.** This is what coastal Maine is supposed to look like, a lobster pound by a working dock. While it used to be little known, at recent visits there was no place to park and the lineup stretched a long way from the outside service window, where we like to pick up our food and then eat at a picnic table on the dock (there's a small dining room as well). The owners are noted for their basket dinners, varying from clam cakes to scallops to shrimp to "just fish," and combinations thereof. Other favorites are a fishwich, clamburger royale and lobster roll. Lobsters can be packed for travel.

Gourmet-oriented places seem to come and go in Brunswick. Lately, the action has been at **The Humble Gourmet,** 100 Pleasant St. Talented chef Chris Toole left the Harraseeket Inn to open this bakery and gourmet takeout place in a strip plaza along Route 1. Although the stress is on catering, Chris and partner Sandra Holland offer lunchtime sandwiches and wraps, prepared foods (from pork tenderloin to shepherd's pie) and great baked goods. The intense lemon bars are to die for. In downtown Brunswick, **Scarlet Begonias** at 212B Maine St. draws locals and students from nearby Bowdoin College to a plant-filled haunt for interesting sandwiches, pastas and pizzas, worthy of either lunch or dinner. **Provisions** at 148 Maine St. is best-known for its wines and cheeses, but also offers specialty foods, breads and a cafe dispensing blackboard specials like Mediterranean fish stew and roasted vegetable lasagna.

In Wiscasset, English cheeses from a Covent Garden firm are one of the strengths of **Treats,** a special store on a prime corner of Main Street. Owner Paul Mrozinski offered a taste of cashel blue and we had to buy some, it was so buttery and delicious. We also had to buy one of the great breads from area bakeries, a crusty olive loaf (one of the others was rosemary and hazelnut). Paul describes the flavors of his farm cheeses much the way he distinguishes among his fine wines. Lately he has expanded his selection of fine New England cheeses. He also offers muffins and scones, sandwiches and salads for picnics, and dinner entrées to go. Across the street at the **Marston House,** Paul and his wife Sharon rent two B&B rooms with private baths in the carriage house behind their home, which is also an antiques shop. The $90 tab gets you a queensize bed, fireplace, private entrance and a hearty breakfast.

Native produce, specialty foods, wine, candies, pâtés, smoked salmon and croissants abound at **Weatherbird,** a gourmet food store and gift shop in a sprawl of a building called Northey Square off Main Street in downtown Damariscotta. There are a few tables out front upon which to partake.

You'll find at least 42 flavors at **Round Top Ice Cream,** Business Route 1, Damariscotta. This is the original home of the ice cream favored by restaurants throughout the region, an unpretentious little spot on the farm where it began in 1924. The choices range from cappuccino to watermelon, from ginger to raspberry. Cones come in three sizes, and you also can get a banana split.

Specialty foods, cookware, kitchen gadgets and fine pottery are among the wares at the rambling **Village Store,** part of the suave House of Logan enterprise in Boothbay Harbor.

Heading toward Rockland along Route 1, look for **The Well Tempered Kitchen,** in the stable of a 19th-century farm at 122 Atlantic Highway, Waldoboro. It holds quite an array of cookware, linens, Maine foods and more of interest to those "who love the process of cooking." The **School House Farm** produce stand, a few miles west of Thomaston on Route 1, displays baskets of fresh vegetables, local cheeses and eggs, jams and jellies, homemade breads, muffins and blueberry pies, as well as the lovely watercolors of flowers and local landscapes by owner Debbie Beckwith, whose gallery may be visited next door.

One of the all-time great places to eat lobster has to be the secluded **Waterman's Beach Lobster,** Waterman's Beach Road, off Route 73 near Spruce Head in South Thomaston. Order a lobster roll, lobster stew or a one-pound lobster dinner (all $7.95, last we knew), or splurge on the lobster-clam combo with sides of coleslaw and corn ($13.95). Take it to one of the picnic tables on an open deck right beside the water and enjoy. No buildings are in sight to mar the view. Owner Ann Cousens also bakes great blueberry, rhubarb and pecan pies. Open daily in summer, 11 to 7. BYOB.

In Rockland, Frances Holdgate and partners stock fine cheeses, house-made deli meats and specialty foods at the new **Market on Main,** 315 Main St. Locally made raviolis, sauces and dips are featured. "Hand-crafted comfort food" is offered for lunch, supper and Sunday brunch in a 40-seat deli/café restaurant, open daily from 9 to 7. The fare varies from haddock-sweet potato cakes and Indian-spiced veggie fritters with cool cucumber-yogurt dipping sauce to spinach-mushroom quiche with goat cheese, spit-roasted chicken and chicken pot pie. Desserts could be pear-cherry crumble and double chocolate baked pudding cake with whipped cream. Beverages from espresso to wine are available, and all is available to go.

The Brown Bag at 606 Main St., Rockland, is another casual spot for breakfast, lunch, supper or a snack. The owners, four sisters, started with a bakery and deli in the middle and expanded into a restaurant on one side and a gourmet food shop on the other. The extensive menu lists healthful selections at prices from yesteryear. Stop here for an oversize blueberry muffin, a lentilburger on a whole-wheat roll, a crab and cheddar melt, a loaf of basil bread or a slice of apple-raspberry pie.

A striking, plum-colored building with lavender trim houses **Miss Plum's Parlour** along Route 1 in Rockport. It's famous for ice creams and yogurts, served at a takeout window and available in changing flavors from red raspberry chip to toffee bar crunch. Sundaes, frappes, root-beer floats, lime rickeys, banana splits and more may be taken to lavender-colored picnic tables at the side. Owners Elaine and Bill Pellechia added a stylish little restaurant and a clever menu for inside dining. Open daily 7 a.m. to 10 p.m. in summer and fall.

In Camden, Maine beers and ales are the rage at **Sea Dog Brewing Co.,** which emerged no-expense-spared in 1993 in one of the former Knox Mill buildings at 43 Mechanic St. and since has expanded to Bangor and Falmouth Foreside. Tours of the downstairs brewery are given daily at 11 and 4 in summer and there's a brewtique for bar ware and apparel. Most visitors gravitate to the fancy tavern – a mix of booths, beams, oriental runners and stone walls that's too atmospheric for words. The splashy waterfall outside the soaring windows adds to the effect. The brewery's Penobscot Maine lager, Windjammer Maine ale and Owl's Head light are featured, along with a variety of snacks and sandwiches. More substantial fare is available at night.

Our favorite shop among many in Camden is **Lily, Lupine & Fern,** lately relocated to Main Street. Owners Gary and Bunni Anderson have augmented its traditional flowers with cheeses, gourmet foods and a selection of wines and microbrewery beers. Their daughter runs Cork, a wine bar and restaurant on Bayview Street.

Tea on the lawn, a Bar Harbor tradition, is served at the Jordan Pond House.

Down East Maine
Lobster, Plus

We know, we know.

You're going Down East on vacation and you can't wait to clamp your teeth around a shiny red lobster. In fact, you can hardly think of anything else. Oh, maybe some fried clams or a bucket of steamers, but lobster is what you're really after.

So you'll stand in line to get into some dive for the $8.95 lobster special. You'll suck out the feelers and wrestle with the claws of your one-and-one-quarter-pound (if you're lucky) crustacean. You'll end up with about three ounces of lobster meat, debris all over your clothes and hands that reek for two days.

And you'll probably gush, "That was the *best* lobster I've ever had!"

Well, friends, we're here to tell you that there is life after lobster in Maine. A lot of fine, creative cooking is going on in the Pine Tree State, and in the last two decades a number of excellent restaurants have emerged Down East along the coast, many of them with young and innovative chefs.

Also available are many suave inns and bed-and-breakfast establishments, which are giving visitors an alternative to the traditional cabins, campgrounds and motels that abound along the coast of Maine.

And, sign of the times, the coffee craze has come to Maine. On a recent trip we discovered the Coffee Express Drive-Thru at the Maine Coast Mall in Ellsworth.

In this final chapter, we meander our way along the coast, peninsulas and islands, hitting the high spots from East Penobscot Bay and Deer Isle to Bar Harbor, Acadia National Park and the Schoodic Peninsula – the epitome of Down East Maine.

Dining

Here, as elsewhere in Maine, restaurants and lodgings are detailed roughly geographically, from west to east.

Back by Popular Demand

Moveable Feasts, Main Street, Blue Hill.

The chef who spearheaded the changes in Down East dining tastes a generation ago is back for an encore.

John Hidake, who launched Blue Hill's acclaimed Fire Pond restaurant in 1977 and led it through its glory years, was converting a rambling old white Maine house on Tenney Hill into a fine-dining restaurant for opening by summer 2000. The house also is headquarters for his Moveable Feasts catering service and a deli/takeout retail business.

"We anticipate filling a few niches here," said John, who developed an avid following both at Fire Pond and subsequently as a caterer with his wife Beth.

The new restaurant seats about 50 in two small front dining rooms and a larger, L-shaped room that doubles as a reception area and bar. It conveys the ambiance of an early 1800s house and is furnished to the period. Each dining area has a fireplace, which permits a longer operating season than at Fire Pond.

The Hidakes sold Fire Pond in 1987 because "we had achieved what we had set out to do" and he wanted to spend more time with his young family. "But I really missed the creativity of a restaurant kitchen, which you can't do in the catering business." He also missed his regular patrons, who had become close friends. His wide following missed him, too – in its earlier days, a trip to Maine without a dinner at Fire Pond was unthinkable. All these factors conspired to prompt his return.

"We'll restore some of our favorite dishes," he said, "but this won't be a repeat of Fire Pond. Chefs evolve with different experiences, and this will be more creative."

John hadn't yet named the restaurant –"we're still sheet-rocking the kitchen," he said at the turn of the millennium – or settled on the menu. "Nouvelle is no longer the way to go, so this will probably mix a lot of different kinds of food. Just say the goal is to provide very fine food at an affordable price."

(207) 374-2441. Dinner nightly in summer, 5 to 9 or 9:30. Fewer days in off-season. Closed six weeks in late winter.

The Best of the Best

Jonathan's, Main Street, Blue Hill.

Innovative regional cuisine, an award-winning wine list and then a cookbook. These are the hallmarks of Jonathan Chase, founder of this trend-setting restaurant now well into its second decade. The cookbook, *Saltwater Seasonings,* written in collaboration with his sister, Sarah Leah Chase, the Nantucket caterer and cookbook author, received accolades from Down East magazine as "quite possibly Maine's best regional cookbook in fifty years."

Although he sold the restaurant in 1998, Jonathan remained very much a presence. "I still do everything," he said, and few patrons were any the wiser. The sale produced an enlarged front dining room with a colorful and sophisticated Mediterranean look in yellow, red and white. The large rear dining room also was due for a facelift in 2000.

The sale also allowed Jonathan to refine his focus on what he calls "progressive Maine cooking, with a huge emphasis on local ingredients." He localized his traditional international reach, offering paella with native shellfish and local free-range chicken, peas and long-grain rice. He deleted the bourbon and Bass from his signature lamb shanks, now braised in Maine microbrew ale and maple barbecue sauce. The house-pickled Maine mussels are served with local sharp cheddar and homemade crackers. The grilled venison burger with smoked cheddar is served on a toasted homemade bulkie roll with rhubarb ketchup and old-fashioned slaw.

The menu has been recategorized under small, medium and large plates and, bucking a trend, the prices have been lowered. But Jonathan has not lost the flair that makes the restaurant a culinary star.

For starters, we've enjoyed his crostini with roasted elephant garlic and chèvre, served with ripe tomatoes, and a remarkable salad of smoked mussels with goat cheese and pinenuts. Also good are the soups, a choice of cold minted pea or hot cauliflower and blue cheese at one visit. Among entrées, the risotto "via veneto" combining shellfish with imported cheeses, and a pasta dish blending sautéed mahogany clams and hot Italian sausage with kale, tomatoes and onions, reflected the owner's tour of Tuscany. Now look for things like "Grange Supper," baked cattle beans with smokehouse ham and old-fashioned slaw, grilled Atlantic salmon with Nervous Nellie's hot pepper jelly glaze and dilled potato salad, and a lobster, peeky toe crab and sea scallop stew. Vvegetarian and vegan dishes also are featured.

Butterscotch pudding with shoofly cream, an old-fashioned oatmeal cookie ice cream sandwich and warm bread pudding with sundried cranberries and whipped cream are among the sweet endings. So are cantaloupe sorbet and a dynamite kahlua mocha mousse. Winner of the Wine Spectator Award of Excellence, the wine list is exceptional and pleasantly priced – when did you last enjoy a Firestone merlot for under $20?

(207) 374-5226. Entrées, $12 to $16. Dinner nightly, 5 to 9. Closed Monday in off-season and month of March.

The Burning Tree, Route 3, Otter Creek.

Tops on almost everyone's list of culinary havens on Mount Desert Island is this pure restaurant in a rural setting south of Bar Harbor. There are tables on the long front porch, one section of which is a waiting area. Beyond are two small dining rooms, cheerfully outfitted in pinks and blues, their linened tables topped with tall, blue-edged water glasses. Local art and colorful paintings adorn the walls.

Such is the summer-cottage setting for what chef-owners Allison Martin and Elmer Beal Jr. call "gourmet seafood" with a vegetarian sideline. The only other dishes are a couple of versions of chicken: roasted free-range breast or a pan roast with sausage, clams, fennel, potatoes and a tangy shellfish broth. But it's seafood that most customers are after – basic like oven-poached codfish in a seafood wine broth and lofty as in pan-seared yellowfin tuna over lemony blue-cheese croustades. Vegetarians relish such treats as a cashew, brown rice and gruyère terrine and pan-fried polenta with pigeon peas, hominy, ceci beans, sweet peppers and a tomato-ginger sauce.

"We're the only restaurant that buys right off the boat," advises Allison. "Elmer

Main dining room at Fiddlers' Green overlooks side deck and harbor.

knows three fishermen who supply him with gray sole, monkfish, flounder and cod." He gets his crabmeat from his cousin in Bass Harbor and his chicken from a farm on Deer Isle.

Our party was impressed with starters of mussels with mustard sauce, grilled scallops and an excellent vegetarian sushi. The cioppino was so highly rated that two of us ordered it. The others chose baked monkfish with clams and artichokes on saffron orzo and the cajun crab and lobster au gratin, a fixture on the menu. The garden out back provides vegetables and herbs, and the owners use organically grown produce whenever possible. Entrées come with fresh vegetables (carrots and snow peas, at our visit) and a choice of garlicky potatoes or three-grain rice salad in a lemon vinaigrette.

Desserts are to groan over: perhaps nectarine mousse cake, Ukranian poppyseed cake, or strawberry pie. A good wine list, chosen with as much care as the menu, is priced mostly in the teens.

(207) 288-9331. Entrées, $18 to $23. Dinner nightly except Tuesday, 5 to 10. Open mid-June to mid-October.

Fiddlers' Green, 411 Main St., Southwest Harbor.

Chef Derek Wilber, son of a local boat builder, and his fiancee Sarah O'Neil opened this stylish restaurant to rave reviews in 1999. They gutted the old Spinnakers family restaurant and created two simple but sophisticated dining areas. One, all in yellow, has windows onto the ocean and a side deck. The other is smaller with rag-rolled walls of burnt orange.

A statue of Neptune and a fountain is situated beside the hostess station, often staffed by Sarah, now Mrs. Wilber. A downstairs wine vault holds more than 160 labels, including rare vintages.

A short menu itemizes changing choices in the new regional idiom. Expect starters like crab cakes with a three-chile honey-mango sauce, mussels steamed

Tiny hanging lamps illuminate meals and artworks at Redfield's.

in Guinness with shallots, grilled venison sausage with an onion sauté, and house-smoked scallops and mussels with a baked brie and walnut pastry basket.

Main courses, served with a house salad, could be seared yellowfin tuna with a tamari-mirin sauce, grilled swordfish with a pineapple-ancho salsa, beef medallions with a brandied apricot demi-glace, and veal stuffed with crab and red pepper and topped with marsala wine.

Typical desserts are honey-mango crème brûlée, cream puffs and maple-nut tart.

(207) 244-9416. Entrées, $17.25 to $19.95. Dinner nightly except Wednesday, 5:30 to 10; Thursday-Saturday in off-season, 5:30 to 9. Closed January-April.

Redfield's, Main Street, Northeast Harbor.

The sign on the door is apt to say "Thank You – Full" at this, the hottest dining ticket on Mount Desert Island. Scott and Maureen Redfield's trendy restaurant, located next to family's Redfield Artisans showroom and beneath their personal quarters, would be quite at home on Nantucket, although the prices and lack of pretensions are refreshingly Down East.

Decor in two small dining rooms is simple yet sophisticated. Tiny lamps hanging from long cords over most tables illuminate some large, summery, impressionist-style paintings and make the rooms rather too bright for our tastes. But they do highlight the food, which is worth the spotlight. We staved off hunger with a basket of Maureen's fabulous focaccia topped with tomatoes and goat cheese, exquisite house salads and a shared appetizer of venison carpaccio as we nursed the house La Veille Ferme wine. Lemon sorbet in a lotus dish prepared the palate for the main dishes: sliced breast of duck with fresh chutney and marinated loin of lamb with goat cheese and black olives, both superb. Strawberry sorbet and a chocolate-almond mint tart ended a memorable meal.

Scott, who used to cook at Cranberry Lodge of Asticou, changes his menus frequently. He might offer an appetizer of grilled bluefin tuna and vegetable timbale with nori and wasabi vinaigrette or entrées of seared tofu with wilted ginger spinach and Chinese black bean glaze, and seared fillet of salmon with dill and lime hollandaise.

He also is his own man, a Renaissance man at that. In 1999, he took the summer off to join the maintenance crew at the Asticou Inn and was building a studio in which to work on his wood sculptures. So Redfield's was closed unexpectedly that summer for dinner, offering lunch instead, doing a land-office catering business and reopening for dinner in the off-season.

For lunch, Maureen and their sous chef offered a panoply of Redfield-style treats, from a blue cheese and garlic caesar salad laced with a choice of grilled beef tenderloin, tamari shrimp or grilled portobello mushrooms, to a "stacked liverwurst" with red onion and dijon on dark rye. Specials included a crab cake sandwich on grilled focaccia and salmon soufflé with crabmeat, roasted red peppers, horseradish and parmesan cheese. Several "small plates" were geared to the wine bar offerings.

(207) 276-5283. Entrées, $19 to $25. Lunch in summer ($ 4.95 to $9.95), Monday-Saturday 11:30 to 4. Dinner, fall through spring, Thursday-Sunday 6 to 9.

George's, 7 Stephens Lane, Bar Harbor.
This hard-to-find restaurant in a little Southern-style house behind the First National Bank has long offered some of the most creative food on Mount Desert Island. Run with a Greek accent by retired local high-school history teacher George Demas, it's a summery place, lately gone glamorous. George is still in the kitchen, never taking a night off, we're told.

The table appointments were stylish and the track lights were draped with white cloths in the piano bar, to which we were assigned at our latest visit. The menu is unusual in that all appetizers are $8 or $12, and all entrées $25. You can graze or order a prix-fixe meal (appetizer, main course and dessert) for $34 to $37. The award-winning wine list is also unusual, in that entries are categorized under full-bodied, medium and light. Precious few are priced in the teens and low twenties.

Four cheese crisps were served as we sat down for our most recent dinner, and then we waited and waited – at least an hour and a half – until our entrées arrived. An appetizer of salmon quesadilla (great tastes, served on an unusual plate with a fish head and tail on either side) and a salad dressed with George's special vinaigrette and feta helped stave off starvation. The wait was worth it for a special of elk medallions; not so for a lamb dish that was overdone, or for a paltry medley of strawberry, pear and orange/passion-fruit sorbets. The waiter, slowed by a large private party in another room, even mixed up our wine order and charged us for an appetizer we never ordered. Ours must have been an off night, since the local consensus was that George's had never been better.

At an earlier dinner, hot crusty French bread and the best Greek salads ever preceded the entrées: distinctive smoked scallops on fettuccine and a special of shrimp on a fresh tomato sauce with feta cheese, rice pilaf and New Zealand spinach with orange juice and orange zest.

The appetizers remain assertive (perhaps kasseri cheese broiled with garlic, lamb and phyllo napoleon with tzatziki, seared tuna loin with pickled ginger and wasabi), and the entrées creative: lobster strudel with chanterelle ragoût, roasted lobster stuffed with spinach and artichoke bread pudding, and char-grilled lamb tenderloin with peach ketchup. Desserts are usually first-rate, from chilled champagne sabayon with figs to fresh peach crème brûlée and, one night, an irresistible blueberry and peach meringue.

(207) 288-4505. Entrées, $25. Dinner nightly, 5:30 to 11. Open mid-June through October.

The Porcupine Grill, 123 Cottage St., Bar Harbor.
Owner Tom Marinke's antiques business provided the furnishings and impetus for this trendy grill. It takes its name from the nearby Porcupine Islands and has given George's competition for top honors in town.

"Everything is real," says Tom, showing the assorted antique oak drop-leaf tables and Chippendale chairs, the rugs on the honey-colored wood floors, the Villeroy & Boch china, and different fresh flowers scattered about the dining areas on two floors. Also, "everything's homemade with Maine ingredients where possible."

Antique bulls-eye glass dividers and period sconces help create a cafe atmosphere in the main-floor bar area, where many like to sip champagne cocktails pairing French sparkling and Maine raspberry wines or Porcupine punch (rum and fruit juices) before snacking on steamed mussels with cilantro and smoked lemons, salmon cakes with minted cucumber vinaigrette and pickled ginger, or a terrine of shiitake mushrooms, crabmeat and cheese with a roasted tomato and sherry sauce, the mushrooms grown by Tom.

We prefer the quieter upstairs, where on a busy night we lucked into a private dining room for two. Our appetizers, smoked salmon and jonnycakes with caviar and sour cream and a signature caesar salad topped with fried shrimp, lived up to advance billing. Among entrées we were smitten with the grilled chicken with ginger-peach chutney and the sautéed shrimp and peas in a light garlic-cream sauce over fresh egg noodles. Other possibilities might be roasted salmon fillet with a wasabi glaze, pickled ginger and udon noodle salad, roasted pork loin with dijon sauce, and grilled New York strip steak with shiitake-red onion marmalade.

A McDowell fumé blanc accompanied our meal, chosen from a well-selected, rather expensive wine list augmented by reserve wines. Desserts included a wonderful pear and rhubarb crisp with homemade ice cream, cantaloupe sorbet, and white chocolate cheesecake with blueberry sauce.

(207) 288-3884. Entrées, $18 to $24. Dinner nightly from 6, June-October; off-season, Friday-Sunday, 6 to 9.

More Dining Choices

Seaweed Cafe, 146 Seawall Road, Manset.
"Natural seacoast cuisine" is the billing for this diminutive newcomer, tucked away in a small Cape Cod-style house in the Manset section of Southwest Harbor. Chef-owner Bill Morrison, whose fare we enjoyed at the nearby Lindenwood Inn before he launched his own venture, arrived on Mount Desert Island by way of restaurants in Aspen and Boston. Here he specializes in the fare of "Asian islands – Japan, Hawaii, Thailand" – as well as China. That gives assertive twists to New England seafood and reflects his personal inclination for organic and natural foods.

From his open kitchen on one side of the house comes a changing array of flavorful fare, served in a simple, low-lit dining room with seven tables and seats for twenty.

The appetizers are a vegetarian's dream: a salad of organic mesclun with Thai basil or miso tahini dressings, or a natural vegetable soup of organic beans, grains and vegetables seasoned with miso and sea salt.

His signature Japanese maki sushi rolls are a carryover from the Lindenwood, where one of us made a meal of his crab with cilantro and lobster with avocado mako sushi rolls as well as Thai mussels steamed in sake with basil, cilantro, ginger and hot pepper.

Here, the entrées might be tuna steak au poivre with wasabi béarnaise and mushrooms braised in lobster broth or tutu-man chicken, roasted with a Hawaiian teriyaki sauce infused with ginger and bourbon. Many make a meal of the dinner chowder or seafood stew – prepared, Bill says, with "whatever's from the ocean that day."

He and his waitress make the desserts, perhaps genoise, fruit tarts and chocolate truffle cake. We found his bourbon ice cream with chocolate biscotti and a strawberry tart with mascarpone to be refreshing counterpoints to such assertive dinner flavors.

More good tastes turn up at Sunday brunch. You might find organic crêpes with roasted five-spice chicken, vegetables and shiitake mushroom sauce; a lobster, avocado and goat cheese omelet; lobster maki-sushi with mango, or egg foo-yung with Maine shrimp or crab.

Bill's wife Mary and young daughter Gillian share hostess duties in this intimate, family-run establishment.

(207) 244-5072. Entrées, $8.50 to $20. Dinner, Wednesday-Sunday from 5:30. Sunday brunch, 10 to 2. BYOB. No credit cards.

Preble Grille, 14 Clark Point Road, Southwest Harbor.

"Regional cuisine/Mediterranean pizzazz" is the billing for Terry Preble's newest venture. Chef Terry, who had quite a following at his Fin Back restaurant in Bar Harbor, sold that to concentrate his efforts in Southwest Harbor – to good advantage, according to local consensus, which felt both venues had suffered by his spreading himself too thin.

The new establishment is considerably larger than his original, and the emphasis has changed from summery seafood to heartier grill fare with Tuscan accents. Pastas vary from sweet and hot Italian sausages with broccoli rabe to shrimp with artichoke hearts and feta cheese over farfelle. The manicotti bears the light Preble touch of old: filled with spinach, caramelized onions, sundried tomatoes, ricotta and asiago cheese and topped with a pink béchamel sauce. Main dishes, served with focaccia and green salad, could be cioppino, lobster sautéed in a Seal Cove chèvre and tarragon cream sauce with polenta, grilled pork chop with dried cherries, and grilled angus steak topped with gorgonzola cheese, roasted garlic and sundried tomato butter.

Starters include an acclaimed lobster ravioli, a grilled pizzette with pesto and shrimp, and Maine crab cakes with a sweet and sour lime sauce and a sour cream-citrus sauce. A dessert of frozen peanut butter mousse pound cake harkens back to the Fin Back days.

All this is served up in a colorful interior with a mix of booths and tables and accents of contemporary art.

(207) 244-3034. Entrées, $14.95 to $24.95. Dinner nightly, 5 to 9 or 10, weekends in spring and fall. Closed in winter.

Seven Tables, 16 Main St., Seal Harbor.

Yanni Antoniadis and his American wife Linda traveled frequently to his native Greece, where she learned Greek-style cooking from members of his extended family. "She'd been trying out the recipes on me for years," Yanni said, as they opened this Mediterranean bistro in 1999 in the space vacated by the late, great Bistro at Seal Harbor.

Yanni operated a small Italian restaurant in New Hampshire, where he did the cooking. Here his wife is the chef and he the genial host, overseeing a small service bar and a charming dining room pristine in white and mint green.

The space holds only seven tables, hence the name. And the kitchen with ten-burner stove is not much bigger than that in a studio apartment. But from that snug kitchen come authentic dishes designed to warm a Greek's heart. Start with the traditional dolmathes (stuffed grape leaves), the tzatziki (diced cucumbers in a smooth garlic-yogurt sauce) or taramasalata, smoked cod roe mousse served with pita bread.

Move on to such main courses as spanakopita, Aegean shrimp in a spicy tomato sauce with feta cheese, a classic moussaka or "frikasse," Yanni's favorite dish prepared by his mother for special occasions. A dill-scented stew, it combines lamb, artichoke hearts, greens and avgolemono.

Linda says she has "toned down the sugar" in dessert favorites like baklava, semolina custard pie and pistachio-apricot frozen yogurt. A handful of Greek wines were on order for the Mediterranean-based wine list.

(207) 276-3077. Entrées, $15 to $18. Dinner, Tuesday-Sunday 5 to 9, July-September; weekends in late June and early October.

Cafe This Way, 14½ Mount Desert St., Bar Harbor.

The food is first-rate and the interior somewhat theatrical at this pleasant cafe down a side street with a sign pointing the way. Chef Julie Harris and Julie Berberian, both from Bar Harbor's former Fin Back restaurant, and partner Susanne Hathaway turned the old Unusual Cabaret dinner theater space into a casual melange of tables and bookcases surrounding a circle of sofas in the center. But for the theater lights overhead, the dining area looks like a large living room.

The contemporary menu features seafood, as in entrées of bouillabaisse with gorgonzola ravioli, grilled tuna with sautéed apples and smoked shrimp, and crab cakes with tequila-lime sauce.. Shrimp and scallops are baked with artichoke hearts and sundried tomatoes and served over a bed of spinach and crabmeat.

Several main dishes also are available as appetizers on this mix-and-match menu. Otherwise the stars are homemade tuna sausage with wasabi and pickled ginger and two kinds of quesadilla, one with goat cheese and roasted red peppers and the other with smoked shrimp, mango and mozzarella.

Folks rave about the salads, perhaps watercress, caesar or baby spinach with grated asiago cheese and prosciutto, or warmed endive with grilled shrimp over greens with citrus vinaigrette.

Chocolate turns up in most of the desserts. Typical are chocolate-amaretto mousse, raspberry-chocolate truffle cake, and peanut butter and chocolate fudge cake.

Some of the best, most reasonable breakfasts in town are offered here year-round.

(207) 288-4483. Entrées, $12 to $19. Dinner nightly in summer, 6 to 9. Breakfast in summer, Monday-Saturday 7 to 11, Sunday 8 to 1. Breakfast and lunch in off-season, daily 7 to 2.

Mandarin red walls of stylish Havana dining room radiate a glow at night.

Havana, 318 Main St., Bar Harbor.

The name and the phone number (288-CUBA) hint that this newcomer is one sophisticated restaurant, with innovative, Latin-inspired fare served in stylish surroundings. Local restaurateur Michael Boland and manager Rob Brown gutted the former Two Cat restaurant space to create a bar and adjacent dining room with votive candles and fresh flowers on white-clothed tables spaced well apart. The walls, painted mandarin red, radiate a glow at night.

Chef Paul Wilson from Augusta changes the menu daily. Among appetizers, the shrimp stuffed with jícama and coconut and served with a sweet-potato purée and peanut dipping sauce, and the crab and roasted corn cake served with red pepper purée and cilantro sour cream were early favorites. Winning main dishes included sole roulades stuffed with crab, almonds and green chiles over a coconut and white wine sauce; cinnamon- and cumin-rubbed monkfish seared with leeks and garlic; rock game hen with chorizo, corn and quinoa stuffing and tangerine glaze, and local organic pork tenderloin stuffed with roasted corn, pickled ancho chile and onions with an orange-ginger glaze. The vegetarian paella dish is geared to vegans.

Desserts are to die for. Consider orange-ginger bread pudding, pineapple cheesecake with a gingersnap crust, mango and tuaca chocolate truffle torte, or mango sorbet.

Selections on the extensive, affordable wine list range around the world.

(207) 288-2822. Entrées, $14 to $22. Dinner nightly, from 6.

Ocean Wood Gallery & Restaurant, Birch Harbor.

Sitting on the porch of this summery restaurant, overlooking colorful gardens bordering a lovely cove, is to us the epitome of the Maine summer experience. A couple of miles from Winter Harbor on the Schoodic Peninsula, this delightful little house doubles as a gallery for the intricate baskets and carvings of the natives of La Palma, a village in the Panamian rain forest, which owner Jim Brunton came

Diners on porch at Ocean Wood Gallery feast on view of flowers and water as well as good food.

to know when he was in the Peace Corps. The small carvings are made from the cocabola nut. All the profits from sales go to the craftspeople.

The restaurant section on a wraparound porch is simple, with white tables, chairs and linens, fresh flowers in vases and huge windows so one can savor the view. We thought the panacea soup (garlic and ginger broth with mushrooms, carrots and chicken) sounded good, but decided instead on the curried chicken salad that incorporated candied ginger and cashews and was delicious (although someone had used rather a heavy hand with the curry powder) and the roast beef sandwich on focaccia. The latter came with vidalia onions and horseradish cream sauce, and was a huge affair. A glass of Bartlett coastal white wine and a tart lemon mousse with two ginger shortbread cookies added up to a perfect lunch for a warm afternoon. Lobster stew, lobster or crabmeat salad and a chicken, bacon and brie sandwich are other possibilities, all in the $5.50 to $9.50 range.

On the evening menu you'll find the same salads and soups, plus smoked salmon and mussels for appetizers, and entrées like finnan haddie pie, lobster alfredo, rack of lamb, and pork tenderloin with bourbon-laced sweet potatoes. Bread pudding with butter-rum-raisin sauce and the bull mousse (deep chocolate with kahlua, Jack Daniels and a mystery ingredient – guess it and you get another one) make worthy endings.

(207) 963-2653. Entrées, $9.50 to $17.50. Lunch daily, 10:30 to 5:30; dinner 5:30 to 9. Open late June to early September.

'Home' Cooking, Garden Accent

The Kitchen Garden Restaurant, 335 Village Road, Steuben.

The name is a natural for this pure restaurant beloved by locals in the know. Partners Jessie King and Alva Lowe love to cook and to garden, and they turned both avocations into a homey restaurant surrounded by gardens on the outskirts of tiny Steuben. Occupants of the snug, 1860s Cape-style house for eight years, the couple built a rear addition off their farm kitchen and opened three country-fresh dining areas seating a total of 30. "We welcome you to our home," proclaims the menu. "Your table is yours for the evening," adds Jessie.

Alva caught the cooking bug from his grandmothers who ran a Mom and Pop restaurant in his native Jamaica. Here he stresses fresh organic ingredients from his own gardens and from Island Acre Farm. "I use local fish, free-range chicken and local rabbit and grow my produce, all organically," he says. He changes the prix-fixe menu every two weeks, offering a limited choice at a bargain price.

Jamaican crab cakes was the chef's choice for appetizer the night we visited. Then came a choice of soups – curried summer squash or corn chowder – served with homemade anadama bread, followed by a green salad. Always among the four choices for entrée is hot and spicy Jamaican curried goat with carrots and potatoes. Others could be homard aux aromates (lobster steamed in white wine, flavored with herbs from the kitchen garden), stir-fried chicken with snow peas, mushrooms and chinese cabbage, and pork tenderloin rolled with prosciutto and parmesan cheese. Alva's range is demonstrated by another fortnight's menu featuring an appetizer of spanakopita and entrées of broiled tuna with capers and tomato sauce, chicken breast stuffed with orange and leeks, rabbit in prune and wine sauce, and beef tenderloin béarnaise.

Jessie oversees the front of the house and is responsible for the simple yet luscious desserts. Rhubarb pudding, chocolate mousse and lemon tart are among her favorites.

The couple moved from her native Connecticut to Steuben "to get away from the rat race," she said. It turns out they worked so hard at their restaurant here they simply had to cut back the hours and shorten the season – no more lunch, no more dinners in fall. "We were doing it mostly ourselves and when our helper quit, we had no choice."

(207) 546-2708. Prix-fixe, $35. Dinner by reservation, July-September, Thursday-Sunday, seatings at 6 and 8; also weekends in June.

Ethnic Gourmet

Jean-Paul's Bistro, Main Street, Blue Hill.

Gaelic charm comes in the summer to Blue Hill in the form of this delightful bistro opened by Jean-Paul Lecomte, taking full advantage of its view onto Blue Hill Bay. In his classic white Maine home with green shutters, the former waiter at some prestigious New York City restaurants, including the 21 Club, offers lunch and tea. Jean-Paul takes care of the front of the house and several relatives, among them his mother, father, brother and sister-in-law, help out.

You can drop in at 11 a.m. for a cup of cappuccino and a chocolate croissant or in early afternoon for a pot of tea. For lunch, the menu might yield a classic salade niçoise, a New Orleans muffuletta sandwich or a baguette with roast beef and brie, a smoked native fish plate and a French farmer's plate of charcuterie and cheeses. We thoroughly enjoyed the croque monsieur with a side salad of mixed baby greens and the grilled chicken caesar salad, layered rather than tossed and served with a baguette. The side terrace with its custom-made square wooden tables topped with canvas umbrellas proved such a salubrious setting that we lingered over a luscious strawberry tart and a slice of midnight chocolate cake that Jean-Paul insisted we taste, calling it a French-Japanese cake – inexplicable, but very good. Other desserts from the patisserie might be blueberry and peach bread pudding, chocolate truffle terrine and the specialty lemon-blueberry madeleines.

Jean-Paul Lecomte on terrace at bistro.

Relax with tea and a pastry on one of the side-by-side Adirondack chairs for two scattered around the back lawn that slopes toward Blue Hill Harbor. Enjoy, as you really can't from any other establishment in town, the pristine view.

Inside, the dining room has cathedral ceilings, local art, white tablecloths, and blue and white spattered Bennington pottery for a simple and fresh yet sophisticated look. And it has big windows for enjoying that view. Wines and beers are available.

(207) 374-5852. Lunch, $6.95 to $11.95. Coffee, lunch and tea, daily except Sunday 11 to 3, July-October.

XYZ Restaurant & Gallery, Shore Road, Manset.

The letters stand for Xalapa, Yucatan and Zacatecas, and the food represents the Mexican interior and coastal Maine. Owner Janet Strong had the West Side Gallery here for a year before opening this enterprise in 1994 with cook Robert Hoyt, who's traveled in Mexico for years and describes himself as "a nut for the food there for a long, long time."

We could easily become nuts for his food, too, after a couple of dinners here. Everything, as Robert says, is "real," from the smoked jalapeño and tomatillo sauces served with the opening tortillas to the fine tequila he offered with dessert as a chaser

Busy hostess Janet recommended we try her partner's sampler plate ($13 each): two chiles rellenos and a chicken dish with mashed potato and pickled cucumber. Thoroughly smitten, we returned another time to enjoy the pollo deshebrada (shredded chicken in a rustic sauce of chiles with cilantro and onions) and tatemado (pork loin baked in a sauce of guajillo and ancho chiles). The menu changes weekly, so you might find camarones ajo (tiger shrimp with garlic, ancho and poblano chiles) or lengua Mexicana (native beef tongue stewed in a mild broth of tomato and herbs), a house specialty.

Desserts range from flan, Mexico's version of crème caramel, to the sensational XYZ pie, layers of coffee and butter crunch ice cream divided by a ridge of solid chocolate covered in warm kahlua chocolate sauce

Part of the main floor of the Dockside Motel, the L-shaped dining room is colorful in white, red and green, the colors of the Mexican flag. The front windows look out onto Somes Sound across the road.

(207) 244-5221. Entrées, $12 to $14. Dinner nightly in summer, from 5:30. Open mid-May to mid-October.

Tea on the Lawn

Jordan Pond House, Park Loop Road, Acadia National Park.

Tea on the lawn, with an incomparable setting in the national park, is a Bar Harbor tradition. Lawns sloping down to Jordan Pond and the Bubbles mountains in the background are the backdrop for a steady stream of visitors drawn by the unexpected novelty of day-long tea (two popovers with butter and strawberry preserves, $6) and, more recently, cappuccino or Oregon chai and popovers ($7).

We're drawn more often for lunch to this storied landmark, which was rebuilt in contemporary-style after fire destroyed the original. The tables of choice are outside on the "porch," which is more like a covered terrace. The last time we enjoyed a fine seafood pasta and a curried chicken salad, garnished with red grapes and orange slices, and shared a popover – good but a bit steep at $3.50, given that it was hollow.

The dinner menu is fairly standard, with the predictable grilled salmon, baked haddock, sautéed Maine crab cakes with a green onion sauce, prime rib, and steamed lobster. If you're hungry, start with lobster stew and popovers. Finish with homemade ice cream, cappuccino flan or – if you're not popovered out – popover à la mode. Flickering candles, fresh flowers and the sunset over pond and mountains create an unforgettable setting.

There's a full bar, and the large gift shop (one of several Acadia Shops on the island) is fun to browse in.

(207) 276-3316. Entrées, $13 to $18. Lunch, 11:30 to 2:30. Tea on the lawn, 11:30 to 5:30. Dinner, 5:30 to 8 or 9. Open mid-May to mid-October.

Lobster Pounds

Union River Lobster Pot, 8 South St., Ellsworth.

Ellsworth got its first "waterfront" restaurant when Brian and Jane Langley opened this sprightly place at the back of a former seafood market. The Langleys had put the Oak Point Lobster Pound in Trenton on the culinary map for ten years. Here they continue the tradition, boiling lobsters outside and serving inside at windows yielding a glimpse of the river. The lobster roll has all the meat from a whole lobster for $10.95; a whole shore dinner is $19.95. Brian's stews and chowders are renowned, as are the blueberry pie and chocolate mousse pie. Although it's a simple place, the menu is fairly extensive and Brian teaches cooking in Ellsworth, so he knows what he's doing. How often have you seen strawberry-amaretto torte on the menu at a lobster pound?

(207) 667-5077. Lunch and dinner daily, 11 to 9, mid-June to mid-October.

Thurston's Lobster Pound, Steamboat Wharf Road, Bernard.

From the jaunty upstairs deck here you can look below and see where the lobstermen keep their traps. This is a real working lobster wharf. And if you couldn't tell from all the pickup trucks parked along the road, one taste of the lobster will convince you.

We enjoyed ours ($7 to $8 a pound, plus $3 for the extras, from corn to blueberry cake). Together we also sampled the lobster stew (bearing tons of lobster), a really good potato salad, steamers and two pounds of mussels (about one pound too much). Oh well, this *was* our first lobster feast of the summer. You wait in line for one of the square tables for four on the covered deck, place your order at the counter and select from a choice beer and wine list (imagine, a lobster pound offering a pouilly fuissé). They provide the candles, and a little wash basin outside the kitchen so customers can wash the lobster debris off their hands.

This is a true place, run by Michael Radcliffe, great-grandson of the lobster wharf's founder, and his wife Libby. A local couple, whose license plate said "Pies," was delivering the apple and rhubarb pies for the day the first time we stopped by.

(207) 244-7600. Open daily 11 to 8:30, Memorial Day through September.

Fisherman's Landing, 35 West St., Bar Harbor.

We've been going to this lobster pound on the working pier, the only one beside the water in town, since the '70s.. From inside a cramped shack come succulent lobsters; you eat at picnic tables on the wharf, inside an enclosed pavilion or on an upstairs deck, sip wine or beer obtained from the adjacent bar, and watch all the harbor activities. For visitors, it's the essence of Down East Maine, all wrapped up in one convenient package. The french fries are especially good, and hamburgers and other items are available.

(207) 288-4632. Open daily in summer, from 11:30.

Dining and Lodging

Castine Inn, Main Street, Box 41, Castine 04421.

A passion for creative cooking led peripatetic chef Tom Gutow – mature beyond his 27 years – to the coast of Maine. There in 1997, in the out-of-the-way village of Castine, he and wife Amy found the inn of their dreams. They quickly elevated the atmospheric Castine Inn into one of the best restaurants in Maine.

The century-old inn, surrounded by a wraparound porch yielding views of prized gardens and the harbor beyond, was a natural for an aspiring chef like Tom, who wanted to do his own thing. After graduation from Connecticut College, where he majored in English literature, the Michigan native apprenticed with three-star Michelin chefs in France and with celebrity chefs David Bouley and Diane Forley in New York. He and Amy, an attorney, tired of urban life and scoured the New England countryside for an inn. Their search ended at Castine, where longtime chef-owner Mark Hodesh and his artist wife Margaret Parker were ready to sell the inn. By sheer coincidence, the Hodeshes were returning to Ann Arbor, where Tom had grown up and their families knew vaguely of each other.

Amy gave up her law practice to become an innkeeper (and mother to their infant daughter). Tom relishes his share of nirvana: "We get to live in one of the most beautiful places in the world. And I get to cook every day."

He gradually transformed the inn's reputation for both creative and traditional Down East fare into one highlighting local, seasonal foods prepared in a refined, metropolitan style. He calls it "the best of big-city cooking in a casual Maine atmosphere." He offers a short à la carte menu that changes daily, plus a six-course tasting menu for the entire table ($50 to $62 per person).

One night's tasting menu illustrates the style. Chilled celery gin soup preceded an appetizer of seared salmon with caramelized endive and summer squash in ginger-tomato water. Lobster with leeks, shiitake mushrooms and fennel came next. The main event was grilled beef tenderloin with asparagus, tomatoes and white wine vinaigrette. Honeydew melon soup with grape granita followed. Dessert was lime mousse and kiwi layered with lemon crisps on a pool of caramelized grapefruit sauce. Each course may be paired with a glass of wine from a small but choice wine list notable for a number of offerings fairly priced in the teens.

The night's à la carte menu ranged from a starter of rolled terrine of foie gras with spiced apple compote and rhubarb syrup to rabbit loin and saddle with shiitake mushrooms and tarragon-chervil sauce. Desserts were light, from lavender crème brûlée to spicy caramelized strawberries with plum sake and phyllo crisps.

At our visit, energetic Tom had just returned from organizing a $75-a-plate chefs' dinner at Arrows in Ogunquit. He teamed with Sam Hayward of Portland's Fore Street and Arrows partners Mark Gaier and Clark Frasier to feature the best in Maine cooking. Tom's contributions were an appetizer of beef carpaccio, seasoned with coriander and cumin and wrapped around tarragon goat cheese, and a main course of grilled elk with pickled fiddlehead ferns, tomatoes and mustard oil. At an earlier event, his lobster and scallop dish with an herbed orange glaze earned him a state designation as Maine's lobster chef of the year.

Culinary treats such as these are served in a spacious, serene, 60-seat dining room graced by the stunning murals of Castine painted by the former innkeeper-artist. A guest parlor and a cozy, convivial pub with hand-painted tables and a fireplace occupy the front of the house.

The Gutows are gradually upgrading the accommodations, which open hotel-style off long, wide corridors on the second and third floors. They first turned two small rear rooms into a large room with a queen poster bed, an armchair and two club chairs and a large bath with an antique sunken tub surrounded by black and white tiles, separate shower and a vanity in an alcove. Decor is modest yet stylish, with understated floral fabrics and window treatments. More rooms were to be given the Gutow treatment as time and funds permit. Tom acquired construction skills by watching the pros handle his early renovations and then undertook the rest himself.

Overnight guests enjoy Tom's creations at breakfast. The menu generally offers three hot entrées: an omelet with goat cheese and herbs, corned beef hash topped by a poached egg and homemade apple bread french toast with Maine maple syrup.

(207) 326-4365. Fax (207) 326-4570. Doubles, $85 to $140, large room $210. Nineteen rooms with private baths. Two-night minimum in summer. Children over 8. Inn and grounds non-smoking. Closed Dec. 20 through April.

Entrées, $20 to $31. Dinner nightly, 5:30 to 8:30 Memorial Day to Labor Day, 6 to 8 to Columbus Day, weekends only rest of season.

Pilgrim's Inn, Box 69, Deer Isle 04627.

An aura of history and an aroma of fine food emanate from this impressive, dark red 1793 house run with great taste and flair by Jean and Dud Hendrick. With a harbor in front and a mill pond in back, inviting common rooms and thirteen guest rooms (plus two efficiency suites in a house next door), it's a quiet place that beckons guests to stay for extended periods.

Jean and her chefs are known for creative cooking, as testified by their recently published *The Pilgrim's Inn Cookbook*. They favor local ingredients and do their grilling on an enormous barbecue on a rear deck. Cocktails start at 6 in the downstairs common room or outside on the deck (where guests nibble on abundant hors d'oeuvres like bluefish pâté and mingle with Jean and Dud, who fixes a neat raspberry daiquiri upon request). A prix-fixe dinner ($31.50 for the public) is served at 7 o'clock. You move into the charming dining room in a former goat barn, with farm utensils and quilts on the walls, hand-hewn beams, mismatched chairs, tables with fresh flowers, big windows and ten outside doors that open to let in the breeze. Self-taught cook Melissa Homann from Brooklyn, who took graduate courses at the French Culinary Institute and teaches Southwest cooking at the New School, has expanded the menu options. Changing daily, they include two appetizers and usually four entrées, one of them vegetarian. One spring night's menu started with a choice of wild rice and mushroom soup with melted fontina cheese or a shrimp taco with jícama-lime slaw. A salad of local greens preceded the main course: a choice of Thai vegetable stir-fry, seared pinwheel salmon with orange sauce and couscous, lemon-rosemary roasted poussin with creamy polenta or chili-rubbed grilled beef tenderloin with a hazelnut-chipotle sauce. Desserts were bittersweet chocolate and orange mousse terrine, peach and blueberry tart with almonds, banana-caramel baked alaska with chocolate sauce, or an assortment of ice creams and sorbets with cookies.

Pilgrim's Inn is in handsome 1793 house.

Never will we forget an earlier Sunday dinner of salad with goat cheese, home-made peasant bread, a heavenly paella topped with nasturtiums (such a pretty dish that it should have been photographed for Gourmet magazine) and a sensational raspberry-chocolate pie on a shortbread crust.

Homemade granola, scones, melon and omelets are typical breakfast fare. French toast and a brioche with grilled vegetables were the choices at our latest visit.

The handsome guest rooms, each with wood stove and ten with private baths, are decorated in sprightly Laura Ashley style. Most in demand are the larger rooms at the back. Two bedrooms on the newly renovated third floor have private baths with vanities topped with Deer Isle granite. Oriental rugs and quilts lend color to the prevailing simplicity. The main-floor library has an exceptional collection of books; another parlor is a showroom for local artists. The Hendricks have added appropriate art to every guest room. It's typical of the TLC they lavish on the inn.

A few years ago they transformed a rear shed into **The Rugosa Rose,** a stylish craft and gift shop. They bought the adjacent property to double the size of their grounds and converted its vintage house called Ginny's into two housekeeping suites that were "proving to be real sweethearts," Jean advised. Each has a living room with sofabed and cable TV, cast-iron stove, queen bed, full bath and efficiency kitchen and dining area, plus a deck overlooking the water.

(207) 348-6615. Fax (207) 348-7769. www.pilgrimsinn.com. Ten rooms with private baths, three rooms with shared bath and two efficiency suites. Doubles, $150 to $17: MAP; efficiency suites, $205. Two-night minimum requested. Open mid-May to mid October; efficiencies open year-round. No credit cards.

Prix-fixe, $31.50. Dinner by reservation, nightly at 7.

Goose Cove Lodge, Deer Isle, Box 40, Sunset 04683.

Some of the most inspired meals in Maine are served at this food-oriented, family-style lodge on 70 acres along the remote shores of Deer Isle. The only problem (?) is that you may have to stay for a week in season to partake or manage to slip in for dinner as a transient via a one-and-one-half-mile-long dirt road through the evergreens, starting in the middle of nowhere and terminating at the open ocean at the End of Beyond.

Joanne Parisi, a former Massachusetts caterer and now innkeeper with her husband Dom, hired Rob Evans as chef to change the traditional lodge format into that of a restaurant. They present healthful, new American fare for up to 90 lodge guests and outside diners by reservation. Sturdy, shiny pine tables are set in summery pink in the handsome **Point Restaurant** dining room wrapping around the ocean end of the main lodge, which has gained a new seaside deck where lunches are served in summer.

The formerly prix-fixe menu at one seating is now à la carte, still innovative as ever and changing every week. Guests gather for cocktails and complimentary hors d'oeuvres in the bar or on the deck before dinner, the hours for which have been made more flexible.

Typical starters might be marinated tuna tartare with wasabi cream, peeky-toe crab cake with mustard beurre blanc, and beef carpaccio with tomato chutney and lemon vinaigrette. Recent main courses included rock crab-crusted salmon fillet with a poppyseed-chive blini and grapefruit-tarragon butter sauce, grilled swordfish with chipotle butter sauce and Japanese noodles, and herb-crusted rack of New Zealand lamb with port wine demi-glace. The pastry chef changes the desserts nightly.

Lunch service inaugurated on the seaside deck in the summer of 1999 proved immensely popular with the public.

One Sunday's brunch fare included pineapple, bananas and nutmeg flamed in spiced rum, homemade granola with yogurt, an assortment of fresh breads, buttermilk pancakes with spiced plum topping and a choice of eggs or omelets prepared any style, served with pan-seared red bliss potatoes and grilled ham.

The Friday night lobster feast on the beach is a highlight of the week for the long-termers, who tend to be repeat guests year after year. Counselors entertain and supervise children during the adult dinner hour. String quartets, folk singers, a lobster fisherman or a local writer may entertain after dinner.

The Parisis offer "simple, rustic and comfortable lodging" in ten rooms and suites upstairs in the main lodge or in the nearby East and North annexes. Most in demand are the upstairs Lookout Suite, essentially a complete two-bedroom apartment, and the nine secluded cottages and four duplex cottages, each with ocean view, sun deck, kitchenette or refrigerator and fireplace. Some of the larger require payment for a three-person minimum.

The lodge property – marked by five trails, sandy beaches and tree-lined shores – is a paradise for nature lovers. At low tide, you can walk across a sand bar to Barred Island, a nature conservancy full of birds and wildlife.

(207) 348-2508 or (800) 728-1963. Fax (207) 348-2624. Twenty-three rooms, suites and cabins with private baths. Doubles, B&B, $140 to $450 in summer; $120 to $239 in off-season. Two-night minimum in rooms and suites; one-week minimum in cabins in July and August, two nights rest of year. Open mid-May to mid-October.

Entrées, $16 to $30. Lunch in summer, Monday-Saturday 11:30 to 3:30. Dinner by reservation, nightly 5:30 to 8:30.

Le Domaine, U.S. Route 1 (HC 77, Box 496), Hancock 04640.

Here is a perfect getaway for gourmets: a country auberge with a handful of elegant upstairs guest rooms, some with private decks overlooking the rear gardens, and a main-floor restaurant and lounge purveying classic French cuisine and fine wines.

The red frame building semi-hidden behind huge evergreens seems as if it were lifted from provincial France and plunked down in rural Hancock, which is even down east from down east Bar Harbor. Inside is an extraordinarily appealing place in which to stay and dine.

Founded in 1945 by a Frenchwoman, Marianne Purslow-Dumas, Le Domaine is run now with equal competence by her daughter, Nicole Purslow, a graduate of the Cordon Bleu School and an advocate of country-French haute cuisine.

Beyond a delightful wicker sitting area where French magazines are piled upon tables is the long and narrow, L-shaped dining room, dominated at the far end by a huge stone fireplace framed by copper cooking utensils. Walls (red above, green below and separated by dark wood beams) are decorated with maps of France and pictures of folks in provincial costumes. A porch room in back, its tables covered with gaily colored cloths from Provence, takes full advantage of the sylvan view.

The menu changes frequently and features local produce from nearby gardens and herbs that grow by the kitchen door. Four or five entrées are offered each night. They could include sautéed fillet of sole with parsley and lemon juice, steak au poivre, and free-range poussin roasted with tarragon and champagne. We'd return any time for the sensational sweetbreads with lemon and capers, the grilled salmon with fennel, lamb chops dusted with rosemary and thyme, and a house specialty, rabbit with prunes marinated in brandy. Zucchini, snap peas and gnocchi might accompany.

The French bread is toasted in chunks and the rolls are marvelous. For starters on various occasions, we've tried malpeque oysters with a shallot-sherry vinegar dipping sauce, coquilles St. Jacques in a heavenly wine sauce, smoked trout, and a salad of impeccable greens and baby spinach, tossed with goat cheese and walnuts.

The cheesecake on raspberry sauce is ethereal, as is the frozen coffee mousse. Another visit produced a raspberry tart and frozen raspberry mousse with a meringue, plus perfect french-roast coffee. The wine list (mostly French, of course) is expensive, but some bargains are to be found.

Relaxing after dinner on wicker chairs in the sitting room with snifters of heady eau de vie, we almost didn't care about the cost. We headed upstairs to our overnight home in the king-bedded Tarragon Room, one of seven attractive, country-fresh guest rooms named after herbs.

All are exceptionally outfitted in chintz. The amenities you'd expect are here, including antiques, clock radios, books, French magazines, bedside reading lamps, French soaps and bath oils (and a night light in the shape of a shell), plus complimentary Perrier water. Behind a studied simplicity are many artistic touches. On our rear deck, for instance, a spotlight shone on a tree growing through it and a piece of driftwood was placed perfectly on the stairs.

The next morning, we admired a circular garden surrounded by large rocks in back, looking casual but probably taking hours to plot. A number of trails had been cleared through a forest of pine trees on 85 acres. We took a long walk to a pond, picking blueberries for sustenance along the way.

A breakfast tray was delivered to our deck, bearing bowls of peaches an

Wicker sitting area and curved bar lead to dining room at Le Domaine.

raspberries, granola, crème fraîche, hot milk in a jug, homemade blueberry preserves, three of the flakiest croissants ever and a pot of fragrant coffee, all on floral china with linen napkins. Sheer enchantment!

(207) 422-3395 or (800) 544-8498. Fax (207) 422-2316. Seven rooms with private baths. Doubles, $275, MAP. Open June-October.

Entrées, $23.75 to $28.50. Dinner nightly except Tuesday, 6 to 9.

Lodging

Blue Hill Inn, Union Street, Box 403, Blue Hill 04614.

This trim white Colonial inn with dark green shutters – a landmark in the heart of Blue Hill for nearly 170 years – has been considerably spiffed up by Mary and Don Hartley.

They enhanced the twelve guest accommodations with plush carpeting, new wallpaper and modernized bathrooms. All come with private baths and four with fireplaces. Some have sitting areas converted from small bedrooms. Our rear bedroom – occupied the previous night by Peter of Peter, Paul and Mary fame following a concert for Paul's hometown fans at the Blue Hill Fair Grounds – was comfortable with a kingsize bed, two wing chairs, colorful bed linens, plump towels and windows on three sides to circulate cool air, which was welcome after a heat wave. The other rooms we saw also were nicely furnished with 19th-century antiques and traditional pieces.

In 1997, the Hartleys added a luxurious efficiency suite next door. The cathedral-ceilinged Cape House offers a kingsize canopy bed plus an antique "bed in a box," fireplace, living room with telephone and TV, kitchen and a rear deck.

Back in the main inn, a small library-game room is furnished in antiques. The larger main parlor, where classical music plays in the background, has a fireplace and a ten-candle Persian chandelier. This is where the Hartleys serve hors d'oeuvres (perhaps smoked bluefish or local goat cheese) during a nightly innkeepers' reception for guests. (They no longer offer the gourmet dinners for which they traditionally had been known.)

In the morning, breakfast is a culinary event. Ours started with the usual juices, a plate of cut-up fresh fruit and a wedge of apple-custard pie that one of us thought was dessert. The main course involved a choice of eggs scrambled with garden chives in puff pastry, an omelet with chèvre or brie and Canadian bacon, waffles with fresh strawberries or blueberry pancakes. Excellent french-roast coffee accompanied.

Outside, guests enjoy the Hartleys' perennial garden with lawn furniture, a hammock and a profusion of huge yellow lilies. The innkeepers occasionally charter a schooner to take guests out on East Penobscot Bay for day trips. They also sponsor seasonal concert weekends, and planned wine-tasting gourmet dinners and visiting-chef weekends in the off-season.

(207) 374-2844 or (800) 826-7415. Fax (207) 374-2829. www.bluehillinn.com. Ten rooms and two suites with private baths. Mid-June through early October: doubles $138 to $165; suites, $190 to $240. Off-season: doubles $118 to $150, suites $160. Two-night minimum weekends. Closed December to mid-May.

The Inn at Canoe Point, Route 3, Box 216-B, Bar Harbor 04609.

Here is one of Mount Desert Island's few small B&Bs right on the ocean, and it is a stunner of a place. Nancy and Tom Cervelli, formerly of the Kingsleigh Inn in Southwest Harbor, acquired a going concern from founder-turned-realtor Don Johnson, who similarly had started with a B&B in Southwest Harbor. Blessed with the best waterfront location imaginable and a smashing deck that takes full advantage, the inn was in the enviable position of accepting bookings a year in advance.

Formerly a private residence, the stucco house with Tudor trim is set well back and below Route 3 in an acre and a half of woods flanking Frenchman Bay. All five guest quarters enjoy water views. We're partial to the front Master Suite with queen bed, sitting area with a gas fireplace and french doors onto a deck and the side Garden Room, which has three walls of glass and its own door onto the garden and sea. The third-floor Garret Suite comes with wicker chairs, a neat captain's chest and a kingsize bed from which you can look out at an endless expanse of water. All are discreetly decorated in exquisite taste and muted colors so as not to detract from the view.

Guests enjoy a handsome living room, which has an elegant grouping of seats around the fireplace, and the waterfront Ocean Room with a huge curved sectional fireplace and stereo. The latter room is where breakfast is served at tables for four topped with candlesticks – when the weather isn't suitable for eating on the spacious deck at water's edge.

Breakfast might be eggs in puff pastry, omelets, waffles or lemon french toast plus a choice of juices and a fruit course. Decanters of port or sherry are in all the guest rooms, and Nancy serves tea, cookies, cheese and crackers on pleasant afternoons on the deck.

The Cervellis had only to fine-tune, adding a fireplace in the Anchor Room and

Waterside deck at The Inn at Canoe Point offers sweeping view of Frenchman Bay.

remodeling the baths in the Garret and Portside. "We've been upgrading one room at a time," said Nancy.

(207) 288-9511. Fax (207) 288-2870. www.innatcanoepoint.com. Three rooms and two suites with private baths. Memorial Day-October: doubles, $160 to $195; suites, $230 and $265. Rest of year, doubles, $80 to $115; suites, $130 and $160.

The Inn at Bay Ledge, 1385 Sand Point Rd., Bar Harbor 04609.

Reindeer fashioned from vines stand sentry at the entrance to this clifftop retreat overlooking Frenchman Bay. They reflect the "upscale country ambiance" that Jack and Jeani Ochtera, former owners of the Holbrook House in town, have imparted since our first stay in this early 1900s house that has been "added to a million times," in Jeani's words.

King or queen canopied and four-poster beds plump with feather mattresses and pillows, Ralph Lauren towels and linens, and colorful quilts with matching window treatments are the rule in the ten guest rooms with private baths, three with jacuzzis. All but one have picture windows affording splendid water vistas. A paneled upstairs sitting room harbors a hidden TV/VCR amidst a decorative scheme of old family fishing gear, hand-carved birds and Jeani's handmade samplers. A porch running the length of the inn offers a fine view of Frenchman Bay.

Rolling lawns and gardens lead to a sheer cliff, where a steep staircase descends 80 feet to the stony beach and a cave along the bay. An expansive, tiered deck stretches along the front of the inn. Here are umbrellaed tables and twig chairs where you may read and relax at this truly relaxing place. A heated swimming pool is on a lower level of the deck, and tall pine trees all around make the salt air even more refreshing. Newly planted roses brighten the lately expanded gardens.

The inn's first floor contains a sauna and steam shower, as well as a new sunroom where Jeani offers fresh fruit, cereal, granola, breads and muffins and perhaps three-cheese and bacon quiche, blueberry buckle or cheese strata. We took ours out to the porch and watched cheeky chipmunks race around, vying for crumbs.

The inn also offers three cottages, one with kingsize bed and fieldstone fireplace, hidden in the trees across the road.

(207) 288-4204. (Winter: (207) 875-3262). Fax 288-5573. www.innatbayledge.com. Ten rooms and three cottages with private baths. Doubles, $150 to $265 in inn; cottages, $130 to $150. Two-night minimum in season. Closed November-April.

Ullikana Bed & Breakfast, 16 The Field, Bar Harbor 04609.

Hospitable owner-innkeepers, creative breakfasts, a quiet in-town location near the water and a guest book full of grateful raves. These are among the attributes of this summery but substantial, Tudor-style cottage built in 1885, tucked away in the trees between the Bar Harbor Inn and "the field," a meadow of wildflowers. Transplanted New Yorkers Roy Kasindorf and his Quebec City-born wife, Hélène Harton, bought it in 1991 from a woman who had turned it into a B&B at the age of 86. They retained many of the furnishings, adding some of their own as well as artworks from artist-friends in New York. In 1998, they acquired the summery Yellow House across the street and added six more guest rooms.

Ten bedrooms in the main house hold lots of chintz, wicker and antiques; some come with balconies, fireplaces or both. One dubbed Audrey's Room (for Roy's daughter) on the third floor contains two antique beds joined together as a kingsize and a clawfoot tub with its original fixtures, from which the bather can look out the low window onto Frenchman Bay. We were happily ensconced in the second-floor Room 5, a majestic space outfitted in country French provincial fabrics with king bed, two wing chairs in front of the fireplace and a water-view balcony upon which to relax and enjoy the passing parade.

Rooms in the Yellow House are light and airy, furnished "in the style of a simple summer home," in Hélène's words. "We saved everything we could from the original." Jack's Room comes with an imposing kingsize pineapple poster bed, mirrored armoire and a marble bath with glass shower. Guests here enjoy a double parlor as well as a wraparound porch.

Back in the original house, the main floor harbors a wicker-furnished parlor with lots to look at, from collections (including two intricate puppets beside the fireplace) to reading materials. It's the site for a convivial wine and cheese hour in the late afternoon. Beyond a dining room with shelves full of colorful Italian breakfast china is the kitchen from which Hélène produces the dishes that make breakfasts here such an event. In summer, they're served outside at tables for two or four on a pleasant terrace with glimpses of the water. Roy is the waiter and raconteur, doling out – in our case – cantaloupe with mint sauce, superior cinnamon-raisin muffins with orange glaze, and puff pancakes yielding blueberries and raspberries. Your feast might start with Hélène's grilled fruit brochettes bearing peaches, strawberries and kiwi with a ricotta-cheese sauce or grapefruit segments in cinnamon syrup, followed by an Italian omelet with homemade tomato sauce and mozzarella cheese or crêpes with frozen yogurt or a rum-cream sauce. All this is served on matching dishes and placemats – a rainbow of pastels, as cheery as the setting.

(207) 288-9552. Sixteen rooms with private baths. Doubles, $130 to $220. Closed November-April.

Chiltern Inn, 3 Cromwell Harbor Road, Bar Harbor 04609.

Lovely gardens surround the outside of this elegant, cottage-style shingled carriage house built in 1906 at the edge of town for the first secretary to the ambassador for France. Inside all is lofty and sumptuous, as transformed by antiques dealers John Shaw and Pat Monhollon. They had met serendipitously when Pat was a guest at John's B&B and pottery studio in St. Andrews, N.B. They honeymooned in Bar Harbor and set about opening an inn to supplement the antiques business. Fire interrupted their restoration, but presented the opportunity for John to design some stunning architectural fillips and Pat to decorate with elan.

The ground level contains an exotic, columned room with an indoor pool, hot tub, sauna and a marble fireplace as well as a low-key antiques shop and guest reception area. The focal point of the second level is an open, soaring great hall, where plants grow in a zinc-lined clawfoot tub that belonged to Pat's mother and a split staircase ascends dramatically to a loft library. Clerestory windows flood the white walls and furnishings with light. An adjacent, skylit parlor is more formal with seating grouped around an ornate manteled fireplace beneath a French crystal chandelier. French doors open to an elegant sun room where Chippendale-style chairs flank small mahogany tables set formally for breakfast.

Breakfast is prepared in a beauty of a kitchen layered in different varieties of cherry, from domestic on the floors to Brazilian on the counters. The fare could be omelets, a rich cheese and bacon quiche or french toast stuffed with raspberries.

Three lavish guest rooms on the second level feature king or queen beds, gas fireplaces, Italian marble bathrooms with double whirlpool tubs and oversize showers, TVs, telephones, overstuffed seating (including a couple of alcove window seats) and rich, understated antiques. A fourth guest room, in the works on the garden level, is similar but lacks a jacuzzi and adds a patio.

John and Pat bill theirs as a small and sophisticated European-style hotel that is "elegant, intimate and luxurious." Although not a hotel in the traditional sense, it's all of the rest and more.

(207) 288-0114 or (800) 404-0114. Fax (207) 288-0124. Four rooms with private baths. Doubles, $295 to $375 in summer, $250 to $325 in spring and fall, $225 to $250 in winter.

Lindenwood Inn, 118 Clark Point Road, Box 1328, Southwest Harbor 04679.
Towering linden trees shade this turn-of-the-century sea captain's home, now grandly refurbished by Australian owner Jim King. Jim, who had opened the Kingsleigh Inn here, returned from traveling around the world in 1993 to purchase the Lindenwood, which had fallen on lean times.

He quickly imbued the main house with his eclectic decorating touch, setting palm trees on the wraparound porch, splashing vivid colors on the walls and spattering collections of shells and stones in the nine bedrooms. "We don't have New England decor here," he asserts, "and people love it."

The two parlors are contemporary, accented with green and white striped upholstered chairs. Potted plants throughout the main floor bring the outdoors inside. Upstairs are nine guest quarters of varying sizes, all with private baths and several with fireplaces. Check out Room 6 with its six-foot-long clawfoot tub. It's one of six rooms with private decks or balconies affording views of the harbor. The ultimate is the penthouse suite with a curved sofa and gas fireplace, opening onto an enormous rooftop deck holding an oversize spa.

Next Jim redid two waterfront cottages and converted an adjacent apartment house into six efficiency suites he called the Lindenwood Annex. He converted another house across the street into yet another annex with six guest rooms.

Outside at the side, screened by a trellis from the street, is a heated gunite pool and a separate spa topped by a sculptured mask spraying a stream of water. We basked in the lap of luxury in the prime pool-side cottage with cable TV in the cathedral-ceilinged living room, an efficiency kitchen and a queensize bedroom.

In the morning, seated in one of the three small dining rooms, we helped ourselves to fresh fruit and raspberry-banana muffins from the buffet and were served a main dish of fruit crêpes. Other days might produce stratas, omelets (vegetarian or with strawberries), or stuffed french toast.

Meanwhile, Jim refers to himself as "the traveling innkeeper." He's venturing into interior design work and turning day-to-day duties over to Esther Cavagnaro, probably Mount Desert's best known innkeeper.

(207) 244-5335 or (800) 307-5335. Fax (207) 244-3643. www.acadia.net/lindenwood. Twelve rooms, two suites, six efficiency suites and three cottages with private baths. July and August: doubles $95 to $155, efficiencies $115 EP, suites, $185 to $245, cottages $1,085 to $1,295 weekly. Rest of year: doubles $75 to $145, efficiencies $95 to $105, suites, $145 to $195, cottages $95. Closed Dec. 15 to March.

The Kingsleigh Inn, 373 Main St., Box 1426, Southwest Harbor 04679.

An unusual pebbledash stucco-stone exterior with a great wraparound porch full of wicker and colorful pillows houses one of the area's more inviting B&Bs.

Ken and Cyd Collins from Newburyport, Mass., have added their own antiques and artworks to the eight bedrooms, some with harbor views. One has a new balcony with chairs overlooking the water, and another a new deck. The Turret Suite on the third floor offers television and a great view from a telescope placed on a tripod between two cozy wicker chairs; the bedroom comes with a kingsize rice plantation poster bed and fireplace. The other rooms are lavishly furnished with queensize beds, Waverly wall coverings and fabrics, plush carpeting, lace curtains, country accents and woven baskets filled with thick towels. Afternoon tea and homemade cookies are served on the porch or in cool weather by the fireplace.

Breakfast by candlelight is taken at tables for two in a dining room with polished wood floors, dark green tablecloths, and pink and green china. The repertoire includes individual egg soufflé with red pepper sauce, ricotta-stuffed french toast with warm blackberry sauce, waffles with different fruits and apple pie coffeecake.

(207) 244-5302. Fax (207) 244-0349. Seven rooms and one suite with private baths. July to mid-October: doubles, $90 to $125; suite, $175. Rest of year: doubles, $55 to $95; suite, $105 to $135.

The Black Duck on Corea Harbor, Crowley Island Road, Box 39, Corea 04624.

This century-old fisherman's house, converted into a B&B in 1990, sprawls across a harborfront property with a variety of intriguing public spaces, eclectic decor and a small menagerie of pets that includes a Vietnam potbellied pig named Dolly Bacon. Barry Canner and Robert Travers, a realtor, share the property with guests in four bedrooms and two cottages.

Theirs is a much-lived-in (and loved) house, from the cozy den off the entry with not one but two fireplaces to the enormous living room with fireplace, a carved Indian in one corner, a dramatic screen in another, assorted carved bird and quite a toy collection in a glass case. A front deck offers sitting areas on either side of the entry for viewing the harbor goings-on across the street. And trail meanders through a portion of the twelve-acre property to a cove in back.

Upstairs are three bedrooms, one in front with a queensize metal sleigh be topped by a bright floral coverlet, sitting area and large private bath. Two with queen or twin beds share a bath and may be rented as a suite. Our favorite is a cu

Fine kitchenware is on display in Rowantrees Pottery showroom.

side room off the main floor with private entrance and deck, good reading lights over the double and twin bed and a private bath. Across the street are two waterfront cottages, one a studio and the other with living room up and bedroom down, available generally by the week. .

A dark and historic looking dining room is the setting for healthful, low-fat breakfasts. Barry says his repertoire doesn't repeat for ten days. The meal might be melon drizzled with blueberry-raspberry sauce, carrot-raisin muffins and a main dish like baked orange french toast with orange glaze and walnuts, eggs Black Duck (like benedict but with horseradish sauce) or frittata made with eggbeaters.

(207) 963-2689. Fax (207) 963-7495. Doubles, $75 to $95. Two-room suite, $145.

Gourmet Treats

Potteries and crafts places abound in the vicinity of Blue Hill and Deer Isle. Foremost is **Rowantrees Pottery,** 9 Union St., Blue Hill, where Sheila Varnum and her associates continue the tradition launched in 1934 by Adelaide Pearson through her friend, Mahatma Gandhi. Named for the mountain ash tree above the green gate in front of the rambling house and barn, Rowantrees is especially known for its jam jar with a flat white lid covered with blueberries, as well as for unique glazes. **Rackliffe Pottery** on Route 172 also makes all kinds of handsome and useful kitchenware.

Local farmers, food producers and artisans gather at the **Blue Hill Farmer's Market** at the Blue Hill Fairgrounds Saturday mornings in July and August to sell everything from fresh produce and goat cheese to handmade gifts and patterned sweaters. It's a fun event for local color and foods.

The renamed **Blue Hill Wine Shop** (formerly Blue Hill Tea & Tobacco), in an aromatic modern shed attached to a home on Main Street, carries an abundance of teas, coffees and rare tobaccos as well as fine wines. "New name, same great stuff," say partners David Witter and William Petry. They also have related gift collections and do an extensive mail-order business.

Nervous Nellie's Jams and Jellies, Sunshine Road, Deer Isle, makes the products you see all over Maine the old-fashioned way. Founded by Peter Beerits, the business puts up 40,000 jars each year in the little house with a big kitchen. So many people were stopping in that Peter decided to serve refreshments as well. His **Mountainville Cafe** offers morning coffee and afternoon tea with homemade scones and breads (with plenty of jams). Included is a frozen drink called a Batido, a refreshing but caloric mix of cream cheese, freezer jam and crushed ice cubes. Besides all the wonderful jams (we especially like the wild Maine blueberry-ginger conserve and the hot tomato jelly), Peter's quirky sculptures on the grounds outside make this worth a visit. We were intrigued by a sculpture of a lobsterman with huge red wooden claws for arms. Lately, Peter cleared the surrounding woods to be peopled with sculptures from his new studio fashioned from an abandoned store he moved to the site. Look for witches, woodsmen and owls among the trees. Open daily 9 to 5, mid-May through Christmas; rest of year, by chance.

Stonington's Main Street has been enlivened by **The Clown,** a seasonal venture combining English antiques, contemporary art and Italian ceramics with Italian specialty foods and wines. The olive oils are produced on the farm in Tuscany of owners Kyle A. Wolfe and Martin Kolk, who opened a year-round offshoot of the same name in Portland in 1999. At the other end of Main Street is **Penobscot Bay Provisions,** a fine gourmet store offering fresh breads made from natural ingredients, soups and sandwiches, prepared foods, smoked fish, cheeses and wines.

Maine stoneware pottery, cobalt blue songeware plates, hand-painted stoneware from Silesia and unusual candlesticks for the dinner table are among the design items of interest to cooks and hostesses at **Harbor Farm**, a store and showroom in an 1850 schoolhouse along the causeway on Little Deer Isle. It features unique, made-to-order home and kitchen accessories, from tinware and tiles to an apple peeler and a maker of toasted sandwiches with sealed edges.

Rooster Brother, 18 West Main St., Ellsworth, is an exceptional store for cooks, serious and otherwise. Occupying a large Victorian building, it has a specialty-food and wine shop downstairs and a wide variety of cookbooks and assorted kitchen equipment upstairs. More than 60 cheeses and an expanded wine selection known for good values are available. Lately, owners Pamela and George Elias have been concentrating on coffee roasting and an expanding bakery, which features its own French bread. We came away with four types of dried chile peppers we have trouble finding in the Northeast as well as a cookbook called *Hotter Than Hell.*

Little Notch Bakery, based in The Shops at Hinckley Great Harbor Marina in Southwest Harbor, is a great bakery producing more than 4,500 loaves of bread weekly for avid customers, including some of Down East Maine's finest inns and restaurants. Specialties include Italian breads, focaccia, olive rolls and onion rolls. Owners Art and Kate Jacobs opened the year-round **Little Notch Cafe** and retail outlet at 340 Main St. in the center of town. Art said the bittersweet belgian chocolate brownie he urged us to sample tasted like fudge, and it sure did. Had it been lunchtime, we'd have gone for the grilled flank steak sandwich with roasted peppers and onions on a French baguette for $5.95.

Little Notch Bakery products and Seal Cove goat cheese are hot numbers at **Sawyer's Market**, the Southwest Harbor grocery with all the right stuff, including a rear deli case of fantastic-looking salads, marinated cooked salmon and other gourmet items prepared exclusively for Sawyer's. You could fashion yourself a delightful picnic here or at the Sawyers gourmet store selling wines, cheeses, pâtés and such just across Main Street.

The grocery store in Bar Harbor is the **J.H. Butterfield Co.**, a fixture since 1887 at 152 Main St. Catering to the upper crust, it has a fine supply of gourmet foods, chocolates, picnic items and luscious fruits, and there are good sandwiches to go for picnics. Never have we seen so many varieties of Walker shortbreads and biscuits. There's also an extensive selection of beers and wines, including those from the nearby Bartlett Winery.

Another place of interest in Bar Harbor is **Porcupine Island Co.** at 4 Cottage St., which claims the largest selection of made-in-Maine specialty foods in the state. Sisters Bambi Mohr and Wendy Scott make the exotic Porcupine Island sauces, including a feisty garlic and horseradish mustard roasting grill sauce, all natural and without preservatives. Ginger is the secret to their addictive wasabi stir-fry sauce.

Worth a stop on the Schoodic Peninsula is the **Chickadee Creek Stillroom** on Route 186 in West Gouldsboro. An array of herbs and everlastings is charmingly displayed in a ramble of rustic little rooms. More than 300 varieties of herbs, spices and seasonings are sold by the ounce. Jeanie and Fred Cook grow some 40 varieties of herbs. They offer a potpourri called "Maine Woods, a walk through the pines and firs," for $3 a scoop, along with closet spices and bath herbs. They also sell garlic bread and logs of herbed goat's cheese. Jeanie will cut fresh herbs while you wait, $1 a bunch.

Award-Winning Fruit Wines

Bartlett Maine Estate Winery, Gouldsboro.

A winery in far Down East Maine? Yes, this with-it operation a half mile off

Route 1 in Gouldsboro, east of Hancock, is in the forefront in producing premium fruit wines. Finding conditions unsuitable for grapes, winemakers Robert and Kathe Bartlett substituted local apples, pears, raspberries and blueberries, and pioneered in making fine wines that have won best-of-show awards in the East (including, in 1989, the most medals of any winery in the New England Wine Competition and a total of 72 medals in twelve years). They employ grape wine techniques in the production of 16,000 gallons annually, and the wines are aged in French oak.

The Bartletts consider their apple and pear Coastal White perfect for a picnic along the shore, and we're partial to the nouveau blueberry, fit for the finest of gourmet dinners. Prices range om $7.95 to $24.99 for blueberry French oak reserve.

(207) 546-2408. Open Monday-Saturday 10 to 5, Memorial Day through Columbus ıy; rest of year by appointment.

Index

A

Aardvark, Yarmouth Port, MA 404
Abbicci, Yarmouth Port, MA 400
Abbott's Lobster in the Rough, Noank, CT 332
Acqua Bistro, Peterborough, N.H. 480
Adams Fairacre Farms, Poughkeepsie, NY 95
Adesso, Providence, RI 386
Aesop's Tables, Peterborough, NH 495
Agora, Providence, RI 381
Al Ducci's Italian Pantry, Manchester Center, VT 267
Al Forno, Providence, RI 372
Alice's Bakery & Café, Norwich, VT 243
Allentuck's New York Delicatessen, Great Barrington, MA 296
L'Alouette, Harwich Port, MA 406
Amalfi, Rockland, ME 541
The American Bounty Restaurant, Hyde Park, NY 68
American Seasons, Nantucket, MA 430
Amos A. Parker House,Fitzwilliam, NH 492
Anago, Boston, MA 466
Anchor Inn, Nantucket, MA 446
Annie Brownell House, Providence, RI 392
Antiques & Accommodations, North Stonington, CT 345
Anton's at the Swan, Lambertville, NJ 22
Apple Gate Bed & Breakfast, Peterborough, NH 494
Apple Pie Bakery Cafe, Hyde Park, NY 68
Applegate Bed & Breakfast, Lee, MA 298
Aquitaine, Boston, MA 470
Ardmore Inn, Woodstock, VT 241
Arrows, Ogunquit, ME 498
The Artist's Palate Cafe, Manchester, VT 262
Ashley Manor, Barnstable, MA 412
Asterix & Obelix, Newport, RI 352
Atlantica, Camden, ME 544
Auberge Bonaparte, Montreal, QUE 200
Auberge du Vieux-Port, Montreal, QUE 201
Auberge Maxime, Ridgefield, CT 310
Aubergine, Hillsdale, NY 272
Aubergine, Portland, ME 520
Aujourd'hui, Boston, MA 462
Aurora Provisions, Portland, ME 537

B

Back Bay Grill, Portland, ME 522
The Back Burner, Hockessin, DE 7
Barnard Inn Restaurant, Barnard, VT 224
Barnard-Good House, Cape May, NJ 60

Bartlett Maine Estate Winery, Gouldsboro, ME 591
The Batcheller Mansion Inn, Saratoga Springs, NY 164
Bean & Cod, Falmouth, MA 422
Bee and Thistle Inn, Old Lyme, CT 333
Beekman Arms, Rhinebeck, NY 88
The Belmont, Camden, ME 554
Belvedere Mansion, Rhinebeck, NY 86
The Benjamin Prescott Inn, Jaffrey, NH 494
Benmarl Vineyards, Marlborough-on-Hudson, NY 94
Beverly's Specialty Foods, Saratoga Springs, NY 162
Bev's Homemade Ice Cream, Lenox, MA 304
Biba, Boston, MA 458
Bibo's Madd Apple Cafe, Portland, ME 523
The Birches Inn, New Preston, CT 278
The Birchwood Inn, Temple, NH 491
Biscotti, Ridgefield, CT 315
The Bistro at Red Newt Cellars, Hector, NY 105
Bistro Henry, Manchester Center, VT 260
Bistro Zinc, Lenox, MA 288
Bizen, Great Barrington, MA 293
The Black Bass Hotel, Lumberville, NJ 37
The Black Duck on Corea Harbor, Corea, ME 588
The Black Pearl, Newport, RI 350
Black Point Inn Resort, Prouts Neck, ME 531
Black-Eyed Susan's, Nantucket, MA 435
Blantyre, Lenox, MA 274
Blue Hill Inn, Blue Hill, ME 583
The Boarding House, Nantucket, MA 428
The Boat House, Lambertville, NJ 32
Bois d'arc, Red Hook, NY 82
La Bonne Auberge, New Hope, PA 24
Boston Harbor Hotel, Boston, MA 476
The Bostonian Hotel, Boston, MA 477
Boulangerie Obelix, Newport, RI 369
Bramble Inn & Restaurant, The, Brewster, MA 407
Brandywine River Museum, Chadds Ford, PA 18
The Brewster Fish House Restaurant, Brewster, MA 405
Bridgeton House, Upper Black Eddy, PA 43
Brockamour Manor, Niagara-on-the-Lake, ON 143
The Brown Bag, Rockland, ME 563
La Bruschetta, West Stockbridge, MA 285
Buckley's Tavern, Centreville, DE 8
Bufflehead Cove Inn, Kennebunkport, ME 512

The Burning Tree, Otter Creek, ME 566
Butler's, Essex Junction, VT 218
Buttermilk Falls B&B, Ithaca, NY 122
Bykenhulle House, Hopewell Junction, NY 90

C

Cabanas On the Beach, Cape May, NJ 57
The Cady House, Providence, RI 392
The Cafe, Rosemont, NJ 30
Cafe at Wharf Street, Portland, ME 527
The Cafe Budapest, Boston, MA 469
Cafe Buon Gustaio, Hanover, NH 231
Cafe Louis, Boston, MA 461
Cafe Lucia, Lenox, MA 292
Cafe Miranda, Rockland, ME 543
Cafe Nuovo, Providence, RI 375
Cafe Pongo, Tivoli, NY 84
Cafe Routier, Old Saybrook, CT 326
Cafe Shelburne, Shelburne, VT 206
Cafe This Way, Bar Harbor, ME 572
Cafe Uffa! Portland, ME 528
Cafe Zelda, Newport, RI 359
Caffe Lena, Saratoga Springs, NY 172
Calico Restaurant & Patisserie, Rhinebeck, NY 79
The Camden Windward House, Camden, ME 559
Le Canard Enchaîne, Kingston, NY 82
The Candleberry Inn, Brewster, MA 413
The Cannery, Canaan, CT 289
Cape Arundel Inn, Kennebunkport, ME 510
The Cape Cod Potato Chip Co., Hyannis, MA 422
Cape Neddick Inn, Cape Neddick, ME 499
Cape Pier Chowder House, Cape Porpoise, ME 517
The Cape Sea Grille, Harwich Port, MA 401
Les Caprices de Nicolas, Montreal, QUE 180
The Captain Freeman Inn, Brewster, MA 413
The Captain Lord Mansion, Kennebunkport, ME 513
The Captain's House Inn of Chatham, Chatham, MA 417
Cascade Mountain Winery & Restaurant, Amenia, NY 78
Castine Inn, Castine, ME 578
Castle Hill Inn & Resort, Newport, RI 360
Castle Street Café, Great Barrington, MA 287
The Caterina de Medici Dining Room, Hyde Park, NY 72
CAV, Providence, RI 388
Cave Spring Cellars, Jordan, ON 150
Centerboard Guest House, Nantucket, MA 445
Centre Street Bistro, Nantucket, MA 436
Chachka, Erwinna, PA 45
Chadds Ford Inn, Chadds Ford, PA 9
Chaddsford Winery, Chadds Ford, PA 20
Chaiwalla, Salisbury, CT 305
Chamard Vineyards, Clinton, CT 348

Le Chambord, Hopewell Junction, NY 85
Chantecleer, Manchester Center, VT 258
The Chanticleer Inn, Siasconset, MA 424
Chapaquoit Grill, West Falmouth, MA 406
Charlotte, Lakeville, CT 291
Le Château, South Salem, NY 314
Château des Charmes, Niagara-on-the-Lake, ON 148
Cheeky Monkey Cafe, Newport, RI 359
Les Chenêts, Montreal, QUE 192
Cherie's Sweet Treats & Other Eats, Kennebunk, ME 516
Chesterfield Inn, West Chesterfield, NH 487
Chez la Mère Michel, Montreal, QUE 190
Chez Lenard, Ridgefield, CT 319
Chez Noüe, Ridgefield, CT 312
Chez Pascal, Providence, RI 384
Chez Sophie Bistro, Malta Ridge, NY 155
Chianti, Il Ristorante, Saratoga Springs, NY 157
Chickadee Creek Stillroom, West Gouldsboro, ME 591
Chillingsworth, Brewster, MA 396
Chiltern Inn, Bar Harbor, ME 586
Chimney Hill Farm Estate & Old Barn Inn, Lambertville, NJ 39
Christian's, Nantucket, MA 434
Christopher's Boathouse, Boothbay Harbor, ME 540
La Chronique, Montreal, QUE 178
Church Street Bistro, Lambertville, NJ 27
Church Street Cafe, Lenox, MA 284
Cioppino's, Nantucket, MA 433
The Clarke Cooke House, Newport, RI 356
Claude Postel, Montreal, QUE 186
Clayton's, Yarmouth, ME 561
Cliff Lodge, Nantucket, MA 445
Cliffside Beach Club, Nantucket, MA 441
Cliffside Inn, Newport, RI 362
Cliffwood Inn, Lenox, MA 297
Clinton Vineyards, Clinton Corners, NY 94
Clío, Boston, MA 465
The Clown, Portland, ME 537
The Clown, Stonington, ME 590
The Club Car, Nantucket, MA 431
Le Club des Pins, Montreal, QUE 188
Coach Farm, Pine Plains, NY 96
Cobb's Cove, Barnstable Village, MA 410
Colby Hill Inn, Henniker, NH 490
Commodore Room, Newport, RI 351
Company of the Cauldron, Nantucket, MA 433
Contrast Bistro & Espresso Bar, Dennis, MA 404
Copper Beech Inn, Ivoryton, CT 336
Cork, Camden, ME 546
The Corner Bakery, Pawling, NY 94
Cornucopia of Dorset, Dorset, VT 262
Cranberry House, Niagara-on-the-Lake, ON 145

Cripple Creek Restaurant, Rhinebeck, NY 79
Crosstrees, Kennebunkport, ME 515
Cucina Rosa, Cape May, NJ 56
Culinary Archives & Museum, Providence, RI 393
The Culinary Institute of America, Hyde Park, NY 68

D

The Daily Planet, Burlington, VT 211
Danforth, The, Portland, ME 533
Daniel's on Broadway, Cape May, NJ 51
Daño's on Cayuga, Ithaca, NY 108
Daño's on Seneca, Valois, NY 106
Deerhill Inn & Restaurant, West Dover, VT 250
Del Rossi's Trattoria, Dublin, NH 483
Della's Catessen, Portland, ME 537
Devonfield, Lenox, MA 299
Different Drummer's Kitchen, Lenox, MA 304
Dilworthtown Inn, Dilworthtown, PA 2
Dr. Konstantin Frank/Vinifera Wine Cellars, Hammondsport, NY 98
Le Domaine, Hancock, ME 582
Dos Amigos, Northport, ME 548
Doveberry Inn, West Dover, VT 257

E

The Ebbitt Room, Cape May, NJ 50
1811 House, Manchester Village, VT 264
Elm Tree Cottage, Newport, RI 364
The Elms, Ridgefield, CT 320
Elms Restaurant & Tavern, Ridgefield, CT 308
Empire, Providence, RI 385
The Epicurean, Niagara-on-the-Lake, ON 134
L'Epicureo, Providence, RI 382
The Equinox, Manchester Village, VT 247
Escabèche, Niagara on the Lake, ON 136
The Escoffier Restaurant, Hyde Park, NY 70
L'Espalier, Boston, MA 450
Espresso Cafe, Nantucket, MA 437
EverMay on the Delaware, Erwinna, PA 33
Everything But the Kitchen Sink, Hockessin, DE 20
L'Express, Montreal, QUE 189

H. Gillingham & Co., Woodstock, VT 243
Whey & Fromagerie, Nantucket, MA 448
Fairville Inn, Mendenhall, PA 14
Fancy's Farm of Chatham, Chatham, MA 421

Fancy's Farm Stand, East Orleans, MA 421
Fans Court, Niagara-on-the-Lake, ON 134
The Farm House Restaurant, Avondale, PA 4
The Federal House, Lansing, NY 122
The Federalist, Boston, MA 478
Fiddlers' Green, Southwest Harbor, ME 567
Fifteen Beacon, Boston, MA 478
Finale, Boston, MA 474
The Fish House, Lambertville, NJ 30
Fisherman's Landing, Bar Harbor, ME 578
Five Gables Inn, East Boothbay, ME 558
Five Spice Cafe, Burlington, VT 210
Flat Road Diner, Manchester Center, VT 267
Fore Street, Portland, ME 519
43 Phila Bistro, Saratoga Springs, NY 156
Fouquet's, Montreal, QUE 193
The Four Columns Inn, Newfane, VT 253

Four Seasons Hotel, Boston, MA 475
410 Bank Street, Cape May, NJ 48
The Francis Malbone House, Newport, RI 366
Frankie & Johnny's, Cape Neddick, ME 506
The Frenchtown Inn, Frenchtown, NJ 25
Frescos, Cape May, NJ 57
Frogwater Cafe, Camden, ME 547
Fromage, Old Saybrook, CT 347

G

The Gables at Chadds Ford, Chadds Ford, PA 6
Gabriel's, Portland, ME 522
Gail's Station House, Ridgefield, CT 317
Gate House Hotel, Niagara-on-the-Lake, ON 138
The Gatehouse, Providence, RI 378
Gelston House, East Haddam, CT 340
Geneva on the Lake, Geneva, NY 118
George's, Bar Harbor, ME 569
Gideon Putnam Hotel and Conference Center, Saratoga Springs, NY 169
Ginny Lee Cafe, Lodi, NY 104
Glenora Wine Cellars, Dundee, NY 99
Globe, Montreal, QUE 182
The Golden Lamb Buttery, Brooklyn, CT 328
Golden Pheasant Inn, Erwinna, PA 36
Goose Cove Lodge, Sunset, ME 581
The Grange at Stonecroft Inn, Ledyard, CT 338
Green Briar Jam Kitchen, East Sandwich, MA 420
Grissini Trattoria & Panificio, Kennebunkport, ME 504
Guido's Fresh Marketplace, Great Barrington, MA 303

H

Hagley Museum, Wilmington, DE 17
Haight Vineyards and Winery, Litchfield, CT 306
Half Moon Restaurant & Saloon, Kennett Square, PA 7
Les Halles, Montreal, QUE 191
Hamanassett, Lima, PA 14
Hamersley's Bistro, Boston, MA 455
Hamilton's Grill Room, Lambertville, NJ 23
The Hancock Inn, Hancock, NH 488
Hannah Davis House, Fitzwilliam, NH 493
Hanover Consumer Cooperative Society, Hanover and Lebanon, NH 244
The Hanover Inn, Hanover, NH 237
Hanshaw House B&B, Ithaca, NY 120
Harbor View Tavern, Thomaston, ME 545
Harney & Sons, Salisbury, CT 304
Harrald's, Stormville, NY 74
Harraseeket Inn, Freeport, ME 549
Harraseeket Lunch & Lobster Co., South Freeport, ME 562
Hartefeld National, Avondale, PA 9
Hartwell House, Ogunquit, ME 511
Harvest Barn Country Market, Niagara-on-the-Lake, ON 152
The Harvest Moon Inn, Ringoes, NJ 29
Hattie's, Saratoga Springs, NY 160
Havana, Bar Harbor, ME 573
Hay Day, The Country Farm Market, Ridgefield, CT 321
Heart of the Village Inn, Shelburne, VT 219
Hedgerow Bed & Breakfast Suites, Chadds Ford, PA 15
The Heights Cafe & Grill, Ithaca, NY 112
Helsinki Tea Company Cafe and Bistro, Great Barrinngton, MA 296
Hemingway's, Sherburne, VT 226
Henry of Pelham Family Estate Winery, St. Catharines, ON 149
Hermann J. Wiemer Vineyard, Dundee, NY 99
High Brewster, Brewster, MA 408
Hillebrand Estates Winery, Niagara-on-the-Lake, ON 147
Hillebrand's Vineyard Cafe, Niagara-on-the-Lake, ON 130
Historic Merrell Inn, South Lee, MA 300
Hobbit Hollow Farm, Skaneateles, NY 123
Home Hill Country Inn & Restaurant, Plainfield, NH 234
Hopkins Vineyard, New Preston, CT 306
L'Hôtel de la Montagne, Montreal, QUE 199
Hotel du Village, New Hope, PA 37
Hotel Inter-Continental Montreal, Montreal QUE 198
Hotel Le Meridien, Boston, MA 475
Hotel Omni Montreal, Montreal, QUE 198

House of 1833, Mystic, CT 344
The Humble Gourmet, Brunswick, ME 562
Hurricane, Ogunquit, ME 500

I

Icarus, Boston, MA 467
The Impudent Oyster, Chatham, MA 405
Inaho Japanese Restaurant, Yarmouth Port, MA 403
The Inn at Bay Ledge, Bar Harbor, ME 585
The Inn at Canoe Point, Bar Harbor, ME 584
The Inn at Charlotte, Charlotte, VT 220
The Inn at Crotched Mountain, Francestown, NH 489
The Inn at Essex, Essex Junction, VT 217
The Inn at Glenora Wine Cellars and Veraisons Restaurant, Dundee. NY 102
The Inn at Harbor Head, Kennebunkport, ME 511
The Inn at Montchanin Village, Montchanin, DE 10
The Inn at Mystic, Mystic, CT 339
The Inn at Ormsby Hill, Manchester Village, VT 263
The Inn at Phillips Mill, New Hope, PA 35
The Inn at Richmond, Richmond, MA 301
The Inn at Ridgefield, Ridgefield, CT 313
The Inn at Sawmill Farm, West Dover, VT 245
The Inn at Shelburne Farms, Shelburne, VT 215
The Inn at Stockbridge, Stockbridge, MA 300
The Inn at Sunrise Point, Camden, ME 561
Inn at the Falls, Poughkeepsie, NY 89
The Inn by the Sea, Cape Elizabeth, ME 530
Inn of the Hawke, Lambertville, NJ 33
Inniskillin Wines. Niagara-on-the-Lake, ON 147
Isaac Stover House, Erwinna, PA 42
Isabel's on the Waterfront, Burlington, VT 208

J

J.H. Butterfield Co., Bar Harbor, ME 591
J.P. Daniels, Old Mystic, CT 329
The Jackson House Inn, Woodstock, VT 23?
Jean-Paul's Bistro, Blue Hill, ME 575
Joe's Boathouse, South Portland, ME 525
John Andrew's, South Egremont, MA 284
The John F. Craig House, Cape May, NJ 63
John Thomas Steakhouse, Ithaca, NY 111
Jonathan's, Blue Hill, ME 565
Jongleux Café, Montreal, QUE 179
Jordan Pond House, Acadia National Park, ME 577
Julien, Boston, MA 464
Just a Taste, Ithaca, NY 113

K

King Ferry Winery, King Ferry, NY 102
The Kingsleigh Inn, Southwest Harbor, ME 588
The Kitchen Garden Restaurant, Steuben, ME 574
Kitchen Little, Mystic, CT 332
Klinger's Bread Company, South Burlington, VT 222
Knapp Vineyards Restaurant, Romulus, NY 103
Knapp Vineyards Winery, Romulus, NY 102
Konzelmann Estate Winery, Niagara-on-the-Lake, ON 148
Krazy Kat's, Montchanin, DE 2
Kristina's, Bath, ME 544
Kurtz Orchards Country Market, Niagara-on-the-Lake, ON 152

L

Lake Champlain Chocolates, Burlington, VT 222
The Lakeview Inn, New Preston, CT 280
Lakewinds, Niagara-on-the-Lake, ON 141
Lala Rokh, Boston, MA 468
Laloux, Montreal, QUE 187
Lambertville House, Lambertville, NJ 38
Lamoreaux Landing Wine Cellars, Lodi, NY 100
The Landing, New Hope, PA 27
Le Languedoc, Nantucket, MA 426
Le Latini, Montreal, QUE 184
Lawnmeer Inn and Restaurant, West Boothbay Harbor, ME 552
Left Bank Libations, Lambertville, NJ 33
Leunig's Bistro, Burlington, VT 211
Lilly's On the Pond, Rindge, NH 484
Lily, Lupine & Fern, Camden, ME 563
The Lincoln Mineral Baths, Saratoga Springs, NY 172
Lindenwood Inn, Bar Harbor, ME 587
Lion's Share Bakery and Coffee Roasters, Manchester Center, VT 266
A Little Dream, Camden, ME 560
Little Notch Bakery, Southwest Harbor, ME 590
The Little Rooster Cafe, Manchester Center, VT 266
Loafers American Bistro, Frenchtown, NJ 31
Loews Hotel Vogue, Montreal, QUE 199
Log Cabin, Bailey Island, ME 558
Longfellows Inn and Restaurant, Saratoga Springs, NY 159 and 168
Longwood Gardens, Kennett Square, PA 17
Louisa's, Cape May, NJ 55

M

MacKenzie-Childs Ltd., Aurora, NY 127
Madeline's, Ithaca, NY 106
Maestro's, Saratoga Springs, NY 161
The Mainstay Inn, Cape May, NJ 59
La Maison Cappellari at Mostly Hall, Falmouth, M 419
La Maison Pierre du Calvet, Montreal, QUE 201
Maison Robert, Boston, MA 460
Manon, Lambertville, NJ 26
Manor House, Cape May, NJ 62
Manor House, Norfolk, CT 302
The Mansakenning Carriage House, Rhinebeck, NY 91
The Mansion, Rock City Falls, NY 166
The Mansion House, Cape May, NJ 55
The Maple Leaf Inn, Barnard, VT 240
Market on Main, Rockland, ME 563
The Market on the Boulevard, Newport, RI 369
Marquis at The Belmont, Camden, ME 554
Martinos, Keene, NH 484
Marynissen Estates, Niagara-on-the-Lake, ON 151
Max's Memphis Barbecue, Red Hook, NY 83
Maxwell Creed's, Kennett Square, PA 4
The May West Inn, Saratoga Springs, NY 168
Mayflower Inn, Washington, CT 277
McEnroe Organic, Amenia, NY 96
McKinney & Doyle Fine Foods Cafe, Pawling, NY 76
Mediterraneo, Montreal, QUE 181
Merrimac Smoked Fish, Great Barrington, MA 303
Mill Way Fish & Lobster Market, Barnstable, MA 420
Millbrook Vineyards & Winery, Millbrook, NY 93
Mirabelles, Burlington, VT 222
Miss Plum's Parlour, Rockport, ME 563
Mr. Shane's Homemade Parlour Ice Cream, Ridgefield, CT 322
Mistral, Boston, MA 453
Mistral's at Toll Gate, Manchester Center, VT 259
Monadnock School for Natural Cooking and Philosophy, Peterborough, NH 486
Mona's, Burlington, VT 214
Mondexo, Montreal, QUE 194
Monsoon, Lebanon, NH 230
Moona, Nantucket, MA 432
Moosewood Restaurant, Ithaca, NY 114
Morgan-Samuels Inn, Canandaigua, NY 116
Mother Myrick's Confectionery, Manchester Center, VT 268
Moveable Feasts, Blue Hill, ME 565

Mrs. London's, Saratoga Springs, NY 162
Mystic Drawbridge Ice Cream Shoppe,
    Mystic, CT 347

N

Nantucket Nectars, Nantucket, MA 448
Nantucket Tapas, Nantucket, MA 436
The Nauset House Inn, East Orleans, MA 415
Neath's, Providence, RI 376
NECI Commons, Burlington, VT 212
Nervous Nellie's Jams and Jellies, Deer Isle,
    ME 590
New Rivers, Providence, RI 374
New Skete, Cambridge, NY 171
The Newcastle Inn, Newcastle, ME 553
Niagara Presents, Jordan Station, ON 153
Nicola's Trattoria, Keene, NH 481
98 Provence, Ogunquit, ME 502
No. 9 Park, Boston, MA 456
Noah's, Stonington, CT 331
Norumbega, Camden, ME 556

O

The Oban Inn, Niagara-on-the-Lake, ON 140
Ocean Wood Gallery & Restaurant, Birch
    Harbor, ME 573
The Old Beach Inn, Newport, RI 366
The Old Court, Providence, RI 391
Old Fort Inn, Kennebunkport, ME 514
The Old Inn on the Green and Gedney Farm,
    New Marlboro, MA 270
Old Lyme Inn, Old Lyme, CT 334
The Old Mill, West Stockbridge, MA 286
Olde Rhinebeck Inn, Rhinebeck, NY 92
Olga's Cup and Saucer, Providence, RI 389
Oliva, New Preston, CT 294
Olives, Charlestown, MA 457
On the Twenty Restaurant & Wine Bar,
    Jordan, ON 129
Once Upon a Table, Stockbridge, MA 295
181 Main Street Bed & Breakfast, Freeport,
    ME 557
Opaline, Burlington, VT 211
Oran Mor, Nantucket, MA 427

P

Pangea, Ithaca, NY 109
Parish Cafe, Boston, MA 474
Les Passants du Sans Soucy, Montreal, QUE
    200
Le Passe-Partout, Montreal, QUE 176
Pasta Unlimited, Deep River, CT 347
Pastiche, Providence, RI 394
Patisserie de Gascogne, Montreal, QUE 204
Pat's Kountry Kitchen, Old Saybrook, CT
    347

Pauline's Cafe & Restaurant, South
    Burlington, VT 207
Le Pavillon, Poughkeepsie, NY 76
Peaches at Sunset, Cape May, NJ 58
The Pearl, Nantucket, MA 428
Peller Estates Winery, Niagara-on-the-Lake,
    ON 151
Peltier's Market, Dorset, VT 267
Penny Cluse Cafe, Burlington, VT 223
Pepperclub, Portland, ME 528
The Percy Inn, Portland, ME 535
Perfetto, Portland, ME 527
Le Persil Fou, Montreal, QUE 189
Peter Piper Market, Nantucket, MA 448
Le Petit Bistro, Rhinebeck, NY 80
Le Petit Chef, Wilmington, VT 261
La Petite Auberge, Newport, RI 355
Phillips Place, Kennett Square, PA 19
Piccolo, Ridgefield, CT 318
Pickity Place, Mason, NH 496
Pilgrim's Inn, Deer Isle, ME 579
The Pineapple Inn, Nantucket, MA 444
Pizza by Elizabeths, Greenville, DE 10
Pizza Grille, Mystic, CT 347
Pizzico, Providence, RI 387
The Place, Newport, RI 350
Le Poissons Rouge, Montreal, QUE 194
Pomegranate Inn, Portland, ME 532
The Porcupine Grill, Bar Harbor, ME 570
Porcupine Island Co., Bar Harbor, ME 591
Portland Coffee Roasting Co., Portland, ME
    536
Portland Public Market, Portland, ME 535
Portland Regency Hotel, Portland, ME 531
Pot au Feu, Providence, RI 383
La Poule à Dents, Norwich, VT 227
Preble Grille, Southwest Harbor, ME 571
Première Rue, Montreal, QUE 195
Primo, Rockland, ME 541
The Prince and the Pauper, Woodstock, VT
    227
The Prince of Wales Hotel, Niagara-on-the-
    Lake, ON 134
Pronto, Newport, RI 357
The Providence Biltmore, Providence, RI 391
Provisions, Brunswick, ME 562
The Pub & Restaurant, Norfolk, CT 297
Putnam Market, Saratoga Springs, NY 170

Q

The Queen Victoria, Cape May, NJ 62
Queen's Hotel, Cape May, NJ 62
Queen's Landing Inn and Conference Resort,
    Niagara-on-the-Lake, ON 136
Queenston Heights Restaurant, Queenston,
    ON 132
Quelli della Notte, Montreal, QUE 182
Quimper Faience, Stonington, CT 348

R

Rachel's Wood Grill, Portland, ME 525
Radius, Boston, MA 452
Randall's Ordinary, North Stonington, CT 341
The Red House Country Inn, Burdett, NY 123
The Red Lion Inn, Stockbridge, MA 281
Red Maples Restaurant, Bennington, NH 482
The Red Pheasant Inn, Dennis, MA 399
The Red Shutter Inn, Wilmington, VT 256
Redfield's, Northeast Harbor, ME 568
The Regatta of Cotuit, Cotuit, MA 402
The Regatta of Falmouth By-the-Sea, Falmouth, MA 398
Reif Winery, Niagara-on-the-Lake, ON 150
The Reluctant Panther, Manchester Village, VT 252
Les Remparts, Montreal, QUE 187
Rempel's Farm Market, Niagara-on-the-Lake, ON 152
Renée's Bistro, Ithaca, NY 110
Restaurant Bouchard, Newport, RI 352
Restaurant Bravo Bravo, Mystic, CT 330
Restaurant du Village, Chester, CT 324
Restaurant Zen, Montreal, QUE 197
Rhode Island House, Newport, RI 367
Ribollita, Portland, ME 524
Rice's Sale and Country Market, New Hope, PA 46
The Ridgefield General Store, Ridgefield, CT 321
Ridgefield General Store Cafe, Ridgefield, CT 317
Ristorante Black Orchid, Boothbay Harbor, ME 545
Ristorante Giardino, Niagara-on-the-Lake, ON 139
The Ritz-Carlton, Boston, MA 476
The Ritz-Carlton, Montreal, QUE 196 and 198
Riverwind, Deep River, CT 343
The Robinhood Free Meetinghouse, Georgetown, ME 538
Robson-Grieve House, Niagara-on-the-Lake, ON 144
Ronnybrook Farm Dairy, Ancramdale, NY 96
Rooster Brother, Ellsworth, ME 590
Rosalie's Cucina, Ithaca, NY 107
Rosalie's Cucina, Skaneateles, NY 107
Rosaly's Farm Stand, Peterborough, NH 496
The Rose Inn, Ithaca, NY 115
Round Top Ice Cream, Damariscotta, ME 562
Rowantrees Pottery, Blue Hill, ME 589
Rowes Wharf Restaurant, Boston, MA 464
Rue de L'Espoir, Providence, RI 387

S

Sài-Gòn Cafe, Burlington, VT 214
St. Andrew's Cafe, Hyde Park, NY 71
Sakonnet Vineyards, Little Compton, RI 370
Salt Marsh Tavern, Kennebunkport, ME 503
Sand Castle Winery, Erwinna, PA 45
Santa Fe, Tivoli, NY 83
Saratoga Arms, Saratoga Springs, NY 165
Saratoga Bed & Breakfast, Saratoga Springs, NY 167
Le Saucier, Boston, MA 479
Savanas' Inn, Newport, RI 368
Sawyer's Market, Southwest Harbor, ME 590
Scales and Shells, Newport, RI 358
Scarlet Begonias, Brunswick, ME 562
'Sconset Cafe, Siasconset, MA 436
Sea Dog Brewing Co., Camden, ME 563
Seascapes, Kennebunkport, ME 502
Seasons, Boston, MA 467
Seasons Restaurant, Watkins Glen, NY 111
Seaweed Cafe, Manset, ME 570
The Sergeantsville Inn, Sergeantsville, NJ 28
Seven Tables, Seal Harbor, ME 572
1740 House, Lumberville, NJ 42
Shannaleigh, Niagara-on-the-Lake, ON 144
Shaw Cafe & Wine Bar, Niagara-on-the-Lake, ON 133
Shaw Festival, Niagara-on-the-Lake, ON 153
Shelburne Farms, Shelburne, VT 221
Shelburne Museum, Shelburne, VT 221
Sheldrake Point Vineyard & Cafe, Ovid, NY 105
Ships Inn, Nantucket, MA 443
The Silo, New Milford, CT 322
The Simmons Homestead Inn, Hyannis Port, MA 418
Simon Pearce, Quechee, VT 244
Simon Pearce Restaurant, Quechee, VT 228
Siro's, Saratoga Springs, NY 159
Smokejacks, Burlington, VT 209
Société Café, Montreal, QUE 196
Something Natural, Nantucket, MA 437
Sonnenberg Gardens, Canandaigua, NY 126
Sonsie, Boston, MA 473
The Southern Mansion, Cape May, NJ 64
Southwest Cafe, Ridgefield, CT 318
Sovana Bistro & Pizza Kitchen, Kennett Square, PA 6
Speeder & Earl's, Burlington, VT 222
Sperry's, Saratoga Springs, NY 158
Spigalina, Lenox, MA 292
Spinnakers, Geneva, NY 112
The Squire Tarbox Inn, Westport Island, ME 550
Stable, The, Niagara-on-the-Lake, ON 145
Standing Stone Vineyards, Valois, NY 101
Star Fish Grill, Brunswick, ME 539

Steamboat Inn, Mystic, CT. 343
Steve's Bagels, Ridgefield, CT 318
Steve's Centerbrook Cafe, Centerbrook, CT 325
Stonecroft, Ledyard, CT 337
Stonehenge, Ridgefield, CT 309, 319
Stonewall Kitchen Company Store, York, ME 517
Straight Wharf Restaurant, Nantucket, MA 429
Street and Co., Portland, ME 521
The Summer House, Siasconset, MA 440
Sundae School Ice Cream Parlor, East Orleans, MA 421
Sunnybrook Farm Estate Winery, Niagara-on-the-Lake, ON 151
Sushi by Yoshi, Nantucket, MA 437
Sutton's Country Store and Cafe, Glens Falls, NY 170
The Swan, Lambertville, NJ 32
Sweet Pierre's, Ridgefield, CT 322
Sweet Tomatoes Trattoria, Burlington, VT 213
Sweet Tomatoes Trattoria, Lebanon, NH 229

T

T.J. Buckley's, Brattleboro, VT 261
The Texas Taco, Patterson, NY 84
Thai Cuisine, Ithaca, NY 113
Thirty Three & 1/3, Ridgefield, CT 315
Thomas Mott Homestead, Alburg, VT 220
Three Mountain Inn, Jamaica, VT 255
Thurston's Lobster Pound, Bernard, ME 577
Tiara, Niagara-on-the-Lake, ON 137
Timothy's, New London, CT 327
Tisha's, Cape May, NJ 54
Tony's Colonial Food Store, Providence, RI 394
Toqué! Montreal, QUE 174
Treats, Wiscasset, ME 562
Tree's Place, Orleans, MA 422
Tremont 647, Boston, MA 472
Trent, Providence, RI 390
Truc, Boston, MA 471
The Trumbull House, Hanover, NH 242
Tucker's Bistro, Newport, RI 360
Twelve Pine, Peterborough, NH 485
21 Federal, Nantucket, MA 426
Twin Farms, Barnard, VT 238
The Twinings Tearoom, Cape May, NJ 66
Two Lights Lobster Shack, Cape Elizabeth, ME 529
Two Tannery Road, West Dover, VT 260

U

Ullikana Bed & Breakfast, Bar Harbor, ME 586

Union Bar & Grill, Great Barrington, MA 293
Union Park, Cape May, NJ 52
Union River Lobster Pot, Ellsworth, ME 577
Union Street Inn, Nantucket, MA 446
Unionville Vineyards, Ringoes, NJ 45
Up for Breakfast, Manchester Center, VT 266

V

Vanderbilt Hall, Newport, RI 361
Vanderbrooke Bakers and Caterers, Old Saybrook, CT 347
Venda Ravioli, Providence, RI 394
Veranda House, Rhinebeck, NY 92
The Village Fare Cafe & Bakery, Manchester Village, VT 266
Village Pump House Restaurant, Shelburne, VT 213
Vineland Estates, Vineland, ON 149
Vineland Estates Winery Restaurant, Vineland, ON 131
The Vintner's Inn, Jordan, ON 142
The Virginia Hotel, Cape May, NJ 60

W

Wagner Vineyards, Lodi, NY 100
Walter's Cafe, Portland, ME 526
Walter's La Locanda del Coccia, Providence, RI 379
The Washington Inn, Cape May, NJ 53
Water Street Cafe, Stonington, CT 327
The Waterfront Restaurant, Camden, ME 546
Waterman's Beach Lobster, South Thomaston, ME 563
Waters Edge, Cape May, NJ 49
The Wauwinet, Nantucket, MA 438
Wedgewood Inn, Yarmouth Port, MA 411
Wellington Court Restaurant, St, Catharines, ON 132
Wequassett Inn, Chatham, MA 409
West Creek Cafe, Nantucket, MA 434
The West Deck, Newport, RI 353
West Lane Inn, Ridgefield, CT 320
West Main at Pocket Knife Square, Lakeville, CT 290
West Street Grill, Litchfield, CT 282
The Westchester House, Saratoga Springs, NY 164
The Westin Providence, Providence, RI 390
The Whalewalk Inn, Eastham, MA 414
Wheatleigh, Lenox, MA 275
Wheatmarket, Chester, CT 346
The Whip and Spoon, Portland, ME 536
White Barn Inn, Kennebunkport, ME 507
The White Horse Tavern, Newport, RI 354

Whitewing Farm, West Chester, PA 12
Wickford Gourmet Foods, Wickford, RI 370
The Willard Street Inn, Burlington, VT 219
Windham Hill Inn, West Townshend, VT 249
Windows on the Water, Kennebunkport, ME 505
The Wine Bar, Saratoga Springs, NY 163
Winterthur Museum, Garden and Library, Winterthur, DE 16
Woodstock Inn and Resort, Woodstock, VT 236
The Woolverton Inn, Stockton, NJ 40

X

Xaviar's, Garrison, NY 73
Xe Sogni, Amenia, NY 81
XO Café, Providence, RI 377
XYZ Restaurant & Gallery, Manset, ME 576

Y

York Street House, Lambertville, NJ 44
The Youngtown Inn & Restaurant, Lincolnville, ME 555

Also by the Authors

Inn Spots & Special Places in New England. The first in the series, this book by Nancy and Richard Woodworth tells you where to go, stay, eat and enjoy in New England's choicest areas. Focusing on 35 special places, it details the best inns and B&Bs, restaurants, sights to see and things to do. First published in 1986; fully revised and expanded fifth edition in 1998. 524 pages of great ideas. $16.95.

Inn Spots & Special Places / Mid-Atlantic. The second volume in the series, this guide by Nancy and Richard Woodworth covers 35 special areas in the Mid-Atlantic region from New York to Virginia. First published in 1992; fully revised and expanded third edition in 1998. 536 pages of timely ideas. $16.95.

Inn Spots & Special Places in the Southeast. The newest volume in the series, this book by Nancy and Richard Woodworth covers 26 special areas from North Carolina to Florida. With its emphasis on fine inns and good restaurants, the series now covers the entire East Coast, from Eastport, Me., to Key West, Fla. Published in 1999. 376 pages of new ideas. $16.95.

Waterside Escapes in the Northeast. This guide by Betsy Wittemann and Nancy Woodworth relates the best lodging, dining, attractions and activities in 36 great waterside vacation spots from Chesapeake Bay to Cape Breton Island, from the Thousand Islands to Martha's Vineyard. Everything you need to know for a day trip, a weekend or a week near the water is told the way you want to know it. First published in 1987; revised and expanded third edition in 1996. 474 pages to discover and enjoy. $15.95.

Weekending in New England. The best-selling travel guide by Betsy Wittemann and Nancy Woodworth details everything you need to know about 24 of New England's most interesting vacation spots: more than 1,000 things to do, sights to see and places to stay, eat and shop year-round. First published in 1980; fully revised and expanded fifth edition in 1997. 448 pages of facts and fun. $16.95.

The Originals in Their Fields

These books may be purchased at bookstores or direct from the publisher, pre-paid, plus $2 shipping for each book.

Wood Pond Press
365 Ridgewood Road
West Hartford, Conn. 06107
Tel: (860) 521-0389
Fax: (860) 313-0185
E-Mail: woodpond@ntplx.net
Web Site: www.getawayguides.com.

ON LINE: Excerpts from these books are found at www.getawayguides.com. Check out this web site for updates on some of our favorite inns, B&Bs, restaurant and attractions in destination areas around the East.